FINDING A PLACE CALLED HOME

A Guide to African-American Genealogy and Historical Identity

FINDING A PLACE CALLED HOME

A Guide to African-American Genealogy and Historical Identity

DEE PARMER WOODTOR, PH.D.

RANDOM HOUSE • NEW YORK

Finding a Place Called Home: A Guide to African-American
Genealogy and Historical Identity

Copyright © 1999 by Dee Parmer Woodtor, Ph.D.

This book is available for special purchases in bulk by organizations and institutions,
not for resale, at special discounts. Please direct your inquiries to the Random
House Special Sales Department, toll-free 888–591–1200 or fax 212–572–4961.

Please address inquiries about electronic licensing of reference products, for use on
a network or in software or on CD-ROM, to the Subsidiary Rights Department,
Random House Reference & Information Publishing, fax 212–940–7370.

Visit the Random House Web site at www.randomhouse.com

Typeset and printed in the United States of America.

Typeset by Allentown Digital Services Division of RR Donnelley & Sons Company

Library of Congress Cataloging-in-Publication Data

Woodtor, Dee Palmer.
    Finding a place called home: a guide to African-American genealogy and
historical identity/Dee Parmer Woodtor.—1st paperback ed.
      p. cm.
    Includes bibliographical references and index.
    ISBN 0–375–40595–X (Hardcover)
    ISBN 0-375-70843-X (Paperback)
    1. Afro-Americans—Genealogy—Handbooks, manuals, etc. 2. Afro-
Americans—Ethnic identity. I. Title.
    E185.96.W69 1998
929'.1'08996073—dc21   98–49673
                                                   CIP

First Paperback Edition
0 9 8 7 6 5 4 3 2 1
November 1999
ISBN 0–375–70843–X
SAP Network #: 10039329
New York Toronto London Sydney Auckland

CONTENTS

CONTENTS

ACKNOWLEDGMENTS

*T*hough it would be impossible to thank every person whose spirit somehow touched this book on its unusual path to publication, the following persons and places must be acknowledged for being at the critical points:

My students, who taught me how to solve their problems,
African American genealogists, who challenged me to think,
Art Andersen and Adrian Capehart, who gave me the first challenge when they came up with the idea,
David Thackery at the Newberry Library, who trained me and held me to some very rigorous research standards,
The Newberry Library itself for allowing me to enjoy its many wonderful collections as well as its ambiance over a four-year period,
James Dent Walker for his wonderful wit and knowledge of the National Archives,
My far-flung relatives, who allowed me to stumble through interviews, especially Cleve Parmer and my father, Willie James Parmer, now deceased,
My ancestors, who gave me a place to call home, and a spirit to get up and "shake a leg" to make something happen,
All three of my former publishers, who backed out for unknown and mysterious reasons,
Myself for deciding that after five years of waiting, it was time to "shake a leg," and do it myself,

Ricardo Cunningham, the connects man,
Manie Barron, who has more than second sight...

And finally, all those who gave me encouragement, support, and information, including: librarians and archivists; Del Jupiter of Atlanta and Fern S. Nix of Oaky Streak; members of Chicago's Afro-American Genealogical and Historical Society; DePaul University's School for New Learning; Lisa Moran, who designed the original book, and all of my family—my mother, Adele Crittenden-Longmire King; my sisters, Hortense Parmer Brice, Twinet Parmer, and Catherine Barner; my brother, James Otis Parmer; my three children for my mental absences; John Ore Johnson and his wife, Nikki Tucker, and Jalea Tucker Johnson; the hope for my future line, Laura Wede Bryant and Saingbey Woodtor; my nephew, Troy Winston Brice for running errands; and my husband, Patrick Saingbey Woodtor, for supporting me in this "great work."

I thank you all collectively, and close with this reminder:

Some liberties I have taken,
Some rules I have forsaken,
All errors, I will claim for the making!

—DEE PARMER WOODTOR

A NOTE ABOUT THE PHOTOGRAPHS

*T*hese photographs invite you, entreat you, to tell a story, perhaps woven from your own imagination or your surviving records, papers and documents. Feel free to stare at them in your own mental privacy and wonder what stories they have woven into existence. Ask yourself who owns the image: the person who took the photograph; the person whose image stares back at you right now; the current owner of the image; or the person's family. Family photographs have a separate life of their own. All too often they wind up in the possession of far-off and distant people who know nothing of the image-owner's history. In the end, the individual owns his own image. What he or she projected, an imbedded message, is preserved for all time. That is what we have to read or decipher in the posture, the eyes, the dress and others in the photograph. May your vision serve the message well.

Cover: Family photographs found in archival collections.
Title Page: The William and Anna Stanley Family in Sparta, Georgia, courtesy of William J. Stanley III.

AUTHOR'S FAMILY PHOTOGRAPHS

*S*cenes from where I was born: A dusty road (102) and St. Luke AME Zion Church (108). My grandfather Ezra Parmer (222) and wife, Callie Nix Parmer (10), brothers, Henry (7) and Randall (83). My mother and father after migrating North (204). World War II veterans, cousins Cleve and Roscoe Parmer (351) Cleve, on right, was a prisoner of war in Italy. Gert Parmer (237) and Cousin Lula Parmer and Uncle John Parmer at Tuskegee (390). Author and two sisters waiting to be dressed for church (396). Members of the Nix family: Adam Nix and family in Pensacola (2); ex-slave, Lucindy Tillman Nix (23); Comer Nix & children (46); Adam Nix

Sr. (213). Other family photos are: Aunt Lou Crittenden Hawkins with husband and son (122) and Amealie Posey Longmire with grandson (246). Cousin Martin de Porres Lewis loaned a photo used in his book, *The History of St. Joseph's Church and Parish, Pensacola* (170).

LOANED FAMILY PHOTOGRAPHS

*M*y genealogy friends and former students have also loaned photos for this book. They are Mrs. Christine Greer Loving, whose photos are: Alice Jacobs and great-grandniece, Willetta Yates Greer and dog, Sailor (16) and Christine Moody Yates (357). Yates was a cartographer for the War Department. Courtesy of Daniel Tyree Callis, Samuel Franklin Tyree and his bride, Caroline Eugenia Blackville (68). Spencer Taylor whose narrative of slavery appears in The American Slave, courtesy of Del Jupiter, great-niece (146). Calvin Boger photo courtesy of Mrs. Jeanne Jones (326). Erreal and Calanthe Hackworth courtesy of Patricia Walker Hackworth Bearden (277). Courtesy of Nettie Nesbary (410).

LOST IDENTITIES

*A*bandoned photos, carelessly sold as part of a deceased's estate often appear in antique shops which is where I found those on pages 22, 267, 304, 354, and 381, all belonging to a family whose surname was Blakley. One piece of identification in the stash of 15 photos was a registration card dated 1939 for an RN named Mary Emma Blakley who lived at 4957 Vincennes Avenue. Another stash of photos of unidentified military men appear on pages 88, 96, 167, 191, 356, and 373. The final photo, bought individually, was taken in Texas (346).

INTRODUCTION

Genealogy is becoming one of the fastest growing hobbies in the nation; and it is growing steadily among African Americans. Certainly we have always remembered our histories. Our legacy has been passed down through oral tradition, through stories told by our parents, aunts, grandparents, and other kin. We were encouraged by the late Alex Haley's search for his ancestry that led him back to the village in Africa. We nodded a confirming "I told you so" when DNA "proved" Thomas Jefferson sired at least one child by his slave, Sally Hemings. We have always known a "truth" about our families; what we may not have known was how to write it down, where to go for supporting evidence. Dee Parmer Woodtor's work *Finding a Place Called Home*, changes all that. We learn where to turn, how to document, how to trust our oral history, and how to question the empirical data of official records.

Documenting one's heritage takes time, a critical eye, a detective's determination, a listening ear. As Africans Americans, those whom this nation has doubted and discounted, we are pressed to prove, to produce records that validate our existence and history. This is made difficult because the very evidence we are asked to bring forth about our enslaved ancestors is that which this nation refused to document. From 1790 to 1840, the federal censuses contain only the names of free heads of households; slaves and others were enumerated in brackets by age. The 1850 and 1860 population censuses tell more of white Americans. Names of slaves appear only if the slave owner considered them a member of the family, or if they were 100 years old. In the Slave Schedules of 1850 and 1860 enslaved Africans can be found enumerated by age, sex, and color under the slave owner's name. Absent even from slave schedules are the names of our ancestors whose lives we are trying to document.

Woodtor understands the challenge awaiting African Americans searching for enslaved ancestors. We want to know when our people arrived in America, the name of the slave ship that brought them over, and if possible, our ancestral homeland—the village in Africa from which we came. Woodtor encourages our search for our place in Africa, but cautions that few records give enough detailed information to help us do so. She directs us to the coastwise ship manifests housed in the National Archives, but notes the information is indexed by port of arrival and departure date, not name of the enslaved, the buyer, or seller. Woodtor takes us through steps to identify unknown slave owners and the records they left behind. She guides us through slave holders' wills, letters, tax digests, deeds, newspaper notices for runaways, or estate auctions—documents that may contain names of our enslaved forefathers. She reminds us that researching one's ancestors under slavery requires delving into the lives of the slave owner. To find "us," you must study "them."

Under freedom, African Americans shed the social, political, and economic definition of chattel and became to others, "people." The 1870 census is crucial in our search for identity. It is the first federal census taken after the Civil War; the first to list us by name. It records names, ages, birthplaces, occupation, value of real estate and personal property, and other information. In the 1880 census, we learn relationships, marital status, birthplace of each individual's parents, and more. The extended family is before us, telling us more of our heritage and genealogy. We read in the records how we lived. We see where we owned land, and the value of our personal property, if family members were illiterate or could read or write. We read enumeration districts, can turn to land records, identify boundaries of the family land. We can now point to a place on the map where freedom began. We read familiar names, places, rivers, townships. The stories our great-great grandparents told, of their parents born right after slavery, now take on meaning. We can touch, feel, and identify the place we now call down home.

Yet for African Americans, "first freedom" was a time of movement and uncertainty. Records can be wrong, memory can be faulty. Surnames change, are spelled differently or dropped and replaced with new ones. Ages are often guessed, descriptions such as "mulatto" given arbitrarily. Kin, who according to oral history, "never moved from that spot" are living in neighboring counties or have moved to other states. Black-owned land appears and disappears. Black men and women are incarcerated, institutionalized, or hanged with or without a trial. Children were taken from parents and hired out. We lose track of relatives who left to find loved ones. Folks marry and move away.

Woodtor's careful eye steers us to detailed and valuable records often underutilized. She wades through voluminous records of the Freedmen's Bureau. She tells of information found in records of the Freedman's Saving and Trust. Woodtor shows how to find Blacks who served in the Civil War, and examines their pension files for genealogical information. She directs us to labor contracts, sharecropper's agreements, marriage records, state censuses, and documents. Our missing ancestors become traceable and we can bridge the gap between slavery and freedom.

Often easier is our search for twentieth century relatives. The censuses and other public documents note more; African Americans are recording our own histories. Black newspapers report on our social events; editors make political commentaries on issues affecting us. Our black churches increase; our names appear in church records, baptismal, marriage, and christening records. We are educated in greater numbers. Relatives remember the train rides to New York, Detroit, and Chicago during the great Migration, and new-found jobs in plants or on the docks. Uncles and brothers engage in a lively debate as to who came North first.

Women proudly discuss how one of their own came to the city, did well, and always had "her own money." Elders pull out old faded photographs—men in overalls or military uniforms; women in chiffon dresses and freshly done hair. They reach for newspaper clippings, funeral announcements, insurance policies, and the like. These people, members of the oldest living generation, are the ones who can give us information we need to tie our present to our most recent past.

It is this kind of lively discussion—family and friends chattering away at kitchen tables, telling tales, remembering weddings, funerals, and graduations—that Woodtor hopes to stir. Memory is critical; so is talk and the photographs and scraps of paper held dear. Woodtor is a strong believer in the power of oral history. She gives tips on how to conduct an interview, how to evoke memories. She implores us to talk to family, jot down names, dates, and important events. Woodtor reminds us to identify people in photographs, and to be prepared for discrepancies and competing points of view. Catch the living history, she urges, ask the important questions now, while the elders are still living among us. Get everybody talking, for their words can unravel mysteries. Silence is disappointing for the family researcher. One may come ever so close to filling in missing pieces of the family history, the silence says "no more."

Woodtor wants us to discover who we are. She wants memory, records, and oral history to work for us, to guide us in our work. Woodtor leaves no stone unturned, no record book unopened. This is the strength of her work: She is relentless. For the novice and those who have been hooked on genealogy for years, *Finding a Place Called*

Home is a gem. In it, cumbersome research is made simple, additional records to scan are revealed. Woodtor shows us which documents to turn to for vital information. She asks us to trust our instincts, to abandon beliefs when they are proved to be wrong. Ultimately she reminds us to study America's history. She renders a moving and informative account of a slave holder's wealth, migration, marriage, and ability to increase his holding of enslaved Africans. She juxtaposes this to the same story as told by one of the enslaved—of promises of freedom broken, of being separated from wife and children, of marrying again, of forever losing track of siblings sold or left behind. Woodtor provides case studies, puts theory into practice, shares her victories and disappointments. With her, we are convinced that finding one's way home becomes quite possible.

Finding a Place Called Home shows how such painstaking work can pay off. Using Woodtor's book as a guide, African Americans can find long lost relatives. We gain better understanding of our lives under newfound freedom. We imagine our lives under the whims and whippings of slavery. We stand proud knowing we forged new lives in the North, and remember, with pride, the ways and traditions of our South. All of us may not be able to trace our ancestry back to the slave owner, the slave ship, or African homeland. But in our search for these answers, we will learn something new. Embrace Woodtor's work as you embrace your family's history. Refer to it time and time again. It will help you discover who you are; it will take you back to a place called home.

Velma Maia Thomas,
Author of *Lest We Forget*

FINDING A PLACE CALLED HOME

A Guide to African-American Genealogy and Historical Identity

Chapter 1

REGAINING OUR COLLECTIVE MEMORY, RECLAIMING A LOST FAMILY TRADITION

K*now who you are before they have to tell you.*

WOLOF PROVERB (SENEGAL)

Frederick Douglass's Letter to His Former Owner and Possible Uncle:

Rochester, Oct. 4th.

Hugh Auld, Esq.,

My dear Sir:

My heart tells me that you are too noble to treat with indifference the request I am about to make. It is twenty years since I ran away from you—or rather not from you—but from slavery, and since then I have often felt a strong desire to hold a little correspondence with you, and to learn something of the position and prospects of your dear children. They were dear to me, and are still. Indeed I feel nothing but kindness for you all. I love you but hate slavery. Now my dear Sir, will you favor me by dropping me a line, telling me in what year I came to live with you on Alliana Street—the year the frigate was built by Mr. Beechem. The information is not for publication and shall not be published. We are all hastening where all distinctions are ended. Kindness to the humblest will not be unrewarded.

Perhaps you have heard that I have seen Miss Amanda that was—Mrs. Searst that is—and was treated kindly. Such is the fact. Gladly would I see you and Mrs. Auld—or Miss Sopha as I used to call her. I could have lived with you during life in freedom—though I ran away from it unceremoniously. I did not know how soon I might be sold.

But I hate to talk about that. A line from you will find me,

Addressed Frederick Douglass,
Rochester, New York.

I am dear Sir,

Very truly yours,
Fred Douglass.

Imagining Our Ancestors

You are going through this book, so you have tried to imagine what your ancestors were like, what they thought, what they felt. But can you imagine your farthest back African ancestor in the United States? What did he or she look like? What language did he speak? Is it possible that you may look just like him or her? Perhaps you imagine a captured "prince" or "princess." Did either of them pass along some quality that has been characteristic of your family since that time? Perhaps it is a name like Phoebe, Cuffee, Annica, Teneh, Arminta, Quander, Cinque—names whose African origins exist now only in their anglicized versions. Perhaps he or she passed along a demeanor that has always made others call your folks "uppity." Imagine, if you will, the possibility that you may look just like him or her despite the fact that African Americans represent a mix of various African, Indian, and European ethnic groups. These questions and more form the basis of the search for an identity that is new, for we are "new people," and an identity that is old, for we are also an African people.

For a moment, put yourself in the shoes of Frederick Douglass. How would you ask a former slave owner for the specifics about your birth or your sale to him? For that matter, how would you ask for information about your enslaved ancestors from the descendants of the slave-owning family? Perhaps you haven't considered these possibilities, preferring instead to leave them as relics of the past.

Even if this is the case, no doubt you have often thought about slavery and discussed slavery as you imagined it. It is quite possible that you knew someone who was born during the last years of slavery, particularly if you were born before 1950! The idea of personally confronting a past that is shrouded in mystery and misinformation is still new for many African Americans. But for a growing number, finding answers to questions about how their ancestors really survived slavery has become a lifetime pursuit. Perhaps, however, you think that you know all the answers, but that is unlikely.

Who are your ancestors, anyway? Can you name them, describe their features, their thoughts? The old photographs that you once peered at on the raw wooden walls of a house now long since torn down somewhere in the Deep South, or those hanging on your citified relatives' walls, neatly arranged in old wooden frames over a mantle, may begin to answer this question. You might even have in your possession an old photograph album of people who look like

you but whose names and other identifying characteristics have long since been lost. You may even think about a grandparent who once told wonderful stories that brought to life ancestors whose memories have long since been forgotten.

Whatever you imagine your ancestors to have been, this is your chance to find out who they really were. You will be surprised when those faces peering down at you take on new meaning. Remote dark eyes will now come to life. Age lines will now become character lines, and expressions once unreadable will now be read.

The possibility of resolving these questions, the possibility of sorting out genetic and cultural identities, is what entices many African Americans to start a quest to understand the past. This is no small matter, but every year countless numbers begin putting the surviving remnants of the past together. They collect stories, talk with relatives, visit places where their people come from, and travel long distances just to find out more about "their people."

A VERY PERSONAL RIDDLE

*T*hink of one question that is asked every day, but which takes a lifetime to answer: "Who am I?" If you think that you already know who you are, read again Frederick Douglass's letter to one of his former owners. Douglass was, no doubt, advanced in years when he wrote this letter, but he was still thinking about this simple question. Of course, when you ask it you are also asking and answering additional questions. What have I been? What patterns have I woven between the moment of my birth and the

days of my maturity to make my life distinct, unique, and meaningful? How have I written my memory for the future? Indeed, how did my ancestors write their memories for me? And that is the point where your genealogy starts.

This very personal journey on which you are about to embark will take you through countless questions about your identity—questions that will be rooted in fact and fancy, speculation and revelation. In the end, you will realize that you represent the totality of your ancestors' experiences and memories, plus those that you have "written" for yourself.

It was once thought that the historical experiences of African Americans could not be "read" or understood. You may even have doubts in your own mind as you read this book. What, after all, is there to know—especially about the history of African American families? And what about your

family and your ancestors? They too have a history, but has that history receded with each passing generation? Hopefully, this book will help you to understand that your family's history is a unique one—its naming patterns, its path of migration, its physical features, its sheer ability to replicate itself from one generation to the next. For woven into the simple cycle of birth, marriage, and death are countless patterns which when all pulled together make your ancestral lines unique. This is your family's collective memory.

Collective memory is like the mortar that holds a brick structure together. Your family's collective memory is rooted in memories that tell stories about key events in the family's history. If at family gatherings your great-great uncle Joe, now dead for twenty years, is remembered as the one who first came to New York from Georgia with nothing but three dollars in his pocket, this set of facts becomes a part of the family's memory. When his wife, great-great aunt Lou Ella, boarded the train to join him, she wound up at the 12th Street Station in Chicago rather than Grand Central Station in New York. This adds to the family's collective memory. If you look at their photographs, you may understand why Aunt Lou Ella might have gotten her directions wrong. She wore thick glasses!

A LONG VIEW OF THE AFRICAN AMERICAN FAMILY

Genealogy is about time, place, and perspective. Your past neither ends nor begins with your own memory. If you count on your family's memory, you might get a bit further. Your family will tell you that it all began with the first generation to live in freedom, generally somewhere in the South. That happened around 1865. If you probe a bit further, you might then begin to get a sense of the cycles of change that took place before and after 1865. Now you're thinking in terms of generations, and that adds the perspective. The year 1865 is a benchmark from which to count backward for the years of enslavement and forward for the years of freedom. Using twenty years as one generation, we are now in the seventh generation of freedom since 1865. Counting from 1865 back to the initial year of arrival in British North America, generally recorded as 1619, our ancestors lived in twelve generations of slavery. African Americans in the United States have spent more years in slavery than in freedom! Furthermore, depending on the generational cycle in your own family, the generations to live in freedom might even be fewer. Each family's generational cycle is unique, because a generation is equal to the amount of time between the birth of a parent and the birth of their children. For my paternal line, my generation is the third to live in freedom. My family had long generational cycles. My paternal grandfather was born near the end of slavery.

If you are of African American ancestry, you should know that most of your ancestors had arrived in the United States by the year 1790. Your American ancestry runs deep—in fact, deeper than that of the majority of Americans. In a sense, you are more "American" than most Americans. On the other hand, many African Americans view our past as a very brief one. There was slavery and nothing more—just as if the

years of slavery were collapsed into an unknown vacuum. Yet, in no small sense did your African ancestors shape America—and not just in terms of their stolen labor. Think in larger terms—of the cultural impact of an African presence in early America, particularly in the South, where Africans frequently outnumbered Europeans. This cultural impact is so intertwined with what we know of southern culture—its beliefs, customs, food, mannerisms, language, and religion. Few of us think in these terms, but when you embark on doing your family's genealogy, your vision expands to a deeper understanding of the presence of Africans in America.

If you still haven't been able to find the words to describe those first African ancestors, then open your mind to a new experience. Any one of your African ancestors was probably a male between ten and twenty-five. He certainly belonged to an ethnic group, and he probably had some identifying marks which Europeans called "marks of his nation." His home of origin was somewhere between present-day Senegal all the way down to Angola and around to Mozambique and Madagascar, from the Atlantic Ocean all the way inland for at least two hundred and sometimes more miles. He spoke a language; he came from a village; he had a large kin group called a clan; he had probably been initiated into his society of peers, and he had a name that described what clan he belonged to, what characteristics he was expected to fulfill in his adult life, often the time of day or the day of the week on which he was born, and even special names that were given to him by a grandparent. He came with a knowledge of his family's genealogy, of farming and crop production, cloth production, trading, fishing, and all the other skills that allow people to survive. Most important of all, he brought with him the ability to survive and adapt and reinvent himself through countless generations up to the generation to which you belong. In imagining your first African ancestor to arrive in the United States, think of him as an extension of a large clan whose fragments or lines probably still exist somewhere in that vast region called West and South Central Africa. Here in America, he established a new clan, and your task as a family historian and genealogist is to rediscover the members of that clan.

IS THERE GENERATIONAL CONTINUITY IN YOUR FAMILY?

The first Africans in this country began to form families right away. But no one knows who the first African American family was, nor is it really known who the first African to be born on American oil was. If we accept 1619 as the first arrival of Africans on the shores of what was to become the United States, then approximately 375 years have passed and that constitutes roughly nineteen generations. If you had ancestors who arrived from the Caribbean rather than directly from Africa—also a good possibility—then the total number of generations from the point of first arrival would be greater than nineteen. Africans had also come to the Americas with the Spanish and settled in St. Augustine, Florida, as early as 1545.

Few African Americans have written genealogies that span all nineteen generations, but consider the case of Agnes Cane Callum, who was able to trace her lineage back to the union of Eleanor Butler, an Irish indentured servant, and a slave called Negro Charles, born in the year 1681 in Maryland. The Quander family traces its lineage back to the 1684 union of Henry Quando and Margaret Pugg, recently freed by one Henry Adams in Charles County, Maryland. It can be done, and that is where your job comes in. To imagine that you will be able to document that many generations is probably difficult, but with ever-increasing numbers of African American genealogists, consider the possibility very real.

But what about generational continuity over time? Do you know how your surname was acquired, what naming patterns exist in your family, which individuals had a special impact on the family for several generations, what special gifts are passed on from one generation to the next, what migration paths were taken, where most of your ancestors are buried, what relationships they had with their slave owners, or even the name of the port where they arrived? Establishing generational continuity begins with taking a deep look at your family's past followed by naming those patterns that make your family distinct.

Most of our ancestors did not tell their stories—at least in written form. They passed along their stories from one person to the next, from generation to generation by word of mouth. These family stories are often told in the form of jokes, short remembrances, anecdotes, and genealogies that can be recited by a family elder. They are focused on the specifics rather than the broad historical experiences that serve to put everything in context. The family historian's job is to bring the two together—to lend credence to the specifics by placing them in the context of the broad historical

experiences of African Americans. In a sense you are writing into existence a story that has only been felt, told, or even hidden by the waves of silence that can beset a people whose past is filled with more questions than can be answered.

THE AFRICAN AMERICAN
COLLECTIVE MEMORY

*T*roubled silence is a part of the African American collective memory: silence about specific events, silence about ancestry, silence about the sequence of events, and even selective "dis-remembering" of ancestry. However, you can't say it with silence. William Still knew this when he chronicled the stories of runaway slaves, and so did many of his contemporaries who tried to tell their personal stories of enslavement, escapes to freedom, and subsequent redemption based on wonderment about their own survival. Many felt that they had lived for only one reason—to tell their stories of survival, often relying on a religious interpretation rather than on their own individual wile and wit.

In large part, the African American collective memory often starts with the first generation to live in freedom. Yet, from the signing of the Emancipation Proclamation to the present represents only six-and-a-half generations—a very small percentage of the minimum number of family generations that could have lived from the time of arrival to the present. Very few families have knowledge of the generations that lived in "slavery times." The burial of this part of our past was almost willfully done by our very own ancestors who lived through its most difficult period. The struggle to lend meaning to a doubtful freedom during the post-Reconstruction period did not include honoring those ancestors who suffered the most. The struggle to gain a new respectability based on the desire to be accepted as Americans meant casting off the past—quite literally—for Africans had referred to Europeans as Americans throughout slavery, by definition excluding themselves. Upon emancipation, they too could call themselves "Americans."

The search for your family's collective memory is all about redefining those terms for your ancestors. The recent attempts to redefine the past by African Americans must almost certainly include a redefinition of family memory and our collective memory in the same way that Frederick Douglass felt in his old age when he saw the nation quickly redefining the meaning of the Civil War.

Collective memory tells a people's story in epic form—a story that everyone can repeat and that covers an explanation of major historical experiences. The epic of Sundiata is one example of collective mem-

ory, for it tells the story of the Mande people of Mali. Every Mande person knows the epic and the genealogy of the founding family of Old Mali. Similarly, every African ethnic group has stories of origin that tell the story of their clan, village, or group over long periods of time. These stories generally include an explanation about the founding family (either mythical or real) and its genealogy with which every member of the clan or village can identify through his or her own kinship.

African Americans do not have one epic story to explain their capture from Africa, their enslavement and subsequent freedom in the Americas. Nor do many of us have family stories that tell the story of our ancestors in epic form. What we have are bits and pieces of stories or many individual stories based on individual achievements. *Roots* came closest to telling this story in epic form, for *Roots* was the story of nearly every African American family. Kunta Kinte was a symbol of the first African and his exploits, trials, tribulations, and victories in the United States. In a major way, *Roots* is our epic story. Yet your family has its own epic story waiting to be told. It just takes a storyteller and a story writer. Perhaps that person is you.

WHO NEEDS FAMILY MEMORY?

We all need "memory of kin," as Mary Helen Washington termed it. Family memory makes us who we are. In *Pride of Family*, Carole Ione discovered that the age-old conflict between mother and daughter had repeated itself over at least three generations of female ancestors and had determined in large part who and what she became. An even more shocking discovery awaited her, however. The influence of one woman, her great-aunt's mother, in large part determined the relationship between her mother, grandmother, and herself. Carole Ione needed family memory to resolve her own struggle to answer the question "Who am I?"

Family memory acts as a behavioral check on many of our actions. If you've ever heard someone say "the Sutwells don't do that" or "we don't do that," then you know exactly what I mean. Even if the whole collective ancestry is not called upon, the memory of one person can act as a tug on one's conscience to the point that trouble is avoided.

Family memory can resolve more than personal questions of identity. It can also bring forth spiritual connections to ancestors whose talents repeat themselves from one generation to the next, as in the case of families of preachers and orators. My own curiosity about my "family" started through a ritual that many people from my generation experienced—the annual trek down South. Having been just a small child of six when we migrated to Chicago, these annual trips were like a new discovery each summer. Everybody seemed to be related, and there were countless visits on front porches with people who were my relatives. Going to church was mandatory, and it was there that I gained an intuitive sense of the African American cultural heritage.

Certain faces fascinated me more than others and, of course, they were faces of polar opposites. My maternal great-grandmother Amealie's character is still felt in my mother's memories of growing up in her household. I remember seeing my maternal grandfather, Kwessie, only once, but I can see his smooth dark face in all of his relatives who are still living. My paternal grandfather Ezra's picture hangs on my living room wall. He was a very handsome man whose strawberry patch and Raleigh tobacco tins are still remembered. His wife, Callie, like most of the women in my father's line, is more remote (my father was very young when she died). But as I look at her photo and its frame stamped with the famous Tuskegee instructor/photographer's name, A. H. Polk, I feel proud that she and my grandfather had established the connection to Tuskegee as so many South Alabama folks had done at the turn of the century. Three of their sons joined other relatives who had gone to Tuskegee when it was a training school.

In my later life, I began to really wonder about all this happiness I had experienced as a child, for it seemed almost totally contradictory to the historical experiences of African Americans. Who then were my people, I wondered. The smiles and graciousness of my cousin, Queen Esther, the patience that my Aunt Neicy showed, the wisdom with which my Aunt Nig's husband, Uncle Oliver, seemingly spoke, the mere wackiness of Aunt Nig herself—all of these people I began to wonder about. They never talked about the horrors of the South. Indeed, it wasn't until we moved North that I learned about separate riding cars on which we had to board once leaving Nashville—the L & N line became segregated at Nashville going South. Now I know something about the generation that produced me. But I want to know more and more about each previous generation. Who were these people whose genes have made me, in part, what I am today? We all need family memory.

Family memory is immortalized by the information that we pass on to our children about their ancestors. Think of the stories that you could tell about your ancestors or even about this generation: How a relative overcame an obstacle in life, how we talk about our kin, what we say and don't say are all pieces of information that shape a child's memory and development. Even family faces form part of our memory, for children can read character too. How many of us can pass on a coherent story that tells of the trials, tribulations, and triumphs of our ancestors who "carried us over"?

CONFRONTING HISTORY: KEEPING FAMILY MEMORY ALIVE

Americans tend to have short memories, because we live in a society that has learned to produce artificial change. Nothing from the past matters much. All that is important is new. But African Americans experience the hidden weight of history every day in a society that denies the importance of the past but uses it to shape its own vision. But that is history written large. Personal history, that memory of kin and their experiences, the kind that helps each generation to survive, is another matter.

African Americans need strong family memory, indeed, to confront history. The African American family is so poorly understood that any documented continuity over generations is still surprising to many people. Perhaps it is even surprising to African Americans too, so misunderstood is our past. However, the more we tell our own stories, the more we will understand that our ancestors were not faceless, anonymous people. Indeed, their struggles were heroic ones, for out of defeat they were able to build a place for themselves and survive.

If genealogy is about time, place, and perspective, for African Americans we can add one more item to this list—resolution. Many of our ancestors left the only home they knew because of the unresolved tension between the past (slavery) and the situation in which they found themselves (servitude). In the process, they left behind a history and a place. When I was very young, my neighbor used to say, "Child, when I left Hattiesburg, Mississippi, I never intended to go back." Yet Mrs. Keyes was big on kin. So too were the relatives of Dorothy Spruill Redford, author of *Somerset Homecoming*, one of the most poignant books written about African American genealogy. Redford's relatives used to refer to their origins as from somewhere "over the river," but she never knew exactly where that was, nor did anybody ever explain. One of her biggest puzzles was to figure out why the family's favorite saying was "Praise the bridge that carried you over." In a sense, her family memory emphasized not the place but the people. They unwittingly separated themselves from their ancestors while at the same time honoring them. For many of us, confronting the past means rebuilding those bridges. Again, it's an example of the tension between the place and the people, a view of the past that is without geography. It's like having a history without landmarks. Redford vividly described her feelings when she finally found the place.

There on a lonely wooden sign no more than a foot high, were printed the words "Site of Slave Quarters." No buildings. No rubble. No remains. Just a sign and an open field. In one hand, I held the names of almost one hundred and fifty slaves I knew belonged to the Collinses. In the other I held a pamphlet that said three hundred slaves once worked on this plantation. And this was their legacy—a rotting sign.

The genealogical pursuit is therefore all about reclaiming the past and rewriting the experiences of our ancestors, both free and enslaved. For African Americans, at least, it is all about rebuilding a lost collective memory. What better resolution could that be?

In Pursuit of Your Family's Past

*B*ecause our ancestors began forming new families from their time of arrival on the shores of the United States, your task is to reconstruct family linkages and ties as completely as possible using the tools and examples provided in this book. You may think that few if any records exist on African Americans. Many beginners have a secret fear that they will not be able to go back very far. They cannot imagine the kinds of records that were kept on their ancestors during slavery. Once you begin, those worries will go away, and you will be asking not whether records exist, but rather how you can spend some extra time on your vacation searching for more. People from all walks of life are doing family history research, and they are succeeding. Imagine documenting some of your family lines back to the seventeenth century, as Agnes Cane Collum did!

This note of optimism has to be taken in perspective, however. You should not expect

to document the ethnic groups to which your African ancestors belonged. Nor should you expect to identify villages, clan names, or any of the other specifics commonly read about in Euro-American genealogy. That is all but impossible for African Americans. You might come as close as identifying a likely port of arrival, but given the nature of the slave trade, you will find that the majority of our ancestors arrived at only a few ports in the Americas. Nor should you expect to document every family line in complete detail during the period of slavery. If, however, you are very skillful and persistent, you can locate where your ancestors lived, how they lived, who they were related to, and what probably happened to them from one generation to the next.

You should expect to find wonderful old people who will now tell all the family secrets—secrets that seem unimportant in this age, but were, nevertheless, guarded in the bosom for so many years. You will also find in-laws who know more about some of your family members than those who lived with the same individuals all of their lives. You will find sad stories, funny characters that you never knew about before, and proud people who despite their years of uncompensated toil managed to live to pass along enough of the story for you to sort out.

Frequently, you will find exemplary stories of struggle and triumph that deserve to be written about separately from your own family story. The story of the Snow Hill, Alabama school started as a family research project, but when the researcher found so much rich material, he decided to write a full-length book. Black family memoirs are increasingly being published because they tell a story that is unfamiliar to many. Often, you will find trunks of old photos, mementos, and documents that have been lovingly preserved by a thoughtful older relative. These surviving documents may indeed form the basis of your own book!

On the downside, you will frequently find that relatives have been negligent in caring for family papers, cemetery markers, and other evidence that might be helpful to you. So much of African American history has been lost in this way. Lack of evidence and documentation has often led to a faulty understanding of the African American past by historians, regardless of their ethnic identity. If you learn nothing else in your explorations, hopefully you will learn how important it is to preserve evidence of the past.

Wherever you begin and end, know that you are in good company. There are stories to be told and ancestors to record because they could not record their own history. When they were finally able to freely sign their names, it was with the mark *X*. When they spoke to each other, it was with the same expression of hope and despair with which you now speak. In the end, what they said to each other and what they said about their condition will have to rest in peace with them. But you can always tell their story by telling what happened to them. If you are a beginning genealogist and family historian, that honor has been bequeathed to you. May this book serve you and your ancestors well.

This book is also for anyone who wants to know how to reconstruct the experiences of African Americans as they lived through slavery and the first century of freedom. It is also for the curious. Indeed, there is something in here for everyone and anyone who needs to know how to research African Americans as individuals and within family groups. It will show you how to reconstruct the past using available records. It will help you to find these records, some of which lie in obscure places that you may not have even thought about. It will help you to imaginatively explore the experiences of your ancestors. May this book serve everyone well.

WHAT DO I NEED TO DO NOW?

- Let your feelings about your family emerge.
- Examine the emotional ties between family members.
- Answer these questions: Why do I want to do this? How important is it to me and my family?
- Let your true feelings about the past emerge.
- Think about how the knowledge you are about to uncover will help you and your family members.
- Begin to read some of the African American memoirs and family stories listed in the bibliography. Also read a standard history of African Americans in the United States.

Chapter 2

BEGINNING YOUR
GENEALOGICAL PURSUIT

Defining Family Traditions

We will die with our cheeks puffed up.

ACHOLI PROVERB

Before You Begin . . .

*T*here are a couple of good habits that you need to acquire starting right now. One of the first things that you need to do is to start writing down what you know about yourself, your parents, your siblings, and your grandparents. Character descriptions might help, but what is more important is to guess at what you know about the family. A second thing is to take notes and write questions as you read along. Eventually, you will answer your own questions, or this book will help you to find the answers. We begin with an overall view of the transformational process that genealogy can be by looking at the phases that your project will go through.

The Phases of Research in African American Genealogy

*T*hese phases roughly correspond to what you are likely to encounter in your research as you proceed from what you know in the present to the past. Some researchers will spend more time on one phase than on others. It merely depends on the information and records that you find in the possession of various family members at the beginning. If you remember that you must attempt to locate and document your ancestors in all known record sources for each period of time, then it will be difficult for you to go astray! Note that the sequence you follow is time; therefore, these phases will frequently overlap with each other, as will the records.

Documenting the Contemporary Family

During this phase, your activities will be focused on collecting documentation and oral histories from family members. At the same time, you will collect other kinds of documentation in the form of written records and memorabilia that will be helpful in sorting through the past. Your activities and record search will basically be confined to the present—your and your parents' generation.

Collecting Evidence from Vital Records

Here you are still in the twentieth century because most states did not have universal registration of births, marriages, and deaths until the early twentieth century. Vital records are of utmost importance in genealogy because they provide the basic starting data for your search of all subsequent public records.

Collecting Evidence on the Ancestral Home

Here you have located a place where your ancestors lived for a long period of time, a place which could easily be called the "ancestral home." In this phase, you are collecting information on the local area, whether it is your hometown or a rural place in a county. Focusing in on the ancestral home allows you to identify things like settlement patterns, geographical features, and the institutions that African Americans built in the area. Making an extended visit to the ancestral home can often save you time. If you are unable to visit, you will be involved in an extensive information collection effort by mail, as well as using local genealogical research facilities and the World Wide Web.

Collecting Evidence from Federal Population Censuses

As error filled as censuses are, you will place great reliance on them in locating your ancestors between 1920 and 1870. Census records represent one of the few sources from which you are likely to document every living person for given points in time, namely every ten years since 1790. For African Americans, the most important available censuses are those that were taken between 1870 and 1920. Prior to 1870, enslaved African Americans were enumerated by slave owner, age, and sex, but not by name.

Collecting Evidence from the Civil War and Reconstruction Periods

Here, your research begins to approach murky waters. It is relatively easy to locate and use the records for the first three phases, but once you begin to approach the period of slavery, you must be prepared to put more effort into locating records. At this point, you begin advanced research.

Collecting Evidence to Identify the Last Slave Owner

If you don't have the name of the last slave owner, there is little that you can do to continue your research. As surprising as it may seem, many African Americans do not know the identity of the last slave owner for any of their ancestral lines. Most automatically assume that they are carrying that person's surname, but this assumption is often incorrect. Expect to spend a considerable amount of time "muddling" through records for this period if you do not have the last owner's name. For those with free ancestry, this point may be reached much later on in your research than for those with slave ancestry. Here, the goal would be to identify the circumstances under which your ancestors gained their freedom.

Slave Genealogy, or Researching the Last Slave Owner

Once you do find the last owner, you will then spend a considerable amount of time researching slave owners, because they frequently left records that name slaves and the kin relationships between them. You should know, however, that not all slaves will be named in records. In addition, not all slave owners left records, or they may have been lost, or they may still be in the possession of descendants. No one can tell you what the chances are of finding your own ancestors named in such records. One general rule is that wealthy literate planters were more likely to have left such records than poor illiterate slave owners. When you reach this phase, you frequently hope that your ancestors were owned by the former rather than the latter, if for no other reason than the chances of finding documentation on your ancestors. In this phase, it is important to point out that you are researching what your ancestors' owners did with or to them and, in some cases, what your ancestors tried to do themselves.

Tracing Your Ancestors over Time as Slaves

You might find documentation on your ancestors during the last phases of slavery. But what about tracing your ancestors over time during slavery? Because most of our ancestors had arrived in the United States by the time of the Revolutionary War, you will be tracing multiple lines of slave owners. But slave owners, whether planters or farmers, were fairly uniform and predictable. They bought and sold slaves and land; they migrated to new lands; they were involved in a network of kinship and business among slave-owning families within the same area and across the whole South. Moreover, they were frequently forced to make an accounting of their most valued "property." It is frequently said with some irony that the African American researcher will probably learn more about the family that owned his ancestors than about his ancestors themselves. In terms of locating documentation, this is true. Therefore, African American genealogy often focuses more on merely revealing and confronting the past rather than documenting the past in a strict genealogical sense.

Finding the First Africans

If you have been able to do a good job in the previous phases of your research, at some point you may find some of the first Africans in your lineages. From my observations, those who have conducted research on their ancestors in Maryland and Virginia have been most successful. This does not mean, however, that if you are researching other states you will not be able to locate your first African ancestors. Finally, if you do locate the first Africans, it is unlikely that you will be able to go any further unless you have found a unique record that provides specifics on their place of origin.

EVERYBODY HAS A STORY: PROBING YOUR FAMILY'S COLLECTIVE MEMORY

W. C. Handy*

. . . William Wise Handy, my grandfather, a Methodist minister after emancipation, became the first colored man to own property there. He built the first colored church in Florence and several others in Lauderdale County. He and his two brothers had run away from their masters in Princess Anne, Maryland, taking advantage of the "underground railroad." One escaped to Canada, the other to some portion of the East. But my grandfather was overtaken and sold into Alabama where, still urged by the desire for freedom, he started an insurrection for escape, and was shot but not killed. Unknown to his masters, he acquired a liberal education and became an honored and respected citizen of Florence. . . . Grandfather's son, Hanson, was another fearless man, who would not let his overseers or his masters whip him. They admired this gameness, but they sold him into Arkansas, just as one would get rid of an unruly mule. He was never heard of again. My own father used to cry in church

*From *Father of the Blues*

whenever anyone raised the familiar spiritual, "March Along, I'll See You on the Judgment Day." Once, quite innocently, I asked him the reason for these tears. He answered, "That is what the slaves sang when the white folks sold Brother Hanson away."

* * *

Imagine being able to tell a story like this to your children and grandchildren. You might think that you can't because you have no heroic ancestors. However, the story that the sum of their experiences tells is the everyday heroism of survival. Having a story like Handy's is sometimes a matter of simply talking to your older relatives. But first, before you talk with them, you start with yourself by writing a short biography that includes information on your family and ancestry. Some composite examples collected from my students follow.

James Overstreet

My name is James Overstreet. I was born on August 20, 1940, in Itta Bena, Mississippi. I have two brothers and three sisters. My parents are Arthur and Maggie Overstreet. When I was five years old, we moved to Chicago, but we always went back to Itta Bena for the summer. We stayed with our Aunt Etta and her husband, Uncle John. They had a farm outside of Itta Bena in an area called Mills Creek. This is where my mother was born. My father was born near Mills Creek in a place called Wyatt, and he swore that he would never go back there. Most of his people have moved away, but his first cousin still lives there. I have never been there, but I suppose it looks like Mills Creek. It's hard to tell where Mills Creek begins and ends because all I know are the dirt roads that seem to lead to nowhere. Along these roads were houses where some of our relatives lived.

Whenever we visited, they always asked about my parents. The only time that I could get a feel for how many people lived in the area was when we went to church on Sunday. I used to wonder where all of these people came from. On Saturdays we would go into town to buy things, and Aunt Etta would always make a point of stopping at the house of a man named Champion. I was too bored to pay attention to what they were talking about; it seemed that they talked most about people who had died a long time ago. As time went by, we stopped going to Mills Creek, but my mother still goes to see about Aunt Etta who is now in a nursing home.

* * *

Fred H. Digsby

I was born in 1930, the only child of Samuel and Elizabeth G. Digsby in New York. My real name is Frederick Heartley, but I never liked such a stuffy name. Everyone knows me as Fred, and I never disclose what the H. stands for. My mother and father met in New York in the 1920s. She was from Atlanta, but she was born near Columbus, Georgia. My father was from Ohio. I've never been to either of these places, and my parents never really talked about where they came from. I do remember that when one of my mother's relatives died, there was a big mess over some land. When my father died, he left all of these papers and old letters, but I haven't gone through them yet. It always seemed to be a mystery to me that my father communicated with his relatives, but they never came to visit us. One time, a man who looked white came to see my father. They talked for a long time, but my mother always carried me upstairs when strangers came, and that was that!

I met someone last year who resembled my mother so much; as it turned out, this woman had the same maiden name as my mother's, and she came from Atlanta too! She said that no one else in New York could have that name without being related. I took her number, but I haven't called her yet. This was shortly before my mother died, but when I told her about my encounter with the lady, she just passed it off. When my father died, I realized that I was alone. I couldn't even provide all the information needed for their death certificates! I have two sons and a daughter, and I would like to be reunited with my relatives so that my children will know where they came from.

* * *

Lavinia Woods

What I know about my family's history is very little. My mother's people came from North Carolina; my father's people came from Louisiana. I knew all four of my grandparents; they were very talkative, and I can tell you nearly every story that they told me, if you had the time to listen. These stories always made them seem like very important people. No matter what the adversity they faced, they always came out on top by using their wits. I wish that I had the same drive they seemed to have had all of their lives.

Even though I have all the things left by my grandparents, I don't have many documents. There are quite a few photographs, but I can't identify most of the people in them. My great aunt in Durham has the family Bible, but she says that I have to come there to use it. She keeps telling me to come talk with her, and now that I'm doing my family's genealogy, I plan to visit her next summer. She says that all of her people are Indian, but I can't see that. They just looked mixed. As for my father's side, it is believed that some of his people came from Haiti. How this could have happened is beyond me; I don't speak French, and I can't ever imagine having to go there just to do research.

* * *

These stories contain many leads—far more than can be imagined by Mr. Overstreet, Mr. Digsby, and Mrs. Woods at the beginning. They are fairly typical ones for beginning genealogists. They represent, in varying degrees, disjointed perspectives on the past because at some point, a disjuncture in family communication occurred where an ancestor decided to hide the past or let the tradition die with them. Sometimes, intergenerational communication dies a quiet, slow death.

Now that you see how people actually begin this search, perhaps you can write a short version of your family's story. Though it should include just what you know now, at the end, identify those things that are unknown or that you want to know more about. Start with your own place of birth, identify your siblings, parents, and grandparents. Then begin to describe your larger family, family origins, and migration patterns. Speculate on who knows most about the family and why. As your story begins to

unfold, you will become aware of how much or how little you know. This lays the basis for your next step.

TAKING A FAMILY CENSUS

Take an informal census of all of your relatives in the city where you now live. Your informal census will list each family (parents, children, and other relatives who live in the same house), their address, telephone number, and the oldest living relatives. Also include their relationship to you or to your parents. Next, take a census of your relatives who live in the place where your people migrated from. Again, list only the essential information. Continue your census taking until you've covered all of the places where your relatives now reside. If you have an address directory from your last family reunion, it will come in handy, and your task will be a lot easier.

The next step involves visualizing where they live in the United States. What may emerge is a map with dots in one or two southern states and many dots in cities throughout the North and West. No matter the pattern, you'll find that your family is dispersed all over the country. If you had taken the same census fifty or one hundred years ago, the pattern would have been entirely different. What has happened is that your ancestors migrated from the South to the North and then began to migrate within the North.

Information from this census will prepare you for the next step, interviewing key relatives to learn more about the family. From this census, you will identify key members of the family to interview.

DISREMEMBERED ANCESTORS: DOES YOUR FAMILY HAVE A LONG MEMORY?

When I look back on nearly all the stories that genealogists have told me, very few that had been passed down from slavery times were coherent. Many had bits and pieces that were fascinating and enticing and often unverifiable. Several told of ancestors who used words and expressions from African languages. Some told of vague escapes from slavery—one involved using the shell of a large tortoise. One student was trying to document a polygamous slave owner who had three sets of African American families. One beginner was trying to prove ancestral connections to a presidential family so that she could qualify for a scholarship from an endowment established for all descendants of the president who could prove an ancestral connection. All snatches, but no coherent stories.

When I interviewed my mother's cousin, she said to me, "Child, pretty soon they won't even be calling it slavery." Then when I turned to one of the slave narratives done by the WPA between 1934 and 1938, I found this quote from a man named Cato who had been a slave in Wilcox County, Alabama: "Everything I tells you am the truth, but they's plenty I can't tell you." And Cato wasn't the only one who expressed this feeling. That last generation of slaves who were born long enough ago to tell the story lived through the 1930s. It is therefore likely that at least one of your slave ancestors lived only sixty years ago. If that is the case, it is also quite possible that your parents or grandparents knew that person and even talked with him or her. Ask yourself this question: Does my family have a long memory?

That many African American families have lost this long memory—at least in terms of a coherent family oral tradition—has a lot to do with the discontinuity that besets families who migrate. The storytellers were there, but often no one was listening. On the other hand, it also has a lot to do with how the first generation to live in freedom perceived the experience of slavery once free. From a careful reading of the WPA slave narratives, many of our ancestors probably decided that it was best to let sleeping dogs lie, particularly when they were still in your yard. In short, they perceived correctly that freedom brought no significant transformation of the terms on which they lived—they had freedom of personhood and community, but their labor was still being stolen. Thus the tradition of family secrecy established during slavery continued through freedom. In effect, some of our ancestors and their stories were simply *disremembered*.

HOW DEEP IS THE FAMILY'S MEMORY? CREATING YOUR FIRST ANCESTRAL CHARTS

Information about your family can accumulate quickly, and if you did the informal family census, you've already begun to accumulate papers. There are many organizing tools that are marketed commercially, everything from software programs like Family Treemaker to charts that you fill out with a pen. In this section, we will talk about three essential charts that you will use throughout your project: the five generations chart, the descendants chart, and the family group sheet. Illustrations of these charts appear on the following pages. Examine these charts and simply copy the form to use as you read this chapter. You can also purchase similar charts, but it might be a good idea to begin to practice frugality in your project. Note that the family group sheet could have been used for your informal family census, but the purpose of that exercise was to help you identify where your relatives now live and who in the family you will interview later.

Your disremembered ancestors will quickly appear on your five generations chart in the form of a blank space. This simple chart is often called a "pedigree chart," but the word *pedigree* is distasteful to many people. In particular, its association with the idea of breeding animals or purity of bloodlines does not often set well with African Americans. The chart is really a generations chart, and its function is to identify individuals in your direct lineage.

Your First Chart: The Five Generations Chart

Examine the chart that I compiled based on simply talking with my parents, my cousin Cleve Parmer, and a few family documents. Now, try to fill in family information on your own chart. Depending on your age, you may want to consult with several relatives. This will help you to begin to get a sense of how much information your relatives know about their ancestry. Note that information is filled in on yourself first, and then you work backward to your parents, grandparents, and so on. Also note that the males will always be on the top line of each branch and the females will be on the bottom lines. In cases of multiple marriages or liaisons where children were produced, simply add a branch. My five generations chart has been simplified for instructional purposes.

The generations chart is named by the number of generations it shows. A five generations chart starts with your generation and covers the four generations before you. My chart indicates that my parents and cousin, Cleve, remembered our grandparents and a few great-grandparents, but not all of them. On my paternal line, it is difficult to believe that although my father and grandfather shared the same living space for nearly forty years, my father could not readily recall his paternal grandmother's maiden name, and things got even more remote with his paternal grandfather! My father readily recalled Grandma Cindy because she was such a dominant force in the local community, and she died when he was eighteen—late enough for him to have a strong memory. On the other hand, my mother could name all of her ancestors for at least three generations on the maternal line using her memory alone! (She had a talkative grandmother.) She knew little about her father's people—partly because her parents were never married, and she chose never to develop a relationship with her father. Therefore, those blank spaces represent silences caused either through lost information or selective *disremembering* of certain ancestors. To fill out your own Five Generations Chart turn to page 446.

Your Second Chart: A Descendants Chart

Another chart that will help you to record your ancestry is the descendants chart. Again, this is a chart you can create yourself. This chart simply lists all of the individuals who share common ancestry or who are

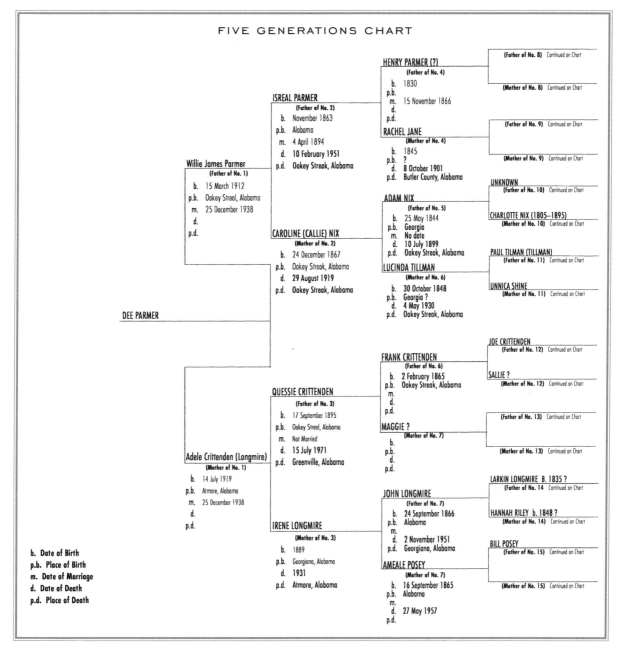

FIVE GENERATIONS CHART

		HENRY PARMER (?)	(Father of No. 8) Continued on Chart
		(Father of No. 4)	
		b. 1830	(Mother of No. 8) Continued on Chart
	ISREAL PARMER	p.b.	
	(Father of No. 2)	m. 15 November 1866	
	b. November 1863	d.	
	p.b. Alabama	p.d.	(Father of No. 9) Continued on Chart
	m. 4 April 1894	RACHEL JANE	
	d. 10 February 1951	(Mother of No. 4)	
	p.d. Oakey Streak, Alabama	b. 1845	(Mother of No. 9) Continued on Chart
Willie James Parmer		p.b. ?	
(Father of No. 1)		d. 8 October 1901	UNKNOWN
b. 15 March 1912		p.d. Butler County, Alabama	(Father of No. 10) Continued on Chart
p.b. Oakey Streal, Alabama		ADAM NIX	CHARLOTTE NIX (1805–1895)
m. 25 December 1938		(Father of No. 5)	(Mother of No. 10) Continued on Chart
d.		b. 25 May 1844	
p.d.	CAROLINE (CALLIE) NIX	p.b. Georgia	
	(Mother of No. 2)	m. No date	PAUL TILMAN (TILLMAN)
	b. 24 December 1867	d. 10 July 1899	(Father of No. 11) Continued on Chart
	p.b. Oakey Streak, Alabama	p.d. Oakey Streak, Alabama	
	d. 29 August 1919	LUCINDA TILLMAN	UNNICA SHINE
	p.d. Oakey Streak, Alabama	(Mother of No. 6)	(Mother of No. 11) Continued on Chart
		b. 30 October 1848	
		p.b. Georgia ?	
DEE PARMER		d. 4 May 1930	
		p.d. Oakey Streak, Alabama	
			JOE CRITTENDEN
			(Father of No. 12) Continued on Chart
		FRANK CRITTENDEN	
		(Father of No. 6)	SALLIE ?
		b. 2 February 1865	(Mother of No. 12) Continued on Chart
	QUESSIE CRITTENDEN	p.b. Oakey Streak, Alabama	
	(Father of No. 3)	m.	
	b. 17 September 1895	d.	
	p.b. Oakey Streal, Alabama	p.d.	(Father of No. 13) Continued on Chart
	m. Not Married	MAGGIE ?	
	d. 15 July 1971	(Mother of No. 7)	(Mother of No. 13) Continued on Chart
	p.d. Greenville, Alabama	b.	
Adele Crittenden (Longmire)		p.b.	
(Mother of No. 1)		d.	
b. 14 July 1919		p.d.	LARKIN LONGMIRE B. 1835 ?
p.b. Atmore, Alabama			(Father of No. 14 Continued on Chart
m. 25 December 1938		JOHN LONGMIRE	
d.		(Father of No. 7)	HANNAH RILEY b. 1848 ?
p.d.	IRENE LONGMIRE	b. 24 September 1866	(Mother of No. 14) Continued on Chart
	(Mother of No. 3)	p.b. Alabama	
	b. 1889	m.	BILL POSEY
	p.b. Georgiana, Alabama	d. 2 November 1951	(Father of No. 15) Continued on Chart
	d. 1931	p.d. Georgiana, Alabama	
	p.d. Atmore, Alabama	AMEALE POSEY	
		(Mother of No. 7)	(Mother of No. 15) Continued on Chart
		b. 16 September 1865	
		p.b. Alabama	
		m.	
		d. 27 May 1957	
		p.d.	

b. Date of Birth
p.b. Place of Birth
m. Date of Marriage
d. Date of Death
p.d. Place of Death

descended from one couple on your generations chart. This type of chart is especially helpful when interviews are being conducted. When I started research on my father's maternal line, I found information in two books written by a descendant of the slave owner's family. This helped me to trace the line back to a slave woman named Susan who lived in Franklin County, North Carolina. The charts below immediately show what information is missing as well as the research tasks that awaited me. Note the recurrence of names. The reason that I labeled the chart "known descendants" accounts for the possibility that during slavery, other kin were not named in the documents used to trace this line.

Now it's your turn to create a similar chart. Start with a couple on your five generations chart. Working down or in descending order, list first the children of this couple. Then next to each child, list his or her spouse. Then list their children and so on until you get to your generation. You can run out of space very quickly, especially for big families. As you work on this chart, you will begin to get a sense of how generations fall in your family, and certain patterns will emerge, such as name-sharing. In addition, you will begin to see which living individuals

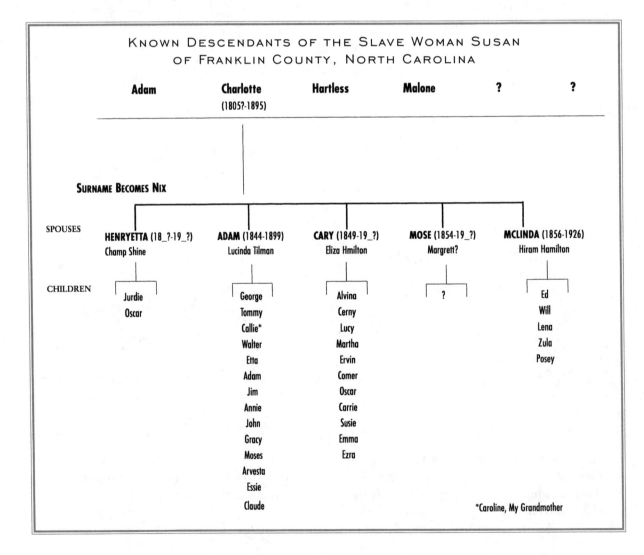

KNOWN DESCENDANTS OF THE SLAVE WOMAN SUSAN
OF FRANKLIN COUNTY, NORTH CAROLINA

Adam	Charlotte (1805?-1895)	Hartless	Malone	?	?

SURNAME BECOMES NIX

	SPOUSES	HENRYETTA (18_?-19_?) Champ Shine	ADAM (1844-1899) Lucinda Tilman	CARY (1849-19_?) Eliza Hmilton	MOSE (1854-19_?) Margrett?	MCLINDA (1856-1926) Hiram Hamilton
CHILDREN		Jurdie	George	Alvina	?	Ed
		Oscar	Tommy	Cerny		Will
			Callie*	Lucy		Lena
			Walter	Martha		Zula
			Etta	Ervin		Posey
			Adam	Comer		
			Jim	Oscar		
			Annie	Carrie		
			John	Susie		
			Gracy	Emma		
			Moses	Ezra		
			Arvesta			
			Essie			
			Claude			

*Caroline, My Grandmother

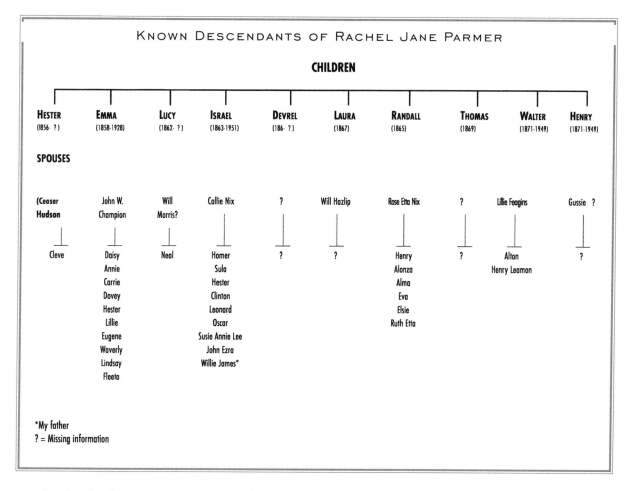

KNOWN DESCENDANTS OF RACHEL JANE PARMER

CHILDREN

HESTER (1856- ?)	EMMA (1858-1928)	LUCY (1862- ?)	ISRAEL (1863-1951)	DEVREL (186- ?)	LAURA (1867)	RANDALL (1865)	THOMAS (1869)	WALTER (1871-1949)	HENRY (1871-1949)

SPOUSES

(Ceasar Hudson	John W. Champion	Will Morris?	Callie Nix	?	Will Hazlip	Rose Etta Nix	?	Lillie Feagins	Gussie ?
Cleve	Daisy	Neal	Homer	?	?	Henry	?	Alton	?
	Annie		Sula			Alonza		Henry Leamon	
	Carrie		Hester			Alma			
	Dovey		Clinton			Eva			
	Hester		Leonard			Elsie			
	Lillie		Oscar			Ruth Etta			
	Eugene		Susie Annie Lee						
	Waverly		John Ezra						
	Lindsay		Willie James*						
	Fleeta								

*My father
? = Missing information

in the family occupy a strategic place in terms of the family's knowledge base. If you're having trouble figuring out whom to interview, this chart will show you immediately. For example, if your goal is to find out more about an ancestor who died in the 1930s, select those individuals first who had some contact with this person. Another option is to identify the older children rather than the younger ones. To fill out your own Descendants' Chart turn to page 450.

Your Third Chart: The Family Group Sheet
A third type of chart that will help you is the family group sheet, a form that lists all of the children or "issue" of one couple. Eventually, you should have a family group sheet for every couple named on your generations chart. A blank family group sheet is provided for you to copy. Now is the time to begin compiling your own family group sheets. Start with your own family and then go to your parents, grandparents, and so forth. Fill in the blanks using your own memory as a source of information or from records that you have at home. Later you will obtain the records to complete the information that the chart calls for. To fill out your own Family Group Sheet turn to page 448.

Note that all of the charts you create

The Family Group Sheet

		Town	State

HUSBAND _____

Birth date _____ Place _____

Marriage date _____ Place _____

Death date _____ Place _____

Burial date _____ Place _____

Father _____ Full Maiden Name of Mother _____

Other Wives of the Husband _____

WIFE _____

Birth date _____ Place _____

Marriage date _____ Place _____

Death date _____ Place _____

Burial date _____ Place _____

Father _____ Full Maiden Name of Mother _____

Other Husbands of the Wife _____

CHILDREN List in order of birth	BORN Day/Mo/Yr.	PLACE Town State	DIED Day/Mo/Yr	MARRIAGE (Spouse's Name)

should be considered preliminary or working charts. Each of the three charts is equally important, but in order of priority, you should work on the family group sheet, then fill in the information on the generations chart. The descendants chart is more of a graphic device because it easily summarizes information in descending order on one couple. As your project proceeds, you will be filling in the missing information or correcting information on all of the charts. Therefore, it is a good idea to work in pencil. Once you have all the proof you need for the information required on the charts, you can then enter it on the permanent charts in ink. Believe it or not, these charts, once completed, will represent the totality of your research. The path to completing them, however, can take years. So don't be alarmed that you have many blank spaces. That's why you're doing this project in the first place—to fill in the empty spaces in your family's memory.

STRONG LINES AND WEAK LINES: DECIDING WHAT LINE TO RESEARCH

When you look at your ancestry, there will be strong lines and weak lines of knowledge. Your charts will help you immediately to figure out which ones are strong and which ones are weak in knowledge about ancestry. Don't discount the possibility that the so-called weak knowledge includes disremembered ancestors or people whose identities are known, but whom no one will talk about on your first query.

In addition, the strong lines are those with which you identify the most—generally the set of relatives with whom you lived during your early years. In my case, it was the Parmers, but I later realized that my inexperience would not allow me to pursue this line. Information on the line stopped with my grandparents, and I did not have the skills needed to pursue it any further. I later switched to the Longmires and then to the Nix line. Because few of us are lucky enough to grow up with both sets of relatives around us, we often have to decide which line to start with based on the criteria

of closeness alone. Though I used a trial and error method to try to figure out which line yielded the most information immediately, the time to decide occurs after collecting the family's oral history. Consider the following case as an example.

Four Grandparents: Giles and Gert Sampson, Wilbert and Neicey Rice

All four of your grandparents (maternal and paternal) lived in the same community of Bates, Georgia, until the 1920s, when Giles and Gert Sampson migrated to Cleveland. Wilbert and Neicey Rice remained in Bates until their deaths. Because you were raised in Cleveland with your Sampson grandparents, you feel more attached to that line. Not only do you carry their surname, but you partly grew up in their household. Wilbert and Neicey are more distant—you can remember visiting, but because there were so many grandchildren around, there was never really a special relationship with them. On the other hand, your mother has kept their memories alive by invoking their names nearly every day of the week. She often tells curious stories about your grandfather Wilbert. He was a community leader and stood his ground in Bates. Once he left Bates and didn't return for five years because he refused to be turned away at the polls. It was said that his father was of the same make, but maybe a bit worse. He once tried to lead a mass exodus of people away from Bates, but no one would follow him. Further, he was a barber and continued to cut hair well into his eighties, when he decided that he would retire. He hung up a sign that said "Gone Fishing but Not to Glory."

Which line should you pursue, the Sampsons or the Rices? Actually, since both families came from the same place and since you have immediate access to both families, you should collect information on both sets of grandparents at the beginning. What you should anticipate, indeed, is that both families were probably associated with each other for a long period of time and potentially have a rich memory base from which to draw. When you begin to reach stumbling blocks for one line, that is the time to make a preliminary decision. At this stage, you're following the path of least resistance until you can make a more informed decision. If your family did not come from the same place, it is best to start with the line that produced the most information when you wrote your family story, took the census, and filled in the charts. The rule is that at the beginning, you will tend to follow the closest emotional ties, but beware. Often these family members have the greatest stake in hiding information. As it turned out in the case of the Sampson and Rice families, the Rices proved to have the most information since the Sampsons tended to be a family of migrants to the North, something the researcher did not know until much later.

Not all families are like the Sampsons and the Rices. The problem of family breaks caused by migration from the South affects both northern and southern genealogists but in different ways. Once they were in the North, marriages occurred between people from different states. Those who remained in the South married across county lines. Both the northern and southern researcher have to ask, Where did all of the people go? Some people really did go off and never return. In addition, beginners who live in the North often believe that when their ancestors migrated, everybody else did too.

They typically say, "We don't have any more relatives down there." Southerners will say, "They went off and never came back." It is more likely that the migrating ancestor simply forgot the bridge that carried him over. Moreover, the typical size of a black southern family during the Great Migration of the 1910s was large. Not everyone migrated at the same time, and in general, few people made a completely clean break with the past. Clues abound, but your task is to recognize and follow them as would a good detective.

COLLECT THE FAMILY'S ORAL HISTORY: DID WE REALLY COME FROM GREASYVILLE, AND HOW DID WE GET TO DETROIT, ANYWAY?

After writing your autobiographical statement, taking the census, and completing the charts based on what information you have now, it is time to begin the first serious foray into your family's past. Collecting the family's oral history is not as easy as it appears—for contained within each family member is only a small part of the family's past. Therefore, it is important to identify those family members who are most likely to be able to tell critical parts of your family's history. Those individuals are the oldest living family members, the busybodies, the gossips, the ones who always stay in touch, and even estranged in-laws. They can all tell you about your family. Select from a vast array of kinfolk, and plan to interview anybody who talks and has a memory, even if it isn't easy! Later, narrow the field to those who seem to know the most. One more thing—get some help. This is not a job to do by yourself.

Questions to Ask and Topics to Cover

Listed below is a long series of questions that you want to ask. Read through them and figure out why it is important to ask them—of course not in one sitting, and not as if you were doing a marketing survey. These are, after all, your relatives, and most will be glad to help you, but still you must be sensitive.

Kin Relations and Naming Patterns

Can you tell me the names of your brothers and sisters and where they now live? Parents? Grandparents, etc.?

What about your aunts and uncles? Do you have the same information on them?

Which adult relatives were your favorites while growing up?

Does your name have any special meaning?

What about your brothers and sisters? Did they have nicknames?

Is there anyone in the family who knows more about the family than anyone else?

Is there any special meaning to (state first or given names)?

Who shares the same given names? Why does the name (insert name) reappear generation after generation?

Did grandparents give names to newborns?

Migration Patterns

How did the family come to live here in ____?

Where did they come from? (Name of nearby town, county, or city.)

Who was the first to leave (name of place)?

Do you know when or about what year?

Who followed after them?

How did they get to (name of place)? By train? Wagon?

Did they leave (name of place) under duress or in conflict?

The Ancestral Home

Are many relatives still in (name the place where you came from)?

Do you stay in touch with them?

How much do you know about where you or your people came from?

Who lived in the old house?

Where did other family members live with respect to the house?

Was the house a log cabin or a newer structure?

What names did people in that area use for certain places?

Can you remember any surnames of the families who lived in that area?

Where was the schoolhouse? The church? The meeting hall?

Is that area now overgrown with trees and bushes?

Linkages to Previous Generations

Did you know your grandparents, or great grandparents?

How well do you remember them?

Were you a child (or adult) when they died?

Do you know where they were born?

Where did they live?

Did they farm, own their own land, or rent land from someone?

How close were they to each other?

Do you remember what they looked like?

Who was your favorite and why?

Did they all belong to the same church (name the church)?

Are they buried there?

Did they ever talk about slavery?

Did they ever talk about former slave
owners?

Did anyone like to tell a lot of stories?

Were the stories about family members?

Were any of the stories tell coming from
another place before arriving here?

Institutional Linkages

Did anyone in the family go off to school?

Did they help to found a church, a lodge, or
a school?

Did anyone own property, a business, or
earn extra money other than through
farming?

Did you ever hear talk about anyone in the
Civil War?

Did you ever hear any stories about the Civil
War?

What about World Wars I and II?

Did anyone belong to a club, union, lodge,
or association?

Was anyone active in politics in the local
community?

First Generations of Freedom

Did anyone ever talk about slavery or the
"Surrender"?

Do you remember what was said?

Who did they work for after freedom
(emancipation)?

How did they get land to farm?

Did anyone ever go off and never return?

Did the old people talk about the Ku Klux
Klan or lynching?

Did anyone ever have trouble with the law?

Did anyone change their surname?

Do you know what surname they originally
had?

Did anyone talk about voting?

Did anyone talk about finding lost relatives
after the Civil War?

Did anyone have a profession like preaching
or teaching?

Records

Was there a family Bible? Who kept it?

Do you have a picture of (name individuals)?

Who kept all of the old pictures and papers?

Do you have school certificates for anyone
in the family?

Did anyone ever buy insurance policies?

Do you have old letters written by family
members?

Other Questions

Don't ignore recreation, homecomings,
reunions, colorful local figures, and others
who may not be related to your family. Also
collect parables, "sayings," and other
famous "last words."

Too Many Questions: How Do I Interview People, Anyway?

Follow these simple rules.

- Record your interview even though it
  may intimidate at the beginning. If you
  do telephone interviews, make sure you
  still ask for permission.
- Use a microphone attachment that can
  amplify wavering voices and minimize
  noises from kids running through the
  living room.
- Take notes just in case your recorder is
  not reliable. Interview your relatives
  several times.
- Learn to interview them as if you're
  having a conversation. Don't just take
  the list above and act like you're the bill
  collector.
- Deference is the rule, even if you are
  older than the person being
  interviewed.

- Decide in advance what kind of interview you will have and what information to look for.
- Allow the interviewee to talk about his or her life and experiences. Invite others who want to talk—at least initially.
- Restate answers just to keep the flow going and keep your head on straight. Learn to listen especially to what *they* think is important. But don't forget your own mission!
- If you don't transcribe or rewrite your interviews as soon as you leave someone's house, you'll regret it.
- One final, final rule—give feedback in the form of a thank-you card, a typed version of the interview, and/or continued communication.

DECIPHERING THE FAMILY'S ORAL HISTORY: SLY AND FAMILY UNSTONED

*I*nterviewing family members can take as little time as one month or as much as several years, depending on your own situation and your age. Your age, however, should not be a critical factor if you concede that younger persons might possibly know more about the family than you do. The critical point about this stage of research is that you must understand that it is an ongoing one in which you collect the information, transcribe it, ask further questions, and then compare each person's account because there will be inconsistencies. You will have to evaluate the information based on where the interviewee falls in his family's life cycle (his or her generation) and what you later find out from other family members or in

records. Each person that you interview has a different view or account of the same event, the same period of time, and even growing up in the same household. Those who told you that they don't know anything will be the very ones who tell you about the murders in the community. If we all experienced things in the same way, it would be a pretty dull world.

The interviews represent no more than the collective experiences of your relatives and what they know about the past. They won't know everything in one interview—that's why you give them feedback and ask for another interview or talk. In addition, the words of a person who speaks authoritatively about events that occurred when he or she was a child of five must be compared with the words of a person who was fifteen at the time. Furthermore, eyewitness accounts of an event outweigh those accounts from individuals who, though they lived during the time, did not actually witness the event or were too young to have known its significance. As your search progresses, you will often find yourself interviewing key people again and again, especially those who misled you by their own ignorance, their vague memory, or their intentional deception about specific events. If they say no, you will find several allies in the family who can help you to ferret out information held back for these reasons. The point is that no stone should be left unturned. You have to commit to this; otherwise you will face problems with researching the records.

Examine two of my first attempts at interviewing older relatives. They are transcribed almost verbatim from the tapes. Your first transcriptions should come as close to verbatim as possible. Make note of interruptions, noise levels, who was there, and so forth. If you are uncertain of spellings or if you are unsure that you took a piece of information down correctly, follow it with a question mark. Later you can write a narrative that organizes the information into logical topics. I used topical headings for the Matthews interview when I transcribed it.

Arthur Matthews had been recommended by a relative, who claimed that Con Arthur knew everything that was to be known. Mr. Matthews passed on before I could get a second interview. Note that I called him a cousin, though I had no idea how we were related before the interview. My uncle Clarence had an excellent memory, but I always had trouble moving beyond the informal stage. Family constantly interrupted or the conversation always drifted away from talking about the past. Before reading these transcribed interviews, prepare to note where I missed opportunities to gain information. Compare the information I gained from each interview, and think about how more distant relatives can give

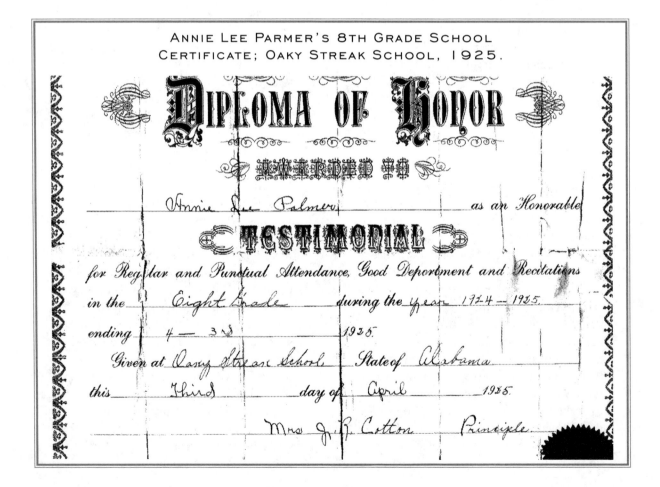

ANNIE LEE PARMER'S 8TH GRADE SCHOOL CERTIFICATE; OAKY STREAK SCHOOL, 1925.

you a better perspective than those who are closer to you.

TWO INTERVIEWS: ARTHUR MATTHEWS AND CLARENCE LONGMIRE

Interview #1: Arthur Matthews, 80 Years Old

September 18, 1991
Niagara Falls, New York
Not Taped

Con Arthur was suggested as a key informant by Cedell Parmer and Bill Matthews, his brother. They both said that his memory is excellent even though he is about eighty years old. That proved to be very correct. In addition to Con Arthur, ____ Shines was present early on. Later Essie Parmer came by. Arthur reminded Mr. Shines that Henrietta Nix Shines was his aunt. [Henrietta married Champ Shine. I had left my charts at home and got the genealogies confused in the course of the interview.]

Arthur Matthews is rather tall and in relatively good shape. He has the deliberative, contemplative speech of Ren Brundidge. It must be a Brundidge trait! I learned that his wife is deceased as are his children. One son died as an adult and the other as a child. He came to the Buffalo area in 1947, and according to him he does not regret it. "Life was hard back then." His parents were sharecroppers, and they lived on the following places when he was young.

#1 Born: At John Watson's place
#2—Walt Sweetie (sp?)
#3—Bob Crittenden

#4—Oscar Stallings
#5—Walt Sweedie
#6—Marvin Stallings

The area where they lived was called Aiken, where there once was a post office on the Stallings place. (There was some talk between Con Arthur and Mr. Shines about where it was moved to.) By now, Mr. Shines is also asking questions, many of which proved to help me. They also talked about people I didn't know.

Con Arthur remembers his childhood as one of the most exciting times in his life because they played a lot of games like Flying Jenny (much like a circular seesaw built on a newly felled tree trunk); swinging from trees with strong saplings; rolling down a hill in wagon wheels! He commented that they used to do some dangerous things. He lost part of his finger while playing. His Aunt Mandy Hamilton fixed it with a concoction of syrup, spider webs, sugar, and some other things. They called a ____? to stop the blood. They looked for the other piece of his finger, but they couldn't find it. Feathers and tar were also used when kids stepped on rusty nails. He and Mr. Shines talked about these things together, but the noise level was too high for me to pick up everything!

Secrecy: The older people didn't allow children to stand around and listen. Mr. Shines said they would tell you ????? (missed it) and, in some cases, if you were too bold, they would spit in your face. They both regretted the failure of the older generation to share. Con Arthur said that when someone in his family died, Samuel Russell (a notary public) said that he, Arthur, was one of the few who could name his grandparents when he completed the forms for his father's death certificate!

Well Digging: Mentioned Adam Nix's death to him, and belief that he had been poisoned. He and Shines started to talk about it. Said that Hester Parmer's first husband, Frank Hamilton, was killed by gas in wells. She later married Caesar Hudson. He said the gas was natural gas. Told a story about his experiences in cleaning out well.

Questions about kin relations followed, and this is what was said between the three with regard to the children of Rachel Jane Parmer as well as others whose names came up. [Note that here, I simply listed the information since I couldn't keep up with where everyone fitted in, especially the Hamiltons.] Cleve Hudson, William Hudson's father, used to say that his grandmother was Hester Parmer, but that her mama was a Hamilton. (Was Rachel Jane a Hamilton? Note: Contact William Hudson!) The Shines: Henrietta Nix Shine was his aunt. Grandpa Ezra (Israel) Parmer: He didn't know all of Ezra's brothers, but he tried to name them in order of age. Randall, Ezra, Henry, Walt, Tom . . . but took him awhile to remember. Tom was in and out and only visited around Christmas and summer. Tom and his Uncle Jonas used to hang around together up around Montgomery where he supposes they were living at the time. He added "Miss" Hester and Emma afterward. Essie added Lucy Parmer, her grandmother. According to Essie, she was married to Will Morris, but her son was Neal Hamilton Parmer, brother (half-brother?) to App Hamilton. Confusing! Amanda Hamilton's (died in late 1920s) children lived to be very old. Had something like a family reunion when he was a child. There were so many people there. Some of her children were Munch, Sally, Kip, Aunt Paige, App Hamilton. Malinda Hamilton was Zola's grandmother. Thinks that she is buried at St. Luke's.

Knew little about Mose Nix and his wife/children. Described him as short (about Uncle Leonard Parmer's height). He stayed with Con Carrie. He was brown skinned, not quite as bright as Carrie who was also short but stout. Carrie was more brown than yellow. Malindi was about my color. Henry Parmer went to Laurel Hill, Florida. Used to come up and visit regularly. He was stout, heavier than Ezra.

Charlie Matthews, his uncle really knew. He would even write down how many eggs the chickens laid in one week. Charlie was his uncle, his father's half-brother. Comment: The whites knew all about kin relations. Walt Sweedie. He could go to him and ask questions when he was young. He lived near Essie and Houston Everidge's house.

Schooling: At St. Luke's school. It used to be on the other side of the road. They then called it Crenshaw school. There was a big mess about whether it was in Butler or Crenshaw county. So, they moved it behind the county dividing line to make it in Crenshaw. Around 1918, a tornado came through and blew it over. Killed two of Will Hamilton's daughters and Russell McLain's son. School hadn't been built properly in the first place. They were all first cousins. A lot of the rest got hurt—the school hadn't been built properly. His step-grandmother wouldn't let them go to school that day. When they awoke right just before day, they could hear it (the storm) coming. It blew the chimney support down and all the dust came in the house. This happened in January. In January and February, they used to get a lot of bad storms. The 1927 tornado blew down Mulberry Church—". . . just slayed timber in its path." There was a flood in 1929 too. Their teacher's name was Mr. Bowen. Fronie Hamilton—she was the most proper woman in county. She also taught school at St. Luke's?

Slavery: Aunt Winnie used to talk about it, but see comments on secrecy.

Grandma Cindy: They used to say that the baby came in the basket. Grandma Cindy would be around carrying a basket. She had scissors in them, but they couldn't see everything. She delivered him. He remembers that she was walking just the way Thera Belle is walking now. She would say to the kids "Y'all better stay out of your daddy's peanuts and bring me some of them." The kids would get a broom and knock a little hole in them so that they would fall out. (They would hang bags of peanuts from the ceiling.)

Interview #2: Clarence Longmire

Uncle Clarence or Uncle Chank as they called him was a short man with very yellow weathered skin, a large beaked nose, dark thick eyebrows and thin lips. He brings to mind Grandma Mealie. He always had his favorite sayings—one in particular about not marrying unless you're sure or something like that. He was saying that even when I was old enough to have been divorced umpteen times.

I can remember their house from childhood. It always had a more citified appearance even though the walls were wooden. When I talked to him last, he was doing well. He had slowed down a bit, but he was

still basically independent and never had the need to have anyone live with and take care of him.

He was born in 1900, at Forest Home? They moved to Industrial (Industry?) from Forest Home in 1909. He's not sure where his father, John Longmire, was born. Around 1910, they moved to Atmore. In 1949, he moved back to Georgiana. Mama was born in Atmore.

Lou was his grandmother. That's all they called her. Her mother was a Posey. His grandmother was sold from one master to another for $1,200. Bill Posey, the master's son, is his grandfather. Lou lived with them and she died in Forest Home when he was a little bitty boy. She was a dark-skinned woman. She might have been about eighty-seven years old when she died. She is buried at Zion Rest (Methodist) Church. Lou had two brothers and two sisters.

Knew his uncles and "aunties." His daddy's mother was Hannah Longmire. They're from Lowndes County. Hannah was kind of an Indian type—not as dark as Lou. She died when they were in Atmore. She would visit from Atmore to Industry. His daddy (John Longmire) kept records on everything. Aunt Nig got rid of those records. Her husband, Uncle Oliver, also had the deed to Christian Light Baptist Church. Eddie Lee Jones couldn't find them—even went into loft of old house where she lived for so long. Couldn't find them. His daddy (John Longmire) built church. They had Sunday school from the Arbor until church was completed. The church was built in 1912.

The above transcribed notes represent the substance of conversations held with two informants. Note how quickly names and references to places appear, not to mention confusing kin ties. In the first case, a distant relative gave critical information about the ancestry of my grandfather. That information is relatively reliable because the informant grew up in the area. In the second case, Uncle Clarence knew bits and pieces of the family's past, knew that the Bible had gotten lost, and he definitely knew the family's migration history, if not his father's true place of birth.

As you transcribe your interviews, make a list that contains (1) things to clarify, (2) additional people to interview, and (3) additional places to search for records, like the family Bible, though you've been told that they were lost.

A Note on Confidentiality

*Y*ou will probably obtain information that few other family members have. You might find documents that reveal information that may cause difficulties within the family. Remember the nature of the information that you are collecting. Health conditions, sexual preferences, inheritances, land conflicts, childbirth outside of marriage or the true paternity of an individual who died sixty years ago—each of these can have repercussions in the present generation. Family secrets, if they are too sensitive to share with everyone for now or if you are uncertain of their implications, should be kept between you and the person providing the information until you can discuss these issues with an older relative or someone else in the family. Though there is really nothing

new under the sun, the family unit is one of the most sensitive institutions in society. Therefore, even when someone tells you that they don't care, be careful with the information. The object of your research is to unite families, rather than to divide them or to add to rifts that seem irremovable. As such, your research really belongs to the family and not to you. Remember this point: The more you involve your relatives in providing information, the more that information becomes the collective property of the family. Bless the ties that bind; figure out a way to cement the strong ties within the family, and build bridges for the weak ones.

Collecting Family Records, Documents, Memorabilia

This ad was placed in the only widely circulated magazine that deals with collecting African American material history. The

COLLECTING FAMILY RECORDS, DOCUMENTS, MEMORABILIA

JOHN EZRA PARMER'S DIPLOMA, TUSKEGEE INSTITUTE

Tuskegee Normal and Industrial Institute

This is to Certify that

John E. Parmer

has completed the Course of Studies prescribed in the

Academic Department

of this Institution, together with the Course prescribed in the

William G. Willcox Trades School

In Plumbing

with a satisfactory record in respect to Scholarship, Labor and Deportment, and is therefore entitled to this

Diploma

In Testimony Whereof, we have appended our names and the Corporate Seal of the Institution.

Given at Tuskegee Institute, Alabama, the twenty-fourth day of May, 1934

_____ President

_____ Chairman, Board of Trustees

point to be made is simply that the records, documents, and other memorabilia that you find in the possession of family members should be preserved, for they are valuable and essential to telling the African American story as well as the story of your family. Most such items, if valuable, do belong in archives, libraries, and museums where preservation is almost guaranteed. Or they should remain in the possession of a trusted family member. But think about the fact that there is a trade in old documents. That means that the people who let go of these documents often did not know their value to the family, let alone their value to the preservation of African American history. Too often, a deceased's worldly possessions are tossed in the garbage. Know the difference between parting with valuable family records to donate to a good cause such as a credible museum—and I emphasize *credible*—versus parting with family valuables by sale. Consider the following stories as a warning.

Charleston, South Carolina, 1935:

A family had recently purchased a house that had a space large enough for kids to crawl under. Two of the children were going about their usual business of playing when they saw some old boxes. They called to their father who then pulled them out. His speculation that they contained old documents was later confirmed. They were letters, the oldest having been written in 1835, by members of the Ellison family, a free black family of Charleston. How descendants of the Ellison family lost the letters is a story that was not revealed in the book *No Chariot Let Down*, which reproduced them in their entirety.

A Small Midwestern Town, 1990s:

A project designed to uncover the pre–Civil War history of blacks in a small midwestern town was seriously damaged when one of the oldest living blacks in the town died. One of the project officials, who waited an appropriate amount of time to show her respect, decided to visit the relatives at the home of the deceased person. Unknown to her as she drove across town, the deceased's great-niece, home from out West, had cleaned out the basement. Upon arriving, she found the great-niece standing over a pile of rubble in the backyard. She had burned all of the man's old documents and papers, some of which dated from the 1840s, including a certificate of freedom and an even rarer piece of correspondence written to a relative from a slave in Virginia.

No need to continue the horror stories. The point should be clear now. Make copies of any documents that you find in the possession of your relatives. Encourage your relatives to donate documents and papers that are historically significant to any credible museum or library of their choice, preferably one that specifically collects African American documents. In that way, you preserve your own family's history as well as African American history. One good way to tell whether the institution is "credible" is to determine what its preservation facilities are like, whether there is at least one qualified archivist/librarian who does nothing but manage the records, and whether there is an internal inventory of the institution's records that you can examine. You won't be out of hand if you ask these questions. If the potential receiving institution acts as if you are being "uppity," move on until you find someone in the same league as you.

KNOWING WHICH FAMILY RECORDS ARE IMPORTANT

*O*ne critical part of each interview should involve looking at old photographs, documents, and memorabilia, items which can often fill up a living room. This is the stuff of family history that hopefully you won't find has been thrown out after your great-grandmother's death or boarded up in the old house which has been sold or rented to someone else. As you talk with your relatives, you are creating an inventory of all the important information that they possess—this includes both oral information (the interviews that you have transcribed) and written information (the documents that you have collected). Listed below are the types of documents that you may find in the possession of family members. Their rarity is based on my experience with students as well as on the current market values of selected black memorabilia found in dealers' catalogues. Finally, the loss of family papers is not only due to carelessness. Remember, many of our ancestors lived in wooden houses that burned easily once they caught fire. The table below should help you to identify records that may be in your family's possession.

Your family's records, though they represent only a small portion of the records that you will use to trace the life cycle of any one of your ancestors, are nevertheless important. An obituary can name an ancestor's children, the spouse, or identify date of death and place of burial. A death certificate can identify your ancestor's parents, a spouse, the cause of his or her death, place of burial, and date of death. A family Bible can, at times, allow you to reconstruct several lineages. School certificates can identify local schools that your ancestors attended. Clues about your family's past abound in surviving family records, no matter how few. Your task is to begin providing dates and

ORIGINAL RECORDS FOUND IN PERSONAL OR FAMILY PAPERS

Fairly Common	Fairly Rare	Very Rare
Birth/Death Certificates	Marriage Certificates Pre-1890	Letters—early 20th Century
Newspaper clippings	School Records Pre-1900	Employment Records Pre-1900
Photographs (1890+)	Photos (1860–1890)	Black Newspapers Pre-1900
Land Deeds	Club and Organizational Records	College Yearbooks Pre-1900
Obituaries	Masonic Papers Pre-1900	Bibles Pre-1900
Insurance Policies	Scrapbooks	Civil War Discharge Papers
WW I and II Discharge Papers		
Marriage Certificates (1920+)		
Church Programs/Bulletins		

*Source: *Where to Write for Vital Records*, U.S. Department of Health.

places for key points in each of your ancestors' life cycles using first the information collected from within the family and later expanding to records housed in many different places throughout the country. As you collect this data, place it on your family group sheets and your generations chart. Most important of all, include the source for every piece of information that you enter.

A NOTE ON PRESERVATION OF RECORDS

*I*f you are lucky enough to have identified a stash of records, photos, and memorabilia, there are a few simple steps that you can take to prevent the catastrophes that occurred in the examples above. The simplest step to preserving records is to make sure that copies are made and stored in different places. First, make a written inventory describing the records in detail; second, copy or photograph the records (photocopying is fine if you do it only once and if the record is not too fragile); third, learn how to preserve the records by using archival-quality storage materials. In the case of old photographs, you might want to restore them if you can afford the cost; if not, take them to a reputable photo lab and they can be photographed for you. Avoid high-priced department stores. The photo lab will give you a print and the negative (ask for a 5 × 7). Keep the photograph and the negative in suitable storage materials. Never, absolutely never, laminate photographs to preserve them. Your local or state historical society or your best public library can assist you in learning more about preservation of family records, papers, and photographs.

A few helpful hints were published in the winter 1996 issue of *Currents*, the newsletter of the South Carolina Department of Archives and History. Some of these hints are reproduced below.

1. Do not repair your documents with tape or glue.
2. Store documents flat when you can, but don't flatten tightly curled or folded paper with force.
3. Keep documents away from sunshine or fluorescent light.
4. Do not use rubber bands, metal paper clips, straight pins, or staples to bind documents together.
5. Do not use wooden or ordinary cardboard boxes to store your valuable photographs and documents.
6. Do not store precious photographs in scrapbooks that use plastic cover pages and sticky adhesive backboards.
7. Do not store photographic negatives or slides in commonly used plastic sheets.
8. Control temperature and humidity in storage areas (70 degrees at 50 percent relative humidity is best). This excludes most attics and basements as suitable storage spaces.

As you can see from this list, the most common materials that we use each day cannot be used to store valuable family documents. One added precaution: Don't believe your local copy shop when you are invited to find yet another use for lamination by laminating your own original photographs! Even documents generated during your own lifetime should be stored suitably for future generations.

What then should you do? In addition

to consulting with your local historical society about preservation, you can find a local art supply company that will show you what an archival storage system involves (namely acid-free paper and boxes as well as appropriate procedures for climate control). The American Association for the Study of State and Local History, based in Nashville, also publishes informational pamphlets about preservation that can be obtained by writing directly to its headquarters.

What Do I Need to Do Now?

*T*he interviews will tell you how much work you will have to do in your research. The more interviews you complete, the less difficulty you will encounter. Having an integrated and nearly complete story that includes a historical perspective for at least this century will make your job a lot easier. Now that you have your interviews, you must take the time to write the family's basic story and compile all the information that you've collected into a notebook. Even if you are using a software program that tells you it can write your history, you must write it in your own words as well. Your story should cover origins, migration paths, and dispersion of family members from an identifiable city, town, or rural area. The story should tell what you know and what you don't know as well as what you

want to know. Once you've written the story and compiled the other information, you'll be able to talk about it more intelligently. The written draft gives you focus, something that you are probably longing for now. As the story emerges from the records that you will next research, you will modify it accordingly. Your story will be a compilation of all the things that you have done up to this point.

The following outline should be used as a guide to compiling the results of your interviews and collection of documents up to this point. This compilation is a sort of working file cabinet that is portable. Your portable file cabinet–notebook should include the following:

Preliminary Ancestral or Generations Chart
Preliminary Family Group Sheets
Family Address and Phone Directory
Statement of What You Want to Know
Family Origins
Family Migration and Dispersion
Significant Events in the Family's History
How Major Historical Events Affected the
    Family (depressions, wars, etc.)
Basic Facts on Each Generation
Family Stories
List of Important Family Records Collected
    During the Interview Process and
    Copies of All Important Documents
    That You've Collected
Your Transcribed Interviews

Chapter 3

TECHNIQUES
AND TOOLS

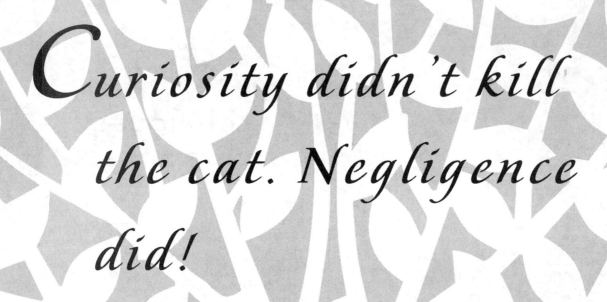

Curiosity didn't kill the cat. Negligence did!

TOOLING UP FOR THE NEXT PHASES

*T*his chapter provides an introduction to the types of materials and institutions that you will frequently use, and it will give you a good sense of what the genealogical research process is all about. The term *research process* should not cause alarm. You will eventually come to understand that records form the foundation of your research, that they come in many forms, are housed in many places, and finally, that the only thing that stands between you and them is knowing how to locate and use them. That is the process.

Genealogical research is all about locating special kinds of historical records. It is finding, using, and evaluating information in historical records that name individuals and their kin relationships. The quantity of historical records that contain names of individuals, both free and slave, should not be underestimated. There are military records, company records, probate records, land records, tax records, institutional records, census records—in short, all kinds of records housed in all kinds of places throughout the United States and even abroad. Part of the fun in genealogical research is finding out about the records themselves, for they have a history of their own independent of the information contained within them. You may even find records that were thought to be lost! This point is particularly important for African American researchers, because some of the most important historical records within the Black community still remain in private hands.

In the course of your research, you will be stumped, dumbfounded, excited, highly motivated—if not downright righteous—and more. You will be guided by your own sense of curiosity and puzzlement. You will even develop outrageous theories that, once you come to your senses, will probably evaporate. Most beginners make the mistake of going too fast because it is easy to become obsessed with finding origins. Don't be like the cat and make mistakes in haste. That will kill your research.

This chapter focuses on genealogy as a research process, specific techniques that are required to successfully accomplish your goals, and the kind of proof needed to confirm that a kin relationship exists between individuals found in historical records.

DEFINE YOUR RESEARCH GOALS

*F*or every phase of your research, your general goal is to locate your ancestors in records for that particular period of time, document the kin ties between them, and preserve this information in a suitable format for both your own family and the genealogical community. There are also some broader goals that African American genealogists should try to achieve. The broadest goal is to reconstruct the lives and kinship ties of your ancestors during slavery and freedom. Because the history of African American families has been so poorly understood, and even maligned, one might think that any reconstruction of family ties would be difficult, if not impossible. Therefore, any evidence of continuity between generations within African American families is helpful in erasing this myth. This is a difficult task because of the nature of slavery and family division; it is also difficult because you won't always find consistent records. But you won't know unless you try. In a sense, your broadest goal is to document African American family heritage.

Your research goals may also change over time. As you collect information, you might find that your own personal research has been sidetracked. Many genealogists develop projects that are an outgrowth of research on their families. You might become involved in the preservation of a cemetery, the designation of a site as a landmark, or the organization of a genealogical and historical society. Dr. Robert Prince probably never thought that his research would stop the construction of a Dallas freeway; nor did he imagine that his efforts would lead to the reconstruction of a Dallas freedmen's cemetery, originally thought to contain twenty graves, that was later found to contain over one thousand! Dorothy Spruill Redford never thought that she would reclaim a whole plantation with the help of state agencies and university faculty. Nor did Lena Ferguson ever imagine that her application to join the DAR would result in a nationwide campaign to construct a monument to Black Revolutionary War soldiers, a campaign led by her nephew Maurice Barboza. These possibilities exist for you because there are so many startling facts about the African American past. You may find an important story—indeed many important stories that will be left untold unless you find and tell them.

Another broad goal is simply that of recording "anonymous" African Americans. Encountering ancestors who lived as slaves gives us reason to pause. They lived their lives without the blessings of freedom, and that is the bottom line. You will have to deal with this on a personal level, and the consequences are far different from merely reading about slavery. Once you discover your ancestors in the place where they served as slaves, you will experience many transformations, including a deeper understanding about the complexity of the human experience.

ORGANIZING FOR A LONG SEARCH

The biggest problem that you will encounter in the early stages of your research is the failure to organize. Organization is the handmaiden of good research. Because your portable file cabinet will soon begin to expand and overflow, you need to plan for handling and storing the amount of material that you will collect. Summarized below are some key organizational points and tasks that you should set about completing early in your research:

- Make an address book or listing that includes contact information on your relatives, libraries, and other facilities (also include their hours).
- Create a filing system to store all records and documents that you locate.
- Use surnames as the major heading and then subjects as the secondary heading, as in *Smith—Death Certificates* or *Smith—Census Research—1870*.
- Create a correspondence log to keep track of your letter writing. Letters should be copied and included in the surname file that you will create or in a separate letter file.
- Create a research calendar that will help you to plan and keep track of your progress.
- Continue to update your genealogical charts.
- Take detailed notes as you research.
- Write down your sources for the following:
  1. Data on your ancestors
  2. Books, articles, and other publications
  3. Quotations
- Do not carry family records with you. Copy and file them away for safe keeping. If they need to be restored, contact a preservation expert at your local or state historical society.

LEARNING TO CONTROL YOUR COSTS

*E*lectra Kimble Price submitted a list of tips to help beginners who subscribe to the Afrigeneas research group on the World Wide Web. Her pointers form a set of pre-cautions and advance warnings that beginners should know about. Getting caught up in the "enthusiasm of the hit" is one precaution. Before you know it, you may spend more money than you planned, thinking that your research progress is measured by the amount of money that you put out. So you need a research budget that starts very modestly. This means that at the beginning, you should avoid purchasing expensive software programs with charts and other organizing tools. At this point, you have little information to place on them anyway. However, as your research proceeds, these programs may increase in usefulness. Know, however, that many genealogists do not use them.

If you spend a lot of time on the Web at the beginning, you might want to watch your costs during this exploratory phase. Another point to remember is that you should avoid paying for research or subscribing to services that you can't use at the beginning phases. Again, these services may become useful to you later, but at present you can't answer that question for yourself. The rule is that if you don't know how a service will benefit you, don't purchase it. Save your money for obtaining the records rather than purchasing the organizing tools and services.

According to Mrs. Price, these are the things you should include in your budget:

1. Repeated and lengthy long distance telephone calls to relatives and government offices.
2. Stamps and postage costs for documents that you request, plus the cost of copying the documents.
3. Subscriptions to journals, magazines,

bulletins, and newsletters plus the purchase of basic genealogy resource books, atlases, gazetteers. In fact, you might need to purchase more shelf space.

4. Membership fees to genealogical societies in the states and townships where you are researching.
5. Tape recorder, a video recorder and/or camera for interviewing and filming family members.
6. Mechanical pencil and eraser for use in libraries and archives. Add to the list a magnifying glass.
7. Three-ring binder for 8″ × 11″ papers, file folders, dividers, and labels. (A file cabinet becomes a necessity.) A three-hole punch.
8. Loose change for feeding parking meters and photocopying.
9. Transportation costs to family reunions, conferences, and other events.
10. Microfilm rental costs.
11. Registration fees for conferences, workshops, and institutes.

TAKING DETAILED NOTES

*T*aking notes as you do your research will save you a tremendous amount of time. As mentioned above, you will need to know where you obtained the information that will inevitably multiply as your research goes along. I have seen researchers with scraps of papers upon which they have written many notes without knowing what source was used to take these notes. I have also seen researchers with well-organized notes contained in a three-ring binder. As

you take notes from sources and records, don't forget the following things to include:

A complete citation for the source (author, title, publisher, year of publication, page numbers, and all other information, such as in which library or archive the source was found). This will allow you or someone else to easily locate or relocate the source.
Your evaluation of the source and whether you need to return to it at a future date.

RESEARCH FACILITIES: WHERE WILL YOUR RESEARCH TAKE PLACE?

*A*sk yourself these questions to determine what research facilities you will be using:

How far do I live from the largest public library in my area?
How far do I live from the county courthouse?
How far do I live from the state archives?
How far do I live from a local or state historical society?
How far do I live from a regional branch (Federal Record Center) of the National Archives?
Is there a stake library of the Latter Day Saints in my area?
Can I use the nearby university or college library?

After answering these questions, you should make a distinction between the resources in the area where you reside and the resources in the area where most of your ancestors lived. Where you now live may have many fine facilities for beginning genealogical research, but ultimately, it is the facilities and resources in the area where your ancestors once lived that you will have to use, particularly as you approach the period of slavery. Suppose you currently live in New York, but your ancestors lived in Maryland. You will start with your research in New York by using the many fine libraries in the area because they will have most sources that beginning researchers will need. At the same time, you may begin to write to various institutions and organizations in Maryland. As your research progresses, you will eventually have to use libraries and archives in the state of Maryland.

Because historical records are spread throughout the United States, your ability to get off to a good start will be affected by the distance between where you now live and the location of good research facilities for beginners. Researchers who are in the best position are those who now live in southern cities near where their ancestors lived. This is a critical distinction to understand. Your research becomes more complicated if you do not have *direct* access to records in the area where your ancestors once lived. You will, therefore, have to compensate for this lack of direct access at the beginning by learning how to effectively use the sources that are closest to you in your local area. If you live in the North, you will have to become skilled in using local facilities, letter writing, and tapping into a network of genealogical information that will help you.

While it is to your advantage to live in a southern city, many of you may live in cities where there are good research facilities for

genealogists, including a regional branch of the National Archives, LDS stake libraries, and large public or private libraries with noted genealogical collections. The effort you put into making a preliminary survey of research facilities in your county, city, and state will pay off later. Listed below are the different types of research facilities that you will use along with the type of information and assistance they are likely to provide.

State Archives

Nearly all state archives offer assistance to genealogists. One of your first steps should be to write to the state archives for an information packet on genealogical research. Indicate that you are also interested in any sources that would assist African American genealogists. Some states have developed special pamphlets designed to help researchers in specific areas, including the area of African American genealogy. State archives are mandated by law to house and maintain (archive) certain records generated by the state government and public institutions. Part of that responsibility includes identifying and maintaining historical records of value. Old vital records, old probate records, census records for the state and neighboring states, and even the family papers of important citizens of the state may be found at the state's archives. In addition, most state archives and libraries will have an extensive collection of books on the state's history and the history of local areas.

State and/or Local Historical Societies

Every state has an official historical society to which a library is attached. In addition, larger cities will also have historical societies with their own collections and libraries.

While most counties do not have a specific facility set aside for a historical society, you will probably find that they do have a historical society at which you will find extremely useful information on the county's history and the genealogies of some of the families housed at a central public library. Historical societies view as their charge the collection and maintenance of significant historical and genealogical information on all aspects of the area's history—whether the area is defined as the state, city, or county. Again, genealogists may use these libraries heavily; therefore, researchers should have little difficulty in accessing records in these facilities. Note also that many historical societies and libraries offer assistance on preservation of old family documents and photographs. If nothing else, they can refer you to a reputable local company or individual who will assist you for a fee.

When you write, request information on the official journal of the society. State historical journals will prove helpful because they always contain articles on aspects of African American history and life in the state. Furthermore, many of these journals discuss research facilities and their collections. It won't hurt to ask if there is a separate list of articles on African American history in the state that have appeared in the journal or a bibliography on African American history in the state. For a small copying fee, you can often obtain these articles without having to worry about where you can find the journal.

Public and Private Libraries with Significant Genealogical Collections

Public libraries in small towns often maintain genealogical collections that beginners will find very useful. Major libraries in larger cities may maintain nationally recognized genealogical collections like the New York Public Library, the Detroit Public Library, the Newberry Library, or the DAR Library in Washington, D.C. While these libraries tend to collect materials for the region or for a specific subject, they will always have an excellent collection of materials for beginners.

College and University Libraries

College and university libraries will have varying policies on library access for the public. Beginning researchers should inquire by phone or letter to determine when and how nonaffiliated researchers may have access. Generally, these facilities will become important to your research later on when you need to use manuscript collections, housed in a special collections department, or historical works written by scholars. Small private colleges, however, will often have genealogical materials that relate to local history.

LDS Stake Libraries

People frequently use the term "the Mormon library," but in order to find out whether such a facility exists in your area, you will need to know that the correct name is the Church of Jesus Christ of Latter Day Saints (LDS), that their local libraries are called *stake libraries*, and finally that the main library, located in Salt Lake City, is called the Family History Library. The stake libraries offer a wide range of microfilmed records and loan sources that can be ordered for use at the stake. Before deciding that you will pack up and do all of your research in

Utah, check a local stake library first. Census records can be ordered, the IGI can be consulted, and most stakes have the *Social Security Death Index*. (See page 82.)

Genealogical Societies

Genealogists are all members of one club; when you go to a meeting of any genealogy society, you will discover a real friendship. It seems that a common interest in those who can no longer harm us eliminates many sources of potential conflict. Most societies do not require that you prove your ancestry to a particular historical period or group of persons. Hereditary societies, like the Daughters of the American Revolution (DAR) or the Society of Mayflower Descendants, may indeed have individuals with African ancestry, but your main interest now is to join those societies that will help you to become an independent and creative researcher. Some genealogical societies have small libraries and resource centers. Some have their own publications such as the *Journal of the Afro-American Historical and Genealogical Society* (Washington, D.C.) or the *National Genealogical Society Quarterly*. Include these societies on your list; join and receive the publications of local, regional, or state societies that are important for your research. Finally, the major journals always include articles on research techniques and methods.

There are other research facilities in your area that you probably never thought you would use. Make sure that you create a list of all libraries and research facilities in the area where you now live to determine what genealogical sources are available for you to begin.

Be Prepared When Visiting Libraries and Other Facilities

*H*ere is a tip from Pearl-Alice, a member of an African American genealogical group on the Web:

There is no getting around sitting in a library looking at microfilm and other materials. By the way, you need a "kit" to do that. I suggest the following: genealogy forms in a spiral binder; pencils (they do not let you use pens in most research facilities); a good magnifying glass (some microfilm is very difficult to read); quarters and dimes for photocopying (saves time with some books); a notebook (for writing down citations, references, etc.) and a few file folders (in case you need to segregate some papers on the spot); a snack and some water (you should spend at least several hours there). Now, I only know this because I went and spent six hours in a research center and didn't have any of this. They even had to lend me a pencil! My notes are in a pitiful little spiral notebook (card size!). And to be honest with you, it is going to be real hard to establish where I left off! But not next time! I'm going to be prepared! So, be prepared the first time!

When you visit libraries and other research facilities, you should also know that you will use on-line (computer-based) card catalogues, CD-ROMS, equipment like microfiche readers and, most commonly, microfilm readers. You might even be directed to the Web, where the library's card catalogue will come up in seconds. If you've never used any of these before, well, you have to learn at some point, as did everyone else. No one on the staff will be shocked to find out that you need assistance. Besides, they would rather help you than see equipment accidentally placed in disrepair because they weren't doing their jobs.

KNOW THE SOURCES FOR BEGINNING RESEARCH

*B*efore you get too far in your research, you will need to know about some basic sources that will aid you. These are the sources that you will look for at a large public library, a genealogical library, or another research facility in your area. They constitute your basic reading list.

Book List of Genealogical and Family History Guides

There are many "how-to" genealogical research guides on the market for beginners.

They will help you to conduct your research, up to a point—at least through the stage of research involving censuses. Few of these publications will include special research problems in Black genealogy, but the basic information contained in these publications will help you to begin.

Your History Reading List

History guides genealogy. It is as simple as that! If you know your history, your research problems will diminish in proportion to the history that you know. There is one catch to this dictum. You should know local and regional history: the history of settlement, agriculture, folkways, ethnic groups, and migration patterns in the area where your ancestors lived. Therefore, you will need to read:

NIX

ADAM
MAY 25, 1844
JULY 10, 1899

LUCINDA
OCT. 30, 1848
MAY 4, 1930

a good history of your county, city or town,
state, and region

a history of slavery in your state of research

a history of Reconstruction in your state of
research

a general history of the African American
experience

Even the history of rivers, as in the case
of the lower Mississippi, will prove important in your research. Do not make the mistake of assuming that histories of local
towns and counties in the South are not relevant to the Black experience. Local histories published prior to the 1960s will rarely
mention Blacks, but you will need to know
about the movements of slave owners to
clarify what happened to your ancestors
during slavery.

Bibliographies

A bibliography is a listing of books and
sources. This means that someone, generally a librarian, has taken the time to sort
through books to determine whether they
are of any value. Annotated bibliographies
describe the contents of each book or article, and of course, these are the best. However, know that most bibliographies are not
annotated. Learning to obtain and study
bibliographies is a very important step that
you will have to take. Because many of my
students have been reluctant to consult
them, their research has often been stalled.
The attitude of "just show me the records"
will not keep your research on track for very
long. There are several essential bibliographies that will help you at the beginning,
and they are listed in the bibliography for
chapter 2. The bibliography compiled by
David Thackery can be ordered directly

from the Newberry Library at a minimal
cost.

Maps, Atlases, Gazetteers

The county will be your geographical unit
of research. Therefore, beginners should
purchase an inexpensive road atlas containing state maps. My old U.S. road atlas containing state maps is used frequently to
figure out the locations of counties, county
seats, and small towns. Many sources exist
for county and local maps. One is your
state's department of highways, from which
you can obtain an accurate state map and
maps for your county of research and the
surrounding counties. The cost of these
maps is minimal.

A standard atlas will perhaps not list
Clantonville, Alabama, but a gazetteer or
historical atlas for that state would.
Gazetteers will not only list Clantonville,
but they will also tell you that Clantonville
was originally settled by a group of planters
from coastal Georgia. The first person to
stake his claim in Clantonville was Stanley
Clanton, who in 1819 got prime land on the
Wallahatchee River for one dollar an acre!
They generally won't tell you that Clanton,
along with the rest of the planters, brought
his slaves with him!

Guidebooks to Research in Your State

Obtaining copies of guidebooks on how to
do historical and genealogical research and
where to locate information in your state or
county of research is very important. These
books are generally written by experienced
genealogists and researchers. For a start,
look for the citations in the most recent edition of *The Handy Book for Genealogists* and
The Source. Your state archives packet will

also contain a list of good research guide-books for the state.

Plan to Use Scholarly Sources Frequently

Because there is not a lot of genealogical source material solely on African Americans, you will use scholarly sources and publications about African Americans in your state of research. These will, in turn, contain additional references that relate to sources for further exploration. In addition to the suggestions above, request that your local librarian help you to access the many bibliographies and computer databases now available to the average researcher. A good start would be to take a look at the *Journal of Negro History* and then subscribe. Finally, the use of material written by scholars should not frighten you. When you get past the seemingly technical terms that some historians might use, you will find that the works on African American history written by scholars within the last thirty years will help you tremendously.

NETWORKING THROUGH GENEALOGICAL SOCIETIES

*T*here are at least thirty African American genealogical societies in the United States. The largest, the National Afro-American Historical and Genealogical Society, publishes a quarterly journal, and most local societies have newsletters. One of the benefits of joining is that your name gets plugged into a variety of mailing lists that relate to genealogy. Don't, however, buy books from direct mail solicitations that tell you the history of your family has already been done, including locating the family crest, and that you can buy it for forty dollars. If you are African American, the term "family crest" should be your clue that this operation is bogus. If you just have to give up your money, maybe it will be worth it to buy an address directory of the people with your surname in the United States. This is what these books contain. Of course, if you are addicted to names, you can get that same information on the Web for a fraction of the cost!

Networking with experienced individuals through the mail or through a society will provide you with valuable insider information. To understand what it was like in the last decade to be an African American genealogist, read Dorothy Spruill Redford's book, *Somerset Homecoming*. It vividly describes what the experience is like to do research without the assistance of genealogical societies and good guidebooks on the basics of research in African American genealogy.

LEARNING TO USE THE WORLD WIDE WEB AS A GENEALOGICAL RESEARCH TOOL

*H*ere's another bit of wisdom from Pearl-Alice, a frequent contributor to an African American genealogical Web site.

It would be great, and sometimes it does happen, if we could just throw names out onto the internet and have all these great connections return. But, genealogy research is not that easy. I think we should encourage as much disciplined research as possible. Methodical research and record keeping is the only way to really come up with reliable results. Sometimes when someone asks for a name that is truly unique, I will send along a contact I know. But, when someone is looking for Smith, Johnson, Washington, etc., most of the online sources can only guide you to physical collections at research centers, libraries, etc. Some sites that do provide actual data are limited, and none of them are comprehensive. You don't get all of the information contained on the original records.

The African American Web sites listed on pages 440–442 contains sites that will help you in the early stages of your research. But know that the Web is only a resource tool and not the final path in your research. At some point in the future, genealogists will have access to certain original records on the Web, but never will they have access to all of them.

UNDERSTANDING PRIMARY AND SECONDARY SOURCES

*I*n genealogical research, you will be working with original records, called *primary sources*, and genealogical sources derived from those records, called *secondary sources*. Original records are those records that document some event or circumstance about an individual at or near the time the event occurred, such as a birth or death certificate. These records are primary sources which contain information that is as close to the facts as you will ever get.

You probably have a birth certificate that was issued by your state's bureau of vital records. The original record is filed with the bureau. If you want a certified copy, it will have the state's seal embossed on the copy

attesting that the information is the same as that appearing in the official record on file at the bureau. Suppose you then photocopy the copy sent to you by the state. Your copy made on the machine can not be certified to be a true copy of the original record, because a number of things could have happened to introduce errors while copying: A paper fragment or debris on the copier's glass plate could have caused a number or a letter in your name to be altered.

Examine the chart below to see how many places and versions of a record might exist for just one event—your birth! While doing that, think of the possibilities for errors and inconsistencies in each kind of source.

The original record may indeed not be the first record filed on your birth. Suppose you were delivered by a midwife who, because she could not write, asked her daughter to record your birth in the family Bible. Because she was a good midwife, one month later she went to the county seat and had your birth legally recorded at the county clerk's office. The clerk then reported it to the state by completing the form used for statewide registration of births. Now, which one is the original record? Is it the one in the Bible, the one that the county clerk completed, or the one on file with the bureau of vital records? It is in the nature of original records that their accuracy can be trusted only if you know how the record was created and what natural and intentional changes were made to alter the original or subsequent copies. Even though a record may be more or less "original" or may have been created close to when the event occurred, you still need to evaluate the content of the record as well as how it

Event	Form of Original Record	Where Located
Your Birth	Midwife's Bible entry	Bible's present owner
	County's register of births	County courthouse
	State's official birth certificate	Bureau of vital records
	Your photocopy	Your files
	Your baptismal record	Your church archives
	Eyewitness account	Person's memory

Event Recorded in Genealogical Source Material

International Genealogical Index (IGI)
Transcriptions of county births
Transcriptions of church records
Microfilmed copies of county records
Compilation of Bible records

was created. Genealogical research is all about the process of locating and evaluating original records or reasonable copies of original records. However, you will not always have access to original records—more often than not, you will spend quite a bit of your time with microfilmed copies of original records, the next best choice. The following section discusses situations in which you will not use the originals, as well as secondary sources that you will use frequently.

SECONDARY SOURCES: GENEALOGICAL FINDING AIDS AND PUBLICATIONS

As mentioned previously, you will find many sources published by genealogists and various genealogical organizations. Most of these sources fall into the category of secondary sources because the information contained in them is derived from the original records. By now, you should be conscious of the possibility that errors can be introduced into your research, depending on the sources that you use. This is especially applicable to genealogical publications, given that many of these publications deal with large masses of records.

Indexes

The first thing that you want to ask about a set of records is: Is it indexed by name or subject? An index will list names and a locator such as a page, section, or reel. As such, indexes are critical to your research. Indexes do not provide you with all the information from a document. They serve the purpose of locating an individual or family surname in a very large record group such as censuses, wills, and deeds. Once you know the location, you can go directly to the original record or write for a copy. Everyname indexes include the names of all individuals named in a record. For this reason, very few publications are everyname indexes.

Abstracts

Abstracts provide more information than do indexes. They generally tell you what kind of transaction occurred between the named parties in a particular record. Wills and deeds are commonly abstracted for selected years. While abstracts do not provide all information, they often provide enough to allow you to make a judgment about a particular record. If you use dates and other information from abstracts, always verify the information by ordering a copy of the original record when possible.

Transcriptions

Transcriptions provide all or nearly all information from a set of records. For that reason, very large groups of records are never transcribed, but rather indexed or abstracted. Transcriptions are frequently done for Bible records, cemetery headstones, and other sets of data that are easily copied and published.

Microtext (Microfilm and Microfiche)

Filming entire sets of records would seemingly give you the best results. But think again! Many, many historical records have been filmed, but there is no finding aid or index for locating individuals in those records. You will encounter this often, and subsequent chapters will be replete with examples. Like all reproductions of original records, there is always the possibility that you, the unwary researcher, can come to the wrong conclusions based on what you do or do not find. Suppose the technician who filmed the records skipped pages while film-

ing? Suppose the microfilm edition of the records does not include all of the records? Suppose the image is blurred or certain letters and numbers are darkened in the filming process? These are all possibilities.

The critical problem in relying on secondary sources and finding aids is the possibility of errors. If you add the possible errors that may have been introduced in creating the original record plus the errors created in the process of indexing, abstracting, transcribing, or filming, then you should understand that evaluating records and source material is just as important as finding that material.

RULES FOR EVALUATING HOW SOURCES WERE COMPILED

African American genealogists should never exclude using any of these finding aids merely on the assumption that African Americans are not in them. Nevertheless, you should be able to evaluate them and be aware of the following possibilities in their use:

- Abstracts, indexes, transcriptions, and microtext may include African Americans, but there is no way to identify them by racial designation.
- Abstracts, indexes, transcriptions, and microtext may include some but not all African Americans found in the original records.
- Abstracts, indexes, transcriptions, and microtext may exclude all African Americans found in the original records.

For every kind of finding aid or microfilm that you use, read carefully how the material was compiled. Credible sources will indicate in an introduction who or what was included or excluded and for what reasons. This introduction should name the location of the records, describe the whole set of records including dates, their condition and general contents, indicate which part was used to compile the information, describe how the information was compiled, and finally, let the user of the compilation know whether the information was validated (checked more than once by two persons or the same person).

Researchers should also be prepared to question original records. Though it is easy to be awed when examining records created 250 years ago, the age or very survival of a document does not make its contents more true or false than when the record was created. If you are having trouble imagining how records could be inaccurate, just think about some of the recent "falsifications" used in official reports involving political scandals, or simply skip to page 72 now to read the story about Chester Blackwell.

GENEALOGICAL PROOF

If historical records can be inaccurate, what about the methods that you will use to trace your ancestry? They too can be spurious. You can easily reach the wrong conclusions if you don't follow the rules in evaluating records and using correct methods. The general method of research in genealogy is to start with the present and work back in time, or *start with the known*

and work back to the unknown. This rule may mean nothing if you are a beginner, but accept the following statement as fact at the outset: If you start your research with the present generation and work back through all the available records each generation at a time, it is unlikely that you will make many errors.

But that is only one rule. For each ancestor in each generation, you must locate and evaluate the appropriate records that document his or her life cycle from birth to death. This is accomplished by linking individuals in records that state the *relationship* between them at a particular time, in a particular place and under a specified circumstance. Preferably, you would want to find records that repeat the same or part of the same information over a long period of time with little change except the ages of the individuals. This helps you to eliminate the possibility that you are researching the wrong line, especially when you find individuals with the same names in the same counties for extended periods of time.

Think of yourself as a lawyer who is building a case using the "who shot Joe" method. Without Mary's confession, you must prove to members of the jury that they have no other choice but to find Mary guilty of shooting Joe based on an overwhelming and convincing amount of evidence. In *all* of your research, you must locate *all* the evidence (that is, all of the possible records for each of your ancestors), evaluate the truth or falsity of the evidence (use good rules for evaluating records), and come to sound conclusions including those which allow you to state that a kin or blood relationship between two individuals could not be verified. One record or source alone is not sufficient to document or "prove" any event or relationship in your ancestor's life cycle.

SOME WORDS OF CAUTION ABOUT GENEALOGICAL PROOF: PROVING WHICH HIP BONE IS CONNECTED TO WHICH THIGH BONE

Genealogical proof is an iffy matter. Ultimately, you are trying to prove with records that all the individuals in one line are linked by blood or some other relationship to a common couple, your great-great-great grandfather and grandmother, for example. A lot of things could have happened in each generation of that line to make it difficult to establish that these really are your blood descendants. One well-known genealogical writer has simply stated that you will never be able to prove that anyone is connected by blood using historical records alone—even if you get a deathbed testimony as some families concerned about lineage have done in the past. In the end, genealogical proof is really proof with records.

For example, people always assume that verification of marriage is proof of bloodlines, or at the least proof of exclusion of lines. Not so. Consider the possible case of bigamy. Let's say that you work in a pension office for a large company and you process pension claims. Upon the death of the pensioner, Joe Doe, you receive claims from Mary Doe and her three children, Sally Doe and her two children, and Frances Doe and her infant. They all claim to be widows of the said Joe Doe. Upon further investigation, you find that Joe Doe happily lived as a bigamist because his job for twenty years

allowed him to do that—he worked as a Pullman porter! Assume that all three widows presented marriage licenses, insurance policies, the birth certificates of their children, their city's telephone book, school records, and two even presented letters from a minister stating that Joe Doe was present at the baptism of his children! If you are one of Joe Doe's descendants, and you did not know that he was a bigamist, your genealogical proof will fall short by two families.

Something as seemingly obvious as the blood tie between parent and child is hardly ever questioned. It is the obvious that is also filled with the most surprises. Some of us go to our graves never really knowing our natural parents, as in the case of many adopted children. Imagine a somber occasion like a funeral where an elderly man is being eulogized. The family is present—his wife, their sons and daughters and other kin. For a moment, imagine that you are one of his sons. Upon reading the obituary, you note that your name has been omitted from the list of his children. Upset, you continue reading and find your name incorrectly entered as one of his grandchildren. Asking your mother, she tells you that this is correct. In the height of your grief, you discover that your oldest sister is your mother, the man you had called "father" all these years was really your grandfather, and finally your mother is really your grandmother! It has happened. Worse things have, too, as in recent cases of mothers not ever telling who fathered their children—unlike the days when confessions were forced in the hushed meetings of church deacons on a quiet Saturday afternoon in a rural southern church. The moral is: Don't count on the obvious, for it can occasionally be untrue. Every claimed blood link should be documented—even those that seem obvious.

THE AMBIGUITY OF ANCESTRY: SHOULD YOU TRACE EUROPEAN ANCESTRY?

At some point, you will have to decide whether your research will end or continue once a European ancestor is identified. Consider the consequences of this dilemma, one which often occurs in African American genealogy. My great-grandmother's father was, according to oral tradition, white. In fact, it is said that her father was the slave owner's son. Furthermore, using the eyeball method of documentation, I could definitely say that she was more white than black. Should I therefore trace Grandma Mealie's presumed line through the European ancestor? The answer is no, because I do not have genealogical proof (documentation with records) that her father was the slave owner's son. Note that such proof depends on finding a record acknowledging her as his child—for example, a manumission record.

Because I don't have that proof, this line remains unexplored, at least through the paternal line. I can still document the maternal line, however. Furthermore, if you really want to take it one step more, Grandma Mealie could have easily been part Indian or even the offspring of two mulattos. Suppose, however, that I had documented proof that her father was of European ancestry. If this were so, then I would have to make a deci-sion about whether to continue research on the European line beyond records kept by the ancestor/slave owner. But since I don't, I have one line that ends, and many researchers will wind up with truncated lines for this same reason. When I look on my chart, I have at least four collapsed lines based on oral traditions of European ancestry. Many of us have to live with the ambiguity of ancestry.

STANDARDS OF PROOF

Example: The Marriage of Lucindy Tillman Nix and Adam Nix

My paternal great grandparents were born near the end of slavery. Adam was born in 1844, and Lucinda was born in 1848. Their household was listed in the 1870 federal decennial census. They also appeared in every subsequent census as husband and wife until their respective deaths. I do not have any documentation on their marriage. Where can I find documentation to verify (1) that they had actually performed a marriage ceremony—either civil, religious, or slave, (2) the year in which the marriage took place, and (3) the location, along with witnesses. Their marriage was not registered in the county courthouse's register of marriages, but Lucinda's death certificate indicated that her husband was Adam Nix. Nevertheless, the family had never discussed them in terms other than husband and wife. Following are a set of questions that I could apply to this problem.

How do I know that they were married rather than cohabiting?

64

How important is it for me to obtain proof
that they were married in either of the
three ways listed above?

What evidence will I accept as proof that
they were married?

What standards of proof will I use to
establish their marriage?

What conclusions can I reach about their
marital status?

First of all, what is the best evidence to
establish that an African American couple
was married during the period of time in
question? Under ideal circumstances, we
could say that the best evidence is to obtain
as many kinds of records where they were
listed as husband and wife. That means
locating: (1) a marriage record still in the
possession of the family and signed by a
minister listing the witnesses, (2) a registration of marriage in the county courthouse,
(3) entries in the federal decennial censuses
for all possible years, (4) a family Bible stating the date and place of marriage, (5) a
church marriage register stating the same,
(6) a record kept by one of their slave-
owning families indicating that they had
married during slavery.

I found only one of the possible six types
of evidence of their marriage: the household
listing in the censuses. Am I to conclude that
they were cohabiting rather than legally
married? In this and many similar cases that
you will encounter, using the standard of
proof that requires written evidence that the
event occurred, we would have to say the
following: "No evidence of marriage found
for Adam and Lucinda Nix." Carrying this
one step further, I could assume that some
ceremony occurred and therefore estimate
their probable marriage date by using the

year of birth of their first child, Gracy, in
1865. Assuming that the dates of birth for
Lucinda and Adam are more or less correct,
I could infer that they were of marriageable
age. Lucinda was at least sixteen to seven-
teen, and Adam was about twenty-one or
twenty-two when they married, ages that
are not unrealistic for that period of time,
though a bit young.

Are there other standards of proof that I
might use? Given the circumstances, I
would suggest that we use the standard
relating to community consensus of the
time. It is likely that Adam and Lucinda
entered into some type of marriage contract
by having a public ceremony. It is also likely
that it occurred near the very last year of
slavery; therefore, we could assume that any
such "record" that exists may no longer be
available. If the marriage occurred after
emancipation, it is likely that the marriage
was not registered at the county courthouse,
because few Black marriages were entered in
the register of marriages for that county
until the 1870s. Yet we know that few couples cohabited without regard for the community standards of that time. Nearly
everybody got married! Adam and Lucindy
Nix may not have known that the State of
Alabama passed a law legalizing all marriages or cohabitations that had occurred
during slavery.

The *proof* used is not hearsay proof or
proof established by oral tradition. (Note
that hearsay evidence is generally not
acceptable as genealogical proof.) Nor is it
preponderance of evidence, where as many
records as possible are obtained that contain
evidence of the event of marriage. Finally,
how important is it to establish a date of
marriage given the conditions of the time?

We are therefore left with a *reasonable* proof. The further back in time, the less likely that the same type of evidence of birth, marriage, and death may be found for African Americans as it is often found for those of Euro-American ancestry. Furthermore, given that many things can happen to destroy historical evidence, not everyone of European ancestry will find similar documentation. You might ask, why do genealogy if you are Black? The reasons have been stated previously. Genealogical investigations help you to understand the paths that your ancestors took. Questions of proving "pedigree" are not always appropriate in the context of slavery.

Another set of standard questions that can be applied to this and other situations that you will encounter are:

Q: Did the event (marriage) occur?
A: Probably.
Q: Was it recorded?
A: Probably not.
Q: Can information about the event be accepted as accurate?
A: Yes.
Q: Is there other evidence about the same event?
A: Yes. Census records, customary practices of the time, and family tradition.

There are other difficult aspects of African American genealogy that cannot systematically be submitted to genealogical standards of proof. While this is also partly true of Euro-American genealogy, the following events will be difficult to establish if we were to follow the strict rules outlined for those wishing to prove, for example, *Mayflower* ancestry: establishing proof for either European or Indian ancestry, estab-

lishing proof of marriage during slavery, establishing the identity of families with changed surnames, establishing proof of African ethnic ancestry, and establishing proof of kin relations between slave communities on neighboring farms and plantations. You might ask, What is there then? The evidence is there, surely. But again, the problem is the proof.

Your genealogical investigations will frequently take you into the area of surmise and indirect proof. Because Black genealogy is still a relatively new field, few have discussed these problems in a straightforward manner. You will find that many of your statements will be preceded by the word "probably," and many of your dates will be estimated dates. The further back in time, the more likely that uncertainties will be encountered. In one sense, this is also true of the work that historians do. While you might frequently get the impression that historians write with a great deal of certitude, if you read a little bit more closely and understand the possible errors in written historical records, you will find the same kinds of problems with evidence and proof.

WHAT DO I NEED TO DO NOW?

*I*n this chapter, you've learned about the resources that you need to know about as your research progresses. You can't do all of the things outlined in this chapter at once. Depending on where you start, you can take a few simple steps now:

1. Inquire about genealogy societies in your local community, attend their

meetings, and join those that are most helpful to beginners.

2. Visit your local public library and take out books on African American history.

3. Explore various sites on the Web that relate to African American genealogy, and decide which lists you will subscribe to, if any.

Chapter 4

YOUR ANCESTORS ON RECORD

The Importance of Documenting the Life Cycle

Of the 1840 census . . . in many northern towns, the census listed insane Negroes where no Negro population existed and in others the figures exceeded the number of Negro residents. . . . It was the census that was insane and not the colored people, stated a clergyman.

LEON LITWACK, *NORTH OF SLAVERY*

Beginning Your Research in the Records

*N*ow that you have created your "portable file cabinet–notebook" and understand some of the research rules, you are ready to begin collecting records that provide the missing information on your charts and in your family story. Your next series of steps will involve a first foray into public records. These records will not be new or strange. More than likely, you have encountered some of them already—birth and death certificates, obituaries, marriage certificates, and other family papers that list name, age, birth, and death. In addition, you've probably encountered several inconsistencies between what was told to you in interviews and what you found in family records. That's all a part of it, and your examination of records from here on out will be to resolve the inconsistencies by finding and using as many different records as possible to arrive at reasonable facts about your family history. This chapter will help you to locate and use vital records and sources as well as to understand what kind of evidence you need to have before engraving information about your ancestors in stone.

On the Vagaries of Public Record Keeping

*A*ny one record can generate a million questions, but the most important question is this: How accurate is the information? The quote that appears at the beginning of this chapter should be a word of warning. The subject of overreporting "insane" Negroes in northern states turned into a big congressional debate about the quality of federal census taking. Yet we often accept as fact whatever is written and official. That's why you have to know what "official" really means. Most public records were created under a legal mandate by state, federal, city, and county governments to record or document information and events for governmental use. The federal decennial population census was created under a mandate by the Constitution for the official purpose of congressional apportionment. Most states were pressured by the federal government to create and maintain a system of vital records (births, marriages, and deaths) at the turn of the century for the purpose of monitoring public health and mortality, and not specifically for the noble act of recording births.

The accuracy of a record depends on the individual who *reported* the information and the individual who *recorded* the information. Consider the following case of Chester Blackwell's "great work." Though officials are always charged with the responsibility of maintaining accuracy in their recording of information and their safekeeping of such records, you will see that to err is more than human when it comes to massive efforts to collect and maintain records.

Chester Blackwell, the Census Taker

The year was 1870. It was one of the hottest Junes that anyone could remember in Amite County, Mississippi, and its surroundings. Chester Blackwell started out early in the morning on horseback; he had a lot of work ahead of him. They had all met with the census marshal for the Southern Mississippi District a few weeks ago; he figured that he had everything he needed. Besides, he knew this whole county like he knew the back of his hand. It hadn't changed much since 1860, when he last took the census for Amite County. The only difference was the surrender, but most of these people pretty much stayed put after that.

As he rounded the bend, he saw a group of people going to the fields. "Where y'all going?" he asked without making the slightest attempt at a greeting. The people said that they were going to weed cotton in the Hayes field, about two miles down the road. As they passed each other, Blackwell muttered to himself, "I know those Percys. I guess when I get to their house, they'll be back. They ain't gon put up with too much of Old Hayes' mess. Everybody is jest about tired of him." All day, Chester Blackwell stopped at different houses to take the census. When he got to the Percys', he didn't see any signs of them. He said to himself,

"Guess they ain't too tired of Hayes yet. Well, I'll give them some time to get back from the fields. I'll go back down the road and check with the colonel. That moonshine looked pretty good. It's been a pretty rough day out here." When he got to the colonel's, he met his wife chopping wood in the backyard. "The colonel here?" he asked. "Nope, down at the still," she replied. Blackwell went down to the still, got to telling stories, drinking, and forgot all about his work. Before he started imbibing, however, he did ask the colonel about the Percys. The colonel gave him this information:

"Well, let's see. There's J. T. Percy. I guess he's about forty. His wife's name is Anna, and she might be a li'l younger. They have about five youngins. One of 'em, her name is Anna too, comes over and helps my wife from time to time. She's 'bout twelve. Now, let's see, the other four, there's Junior, Betsy, Lil Bob, and Caroline. I tell you, looks like to me, she had 'em one right after the other. Anna is the oldest." This is what Chester Blackwell entered onto his census sheet for the Percy household:

PERCY HOUSEHOLD, 1870 CENSUS, AMITE COUNTY

J. T. Percy, male, Black, age 40, place of birth = Mississippi
Anna, female, Black, 35, Mississippi
Anna, female, Black, 12, Mississippi
Junior, male, Black, 10, Mississippi
Betsy, female, Black, 8, Mississippi
Bob, male, Black, 7, Mississippi
Caroline, female, Black, 5, Mississippi

What Blackwell entered sounds plausible as a best estimate of the Percy household. But think again.

WHAT THE PERCYS KNEW TO BE TRUE OF THEMSELVES

J. T. Percy	M, B, 38, Georgia
Anna Percy	F, B, 30, Georgia
Anna Belle Percy	F, B, 12, Georgia
James Percy, Jr.	M, B, 10, Mississippi
Betty Percy	F, B, 8, Mississippi
Anthony Percy	M, B, 6, Mississippi
Carrie Percy	F, B, 4, Mississippi
Alma Bivans	F, B, 68, Virginia

The five children are J.T.'s, but they are not Anna's. In fact, Anna is his sister, not his wife! J.T.'s first wife, Amalie, died before he came to Wilkerson County with his slave owner. He came from Georgia, where he was born in 1832. His first child, Anna, was also born into slavery in Georgia in 1858. She was named after J.T.'s favorite sister. Amalie was Anna's mother, but the other four children were by a second wife who died before he moved to Amite County in 1866. Since his sister was not married, he asked her to come help him take care of his children. Furthermore, there is a grandmother who was not listed at all. The colonel totally forgot about her. And Blackwell, assuming that no one was at home, didn't bother to knock. To add a final touch to this story, the grandmother was, in fact, born in Virginia! This story goes to show you how gross errors can be introduced as official census records. Had Blackwell asked the Percys' friends, a little further down the road, perhaps he would

have gotten more accurate information. Of course, he should have asked the Percys. The colonel acted as if he knew the family when he said, "It looks like she had them one after the other." After all, he was the colonel.

DOCUMENTING THE LIFE CYCLE WITH PUBLIC RECORDS

*T*he core of your research is all about finding records with certain evidence, namely, those records that document vital events (birth, marriage, divorce, death) in the life cycle of each of your ancestors and that state a kin relationship between your ancestors. In African American research, you will not consistently find records for each of these events, and you will often have to use estimated dates. The following discussion will help you get started in official vital records that are available for the twentieth century. We will start out with an instructive case study.

Case Study: Why Vital Records Are Important

One of my relatives had planned to retire, but in order to receive her benefits through Social Security, she had to prove her age. No birth certificate was available, nor had her birth been recorded in the family Bible. When she reported that she was born in 1929, she was denied. She had lived all of her life with the year 1929 as the official year of her birth, but she was told that her year of birth was 1931! What the Social Security Administration had done was to use the 1930 and 1940 censuses to verify her age. She was not listed in her father's household in the 1930 census, but she was listed in

1940 at nine years old. In an attempt to prove 1929 as the correct year of birth, she wrote to the Piney Woods School in Mississippi, where she and her sister went to school for some time, obtained copies of her father's American Woodworkers insurance policy, and she even tried to locate a baptismal record. She searched high and low, but to no avail. She resigned herself to accepting the "official" year of birth as 1931, though it is her belief that her father certainly knew the correct year of her birth.

We only need vital records for major transitional points in life, but it is often at these points that they cannot be located. We have to stop and ask, why do such important documents get lost? In my relative's case, she could not locate any record with her correct birth date—at least no record that would be accepted as alternative proof. For the Social Security Administration to accept 1929, she would have had to produce a record that was generated near the time of her birth, a record like a Bible entry or a baptismal record, or a school record. Could it be that her father falsified her age so that she could attend Piney Woods school with her sister? Why wasn't there an official birth certificate on file? Her county of birth had begun to keep fairly consistent birth registrations by the year 1929. No one will ever know the answer. This case is instructive for genealogists, because it outlines what a typical search might involve in trying to locate evidence of an ancestor's birth, marriage, or death in the twentieth century when no official record exists.

WHAT ARE VITAL RECORDS?

*M*any people confuse vital records with vital statistics. Vital records are kept on the births, deaths, marriages, and divorces of individuals; vital statistics are aggregate totals of all vital records. Vital statistics appear in official government reports that are published; an individual's vital record (birth, death, or marriage certificate) is never published by state or local agencies. Vital records are generally housed in a state department of health or bureau of vital statistics within that department. The bureau's responsibility is to monitor and publish statistical figures about these events as well as to serve as the official keeper of vital records on individuals who were born, married, or died in the state. To obtain a record of a vital event, an individual must write to the state's bureau of vital records for the appropriate form and pay the fee. These records are generally open to individuals with bona fide needs—to have a copy of their own record or to do genealogical research.

Vital records often state kin relationships between individuals. Those genealogical records that state kin relationships are always more valued than those that simply report an event about an individual. Therefore, birth certificates are valued because they establish the names of parents, including the mother's maiden name. Marriage records (licenses and bonds) may identify the parents of a couple. Death certificates, perhaps the best kind of vital record for African American researchers, identify spouses, parents, and other data of value to genealogical researchers.

STATEWIDE REGISTRATION OF VITAL EVENTS

*U*niversal registration of vital events got off to a late start in the United

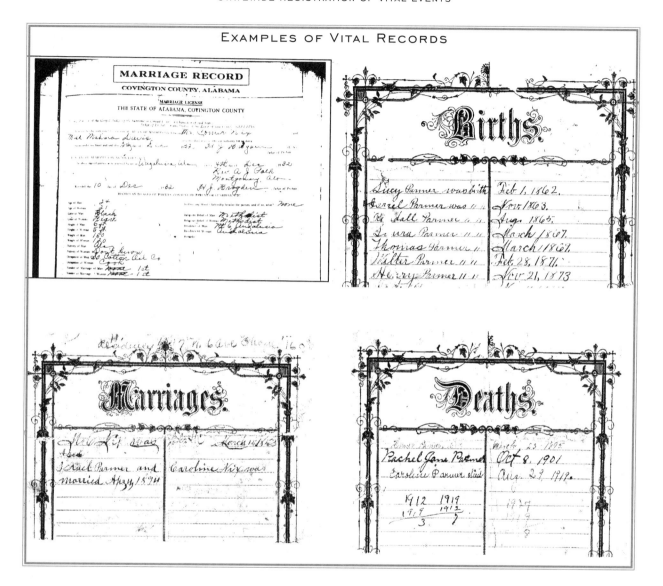

EXAMPLES OF VITAL RECORDS

States. It was not until the early twentieth century that the country could say that a universal system of registration of vital events (births, marriages, deaths) was in place. Even with such a system in operation, the actual registration of these events often depended on a simple matter of how far an individual lived from the local courthouse. Prior to universal registration of vital events at the turn of the century, the registration of births, marriages, and deaths was uneven and ultimately depended on local laws and traditions in a given county courthouse where these events were recorded in various registers. The following chart will give you an idea of the availability of official vital records for most southern states.

ALTERNATIVE RECORDS FOR ESTABLISHING THAT A VITAL EVENT OCCURRED

*R*ecord keeping on African Americans varied from place to place and time to time. In general, for those states with a strong tradition of local record keeping, the typical African American genealogist will fare better in finding records for an ancestor than in those states where such a tradition was absent. No authoritative survey has been done to really determine the extent to which local areas and counties kept good vital records on African Americans.

Almost any record that consistently lists a birth or death can be used to verify that the event occurred, where it occurred, and when it occurred. The absence of an official record only makes the researcher's job more difficult rather than impossible. Note, however, that estimated dates or dates based on an oral tradition or a lost record will have to be used often. Such was the case with my relative who could not find any valid alternative sources to verify her birth. She checked insurance papers, school records, looked for a family Bible without any luck. The one source that she could have used in lieu of the birth certificate, the federal census, was in error, an error that was used against her. Listed below are some alternative sources for establishing that a vital event occurred and that a record might exist to document it.

BEGINNING DATES FOR STATEWIDE MAINTENANCE OF VITAL RECORDS*

State	Birth	Death	Marriage	Divorce
Alabama	1908	1908	1936	?
Arkansas	1914	1914	1917	1923
Georgia	1919	1919	1952	1952
Kentucky	1911	1911	1958	1958
Louisiana	1914	1914	none	none
Maryland	1898	1898	1951	1961
Mississippi	1912	1912	1942	1942
North Carolina	1913	1930	1962	1958
South Carolina	1915	1915	1950	1962
Tennessee	1914	1914	1945	1945
Texas	1903	1903	1945	1945
Virginia	1912	1912	1853	1918
West Virginia	1917	1917	1921	?

*Source: *Where to Write for Vital Records*, U.S. Department of Health and Human Services (Washington, D.C.: U.S. Government Printing Office, 1990). This booklet should be available at your local public library. Note that some states may have records prior to the above dates.

- Cemetery headstones
- Family Bibles
- Funeral obituaries
- County courthouse registers
- Cemetery records
- Funeral home records
- Newspaper notices
- Church records
- Census records
- Institutional records
- Original Social Security Application
- Databases, genealogical compilations, and sources
- Indexes and abstracts for births, marriages, and deaths
- Biographical compendia
- *International Genealogical Index*
- *Social Security Death Index*

Cemetery Headstones and Cemetery Records: Family reunions, if held in the South, are always good occasions to visit church and other cemeteries. There you will see a wide variety of headstones. Some will have names but no dates; some will have nothing at all; and some will have inaccurate information even when dates are given. These are the things to look for in small church cemeteries in the South: naming patterns, patterns of burial, earliest dates of birth and death, aging and styles of headstones. You might want to make a map of the cemetery, because it is unlikely that the church has surviving records. Once you make the above observations, you can readily determine the age of the cemetery as derived from the oldest date of burial. Also take note of those family members who are not buried in the cemetery and those who were born in slavery. This should lead you to examine other local cemeteries, both black and white.

Finally, private family cemeteries in some parts of the country were often used by both Blacks and Whites. If your ancestors served as slaves on large plantations, it would be worth your time to try to locate the slave burial grounds as you sift through the slave owner's records. Slave burial customs varied, but often a separate burial ground existed in the vicinity of these plantations. If you find your ancestors buried at a local white church cemetery, you might surmise that many of the unmarked graves are those of slaves. In certain areas, you might find unusual headstones designed by slaves themselves. In the process of collecting this information, record (including taking photographs) all of the information that you can! You may even find that your ancestors' burial grounds have been excavated by archeologists.

Large private or public cemeteries in major cities will often have a sexton's office in charge of keeping records, and it is here that you will find records on plots and burials. If such records have been kept, you may be lucky to find an index to burials. In other cases, you may find a pile of loose records that have not been maintained at all. Finally, you may find that no such record exists, even though the death certificate indicates that the individual is buried there, as in the case of one of my diligent students, who contemplated suing a cemetery when the plot where her ancestor had been buried could not be found.

Church Records: Church records that contain evidence of vital events are likely to be scattered among the descendants of all former secretaries, pastors, and important church figures. Thelma Eldridge of Chicago found on her visit to Arkansas a complete set

of church records starting with 1866—all in the hands of a ninety-year-old former church secretary. This luck is rare for many African American genealogists. The truth is that African American church records are so dispersed, no one source can tell you where you are likely to find surviving records that might have recorded births, christenings, baptisms, memberships, and deaths.

Funeral Home Records: Funeral homes are good places to locate records that contain vital data on your ancestors. Write or visit the funeral homes in the area where your ancestors lived before migrating North. Most African American funeral homes were started at the turn of the century. There are a few, however, that existed prior to that time, such as the Joseph A. Jackson Funeral Home in Chicago, which dates back to the 1860s. Even for funeral homes as old as this, you might find that sur-

viving records are dated no earlier than the 1900s. There will be many disappointments in your research. There will also be surprising facts, as in the case of white funeral homes handling African Americans. Do not neglect any possibilities in your research.

Funeral Obituaries: Many churches ought to be more diligent in maintaining obituary files. However, everyone kept obituaries as testaments to the life of an individual, and in recent times, obituary writers have become more conscious of both the quality and content of an obituary. Because family members presumably know the most about the deceased, the accuracy of these documents is fairly high. Of course, researchers have to remember that what is not stated in an obituary is as important as what is stated. Examine excerpts from the following obituaries to see why they are important. Mrs. Maggie Shine was certainly the child of slaves, and carried many memories and much information with her when she passed. The second, Aytah Nix, reveals typical migration paths of many African Americans.

Obituary for Mrs. Maggie Shine

The late Mrs. Maggie Shine, daughter of the late Mr. and Mrs. Jack Reid, was born in Butler County on April 15, 1886—99 years, 11 months, and 25 days ago. She departed this life April 8, 1986, 2:30 P.M., at Stabler Memorial Hospital. She joined the Mt. Moriah Baptist Church. Later she joined the St. Luke A.M.E. Zion Church and remained until her passing. She was married to the late Mr. J. B. Shine who preceded her in death. To this union ten children were born; two preceded her in death. She was a devoted wife and mother who loved her family and made many sacrifices for them and to all who were around her. She leaves to cherish her memory six sons, Autrie Shine of Baltimore, Eskimo and Roy of New York, Samuel of Panama City, Oscar and Booker of Greenville, Alabama, Trudie Durham of Florida, and Eolene Shine of New York; 29 grandchildren, 17 great-grandchildren and one great-great-great grandchild; one sister, Mrs. Jerusha Reid; a host of other relatives and friends.

Obituary for Aytah Wood Nix (1905–1978)

Brother Aytah Wood Nix was born in Pensacola, Florida, October 19, 1905, to the late John and Rosetta Nix. He confessed Christ at an early age and was united with Mt. Olive Baptist Church in Tuskegee, Alabama. Later he moved back to Pensacola and then to Chicago, Illinois, where he was united with the Vernon

Baptist Church. After he retired, he moved back to Pensacola where he united with St. John Divine Baptist Church. He served with the Trustee Board and was Vice President of the Senior Usher Board. Brother Nix was united with the late Bessie Martin. To this union was born four children. Later he married Ester Nix. He leaves to mourn (names and residences follow). ✳ ✳ ✳

Family Bibles: Because church life was so important in African American communities, nearly everyone belonged to a church from emancipation well into the twentieth century. Likewise, nearly every family owned a Bible that was kept almost as a centerpiece in the home. Many of these Bibles have long since disappeared, along with the vital data that had been recorded in them. As you conduct your interviews, be sure to inquire about family Bibles for all of your lines. Copying the information into your own set of notes is extremely important. Two significant Bibles in my family have been lost—one belonged to my maternal great-grandfather and the other to my paternal great-grandmother, who, because she was a midwife, had entered the births of many children in the local area. Collecting birth, marriage, and death data from Bibles and obituaries will help you with subsequent searches.

Newspaper Notices: African American newspapers contain a tremendous number of marriage and death notices. Because many of the early papers have been microfilmed and placed in a variety of archives, college and local libraries throughout the country, their accessibility to most researchers will not be a problem. If your ancestors were socially or politically prominent or lived as free persons during slavery, a newspaper search is in order. If you have the year of death or an approximation, it will not be difficult to go through these papers because the earlier ones typically did not exceed ten pages. In addition, white newspapers located in small communities often featured the life stories of elderly black individuals in columns that dealt with bygone days. Local historical societies will often have indexes or clippings files from these papers. Note that there are very few major compilations of genealogical indexes to early Black newspapers.

Institutional Records: Hospitals, schools, unions, factories, lumber companies, Black-owned insurance companies and banks, schools, colleges, and universities are just a few institutions that might have records on your ancestors. The problem with large institutions, however, is that their historical records on individuals are frequently not archived, but rather stored in remote warehouses or simply lost. If you had urban ancestors at the turn of the century, particularly in the larger cities, you might want to check with the local historical society to see if any attempt has been made to archive such records. Company records, including railroad records, may indeed be more accessible than the records of a large public school system. One scholar based his history of migration to Pittsburgh on the study of a company's employee files, each of which contained significant genealogical data. Railroad employee records may be relevant to African American researchers because of the large number of African American men who served as Pullman porters. The fact that death benefit claims may still be pending has encouraged many companies to keep their

personnel or employee records in a relatively intact state.

County Registers: As mentioned previously, many counties in the United States had some form of vital record keeping prior to the emergence of statewide registration of vital events. It appears, however, that recording these events for African Americans was uneven and varied from county to county and state to state. As a good researcher, you will want to directly determine whether your ancestors appeared in these records by examining them yourself.

Census Records and Mortality Schedules: In the case of my relative who could not find valid evidence of her birth, Census Bureau records were used as the *official* validating source for her birth. Likewise, many African American researchers will wind up using information from census records as the only source on an ancestor's birth, marriage, and occasionally, his or her death. This will especially be the case in situations where no other vital evidence or vital records were located in the course of research. For slave-born ancestors who lived into the twentieth century, this will definitely be the case for *approximate* dates of birth and marriage. Census questions about number of years of present marriage, age, widowhood, number of children ever born and how many now living can be used to infer approximate dates and ages as well as other vital data, particularly if the information is consistent from one census to the next.

The body of records called Census Mortality Schedules may be of assistance to research during the period from 1850 to 1880. Using a mortality schedule, each census enumerator inquired about deaths that occurred in the twelve months preceding the census, and that is one critical limitation of the schedules. Another is that the surviving schedules were never collected and archived in one place; some are now archived at the various state archives while others are at the National Archives. No complete microfilm set has yet been published. These schedules will be discussed in the chapter on censuses.

Original Social Security Application: Every governmental agency has a person designated to handle inquiries about individual records on individuals. This has been mandated by the many freedom of information laws that have been passed by all levels of government. The Social Security Administration has such an office, and when I received a response to my original letter, I was shocked to find out that deceased individuals "have no rights to privacy"—in this agency's view, at least. I was, therefore, entitled to the information contained on the original Social Security application of any of my ancestors who had a Social Security number. (Note that this rule is not true in the case of a person's surviving papers housed at a library or archives.)

The original form that an individual completed to receive a Social Security card contains critical information: name of parents, including mother's maiden name, the applicant's date and place of birth, the date the card was applied for, and on occasion, his or her place of employment. If you cannot establish this information from any other source, especially name of parents or a mother's maiden name, then immediately request the appropriate forms from the SSA. The waiting period to receive this information is quite lengthy (two to three months),

so do it early if you don't encounter this information at the beginning stages of your research. The SSA charges a fee based on whether or not you know the deceased's Social Security number (which you should try to get from the *Social Security Death Index* as discussed below in the section describing the index). In your letter of request, and this is true of most queries about deceased individuals, make sure that you provide information that establishes a unique identity such as place of birth, date of birth, race, and so on. The more common the name, the more information you need to provide. You might think his or her name is unique, but nearly all such queries will require specifics.

Genealogical Compilations and Sources
In lieu of obtaining a copy of the original record, many genealogists rely on a variety of publications of compiled vital data and information. These compilations appear in the form of indexes, databases, abstracts, and transcriptions of massive amounts of information, thereby making it easier for researchers. The following sources can also be used by African American genealogists, followed by obtaining a copy of the original record when necessary. Because no compilation can ever be complete or completely accurate, or for that matter always procedurally sound, researchers will want to closely evaluate the information derived from such publications.

Indexes and Abstracts for Births, Marriages, and Deaths: Suppose you visit your county's local historical society or a large genealogical library, and you find a book entitled *Births, Marriages and Deaths Reported to the Pineville Observer Newspaper, 1890–1920.* This book would represent a compilation of *some* but not *all* vital events for your county of research during that period of time. Perhaps a resident of Pineville abstracted this data over the course of five years while searching for information on her own ancestry. This scenario is a typical one for how genealogical publications come about. In this case the genealogist has derived information from a secondary source and not from the original records. Because the *Pineville Observer* was not a Black paper, you could also easily assume that your African American ancestors are not included. Nevertheless, since the book is in your hands, to look would only take a few minutes, and that is exactly what you should do. You should be concerned chiefly with the accuracy of the genealogist's work as well as the accuracy of the newspaper's reporting, since neither publication derived its information from the original marriage, birth, and death records. Even if they had, errors could still abound, including errors of willful exclusion (African Americans), omission (accidental), and misspellings (unavoidable). In addition, judging by the title, the researcher should not assume that all births, marriages, and deaths in Pineville were actually reported to the newspaper.

Social Security Death Index: Imagine having access to millions of names to search using the speed of a computer—in fact, everyone who died and was eligible for Social Security benefits since the program's inception. That's what the *Social Security Death Index* is. The sheer volume of this database guarantees that the information will be limited. The index simply lists the name of the deceased, his Social Security number, local address, and year of birth and death. However, search these records for your ancestors if you think they participated in the Social Security system (cards were first issued beginning in 1936). The search will yield the Social Security number itself, thereby allowing you to obtain information from the original application on file at the Social Security Administration. Those researchers whose ancestors had names like John Smith will have to use this index with caution. The database will pull up hundreds of thousands of John Smiths, and if you do not have any other information to tell you that this is your John Smith, the database is of little utility to you until you get additional information about his place of residence or approximate dates of birth and death.

The IGI—*International Genealogical Index:* The IGI is a publication of the Genealogical Society of Utah (affiliated with the Latter Day Saints or the Mormon church). This microfiche publication is indexed by state and then by surname. It is one of the largest compilations of vital data available to researchers, but it does not include all vital events ever recorded in the United States. Entries on African Americans will appear if African Americans appeared in the records from which the data for the IGI was compiled.

Cemetery Surveys and Transcriptions: Transcriptions of official cemetery records or headstones constitute a large portion of genealogical publications. African American researchers should know that few publications exist on African American cemeteries. African American genealogy is still a relatively new field, after all. Many genealogical transcriptions of cemetery records and headstones may purport to cover all cemeteries in a county, but at the same time exclude African American ceme-

teries. On the other hand, there are more recent publications that (1) indicate whether African American cemeteries are included or (2) actually include them in any transcriptions. It pays to check all sources before making a judgment. In the end, of course, you would want to actually visit any cemetery included in such publications, particularly if many of your ancestors are buried there. If you have access to a Works Progress Administration (WPA) inventory for your state, frequently on file at the state's archives, you might find that in some cases, cemetery records and headstones were transcribed by this project. The WPA conducted many surveys of churches and cemeteries throughout the country, including the South, during the Depression era.

Biographical Compendia: Finally, if you had an ancestor who was socially prominent, owned a business, had a profession, or may have been politically active, you may find a biographical profile in the many biographical compendia published at the turn of the century. These biographical books, often called "mug books" but more appropriately termed biographical dictionaries, are equivalent to *Who's Who* directories. Because there was an active religious and secular publishing movement in the African American community at the turn of the century, you will find these publications for major cities as well as for some southern states. I found, for example, one such book for Alabama by a Joseph H. Moorman entitled *Leaders of the Colored Race in Alabama* published in 1928 by The News Publishing Company of Mobile, no doubt an independent Black publishing company. More recently, an attempt has been made to identify and reproduce all extant copies of such publications in the *Black Biographical Dictionaries* project.

THE WORLD WIDE WEB AND NAME INDEXES

So you've become addicted to names? That's one of the worst genealogical curses because a name is just that and no more. But if you're on the Web, then that's the right place for you to satisfy your addiction, sitting for five hours searching the many databases that are now available. The Ancestry home page (www.ancestry.com) has an ad that refers to searching their database of 90 million names. Try it. The minimal information that you will find is the *Social Security Death Index* information for an ancestor who had a Social Security number. Many of our ancestors who lived in rural areas did not have numbers unless they were employed in nonfarm occupations, or had been in the military, or had moved to the North where they were employed by a company. Even some Northerners went without the benefit of "social security" given that domestic workers were the most neglected group of people with regard to employee benefits.

Just to show you how confusing name searching can be, enter a general search phrase using one of the surnames that you are researching such as "Oglesby Family." Were any of the families that you pulled up connected to your ancestry? At this stage, you will probably answer no. But you've spent hours looking for the Oglesbys. It's not that they don't exist, it's just that either they haven't made it to cyberspace or you, the researcher, do not have reasonable specifics or guesstimates about their identity.

The Web is just that, a web to tangle the unwary. It is yet another layer of information and resources that you will learn to penetrate, hopefully to your benefit. At this point, you can still do your research without using the Web. Yet, if you learn how to use it without getting diverted, the Web can save you the time that you would have spent on writing or calling various places for information. At present, the Web is more of a resource tool for African American researchers rather than a source for extensive information to be found in databases (with the exception of the few that will be noted as we go along).

In addition, very few original records have been posted to the Web. What this means for beginners is that you might easily spend too much time searching for things that do not yet exist on the Web, for example, your own family history. It is more likely that you will be the one to post your family history to various Web sites or to your own Web site.

I've seen many postings that ask the question, believe it or not, "Can you help me find my ancestors, Jake and Fannie Simms?" This question is equivalent to entering the search term "Smith Family." But do use the Web, selectively, until you become familiar with how to do standard genealogical research. This book contains website listings at the end to help you, but know that sources as they currently exist on the Web are sometimes insufficient.

What you will find, however, are many resources to help you do your research as well as many compilations of genealogical data posted to a vast array of sites. The same rules about genealogical compilations discussed above apply to the sources you find on the Web. You must always be prepared to locate the original record when in doubt. Finally, know that libraries and archives still contain most of the information that you are seeking, but if you learn how to use the Web, it can become a wonderful resource tool. Having access to a good genealogical library and being connected to a genealogical network through membership in a society or membership on an African American list on the Web is still your best bet.

One final note about name indexes as they currently exist for African American genealogical research. Most published genealogical name indexes contain information on Europeans, and incidentally African Americans who appeared in the same records. The sources cited in this chapter are those with which you will have the most luck. Study carefully comments made about them before plunging into a mass of data that will leave you frustrated and with a pile of notes on people who may not be connected to you. If anything, you will be one of the people to begin publishing name indexes for African American genealogy. That's exactly how European genealogists wound up with so many publications; they did it themselves.

MARRIAGE RECORDS

Obtaining marriage records can be far more difficult than obtaining death certificates. Most state laws require that marriages occur in steps. That is, couples must apply for a license to marry (marriage license). Once the license is approved and issued by the county clerk, he may report the names of individuals applying for marriage licenses to the local newspaper. The notices may then appear in the local paper prior to the marriage. When the couple marries, they present a copy of the license to the minister or justice of the peace who then returns it to the appropriate authority (generally the county clerk) after the ceremony. The clerk files the record in a volume along with all other marriages for that period of time. Before returning it, the section of the license requiring signatures of witnesses and the minister or justice of the peace must be completed. After the ceremony, a marriage certificate is generally issued by the minister or the presiding individual. Note the number of records that have been generated in this whole process. The best record will often be the license on file at the county clerk's office and not the certificate, which generally states the names of the couple, the minister, the date and location of the marriage and witnesses. The certificate does contain clues to the extent that the witnesses are often relatives.

A NOTE ON THE RECORDING OF VITAL EVENTS DURING AND AFTER SLAVERY

Historical records are filled with examples of estimated dates of birth for African Americans born during slavery. Researchers, therefore, need to know about the problems to expect in using dates to mark these events in their ancestors' lives. One is the exactness of dates of birth. Even when you find a stated date of birth in a record, you should know that the further back in time, the more likely that these dates will not be precise. If you find a complete date of birth for someone born in slavery, for example, you should question its accuracy. If he or she was born near the end of slavery, you can perhaps trust the accuracy more than dates occurring in the early nineteenth century.

In some cases, however, you might eventually find a record kept by a slave owner listing births and deaths. You will note that complete dates are frequently missing. A descendant of the family that owned my ancestors (my maternal grandfather's line) gave me a copy of a Bible record that had been kept by members of her family. You might think that this would be the most accurate source, but this is not always the case. In this case, the births were not recorded as they had occurred. Each birth was entered in the same handwriting, a good sign that someone sat down and recorded these events all at the same time. I was astounded and happy that such a record survived. Of course, it raised more questions than could be answered with the evidence that I did find, and this should always be expected in genealogical research.

For the period of slavery, there is also the possibility that some of your ancestors belonged to the slave owner's church and were buried in the slave owner's family plot at a local church. The practice of keeping lists of slave members of a particular church was often characteristic of the Catholic church in Louisiana, but it was also true of all denominations throughout the South.

Religious worship was sometimes encouraged by slave owners, and this tradition certainly helped your ancestors to build their own churches right after slavery, often with the help of a former slave owner. Once you reach this stage of research, you will eventually find out if this was the case for your ancestors. On your visit to the local area, you might be given a transcription of church membership rosters for local churches and find, for example, that slaves were entered. One or some of those individuals might be your ancestors, but you might not recognize them until you get to that period of research. Don't turn down the information; merely record it in your notebook for reference once you reach the period of slave research.

A Note on Slave Marriages

During the early years of Reconstruction, some states passed laws that addressed the issue of marriages that had been formed during slavery. In the state of Alabama, the legislature simply passed a law making all such marriages legal. On the other hand, the North Carolina state legislature required such couples to register their marriages at a nearby courthouse. As a result of this law, "cohabitation bonds" were issued by various counties, and records of these marriages exist under various titles such as "Freedmen's Marriage Record," "Acknowledgment of Cohabitation," "Marriages of Freedmen," and "Cohabitation of Negroes." Researchers should make a point of checking to see what kind of mechanism was set up by the various Reconstruction state legislatures to legitimize and register marriages that were formed during slavery. Local officials and agents of the Bureau of Refugees, Freedmen, and Abandoned Lands formalized marriages that had occurred during slavery, as did army chaplains attached to various Civil War regiments. Therefore, researchers would want to examine these records when they reach the early Reconstruction years, particularly if their ancestors lived in areas where there was an extensive occupation by the Union army. The chapter on records of the Freedmen's Bureau will assist you in locating such records.

Marriages were generally condoned and encouraged by planters, but only occasionally will researchers find *written* evidence that such ceremonies actually took place. (Ironically, recognition of slave marriages among planters bought a certain amount of peace, and actually proved beneficial to keeping order within the slave community.) Researchers will often find family groups entered in various record books and probate records of slave owners. From these family groups, you will have to assume that the couples were married in the context of what was permissible under slavery. That freedmen moved to quickly validate their marriages before the law suggests that marriage during slavery was an important institution within the slave community. Yet it would be unrealistic to assume that every slave marriage was of free choice. The interests of the slave and the slave owner were the same on this issue, at least, though their motivations were certainly different. Some scholars believe that many slave marriages were forced by planters to increase the size of their slave holdings. There is certainly evidence for this, but scholars cannot tell us

how extensive it was. Consider this report from a freedman, Harry McMillan, to the American Freedmen's Inquiry Commission in 1863 at Beaufort, South Carolina:

Well, since this affair [Union army occupation and freedom] there are more married than ever I knew before, because they have a little more chance to mind their families and make more money to support their families. In secesh [past] times there was not much marrying for love. A man saw a young woman and if he liked her he would get a pass from his master to go where she was. If his owner did not choose to give him the pass he would pick out another woman and make him live with her, whether he loved her or not.

CASE STUDIES: THE USE OF VITAL RECORDS

What Is a Fact? The Use of Death Certificates in Making Inferences

Death certificates are some of the best sources to use for information on your ancestors who died after states began to keep official records in the first decade of the twentieth century. However, it is commonly said that the information contained in death certificates is only as good as the credibility of the individual who provides the information or the informant. Since you will generally not know how the informant obtained his information nor his state of mind when he gave the information on the deceased, you will assume that this information is tentative until you find other records that are consistent with the information given in the death certificate.

Case Study #1: John and Amealie Longmire

The following data was extracted from John and Amealie Longmire's death certificates. John and Amealie are my maternal great-great grandparents, and Amealie was the one who passed down to my mother terms like "as happy as a dead pig in the sunshine." Yet, she too died with her "cheeks puffed up," for based on what she did tell my mother, she certainly knew of the institution of slavery, though she was not a part of it.

The first thing that you need to know is the identity of the informant or the person who provided information needed to complete the record. The informant for Mealie (she was never called Amealie) was Mary Louise Foreman of Georgiana, Alabama. The informant for John was Clarence Longmire, his oldest son. Mealie's informant did not know her mother's name because she was not related to the family; Mary L. Foreman was the local funeral director. John's oldest son knew the names of his grandparents, and he also had access to John's Bible, which has since been lost. Note the years of birth for each (1866 and 1867). According to family lore, Mealie always said that she was born the year slavery ended (in her area, that would have been 1865). The question arises, was Mealie born in 1865 or 1867, or the year that she was actually set free (a date that we really don't know)? Could it be that the informant, the funeral director, skipped over the question? Who was the real informant anyway?

Furthermore, was Mealie really born in Lowndes County? Everyone says that she came "up from around Forest Home," which is in Butler, not Lowndes County. John's birthplace is listed as Butler County, but my research later suggested that he was born in either Monroe or Wilcox County. He was, however, in Butler County around 1868, and perhaps this is the source of confusion. Both John and Mealie were buried at Olive Branch Cemetery, although they had been members of Christian Light Church, a church which John himself helped to build. I learned later that Christian Light Church did not have its own cemetery, and its members were always buried at their sister church, Olive Branch.

There will always be inconsistencies between what is reported and what the family believes to be true. All the more reason to find all surviving family records. The critical role of the informant is also shown. Would you trust an oldest son's word more than that of an unknown informant who gave the information to the local funeral director? The original informant was not identified for Amealie. Note also that the medical information contained in death certificates can also provide insight on the family's medical history.

	John Longmire	Amealie Longmire
Death	2 November 1951	27 May 1957
Birth	26 September 1866	16 September 1867
Birthplace	Butler County, AL	Lowndes County, AL
Father's Name	Larkin Longmire	Bill Posey
Mother's Name	Hanna Riley	Unknown
Informant's Name	Clarence Longmire	Mary L. Foreman
Cause of Death	Organic Heart Disease	Arteriosclerosis
Date of Burial	11 November 1951	31 May 1957
Place of Burial	Olive Branch Cemetery	Olive Branch Cemetery
Funeral Director	Johnson's Funeral Home	Foreman's Funeral Home

The best vital records are those that link individuals to a previous generation or those that include at least two generations of the same family. If John and Mealie were born in the mid-1860s, then we can assume that their parents were born no later than the mid-1840s. From the years of John and Mealie's deaths to the years of their parents' estimated births is at least 110 years, or five generations. The death certificates link us back that far, but researchers should know that the next step is not to try to document the lives of John and Mealie's parents. The next step is to complete research on John and Amealie's generation.

Case Study #2: Rachel Parmer's Maiden Name and the Identity of Her Spouse

My great grandmother, Rachel Parmer, had ten children. I had reached a block in trying to extend the line back because I did not have a "correct" maiden name, nor did I have her spouse's first name. Older family members in my father's generation who should have known the identity of their grandparents did not seem to remember

ever hearing any "talk" about their grandparents. I had my grandfather's death certificate, and it listed Jones as her maiden name. I had never heard of any Joneses in the local area, and I was quite surprised. I had first assumed that perhaps the Jones was actually Jane because the family Bible had listed her as Rachel Jane. The family Bible did not include her spouse's name. The question that continued to overwhelm me was why no one knew. I had at least one family Bible, though the information reflected only one generation; they had certainly left plenty of descendants with ten children; there was a church cemetery filled with graves, but there was no living memory of Rachel Parmer and her spouse. The information given to me during one of my interviews had suggested that her maiden name was Hamilton. (See the chapter 2 interview with Arthur Matthews.)

I decided that the first line of attack would be to obtain death certificates for some or all of her deceased children. I first assumed that all had lived past 1908, the year death certificates began to be collected by the State of Alabama. I had several reasonable choices. I could order all of the certificates, or I could order one for the oldest and one for the youngest. My grandfather was more or less in the middle. If I ordered all of them, it would cost a whopping $120. (The cost of obtaining a death certificate had increased from $5 to $12.) Since I had no cheaper way to do this, I eventually ordered a total of five, three of which focused on the oldest (all females). In addition, I continued to try to find someone who knew more about the family's history.

This is what I found for three of the death certificates:

The object, to identify the name of Rachel's spouse and her maiden name, was not entirely successful using the evidence from three of her children's death certificates. Only one of the certificates indicated the name of a spouse, and one indicated her maiden name which I assumed to be incorrect. Rule: No one source alone should be used to establish an event or a fact. The remaining certificates should be ordered.

Note: Missing Information Is as Important as Found Information

Often, you will receive a notice called a "Certificate of Failure to Find Record." In the state of Alabama, I received two such certificates, one for Hester, the oldest child, and the other for Lucy, the third oldest child of Rachel Parmer. This is what I found for Hester:

This certificate verifies that a diligent search of the records in my custody has been made covering the period 1933 to 1943. No record was found to exist of the death of Hester Parmer Hudson in 1935 in Crenshaw/Butler County, Alabama.

This is not useless information. Early in my research, I had taken a chance at estimating the date of her death because I had not completely transcribed the cemetery headstones in the local churches! Big mistake! Nevertheless, since I knew that deaths were nearly always reported for these counties, this tells me that Hester probably died before 1933. Failure to find information is

Name:	Emma Champion	Israel Parmer	Walter Parmer
Date of death:	17 March 1928	10 Feb 1951	16 April 1949
Age at death:	70	88	76
Informant:	Not listed	James Parmer	Searcy Hospital
Name of father:	Henry Parmer	Unknown	Unknown
Name of mother:	Unknown	Not asked	Unknown
Her maiden name:	Unknown	Rachel Jones	Unknown
Spouse's Name:	Wesley Champion	Not asked	Not asked
Funeral Home:	Not listed	James Herbert	Christian Bene.
Where Buried:	Conecuh County	Pigeon Creek, AL	Greenville, AL
Cemetery Name:	Oldtown	St. Luke Church	Not listed

not a complete failure. It helps you to eliminate certain possibilities or facts. Going fishing in the records with estimated dates and incomplete information had cost me quite a bit of money!

Comparing Local and Family Information with the Record

Sometimes knowing the name of the registrar is important. In the case of Israel Parmer's death certificate, the local registrar had some kin connections with the local community, and she, therefore, may have known Rachel Parmer's correct maiden name. In fact, because Rachel had been a slave, the registrar might have either known more about the family than the family was willing to admit itself—or more than the surviving generations of the family knew about itself! This explanation would certainly seem to fit given that my father and grandfather had never lived more than a few miles from each other before my grandfather died! Surely they had to have talked about the past at some point, though in my grandfather's case, it must have been a painful subject.

Suppose Rachel and her spouse had been slaves on the same plantation or farm, and both of their families had left slavery with the surname Parmer. The maiden name of Parmer would have been correctly reported, causing the unwary researcher of today some confusion, to say the least. Researchers will encounter this problem, but it is only an obstacle rather than a complete block. First of all, slaves rarely married cousins or kin. In this case, the maiden name of a female slave being reported as the same as her spouse's surname on a death certificate merely indicates that neither family

knew any other surname and merely hid the fact that this was the case! The more likely scenario, however, is that surviving relatives would not have reported it at all. One of the oldest children, Emma, certainly had some direct knowledge of her father, knowledge which she apparently passed to the person who was the informant on her death certificate. Her brother, my grandfather Israel, perhaps had no such direct knowledge. Rule: Check the position of the informant in the family's cycle—older children have more direct knowledge than do younger children! Knowledge of ancestry can be easily lost depending on the position of children and their children in the lineage. Note on the Parmer chart that my father was the youngest child of Rachel's fourth child. While he was in a position to know the names of his maternal grandparents and great-grandparents, the fact that he was the youngest may well have had an impact on his ability to know. Furthermore, it is quite possible that my grandfather's apparent reticence about his ancestry may be rooted in other factors—namely the question of his own paternal identity. Had he known his father, he would certainly have passed his name on to his children. This was a relatively close-knit, but quiet, family. Had he been uncertain about his father's identity or wanted to hide that identity, he would have remained silent—and gotten away with it, dying with his cheeks puffed up. Finally, I cannot make any firm inferences about the father of all of Rachel's children, except that he was probably named Henry Parmer.

What I Found Later

The county courthouse marriage register provided the following information: "Henry

Parmer and Rachel Parmer were married on November, 1866 at the home of E. H. Matthews." No maiden name was listed, nor were their ages.

Perhaps her last name was Matthews since it was the custom for daughters to marry in their father's house. Now I have four possible "maiden" names: Jones, Hamilton, Matthews, and Parmer.

Case Study #3: The Family Bible

Imagine your great aunt Etta sitting on the front porch one Sunday afternoon after your family purchased its first Bible from a traveling salesman in 1896, over one hundred years ago. She will record all of the marriages, all of the births, and all of the deaths for her immediate family and for the grandparents if they are living nearby. Depending on how important keeping records was to your family, your great aunt Etta might have entered names and dates one year later or she might have entered them as they occurred. She probably had to ask her grandfather when he was born. He might have said, "Back in those days, child, they didn't tell you. But I reckon I was born about 1810. Your great grandmama used to say it was around Christmas because she can remember how everybody congratulated her on her Christmas present." Aunt Etta's grandfather's birthdate could be accepted as a relatively accurate one, but since she wasn't there, she decided for all of posterity that her grandfather was born December 25, 1810!

If you are lucky enough to find a Bible, having a date like the above is the least of your problems. At least you have an estimated date. You should also know that people took entering dates into the Bible

seriously enough that the motivation to lie was not present. They lied more often by omission (as in the case of my family Bible) than by misstating the estimated dates given to them by a grandparent! Nevertheless, be careful about a wide range of dates entered in the same handwriting. This would indicate that one person recorded the information at one time. Ideally, the events should have been recorded around the time they occurred, and differences in the handwriting are one good measure of this, though it too is problematic. Finally, events that occurred prior to the Bible's date of publication are likely to be less accurate than those that occurred after the date of publication. If the Bible was published in 1900, and dates of birth or marriage are entered for 1890, 1850, and 1805, you should automatically question their accuracy because they were recorded way after the event occurred.

ILLUSIONS ABOUT AFRICAN AMERICANS IN PUBLIC RECORDS

As your research proceeds, you will be beset with your own interpretations and theories. Some of these may be illusory, and may reflect your own sense of uncertainty about digging up the past. You will face enough obstacles with family interviews and finding vital records; therefore, it is important not to create additional obstacles in your own mind. Be assured that the records that have survived to tell your family's story are plentiful, though often requiring quite a bit of your time to locate. Don't assume otherwise. By law, public records are available and accessible to anyone who wants to examine or copy them—even in their original form. Access to some individual public records, however, is limited. If records on individuals fall under the various privacy acts created by governmental agencies, a certain period of time must pass before the general public can have access to them. For example, federal census records for any censuses taken after 1930 are not yet part of the public record because the federal government is obligated to protect the privacy of living individuals from whom they collect records. The same kinds of restrictions might apply to libraries, archives, and institutions that house the personal and family papers of individuals. If you are a writer or researcher who plans to write about a living person or a recently deceased person, and you know that the family papers have been donated to a local library, generally those parts of the papers that might relate to the affairs of still living individuals (personal letters, diaries, financial records, etc.) will also have privacy restrictions attached to them.

However, you may gain access to closed governmental records that apply only to you or a deceased member of your family by proving your identity or your relationship to the deceased. Local public records like those found in a county courthouse do not have such restrictions except in those states and cities where all birth records have been closed to the public. In the case of birth records, you may gain access to some closed records if the purpose of your research, genealogy, is known. These concerns should not be a problem for you because nearly all historical records are open to those who have the following three things: patience, time, and the strength to go through them!

SAME RECORDS—DIFFERENT METHODS—SAME RESULTS

*T*here is some confusion about how Euro-American and African American genealogical research differ. The difference is essentially in methods and not in the records themselves. In African American genealogical research, the typical researcher will not use compilations of genealogical source material and data as frequently as Whites do. This relates to the lack of plentiful genealogical compilations on African Americans. The records are there, but very little of this information has been transcribed or indexed and then published for the genealogical community. Much of your effort will involve locating the original records and making your own transcriptions and abstracts rather than counting on finding them in genealogical collections and libraries.

In addition, African American researchers will find that they will use the same records as Euro-Americans but often in a different way. At the beginning, everyone uses vital records and census records in much the same way. The differences in methods begin to occur when our historical experiences significantly diverged, and that means for the period 1870 and before. While some of the same pre-1870 records will be used by both groups, African Americans will have to wade through a large body of records on slave owners and other genealogical source material which Euro-American genealogists will not, of necessity, have to do—primarily because much of that information has been sifted through, then indexed or abstracted and published by Euro-American genealogists already. That is only now beginning to happen in African American genealogy.

MYSTERIOUS HIDDEN BLACK RECORDS

I've often talked to beginning genealogists who believe that somehow libraries and archives are hiding certain records that pertain to Blacks, particularly those on slavery and especially those relating to mixing. This is rare, and the problem is really linked to the problems posed in the previous section. However, some records have reportedly been excised when Black ancestry is discovered by White genealogists. While there are still some individuals to be found at libraries, historical societies, and archives who feel it is their purpose to glorify only one part of American history and even to hide it when it is negative, particularly as it pertains to the treatment of Blacks, you should know now that this indeed is a new day. Fifty years ago, some of these places may have been inaccessible. Not today. You will not be the first person of African ancestry, known or unknown, who uses these institutions and their records. Furthermore, the new mission of these institutions is to collect all of American history. Things have indeed changed.

Finally, records and documents are more likely to be not hidden but stored in basements, attics, and all other such places that do not protect their longevity. Visit any county courthouse, and you will find volumes of records stored in places where they should not be. The value placed on historical records in the United States has not been very high. The National Archives was estab-

lished in 1934—very late for a country with such a significant history. Finally, if anyone has anything to hide, they do not donate their personal and family papers to libraries, or they place restrictions on their use. Even in the case of personal family papers of slave owners retained by their descendants, papers which you will find useful once you research slavery, you will generally not encounter secrecy. Many genealogists have obtained assistance and records from the descendants of slave-owning families. In some cases, your research will help those descendants, who know little about their own ancestry. History is a complex matter. Remember that your primary purpose is to write into memory those of your ancestors who could not do it for themselves.

A QUESTION OF COLOR: SEGREGATED RECORDS

*I*n the South, records on African Americans were often segregated, and this makes your research somewhat easier. However, caution is the word! This applies generally to vital records and not to deeds, wills, and probate records, except during the period of slavery, when records on free Blacks may have been kept in separate registers and books, particularly those that relate to their emancipation. For the post-slavery period, there may indeed be a colored birth or marriage register at the end of a volume that reads "Register of Births" or "Register of Marriages," but most records, if they were identified at all, would have to be read first to find out whether the individuals were African American. Therefore, assume that your African American ancestor's record is interfiled with all other individuals unless you know otherwise. And most important of all, ask if separate records exist, particularly in the case of marriages.

WHAT MUST I DO NOW?

You've read through quite a bit of information, and it may seem overwhelming. The purpose of this chapter is to introduce you to the possibility that records to establish birth, marriage, and death can be obtained from many sources, all of which contain information about vital events. The more difficulty you encounter in finding information on an ancestor, the more likely you will check more than one of these sources. Of course, as a matter of good research, you will always compare the information from all sources to see if it is consistent. If it is not, then you will have to weigh which records are most likely to be accurate. For now, simply enter into your notes and your family group sheets the data that you have located from the interviews and records in the family's possession. Listed below are some procedural steps that you need to take next:

- Focus on collecting vital records for your generation first, then your parents' generation and then your grandparents' generation. As you go back in time, you will begin to encounter missing pieces of information.
- You will then need to request copies of birth and death records housed at the state's bureau of vital records. Don't forget that you write to the state in which the event occurred and that you must first write to obtain the appropriate forms.
- For marriage records, you must write to the county clerk where the marriage occurred. Here you will have to assume that the marriage occurred in the county where you know that your ancestors lived. All you need is two sentences (clerks are overwhelmed with similar requests). Those two sentences are: (1) Do you have a marriage record for Benjamin Smith and Bertha Edwards for the period 1940–1941? (2) If so, please let me know how much it will cost to obtain a copy. Of course, a quick call to find out the cost will expedite a response, and you might luck out and find a clerk who will verify whether such a record exists. A third sentence might be: Please check the "colored" register for the above individuals. If the term offends you, you can use African American, but know that they were called "colored" or "Negro" registers until the era of segregation ended.
- If these sources yield nothing for a particular individual, then you will set aside that question until you become familiar with other records listed in this chapter. It is likely that when you reach census research or when you visit the ancestral home, you will find the missing pieces of information.
- Compile your own personal resource directory from websites. It should at least include information on vital records for all the states where you think your research might lead you.
- Don't forget to check the bibliography and resources pages at the end of this book for critical information.

Chapter 5

A PLACE CALLED DOWN HOME

In Search of the Ancestral Home

It is the story of a mostly landless people, the coloreds, who lived in Glen Allan and other small southern towns . . . [a story] to recall a treasure more valuable and enduring than land ownership. It is the treasure that stood out in my colored childhood when there was so little else, and it has been a source of strength to me in all the years since then. That treasure is the nourishing love that came to me from my extended family. . . . This congregation of black maids, field hands and tenant farmers worked the cotton fields, fished Lake Washington, gathered at St. Mark's Missionary Baptist Church to sing and pray, and gathered at the Greenville train station to bid farewell to loved ones moving north. In ordinary daily living through very difficult times, they showed themselves to be a great people.

CLIFTON TAULBERT, *ONCE UPON A TIME WHEN WE WERE COLORED*

Gladys Collins Pritchett is searching for descendants of George Collins and Mary Elizabeth Pride, who lived in or near Eastville, Virginia, from the 1850s to the 1880s, before moving to New Jersey. If you can be of assistance, write to Gladys Collins Pritchett . . .

FROM *AMERICAN VISIONS MAGAZINE*, AUGUST/SEPTEMBER ISSUE 1993

Charles Edward Washington was born in Portsmouth, Virginia, March 29, 1892. After migrating to Wilmington, North Carolina, he married Ella Johnson. Does anyone know about this man or have other information about this family?

FROM *JOURNAL OF THE AFRO-AMERICAN HISTORICAL AND GENEALOGICAL SOCIETY* , FALL/WINTER 1991

Everybody Has a Home

*T*hose far-flung families that you placed on the map of the United States are all connected by common origins. They share more than they know, at least until you begin to tell them all about themselves. They or their ancestors come from somewhere like Greenville and its environs. They come from people just like those "colored" people who boarded the train at the Greenville station. They have common ancestry and a common place of origin somewhere in the South to which they can attach the word "home." It doesn't matter that it may only reflect a state of mind. Nor does it matter that its name is not on the map, and that there's not one building, log cabin, or shack to which they can proudly point. It still reflects the lives of the community of kin that once made it home for better or worse.

Between 1865 and 1914, the majority of African Americans lived in small rural communities among their extended kin. They remained tied to the land as either sharecroppers or small-scale farmers. It was a transitional period, however, and for many of your ancestors, this period would be the last one in which they lived so closely among people who had come such a long way together. Some left as early as the 1880s, as indicated by the ad Gladys Pritchett placed in the genealogy section of *American Visions Magazine* or around the turn of the century like Charles Edward Washington. Most likely these individuals did not leave a traceable path; they cut their ties early. Like them, many others left well before the official commencement of the Great Migration in 1914. Those who migrated before the turn of the twentieth century left in some rather unique circumstances, and they were brave indeed. Knowing about these late-nineteenth-century migrations will help researchers like the ones discussed above. In addition, the following examples will serve as a word of caution to researchers who might assume incorrectly that the path from the South to the North was a direct one.

In this chapter, you will become familiar with the records that are available in your ancestors' places of origin. For those researchers who frequently visit "home," this chapter should be considered one in which you begin to collect a considerable amount of information that will help you at the next stage—finding your ancestors in the census records. For those who will have to go directly to census records as the next big source of reliable information, know that you cannot skip this chapter, for two reasons. One reason is that you will eventu-

ally have to go "home." The second is that information in this chapter is necessary to help you bridge the gap between (1) using the resources that you have been able to locate through a genealogy facility in your home and (2) the next step, which is census research. If you are not near the ancestral home, you will have to try to obtain the information by writing to various places in the county as well as using genealogical sources that you find at a research facility where you now live. In sum, the information in this chapter is to be used as a preliminary survey of what's available in the counties where your ancestors lived.

EARLY LABOR MIGRATIONS: ENTER THE LABOR AGENT

The surplus of slaves in Maryland, Virginia, North Carolina, South Carolina, and Georgia that fed the domestic slave trade before the Civil War was transformed into a free labor reserve of individuals and families after the war's end. Ironically, now they were free and willing to migrate to places whose very names had struck terror in the heart if even spoken before slavery ended. The state of Virginia still had the largest number of African Americans in any one state by 1870. The hunger for labor still existed in the Deep South's former slave states—Mississippi, Louisiana, Texas, and Arkansas—states that bought slaves during the domestic slave trade but had not had to hire free labor. For those freedmen who migrated from the Carolinas and Georgia to Mississippi and Texas, the sheer lure of better opportunities was one motivation for continuing this antebellum movement. Instead of migrating to Kansas, they moved to the labor-starved Mississippi Delta (along with migrants from other Mississippi and Alabama counties).

They didn't migrate without help, and that help came from labor agents. These labor agents were a mixed bag of individuals—those who recruited right after the war may indeed have been former slave traders or former Union army officers who had worked as field agents for the Freedmen's Bureau. Later, African Americans recruited laborers during the Great Migration. Records kept by these agents may, on occasion, be found, but for your research they are essentially unavailable.

THE EDGEFIELD EXODUS

You may not have heard of the Edgefield Exodus, but it is symbolic of the early migrations away from the South that were organized by groups of African Americans during Reconstruction and the early years of Redemption, or the consolidation of power by Whites in the South. Both African American and White-owned newspapers commented on the migration out of Edgefield County, South Carolina, to Arkansas and Tennessee. By 1881, over five thousand had left. But many Black South Carolinians, radicalized by the war and the early years of Reconstruction, were looking for more than just forty acres and a mule. They wanted complete autonomy. Thus, in April 1878, the Liberian Exodus Joint Stock Steamship Company, organized and owned by Blacks way before Marcus Garvey initiated his Black Star Line, departed Charleston harbor en route to Liberia with two hundred African Americans on board. They were led by one Harrison N. Bouey. It doesn't matter that some returned. Interestingly, at the end of the Civil War one thousand Blacks from

Georgia and South Carolina had sailed for Liberia out of the same port.

ENTER THE EXODUSTERS

For those who wanted to own their own labor, free and clear, the appeal of having land as an added bonus must have been a key factor in the migrations from southern states that formed the Exodus movement of 1878 and 1879. While the initial goal was Kansas, some also wound up in Indiana, Ohio, Illinois, and Missouri in pre–Civil War African American settlements and neighborhoods of cities. The Exodusters movement caused such an uproar in the South that it prompted a Senate committee investigation. This report can be obtained from larger public libraries that have been designated to receive official publications of the U.S. government. The report was entitled *Report and Testimony of the Select Committee of the United States Senate to Investigate the Cause of the Removal of the Negroes from the Southern States to the Northern States* (U.S. Senate Reports, 46th Congress, 2d session, No. 693, 3 parts). The committee solicited testimony from a wide range of individuals, including many of the migrants themselves. You may even find an ancestor's testimony!

THE GREAT MIGRATION

The year 1914 was a critical year for nearly everyone in the world; where you were at that time determined what changes the year would bring in your life. For some it meant eventual military service—367,710 African Americans served in

World War I. For young men in Europe, it meant dashing their plans to migrate to the United States; instead of carrying their important possessions in cheap suitcases or laden trunks, they carried guns. For northern industrialists, it meant a shortage of labor but also an opportunity to make money. The onset of World War I helped or forced people to make some very crucial decisions indeed.

Booker T. Washington's vision of a southern Black class of artisans and farmers had yet to come to fruition. Thousands of African American men and women who had become educated enough to know about opportunities elsewhere, those poised in the cities and towns of the South and therefore part of a communications network that barely reached the rural folks, were not part of that class anyway. They therefore responded to the recruitment efforts of northern companies and the ads placed in the *Chicago Defender* by labor agents. Booker T. Washington was in his grave when Robert S. Abbott, the founder and publisher of the *Chicago Defender*, turned his philosophy completely upside down. The would-be "Black artisans" of the South voted with their feet; they went North and West rather than remain in the South to form that class of working men upon which the Washington philosophy based its dreams. Every issue of the nationally distributed *Chicago Defender* encouraged men and women to leave a South that refused to recognize their rights to political participation and the benefits that derive from it. Many did leave for these reasons, especially reasons relating to local violence against Blacks, but most perceived their departure as a chance to make a decent living.

For a people who have experienced some of the most significant *internal* migrations in the Western world, our collective memory has little to say about them. We haven't had time to look back at what a phenomenal transformation it really was to be a part of the migration of one million people from the South to the North and West between 1914 and 1920. At the end of the Civil War, four million African Americans lived in a rather narrow band of geographical space starting in Maryland and Virginia and making a long swath through the Southeast and all the way across to Texas. This was the Black Belt, named for its high-quality soil and capacity to produce cotton and other food crops. In the course of sixteen years, it must have been extraordinary to see its population reduced by one million—even more, it must have been phenomenal to have experienced it.

Part of your journey into the past is to re-create that place—the land, the people, the kin and who they married, where they struggled and died, and finally where they were buried. This task is not an easy one, but it is a rather natural extension of your family's collective oral history. But before you get there, you need to know why they left. That in turn will partly answer what you will be looking for once you arrive.

WHY THEY LEFT AND WHERE THEY WENT

*I*t was almost inevitable that some Black folks would leave the South. Between the end of the Civil War and the turn of the century, there was a considerable movement of Blacks throughout the South. The depression of the 1880s partly helped to spur this initial out-migration. The old as well as the newer industrial southern cities were the places where these early migrants found opportunities. Cities like Atlanta, Birmingham, Richmond, Charleston, Memphis, New Orleans, Baltimore, and Washington, D.C., already had significant numbers of African Americans whose presence predated the Civil War. Baltimore and Washington were once considered meccas for African Americans who aspired to lead better lives. Mid-sized towns like Pensacola, Florida, or Orangeburg, South Carolina, had also drawn a sizable population of blacks. Contrary to most of what has been written about the Great Migration, it was hardly a field-to-factory movement at the beginning. These southern towndwellers were the people who left to go North first.

The Great Migration cast a wide net and eventually did become a field-to-factory migration. Companies hired labor agents to recruit Black workers. Where there were no labor agents, Blacks took it upon themselves to write thousands of letters of inquiry. They wrote to the *Defender*, to the Urban League, and to relatives who had already gone. This is the group that laid the foundation for the early northern Black middle and working classes—they were the ones who attained whatever little upward mobility there was to be had. They were the ones who provided the engine for the rise of a significant class of professionals and businessmen. They were the ones who formed stable communities and organizational life in the newly forming ghettos, though they perhaps

saw themselves fighting a losing battle as restrictions began to be built around them in the same way they were during slavery and Reconstruction.

The Great Migration turned out to be a migration to eight principal northern industrial cities: Detroit, Chicago, Columbus, Cincinnati, Cleveland, New York, Philadelphia, and Pittsburgh. These cities contained 40 percent of all African Americans living in the North by 1920! Though much is made of the Great Migration to the North, remember that more blacks migrated to cities in the South than to the cities of the North for roughly the same period of time, an in-migration. The southern cities with the largest black populations by 1920 were Norfolk, Atlanta, Baltimore, Birmingham, Charleston, Houston, Jacksonville, Memphis, New Orleans, and Richmond. Baltimore and New Orleans had the greatest number with Birmingham, Memphis, and Atlanta trailing.

As you figure out why and how your ancestors left the South, you will collect migration stories in the process—wonderful, amazing, amusing, and sometimes sad stories about families working together. The story will be told, of course, from your own perspective. Hopefully your relatives will not have to repeat what one of the informants told Nicholas Lemann, the author of *The Promised Land:* "You didn't ask me the right questions. I've had a very interesting life, and have lots of stories to tell." The perspective that you carry on your ancestors' experiences should, of course, help you to ask the right questions so that no one has to tell you what to ask. Know who you are before someone else has to tell you!

WHAT THEY FOUND UPON ARRIVING

What migrants found when they arrived in northern and western cities was a group of earlier African American settlers, many of whom were prosperous and resented the throngs of their kinsmen making land, housing, and everything else scarce overnight in the countless confined areas in which they settled. Some believed that they were destroying the progress of the "race." Some set up social barriers—thin though they were—which must have had a lasting effect on aspiring newcomers. In Chicago, a group of black citizens established an Old Settlers Club in which membership was based on the requirement of having been in Chicago for at least thirty years. The club was founded in 1902, just when the trickles of migrants had begun to increase to a steady flow. Others responded more positively, especially those who came to Chicago with their own special skills—indeed, they recognized that these migrants would become the source of new circulation for Black-owned newspapers, the clients for a growing professional class of doctors, lawyers, Black-owned insurance companies and hospitals as well as other businesses whose growth depended on the Black consumer. Nearly all of these new enterprises in Chicago were established by educated migrants to the city and not by early settlers!

RE-CREATING YOUR ANCESTORS' GREAT MIGRATION

If your ancestors migrated during this period (1914–1920) or even later, the first thing that you want to re-create is their migration experience. Ideally, this is done in the course of collecting the family's oral history. That means asking for details as small as the train taken and the station where they disembarked as well as any surviving letters written by relatives, old bank books and employment cards, World War I discharge papers, and even street addresses. Employment records and military discharge papers in particular provide clues about your ancestors' migration experience. The migration of Pullman porters is still an untold story, partly because their employment records, part of the massive amount of papers left by the company, are still being organized at the Newberry Library in Chicago. Once your research leads you to your ancestors' point of departure, it is then time to take a visit either physically or through correspondence. You are ready to retrace your ancestors' path back down home.

WHAT YOU ARE LOOKING FOR ONCE YOU ARRIVE

Your search should always be guided by the thought that you are re-creating the past. A return to the ancestral home—whether by using sources and records where you now live or through an actual visit—is part of the territory. Depending on how old you are and where you fit in your family's kinship structure, this experience can be immediate or a very distant one. Your interviews with kin can make part of that experience more immediate even if you didn't experience it yourself.

Remember, you are always looking for two things—the experience and the records or documents to verify and interpret that experience. Often the search for records can come to symbolize your search for the ancestor, particularly when the record reveals far more than you expected. And, for African American genealogists, the search for a record is deeply entwined with all sorts of meanings, particularly that of making one's ancestors legitimate, providing them with a place in the world when their own experiences denied them that essential part of their humanity.

NOT EVERYBODY LEFT: WHAT TO DO WHEN YOU FIND THE RELATIVES YOU NEVER KNEW

Your visit, hopefully of at least two weeks' duration, will invariably put you into contact with relatives and family friends. Many of them will be relatives that you have never seen or relatives with whom you will establish a new relationship based on questions that relate to the family's history. If you are their junior, you will definitely be on new ground. Following are the major places that you should visit, the records that you should look for, as well as some themes that will keep coming up to "haint" you.

Finding a Guide

If you are not traveling with relatives, it is recommended that you recruit someone to assist you in identifying individuals to visit. Having a guide to the local area will save you time and, most important, provide you with an entrée into the local community. It is difficult to knock on someone's door asking about kin relations despite the open friendli-

ness that you will encounter. This is especially important when you need an entrée for some of the more sensitive visits that you might have. Finally, your guide can expand the possibilities of people to interview. You may drive by Mr. Ferguson's house ten times and wave even more than that before you find out—on the day you leave, no less—that Mr. Ferguson knows every event in the local community's history.

The Ancestral Church

Dotted throughout the South are thousands of small African American churches of every known Protestant denomination. If there are now approximately 65,000 African American churches in the United States, over half of them must be in the South. A recent survey reported that 70 percent of African Americans attend church. In each and every county of the historical Black Belt and in every small place where Black folks lived during slavery, you will find that they established independent churches within a few decades after emancipation. Many were extensions of churches established during slavery or through a bequest by a former slave owner. The first African American church established in this country cannot be identified with any certainty. But Silver Bluff Baptist Church outside Augusta, Georgia (Edgefield district), claims to be the oldest black church that has continuously operated on its own since its founding—in 1750. The church more than anything else was and still is the central institution in African American life outside of the family. Living without church membership was unimaginable for your ancestors—nearly everybody belonged.

Therefore, on your return, if you find

nothing else, you will find a church to which your migrating ancestors belonged before leaving—perhaps no more than a small building that looks like a one-room schoolhouse, but often a newer brick structure, a certain sign that the congregation is still active and maintaining the tradition. You may also find the original church as it was constructed in the 1880s, with improvements added over the years. Many churches in this seventh generation of freedom are now celebrating their one-hundredth-year anniversaries, for it was a little over a century ago that the majority of currently existing congregations formally organized, obtained land, and built permanent church structures.

My home church, St. Luke A.M.E. Zion near Greenville, Alabama, was organized in 1889. In the 1970s, a new brick structure was built, and a church marker names the founding families.

FACSIMILE OF CHURCH MARKER AT ST. LUKE A.M.E. ZION

St. Luke A.M.E. Zion Church Founders
Greenville, Alabama

Henry & Sallie McClain	W. T. & Annie Nix
C. G. & Elijah Nix	Abb & Marie Hamilton
Glen & Mary Mathews	Henry Crittenden
Tom & Mellie Hamilton	Sandy Florence
A. W. Nix	

Sustainers

Claude & Annie Lee Ewing	Caesar & Hester Hudson
Judie & Maggie Shine	Sula, Maude, & Fronie Everett
Arthur & Cleo McClain	Herbert & Eppie Mathews
Will and Maggie Hamilton	George Nix
Dave & Clodia Owens	Walt & Lillie Parmer
Claude & Lela Florence	Randall & Rosetta Parmer
Adam & Lucindy Nix	Rich & Annie May
Ed & Estelle Daniels	Richard A. May
Neal & Jennie Parmer	Dura F. Owens
Clinton & Neice Parmer	Sylvester & Gatsie Nix
Israel & Callie Parmer	Irving & Carnie Nix
Alonza & Dorothy Parmer	Oliver & Lena Everett
Oscar & Oleta Shine	

These names really represent families that have constituted St. Luke's congregation throughout seven generations of freedom. The land on which the church was built was owned by Henry McClain, who acquired it on January 6, 1868, from D. R. Nichols. Therefore, the whole history of this one small community can almost be told by studying these families. They married one another, worshiped together, and shared each other's trials and tribulations. Some also migrated away—at first to places like Pensacola, Andalusia, and Montgomery, then later to Buffalo, Chicago, Los Angeles, and Detroit. Perhaps you will not find a marker or physical evidence of this sort, but certainly you will want to know the names of the church founders and church "sustainers." Note that if the church was founded in the 1880s, it is likely that its founding members were born during slavery and may have been old enough to remember it. Your early research may take you back to the period of slavery more quickly than you can imagine!

Once our ancestors had begun to acquire literacy, they also began to keep records. But often a rise in historical consciousness did not occur at the same time except among those who had received formal schooling in the new training schools away from home. Thus, your return will be marked by a combination of surprise at what you find and profound disappointment that the records are not always there. If you find no surviving records, that doesn't mean they have been destroyed. It could also mean that they were never created or that they were kept sporadically. Your job becomes a little bit more difficult now. You will have to locate the descendants of former church secretaries, identify the ministers who were assigned to the church, and talk with elders in the church. Your task becomes one of reconstructing the history of the church and its families.

Better Luck at the Church Cemetery— Maybe

You will find cemeteries throughout the South that are attached to the churches your ancestors attended. Don't shy away. In places like Virginia, Maryland, and North Carolina, you may find private family cemeteries. You will also find segregated African American graves in cemeteries that are maintained by towns. Sometimes you will find cemeteries reserved only for Blacks— such as the colored cemetery Dr. Prince found in Dallas—with few or no surviving tombstone inscriptions. The colored burial ground recently discovered in New York is not really unique—unique to New York City perhaps, but there are countless such burial grounds spread all over the country, wherever African Americans once lived in large numbers. What you will find depends on whatever clues your ancestors left for you to read their history. Finding a cemetery where graves are marked but the headstones have been weathered away, or finding that a cemetery exists somewhere in the woods,

overgrown without any remaining headstones or markers, is not always the end of the search.

If the home church does have a cemetery, you will want to copy into your notebook every inscription from the headstones. This assumes that the cemetery is not very large. Copy the inscriptions in your notebook using the same order that they appear in the cemetery so that it reflects the family plot arrangement typical of most cemeteries. In larger city cemeteries, you might find that records have been kept by a sexton or the equivalent. Finally, for those headstones whose inscriptions have been partly worn away, you must try to trace the words with your hand or with chalk. My first genealogical research trip involved just such a measure. I had to kneel and use my hands just to make sure. As you meet more genealogists you will hear many cemetery stories, so I won't destroy the excitement for you.

Training Schools and Institutes

The many country schoolteachers who taught your ancestors were almost like itinerant preachers. They had a little education—enough to teach primary grades—and they later took leave for further study. Often moving from school to school, wherever a community could board them and pay a small stipend, they were a courageous bunch. They themselves had often been educated by that generation of teachers who came from the North during Reconstruction. Once married, they settled into a local community where they served as letter writers, church secretaries, and general community leaders. Unfortunately, this generation of schoolteachers left few written memoirs of their service and even fewer records on their pupils, whose labor had to be balanced with farm work. Only the determined and the gifted pupils left those countless little rural areas to attend schools and institutes like Piney Woods, Calhoun, Snow Hill, and Lomax. Those who were even luckier found their way to Atlanta University or Hampton or Tuskegee.

The Local Funeral Home

We've talked about death certificates, so you know how important funeral homes can be. Many funeral homes, however, didn't start keeping formal records until late in the twentieth century. I visited the oldest Black funeral home in my area, but I found out that records hadn't been kept until recently. I did find that the history of the first owner was important, though ancillary to my own research goals. If you do find such records, they will often contain information on kin, how the funeral was paid for, names of insurance companies, and where your ancestor was buried. Always check the oldest White funeral homes in the area to find out whether they might have records on Blacks. Don't be surprised to find that White funeral homes in your home area generally hired a Black undertaker to handle Blacks.

UNDERSTANDING THE LAY OF THE LAND: RECONSTRUCTING NIXTOWN, A LOST COMMUNITY OF KINSHIP

Where I was born used to be called Nixtown, according to family lore. It was a settlement of no more than a few hundred people all linked together by a common history, kinship, and marriages that, I discovered some one hundred years later, had taken place before and after slavery. The place Nixtown occupied still exists, but no one calls it that anymore. In fact, it had never found a place on any map. It is only a state of mind and, as for that, it only exists in the memories of a few people still living to tell the story. When they stopped calling it Nixtown, I don't know. Perhaps it happened in the 1940s, when migration to Andalusia and then Pensacola, Tuskegee, Chicago, and Buffalo had taken its toll. My own personal realization that this was a community of kinship linked to land ownership came late in my research, because I had made the common mistake of focusing on a progenitor whose impact on the family memory had been negligible.

The focus of this small settlement was my great-grandmother Lucindy Tillman Nix, the midwife, landholder, community leader, and matriarch who stood in her husband's shoes when he prematurely and mysteriously died after digging a well. (I was told that he accused one of his relatives of poisoning him. Yes, we had our "root men" too. It is more likely that the gas killed him, according to one of my interviewees; see my chapter 1 interview with Arthur Matthews.) Because genealogy is never a cut-and-dry affair, it often turns into a matter of reconstructing kinship ties about which you know little. As you research your ancestors in the small places where they came from, you will find the same surnames clustered in one area of a county. You will begin to wonder about other families with that surname—families perhaps not in your direct line, but families who are probably related in some way. You will begin to wonder about their daily existence, what kind of recreation they had outside of church activities, or why some families intermarried but others did not. You are unearthing a story as well as kinship ties. Like all stories, it can be told in narrative form. Families are never simple affairs, nor are the relationships that exist within families and between families all that simple. The enticement in genealogy is *reasoned* speculation based on the facts.

On one of my visits to my ancestral home, I created a map of the area where I was born. I later asked my mother to help me because her perspective would be that of a newly arriving person who married into the community in the late 1930s. Using the county maps that I had ordered from the Alabama State Highway Department, along with knowledge of the township and range numbers culled from the deed and mortgage books at the courthouse, allowed me to place this settlement on an official map (see pg. 114).

Saturday Afternoon at the Courthouse

*G*oing to town was a Saturday ritual for many of our ancestors. The courthouse square is where, outside of Sunday church services, people congregated to find out about the local news in other communities. But your ancestors' encounters with public authority were not always positive—for if the local courthouse was the symbol of authority in most rural communities, it often represented personal pain for them, its stately brick structure only reinforcing their sense of powerlessness. The courthouse was at the center of power in the South for it was there that all things of value changed hands. Trials were held and the guilty sent off to the county jail, crop liens were registered, land and poll taxes were paid, voters were registered, returning soldiers were dutifully entered into record books, land was deeded over or forfeited for taxes, slaves were registered as having been bought, sold, and mortgaged, and finally it was at the courthouse where your ancestor's will and estate were handled by a judge of probate—if your ancestor owned property.

But times have changed. Before you leave, a visit to the county courthouse, where your ancestors may have experienced pain on signing a crop lien or joy at obtaining the deed to a small parcel of land, is mandatory. Now you are returning to see what events in their lives were recorded and why they were recorded. Courthouse records are open to the public, and the clerk will simply show you where the record books are. You never know what you will find, so set aside enough time. On my first visit, I didn't find many of my ancestors entered into late-nineteenth-century registers of marriages, births, and deaths. But I did find them in deed and mortgage books all the way back to the post-emancipation period. I found it hard to believe that such small parcels of land could generate so many transactions. Here are examples of what I copied into my notebook:

MY COURTHOUSE NOTES

Direct Index to Conveyances of Real Estate, 1925–1936, Book L–R
Date: 27 January 1936
Land Description: 11-1/2 acres, Part of Township 7, Range 15, Section 14
Grantee: Etta Parmer
Grantors:

Annie May and husband, Richard May	Tom Nix, a single man
George Nix and wife, Nellie Nix	John Nix, a single man
Walter Nix, a single man	James Nix and wife Fannie
Lillie Dawkins and husband Gus Dawkins	Lucindia Moorer and husband Ed Moorer
William Daniel and his wife, Daisy Daniel	Man Cook, single
Sula Hamilton and husband, Columbus	Isreal Parmer, a single man
Hester Parmer, a single woman	Clinton Parmer and wife Nessie Parmer
Leonard Parmer, a single man	Oscar Parmer and wife Eunice Parmer
Annie L. Reid and husband Gideon Reid	John Ezra Parmer, a single man
James Parmer, a single man	Victoria Nix, a single woman
Leona Nix Harvey and husband Henry Harvey	Masue Nix, a single woman
Willie C. Nix, a single man	

Note: The grantee is the person to whom something is conveyed or sold. The grantor is the person who conveys, sells, or gives something. Note also that the direct index names only the grantor(s) while the indirect index would name the grantees.

Lumber/Deed Book 36, p 431
Filed 8 October 1923   Date of Deed: 25 January 1879
Grantor: Adam & Lucindy Nix, sale of 80 acres @$240
Grantee: J. J. Rainer
Description of Land:
Township 7, Range 15, Section 22
SW 1/4 of NW 1/4 and SE 1/4 of NW 1/4
Lumber/Deed Book 36, p 95
Filed 14 April 1923
"Timber Mortgage" for $700 on 217 acres
Grantor: Adam & Lucindy Nix
Grantee: W. T. Smith Lumber Company
Description of Land:
Portions of Township 7, Range 15, Section 14 and
Township 7, Range, 15, Section 15

Deed Book, Volume 8   Date: 30 January 1892
Tillman sisters sell land to Elizabeth J. Whittle for $51
Lucindy Nix and Adam Nix, Sarah Tillman, Caroline Tillman, Lizza Davidson and husband Henry Davidson, Henry Shine. Lucindy, Sarah, Caroline each 1/6th interest (or 1/2) and Lizzie Davidson and Henry Shine jointly 1/2
Description: Township 8, Range 14, Section 12, 76.5 Acres

11 Feb 1893
Champ Shine sells 180 acres to William T. Rogers for $600
Description: Township 7, Range 15, Section 14
Section 14: NW 1/4 of NW 1/4 and W 1/2 of SW 1/4
Section 15: NE 1/4 of SE 1/4 and West 1/2 of SE 1/4 of SE 1/4 and SW 1/2 of the SE 1/4

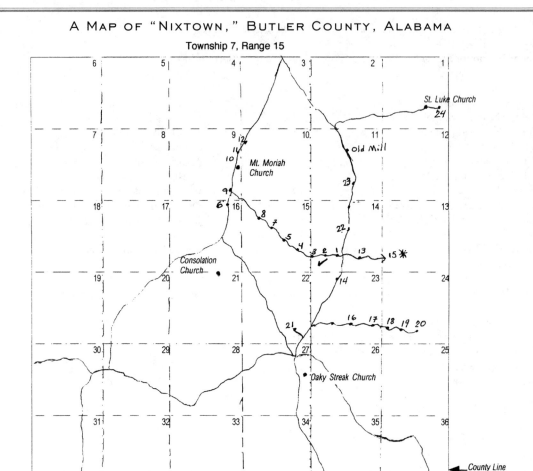

A MAP OF "NIXTOWN," BUTLER COUNTY, ALABAMA

Township 7, Range 15

Key

1	My birthplace	9	John/Annie Crittenden	17	Clint/Nessie Parmer
2	Etta Parmer	10	Ples Ferguson	18	Bill Ray Little
3	George Nix	11	Tyson Ewing	19	Aubrey Carter
4	Aunt Anne May	12	Eppie & Hubbard Matthews	20	T. & Lou Crittenden
5	Grandma Cindy's Old Cabin	13	Pecan Orchard/H. Little	21	Grandpa Israel
6	Old Plantation (Now Store)	14	Ola Mc Clain	22	School House
7	Jess Bones	15	Old Route to St. Luke	23	Henry Parmer
8	Walter Parmer · · · ·	16	Claudie & Arthur Parmer	24	Matthews/Hamiltons
*	Old Slave Cemetery?	✓	Baseball Field		

Note: I was born in Township 7, Range 15, in the SE Quadrant of Section 14 where the Crossroads meet.

Source: Butler County Courthouse: Greenville, Alabama

EXAMPLE OF WWII DISCHARGE RECORD

Army of the United States
Honorable Discharge

This Is to Certify, That .... Cleveland Parmer 34 405 290 Sergeant

.... Co L 370 Infantry 92 Division APO 92 New York ....

Army of the United States

is hereby HONORABLY DISCHARGED from the military service of the UNITED STATES OF AMERICA.
This certificate is awarded as a testimonial of Honest and Faithful Service to this country.

Given at ___ Separation Point ___ 1326th SCU ___ Camp Lee Virginia ___

Date ___ 20 October 1945 ___

John L. Hill Lieutenant Colonel QMC
Commanding

ENLISTED RECORD AND REPORT OF SEPARATION
HONORABLE DISCHARGE

1. Last Name — First Name — Middle Initial		2. Army Serial No.	3. Grade	4. Arm or Service	5. Component
Parmer Cleveland		34 405 290	Sgt	Infantry	AUS
6. Organization		7. Date of Separation	8. Place of Separation		
Co L 370 Inf 92 Div APO 92 N Y		20 Oct 45	Camp Lee Virginia		
9. Permanent address for mailing purposes		10. Date of Birth	11. Place of Birth		
Pigeon Creek Ala Rt 1 Box 96		2 Feb 22	Pigeon Creek Ala		
12. Address from which employment will be sought		13. Color Eyes	14. Color Hair	15. Height	16. Weight	17. No. Depend.
See 9		Brown	Black	5-10	170 Lbs.	1

18. Race			19. Marital Status			20. U. S. Citizen		21. Civilian Occupation and No.
White	Negro X	Other (specify)	Single X	Married	Other (specify)	Yes X	No	Angle Cutting Machine Operator 9-65.45

MILITARY HISTORY

22. Date of Induction	23. Date of Enlistment	24. Date of entry into Active Service	25. Place of entry into Service
6 Oct 42		21 Oct 42	Greenville, Alabama

Selective Service Data	26. Registered Yes X No	27. Local S.S. Board No.	28. County and State	29. Home Address at time of entry into Service
		2 Georgiana	Butler Alabama	See 9

30. Military Occupational Specialty and No.	31. Military Qualification and Date (i. e., infantry, aviation and marksmanship badges, etc.)
Asst Squad Leader	None

32. Battles and campaigns
Rome- Arno   North Apennines

33. Decorations and citations
European African Middle Eastern Service Ribbon

34. Wounds received in action
None

35.	Latest Immunization Dates			36.	Service Outside Continental U. S. and Return		
Smallpox	Typhoid	Tetanus	Other (specify)	Date of Departure	Destination	Date of Arrival	
Apr 45	Apr 45	Aug 45	None	15 Jul 44	Italy	27 Jul 44	

37. Total Length of Service						38. Highest Grade Held		
Continental Service			Foreign Service					
Years	Months	Days	Years	Months	Days			
2	1	2	0	10	28	Sergeant	2 Jun 45	USA	12 Jun 45

39. Prior service
None

40. Reason and authority for separation
Conv of Govt AR 615-365 15 Dec 44 & TWX 40094 AGOBG24 Sep 45

41. Service schools attended	42. Education (Years)		
None	Grammar	High School	College

PAY DATA

43. Longevity for Pay Purposes			44. Mustering Out Pay		45. Soldier Deposits	46. Travel Pay	47. Total Amount, Name of Disbursing Officer
Years	Months	Days	Total	This Payment			
3	0	15	$300	$100	None	$39.65	139.65 I D Waltz Maj FD

INSURANCE NOTICE

IMPORTANT: IF PREMIUM IS NOT PAID WHEN DUE OR WITHIN THIRTY-ONE DAYS THEREAFTER, INSURANCE WILL LAPSE. MAKE CHECKS OR MONEY ORDERS PAYABLE TO THE TREASURER OF THE U. S. AND FORWARD TO COLLECTIONS SUBDIVISION, VETERANS ADMINISTRATION, WASHINGTON 25, D. C.

48. Kind of Insurance			49. How Paid		50. Effective Date of Allotment Discontinuance	51. Date of Next Premium Due (One month after 50)	52. Premium Due Each Month	53. Intention of Veteran to
Nat. Serv.	U.S. Govt.	None	Allotment	Direct to V.A.				Continue	Continue Only	Discontinue
X				X	30 Sep 45	31 Oct 45	6 50			X

54.

55. REMARKS (This space for completion of above items or entry of other items specified in W. D. Directives)

Lapel Button Issued
No time lost under AW 107
Inactive Service ERC 6 Oct 42 to 21 Oct 42
Adjusted Service Record Score (2 Sep 45) 56

RIGHT THUMB PRINT

56. Signature of person being separated	57. Personnel Officer (Type name, grade and organization—signature)
Cleveland Parmer	John R Cawelti 2nd Lt QMC

WD AGO Form 53-55
1 November 1944

This form supersedes all previous editions of WD AGO Forms 53 and 55 for enlisted persons entitled to an Honorable Discharge, which will not be used after receipt of this revision.

Note: You will find similar discharge records in your county of origin.

Understanding Land Descriptions

Remember Township 7, Range 15! If you find certain land descriptions that are always associated with your ancestors, hopefully you will have taken some note of it. In the cases above, you probably noticed that Township 7, Range 15 appeared in all of the documents. Nearly all of the land in the Deep South states fell into the public domain prior to its settlement by Europeans. That is, the federal government claimed ownership after the many treaties of cession were signed by Native Americans. The land was then surveyed and conveyed to white settlers on a variety of terms—cash, grants for military service, and sheer occupancy. You have probably seen maps that contain legal descriptions of land, but perhaps you never noticed them. Now is the time to learn, because if you can geographically situate your ancestors within a county, your research can reveal a lot more information about them.

Counties in the public domain states (most U.S. states excluding the original colonies) were surveyed and laid out in sections by township number, range number, and then section number. Each township had 36 square sections, and each one of the 36 sections contained roughly 640 acres. The total number of acres in the 36 square sections equals 23,040 acres. To see what Township 7, range 15 looked like on the county map I obtained from the Highway Department, see the map on page 117.

To locate section 14, simply look for that number in one of the little squares, which will always be approximately one mile on each side. Also examine how the sections are numbered. Note that sections 1 and 9 contain Black churches (one Baptist and one A.M.E.) while sections 21 and 27 contain White churches (one Baptist and one Methodist). Finally, notice that this section of the county borders Crenshaw and Covington counties. When your ancestors live close to county borders, you will have to actually check the records of both counties. Using just one map and the deed records obtained at the courthouse, I was able to locate in space the physical reference point for my ancestors—a reference point which lay in between St. Luke A.M.E. Church, Mt. Moriah Baptist Church, and Oaky Streak United Methodist Church!

States outside the public domain system had more complicated systems of surveying land, and this makes it all the more important to learn the system for surveying and recording land used in your own state of research. Local maps or land ownership maps as well as historical maps will help you to understand the task ahead of you.

Analysis of My Courthouse Notes

The above transactions were found by checking the indexes to all possible conveyance volumes in the courthouse starting with the present and working back. The general term *conveyance* refers to transactions where property or something of value is being transferred between two or more people, generally in the form of a sale, a mortgage, or by gift. A more common term would be "deed books," but if you use only that term, you won't know that other kinds of conveyances are recorded in separate volumes like mortgage books, and timber books if timber was a big commodity in that particular county. If you think your ancestors were poverty stricken and owned nothing to transfer or mortgage, then think

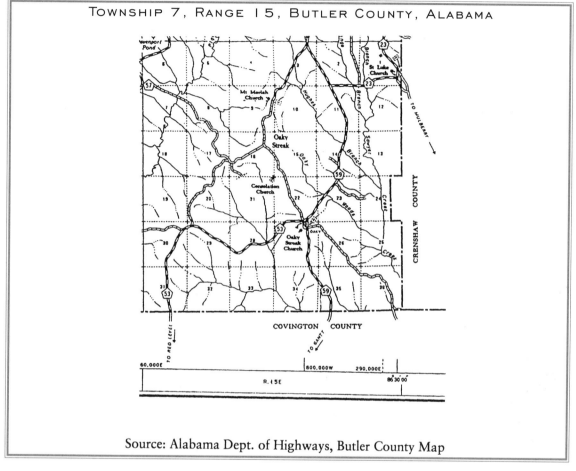

TOWNSHIP 7, RANGE 15, BUTLER COUNTY, ALABAMA

Source: Alabama Dept. of Highways, Butler County Map

again. One of my students found that her ancestor borrowed money on a mule, and the transaction was recorded in the deed records.

When you visit the courthouse, this is what you must also do. If you feel uncomfortable walking around peeking at transactions that involve people that you know or even people that you do not know, don't worry. This is all a matter of public record. If you use the term "indexes to real estate conveyances," then the clerk can help you to locate all of them. But you must ask first. Of course, you also have your own eyes too, and

you should use them. Because this is an exploratory visit to get a sense of the lay of the land, you should take note by name of all volumes so that when you have to write, you'll know where the volumes are and what they are called at that particular courthouse.

The indexes to the real estate conveyances helped me to locate the names of many of my ancestors as grantors (persons conveying real estate or property) or grantees (persons receiving property). Note that each volume must be checked starting with the more recent date, and you then work back because (1) some deeds are not registered in the same year that they are drawn up, (2) few courthouses have a single compiled index covering all years, and (3) in general, you must check all records available as a matter of doing good research. Even at the courthouse, you can't completely trust the compiled indexes. This is why you have to be even more cautious about published indexes. Did they transcribe the information just from the general index or did they examine the indexes to each separate volume, or finally, did they cross-check the actual entries (transactions as they were entered) to see if they matched the pages listed in the index? Worse, did they skip some of the entries?

When I located the first deed, I found that of more consequence than the land transfer was the listing of about thirty-five of my relatives and/or ancestors including those I did not know were in my direct line. I also found the names of two of my great-grandmother's siblings and the names of their spouses. In addition, some of them had to sign and submit affidavits using a local notary where they lived, thereby providing clues to migration paths. Some had moved out of the area to places like Tuskegee and Pensacola as early as 1900.

The other transactions revealed that my great-grandmother Lucindy earned a small bit of money on timber land. I had to then figure out what she may have done with that money. She ginned her own cotton, I'm told, and she knew how much she would get for every bale when it was taken into town. She was illiterate, but she was numerate, an important point to understand as you do your own research. Finally, deeds should be evaluated for possible kin relationships, as in the case of Deed Book 8, Volume 8, which

helped me to identify the relationship between the named Tillman sisters and the Whittles and Shines. This cluster of names, as it turned out, helped me to locate Lucindy's former slave owner, his place of origin, and some of her kin during slavery. What a giant step from just one search early in my research.

Will Books

Will books should not be excluded as part of your preliminary search, particularly after the death of one of your ancestors. Do not assume that your ancestors were too poor to have written wills—if they owned any amount of land, then almost certainly you will find that this property was a subject of concern to the judge of probate. Like deed books, will books also have name indexes which identify the person whose will was probated as well as any named beneficiaries. The will contained in the will book volume is a copied version of the original will written by either your ancestor or an individual to whom it was dictated. Because the will book version is copied *into* the will book by a clerk, consider the possibility of errors, but this concern is less important for now when other problems can cause you to make some errors of inference in reading the will.

Care should be taken in *interpreting* wills because (1) family relationships are not always spelled out, (2) the will may refer to part of the estate having been already transferred to an heir (in which case deed books must be checked), (3) they cannot be used to determine exact date of death, and (4) the will is only one document that forms a part of the deceased's estate papers, on file in a separate location at the courthouse. If you don't know to ask for the deceased's estate packet or papers, then you will lose some important genealogical information. Finally, transactions that relate to the disposal of the deceased's estate have to be reported to the judge of probate, and these transactions may be filed in subsequent will and deed books. Therefore, it's important to check all indexes for your ancestor's name after the will was written into the will books.

You will find other records at the courthouse, as in the case of my cousin's World War II discharge record. The point about your first and not last visit to the courthouse is that you identify all available volumes commonly used by genealogists to understand how they are organized, whether they have indexes, and any other peculiarities that might be unique to the system of record keeping. I went to the Russell County, Alabama courthouse as I was driving through, only to find that all of the records genealogists commonly used had been microfilmed. You will have many courthouse stories to tell as you begin to understand that even record keeping in this country was a very local, rather than uniform, practice.

A Visit to the Local Historical Society Library

*I*n addition to your courthouse visit, a survey of the holdings of the local public library or the county's historical society will also pay off. I found maps, cemetery transcriptions, family histories—even old photographs (including photos of Blacks) at the Butler County Historical Society's collection. You may not find anything on your ancestors, or you may have the luck of one of my students, who found a local library

containing photographic negatives of both local Whites and Blacks dating back to the nineteenth century—with name identifications! Resources at a local historical society or a local library will help you to collect some basic information that will aid you in the later stages of your research. (If there is no local historical society, you should ask for the genealogy section at the county library.) Typically, local libraries maintain newspaper clippings files that contain obituaries of notable local Blacks who lived a very long time or clippings on prominent White families, many of whom may have had ancestors who were slave owners.

I found that members of the local society had indexed and/or transcribed some courthouse records, cemetery records, tax lists, and early tract books. I encountered a member of the Butler County Historical Society at the courthouse. He proudly pointed out that Butler County was the setting for part of Margaret Walker's book *Jubilee*, a fictional account of her grandmother's life story. Walker had spoken to the society about the book and her research. If you haven't read *Jubilee*, now is the time to do it, paying close attention to the details, many of which provide clues to research. Finally, because you will probably need to do so later on, obtain a list of local researchers who will research local courthouse records for a small fee.

Visiting the Ancestral Home by Mail or on the Web

*Y*our visit to the ancestral home is a necessary step in your research—it should not be skipped, for it is the easiest way to collect information on your family. On the other hand, many genealogists cannot do this at the outset. Perhaps sufficient information was not collected in the course of your interviews, or perhaps you have no idea about the origins of the ancestor that you are researching except his or her state of birth. If you are a beginner, hopefully you will not face the problem of tracing a lost or migrating ancestor who may have tried to cut all ties with the past.

In addition, you will not be able to accomplish everything on your first visit. Therefore, you will wind up doing quite a bit of your research from the community where you now live and writing to various places for information. You will need addresses for the county courthouse, the state's archives, local historical societies, and the state's division of vital records. Any letter should be brief and to the point, ideally no more than five to ten sentences.

This is where the Web begins to pay off. Many genealogy and general sites can provide information on your county of research, and you should consult the bibliography for a list of sites to explore: maps (both historic and contemporary), important addresses and telephone numbers, help lists, and lists of extinct towns. Note that these are all resource tools to help you get around a little bit easier. Few of these sites contain the kind of information that you will find when you make a visit to the place where your ancestors called home.

What Must I Do Now?

*I*n this chapter, you've become acquainted with the kinds of records that will help you fill in the missing pieces in your vital records search. You've also come to understand that a visit to your ancestors' place of origin will eventually become necessary, but that if you are unable to do so, you can begin to explore the same resources from where you now live. The following resource checklist should be used as a guide to the kinds of original records as well as genealogical resources that you can find in the county and locality where your ancestors once lived. In effect, this chapter guides you to the importance of the county as your unit of research.

- Compile a resource kit on the county of origin. Your personal resource kit should include all important addresses of genealogical institutions as well as places where you can find records on your ancestors. That includes the places discussed above such as cemeteries, old schools, churches, and the like.
- Add to your resource kit a set of maps obtained either from an atlas, the state's highway department, or the Web. You will need several maps: a state map showing all counties, a detailed map showing localities in your county of research, as well as maps that show churches that still exist and townships and ranges or other systems of land division.
- Begin your letter writing campaign to let people know that you are coming or to find out general information such as facility hours, resources available, and individuals that you might have skipped during your family interviews.
- Begin to focus in on county courthouse

research, particularly records from the late nineteenth century up through the mid-twentieth century. Again, those records are the standard vital records as well as wills, deeds, and other conveyance records.

- If you can't visit, you should make sure that you write to the local historical society for a list of publications that deal with the county, including a county history. Not every county has a formally published history, but a member of a local genealogical or historical society has almost certainly written an outline of the county's history.

Know that you are only limited by your own imagination. If you pursue all roads, your journey may be long, but you will eventually reach home.

Chapter 6

UNRAVELING THE
TIES THAT BOUND

1870 to 1920

I just want to know what happened to my great-grandfather—who his people were. My grandmother used to tell me that his family was from Tennessee because she remembers visits by her father's people. That's about all anyone knows, because my grandmother moved to Clevelend when she was a small girl.

FROM A BEGINNING GENEALOGIST

CENSUS RECORDS, YOUR BASELINE

Often, beginning researchers start with a purpose as narrow as knowing one ancestor. But if you find one ancestor, you find nearly all of them—living in an extended kinship network that is larger than the two-parent household and smaller than a clan. The methods in genealogy require you to prove a relationship by linking individuals in different records for the same period of time and over their life cycle. So, when you use genealogy to find one ancestor, the very methods that you use require you to find them all.

During this period, family ties bound our ancestors far more than they do today. It may be said that people during your grandfather's and great-grandfather's times had no identities separate from their places in a family. But even if you go South today, you'll meet someone who'll say, "Yeah. I know the Brewers. They live around about Bent Fork. Ol' man Tom Brewer. Yeah. He's some relation to me. He was married to one of my cousins who lived back over there near Bent Fork." It doesn't matter that you asked where Sadie Brewer lives. You were told about Tom Brewer though you don't know him and probably don't want to see him

either. But when you get to Sadie Brewer's house, you'll find ol' man Tom rocking on the porch. He's Sadie's great-uncle; he's related to you, and he knows more than she does anyway.

So ingrained is this tradition of extended kin among some Black folks in the South that it should hardly be a surprise that it continues to exist today. Down the road from my uncle Clint's house, there lives a "clan" of extended kin. The main house is occupied by Dempsey and Lucindy Bones. Their daughter built another house next door about ten years ago for her family. There are four trailer homes occupied by other adult children and their families. There are at least four generations of this family living in this one place. And they have lived there for a very long time! So long that Dempsey Bones can hunt at night alone, a practice his wife is trying to get him to stop.

Though everybody did know where they fit in a network of kinship, it doesn't mean that this information was passed down to their descendants now living in the late twentieth century, especially those who migrated. If you haven't interviewed all of your relatives who were born in the 1920s, you won't understand how this can happen. Think of it this way. People born in the 1920s are now in their seventies. During their youth, they came into contact with former slaves born as early as 1840, possibly as their grandchildren. Furthermore, they lived as children to parents who probably married between 1890 and 1920. If you examine your partially completed ancestral chart, you might very well find that you don't know the maiden name of your great-grandmother although she died around 1910, you don't know where she was buried even though the family's church is filled with graves, and in fact, even your ninety-year-old relatives don't know anything about her. That's why you're searching now.

Despite these possible losses of information, the ties that bound your kinfolk are partly reflected in records for this fifty-year span of time. It also happens to be the most difficult period of research that you will encounter—fifty years is a long time in the human life cycle, time enough for someone to be born, have their children, and even see their grandchildren. In addition, this period represents a significant generational shift in lifestyles, expectations, and family migration patterns. Finally, it is the period in which those critical documents on the vital events in the lives of your ancestors are likely to become scarce or, if they exist, it will take some effort for you to find them. The effort you should have spent in collecting information on all of your ancestors and relatives between the Great Migration and the present will pay off now.

MINING THE CENSUSES

As you've worked your way through the records up to this point, you've probably noticed that few of them have listed complete household units or even families. Indeed, most historical records do not list complete families and households together unless it is a census, and that is what you are about to tackle next. This stage of research offers a kind of reprieve from working on one ancestor at a time. Now you will be dealing with your ancestor as he lived with a group of people under one roof (a household), most likely his immediate kin or some of your ancestors that you haven't even thought about yet. You will be researching family units and your key is the likely head of household for each census year. Note that a household is everyone living under one roof, but a family is everyone who is related by blood. There can be two or more families in one dwelling unit or under one roof. Your ancestor might have been the head of his family of three, but he might have been living in his father's house, in which case his father is the head of household. During this stage, you will be dealing with census records for the period 1870 to 1920, tracking the family unit as it changes over time. You will find out that this time period and this set of records is extremely critical to bridging the information gap between slavery and freedom. The families that you find in census records will form a baseline with which to reference the past (slavery) and the post slavery period (1865 to the present). This baseline should connect the twentieth-century generations with generations that lived before the Civil War. Therefore, it is important that you use census records to your best advantage—for you may find nowhere else the information that you need in such great detail.

What you will need to carry with you when you go to a research facility is a list of

HOLMES COUNTY, MISSISSIPPI 1870 CENSUS SHEET

Page No. 2

Schedule 1.—Inhabitants in _Richland District_, in the County of _Holmes_ State of _Mississippi_ enumerated by me on the _6_ day of _July_, 1870.

Post Office: _O'Finger_ _76. 2. Bar_ Ass't Marshal.

1	2	3 The name of every person whose place of abode on the first day of June, 1870, was in this family.	4 Age	5 Sex	6 Color	7 Profession, Occupation, or Trade of each person, male or female.	8 Value of Real Estate.	9 Value of Personal Estate.	10 Place of Birth, naming State or Territory of U.S.; or the Country, if of foreign birth.	11	12	13	14	15	16	17	18	19	20
1	386 425	Mercer Eliza	63	F	W	Housewife	1000	300	Miss.										
2		— Jane	20	F	W				Miss										
3		— Eliza E.	17	F	W				Miss										
4		— Margret	15	F	W				Miss										
5	387 426	Phillips Saml	46	M	B	Farmer			N.C					1	1			1	
6		— Silia	30	F	B	Housewife			Va					1	1				
7		— Samuel	16	M	B	Farm hand			Miss					1	1				
8		— Elizabeth	14	F	B	Farm hand			Miss					1	1				
9		— Di[l]a	80	F	B	at nice			Va					1	1				
10	388 427	Brooks Thomas	40	M	B	Farmer			Va					1	1			1	
11		— Jane	30	F	B	Housewife			Miss					1	1				
12		— Harmon	16	M	B	Farm hand			Miss					1	0				
13		— Edgalia	14	F	B	Farm hand			Miss					1	1				
14		— May	7	F	B				Miss										
15		— Charles	1	M	B				Miss										
16	389 427	Stewart Josiah	58	M	W	Farmer	11740	2,635	Ga									1	
17		— Elizabeth	42	F	W	Housewife			Miss										
18		— Richard D.	20	M	W	Farmer			Miss										
19		— Bettie	10	F	W				Miss					✓					
20		— Mattie	8	F	W				Miss					1	(×)				
21		— Lucy	1/2	F	W				Miss				Sep						
22	340 428	Barnes Hardy	79	M	W	Farmer			Miss								1 ×		
23	341 429	Stewart Jack	65	M	B	Farmer		175	Miss					1	1				
24		— Polly	64	F	B	Housewife			Miss					1	1				
25	342 430	Stewart Eli	30	M	B	Farm hand			Miss		1			1	1			1	
26		— Henrietta	26	F	B	Farm hand			Miss					1	1				
27		— Lavina	8	F	B				Miss										
28		— Taylor	6	M	B				Miss										
29		— Monroe	4	M	B				Miss										
30		— Pattie	1/2	F	B				Miss				Jan				—		
31	343 431	Stewart Harris	30	M	B	Farmer	93	200	La					1	1			1	
32		— Marinda	20	F	B	Housewife			Miss					1	1				
33		— Samuel	7	M	B				Miss										
34		— Frank	5	M	B				Miss									1	
35		— Willie	3	M	B				Miss										
36		— Georgiann	1/2	F	B				Miss				Sep						
37	344 432	Morris John	87	M	W	Farmer		280	N.C									1	
38		— Rebecca	76	F	W	Housewife			N.C										
39		— Elias	24	M	W	Farmer			Tenn									1	
40		— Martha	20	F	W	Housewife			Miss										

family members who lived during 1920 and 1910. Note that you will start with the 1920 census and work back. At the minimum, you will need the name of the head of household for either 1920 or 1910.

Using census records is rather straight-forward. There are thirteen regional federal record centers, now oddly called regional records services facilities, spread through-out the country, all part of the National Archives and Records Service based in Washington, D.C. Each center has available for public use microfilm copies of all federal population censuses that were taken at ten-year intervals and that are extant for the period of time between 1790 and 1920. Note that a large portion of the 1890 census was destroyed in a fire; therefore, you shouldn't expect to find the population schedules available for your use. Occasion-ally, a few surviving parts may be found somewhere in the dust bind of a county courthouse!

If you do not live near a federal record center, you have additional options available to you, through a local facility though they do not have complete sets. You may order the film you need through an LDS stake library or directly from the National Archives; you may also use those copies that are available through your state archives, a genealogy library, or a historical society. Generally, the latter three facilities will only have copies of the censuses taken for the region in which they are located.

Your first visit to any facility that houses consensus will be filled with a bunch of details and steps that seem bewildering. To save yourself some of the initial agony, always call first and always carry with you (1) the names of your ancestors who were heads of their households for each census year that you want to research, (2) the cities, counties, and states where they lived, and (3) at least the names of a few of their dependents, including wives and in-laws who might have lived in the household at the time.

Once you learn the mechanics of using census records, and this will take some time, your confidence in using historical records will be tremendously boosted. If you master this mass of data, if you don't get lost won-dering about curious names (like the sur-names Chinese and Negro, found in the 1870 index to the Mississippi census) or the individuals enumerated in prisons or even less savory places, you will survive the seem-ingly complicated instructions about using indexes, microfilm readers, and all the other details that need to be known before you find your ancestors. Once you do find them, don't run to the copying machine. Photo-copies last only a little while. Write the information down in your notebook—*all* of the information, especially that which will help you to find it again.

For the censuses taken between 1870 and 1920, you will find the following basic information although some minor varia-tions in questions asked did occur from one census to the next: (1) name of head of household, his wife and their children, (2) age, sex, and color for each member of the household, (3) relationship of each individ-ual in household to the head (except for the 1870 census), (4) occupation, (5) schooling or literacy, (6) place of birth for the individ-ual being enumerated and his parents, (7) value of real and personal property, and (8) date and geographical unit where the indi-viduals on each page were residing (post office, street address, beat, township, etc.).

WHICH CENSUS RECORDS?

*L*isted below are most of the censuses that will help you in your research.

Federal Decennial Population Censuses for 1870, 1880, 1900, 1910, 1920
Federal Decennial Agricultural Censuses for 1870, 1880, 1900, 1910
Slave Schedules for 1850 and 1860
1866 State Censuses for selected southern states
Special Censuses taken by states and cities

NAME INDEXES FOR CENSUSES

*H*ow will you find your ancestors when millions of people could have been enumerated in one state alone? You won't go directly to the microfilm copy of the county census and search line by line for your ancestor. Line by line searching is only for situations where you haven't located your ancestors. One county alone could contain between six thousand and forty thousand people depending on the census year. What you will do is to use a name index which will tell you on what page and in which enumeration district the household can be located in the actual census.

Nearly every census between 1790 and 1870 has some kind of name index which can be used to locate your ancestor's household. Most of the critical censuses for African Americans, those between 1870 and 1920 in the southern states, have been indexed. The 1870 census indexes are printed in volumes by state. The remaining indexes, 1880 through 1920, have been microfilmed, and it is the microfilm copy of the index that you will use to find out in which enumeration district and on what page your ancestors appear in the actual census for their county or city of residence.

In order to use the microfilmed census indexes, you will have to convert your ancestor's name into a code based on the sound of the name rather than the actual spelling. This is called a Soundex code, and the indexes are often called Soundex indexes because the records are organized by how a name sounds phonetically rather than how it is actually spelled.

Learning how to convert the name to Soundex code can be as simple as looking at your driver's license. The first letter plus the three numbers that follow is a Soundex code for your surname. However, you will have to learn how to write a Soundex code for all of the surnames that you are researching. Instructions for coding your name in Soundex form appear in many National Archives publications relating to census records. It is also something that you can learn on your first visit to a federal record center. Better that you learn it now, for there will be many other steps not named in this text that you have to go through. A simplified version of the Soundex coding system, adapted from a sheet used by the Newberry Library, follows. Practice by converting the surnames that you are researching.

Soundex Instructions

Surname _____ ◻◻◻◻

- Step 1: Write the last name (surname) on the line above.
- Step 2: In the first box write the first letter of the surname.

- Step 3: Cross out the letters (a, e, i, o, u, y, w, h) in the last name. Ignore the first letter because you've already used it.
- Step 4: Code the next three remaining letters of the surname using the chart:
  1 for the letters B, P, F, V
  2 for the letters C, S, K, G, J, Q, X, Z
  3 for the letters D, T
  4 for the letter L
  5 for the letters M, N
  6 for the letter R
- Step 5: Insert the three numbers into the last three boxes.
- Step 6: In case you don't have enough numbers, add zeros to bring the code to three numbers.
- Step 7: Carry the codes with you on your first visit to research census records. You will look up the code to find out which reel of film to request.
- Step 8: Ask for help. Most facilities provide some assistance for beginners.

Additional Rules

1. Some short names cannot be coded. Use zeros for all three digits.
2. If you have double letters, use only one of them to code.
3. In general, disregard name prefixes like De, Van, Von, Du. Mc and Mac are not considered prefixes in this system.
4. If there are letters that convert to the same number, code only the first letter as in CKS of the name Jackson. Code only the C because K and S convert to the same number.

Here are some examples of how surnames are coded. If you prefer, practice on your surnames, but study the rules above to understand why the codes turned out that way.

Surname:	Jacks	McArthur	Adams
Letters to Code:	c	crt	dms
Final Code:	J200	M263	A352

Summarized below are the steps that you will take before examining the census record for your county. Don't forget that all of the census records have been microfilmed, and that is the form in which you will most likely use them. The following flow chart indicates the steps that you will take before you actually examine the microfilmed copy of the original census record for censuses between 1880 and 1920. The 1870 census index is not on microfilm; it will appear as a printed volume shelved with other books at the facility where you are doing your research.

Summary of Steps in Census Research

1. Determine which type of index (printed or microfilm) you will need. (If the census year is 1880 and after, you will use the microfilm indexes.)
2. Code surname in Soundex code.
3. Use Soundex code to look up name of head of household in the microfilm index for the state.
4. Copy into your notebook the information on the index card including (1) county name, (2) enumeration district, and (3) page or sheet number.
5. Obtain the reel of film you need for the county.
6. Scroll to the page number you need, making sure that it is the same enumeration district you listed in your notes.
7. Examine the page to find your

ancestor's household. List all of the information in your notebook.

READING THE RECORD

*C*ensus records can often encourage the unwary to misinterpret reality. Think of the census as what the census taker recorded—not necessarily what the truth is (remember Chester Blackwell). Listed below are some sources of errors and misinterpretations commonly associated with census records. Not knowing these possible sources of confusion will limit your ability to continue your research.

The illustration in this chapter shows you what a census sheet looks like. But you might also need to know that the census administration, because it involved such a large-scale effort to record everybody, had to divide this effort into convenient geographical units based on states and within each state enumeration districts, and within each enumeration district there were a variety of units such as postal beats and wards. The main unit, however, is the enumeration district. The following section explains some of the errors that you might make if you don't know about them in the first place.

Problem: Changes in Enumeration Districts

Solution: Enumeration districts were used to geographically divide each state into census administrative units beginning with the 1880 census. You might be tempted to assume that the enumeration boundaries for each and every census year remained the same, but that would be a mistake. Enumeration districts do not necessarily cover the

same physical space for every census even though the same enumeration district numbers or names may have been used. For example, one county or area may have been divided into fifteen enumeration districts for the 1880 census, but because of population decreases, it may have ten in the 1900 census and eight in the 1910 census, all the way down to one in the most recent census. The only time that you can be relatively sure that the boundaries for an enumeration district did not change from one census to the next is when a township and/or range number is given for each census year as in the case of enumerating inhabitants in Township 7 of Butler County for the years 1870 through 1920. Note that you will find that post office names and plantation names were also used, particularly for the 1870 census.

Problem: Inconsistent Spellings of Surnames

Solution: Know all the variations of a surname's spelling. Using the census indexes (printed indexes as well as the Soundex) will give you an idea of how many different ways your surname can be spelled. Returning to the case study on Chester Blackwell, the census taker, suppose J. T. Percy had always spelled his surname Piercy or Parcy. That is, after all, quite possible. Well, Chester Blackwell spelled it as he heard it and as it was commonly spelled. Chester Blackwell might have been a near illiterate himself, but the more probable case is that of all the words in the English language, surnames are the least likely to be standardized or spelled the same.

Some names more easily lend themselves to spelling changes than others. But even with a common name like Smith, you

A Study of the Longmire Surname—1900 and 1910 Census Indexes Soundex Code: L525

Spelling	Given Name	Age	County	ED/Sheet
Longmire	Adam	18	Conecuh	47,3
	Albert	60	Wilcox	139,9
	Alek	35	Monroe	168,6
Longmir	Ben	63	Wilcox	124,6
Longmire	Bradford	54	Clarke	29,5
	Carline	12	Clarke	25,11
Longmier	Charles	40	Wilcox	144,3
Longmire	Charley	33	Escambia	150,8
	Cora	31	Mobile	113,34
Longmile	Eli	56	Wilcox	141,1 or 7
Longmire	Eliza	50	Pickens	78,4
Longmaier	Ellen	3	Clarke	25,11
Longmire	Emma	13	Wilcox	134,12
	Emma	27	Clark	39,4
	Frank	44	Monroe	165,4
	George	36	Butler	22,20
	Henry	11	Escambia	150,6
Longmyer	Isam	73	Conecuh	50,8
Longmire	Isiac	43	Conecuh	48-16
	Jack	46	Mobile	113-34
Longmeyer	Jacob	44	Mobile	95,23
Longmire	James	55	Butler	22,22
	Jane	60	Monroe	167,4
	Jim	26	Monroe	162,8
	Joe	26	Monroe	162,8
	John	38	Butler	23,10
	John	25	Monroe	166,3
	Joseph	55	Conecuh	52,20
	Judge	20	Monroe	157-17
Longmeyer	Lee	25	Clarke	25-10
	Leola	9	Escambia	150,6
Longmier	Lewis	48	Conecuh	48,17
	Loursa (?)	47	Escambia	150,10
	Mark	18	Monroe	165,3
	Martha	85	Monroe	168,1
	Mary L.	8	Escambia	150
	Mat	50	Monroe	168,30
	Missy	30	Conecuh	54,11
	Mose	50	Mobile	87,15
	Nathan	50	Butler	10,20
	Nicholas	32	Conecuh	55,6
Longmeyer	Patti	39	Mobile	95,18
	Robert	50	Monroe	161,5
	Samuel	21	Escambia	150,12

can probably think of at least four possible variations—Smithe, Smythe, Smitz, Smits. Some names can have as many as thirty possible spelling variations without a hint that they are spelled differently when they are pronounced.

A Census Study of the Longmires—1900 and 1910

	Scot	27	Wilcox	140,8
	Seler	23	Monroe	165,8
	(G?) Sussie	32	Butler	22,20
	Timothy	18	Monroe	170,17
	Viney	19	Butler	2,20
Longmyer	Wade	31	Conecuh	50,8
	Mary	3m	Lowndes	118,10
	Mary	30	Monroe	127,14
	Mary	50	"	130,12
	Mary Jane	1m	Monroe	128,22
	Mary L	20	Escambia	78,1
	Matthew	55	Monroe	118,12
	Mick	4	Monroe	127,14
	Minnie	25	Escambia	78,5
	Mollie	20	Butler	30,4
	Nathan	60	Butler	30,11
	Nick	45	Conecuh	45,11
	Peggie	63	Monroe	119,21
	Sally	19	Escambia	78,20
	Sarah Ann	7	Clarke	31,4
	Scot	30	Wilcox	162,2
	Seeley	50	Butler	30,17
	Suanna	4	Monroe	128,22
	Sue	60	Wilcox	163,4
Longmeyer	Susie	42	Conecuh	34,5
Longmire	Tim	28	Monroe	120,13
	Wade	45	Conecuh	39,5
	Will	36	Butler	30,2
	Will	50	Wilcox	163,4
	William	18	Monroe	127,7
	Willis	12	Escambia	78,8
	York	37	Escambia	82,29

Many circumstances account for variations in spellings. Newly arriving immigrants often changed their names by shortening them; sometimes, their names were changed by immigration officials who hadn't the patience to adhere to the protocols of good record keeping, thereby causing immediate switches of nationality. The same applied to your ancestors, many of whom could not write or spell their surnames. *Someone else wrote what they heard.* Often, individuals with common ancestry will wind up spelling their surnames differently. These name changes should not be a matter of shame. How many times can you or must you try to tell the "official" record keepers how your name is spelled when they have the power of the pen in their hands? In doing your research, know how many different ways your surname can be spelled, especially the further back in time you go.

Problem: Incorrect Color/Racial Designations

Solution: Don't use race as a criterion in scanning through census records. The Census Bureau never figured out how to tell who was mulatto and who was not. They essen-

UNRAVELING THE TIES THAT BOUND

A Census Study of the Longmires—1900 and 1910
1910 Alabama Soundex, L525, Longmires

Spelling	Given Name	Age	County	ED/Sheet
Longmire	Abe	49	Lowndes	118,10
	Adam	27	Conecuh	36,5
Longimeyar	Ben	68	Wilcox	144,13
Longmile?	Bob	58	Monroe	132,22
Longmire	Brad	65	Clarke	20,5
	Carrie	2	Monroe	130,3
	Charley	43	Escambia	78,15
	Cilles	50	Monroe	127,14
	David	34	Conecuh	37,20
	Dee	28	Monroe	130,12
	Della	27	Monroe	128,22?,32?
	Decie	40	Escambia	78,8
Loungmire	Eli	70	Conecuh	37,22
Longmire	Eliza	62	Pickens	102,7 w/JoelPuckett
	Ellen	70	Wilcox	145,17
	Ellis	53	Monroe	130,1
	Emma	32	Clarke	31,3 w/ D. Tait
Longmeyer	Erbia	52	Wilcox	144,22
Longmayer	Etla	75	Wilcox	144,9
Longmire	Frank	52	Monroe	127, 14
	George	46	Conecuh	35,5
	George	23	Clarke	20,8
	Hattie	22	Escambia	78,18
	Hattie	2mos	"	78,8 w/ Decie L
	Hattie	38	Monroe	130,3 w/ John
	Henry	28	Lowndes	118,11
Longmoer	Hough (W)	73	Lrdale	59,6
Longmire	Isaac	52	Conecuh	37,2
	Isaac	23	Escambia	75,11
Longmmeyer	June	68	Conecuh	34,5
Longmire	Jessie	37	Escambia	82,28
	Joe	45	Monroe	130,3
Longmeyer	John	38	Conecuh	34,5
Longmyer	John	43	Butler	17,11A,??
Longmire	John	34	Monroe	120,7
	John T. (w)	30	Pickens	102,2
	Josh	11	Escambia	78,8 w/ Decie
	Judge	29	Monroe	120,7
Loungmire	Lee	35	Conecuh	37,14
Longmire	Lewis (w)	30	Escambia	78,7
	Lillie	3	Monroe	122,14
	Lizzie	29	Escambia	78,14
	Mark	30	Monroe	127,14
Longmire	William	60	Mobile	111,22
Longmeyer	Woodie	23	Mobile	104,10
Longmire	York	26	Butler	23,10

tially used the eyeball method. Not all mulattos look white or Indian. Nor are all fair-skinned people technically mulattos, a point that the current members of the biracial movement don't seem to understand. We are all old "new" people. This problem is further compounded by incorrectly entering racial designations in both directions. Free blacks in the pre-1860 censuses are variably entered as mulatto in one census and white in another. Look at the following errors found just in a cursory review.

EXAMPLE OF MISREPORTED RACIAL IDENTITY: 1870 CENSUS OF BUTLER COUNTY

Page 396, Visitation #536, Family #538
Name: Alfred Whittle   Spouse: Lucinda Whittle
Age: 50   40
Race: **Black**   **White**
Occupation: Farmer   Keeping House
Value of real estate: $700
Value of Personal Estate: $400
Place of Birth: South Carolina South Carolina
Education: Literate
Children: All listed as white.

This clearly is a mistake that is commonly made. The household listed immediately before the Whittles' was Black and the census taker simply continued to insert "B" for Black. In subsequent and previous censuses, Whittle was probably listed as White.

Problem: Misinformation or Inconsistent Information on Individuals
Solution: This is certainly a common problem, and it is often difficult to tell whether the error was that of the census taker or that of the informant who (1) may not have reported the information himself, (2) may have willfully given incorrect information, or (3) may have given incorrect information unintentionally. This will certainly be the case with ages and places of birth. Many former slaves did not have knowledge of their precise dates of birth. Even some whites did not have knowledge of their precise dates of birth. Knowledge was a function of literacy in a time when ages were often preceded by the term "about." Ages, therefore, are to be considered estimates and will often vary from census to census. Note also that the spelling of names varied considerably.

Listing the names of all heads of household found in the census indexes as a preliminary step can help you to explore migration patterns, the formation of families, and the disappearance of others. This technique should be avoided if the surname search is based on names that might have been shared by nonkin. Though my Longmire ancestors had a relatively unique surname that clustered in just a few counties of the state, I generated a massive amount of data in the process of figuring out how they were connected! Out of curiosity, I checked the Mississippi census index and found yet another cluster of Longmires. My task then was to figure out whether they were connected. The uniqueness of the name and Alabama's proximity to Mississippi suggested to me that there was a strong possibility that some relationship existed between these Longmires, even if it was nothing more than having left slavery with the slave owner's name.

Problem: Incorrect Places of Birth

Solution: This is a real problem for African American research. The censuses taken between 1870 and 1920 asked for places of birth for the informant only, and between 1880 and 1920, the place of birth for the informant's father and his mother was asked. Place of birth for parents is one of the most critical leads, but it is often inaccurate in favor of the state in which the census is being taken or in favor of the information given for the head of household. Careless census takers tended to use ditto marks for places of birth. You can spot these errors, especially in (1) inconsistent information on place of birth in two or more censuses, and (2) very old individuals in the Deep South who report their place of birth as a state that had not been admitted into the Union when they were born. On the latter point, be cautious. You have to know what the possibilities are for this person's place of birth.

Problem: Failure to Locate an Ancestor's Household

Solution: The African American population has been consistently undercounted in all censuses: about 12 percent in 1870 and 1890, about 9 percent in 1880, and about 11 percent in 1900. The undercount in southern states may have been higher than in northern states. Don't assume that you won't find your ancestors in any census, however. Before you assume that they were not counted, first make sure that you've followed all the appropriate steps in doing a census search for the census under question. Also remember that complete indexes for some census years are not available, as in the case of the 1880 census; only households with dependents ten and under were indexed. If unable to locate them, check adjacent counties and states, examine tax rolls, and use the agricultural censuses (1870–1910) for the enumeration district in which you found most of your ancestors living for the census year you are researching.

Problem: Handwriting

Solution: Nineteenth-century cursive handwriting can be difficult to read, especially the letters *l*, *t*, *s*, *f*, and *j*. Since one census taker was responsible for a fairly large area, you will be able to familiarize yourself with his handwriting style. Finally, words and names that you can read should be compared with those that you cannot. Alphabet keys of cursive writing samples are often available for researchers at the various federal record centers as well as other facilities. Ask for them or ask for help.

Problem: Name Reversals/Name Changes

Solution: If you fail to find an ancestor in any of the available censuses, consider the possibility that he or she changed his name or that the name was reversed by the census taker. Often given names and surnames are interchangeable—Washington, Brook, Samuel, and even a name like Hannah, which is also a surname. Remember that after emancipation, names like Washington Smith were not uncommon. Name changes may go undetected, but between the 1870 and 1880 censuses, some African Americans did change their surnames. If an ancestor is found in 1880, but not in the 1870 census, there may indeed have been a name change or a name reversal, though it is more likely that your ancestor was not enumerated.

Problem: Misreading the Record

Solution: Avoid unusual interpretations and wild theories. Study the following case. The man who sat next to me let out a sound—I knew it. He had found something. I peeked over and asked, "What did you find?" He commented, "Look at this. They must have been in jail!" I scrolled through several pages that listed single African American males of all ages. "What could this be? I asked. "I don't know. You tell me," he replied. "Where are their families? Wait a minute. Did you read the top of the page?"

I scrolled to the top, but I couldn't find anything. "But this has to tell you where. What state is this anyway? Illinois? Chicago?" "Yes." Just then, a friend had joined us. He continued to scroll back until the first page in the series was found. It said: "Enumerated this 26th of June, 1880 at the La Salle Hotel, Chicago, Illinois." The first line of the first sheet listed the occupation, and all subsequent spaces for occupation had ditto marks. In the man's excitement, I lost my own good sense, wanting to believe that he had been correct about their being in jail. It turned out that they were all living in a boardinghouse provided by the hotel for which they worked—as waiters! The record can be misread easily if you are predisposed to do so.

Problem: Changes in County Boundaries and Names

Solution: Know the history of the county. County boundaries have changed frequently over the course of the history of any one state. You should know that the geographical unit of research in genealogy is the county. Be careful—your ancestors may appear in different counties but they may not have moved one inch. Instead the boundaries moved to include or exclude their residence in a county. As I stood watching the huge turkeys in the Matthews'

backyard, my cousin Stanley said to me, "You see that fence. As soon as you step across the fence, you're in Crenshaw County. The county line runs right through our yard." It finally dawned on me that my grandfather Israel had lived in Crenshaw County in his youth, but later moved to Butler County in the small settlement where he died—no more than five miles away! In order to understand the geography of your county, use your county map from the department of highways and Everton's *Handy Book* to identify county name and boundary changes.

Problem: Failing to Identify Your Ancestors' Neighbors

Solution: The visitation sequence number is always printed in the far left margin of the census page. You can often make some assumptions about residence patterns by examining the visitation sequence. Those individuals *listed* next to each other in the order of visitation by the census taker also *lived* next door to each other, or in large cities in the same building or in the same square block or across the street from each other. Neighbors used to be a lot friendlier, and for some communities, you may find that the neighbors are really cousins or share a common experience like migrating North together from the same place.

WHAT THE RECORD WILL TELL YOU ABOUT YOUR ANCESTORS

Generational Changes, Glitches of Time, and Hidden Customs

As you can see, census records can open up many possibilities for identifying your ancestors, their kin, and the communities in

1870 AGRICULTURAL CENSUS SHEET, MONROE COUNTY, ALABAMA

SCHEDULE 2.—Productions of Agriculture in *Beat 12 Midway* in the

enumerated by me on the *17th* day of

THE NAME.	OF THE PERSON WHO CONDUCTS THIS FARM.			ACRES OF LAND.				FARM VALUES.			FENCES.	
		TENURE.		IMPROVED.		UNIMPROVED.						Cost of fertilizers purchased in 1879.
	Owner.	Rents for fixed money rental.	Rents for share of product.	Tilled, including fallow and grass in rotation, (whether pasture or meadow.)	Permanent meadows, permanent pastures, orchards, vineyards.	Woodland and forest.	Other unimproved, including "old fields" not growing wood.	Of farm, including land, fences, and buildings.	Of farming implements and machinery.	Of Live Stock.	Cost of building and repairing in 1879.	
				No.	No.	No.	No.	Dollars.	Dollars.	Dollars.	Dollars.	Dollars.
1	2	3	4	5	6	7	8	9	10	11	12	13
1 *Mowry Andrew J*			1	31						100		
2 *Snowden John J*	1			40				210	5	310		
3 *Smith Lorenzo*			1	50						70		
4 *Snowden James E*			1	40						100		
5 *Masdan William J*			1	125						500		
6 *Hale James*			1	20								
7 *Kirby Charles A*			1	20								
8 *Ramsay James*			1	25								
9 *Anderson Jefferson*	1			40						150		
10 *Longmire Larkin*			1	23								

NEAT CATTLE AND THEIR PRODUCTS.										SHEEP.					
On Hand June 1, 1880.	MOVEMENT, 1879.									On hand June 1, 1880.	MOVEMENT, 1879.				
	Cattle of all ages										Sheep and lambs				
Working oxen.	Milch cows.	Other.	Calves dropped.	Purchased.	Sold living.	Slaughtered.	Died, strayed, and stolen, and not recovered.	Milk sold, or sent to butter and cheese factories in 1879.	Butter made on the farm in 1879.	Cheese made on the farm in 1879.		Lambs dropped.	Purchased.	Sold living.	Slaughtered.	Killed by dogs.
No.	No.	No.	No.	No.	No.	No.	No.	Gallons.	Lbs.	Lbs.	No.	No.	No.	No.	No.	No.
25	26	27	28	29	30	31	32	33	34	35	36	37	38	39	40	41
	5	12						100								
2	3	1	3													

which they lived. Census records can provide a good measure of who your ancestors were. They also point to new directions and new records to look for. Finding your ancestors in census records is not the end of your search. There is a good chance that some of your ancestors did not appear in census records, and this should also lead you to a search for alternative records sources and census substitutes to document their presence in a particular area. As you look for these new sources, you must keep in mind that your ancestors were not static people—they aged, they had additional children, they moved to different places, and some even changed their names.

Case Study: Generations Shift with Hardly Any Notice

Your census research should start with 1920 and proceed back to locate each household in each census ending with the 1870 census. Assume that you are researching your grandfather Isaam Thomas who at the age of sixty-three lived in Dinwiddie County, Virginia, in 1920. This is what you will happen as you trace his household back in time.

Grandfather Isaam Thomas, Dinwiddie County, Virginia

1920 Census: Age 63, head of household, no children listed

1910 Census: Age 53, head of household, widower, no children

1900 Census: Age 43, head of household, 1 spouse, 3 children at home

1890 Census: Not available unless enumerated as veteran of Civil War

1880 Census: Age 23, may be head of own household

1870 Census: Age 13, living in his parents' household

1860 Census: Unnamed but counted as a slave at age 3 in slave schedule under slave owner's name or free person of color

1850 Census: Not born

Born in Africa?

Roma Jones Stewart compiled a list of all those born in Africa for the 1870 Georgia census. From her book, titled *Africans in Georgia*, one Patrick Lawrence, age thirty, told the census taker that he had been "imported in 1860." Another was called "George African," and a few reported their place of birth as Upper Guinea! You might find such an ancestor as well. Because high mortality was one of the characteristics of slavery, it is often a surprise to see someone old enough to have been born in Africa who survived to be counted in the 1870 census. (The 1870 statistical report for the census indicated that under seven thousand individuals living in the United States reported Africa as their place of birth.) I found several such individuals just by chance—two in my county of research and one in a county that borders Georgia. Rosie had reached the age of one hundred according to the 1880 Butler County Census (page 507). Finally, an unbelievably young man of thirty named Joe Goldsmith claimed Africa as his birthplace in the 1870 Butler County census census (page 363). One wonders whether Mr. Goldsmith's age was correctly reported.

Age Differences Between Spouses

In the 1880 Butler County census (ED 42, page 21, line 7) Solomon Bolling, age seventy-four, is married to Celer, age forty-four. Is this an error in reporting ages? Perhaps not. Even though individuals born during slavery may not have known their precise ages, there was a tendency for husbands to be older than their wives, generally by five to ten years but not, as in this case, thirty years. Whether or not there truly was a thirty-year difference depends on how much information the researcher can bring to bear on his Bolling ancestors.

Adoptive Kin

African American families have a long tradition of taking in the children of kin without formally adopting them. The 1870 and 1880 censuses should be studied carefully because children named in these households may, on occasion, be adopted kin.

Indentured Childhood

You will occasionally encounter young children living in a White household. In many instances these children were legally bound to Whites, and families often had trouble reclaiming their children. This arrangement is especially noticeable in the 1870 census, though it had started to decline by 1880.

Sharecropping and Land Ownership

The various agricultural census schedules (1870–1910) are not readily accessible. You can, however, obtain them through interlibrary loan or through an LDS stake library. Some are housed at National Archives federal records centers. Those for the Deep South can be located at the center in Atlanta. They are not indexed, but if you know the name of the enumeration district in which your ancestors lived, you can easily find them on the agricultural schedules. Individuals who farmed at least three acres either on land they owned or as share tenants (farming a plot of land owned by someone else with their own tools and seeds) can be located on these schedules. Farm laborers, or what we commonly know as sharecroppers, would not be found on these schedules.

Once your ancestor is found, it is likely that he will be listed on the same page with the landowner from whom he is renting the land. The agricultural schedules provide a detailed view of how much your ancestors really owned and how many acres they farmed. It can even tell you if your ancestors themselves hired farm laborers in the year preceding the census year. For African American researchers, the agricultural schedules are almost certainly an untapped and underused resource. I even found one of my ancestors who was not enumerated in the population schedule!

Name Sharing with Whites

Scroll the pages of any census taken between 1870 and 1920, and you will frequently find that some African Americans carried the same surnames as Whites in the same area. This is especially important to do for the 1870 census schedule. This pattern of surname sharing or name adopting especially becomes relevant for your research on slavery. It implies some relationship between Whites and Blacks, generally former slave and former slave owner, but this possibility is something that will have to be verified through your research.

Surname Clusters Reveal a Hidden Story

You will also find that the same surnames reappear on a number of pages. Never merely look for your ancestor's household without scrolling ten pages on either side of the page where it appears. In that way, you can easily note other households and relatives for your ancestor. In some cases, you can identify siblings, parents, and grandparents all living in the same area. Of course, good use of the census indexes will also help you to identify families and households that share the same surname in the county and state. If you carry a fairly common surname such as Johnson or Smith, you would not automatically assume that all of these individuals are connected by kinship, and you may want to limit your search to just those Johnsons or Smiths who were enumerated in the same area where your ancestor lived.

The Longmire chart on page 134 shows how lists can be generated to identify name clusters within the same area.

Tracking Vital Events with the Census

Mortality schedules were completed by census takers between 1850 and 1880. The chances of finding an ancestor in these schedules depends on a series of "ifs," which when taken together would seem to relegate them to the category of minimal utility. However, for 1850 and 1860, some schedules named slaves along with their causes of death, occasionally their surnames, age, sex, color, and marital status. Many of these schedules have been abstracted and published in book form, but be careful, because some excluded slaves whose names appeared in the mortality schedules, as in the case of the published indexes to the mortality schedules for the state of Georgia. For any death to have been reported on a mortality schedule, the Census Bureau stipulated that it should have occurred one year preceding the date the census was taken. (Remember most censuses were taken in June and July.) Finally, not all states collected information for this effort, but for those that did, you might find the remaining schedules housed at your state's archives.

The 1900 through 1920 censuses ask questions with regard to number of years married, month of birth, and finally, number of living children out of total children ever birthed. This information is also a form of reporting vital events. Indeed, census records will constitute one of your primary sources for obtaining information on approximate dates of birth and marriage. For African Americans, this information is especially important if no other records can be located to provide estimates of month and year of birth or year of marriage.

OTHER CENSUSES AND CENSUS SUBSTITUTES

Census records are invaluable, but they tell a story only every ten years. What happens in between can be documented with other sources. City directories are especially important for tracing your ancestors who migrated to the mid-sized towns of the South and to larger urban centers of the North. Often published yearly, most listed head of household, his or her occupation, an address, and any dependents. Lucky for you now that segregation paid you a dividend years later—a large number of these directories used asterisks or some other mark to identify African Americans.

County records, especially tax lists and tax digests, can document a continuous residence in a particular county for years in between the decennial censuses. Most counties in the South taxed individuals way before income taxes became a permanent part of our existence. Furthermore, tax lists predate the first federal census of 1790—an important point to remember for colonial research.

School censuses are frequently used by researchers, if they are available. For example, the Mississippi state archives has selected school censuses that were taken at the turn of the century. Other states may also have such censuses, and good researchers should always inquire through the state archives for the state in which they are conducting their research.

The 1890 Census of Surviving Soldiers of the Civil War

Researchers frequently ignore the 1890 *Schedule of Surviving Soldiers of the Civil War,* part of which survived the fire. If you had an ancestor who was eligible to serve in that war as part of the United States Colored Troops division, then you should certainly check this schedule. Note that it is a schedule of *surviving* soldiers. It therefore will not reveal names of those who died before the census was taken. That part of the remaining 1890 schedule covers, in alphabetical order, half the state of Kentucky and all other states whose first letter begins with *L* through the end of the alphabet plus the District of Columbia, effectively covering most states where African American soldiers were heavily recruited. The one drawback to this schedule is that not all surviving USCT soldiers were actually enumerated or identified. You will find the names of many Confederate soldiers who were mistakenly entered. The Census Bureau later drew a line through their names.

State, City, and Other Censuses

Dubester's volume on state censuses should be consulted to determine whether additional censuses were taken by individual states in years between the federal census. Florida, Ohio, and New York took censuses in 1885. Many of the Reconstruction governments of the South took censuses in 1866, most of which are housed in states' archives. While the Reconstruction censuses are not entirely reliable and inclusive, they may prove critical to your own individual research, particularly in placing your ancestor in a given county during this turbulent year. Censuses can be taken by any governmental body or private organization for that matter. Occasionally, there are rare finds like the census that a scholar took in 1880 for his own research. The scholar enu-

merated all (or nearly all) African Americans living in Dinwiddie County, Virginia, in 1880, but his surviving records (housed at the University of Iowa) have not been made available for widespread use. They are available for those willing to use the university's collection in person.

Slave Schedules

While the 1850 and 1860 slave schedules will be discussed in more detail in subsequent chapters, they will be briefly covered in this chapter to alert you to a few mistakes that beginners make. No other federal census prior to 1870 enumerates African Americans by name unless they were "free persons of color" or free. Slaves were enumerated statistically (age, sex, and color) under the names of their owners. Exceptions to this rule occurred: When a slave had reached the unlikely age of one hundred, the census taker was instructed to enter his or her name on the 1850 and 1860 schedule, *or* when a mistake was made by the enumerator, the names of slaves were entered next to the blank spaces where names could have been entered but were not.

You might wonder why slaves were enumerated at all. Article 1, Section 2 of the U.S. Constitution stipulated that all "other persons" (an indirect reference to slaves) would be counted as three-fourths of a person for purposes of apportionment! To be taxed without representation was one thing that created this document, but to be counted as three-fourths of a person with representation by your slave owner was indeed phenomenal. With that said, researchers should know that the year 1870 pretty much terminates research for the first generation of freedom. Your research in all subsequent records will involve records that document how, when, and where your ancestors gained their freedom.

Other Problems Related to Methods of Research

*T*he method of census research is rather straightforward. You are tracing the same household from one census to the next. As in the case of Isaam Thomas, changes will occur over this fifty-year period, but if you start with the 1920 census and work back, you will almost always discover the Thomas kin network in each census. By the time you reach the period when Isaam Thomas was a minor in his parents' household, you will not have any difficulty locating that household even if you don't know the names of his parents. (Note: Since you don't know the names of his parents, you won't be able to use the census index, but you will be able to determine from the index the name of the county, the enumeration district, and the pages where the Thomas kin network was listed.

Taking Notes

*S*tudy the format of the notes that I took on the Longmire family for an 1880 census search.

My Notes

Surname: Longmire
Records: 1880 Population Census, Monroe County, Alabama
Date of Research: September 1993

Results:
Enumeration District 156, page 25, Monroe County
   Larkin Longmire, Mulatto, male, 47, farmer, AL, AL, SC*
   Hannah Longmire, Black, female, 27, keeping house, AL, AL, AL
   John Longmire, Black, male, 18, son, works on farm, AL, AL, AL
   Julia Longmire, Black, female, 11, daughter, works on farm, ibid.
   James Longmire, Black, male, 9, son, AL, AL, AL
   York Longmire, Black, male, 7, son, AL, AL, AL
   Mary Longmire, Black, female, 5, daughter, AL, AL, AL

*State abbreviations refer to (1) his place of birth, (2) his father's place of birth, and (3) his mother's place of birth.

Observations: In the same enumeration district, see Abe Longmire (age 25) on page 16, Albert Longmire (28) on page 18, Andrew Longmire (37) on page 3, Ellis Longmire (age 24) on page 19, John Longmire (age 22) on page 3, Nathan Longmire (38) on page 17. Note also that Soundex index includes Longmires in Conecuh and Wilcox. Highly likely that they are related to each other. Find other Longmires born in South Carolina. Found no Longmires who could be parents of Larkin. Saw Rileys in same area as Longmires. Hannah's relations?

Problems: Hannah, John's mother, is listed as 27 years old. Check other records. Couldn't be his stepmother? Possibly incorrect age.

To do next:
(1) Research Larking Longmire in Agricultural Schedule for 1880.
(2) Reinterview Uncle Clarence about his grandfather and Monroe County origins.
(3) Take a chance and see if can find a death certificate for Larkin.

ISSAQUENA COUNTY SLAVE SCHEDULE, 1850

SCHEDULE 2.—Slave Inhabitants in _____ in the County of _Issaquena Co_ _____ of _Mississippi_, enumerated by me, on the _24_ day of _August_, 1850. _George F. Johnston_ Ass't Marshl

NAMES OF SLAVE OWNERS.	Number of Slaves.	Age.	Sex.	Colour.	Fugitives from the State.	Number manumitted.	Deaf & dumb, blind, insane, or idiotic.			NAMES OF SLAVE OWNERS.	Number of Slaves.	Age.	Sex.	Colour.	Fugitives from the State.	Number manumitted.	Deaf & dumb, blind, insane, or idiotic.
1	2	3	4	5	6	7	8			1	2	3	4	5	6	7	8
Hector S. D. Thristin (est.)	1	3	F	B				1	1	Melissa J. MacQuillen	1	45	F	B			
	1	23	M	B				2	2		1	23	M	B			
	1	28	M	Mo				3	3		1	19	F	B			
	1	25	F	Mo				4	4		1	10	M	B			
	1	35	M	B				5	5		1	3	M	B			
	1	28	F	B				6	6	Est of B. C. McQuillen	1	31	M	Mo			
	1	32	M	Mo				7	7		1	30	F	Mo			
	1	22	F	B				8	8		1	22	M	Mo			
	1	24	M	B				9	9		1	15	M	Mo			
	1	39	M	Mo				10	10		1	11	M	Mo			
	1	60	F	B				11	11		1	10	M	Mo			
	1	30	M	B				12	12		1	30	F	B			
	1	27	M	B				13	13		1	60	F	B			
	1	10	M	B				14	14		1	16	F	B			
	1	60	M	Mo				15	15	James B. Woolfolk	1	30	M	B			
	1	12	M	B				16	16		1	50	M	B			
	1	18	M	M				17	17		1	22	M	B			
	1	10	M	B				18	18		1	18	M	B			
	1	05	M	Mo				19	19		1	16	M	B			
	1	30	F	B				20	20		1	25	F	Mo			s
	1	10	M	B				21	21		1	28	F	Mo			s
	1	8	M	B				22	22		1	16	F	B			s
	1	25	M	B				23	23		1	8	F	B			s
	1	25	M	B				24	24		1	8	F	B			s

Note: (1) Absence of names of slaves, (2) Blank columns, (3) Deceased slave owners listed as an estate.

(4) Call lady in Monroe County to see if there are any Longmires still in area.
(5) Find out what kinds of records are available in Monroe County, including courthouse records.

THE 1890 CENSUS

Most of the 1890 census was destroyed in a fire. After you complete the 1900 census, you will have to jump twenty years to the next available one, the 1880 census. Twenty years is long enough to "get missing" from a household. Families that were just beginning to produce children around 1880 will not appear as intact households in the 1900 census. In effect, twenty years is long enough to have children and for the children to be gone. Consider the case of a female who was born after the 1880 census, who married and left her parents' household before the 1900 census was taken, and you have no idea about her existence since you know little about this line of the family. Researchers should routinely check spacing between children's ages in a household and carefully study responses to questions about the number of children born. Big gaps in spacing of children frequently indicate (1) high rates of miscarriage or (2) children who did not reside in the parents' household or (3) females who married in between censuses. Another way to deal with the 1890 gap is to use county tax lists, city directories, and other census substitutes if they are available. Finally, the 1890 gap in family information is all the more reason that researchers should go into census research with more than just a name. But if a name is all you've got, you often have no choice!

"Jumping Around," or Failure to Follow the Sequence of Time

*R*esearchers often skip around in census records. This is not recommended for beginners, who should attempt to start with the 1920 census and systematically work back. This, however, is not an ironclad rule. Nor is it improper to do census research at the same time that you collect vital records and locate substitutes for vital records. The critical point is that you absorb, integrate, and interpret the often massive amount of information that you can collect in a short span of time.

This all too brief discussion of census research should get you started. Remember that census research will be with you throughout your genealogical project. There will always be people you missed or didn't locate the first time; and there will always be unidentified ancestors who will be unearthed later, after you begin to extend your lines beyond the generation that lived at the turn of the century.

Summary

*T*his chapter has provided you with the basics of tracing your ancestors in family units between 1870 and 1920 using the federal population censuses as well as other censuses that might help you. This is one of the easiest and most enjoyable phases of your research, but it can be filled with pitfalls and frustrations if you don't follow the basic precautions as outlined above.

Chapter 7

FINDING FREEDOM'S GENERATION

Your Ancestors During the

Civil War, 1860–1865

Anoder ting is, suppose you had kept your freedom without enlisting in dis army; your chillen might have grown up free and been well cultivated as to be equal to any business, but it would have been always flung in dere faces— "Your fater never fought for he own freedom."

PRIVATE THOMAS LONG, FIRST SOUTH CAROLINA VOLUNTEERS,
CITED IN BENJAMIN QUARLES, *THE NEGRO IN THE CIVIL WAR*

Letter from Judge of Probate, Bullock County, Alabama

December 12, 1912

Hon. C. B. Smith, State Auditor, Montgomery.

Dear Sir:— In re Pensioner No. 24655, James Young.

Replying to your favor of this date, just receive, I beg to advise that Judge Singleton is at present out of the city, but I think I can give reply to the inquiry.

Yes, James Young is a negro, one of those good, old, true, Southern darkies, and the record shows that he was a private in Company "K", 29th Ala, enlisted the 21 of February, 1862 at Clayton, discharged 15 May, 1865, has been drawing a pension since 1902, when he was 69 years of age, and the general sentiment among all the white people who know him is, he not only deserves the pension for actual fighting service rendered, but as he is now almost eighty years old, he deserves to be advanced into a higher class.

Don't disturb old Uncle James, or Jonas as we call him. He is a Confederate Veteran, and the laws intent is to reward service, without regard to color, and I am informed by those who say they know, that he gave the service.

With best regards, I am,
Very truly yours,
P. F. Miles, Probate Clerk

Who Remembers?

Private Thomas Long certainly had the right idea. He was the last African American in his line to have lived under slavery. No doubt, he had in mind more than the preservation of his lineage. Perhaps he planned for future generations to remember him as a man who had earned an equal place in the world because he fought for his freedom. We can only wonder now if Private Long's descendants have a copy of his discharge papers from the United States Colored Troops. Perhaps they have letters from the Pension Bureau or even a photograph of him sitting proudly in his uniform.

But what about the memories of the 180,000 or so men who fought with the United States Colored Troops and the 30,000 who fought in the U.S. Navy? How much of their memory survived, and how much did they themselves pass down in the form of family oral history? Have their descendants also remembered? Few African American families seem to have a memory of their Civil War ancestors. Even fewer seem to have surviving documents and memorabilia relating to the war.

If the inevitable result of the Civil War was freedom for slaves, how could Mr. Young's involvement in the war have made a difference in his own freedom? Moreover, how, as the state auditor must have asked, could a "negro" serve in the Civil War on the Confederate side? It was actually quite easy. He also must have smiled to himself every month when his check was delivered. Of course, had the war started turning in favor of the Confederates, he might have been doing some recalculating.

If Mr. Young were your ancestor, under what circumstances would you have found out about his service? If you had a family story that had been passed down—a very likely situation, since Mr. Young was still living in 1912—would you have thought that your relatives meant service in the Confederacy when they told you that he had fought in the Civil War? It is more likely that you would have assumed that he fought on the Union side. Furthermore, you would have assumed his service was in the United States Colored Troops division rather than in the regular army, which was assumed to have no Blacks, or the volunteer army, which was prohibited from enlisting Black men even though some did serve. This letter is used as an example to suggest to beginning researchers that Civil War research can often lead to fascinating and complicated stories about your ancestors—even those who never officially enlisted on either side. It represents the other side of *Glory*.

In thinking of the Civil War (1861–1865), the genealogical researcher should first and foremost consider that this is the period in which our ancestors struggled to work their way through to freedom from slavery. For some, the wide chasm between freedom and slavery was crossed in a matter of days from the inception of the war, and for others it may have been a matter of finding out some months after its end!

How Did the War Affect Your Ancestors?

*T*he best way to approach this entire period is to try to answer this question. When I talk to genealogists, I ask them what impact the war had on the local area where their ancestors lived. Generally, they cannot answer. Very few of us think in historical terms. The complexity of the Civil War experience for African Americans is still an unfolding story, one you will have to help reveal by studying your ancestors' experiences. Because this war had such a far-reaching effect on every individual who lived during this era, the documents and sources that tell this story will contain unique experiences for nearly every one of your ancestors. If you find nothing else while researching this era, you will find countless human stories that leap from the pages, asking to be told. There will be many human tragedies, and there will be many stories showing how so many managed to survive.

If you consider that approximately 180,000 African Americans served as enlisted men in the United States Colored Troops alone, then there is a high probability that you have at least one ancestor among that group. Furthermore, there is a high probability that a sizable number of these men survived well into the twentieth century. If your ancestors lived in some of the areas where men were heavily recruited, especially the states of Kentucky, Louisiana, Mississippi, and Tennessee, as well as states in the North with sizable populations of free blacks, there is more than a good chance that one or more served. While the probabilities are high, the one obstacle to your research is that few families seem to have a surviving memory of their ancestors' Civil War service. Even fewer seem to have surviving documents and memorabilia relating to the war such as uniforms, photographs, and discharge papers. Therefore, a routine check of the records is always mandatory.

When the order to enlist men to fight in the war under the United States Colored Troops division was issued in May 1863 (War Department General Order 143), several units had already been raised, trained, and had seen battle. Those units in New Orleans, South Carolina, and Kansas whose formation had preceded this official order were eventually incorporated into the USCT. The following chart provides an official state-by-state count of men who enlisted:

UNITED STATES COLORED TROOPS ENLISTMENT BY STATE*

South		North		Mid-Atlantic		Mid-West		Border		Other	
VA	5,919	ME	104	NY	4,125	OH	5,092	DE	954	CA	1,918
NC	5,035	NH	125	NJ	1,185	IN	1,537	MD	8,718	OR	38
SC	5,462	VT	120	PA	8,612	IL	1,811	MI	8,344	CO	5
FL	1,044	MA	3,966	DC	3,269	MI	1,387	KY	23,703	NE	15
GA	3,486	CT	1,764			WI	165			NV	27
AL	4,969	RI	1,837			MN	104			NM	16
MS	17,869					IA	440			UT	5
LA	24,052					KS	2,080			WA	17
TX	47										
AR	5,526										
TN	20,133										
Total	93,542		7,916		17,191		12,616		41,719		2,041

Others not attributable to correct states: 3,950

*Source: Table 1, Berlin, et al., *Freedom: A Documentary History of Emancipation, 1861–1867*, Series II, The Black Military Experience, page 12. Berlin's figures were compiled from *Official Records of the Bureau of Colored Troops*, series 3, volume 5, page 138.

These figures mask some critical points about the military experience of African American men in the USCT. Soldiers were not recruited in proportion to the black population for each state. Recruitment was done in the context of the war itself. African Americans in certain states, therefore, bore a disproportionate burden with respect to the percentage of draft-age African American men in their state and in the nation. Northern or free states contributed approximately 24 percent of total enlistments. Border states critical to the Union effort were also placed in the same position. Recruits from Kentucky and Tennessee contributed a resounding 24 percent of USCT enlistees, representing 47 percent of the total black population in both states, slave and free.

Ironically, enlistments from the Deep South states reached these levels only for certain areas—namely, the Mississippi Delta and Louisiana. Enlistment hardly reached Alabama and Georgia. Even though many of these enlistments represent slaves who crossed the borders from neighboring states, that such a sizable percentage was drawn from a few states suggests that slaves knew the importance of this burden—not just for their individual freedom, but for that of the whole African American population. These figures do not include men who served in the navy, primarily from Virginia and Maryland where there was a tradition of seafaring already established among free blacks as well as slaves. Figures for black naval enlistments vary from 10,000 to 25,000 depending on the sources used.

Another group that is not so well documented actually equaled in number those men who served in the USCT. They either were impressed into the Confederacy or worked for the Union in nonmilitary capacities. The Confederate effort needed laborers, body servants, miners, cooks, munitions plant laborers, and other workers, particularly near the end of the war. Slave owners were requisitioned to supply a certain percentage of the slave population to the war effort. Slave artisans were particularly in high demand, as were those who had some special skill or knowledge that had gone untapped during slavery. Benjamin Quarles in *The Negro in the Civil War* cites many fascinating cases of men who acted as scouts, spies, and laborers for the Union effort without being enlisted. It was often fugitive slaves who provided John Pinkerton, later of

Pinkerton detective fame, with critical information on Confederate troop movements.

Some obtained freedom by virtue of being "abandoned." For example, planters in the Sea Islands left their homes and plantations or farms early in the war due to Union victories. The Port Royal area in South Carolina (St. Helena's Island) is one such area where this occurred. In her book *Rehearsal for Reconstruction*, Willie Lee Rose documents the early years of freedom for African Americans who lived in this area. Some slave owners who had large vested interests constituted a class of "absentee" planters. Stephen Duncan, a Northerner by birth, was one such planter who left his vast interests in Mississippi Delta plantations under supervision after having nominally freed his slaves. Duncan was one of the largest slave holders in the South, having owned over his lifetime at least fourteen plantations in Mississippi and Louisiana.

The war created a large body of fugitive slaves who effectively obtained a jump start on freedom. Early in the war, heavy military engagements occurred in places like Virginia and South Carolina. Slaves perceived the opportunity and ran behind Union lines. Though they would have been considered fugitives in earlier times, it was in Virginia that they were declared "contrabands" of war. In the field, commanding officers had to make decisions on the ground rather than wait for clarification from Washington. The ensuing battle between slave owners seeking the return of their slaves and various army commanders who acted individually on this issue was eventually clarified under the first Confiscation Act of 1861. It effectively granted freedom to "contraband" or fugitive slaves, but as with all laws, its simplicity of wording turned out to hide a complex maze of behavior.

There was the experience of dislocation for part of the slave population in each state. This movement of "refugeeing" slaves was brought about as a result of planters fleeing with their total slave labor force to remote places in their state and even across state lines to Texas, for example, where it was believed that slavery would remain in the event of a Confederate defeat. A small band even wound up in Brazil, of all places, where slavery wasn't abolished until 1885! This phenomenon should be considered a possibility for your ancestors if you run into difficulties explaining how your ancestors got to Texas and other far-flung places.

Those who gained freedom early on in the war formed a vanguard, particularly those men who were recruited to serve in the United States Colored Troops. The role of this large body of African American men, almost all of whom fought under white commanding officers, has been sorely underestimated in its contribution to postwar leadership of African American communities. These men often started their road to literacy in the USCT, and their exposure to a panoramic view of the condition of African Americans in those communities through which they passed encouraged a vision that had not previously been possible.

The war really has not been so long ago, yet little of the war experience remains in our collective memory. That White Southerners kept the memories of the war alive has a lot to do with your ancestors' burial of theirs. Small wonder that when the 1890 U.S. census takers had to enumerate surviving Union Civil War veterans, African

American veterans were undercounted, particularly if they lived in the Deep South states. Furthermore, the first bitter lessons of freedom may have made these events unworthy of memorializing for some African Americans, no matter how courageous their service may have been.

At this point, your task as a genealogist and family historian is to pick up the idea where Private Long left off—to document your family's first generation of freedom. This will be one of the most difficult phases of your research, for much has been buried. Moreover, the complexity of the war and Reconstruction period is only surpassed by the complexity of the documents that survived from that period—a great many of which contain some references to individual African Americans who seized the opportunities for freedom.

STARTING A CIVIL WAR SEARCH

*T*hose researchers who do best are those who understand that it was both a war and a struggle for individual African Americans to seize the immediate opportunities presented to them to gain their freedom. In order to understand the range of experiences that your ancestors may have had, your research should be guided by the following specific goals: (1) understand how the war affected African Americans, (2) understand how Union and Confederate policy affected the recruitment of soldiers and military labor, (3) understand war developments in your state and local area of research, and (4) understand what genealogical and historical sources exist on Civil War records. Therefore, understanding the progression of the war, the methods used to recruit African Americans, the impact of Union and Confederate troops in an area, the methods devised to deal with refugees and contrabands, and even the organization of the war effort (the military command structure) on both sides will help you to understand what may have happened to your ancestors. See the bibliography for a basic reading and reference list.

The easiest entrée into the massive amount of documentation on the war is to first answer this question: "Did any of my ancestors serve in the USCT?" In order to answer this question, you will need at a minimum the names of all male ancestors who were between the ages of twelve and fifty during the war and their probable places of residence, using residence before the war or immediately after the war as clues if you are unsure of the exact location. Once you reach this point, you should have completed your census searches and you should have most of the households that existed between 1865 and 1870. The second thing that you need to establish is whether your ancestor applied for a pension or whether his wife and children received any benefits as his survivors (widows' and dependent children's benefits).

To determine whether your ancestor enlisted, the alphabetical *Index to Compiled Service Records of Volunteer Union Soldiers Who Served with United States Colored Troops* (National Archives Microfilm Copy #589) should be consulted. If you locate an ancestor, form NATF 80, available from the National Archives, should be completed indicating that you would like a copy of the veteran's military service record and pension record. While this procedure is relatively simple, many unanticipated difficulties await you. One difficulty is locating a facility

that has a copy of the USCT index on microfilm. Note that you could also use the index on the Web because it has the essential information found in the index on microfilm above. (See pages 441–442 for Web addresses.) Do remember that this massive project will contain errors, including errors of omission, as with all major efforts to index large bodies of records. Also note that the index does not cross-reference aliases, of which there were many. When I used it, I could not find one Samuel Nix, whose pension file and enlistment record I had examined at the National Archives some years ago. But do use the Web index and back it up with the microfilmed index.

This brings us to yet another issue, the problem of surname usage and reporting. Many soldiers served under assumed names or aliases. Some may have been enlisted under a slave owner's name. The spelling of the surname may have changed from the time of enlistment. Finally name reversals may have occurred, as in the case of Johnson Alfred becoming Alfred Johnson. Search the records using all possible variations of the name's spelling.

Additional sources might help you to determine whether an ancestor was officially enlisted. One is the 1890 Census, *Special Schedule of Surviving Soldiers, Sailors, and Marines, and Widows* which was discussed in the previous chapter. These schedules have been microfilmed and some have also been indexed. They can be easily obtained through the National Archives microfilm rental program, a genealogical lending library, or a library with a large genealogy collection. Caution is important in using this as your only source of evidence for service. This census is based on survivors; therefore, you will not find an ancestor who died prior to the date the census was taken. Furthermore, you may not find an ancestor who lived in the South. Census takers enumerated surviving Confederate veterans despite the fact that the schedule was designed for Union veterans. Confederate names will have a line drawn through them. In addition, the political tensions in the South and the vagaries of poor census taking probably led to omission of many surviving Black veterans.

Despite this, if you find an ancestor on the 1890 schedule, it will provide some of the essential details to be found in the official service record: dates of enlistment and discharge, rank, name of company, and name of regiment. This census also asked for a post office address, whether any disabilities were suffered, and the pension number. This number is the same number that appears in the *General Pension Index*, an alphabetical index of all pension applicants and claimants dated between 1861 and 1934. The *General Pension Index* has been microfilmed (T288), and each card in the index contains military service information, names of dependents, the pensioner's application number and certificate number. Soldiers who served in the USCT would also appear in this index.

The last columns of the 1900 and the 1910 censuses ask if the person being enumerated is a survivor of the Civil War. Again, this possibility should not be overlooked when you do your census work; however, the same limitations suggested for the 1890 schedule apply here. These censuses should not be your only source to determine the possibility of military service during the war.

Once you find a name in the index that you think might be the ancestor that you are looking for, make sure you write down all the information that appears in the index, especially the soldier's assigned regiment and company and any previous units he might have served in as well as any aliases. That is about all that will appear on the index card. But with that information, you can obtain your ancestor's compiled military service record by completing form NATF 80 and mailing it to the National Archives. The compiled record will report on his service history, including movements, battles, injuries, etc. But, more often than not, you will not be certain enough about the individuals you found in the index, so you will want to examine a quick reference guide on regimental histories, which will tell you the same kind of information in capsule form.

Indeed, an article in a scholarly or genealogical journal or a regimental history may have been published for your ancestor's regiment. Though there are still relatively few full-length books on USCT regiments, researchers should stay current with genealogical publications because research on various units is now being conducted by both historians and genealogists. In lieu of this information, however, you can check the regimental history on the Web (at the same site as the index) or you can use *Dyer's Compendium*, readily available in most libraries. This source will state all critical information on the regiment—where it was organized and discharged, battles fought, casualties, and the names of preceding or succeeding units of which it may have been a part. The National Archives has compiled unit histories (*Service Histories of Volunteer Units in the Union Army*, Microcopy 594), and they can also be purchased by unit.

This procedure is fairly simple and straightforward, but when you examine the

USCT index you will, of course, find that many people shared your ancestor's name. How will you tell which one is your ancestor, if any? The use of *Dyer's Compendium* will help because it indicates where each unit was raised and discharged. If you find three people with the name Samuel Pompey, you will be able to eliminate all those who never lived or passed through your ancestor's place of origin. Now you're ready to fill out form NATF 80 requesting the military service record of Samuel Pompey who was recruited in Mobile, Alabama, and not Newport, Rhode Island. Of course, a visit to the National Archives in Washington, D.C., will save you a lot of guessing and money for submitting each form for all those who might be your ancestors, and that is what is recommended for African American researchers. (See special section on the National Archives.)

Pension Records

Nearly every pension file for former USCT soldiers can tell not only a life story, but also about individual war experiences. While it has been estimated that 80 percent of all servicemen applied for a pension, the figure for men enlisted in the USCT is considerably lower. Pension records contain an astounding amount of information even when claims were denied. The original records (Union army, including the USCT) are housed at the National Archives, and you may request copies of documents from a file using the same form (NATF 80) used to request a military service record.

Items that appear in these files are fre-

quently the very kinds of things genealogists are looking for; pension applicants had to prove their own identity (service, age, disabilities, marriages, ages of children). Remember, this may have been difficult in an age when few could read or write or when establishing a person's identity depended on verification through a local county clerk or reputable individual. Therefore, the applicant had to name individuals and collect documentation in order to prove his identity and his service in the military, often with the aid of a local lawyer or agent. Agents were often stationed throughout the country to service applicants, and many a lawyer earned his income by serving as an agent.

Pension files contain depositions given by or on behalf of the applicant, his relatives (including parents of unmarried servicemen), neighbors, and fellow soldiers who served in the same company. A deposition is a statement of the basic facts of the case, and it generally shows the relationship between the soldier and the person giving the deposition. Thus, evidence in the pension file will identify people with whom the veteran had very close ties before, during, and after the war. That would also include fellow soldiers, siblings, and in-laws. The standard questionnaire completed by all pension applicants states circumstances of birth, enlistment, marriage, places resided since discharge, name changes, and name of former slave owner (if a former slave) depending on the date of the claim or the length of the pension. Some applicants submitted copies of marriage certificates, divorce papers, baptismal records, and their discharge certificates.

Widows and/or dependent children submitted death certificates and claims from

USCT PENSION FILE, WIDOW'S APPLICATION FOR ARREARS
OF PAY & BOUNTY

WIDOW'S APPLICATION FOR ARREARS OF PAY AND BOUNTY.

State of *Alabama*
County of *Butler* } ss:

On this *3rd* day of *November*, 1866, personally appeared before me, a *Justice of the Peace* in and for the County and State aforesaid, *Mary Mosley* of *Greenville*, in the County of *Butler* and State of *Alabama*, who, being duly sworn, deposes and says that she is a *free* person of color: that her age is *22* years; that she is the widow of *Silas Mosley* deceased, late a resident of *Greenville* in the State of *Alabama*, who was a *Private* in Company "*K*" of the *96th* Regiment United States Colored Troops, who enlisted at *Fort Morgan*, in the State of *Alabama*, on or about the *21st* day of *August*, 1863, and who died in ~~the service of the United States~~ at *Greenville, Alabama* on or about the *17th* day of *October*, 1866. That her maiden name was *Mary Davis* and that she was married to the said *Silas Mosley* on the *6th* day of *October*, 1860, at *Bascos Randolph Co* in the State of *Alabama*, by *John Savors*, and that she ever afterwards lived with and deported herself as the lawful and dutiful wife of the said *Silas Mosley*; that she has had by her said husband *One* children, named and aged, respectively, as follows: *Silas Mosley, Aged four Months. (said child being now dead)*

The further makes oath that her said husband was a *free* person at the time of entering the service of the United States, and had been *free* since the *1st* day of *July*, 1862. The makes this application to recover all arrears of pay, bounty, or other allowances due the deceased from the United States, and desires that the Certificate of Pay, when issued in satisfaction thereof, may be sent to her at *Greenville* P. O., County of *Butler* and State of *Alabama*.

funeral homes to cover burial expenses. The declaration for a widow's pension will frequently state information about the veteran's previous marriages, if any, and children born of those marriages. Even the moral character of the veteran or his widow comes under scrutiny. Widows often had to obtain statements from reputable locals (ministers, the sheriff, and others) attesting to her "widowhood." I found one deposition given against a widow based on charges that she was running a boardinghouse of ill repute!

Finally, medical statements provide a considerable amount of detail with regard to the veteran's health and specific medical condition, whether the condition was related to military service, and the course of an illness, all of which provide insights into the veteran's medical history. Doctors often submitted examination reports, and of course, the veteran had to describe how his condition was caused by some war-related incident or illness.

Pension files can be quite lengthy, particularly if the application process was drawn out, if increases in payment were made repeatedly, if applicants had to submit additional statements, or if the veteran's widow(s) and children also received benefits. Therefore, you should always request that the archives staff quote an estimate for photocopying the entire file when you complete form NATF 80. The following case study is used to show researchers what the possibilities are.

Nicodemus Parmer's Life as Seen Through His Pension File

Below is a portion of the deposition of Nicodemus Parmer, completed some fifty-six years after the war's end. He had reached the venerable age of eighty-two, had been married three times, and had lived in three separate states! He was not the typical USCT veteran. After each paragraph, comments are provided to show what evidence and clues are included and excluded.

Nicodemus Parmer's Statement, 1921

Introductory Paragraph

On this 11 day of April, 1921 at Memphis, county of Shelby, State of Tennessee before me, W. L. Sullivan, a Special Examiner of the Bureau of Pensions, personally appeared Nicodemus Parmer, who, being by me first duly sworn to answer truly all interrogatories propounded to him during this special examination of aforesaid claim for pension, deposes and says:

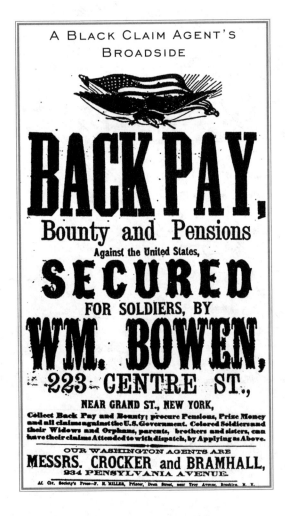

A BLACK CLAIM AGENT'S BROADSIDE

BACK PAY, Bounty and Pensions Against the United States, SECURED FOR SOLDIERS, BY WM. BOWEN, 223 CENTRE ST., NEAR GRAND ST., NEW YORK. Collect Back Pay and Bounty; procure Pensions, Prize Money and all claims against the U.S. Government. Colored Soldiers and their Widows and Orphans, parents, brothers and sisters, can have their claims Attended to with dispatch, by Applying as Above. OUR WASHINGTON AGENTS ARE MESSRS. CROCKER and BRAMHALL, 234 PENSYLVANIA AVENUE.

Second Paragraph

I am 82 years of age: my post office address is Marion, Crittenden Co., Arkansas. I served in Co. I, 71 U.S.C. Inf. in the Civil War. I have not rendered any other service in any branch of either the U.S. Army, Navy, or Marine Corps.

Comments: Current residence, estimated year of birth, current address, and name of company and unit.

Third Paragraph

My mother was Judy Watts; she died when I was but a child. My father was Reason Bowen. My mother belonged to Gov. Watts' mother in Butler County, Alabama, and father belonged to Col. Bowen of the same county. I never belonged to any one but the Watts folks.

Comments: Names of parents and former owners, noting herein that names were same as owners. No explanation why he does not carry surname Watts or Bowen. No indication who cared for him after mother's death since his father was on another place.

Fourth Paragraph

I had brothers as follows: Reece Steen, Caesar Steen, David Murphy, Allen Watts, Sandy Watts and Peter Watts. The different names are because some of my brothers belonged to other folks. My brothers were in Alabama the last I knew of them except Caesar who went to Texas with his master. I have not heard of any of them since the Civil War.

Comments: Names of siblings, their owners, and postwar family separation. No

female siblings? No explanation on non-communication with family since the war. No explanation why surnames differ. You would have to study relationships between the Steen, Murphy, Watts, and Parmer families.

Fifth Paragraph

The first place I lived after my discharge was at Austin, Tunica Co., Miss., on Judge Wrights for awhile, and then I lived in that same vicinity till I came to Arkansas about four years ago. Mr. Bob Tate, Hollywood, Miss.; Prince Jones, col., Hollywood, Miss.; Charley Grandberry, col., Hollywood, Miss.; Mr. ____ Flynn, w., Mr. Jim Anderson, w., Hollywood, and Mr. Ellis Woodford, sheriff, Tunica, Miss., all have known me for years. The following persons have known me ever since I have been in Marion, Ark.: Jim Felix, col., Willis Washington, col., George Taylor, col., Mr. Rhodes, Banker; Mr. White, in the bank; Mr. Coseley.

Comments: Possibly discharged in Mississippi and never returned home. Note that col. = colored, w. = white, and that "Mr." is reserved for whites. Individuals mentioned may have been in same USCT unit. Note also that names of important local Whites are given for "character" references and that he lived in Tunica from time of discharge until 1917.

Sixth Paragraph

I had a slave wife Leah, who was on the Steen place where my brothers Reece and Caesar lived. My owner did not know that I had Leah. I was at that time working on the Steen place. My young mistress married Mr. Steen. I had not child by Leah. We did not have any sort of slave marriage ceremony. I have not seen or heard of Leah since I went into the army. I did not have any other slave wife, but one of the women called Charlotte laid a child to me. She belonged to the Steen family. I never lived with her as her slave husband and have not seen her since the war.

Comments: At first it appears that he was hired out to the Steens, but later a more likely explanation occurs, particularly in light of his surname usage. His mistress (i.e., owner) was a Parmer who married a Steen, and they then combined their operations since they owned slaves collectively. Note that he doesn't count his "slave" marriage to Leah in his total number of marriages, and that a woman with whom he had an affair "laid" (i.e., named) a child to him which he disclaimed without giving a reason.

Seventh to Ninth Paragraph

The first wife I got after the war was Sophia Settles. We married in Tunica County, Miss., about two years after my discharge from the army. We had a marriage license from Tunica, Miss., and a colored preacher, Billy Grandberry, said the marriage ceremony. I had two children by Sophia; both are dead. We lived together for five or six years, when she left me and went to St. Louis, Mo. I have not heard of her since she left me. . . . The second wife I got was Amanda Barnes, daughter of Anderson Barnes. I married Amanda at Tunica, Miss., about 7 or 8 years after Sophia left me. Amanda had not been married prior to her marriage to me. Amanda is still living with me as my wife; we have not been divorced or separated. She is now about 52 or 53 years old.

* * *

Comments: Note that the pension officer is asking whether such a marriage can be verified in local records in the event of future claims. Parmer later states that he was divorced from Sophia in Austin and used a local lawyer, Jim Perkins, who is no longer living. He also stated that Sophia's only kin, a sister named Callie Williams, had died some years later but that other individuals named in the deposition knew Sophia. Sophia's marital fidelity was also questioned by the interviewer, a point that should be noted as not unusual when Whites had the chance to find out about the sexual lives of Blacks. Of course, character and reputation were also used as substitutes for other evidence in granting pensions to widows, but since Parmer had already informed the examiner as to the place, date, and record of his divorce, we will assume that the examiner's question referred more to the latter than the former concern.

A second deposition relates that he and Amanda had one son, also named Nicodemus, and that they adopted a boy of about seven or eight years old. He also stated that he had a "misery in my left side and it prevents me from working to amount to anything. I still try to raise a little cotton. I have not ploughed any this Spring." (One wonders how much work can be done at eighty-two!) He later stated that he had been treated by a "Dr. Dickens, col."

The evidence provided in this one document will allow a researcher to reconstruct Nicodemus Parmer's life starting with his birth during slavery. Indeed, it provides enough leads to reconstruct his family ties between 1860 through the postwar period.

USCT DEPOSITIONS

(Jennie Nix, a widow, applies for benefits)

DEPOSITION _a_

Case of _Jennie Nix_, No. _335,609_

On this _Fifteenth_ day of _April_, 1889, at _Lima_, County of _Allen_, State of _Ohio_, before me, _J. W. Abel_, a Special Examiner of the Pension Office, personally appeared _Jennie Nix_, who, being by me first duly sworn to answer truly all interrogatories propounded to her during this Special Examination of aforesaid pension claim, deposes and says: I am also known as Jennie Nicks, but the correct name is Nix. I am 38 years of age, housekeeper and my post office address is Lima, Allen Co. Ohio. I claim a pension as being the widow of Samuel Nix, who served as a Corporal in Co. "H" 15th Regt U.S.C.T. Infy, and who enlisted as a substitute at Lima, Ohio in the fall of 1864 and was discharged the following year. he died at Lima, Ohio September 20, 1878, he died from the effects of Chronic Diarrhoea, he was thirty three years of age at the time of his death. I became acquainted with Samuel Nix about one year before he went in the army as a substitute, he claimed to me that he had been born at Natchez, Miss, was not a slave but not free born and during the war had went as a cook for some of the officers of the Confederate Army and afterwards as a cook for the Union Army officers and came here with some of the officers, he then remained here about one year when he went as a substitute, I do not know for whom he went as a substitute, excepting that his name was Jones, when I first became acquainted with Samuel Nix he was about 19 or 20 years of age in 1864, he was about five feet four inches in height, I heard from the undertaker

Page 5   Deposition A

Henry Tolbett Statement on Behalf of Jennie Nix's Claim

DEPOSITION _a_

Case of _Jennie Nix_, No. _335,609_

On this _Fifteenth_ day of _April_, 1889, at _Lima_, County of _Allen_, State of _Ohio_, before me, _J. W. Abel_, a Special Examiner of the Pension Office, personally appeared _Jennie Nix_, who, being by me first duly sworn to answer by all interrogatories propounded to her during this Special Examination of aforesaid pension claim, deposes and says: I am also known as Jennie Nicks, but the correct name is Nix, I am 38 years of age, housekeeper and my post office address is Lima, Allen Co. Ohio. I claim a pension as being the widow of Samuel Nix, who served as a Corporal in Co. "H" 15th Regt U.S.C.T. Infy, who enlisted as a substitute at Lima, Ohio in the fall of 1864 and was discharged the following year. he died at Lima, Ohio September 20, 1878, he died from the effects of Chronic Diarrhoea, he was thirty three years of age at the time of his death. I became acquainted with Samuel Nix about one year before he went in the army as a substitute, he claimed to me that he had been born at Natchez, Miss, was not a slave but not free born and during the war had went as a cook for some of the officers of the Confederate Army and afterwards as a cook for the Union Army officers and came here with some of the officers, he then remained here about one year when he went as a substitute, I do not know for whom he went as a substitute, excepting that his name was Jones, when I first became acquainted with Samuel Nix he was about 19 or 20 years of age in 1864, he was about five feet four inches in height, I heard from the undertaker

Page 5   Deposition A

Nicodemus Parmer's wife Armandie moved to Chicago after his death, and in a letter submitted as part of the evidence required to obtain a widow's pension, she asks that her papers be sent to her in Chicago at her place of residence (1047 Maxwell Street). By then, her name is spelled _Palmer_ rather than _Parmer_.

Finally, without this pension file or a good oral history, it would have been diffi-cult to trace Parmer's story in the records. Had you been a descendant of his son living in Chicago, you would have first had to know that _Palmer_ can also be spelled _Parmer_; that he may not have been a slave in Mississippi since there was continued migration to the area after the war, and finally that you would have had to check a number of records before realizing that perhaps an ancestor had served in the Civil War.

Parmer's migratory path is not unusual or rare.

RESEARCHING OTHER PATHS TO GLORY

*N*ot all of our ancestors were officially enlisted in the USCT or the U.S. Navy. Indeed, some fought for or were forced to serve the Confederacy. This fact is increasingly being recognized as more research is being done on African American history. The Museum of the Confederacy, for example, recently arranged a major exhibit on African American life in the pre–Civil War period and sponsored a conference on African Americans in the war taking special note of their role in the Confederacy. Also consider the Regiment of Native Guards of New Orleans, which consisted of two units (mainly free blacks) that were raised to fight for the Confederacy. These two units are the only fully mustered-in units of individuals of African American descent. They were never called into active duty. The Confederacy, though it considered forming Black units, never quite got around to this question until the war's end.

There have been cases of individuals being recruited and mustered in with locally formed troops (both Confederate and Union), and researchers should not ignore these sources, particularly if there is a story that has been passed down in the family. One expert suggests that those men who actually fought with these units were connected to enlistees by blood, a possibility that cannot be ignored. In South Carolina, John McKindlay, the son of a free black, enlisted in the 17th Regiment Infantry for which he was granted a pension in 1923 when the state legislature passed a bill granting pensions to Blacks who served as loyal "servants, cooks, or attendants." Henry Brown, a drummer for the Darlington Guard's militia unit, also received a pension. The states of Mississippi and Tennessee also granted Confederate pensions to Blacks who served in a variety of capacities. Note that because individual states of the former Confederacy awarded pensions (and not the federal government), this policy varied and even official policy may not have reflected reality. A tremendous amount of localism came into play in awarding pensions.

IMPRESSED LABOR— CONFEDERATE STYLE

*T*he more likely kind of service that your ancestors gave to the Confederacy was in the form of impressed labor, about which profuse evidence exists. Impressed labor involved hiring slaves from planters and farmers who were then compensated in cash payment for their slaves' labor. James H. Brewer's work *The Confederate Negro: Virginia's Craftsmen and Military Laborers, 1861–1865* is an exemplary one on this aspect of Black conscripted labor, and researchers who have ancestors living in areas where there was heavy military activity should consider the possibility that some of their ancestors were indeed "impressed." For the states of Virginia, Georgia, and Alabama, it may well be that more Blacks were used for the Confederate cause than the number who officially enlisted in the USCT.

The National Archives houses some, but not all records of the Confederacy in Record Group 109 (War Department Collection of Confederate Records). One of the most important series of records within this collection relates to the impressment of slave labor for Confederate fortifications, railroad construction, and war supplies. Various acts of the Confederate Congress empowered officers and commanders to impress slaves in addition to the slave cooks and musicians to which each company was entitled and for which their owners were compensated at the rate of fifteen dollars per month plus clothing and rations.

The Confederate impressment records, housed at the National Archives, are arranged by state and then under the name of the slave owner. These records are simply called "Slave Rolls," and the staff of the Military Reference Branch of the National Archives can assist researchers in determining whether an individual slave owner ever "hired out" and was paid for slaves that he owned. The Archives staff uses an internal index keyed to the name of the slave owner and the county in which he resided. Researchers must, therefore, know the name of the slave owner and the county of residence prior to requesting these records.

Subsequent columns indicate rate of wages (left blank), amount for each slave (mainly blank), and the amount received (most received $32.00 per slave). The form is signed by Thomas B. Stauart, attorney. These records are massive, and it is unfortunate that they, like many other records, will probably not be microfilmed despite their faded condition.

Because Confederate records are dispersed, researchers may also find that state archives and county courthouses have records on military laborers during the War. A letter of inquiry to the state archives in which your ancestor lived will help you to begin your search at this level. What you need to determine is (1) whether there are any surviving rosters of free or slave military laborers for Confederate installations and (2) how the records are organized at the archives. Because these questions haven't been treated in a broad way, it is difficult to determine which states impressed the most slave labor, but Virginia seems to have used impressed labor extensively. Again, the answer for your particular state may be found by knowing the military organization of the Confederate army in your state and the various sites and dates where troops were stationed during the course of the war.

IMPRESSMENT—UNION STYLE

Union troops also impressed African American laborers. The employment of slave labor by advancing Union troops may surprise you; however, federal policy makers attempted to establish an ideological or political framework for the war that denied slavery as the central issue. Simply put, they thought the war could be fought without African American involvement. But field conditions, particularly as the war progressed, dictated otherwise. Soon military commanders were "conscripting" labor for which they either paid slave owners, paid no one, or paid small wages to slaves who at that instant became freed men, sometimes. African Americans were willing to work under horrendous conditions to gain their freedom—for example, digging a trench to

FACSIMILE OF A CONFEDERATE SLAVE ROLL OR IMPRESSMENT RECORD COVER PAGE

1131
Franklin County
Brooke Defenses
No. 404

SLAVE ROLL
For Dec 1862, Jan 1863
Stamp: Adjutant General's Office
    Division, Confederate Archives
$613.00
Verso
Virginia
Slave roll:

The subscribers, acknowledged to have received of J. B. Stuart 1st Lt. Corps of Engineers, the sums set opposite our names respectively, being in full for the services of our slaves at Brooke Defenses during the months of Dec 1862, Jan, Feb 1863, having signed duplicate receipts.

From Whom Hired	Name and Occupation		Time* Employed
Preston Stephen	Doc	Laborer	
Dickinson Stacy	Ben	"	
Parker Bluford	Wesley	"	
Pinckard _____	Henry	"	
Jemerson Marshall	Alexander	"	37 days
Wade John Sr.	Bob	"	
	Moses	"	
	Allen	"	
Wade Sackfield	Stephen	"	
Patterson, James R.	?	"	
Wade, John Jr.	Sam	"	
Edmonds, Wm H.	Walter	"	
	Giles	"	33 days
	Robert	"	
Murphy, Edward C.	Silas	"	
Dickinson, Martha C.	Charles	"	
Edd, Joseph	Moses	"	
Fralin, David	Moses	"	
Brown, Fred K.	Bill	"	

*All served 60 days unless indicated.

divert the Mississippi River during the Vicksburg campaign. While they were officially engaged as laborers, they had not been emancipated. The project failed, and the notorious commander, General Thomas Williams, eventually returned them still unfree to their plantations along the Mississippi River!

PERSONAL BODY SERVANTS, COOKS, AND OTHERS (UNION AND CONFEDERATE)

*B*ody servants for Union soldiers were generally not officially enlisted, and the literature indicates a considerable amount of chicanery where soldiers took advantage of slaves' vulnerability as servants to Union army officers. In some instances, former slaves believed that they had been enlisted, and they therefore subsequently applied for military pensions. These claims were invariably turned down, but documentation on denied claims also exists. In other instances, body servants migrated to northern states after the war with their employers.

Evidence about the experiences of your ancestors who might have served as body servants with a slave owner will often turn up in the personal papers of the slave-owning family. My maternal great-great-grandfather was a personal body servant, and I found reference to him in copies of letters included in a book about the history of the area and its families.

The complexity of military records can frequently befuddle researchers. Searches for evidence of military service are relatively easy when your ancestor appears in indexed

records. However, once you venture beyond these records, you will have to do a considerable amount of research using other records housed at the National Archives and in other institutions.

Based on the experiences reported in the above documents, a number of justifiable reasons exist for you to expand your Civil War search. Even if you find that one of your ancestors served in the USCT, you will need to place his experiences in some kind of historical context. If your ancestor served in another capacity, such as an impressed laborer, you may be able to find documentation on his experiences. If you've reached an impasse in your research associated with this period of time, you may find that searching the records generated by the War Department might provide clues.

UNION CONTRABAND CAMPS

*C*ontraband camps were a by-product of military field commanders' attempts to deal with the thousands of slaves (both individuals and family groups) who fled behind Union lines during and after military battles or the establishment of military posts in key areas in the South. The posts along the Mississippi River from Cairo to Vicksburg, in low-country South Carolina and Georgia, western Tennessee, Kentucky, and some parts of tidewater Virginia and North Carolina had camps.

The story of the contrabands of war and those whose labor supported military efforts is an aspect of your ancestors' experiences that should not be ignored, particularly if they lived in areas where the Union army established a permanent presence. These records will often reveal the migratory patterns of those who fled from their slave owners during the war and after the war to other places—possibly not returning to their "homes" or families. In order to determine whether your ancestors were considered contrabands of war, you might construct a search strategy that uses some or all of the following steps:

Determine when Union troops arrived in your area
Determine what impact their arrival had
Determine the nature of the local operations
Identify which records to examine using National Archives inventories and published reports of the superintendents of the contraband camps

The critical points to remember about these camps or settlements is that they tended to be in a constant state of flux, consisting of slaves (1) who had fled plantations and farms, (2) who had been left on abandoned plantations, or (3) who were families of USCT recruits. They had to be supported financially, and as a group, they formed a pool of labor from which many men were recruited for enlistment in the army or to work on military installations. They were the main focus of wartime relief efforts financed by northern aid societies. Little of the land on which contraband camps were constructed was sold to freedmen, nor did the camps evolve into permanent settlements or Black towns after the war, except for a few in coastal Virginia and South Carolina.

CASE STUDIES

Two Genealogical Puzzles: The Migration of Contrabands North

The following article appeared in the *Aurora Beacon* in 1932 under the "Now and Then Column." Aurora is a small town some twenty-five miles west of Chicago. Ms. Jeanne Jones, one of my genealogy students, shared a copy of this article which quickly became a puzzle to solve. (Ms. Jones had obtained a copy of the article from the Aurora Historical Society.) Cal Boger was her grandfather, and though she had memories of him, she had no idea about his family of origin in Georgia.

Cal Boger's Story from the Aurora Beacon

"Cal" Boger was a mason and contractor, who overcame obstacles that would discourage—and did discourage—many in his position. He was born in slavery, and with practically no education, came to Aurora in 1865, a lad of 17 years, to make his own way in a strange country, with the new birth of freedom. He was Aurora's fourth colored pioneer; a youth with a credible war record, whose stock in trade was health, strength, a happy disposition, a faculty of making friends, and a heritage of common sense and good judgment.

The subject of our story was born in bondage on a plantation in a territory known at that time as "Hickory Flats" not far from Atlanta, Georgia. He was one of 13 children who went by the name of McDonough, after the master. At the age of 12 years, just previous to breaking out of the war Calvin ran away, to make his way to the northern land of freedom. As all refugees did at that time, he changed his name to conceal his identity and adopted that of "Boger."

When the war broke out "Cal" found himself

within the Union lines; just a boy with no particular destination and with nothing to do but follow the army. In his wanderings he met with two different officers, who were to have an important influence on his future life—Dr. Abner Hard and Captain Hattery, both from Aurora. The former was regimental surgeon of the 8th Illinois Cavalry, and as the story goes, "Cal," a bright lad of 13 years, was unofficially appointed orderly or personal attendant of Dr. Hard. He had also been with Captain Hattery and others in the same capacity.

While he served his country faithfully during the war, he was never enlisted officially, on which account he was not eligible to membership in the G.A.R. (Note that this stands for the Grand Army of the Republic, the Union side.) After the war Cal Boger came to Aurora a lad of 17 years. To the best recollection of the family today, he was brought to Aurora by Captain

Hattery as an attendant, and henceforth made his home.

Though Cal came to Aurora with Captain Hattery, it may have been the influence of Dr. Hard's career that led Boger's son to eventually become a doctor. Many such articles (often printed at the time of the subject's death) about former slaves were published by the White press in both the North and the South. Those in the South tended to memorialize aspects of the past that emphasized stereotypes, but in this instance, Boger's tenacity and industriousness are highlighted. He was a leading citizen of Aurora and well known by everyone.

As a genealogist, think about what you would do to extend Boger's line so that you could at least verify his story and possibly identify some of his relatives, some of whom would almost certainly show up in the 1870 census—with that many siblings, it should not be difficult. The partial solution to Boger's origins appears in a subsequent chapter.

The following is an extract of a biographical statement compiled by an archivist at the Evanston, Illinois Historical Society.

The Migration of Corporal Andrew Scott

Corporal Andrew Scott was born in Stafford County, Virginia on June 16, 1840 to Mr. and Mrs. Philip Scott. He grew up there and was married to Miss Susan Jane Davis by Reverend Washington Stephens in August, 1861. The tides of war caused upheaval and change with many black people relocating to the North. Andy, Susan and baby James made their way to Chicago, Illinois by 1864. Andrew found employment as a hostler. However, a Captain James induced him to enroll as a substitute on January 6, 1865. The enlistment papers indicate he had black hair, black eyes, black complexion and stood five foot nine inches tall.

Private Scott initially joined the 67th United States Colored Infantry, Company B, but was transferred on August 15, 1865 to Captain Thomas Montgomery's Company I of the 65th United States Colored Infantry. Private Scott encountered the typical hazards of soldiering including a bout with diarrhea in mid October, 1865, and a case of bronchitis at the end of the same month. A promotion to Corporal came on November 16, 1865. While stationed in Baton Rouge, Louisiana, the regiment was assigned to unload heavy ordnance and ammunition from steamboats. This task, during the summer of 1866, resulted in the Corporal receiving a rupture. The military records state, "No record found of any unauthorized absence, arrest, confinement or trial" which along with his honorable discharge on January 8, 1867 indicates Scott's loyal service to his country.

Corporal Scott's story was such an unusual one because he migrated to the North and returned South as a substitute in the service of the USCT. (Substitutes were often paid to enlist in place of an individual who had been drafted, and northern states were allowed to use Blacks to meet their quotas of draftees.) The fact that Scott became a corporal attests to his leadership skills. He later settled in the then-small town of Evanston and helped to found not one, but two of that city's oldest Black Baptist churches.

These stories only point to several of the many possible migratory paths that your ancestors may have taken during the war and Reconstruction. Because many veterans of the USCT did migrate (remember Nicodemus Parmer's path) after being discharged, don't be surprised if your ancestor was among that group.

WHY JUNETEENTH AIN'T JANUARY 1: THE VANGUARD OF FREEDOM

*O*ver the four-year course of the Civil War, freedom came at different times and under different circumstances for your ancestors. Those slaves freed under the Emancipation Proclamation on January 1, 1863, were all slaves owned by individuals still considered rebels. The proclamation effectively freed people still in Union enemy territory. To that end, it was more of a declaration of intent. It excluded nearly one million slaves who were in the border states or whose status hadn't been resolved as contrabands of war. In a sense, freedom stood at a stalemate except for those who were able to seize the opportunity to gain their own freedom either through enlistment in the United States Colored Troops or by running behind Union lines, automatically becoming contraband of war until they were granted their formal freedom.

For years, African Americans have celebrated Emancipation Day, and not always on January 1. Juneteenth celebrations are frequently held on June 15 or at some other time in the summer months. A recent writer suggests that the traditions behind many of the differing Emancipation Day celebrations have been forgotten. It can be surmised that the differing dates are not just a matter of convenience but may, indeed, refer to the actual time when freedom occurred in the many local communities that still maintain this tradition. Most important, Juneteenth celebrations attest to the equivocation of the proclamation itself. The fact that emancipation is celebrated at different times, if it is celebrated at all, attests to the absolute ambivalence of this document with respect to those slaves who remained in bondage. Alas, the Emancipation Proclamation, when signed, was more symbol than reality for the majority of African Americans.

This introduction to records generated by the Civil War period should provide you with a basic start, as well as a perspective that encourages you to consider the full range of possibilities that existed for your ancestors' lives. Not everyone's ancestor served in the USCT or had direct Civil War experiences; nevertheless, failure to take advantage of the profuse amount of records generated during this period will leave a gap in your research. If there is no evidence of service, the sweep of the Freedmen's Bureau agents throughout the South left records on many of your ancestors, and it is likely that contained in the records left by the Bureau you will find some of your ancestors. This subject is covered in the following chapter.

A NOTE ON METHODS AND RECORDS

From an African American perspective, the experiences of the war and Reconstruction were very deeply intertwined. Therefore, the direction in which your research will go for this period very much depends on what kinds of experiences your ancestors encountered. Between the beginning of the Civil War and the end of Reconstruction is roughly fourteen years, and you will definitely have to figure out where your

ancestors were and what happened to them. You cannot skip over this period until you focus in on the local area and get a good sense of what happened, for that had a considerable impact on your ancestors, even those who did not enlist in the USCT. You will, of course, start with the assumption that most of your ancestors remained on or very near the places where they were last slaves. Note that the 1870 census will help you a lot by giving you clues to where they might have been during the war. However, for a fairly large segment of the black population, both slave and free, the war laid the basis for their dispersion away from those places where they had been prior to the onset of the war.

Fortunately, the major records that you will use are housed in one place—at the National Archives in Washington, D.C. The records from the Civil War and Reconstruction periods are vast, and for any one of your ancestors, you may find information in records of the War Department, the Colored Troops Division, the Veterans Administration, the Bureau of Freedmen, Refugees, and Abandoned Lands, the Southern Claims Commission, the Freedmen's Inquiry Commission, and the Treasury Department. So vast are the options for individual researchers, it is imperative that you understand first how the war may have affected your ancestors. That understanding comes from taking one preliminary step— knowing the overall course of the war and its impact on slaves or free blacks who lived in the state and county where your ancestors lived. Finally, once you get your feet wet with the prelimnary record searching, the basis will have been laid for more sophisticated searches in more complex and voluminous records.

Chapter 8

CLOSE TO KIN, BUT STILL WAITING FOR FORTY ACRES AND A MULE

Searching for Your Ancestors During Reconstruction

The land in question has been, under my direction, divided into forty acre tracts and settled upon by freedmen who had been promised it in accordance with the provisions of the Sherman Field Orders.

GENERAL SAXTON TO GENERAL OLIVER O. HOWARD

The former owners of the land in the Sea Islands on the coast of South Carolina and the owners of the land on the Main embraced in General Sherman's Special Field Orders will be permitted to return and occupy their lands.

ORDER OF MAJOR GENERAL ROBERT K. SCOTT,
SUCCESSOR TO GENERAL SAXTON, AFTER HIS REMOVAL FROM OFFICE

CITED IN DOROTHY STERLING,
THE TROUBLE THEY SEEN: BLACK PEOPLE TELL THE STORY OF RECONSTRUCTION

THE POST-CIVIL WAR PERIOD

*R*econstruction was one of those periods in the lives of your ancestors that generated uncertainty and optimism. Land was granted by one military commander and then rescinded by another. The South was occupied by the Union army, and the post-Civil War period was one in which deep emotions raged during what is called Reconstruction, and eventually settled in what the South called Redemption, the turning point and end of Reconstruction in 1874. For a period of approximately nine years, and in some places more, African Americans had a small window of opportunity to define the meaning of their new freedom, but always in the context of the political uncertainties that continued to prevail between the North and the South.

In one sense, the war was a forced national referendum on the status of African Americans—not just on slavery—where the vote was taken in countless administrative decisions, proclamations, military commands, actions, and battles—all on the field. African Americans voted for themselves and seized the moment, certainly knowing that the opportunity would not come again. The by-product was freedom, but it was a freedom that was confused with the national goal of saving the Union. The reason that the Civil War remains such a fascinating, debate-provoking subject of discussion is that it represents one of the few times in the nation's history when so many men acted with such a single purpose but with such contradictory goals. There was a private battle and a public battle, the private one being the grand referendum on the status of African Americans, the public one a fight between Americans—White Americans, that is. This debate even continues today, as evidenced by Ken Burns's relatively poor treatment of this issue in his much-acclaimed documentary on the Civil War.

In the war's aftermath, freedmen couldn't strike out in large numbers to a new frontier, for much of the frontier was no longer there, nor were they really welcome to what was left of it, even though some tried. They could not settle on the vast amount of land that lay abandoned in the South for they entered a market with little money and without willing sellers. The thousands of slaves who had been settled in contraband camps away from many of their kin found no permanent homes there, and they struck out to rejoin their kin. At war's end, slaves became free but essentially homeless and landless. What a victory! Freedmen without land and without homes were in the same position as some planters, with their valueless Confederate money, burned-down plantation houses or farms, and 90 percent of their wealth (slaves) having disappeared—for some, overnight. Really neither had anything to celebrate, and this was the reality that soon beset freedmen in the South. The images of the defeated planters and the jubilant freedmen are indeed overdrawn. For despite the days of Jubilee, freedmen realized that celebration had its ironies—that indeed, freedom had to be actualized in a very confined space of possibilities. Former slaves, African Americans entered a modern industrializing world where citizenship virtually rested on land ownership. In large measure, citizenship was retained for those who already owned the land.

This reality that African Americans faced is one that had little to do with the grand politics of the war and the Reconstruction era. For at no time during this period did African Americans have any power to formulate or affect the decisions about their fate at the national level. If anything, they voted with their feet during the war by forcing every command and political decision emanating from Washington. They didn't wait for compensation, for it wasn't even on the national agenda. Lincoln considered an emigration plan, and some Blacks did emigrate to Haiti only to be bailed out from this catastrophe. The last trickle of Blacks left for Liberia, Thaddeus Stevens argued for legislation in Congress granting land to freedmen, and finally Frederick Douglass did speak up in his characteristic brilliance. The only compensation for slavery was paid to loyal *slave owners* in the border states of Maryland, Missouri, and Kentucky as well as those who owned slaves

in the District of Columbia. You will find this evidence in the records if one of your ancestors gained his freedom in this manner.

BUILDING A PERSONAL FREEDOM

*F*reedom is not an object, nor is it a state of mind. It is a state of being where in our day-to-day behavior we have choices and some degree of control over our own affairs. In the course of building their freedom after the Civil War, our ancestors faced many critical decisions about their family life and their personal identities. How African Americans defined themselves in the first generation of freedom depended on the circumstances in which they lived, such as those evidenced by the two field orders, first granting land in forty-acre lots and then rescinding the grant under the presidency of Andrew Johnson.

WHAT'S THE MEANING OF THE NAME? YOUR ANCESTORS' SURNAMES

I used to be proud of my name. . . . I have ceased to be so. I fear it will no longer be spotless as the two meanest Negroes on the place have appropriated it.

CAROLINE RAVENEL, FORMER MISTRESS OF A LOW COUNTRY SOUTH CAROLINA PLANTATION, QUOTED IN LEON F. LITWACK, *BEEN IN THE STORM SO LONG: THE AFTERMATH OF SLAVERY*

Can you explain why the two "meanest"— and we don't doubt that—Negroes on the

Ravenel plantation took that name? One area that may cause you grief, if you don't analyze it, is that of the names with which African Americans entered freedom, particularly their surnames. Given names are also important, but understanding those names will be best dealt with during the period of slavery. For now, the focus is on the surnames that your ancestors had to declare in their transactions with the rest of the world as free men during the war and Reconstruction. You will assume that your ancestors used surnames during slavery, that these names were entered into the public record by 1866, and that they did not change over time or at least had not changed by the time the 1870 census was taken. If this is the case, you will not have the problem of discontinuity in surname usage, a problem which we will soon see faced Nicodemus Parmer and David House.

THE TRUE MEANING OF "X"

*Y*ou are carrying the surname that your ancestors gave you, for even as slaves, they had their own identities. And because they gave you a surname, you might just want to know why it was Adams rather than Ademoya or *X*. Though a powerful symbol, *X* has been partly used to convey a number of messages. For some, assuming the surname of *X* is not just the rejection of a slave owner's name; it is also a complete break with the past. Its adaptation is something with which a younger generation can identify. Once upon a time, however, it simply meant that a person was unable to write his surname, or as will be seen shortly, hadn't the power to enforce recognition of his

name. It meant no more than that—not even that the person could not read. Note that a signature is not necessarily a measure of literacy. Caddy Gordon's husband in *Children of Strangers* practiced writing his name before he opened his bank account because it was a matter of pride for him! Certainly today, wearing an item of apparel with an *X* doesn't mean the same thing. Nor does it seem to invite any significant understanding of our ancestors' lives.

Ironically, our ancestors didn't have to wear an *X* for the rest of the world to know that most of them could not read, nor sign their own names in the form of a signature, nor really know what names their African forefathers used. Only a small percentage (approximately 10 percent) of slaves entered freedom with the ability to read. Literacy as we know it today was a function of the spread of free public schools. Thus, many Americans at mid-nineteenth century also signed their names or made their marks with an *X*. Any transaction that called for entering a person's name on record required that the name be spelled and written by a second party. This too caused confusion, as in cases of name reversals and misspellings.

If you subscribe to the theory of *X* as the unknowable past, some surprises await you. For it is in the process of *naming* your ancestors—assigning them individual identities within their families—that *X* becomes a symbol for an unknown in an equation that can be solved. Replacing the *X* with a once living, breathing individual, your ancestor, is the real challenge and the source of your transformation.

Surnames were widely used among slaves, and those surnames, though not always recognized by slave owners, continued to be used after freedom. Therefore, it is likely that the majority of freedmen did not carry into freedom the surname of the last slave owner, though many did. Simply put, they carried the surnames their parents carried in the same way that we now carry the names that our parents gave to us at birth. Freedmen's surnames, however, do reflect the acquisition of a *non-African* surname and generally a European surname at some point in the past, perhaps even the surname of an earlier slave owner. The following discussion will help you interpret how your ancestors dealt with such a critical transition—the introduction of their surname to the rest of the world.

ACQUISITION OF THE LAST SLAVE OWNER'S NAME

*M*ost of my ancestors who lived after the Civil War adopted the surnames of their last owners. I do not know the circumstances or decisions that led to acquiring them. Here are several possibilities.

1. They were closely associated with their slave owners and continued this relationship after slavery.
2. Some, according to oral tradition, were the natural children of the slave owners and continued to use the name.
3. Some may not have had the opportunity to select another name because their surnames had already been entered into the public record as that of the last slave owner, the recorders' assumption being that the person's surname would continue to be one that linked him to

his former owner for purposes of identification.
4. They may not have known any other surname, having been in the same family of slave owners as their ancestors before them, or they may have been descendants of slaves who were sold South when they were very young, too young to know their origins.
5. Their former owners were part of the small-scale slave-holding class in the country where relationships between owner and slave were relatively close, often inviting certain types of control after freedom that did not exist in areas where large-scale plantation slavery combined with absentee ownership existed. Slaves on these plantations, some exceeding two hundred, did not leave slavery with the owner's surname unless there had been close ties prior to emancipation.

These reasons partly explain the surname sharing patterns between Blacks and Whites that you found in the 1870 and 1880 censuses. But what of your ancestors who lived on large plantations—say, a plantation with one hundred slaves? Would they have also adopted the slave owner's surname? It is unlikely, for none of the conditions that facilitated close communication and living arrangements would have applied on large-scale plantations. In addition, slaves on large plantations often shared historical experiences that were quite different from those found among slaves on smaller plantations. It was on the larger plantations that multigenerational slave communities formed, and it was in these communities that surname usage was encouraged. Surname usage symbolizes continuity with a defined past, and slave communities on many large plantations were often stable enough to support that continuity.

SURNAMES AS ARTIFACTS OF CIRCUMSTANCE AND PLACE

*A*s your ancestors increased the number of their public transactions after freedom, their surnames had to be written into a record—whether as depositors in one of the Freedmen's Branch Banks or as signators on a labor contract or as couples getting married by a county clerk. Suppose your ancestor did all three of the above in the span of a year. If he could neither read nor write, he had to sign his name with an *X*. His labor contract, if drawn up by a Freedmen's Bureau agent, may have used the planter's surname without even asking, or worse, no surname at all. If the year was close after 1865, the county clerk may have affixed the planter's surname to that of your ancestor's given name. But at the Freedmen's Bank, your ancestor may have felt the need to declare his surname since the records maintained for purposes of identification required a wide range of information on each applicant, and since most depositors— unlike Caddy Gordon's husband, who practiced writing his name before opening up his bank account as a matter of manly pride—signed their names or "made their marks" with an *X*. The first two instances where your ancestor appeared with the surname of the slave owner were artifacts of record keeping combined with customary practices of the time—the practice of assigning to slaves their owner's surname as

a matter of identification in their interactions with the world around them, a practice which continued through the early years of freedom.

REJECTING THE LAST SLAVE OWNER'S SURNAME OR RECLAIMING THE FAMILY SURNAME

*I*f during the early years of freedom, some freedmen continued to carry a slave owner's name whether by choice, by imposition, or by custom, at some point a decision had to be made about the use of that owner's surname. Between emancipation and the 1870s, some surnames may have been changed from that of the slave owner to a new name. Orville Burton's article, listed in the bibliography, should be studied closely to understand why a man named Calvin Barrow in the 1870 census and other records appeared as Calvin Parker in 1880 without having moved very far from the original site of the Barrow plantation. Perhaps by 1880, his identity had been firmly established since he then owned a ninety-five-acre farm. It is unknown how or why the surname Parker appeared on the 1880 census. He could have always had that surname, even during slavery and after, but it was never recognized; he could have decided to adopt a new surname to express the independence that owning land gave; he could have finally corrected his name in the 1880 census, having gone along with the Barrow surname in 1870.

For those freedmen who felt the need to declare a new name, a name other than that associated with the last or any former owner,

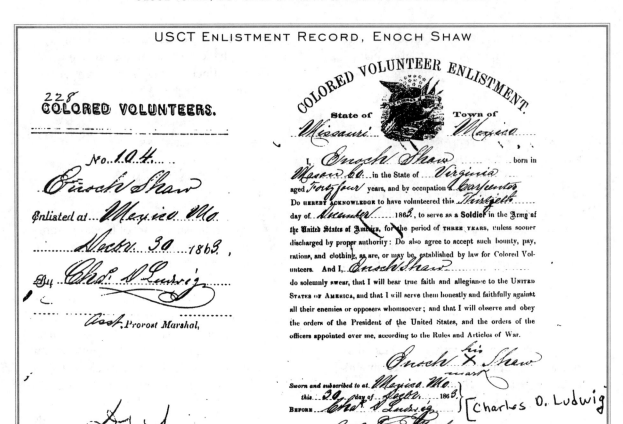

USCT ENLISTMENT RECORD, ENOCH SHAW

there exist as many reasons for doing so as there were individuals who changed their names. One obvious reason, of course, is to express continuity in bloodlines, some of which may be remote, as in the case of Martin Jackson, who stated: "The government seemed to be in a almighty hurry to have us get names. We had to register as someone, so we would be citizens . . . I made up my mind I'd find me a different one. One of my grandfathers in Africa was called Jaeceo, and so I decided to be Jackson." That more freedmen did not look to Africa for their surnames tells us a lot about the extent of intergenerational memories of Africa. In 1865, many freedmen could remember an African ancestor, but perhaps many could not remember their African names. This question deserves exploration on your part to come up with an answer.

Rejecting a slave owner's surname is not the same as reclaiming the family's surname. Rejection is similar to Mr. Jackson's case, where there was a conscious decision not to assume the last owner's name. Such cases are often passed down as part of a family's oral tradition. If not, you will be faced with the situation of explaining where an ancestor's surname came from and how it was acquired. One obvious explanation is that

USCT PENSION FILE QUESTIONNAIRE

3—474

AGENCY INQUIRIES

Cert No. 976939   DEPARTMENT OF THE INTERIOR,

Sam'l Hause & Farmer   BUREAU OF PENSIONS,

Co........., ...Reg't ....

WASHINGTON, D. C. OCT 26 1912., 191

David L. Hause

Dist Snowhill

Ala.

SIR: To aid this Bureau in preventing anyone falsely personating you, or otherwise committing fraud in your name, or on account of your service, you are required to answer fully the questions enumerated below.

You will please return this circular under cover of the inclosed envelope which requires no postage. Very respectfully,

A. W. Boome

Special Examiner.

1. Where were you born? Answer. *Carlouville Ala.*
2. Where did you enlist? Answer. *Moblie Ala.*
3. Where had you lived before you enlisted? Answer. *At Snowsfill Ala.*
4. What was your occupation? Answer. *Farming*
5. Were you a slave? If so, state the names of all former owners, and particularly the name of your owner at the date of your enlistment. *Ira Skinner*
6. State your rank, company, and regiment. *Private Co. D. 61 Colored Inf*
7. Where were you discharged? Answer. *Batton Rouge La.*
8. Where have you lived since discharge? Give dates, as nearly as possible, of any changes of residence. *I lived at Sommerville Tenn from 1866 to 1869*
9. Did you serve in the Confederate Army or Navy? Answer. *No*
10. What is your present occupation? Answer. *I am farming*
11. What is your height? *5* feet, *10* inches. The color of your skin? *Brown* Are there any permanent marks or scars on your person? If so, describe them. *My left little finger is cut off*
12. Were you in the military or naval service under a name different from that by which you are now known? If so, state what it was. *I was not onmone*
13. Have you ever been known by any names other than that given in your application for pension? If so, state them in full. *My name was David Skinner before tho war*
14. By what name are you now known? State in full. *David Louis Hause*
15. What is your actual residence at the present time, and what is the nearest post office? Answer. *Snowsfill Post office box no 5.*

WITNESS:
1. *David L. Hause*   *Plea David Parmer*
2. *Isadore Locke*   Date, *Oct 29th*, 1912

(Witnesses who can write sign here.)   6—3022

the surname was always carried even during slavery and prior to being sold to the last owner. The name may reflect that of a slave owner who lived many decades ago—per-

haps an original owner. It may also reflect a conscious decision to adopt the surname of a local white not associated with your ancestor or a famous person like Washington,

Lincoln, or Jefferson without having ever been associated with the family.

HIDDEN MEANINGS BEHIND MULTIPLE SURNAMES WITHIN ONE FAMILY

*C*onsider the following statement, which appeared in the pension application for one USCT soldier:

I served in Company I, 61st Regiment, USCT under the name David Parmer. That was my name when I was a slave and when I enlisted, the name of David Parmer was put on the company roll. After the close of the war, all of my family took the name of my father, and I did so at his request, so that my name was changed to D. L. House.

STATEMENT OF DAVID L. HOUSE

David House had entered the war under the surname Parmer, but changed it at the request of his father whose surname was House. Nowhere in House's pension file was there an explanation with regard to how he acquired the surname Parmer, except that it was his slave name, presumably meaning that he was owned by a Parmer. Acquiring the surnames that their ancestors used represents the most common way for freedmen to declare their surnames.

Nicodemus Parmer's case, in chapter 7, is more complex. His family left slavery with five different surnames, which he explained as a function of having been owned by different slave owners. If they all appeared on one page in the 1870 census, but in *separate* households, there would be no way to know that they were related unless you discovered

his pension application or unless you studied the whole community of individuals. A name represents a whole host of historical experiences all wrapped up in one word.

A TRANSITION TO FREEDOM THROUGH THE FREEDMEN'S BUREAU

*I*f the Civil War was one of the most tragic periods of American history, then the period of Reconstruction which followed turned out to be equally tragic for African Americans. Had any serious consideration been given to freedmen and their desire for land, which they knew how to manage and cultivate, the lives of African American families would be entirely different today.

The period of Reconstruction really began when the first fugitive slaves crossed Union lines to settle in contraband camps. Once contrabands were declared free under the first Confiscation Act, slaves found it increasingly attractive to escape behind Union lines. Superintendents of these camps were appointed, and this laid the basis for the eventual establishment of the Bureau of Freedmen, Refugees and Abandoned Lands in 1865. At the same time, thousands of northern teachers sponsored by the Freedmen's Aid Society went South to help in the contraband camps. Their primary accomplishment was the spread of literacy among soldiers and ex-slaves.

The Freedmen's Bureau, under the supervision of the War Department, became the primary structure through which freedmen sought aid, protection, and assistance when needed. Had freedmen obtained their forty acres and a mule, the primary purpose of the bureau would have been that of passing out seeds rather than sacks of meal and corn to destitute freedmen and White refugees. While the bureau had many accomplishments in education and welfare, its primary accomplishment was the creation of a mechanism for returning freedmen to the fields. That mechanism was the labor contract, which so many of our ancestors signed with their *X*'s, for they had no other choice. No one knows how many contracts were signed nor the number of freedmen who signed them. What is known is that thousands of these contracts survive and are available for your examination in record books and loose sheets left by approximately nine hundred agents employed by the bureau to act as ombudsmen between Blacks and Whites in local communities in the South.

A great number of the surviving letters and reports written by these agents attest to their singular effort to follow orders from headquarters, orders which dictated that the freedmen were to be convinced that it was in their interests to sign such contracts. Of course, some contracts were declared illegal when it was realized that planters wanted to control the labor force in the same ways that they had prior to emancipation. These contracts represent a tug of war between freedmen and planters—the freedmen negotiated for shorter work hours, freedom of their wives from having to work in the fields, freedom of their children from an apprenticeship system, and finally, freedom of space.

Signing one's name with an *X* to a labor contract that continued the dependency relationship between slave and master merely meant that the individuality of every

freedmen was denied—at least with respect to the rights of full citizenship in a country that equated citizenship with land ownership. And most of our ancestors did this relying on the pragmatism that they had used so many times before to survive slavery. The acquisition of land and living space away from the domination of their former masters took some time to negotiate, particularly in a hostile and often violent environment, an environment which appeared mean-spirited when erstwhile friends of the freedmen were more concerned about their potential dependency and destitution than about helping them to make the transition to freedom.

CASTING THEIR BUCKETS WHERE THEY WERE

Why did the majority of African Americans remain in the South and near the places where they had been slaves? That is a question that you will have to answer for your ancestors. However, the simplest answer is that most were landless. Land, not education, was the mark of citizenship in mid-nineteenth-century rural America. The Southern Homestead Act of 1866 seemed to forecast good news for most freedmen. Public lands in the states of Alabama, Arkansas, Florida, Louisiana, and Mississippi were opened for sale to freedmen and loyal Whites. Disloyal Whites were effectively ineligible to purchase land for six months because they had to sign an oath attesting that they had not rebelled against the United States.

By 1870, only one thousand of the original four thousand families who purchased land under this act still owned it. Most of the land that was purchased was in Florida. The act ignored the fact that most good land near waterways and transportation routes had already been settled during the prewar years and was, therefore, no longer in the public domain. It's hard to farm swampy land, and it was certainly impossible to settle on timber land without the capital required to operate even small timber concessions. For most African Americans, the only way to make money in the South during Reconstruction was to sell one's labor. The Bureau of Refugees, Freedmen and Abandoned Lands, which operated between 1865 and 1872, had no agricultural program except that of making sure cotton and other cash crops continued to be produced. Without land, the mutual support that kinship provided did help families to survive. But while freedmen placed a high value on kinship, there is no doubt that, if they had been given a choice, land would have won out over kinship.

THE FREEDMEN'S BUREAU AND ITS AGENTS

*H*oused at the National Archives in Washington, D.C., are literally thousands of documents generated by the Freedmen's Bureau's nine hundred field agents who were stationed throughout the South as part of the bureau's mission. (Many of these agents were former Union army officers.) These records reveal a complex bureaucracy which has been dubbed America's first social service agency. This analogy is a bit overdrawn because the bureau was an agency of the War Department, and its organization in

each of the southern states mirrored that of a military command, with power vested in state commissioners who supervised assistant commissioners and field agents (called sub-assistant commissioners) assigned to counties and towns. The bureau operated under a law that granted it supervisory power over all affairs in local areas relating to freedmen, refugees needing relief, and abandoned plantations. The bureau operated in Maryland, Virginia (including West Virginia), Tennessee, Kentucky, North Carolina, South Carolina, Florida, Georgia, Alabama, Mississippi, Louisiana, Arkansas, Missouri, Texas, and the District of Columbia.

The bureau's activities incorporated and extended the combined relief efforts of federal and private relief efforts established during the war. The work of the superintendent of contraband camps, the Freedmen's Aid Society, and the Freedmen's Division in the Treasury Department was eventually taken over or coordinated by the Freedmen's Bureau, which was put under the War Department and headed by General Oliver O. Howard. Therefore, researchers will find that the records compiled by the staff of the National Archives some years later reflect the blurred line between military operations and relief efforts. For example, what did taking a census of Blacks in a local area have to do with the war effort? Yet you will also find that censuses were taken, though not uniformly, as directed.

THE RECORDS

A National Archives staff member has estimated that approximately one-fourth of these records contain references to individual freedmen—by name. The following kinds of records, mainly in the form of registers, will be of most benefit to genealogical researchers:

- Hospital registers of patients and surgeons' reports
- Labor contracts between planters and freedmen
- Registers of transportation
- Freedmen's schools established in your local area
- Correspondence and registers of outrages or violence against freedmen
- Marriage registers
- Bounty applications for soldiers discharged from the USCT
- Registers of claims for USCT soldiers, their families, and others
- Lists of rations issued by the bureau and private relief agencies to both former slaves and Whites in a specific area
- Reports on local conditions in the following areas:
  Abandoned and confiscated land owned by former slave owners
  Conflict between freedmen and Whites (reports of "outrages," disputes, local court cases, and correspondence)
- Reports on crop production and crop failures
- Reports on camps and resettlement of camp inhabitants
- Censuses and censuslike lists of freedmen and their families
- Correspondence written by local field agents and local residents

The following reproductions of labor contracts show what you might expect to find.

EXAMPLE 1: LABOR CONTRACT IN BOUND VOLUME

Contract Between John Crittenden
and Former Slaves
Volume 120, page 145, Contract #463
State of Alabama, Butler County

Articles of agreement made and entered into between John Crittenden and the following named negroes—to wit—Joe, Morgan, Louisa, Julia, Lewis, Amy, Dick, Frank, Sukey, Silas, Agnes, Charles, Mary, Ross.

The said negroes agree to cultivate the crop of the year 1866 on the plantation of said John Crittenden and to attend well to the stock and to observe and obey the orders of said John Crittenden or whosoever he may employ to superintend said plantation and to keeping the plantation and tools in good order and attend to the interest of said John Crittenden agreeably. The said John Crittenden agrees to pay said negroes one third of the produce of said plantation for year 1866. The said John Crittenden agrees to furnish said negroes with provisions for the year 1866 the same amount to be repaid out of the produce of the proportioned part of the crop on said plantation of the year 1866.

Attest: John Crittenden
O. Crittenden   (His signature)
C. C. Crittenden

[Signatures of freedmen follow Crittenden's signature. All signed with an X.]

Joe	Julia	Amy	Silas	Mary or May
Morgan	Lewis	Dick	Agnes	Ross
Louisa	Sukey	Frank	Charles	

Joe is my great-great grandfather; Frank is the one who saw Antietam with his owner; and the rest are all their kin. Note the absence of surnames, a problem which

LABOR CONTRACT BETWEEN ANDREW JACKSON AND HIS FORMER SLAVES

Know all Men by These Presents, That *Andrew Jackson* of the County of *Panola* State of *Miss.* held and firmly bound to the **United States of America** in the sum of *Five Hundred* Dollars, for the payment of which *I am* bind *myself* heirs, executors and administrators, firmly, by these presents, in this **Contract**: That *I am* to furnish the persons, whose names are subjoined, freed laborers, Quarters, Fuel, substantial and healthy Rations, ~~all necessary Medical Attendance and Supplies in case of sickness,~~ and the amount set opposite their respective names per month, during the continuation of this Contract—the laborers to be paid in full before the final disposal of the crop which is to be raised by them on *Miss My* plantation, in the County of *Panola* State of *Miss*

NO.	NAMES.		Age.	Rate of pay per month.	NO.	NAMES.		Age.	Rate of pay per month.
1	Henry	Brown	34						
2	Celia	Brown	30						
3	Mary	Brown	30						
4	Jane	Brown	16						
5	John	Brown	12						
6	Harriet	Brown	37						
7	Cornelius	Brown	24						
8	Reese	Brown	19						
9	Willie	Brown	6						
10	Fayette	Brown	1						
11	Isabella	Brown							
12		Brown							
13	Fred Henry Morris								

The planter furnishes the land farming implements teams & feed for teams and feeds the laborers. They (the laborers) to receive the one fourth (1/4) part of the Corn & Cotton crop and all that they may raise on the plantation, and are to receive just compensation for all labor done outside of the work.

can be easily overcome for most researchers through good use of census records.

The next contract is from a large plantation in Issaquena County, Mississippi. It is quite similar to lists of slaves that you will encounter. Again, only a few surnames are given, and most of the individuals are men who appear to be listed in no particular order. But, before you make that assumption, consider the possibility that they may be listed by family groups or by residence. Wives and children will also be named on labor contracts if their work was contracted or if the contract provided for the support of the family. Note that the numbers appearing in the "Class" column refer to the amount of work to be expected, with the number 1 being equivalent to the term "full-hand" (from the slavery period) or the amount of work that a male in his prime could be expected to do.

You might ask, What good are contracts with first names only? Many of these contracts can be linked or matched with individuals in the 1870 census. You might even find that the individuals listed on this contract are also listed in the same sequence on the 1870 census. Taking the Crittenden case, let's assume that I found my Crittenden ancestors in the 1870 census listed by household groupings. By matching their first names from the contracts with all the individuals listed in African American Crittenden households, I am able to link them to John Crittenden as their possible last slave owner—especially when I find that his residence was listed near theirs in the 1870 census. In the case of the Duncan plantations, researchers would also do the same—that is, match the first names of individuals appearing on the contracts with ancestors who are listed in the 1870 census within household groupings. This exercise can lay the foundation for further name/age and household linkages with lists found before 1865 (during the period of slavery) and after 1870 (subsequent censuses). This type of exercise can quickly identify specifics about the generation of ancestors that lived during this momentous transitional period in the lives of African Americans.

WHY BLACK BANKS LOST A HEAD START

The Freedman's Bank was the black man's cow but the white man's milk.

FREDERICK DOUGLASS

Frederick Douglass made this comment when he realized that his appointment as a trustee and his investment in the soon-to-be-bankrupt Freedmen's Savings Banks were all for naught. If you find in your ancestors' surviving papers a bank book whose balance is zero and whose cover reads "Freedman's Savings and Trust Company," at least you will know that your ancestor was not one of the thousands of defrauded African Americans who turned their bank books in, hoping to obtain the balance that was forfeited as a result of the bank's failure.

The Freedman's Bank was founded as an independent entity (not under direct supervision of the Freedmen's Bureau) in March 1865 as a bank where USCT soldiers and other freedmen would deposit their savings, military pay, and bounty pay at the close of the war. And thousands did so, including many early schools, churches, and organizations. Eventually branches were established in thirty-seven cities, but those that survived at the bank's demise in 1874 numbered twenty-nine, with 61,144 accounts. After the bank's failure, freedmen who submitted their claims were eventually given their dividends over a nine-year period between 1874 and 1883. The last payment was made, however, in 1918, with

DISAPPROVED DUNCAN CONTRACT, ISSAQUENA COUNTY, MISSISSIPPI

"Disapproved for insufficient compensation to freedmen. . . ."
Seth Stoughton and H. W. Scott, agents for W. P. Duncan and
the Negroes on Duncansby, Ellislee, and Homochitto.

Date: January 1, 1865

Homochitto Plantation

Name	Age	Class	Name	Age	Class
David	43	1	Dave	10	
Henderson	21	1	Dan	10	
Lazarus	20		Gabriel	10	
Big Frank	27		Josey	15	2
Freeman	28		Lit Patty	26	1
Emanuel	14	2	Grace	28	1
Antony	62		_____	20	
Joe Murray	15		Lil Polly	16	
Old Branch	65	3	Big Jane	24	2
Lit Pete	23	1	Charlotte	22	1
Frank	29		Francis	15	2
Sam	23		Williams, Diana	17	1
Nathaniel	16		Thomas, Diana	23	3
Flemin	18		Anna	47	1
Wilford	32		Elinor	14	3
John	61		Susan	10	3
Gabriel	55		Rachel	40	2
Lit Branch	25		Lit Laura	13	2
Nat	28		Big Laura	20	1
Abram	34		Whitty, A	44	2
Dick	33		Julia	40	3
George	22		Old Jack	65	2
Lit John	23		Jim Brown	52	1
Old Pete	45		Jan Robinson	38	2
Lit Jake	10		Jim Boyd	19	1
Henry	11		Lit Kitty	22	3
Jim	10				

*Source: Records of the Assistant Commissioner for the State of
Mississippi, Bureau of Refugees, Freedmen, and Abandoned Lands,
1865–1869 (NATF, Microcopy 826, Roll 43, Frames 60 to 66).

fully 31,000 of the original depositors not having requested or received a dividend.

Unfortunately and strangely, many of the surviving records were destroyed in the early 1950s by an administrative decision at the National Archives, according to one expert, James Dent Walker. What remains are signature registers (a bank's method of identification) and indexes to deposit ledgers—not the ledgers themselves, but the indexes—and finally, dividend payment records covering the period 1882–89. It is in these records that researchers can find plentiful evidence of the optimism and trust that this generation of freedom felt toward institutions. Those who were in charge of managing the affairs of the bank—its commissioners—turned out to have been financial speculators, negligent in their responsibilities or simply unfamiliar with financial institutions. Only two Blacks sat as trustees throughout the bank's history, and Frederick Douglass was appointed at its close only to come to the conclusion this section started with.

The remaining records, in the form of deposit and signature ledgers, can be extremely useful in locating some of your ancestors. Though they do not reflect all depositors, those who do find an ancestor in the records can obtain a significant amount of information about the depositor's relatives, a physical description, the usual descriptive data (age, sex, marital status), and even the name of a former slave owner.

Unfortunately, the signature registers and the deposit registers are not indexed. To locate an ancestor in these records, researchers often check the index to the deposit ledgers first. Each individual's account number is listed next to his name.

Using the account number, the signature registers for a specific city can be searched for the account number. Once found, the name should match the name found on the deposit ledger index. This still takes some time, however, because the records are organized by state and then by city. For the deposit ledgers, there is a rough alphabetical order, and for the signature ledgers, the records are organized by account number. This method is not fail-safe; both sets of records should be studied.

Copies of the deposit and signature registers can be found on microfilm in most major genealogical collections. Additionally, some researchers have begun to abstract records for selected states. The dividend payment records have not been microfilmed. However, the account number on the deposit ledger can be used to access these records, an important point to remember when you visit or write to the National Archives.

RECORDS OF THE FREEDMEN'S BUREAU ON MICROFILM

Access is always a big problem when you begin to research records like those of the Freedmen's Bureau. The National Archives, however, has an active microfilming program, and some of the records of the bureau have been microfilmed. Researchers should know that the microfilmed records represent only a *small* part of the entire set of Freedmen's Bureau records housed at the National Archives. To determine what kinds of records were microfilmed for your state of research, the booklet *Black Studies: A Select Catalog of National Archives Microfilm*

Publications should be purchased from the publications division at the National Archives. This guide lists by state all records that were microfilmed, and researchers should especially look for records on labor contracts, marriage contracts, and reports for the commissioner of education for genealogical information. The correspondence files have also been partly reproduced though they relate, for the most part, to administrative matters. Some marriage records were microfilmed, especially for the states of Mississippi and Louisiana. Labor contracts for the states of Mississippi and Arkansas were also filmed. Still, a visit to the archives is often absolutely necessary. This visit should involve examining the original records of the bureau's field agents, described in a subsequent section under "Your Visit to the National Archives."

RECORDS ON EDUCATION AND SCHOOLS

*T*he Freedmen's Bureau was very active in helping to coordinate efforts of local freedmen's schools, some of which were established by freedmen and some by the American Missionary Association. Each state had a superintendent of education who reported to the commissioner of education. Because most of these records were microfilmed, researchers should also plan to examine them. On relatively rare occasions, pupil lists will be found. But researchers will certainly be able to identify most schools that were established in a local area because teachers and local agents had to submit monthly reports. In no small measure, the activities of the bureau in this area helped to spread the idea of free public education in the South.

A NOTE ON FREEDMEN'S MARRIAGES AND MARRIAGE CONTRACTS

*G*eneral Howard issued an order in May 1865 authorizing commissioners to formalize freedmen's marriages that had been formed during slavery. These marriages were to be recorded by officers appointed by the various commissioners in the states. This policy actually continued a practice established in contraband camps when freedmen were married by army chaplains behind Union lines. Note that freedmen often felt it necessary to formalize their marriages even though they had been married for years during slavery.

The following points should be noted before looking for marriage contracts in the records of the bureau, according to staff at the National Archives. Implementation of Howard's policy was neither uniform nor consistent. Therefore, the records for each state will vary based on the interpretation of orders by assistant commissioners, who carried out orders from headquarters at the state level. Marriage records for the following states are very sparse: Alabama, Florida, Georgia, North Carolina, and Texas. Records for Arkansas and Mississippi exist in large quantity even though the content of the information on each marriage may vary. Bureau officials were involved in at least creating registers and issuing certificates for parts of some states, namely South Carolina, Tennessee, Kentucky, Louisiana, and the District of Columbia.

Researchers should know that the marriage registers for Mississippi are part of the microfilm series, and that most of the marriages took place at Davis Bend, Natchez, and Vicksburg, mainly for the years 1864 and 1865. The Mississippi marriage records include a large number of former USCT soldiers as well as freedmen who lived in Louisiana, and they were included in the microfilm edition because they happened to be part of the records of the assistant commissioner for Mississippi. Many additional marriage records exist but were not filmed because they remain part of local rather than headquarters records. For those, you will have to consult the original records at the National Archives.

Remember that some states had their own system of formalizing slave marriages. For example, the State of North Carolina created its own system by registering and legalizing previously consummated slave marriages. Called Cohabitation Records, they were issued and maintained at the county level. Other states simply informed freedmen about their rights, or in the interesting case of Alabama, Commissioner Swayne published the resolution adopted by the state convention of Alabama validating all slave marriages. In the state of Georgia, the law read:

Persons of color living together as husband and wife on and since March 9, 1866, are legally married, unless one of the party had two or more reputed wives or husbands, in which case the husband or wife should immediately select the one he or she wishes to marry, and have a

marriage ceremony performed. In cases where persons who were previously forced to marry or contract against their will (a void marriage) later contract and agree to the marriage and cohabit with one another, the marriage is no longer void.*

RESEARCHING FREEDMEN'S BUREAU RECORDS AT THE NATIONAL ARCHIVES

*O*nce you realize that these records contain information on the daily lives of some of your ancestors after the Civil War and once you discover that some of the volumes have begun to fade or, —badly, at that—you will immediately plan a visit. On my first visit, I had obtained a copy of the inventory to the records of the field offices. In that way, I had some idea about what to look for and what to expect. The inventory contained thirty pages for my state of research, and I checked every entry to make sure that I found my county of research. For a small fee, you can request a copy for your state of research by writing to the archives. The inventory is formally called *Preliminary Inventory of the Records of the Field Offices of the Bureau of Refugees, Freedmen, and Abandoned Lands, Record Group 105.*

There is also an inventory for the records of bureau headquarters, but for now you want the one that deals with those nine

*Source: *Documenting Marriages in Georgia*, Georgia Department of Archives and History

hundred agents who collected information and named some of your ancestors. Once I looked through the records, I didn't find the expected marriage contracts or substantial lists of freedmen. But I did find my great-grandfather, John Longmire, at the age of two, and his parents, who in 1868 had been patients at the Garland clinic for freedmen! (Note: I couldn't find any evidence of this site when I visited the area.) I also found the relatives of my great-grandmother, Lucindy Tillman, obtaining sacks of meal, and I found many labor contracts copied into bound volumes. In fact, the labor contracts represented the most abundant records for my county. I became excited when I found a census of all African Americans who lived in Huntsville, Alabama, between June and July 1868—all 2,200 of them. This census even included the names of former slave owners! I hoped that I could find a similar census for where my folks lived (same state but far from Huntsville). I've yet to meet a genealogist who has used the Huntsville records, but surely some have already done so. I didn't find a census, nor the many lists that were drawn up in preparation for extending the right to vote, but the information in these records helped me to get a capsule of the lives of my ancestors between 1865 and 1870, one of the most critical transitional periods in African American genealogy. When combined with the Alabama census of 1866 (see "Census Records"), the census of 1870, and the courthouse notes outlined in chapter 4, a picture of a larger and more extended family network began to emerge. This was so incredibly easy, but note that I picked up far more information and people to identify than I was able to analyze. The

analysis takes longer than the search for records, believe it or not!

SEARCHING FOR LOST KIN

No story is more dramatic during this period than the attempts of freedmen to reunite with their families who had been separated by slave sales. That seemingly aimless wandering was no wandering without purpose. One of my genealogy students told the story of his ancestors, two brothers, who returned to Virginia from Mississippi with gold that presumably belonged to a former slave owner. Many attempts at reunion did not meet with success. Most African American newspapers well into the twentieth century carried personal ads in which former slaves were still looking for anyone who had knowledge of the whereabouts of their lost kin, as in the following case.

$200 Reward. During the year 1849, Thomas Sample carried away from this city, as his slaves, our daughter Polly, and son, Geo. Washington, to the State of Mississippi, and subsequently to Texas, and when last heard from they were in Lagrange, Texas. We will give $100 each for them to any person who will assist them, or either of them, to get to Nashville, or get word to us of their whereabouts, if they are alive. Ben and Flora East.

TAKEN FROM *THE COLORED TENNESSEAN*, CITED IN LITWACK, *BEEN IN THE STORM SO LONG*

* * *

Williams Family. Mrs. Louisa Wade, 113 Williams Street, Hopkins, Kentucky, wants to locate her family, separated during slavery. She lost them at Little Rock, Arkansas. During slavery, they belonged to Joe Williams, whose wife's name was Sarah. There were eight children, including Mrs. Wade, Mattie and Narcissus, sisters; Henry, Moses, Bob, Tommie and Isaac, brothers, mother's name was Millie; father Flanas. If any of them live, write their sister, Mrs. Wade at above address (May 24, 1924).

FROM LORI HUSBAND, *LOST KINSMEN*

While you might only find this kind of information if a genealogist has made it a project to abstract it from the Black press at the turn of the century, as did Lori Husband's project, hopefully more genealogists of the future will see the necessity to do so.

THE BUREAU TRANSPORTS FREEDMEN

*H*idden within the records of the Freedmen's Bureau are records showing how the bureau aided postwar Black

migration to other parts of the South or to urban centers in the North. In 1867, William and Dorothy Selden arrived in Chicago by train from Washington, D.C. Both of the Seldens had been born in Virginia. No doubt they were a part of that group of freedmen who were encouraged to migrate to the North because officials feared the influx of Virginia migrants into the District of Columbia. The Seldens appeared on a transportation register as part of the *Records of the Assistant Commissioner for the District of Columbia* (Microcopy #1056). The Seldens, like the nearly thirty thousand reported cases of the bureau providing transportation for freedmen, represent only a small fraction of those who needed to, wanted to, or were forced to relocate. It is believed that many more received transportation assistance or were relocated, particularly from contraband camps and Freedmen's Bureau colonies. (Note that the Selden case was the first genealogical reconstruction that the author did. See the complete study in Thackery and Woodtor's work, *Case Studies in Afro-American Genealogy*.)

Negotiating the Meaning of Freedom

*H*ow your ancestors negotiated the meaning of freedom for themselves and their families between the end of the War in 1865 and the end of Reconstruction in 1874 tells a story that is dramatic and filled with revelations. It is an individual story, set against the limitations defined by the broad structures outlined earlier. Ironi-

cally, much of that story can be culled from the records left by the Freedmen's Bureau and the organizations associated with its efforts, as well as from the records generated by the War Department. The records of the bureau and its affiliated agencies constitute the few sources in which you, the researcher, can find specific documentation on individual freedmen and the Whites who lived near them.

These individual stories of Reconstruction have been amply revealed in such documentary collections as Dorothy Sterling's *The Trouble They Seen: Black People Tell the Story of Reconstruction*, Leon Litwack's *Been in the Storm So Long*, and Ira Berlin's *Freedom: A Documentary History of Emancipation*. These stand as recommended reading so that you can understand the human drama of survival that faced your ancestors every day. Their story is set in a milieu that is quite different from the rages of politics—in fact, so dismal was the failure of Reconstruction to deal with the poverty of slavery and its aftermath that you may find this period of research to be quite disappointing. Nevertheless, there are stories to be told and families to be traced. The disappointments of this period can be more than offset by your prodigious research efforts to wade through the massive amount of documentation that awaits you, much of which is unindexed in the genealogical sense. But, if your ancestors lived anywhere near the theaters of war, you will certainly find documentation that you need. I found specific information on every line that I was tracing in just a two-day review of volumes at the National Archives, and there were no significant military conflicts in my home county. Who knows what awaits you?

SPECIAL TOPIC: DISCOVERING THE RECORD KEEPER FOR THE NATION USING NATIONAL ARCHIVES RECORDS IN GENEALOGICAL RESEARCH

A Precautionary Tale

On my second visit to the National Archives, I noticed that a young man was reviewing the same records that I was examining. Out of curiosity, I approached him to find out what topic his dissertation covered. He said that he was not a student. Rather, he was trying to find information on his great-great grandfather, who he believed would appear in these records. His ancestor had arrived in Mississippi via the port of New Orleans sometime during the domestic slave trade. He had no idea what year, nor did he have any idea who the slave owner had been. I suggested to him that his problem was really a conceptual problem (thinking through a strategy before using records), and that unfortunately, he would probably never find his ancestor until he had collected information on his ancestor's line. I gave him a quick lesson in genealogy, and later sent him materials on doing genealogical research.

I hope that he has found his ancestor by now because these records, called *slave manifests* for the domestic slave trade, list countless slaves being shipped from all Atlantic coastal ports to New Orleans! There are literally thousands of slaves whose first names appear on these manifests. Without the connecting links—who purchased his ancestor and who sold him from Virginia or elsewhere, as well as a probable year of shipment—this researcher could still be looking. His efforts attest to the strong impact surviving family stories can have on individuals, as well as the lack of support he had to pursue this story in a reasonable fashion. Hopefully, when you visit the National Archives, you will not make the same mistake.

A good number of the records discussed in previous chapters are housed at the National Archives in Washington, D.C. Censuses, military service and pension records dealing with the Civil War, and records of the Freedmen's Bureau are all housed at the National Archives. As the record keeper of the nation, it is by nature a huge facility. Indeed, not all records that fall under the safekeeping of the Archives are located in the capital. There are the twelve federal record centers located in major cities throughout the country, the presidential libraries and other specialized branches. (For example, the records of the Bureau of Land Management are located in Maryland.)

Access to these records for genealogists and other researchers has been facilitated by (1) a microfilming program, (2) a microfilm rental program, (3) the publication of various guides and inventories, and (4) a staff of archivists who will respond to correspondence and provide reasonable consultations when you visit in person. In order for you to tap into these vast resources, you will need to know more about how the records are organized. The National Archives system is easy to navigate once you learn it. Furthermore, understanding this system will also help you to navigate through other institutions with large manuscript holdings.

The Organization of Historical Records

The National Archives is responsible for maintaining federal government records of historical significance as well as the papers of private individuals whose papers have been donated to them. It also has to decide which records should be donated to other institutions or, in many cases, which ones to discard. The Archives has an internal system of organizing and storing these records much as your public library has a system for organizing and storing its books called the Dewey decimal system and a finding aid called a card catalogue. Instead of the library system, the National Archives has an archival system which organizes materials (papers, letters, and documents) into record groups named after the federal agency that deposited the records and to which a number has been assigned. For example, the records of the Freedmen's Bureau have been designated Record Group 105. The various documents, papers, maps, photographs, and whatever else was left after the bureau was phased out were plentiful enough to have them placed under one record group. As the records were organized, descriptive inventories were created.

There exists a descriptive inventory for most record groups, and this serves as a finding aid like the library's card catalogue. For example, the inventory for the Freedmen's Bureau is actually not one, but two. One is titled *Preliminary Inventory of the Records of the Field Offices of the Bureau of Refugees, Freedmen, and Abandoned Lands, Record Group 105* (3 volumes), and the other is titled *Preliminary Inventory 174: Preliminary Inventory of the Records of the Bureau of Refugees, Freedmen and Abandoned Lands: Washington Headquarters* (1 volume). The two inventories make a distinction between those records that were generated by the bureau's headquarters in Washington,

D.C., and those generated by the field offices dispersed throughout the southern states.

The actual records are stored in folders, and the folders are placed in archival boxes on which some identification is marked so that the staff will know how to retrieve them. In order for you to use any of these records, you will have to complete a form and give the staff adequate time to bring the records from their storage place. (Records are stored on shelves to which the public does not have open access.) Your request will be delivered to the General Reading Room where you will be assigned a seat. From that point, you are free to go through box after box of records—as many as you wish as long as the Archives is open.

The search process may take some time. Even though the records have often been organized chronologically, you will not find the surname indexes that genealogists often look for. The only indexes that you may find are those that were created by the record keepers themselves, as in the case of correspondence indexes kept in bound record books during the nineteenth century. This makes it even more important for you to understand how to identify and locate inventories compiled by archivists as well as guidebooks that may discuss the use of the records that interest you!

To obtain copies of inventories, write to the National Archives, Publications Division, Washington, D.C. 20408. Because some inventories have not been officially published, you must write your letter to the attention of the Reference Services Branch asking if a preliminary inventory has been compiled and whether it can be copied for your research needs.

Guidebooks to Using the National Archives

In addition to the published and unpublished inventories that can be obtained by request, a number of publications can help you to do some preliminary sorting before visiting the archives. Guidebooks are more general than inventories—they summarize the contents of major record groups and offer the researcher a broader historical view on how the records were generated, how they were collected, and how they were organized. The standard volume, *Guide to the National Archives of the United States*, is a must once you decide that your Civil War and Reconstruction period research needs to be extended. There is a guidebook for genealogical research *(Genealogical Research in the National Archives)*, but it should never be used alone. In addition, the journal published by the Archives, *Prologue*, contains articles written by researchers who have used the Archives to do their research. Articles describing selected records also appear.

Guides for specific records that fall under one topic are also of importance. The two standard guides on the Civil War, *The Union: A Guide to Federal Archives Relating to the Civil War* and *The Confederacy: A Guide to the Archives of the Confederate States of America*, should always be consulted for an overall view of Civil War records.

The archives has yet to publish a general guide on records that pertain to African Americans. This is partly due to the nature of African American history—nearly every set of records contains references to African Americans. However, there are several specialized guides that will assist you. One is the guide to microfilmed records that relate to African Americans, *Black Studies: A Select*

Catalog of National Archives Microfilm Publications, and the other was compiled by Debra L. Newman, *Black History: A Guide to Civilian Records in the National Archives. Black Studies* does not include references to *all* microfilmed records that contain information on African Americans, nor is it a guide to all records that pertain to African Americans housed at the National Archives. The Newman book is a survey of records generated mainly during the twentieth century, and it is therefore of less genealogical significance.

Regional Archives Guidebooks

The contents of microfilmed records housed at the regional archives are described in four separate publications, organized by geographical region: New England, Chesapeake/Mid-Atlantic, South and Southwest, Central States and the West. For records housed at specific federal record centers, you may write directly to the center asking for a copy of their catalog. The centers at Atlanta, Philadelphia, and Fort Worth would contain materials of interest to African American researchers—especially federal court records, which are routinely deposited at the regional archive that the court's jurisdiction covered.

Microfilm Catalogs and Guidebooks

The Archives also publishes microfilm catalogs by subject area and a master catalog which lists all microfilm publications up to the date of publication (*Comprehensive Catalog of National Archives Microfilm Publications*). Since the microfilming program is an ongoing one, it would be a good idea to check directly with the Archives when there is a question about other records, parts of which may have been microfilmed.

Correspondence

Most correspondence relating to specific records should be directed to the Reference Services Branch, National Archives, Washington, D.C. 20408. If you want the name of a specific archivist who is in charge of the records that you would like to research, you may call the Archives and ask. This is especially important if you are researching records other than censuses, pensions, and military service records. Archivists respond to specific questions and it is difficult to respond to general questions about your research problems. Use this question as your guide: "Is it possible that the records of the assistant secretary described in Inventory #10, page 36, contain references to specific individuals, lists of individuals, or other information that might be of interest to a genealogist?" If the archivist knows the records well, you will get the information that you need. If the archivist doesn't know the records well or if you did not succeed in stating your question properly, the answer may not be adequate. Consider the following options.

Hiring a Researcher

You may obtain a list of researchers who are registered with the Archives. Note that the Archives cannot endorse any of these researchers. The researcher's role is equivalent to that of the archivist's role except that this time, you are paying. The better you state the research problem, the better the researcher can do his or her job. Hiring a researcher to search for you is recommended only after you have made one visit

yourself. There are many steps in the process of using records at the National Archives, and you will forever feel overcharged if you don't know that it takes time to register, check your belongings in a locker, review inventories and other sources, wait for the records to be delivered to you, sift through boxes and files of material not directly related to your research problem, take notes, photocopy materials, and so on. Of course, experienced researchers know the shortcuts, but you will still pay for their time. This is why at least one visit is mandatory.

Your Visit to the Archives

Preparation for your visit should involve correspondence (to obtain inventories and other information) and the compilation of a list of records that you would like to review. The list should be taken from the inventory, and not from one of the more general guidebooks. If you ask to see, for example, the Freedmen's Bureau records for the state of South Carolina, you will be asked to make your request more specific—or *worse*, your request will be honored. Two carts with about thirty boxes will be delivered to you with an indication that when you finish with those, please let the staff know so that the others can be brought out. You might be there for at least a month, if you skim the material. If you read every letter, every register, every volume, you may be there for about six months! Of course, you may also request to see an archivist or someone who can help you narrow down your research problem when you arrive. In that way they can help you to sort through what it is you really need, saving everybody's time.

Doing research is all about knowing

what questions to ask and how to ask them, and being prepared before you visit a library or archive. Even if you ask the question, "Does the material contain genealogical information?" you might be told *no*, when in fact your idea of genealogical information is merely finding your ancestor's name in any record for the contextual meaning of his experiences. In the strict sense, a genealogical record shows kinship ties between two or more individuals. A list of names is generally not understood to constitute genealogical information. A list of names that shows how the individuals on the list are connected is genealogical information. Your goal, however, may be as simple as locating an ancestor in a particular place at a particular time.

Be careful to focus your goals so that you don't exhaust yourself trying to see everything in your one-week stay in the capital. It's impossible. Plan a series of visits based on realistic goals, and don't get diverted. For example, set aside two days to collect copies of Civil War pension records for your ancestors, about two days to obtain and review Freedmen's Bureau records for your home area, and about one day to evaluate what you've found so that you can perhaps complete all the forms necessary to have copies of other records forwarded to you back home. By all means, plan to stay longer than a week, and good luck. As an addendum, I've included a case study of the Alabama records.

Your Research Strategy for Freedmen's Bureau Records

The following strategy is suggested for researchers who use these records. As mentioned previously, they are of critical impor-

tance in filling in the many gaps that occur between the 1870 census and the period of slavery. These instructions, of necessity, are lengthy because the records of genealogical value may have been compiled and filed with various offices within the bureau's headquarters and not with the field agents' records. This is further compounded by the confusions that may occur in using the microfilm edition of the records. The microfilm edition represents only a sampling of the thousands of feet of records housed at the National Archives in Washington. Remember that the bureau was a massive bureaucracy, and its surviving records reflect this fact. Here are the things that you need to do before your visit to Washington.

1. Locate historical sources on the Reconstruction period for your state of research. Almost all historians who write about this period use these records. The four-volume documentary series compiled by Berlin would be a good start just so that you can be convinced of the wealth of information about individual freedmen contained in these records. Be sure to include articles on your reading list.

2. Understand how the bureau was organized. You need at the minimum a sense of how the bureau was organized. Some of the standard histories on the bureau can be rather vague, but nevertheless, it's important to get a general sense of the administrative hierarchy. Note that the primary difference was the division between the headquarters and the field.

3. Review the following finding aids to

understand where different records are located. Note that some of the descriptions may appear on the National Archives' web page, but you can order a real copy very cheaply.

Black Studies: A Select Catalog of National Archives Microfilm Publications

Preliminary Inventory of the Records of the Field Offices of the Bureau of Refugees, Freedmen, and Abandoned Lands, Record Group 105

Preliminary Inventory 174: Preliminary Inventory of the Records of the Bureau of Refugees, Freedmen, and Abandoned Lands: Washington Headquarters

4. Determine for your state of research which records are on microfilm and which are not. Note that most will not be on microfilm.

5. Create a checklist of records to be examined.

6. Use first the microfilmed records, if they are available at a nearby library. This will give you a feel for the types of records you will examine once you visit the National Archives.

7. Create a list of all of your ancestors who lived during the period of Reconstruction.

8. Plan a trip to the National Archives to examine the records directly. Plan for at least one week to thoroughly examine the records.

To obtain copies of the above publications, write to the National Archives. For the preliminary inventory for Record Group 105, the one inventory that is of most importance to your research because it is the inventory to the records left by the nine hundred field agents, request (1) the table of contents pages and (2) the pages for your state only, particularly if you want to minimize your copying costs. Otherwise, feel free to request that the entire inventory be copied, requesting in advance an estimate of the cost. Also check *Preliminary Inventory 174* to determine if any records of genealogical value were compiled with headquarters' records rather than with the field agent's records.

Organization of the Bureau

The following description of the structure relies heavily on the official publications of the National Archives as well as the various publications by Elaine Everly, one of the many archivists who helped to organize the records, a task that was just completed twenty years ago. Consult the bibliography for Everly's articles on the bureau and her assessment of their contents.

HEADQUARTERS: WASHINGTON D.C.

Supervising Department: The War Department, Secretary of War

Bureau Head: Commissioner, General Oliver O. Howard

Staff Officers: Assistant Adjutant General, Assistant Inspector General, Chief Medical Officer, Chief Quartermaster, Chief Disbursing Officer, Officers in Charge of the Claims Division, Education Division (Superintendents), Land Division, and Assistant Commissioners in charge of each of the organizations in the following states:

Maryland, Virginia, Washington, D.C., West Virginia, (Under Virginia), North Carolina, South Carolina, Georgia, Florida, Alabama, Mississippi,

Louisiana, Texas, Arkansas, Tennessee, Kentucky, and Missouri.

STATE AND LOCAL LEVELS: DISTRICT OR SUBORDINATE FIELD OFFICES

For every state: Assistant Commissioner, generally a military officer plus his staff consisting of an Assistant Adjutant General, Assistant Quartermaster, Disbursing Officer, Superintendent of Education, Chief Surgeon, and a Military Superintendent

Within each state: Several Subassistant Commissioners and Assistant Commissioners assigned to subdistricts (one or more counties)

Subassistant Commissioner: Assistant Subassistant Commissioners and Field Agents

As you can see by these titles, it can get to be confusing. Just remember that you want to focus on the local areas first and then work up to examining other records in a systematic manner. Don't dare to ask if any of these records are indexed. The correspondence books are, but that won't help you very much. This is a page-by-page affair, but you will find it absolutely fascinating as your sense of the historical context in which your ancestors lived emerges. Also know that this is one of the few chances that you'll get to experience this rich documentation. The records after this are short on context.

Content of Records

The above titles, though cumbersome, are keys to understanding records that you will find. They also help you to evaluate the likelihood of finding genealogical data when there are volumes and volumes of record books and files to examine. Looking first at offices that generated lists rather than letters would be one way to tackle the massive amount of information. Examining letters, many of which are indexed but many also loose and filed in folders, would be a second priority. The bureau was always understaffed; therefore, certain functions were not uniformly executed throughout all states. For example, while the above structure suggests that every county fell into a subdistrict, this is not the case. Furthermore, the bureau's activities with regard to freedmen fell into two major areas: supervising and executing labor contracts, and schooling. The bureau was abolished in 1872, and its remaining obligations were turned over to the Office of the Adjutant General, Freedmen's Branch within the War Department. The Freedmen's Branch was responsible for the remaining bureau activities through 1879; thereafter, all of its remaining activities were assumed by the Colored Troops Division within the Office of the Adjutant General.

As the bureau was being phased out, some local records (including labor contracts) were often compiled with headquarters records, where they remained. Note also that the records of the assistant commissioners, in charge of each state, were consolidated and compiled with the headquarters records. For that reason, some but not all researchers will find that the microfilmed headquarters records will contain contracts, marriage records of freedmen, and other genealogical data. The guide to the microfilmed records as well as the essential Thackery bibliography point out which of the microfilmed records by state contain important genealogical data.

Labor Contracts

According to Everly, the following labor contracts were consolidated in the assistant commissioners' records and are available as part of the microfilm series: South Carolina, Louisiana, Arkansas, Mississippi, Tennessee, District of Columbia, and some Maryland counties.

Labor contracts for the remaining states may be found in records of the subordinate field office records. They are not on microfilm.

Case Study: Survey of Contents of Field Office Records, South Central Alabama

The following transcription from my notes should provide insight into the contents of the records that you might find for your state and area of research.

Preliminary Inventory, Record Group 105

This inventory will indicate the locations of field offices (subordinate field offices) in your state of research. Part of the entry from the inventory for Alabama appears in the chart on the following page. Once you begin to examine the records, you will find that records for nearby counties and towns were compiled together, particularly for the volumes that contained labor contracts. Agents often carried their record books with them to new assignments and continued to keep records in the same volumes. If your area of research does not have a subordinate field office, then check nearby towns and counties. Note that some of these towns no longer appear on modern maps, therefore necessitating the use of a historical atlas or a book that lists dead towns.

VOLUME 122: COMPLAINT BOOK

Office of Sub-District Commissioner, Greenville
Notes: Indexed. Many cases referred to the local judge's hearings in court. Cases included violence against freedmen for attending political meetings, misuse of apprentices, etc.

VOLUME 129: SERIES 104: REGISTERS OF CONTRACTS

Greenville Sub-District
Notes: Badly faded contracts for southeastern region of state including Russell, Tallapoosa, and Montgomery counties. So badly faded, will take too much time to go through. Also contains many registers of contracts rather than contracts themselves. Locate the contracts that are listed but not contained in volumes.

VOLUME 127: SERIES 106

Miscellaneous Record Book
Notes: The following entries were found.
June 21, 1865: A few cases of violence including hanging of a David in Conecuh County. David had been told that he would be killed if he ever returned home to a neighboring plantation. Jane was listed as David's mother.
Page 177: New York Famine Relief Association delivers corn to Crenshaw County, list of 16 people receiving corn.
Pages 182–184: Corn delivered to Pike, Coffee, and Covington counties.
Page 191: Account of bacon received from New York Famine Relief Association distributed to freedmen at subdistrict of Greenville.

LOCATION OF FREEDMEN'S BUREAU FIELD OFFICES AND THEIR RECORDS, SOUTH CENTRAL ALABAMA

Town	Present County	Records Reported By:
Ashville	St. Clair	Union Army Commander
Athens	Limestone	See Huntsville
Bluffton	Lee	Subassistant Commissioner
Cahaba	Dallas	Not Indicated
Claiborn	Cleburne?	Subassistant Commissioner
Demopolis	Marengo	Subassistant Commissioner
Elyton	?	Subassistant Commissioner
Eufaula	Barbour	Agent
Eutaw	Greene	Agent
Garland	Butler	Freedmen's Hospital
Girard	?	Agent
Greenville	Butler	Subassistant Commissioner
Haynesville	Lowndes	Assistant Subassistant Comm.
Huntsville	Madison	Subassistant Commissioner
Huntsville/Athens		Claims Agent
Huntsville	Madison	Freedmen's Hospital
Jacksonville	Calhoun	Subassistant Commissioner
Livingston	Sumter	Agent
Mobile	Mobile	Subassistant Commissioner
Montgomery	Montgomery	Subassistant Commissioner
Montgomery	Montgomery	Home Colony Hospital
Opelika	Lee	Subassistant Commissioner
Selma	Dallas	Subassistant Commissioner
Selma	Dallas	Freedmen's Hospital
Talladega	Talladega	Subassistant Commissioner
Talladega	Talladega	Freedmen's Hospital
Tuscaloosa	Tuscaloosa	Subassistant Commissioner
Tuscumbia	Colbert	Subassistant Commissioner
Tuskegee	Macon	Assistant Superintendent

Source: Preliminary Inventory for Record Group 105

Page 192: June 27, 1867. Caroline Tilman received five pounds of bacon. Note that Berry Tilman, Caroline's brother, received one sack (112 pounds) corn. Page 133, one Henry Tilman received one sack of corn. Had one wife and two small children. Berry Tilman was my great-grandmother's brother. Are Caroline and Henry her siblings?

Other Observations: Titles of Mr. and Mrs. given to Whites only. Page 201–203, found a series of interesting comments as in the following:

> Mrs. _____, married, able bodied relatives. Bad repute.
>
> Mrs. _____, married, behaved badly after U.S. Troops passed through.
>
> Mrs. _____, widow, is well off. Keeps 100s? house.
>
> Mrs. _____, married, not to receive rations for her negroes.

Other references were to white widows living by prostitution, a sensitive subject that I will let rest in the records until their descendants find them. Note that this is where you begin to understand how the war devastated the social and economic fabric of the South.

VOLUME 123: SEPTEMBER 1865 TO OCTOBER 1866

Series 101, Greenville, Letters Sent

Notes: Roster with remarks as in following: Mr. J. Medley, undertaker and gravedigger for refugees, freedmen, and destitute. Often remarks contain assessments with respect to present economic conditions and assessments of personal wealth as in the following: "Mrs. P_____ has two wealthy brothers-in-law, well off, has two grown-up daughters. Can support herself, no more rations."

Page 19: Names of persons reported as not having registered.

Pages 50–56: Roster (actually register) with first names only. Freedmen?

Series 117: Docket Trials

Notes: Only few trials, rest of volume is empty.

Series 107: Miscellaneous Records (Boxed Letters)

William P_____ shoots black man with whom he is raising a crop in the Pigeon Creek area. Letter to McCogy referring to monthly returns of freedmen. Figure out what "returns" means.

Series 98: Boxed Letters

Has some interesting documents, especially for Demopolis. Lease of plantation for "asylum," purchase of cotton from freedmen, list of freedmen and portion of cotton they will raise.

Other information: Found my great-grandfather John Longmire, age 2, listed with his parents at Garland, Alabama Hospital as patients. Volume 79, Series 123, Census of Black Citizens and Registers of Bounty Claims Received and Forwarded, 1865 to June–July 1868. Approximately 2,200 people enumerated by household and descriptive information: name, age, sex, street, former owner, occupation, present county, present employment, and remarks. Very few bounties applied for. Great evidence of early urban migration. Basically a census of all freedmen living in Huntsville between June and July, 1868!

As indicated from my notes, the records contain a wealth of information, some of which you want to know and some you would have never known without this microscopic view of people who lived in small communities dotted throughout the South starting with the year of emancipation and ending only a few years later. These records represent a window of opportunity that no good researcher can ignore.

Your foray into records left by the Freedmen's Bureau will prepare you for the subsequent stages of research into other types of manuscript collections, housed at various libraries and repositories throughout the United States.

Chapter 9

A LONG WAY
TO FREEDOM

The Genealogy of Your

Slave Ancestors

*Tangled are the skeins
of slave genealogy....*

HARRIET JACOBS, INCIDENTS IN THE LIFE OF A SLAVE GIRL

Obe nykere obi ase.

One does not disclose another's origins.

R.S. RATTRAY, *ASHANTI LAW AND CONSTITUTION*

The Last Generation of Slaves

*T*his is a stop, pause, and think chapter. You've covered quite a bit of territory, and now you are ready to explore the records of slavery. Before you do that, this chapter will help you with perspective. Understanding some of the basic facts about slavery, the kinds of records that exist and what inferences can be made from those records is especially necessary at this stage of research. The reason? Slavery continues to be an ever-present theme in our lives. Unfortunately, we often misinterpret the experiences of our own ancestors, for just as slave genealogies are tangled, so too are the skeins of our own memories. Further, they are clouded with the fact that one does not discuss another's origins, an approach that was used in some Ghanaian societies to deal with slave lineages. Of course, slavery as it evolved in Ghana and in Africa allowed for integration of slave lineages with those that were not. Secrecy served a protective function. In plantation slavery in the Americas, secrecy was used as a self-protective measure for a group who had gone through a painful history of servitude.

Two and one half centuries later, the year 1619 must have been a remote memory to the last generation of slaves to live in the United States. The collective experiences of those slaves whose ancestry reached back that far must also have been seen through a very dim lens, for much had happened to transform those first Africans. The four million slaves who became free by 1865 had become what historian Joel Williams called "new people." Though Williams used this term to refer to racial mixing, which had changed the genetic makeup of Africans in America over twelve generations of enslavement, it can be expanded to include the sum of African experiences that, when combined, represented a cultural transformation into a "New People." How this transformation occurred is part of what you will discover while doing your research.

There are many records that contain names of slaves and their owners for the duration of slavery. There are records that show the transfer of slaves from one party to another by sale, by gift, by mortgage or some other mechanism. There are records listing the name of every slave owned by a planter. There are even records that show slaves inventing a new device or being used for medical experiments or being inoculated against yellow fever. Slavery, at one time, was art and parcel of every thread of the American fabric. Nor was it solely a southern institution. The records of the New England and the Mid-Atlantic states attest to this. No American escaped its impact or consequences. Nor was slavery just a matter between owner and owned. It was a public matter that was duly recorded in record books, planter's accounts, diaries, and travelers' accounts. And there was no wide-scale attempt to systematically destroy these records at the end of slavery. You will occasionally come across examples of records being destroyed through negligence or ignorance, but it is a rare occasion when you encounter willful attempts to hide records on slavery.

Accept the fact that records are plentiful. Philip D. Morgan estimated that 80,000 slaves were named and described in the probate records of low-country South Carolina for the period between 1760 and 1799 alone (all probated estates). If by 1790, the slave population was approximately 107,000 in South Carolina, then a very rough estimate of your chances of finding your slave ancestor's name in the estate records for that period would be approximately 80 percent. Further, the three generations of Windsor and Angola Ame's family dating from the early 1700s to 1796, constructed by a scholar using a set of plantation records from that region, should let you know that your research could yield similar results.

If this then is the case, you might ask, Why is research on slaves so difficult? It is difficult because these records are organized by the names of slave owners and not slaves. If you do not know the name of the owner for each and every one of your ancestors, these records will remain closed to you. *Thus researching your ancestors during slavery becomes researching the owners of your ancestors.* Ironically, you will learn as much, if not more, about your ancestors' owners than about your ancestors. Nevertheless, what you learn about slave owners can help you to directly

understand, often for the first time, the conditions under which your ancestors lived.

Because your slave ancestors left few records written in their own hands, their lives were not documented as well as the lives of free Americans. As you conduct your research, you will begin to understand that the story you are unraveling will be quite different from the stories that can be unraveled using records on free persons. You will not be able to create a neat genealogical chart or table showing the continuity from one generation to the next in terms of places and dates for all marriages, births, deaths, and even places where they might have lived. Furthermore, some groups in American society, in terms of their historical experience, are just as difficult to document. Women during the colonial period, indentured servants, Indians, and poor Whites were not as extensively recorded in historical records as land-owning White males. While free-born, propertied, and literate White males were far more likely to be documented, this fact makes your job only slightly easier.

The nature of the records that you will encounter during the period of slavery attests to what happened to your ancestors, and not what they did or said themselves. Thus, even if you find a letter written from a slave (more likely to have been written by a third party) to his or her former owner or to a relative still owned by the planter, and there are such letters, you will have to carefully weigh its contents. Rare is the occasion where you will find a letter that expresses the honest feelings of a slave—perhaps *former* slaves, as in the case of a letter written by a runaway who eventually settled in Canada and wrote a candid letter to his former owner wishing that his wife were in hell.

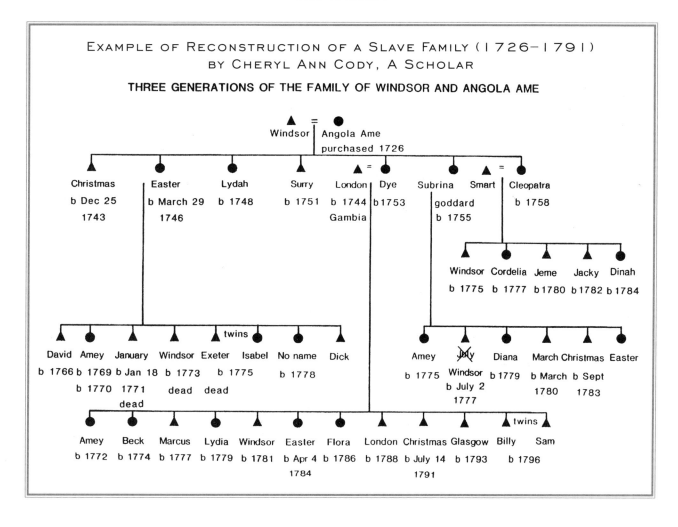

Historians have spent many years trying to infer the beliefs, values, and behavior of slaves in their day-to-day existence—their relationships to one another and to Whites. This effort is often a difficult task because the individual experiences of slaves, despite the unending monotony of laboring, were often unique enough to override the norm. Hopefully, your thorough research will inspire you to find the words to lend credence to the very uniqueness of your own ancestors' experiences.

WHAT TO EXPECT

When you research your ancestors during slavery, you should know that the techniques you will use involve making a series of inferences, many of which may be weak. One reason is that generational change in the slave-owning family may change the whole composition of a slave family. A second reason is that the surnames of slaves did not always appear in records. Often, you will be working with given names, a problem that is compounded when there is little evidence elsewhere. Thus, your research is predicated on a series of contingencies or assumptions that have to be made about slave owners and the records they left behind. Even though this is the case, the rules for evidence remain the same—you must try to link individuals together and over time by locating as many documents as possible, the goal being to show that they were related by kinship or some other relationship. In the process, you may wind up reconstructing family lines that are not yours because of the nature of the records that you will find. Because this aspect of African American genealogy is relatively new, you will not always benefit from other genealogical research. There is a strong possibility that you can benefit from historical research. However, by and large, you will be the path breaker this time.

IMAGINING THE LIVES OF YOUR ANCESTORS AS SLAVES: THE SLAVE COMMUNITY

*I*f this term sounds strange to you, perhaps it is because you may wonder how slaves could have formed communities. The simplest answer is that all human beings struggle for community even in the most dire circumstances. Without community and kinship, it is difficult to produce subsequent generations. In your research on the ancestral home, you may have found the remnants of a slave community without really knowing how to define it. Those ancestors who appear on your chart during the generation of freedom lived in slave communities.

Think of the slave community as one bound by kinship ties and/or a set of com-

mon historical experiences, either on a large plantation or within the confines of a local community composed of slaves from neighboring farms and plantations also bound by kinship ties. Kinship is the basis of slave communities—not slavery itself, a subtle point that you will come to understand as your research evolves. Yet there was more than kinship to bind slaves together. The key focal point of the slave community was the community of slave owners who among themselves also shared kinship ties, common origins and migration paths, and the same worldview.

THE LIFE CYCLES OF SLAVES AND SLAVE OWNERS

*I*f slaves lived within communities, you might ask how "stable" these communities were. The answer is that they were as stable as the lives of slave owners. Therefore, the life cycle of any given slave was directly entwined with the life cycle of the slave owner as seen in the generational cycles of the slave-owning family. Presented below are two composites based on the generational cycles in a slave-owning family. One tells the planter's story while the other tells the story partly from the perspective of his slave.

The Planter's Story

Samuel Goosby was born the third son and the fifth child of Matthew and Luella (Parker) Goosby in 1760, Fairfax County, Virginia. The young Goosby fought in the Revolutionary War, and like so many in his generation, he decided to move to Wilkes County, Georgia, where he had purchased land under a system of land grants set up for veterans of the war. He later sent for his brother, Henry, who joined him in Georgia in 1789.

When their father, Matthew, died in 1792, leaving ten slaves to each of his children, Samuel and Henry returned to Virginia to claim their slaves. Their oldest brother had inherited the old homestead. Back in Georgia, with ten slaves each on neighboring farms, the Goosby brothers began to prosper. By the turn of the century, they owned a sizable tract of land and one hundred slaves combined.

When Samuel died in 1834, his oldest son, Samuel Junior, inherited the homestead and forty slaves. Amanda, his daughter, who had married her first cousin (Samuel's nephew) inherited fifteen slaves. The youngest son, Matthew, inherited twenty-five slaves and, always having been ambitious, decided to move to Mississippi. He had heard about the Alabama fever, the Texas fever, and the Mississippi fever. Matthew headed to Natchez, Mississippi, in the late 1830s. He traveled overland, stopping at frontier trading posts for respite, and he took his slaves, by now totaling sixty, with him.

Though arriving late for this well-settled country, Matthew Goosby was well prepared; he had already purchased a tract of land in Adams County, Mississippi. Goosby continued to add slaves and land to his wealth, and when he died in 1863, he owned one of the largest plantations in Adams County as well as several upriver plantations in Warren County and across the river in Concordia Parish, Louisiana. His oldest son, Matthew III, took over the operation of the plantation. Matthew III had married Amelia Sanders, and she had also brought to her marriage a considerable amount of wealth, including slaves. Their combined wealth at the beginning of the Civil War was close to $500,000 (including slaves valued at $250,000), a sum not to blink at in those days.

Senah's Story

Senah was one of the first slaves that the elder Matthew Goosby had purchased from his neighbor, Benjamin Brody, five years after arriving from England. In fact, without each other's knowledge, Senah and Goosby had arrived in Virginia the same year. By the time of the Revolutionary War, Senah had a wife (Mahala) and two children, all of whom lived on Benjamin Brody's farm, about three miles from the Goosby place. Senah watched Goosby prosper by buying slaves from his neighbors over the years. By the time of the Revolutionary War, Senah had considered escaping and joining the British cause, but his chances kept slipping away. Moreover, there would be no sure way to come back and get his family.

When Matthew Goosby finally died, Senah had hoped that he would gain his freedom as promised. He had been the chief carpenter for Goosby and his neighbors and had earned some measure of respect for his skill. When the division of Goosby's estate was made in 1792, Senah discovered that the elder Goosby had gone back on his promise. He was one of the ten slaves given Samuel Goosby.

Arriving in Georgia with Samuel, his brother Henry, and their inherited slaves, Senah discovered how bad frontier life could be. The closest farm was ten miles away and the Goosbys' provisions for their slaves amounted to no more than a few huts. With his skills in carpentry, a skill the Goosby brothers had bartered for during the division of their father's estate, Senah helped to construct modest homes for the Goosbys and improved cabins for their slaves. Senah also took a new wife, Sukey, this time from among the slaves inherited by Samuel Goosby. Periodically, the Goosbys reported on happenings back in Virginia. One letter arrived informing the Goosbys that smallpox had killed a number of slaves on Brody's plantation, one of whom was Mahala, Senah's former wife. Senah had already despaired of ever seeing their children again—a sentiment that led him to form a new family with Sukey from which four children were born.

When Samuel Goosby died in 1834, his will stated that Senah and his family were to remain on the plantation in Georgia with his oldest son Samuel Junior, who had inherited his father's homestead along with forty slaves. Senah died in 1835. His wife and their four children remained in Georgia for a while, at least. But by 1840 Samuel Junior had encountered financial difficulties and looked to his wealthier brother, Matthew III, now living in Mississippi, to bail him out. Matthew purchased Sukey, her children, and several additional slaves. Sukey and her children wound up in Warren County, Mississippi, but her brothers and sisters were already in Adams County. They had been carried there earlier as part of the young Matthew's inheritance. They all reunited after the Civil War, but never returned to Wilkes County, Georgia, to look for their other relatives. They had made inquiries through the Freedmen's Bureau agent stationed in Warren County, but they never got a response.

Analysis

These two stories reflect the impact of generational change and migration on both slave and planter families. Senah's story is not altogether an atypical one in the sense that families were frequently broken up. Despite this, it appears that the majority of slaves owned by all of the Goosbys remained within the widely dispersed Goosby family, except for those whom Matthew Goosby might have purchased in Mississippi. Imagine identifying by name, age, sex, places and dates of birth, marriage, death, and burial all slaves ever owned by all of the Goosbys over a period of time approaching a century. The total may be close to a thousand! Which are your ancestors, and how will you find out?

Researching slaves on plantations or farms owned by your ancestors' various slave owners can become expansive the further back in time you go even if all of your ancestors were owned by one family. Your results would depend on acquiring knowledge of records in four states—Virginia, Georgia, Mississippi, and Louisiana. Do not think that this will happen overnight. You will have to work at it in a systematic effort to obtain reasonable results. Depending on how well the Goosbys kept records, reconstructing the kinship ties within those slave communities that formed on their plantations can be done.

The most significant juncture in the generational continuity of the slave community and slave families was the death of an owner. At this point, the greatest number of slaves were affected for they may have been sold or divided among the owner's children, many of whom lived considerable distances from each other. This was certainly the case with slaves owned by the Goosbys. Like the descendants of the original Goosby, Senah's descendants, at the end of slavery, lived in Virginia, Georgia, Mississippi, and possibly Louisiana.

WHAT YOU NEED TO KNOW ABOUT SLAVERY

There are many myths about slavery that have now been disproven by careful historical research. However, many of these myths have continued to plague even the most informed people. Just because slavery is your heritage, that doesn't mean that whatever you say about it is true. By and large, the experience of slavery was one that our ancestors were anxious to leave in the past. Thus, the shallowness of the oral tradition within many African American families may be attributable to this desire. Our ancestors, however, knew their own ancestry. These constitute some of the best reasons to do African American genealogy. Understanding the limitations on interpreting your ancestors' experiences will ultimately enable you to come to a deeper understanding. Outlined below are some aspects of slavery that will help you to do a good job in using the evidence to be found in historical records.

SOME PRECAUTIONS IN FORMULATING YOUR VIEWS OF SLAVERY

No doubt you have come to this research with your own views about slavery. When I first started my research, I had no knowledge of how my ancestors lived under slavery, partly because there was no strong oral tradition and partly because for all practical purposes, my family history started with the first generation to live in freedom. Our family founding myth centered around Grandma Lucindy, who, along with Adam, ushered the family and perhaps the whole community into its first years of

freedom. She outlived her husband, and she certainly must have been a force to deal with.

Furthermore, my views had been shaped by reading the general literature on slavery. The specifics were missing: What did they eat? How did they name their children? Who owned them, and what was their relationship beyond that of slave and slave owner? These questions, somehow, were off-limits. I sometimes think that my parents' generation, like the generations before them, had been trained to keep silence so well that they had lost the ability to even think such questions were permissible. Thus they had been trained to *act* the response without giving one—it made me think they knew far more than they actually did! I realized how little I really knew when the day came for me to actually look at real records with the names of real slave owners—those who owned my ancestors and those whose name I carried. That may be the uneasy turning point in your own research.

There exist some unusual theories about slavery that are primarily derived from imagination and the "faceless slave" view of history. A high school student once asked me—in fact argued with me—whether there had been a lot of incest among the first Africans to arrive in the United States. I tried to explain to him why that was almost certainly not the case, but he had in his view of slavery a type of "herding" image gone berserk. In other words, his ancestors were nameless, faceless people without languages or anything else that marked them as individuals and as members of social groups. He had never been taught that Africans were multiethnic and multilingual, having the ability to recognize members from their own groups. For all practical purposes, his ancestors were animals because he had an "animalized" view of slavery—a case where imagery and rhetoric had overcome a sound knowledge of history. View your research as "slavery with a human face"—that of your ancestors. Doing otherwise, ironically, puts you more in the camp of those who found arguments to support slavery. There is a difference between ignorance and not being able to tell the truth.

RECORDED TRANSACTIONS OF PLANTERS AND FARMERS

*T*he records that you will search for will vary according to the type of slave owner (large versus small), and also by state. The key is to know the types of transactions that slave owners made and where evidence of these transactions may be found. The following examples should lead you in the right direction once you find the slave owner. Of course, by the time you begin looking for these records, you may already know quite a bit about the slave owner.

- Slave owners died and left directions for the division of their property. Their estate papers may include an inventory that names slaves and lists their values, a will that names slaves, a division of slaves by named heirs, and manumission papers.
- Slave owners and their overseers frequently kept records in account books and day books that indicated: (1) the issuance of clothes, shoes, and cloth, (2) medical treatment including smallpox vaccinations, (3) birth registers naming the child and mother but rarely the father, (4) death records listing the name and date of death, (5) accounting lists that record slaves at the beginning of the year, and (6) records showing daily activities including work assignments and amount of labor performed.
- Slave owners frequently entered into financial transactions involving slaves such as (1) mortgaging slaves, (2) insuring the lives of slaves, (3) hiring out slaves to neighboring planters, (4) paying slaves for a variety of services, and (5) in several documented cases, using their talents as entertainers and sportsmen.
- Slave owners frequently kept diaries and wrote letters in which slaves were mentioned in passing references or were even the subject of long entries— generally those who continued to cause difficulty.
- Slave owners frequently appeared in local newspapers, where they advertised runaways or may have acquired slaves as a result of an advertisement for the sale of slaves on a neighboring farm or from a slave dealer.

- Slave owners frequently bought slaves and sold slaves using handwritten bills of sale or, less frequently, entering their transactions in courthouse deed books.

- Some slave owners buried their slaves in the family plot or in their church's cemetery. Some baptized slaves, particularly if they were Catholic. Some allowed slave preachers to hold services. Some required that their slaves attend church service with them. Some manumitted their slaves because slave ownership conflicted with their religious beliefs. The professed religion of the owner can be important.

- Some slave owners frequently kept concubines in the slave community. Some frequently took liberties with slave women. Some frequently moved their second families into the kitchen. This aspect of slave genealogy is one of the most difficult to document. Proof will often rest on the family's oral tradition and on strong circumstantial evidence. It is rare to find a deed of manumission similar to the one that Del Jupiter found for her slave ancestor, who was manumitted while still in her mother's womb!

- The descendants of slave owners will frequently have in their possession personal papers left by their ancestors. These papers will not always wind up in historical collections, but rather may remain in the hands of a family member. One of the largest collections of personal papers to come to market in recent times was auctioned off in the past ten years. The papers had become separated at auction, but once the University of Texas found out, they paid close to one million dollars for their acquisition. These papers belonged to the slave-owning Dabney family of Texas and Virginia.

- Some slave owners left few, if any, records. This is especially true of small-scale slave owners, some of whom were illiterate. The most that the researcher may be able to find initially would be records left in county courthouses.

- Slave owners had a joint interest in maintaining the institution of slavery. As such, they created a "prison of local laws" to maintain control over local slave populations. The surviving court minutes, court order books, and jail records attest to the extensive creation of laws on everything from policing the movement of slaves to their taxation to their use on public road construction to whether they could be privately manumitted by their owners.

THE SLAVE/SLAVE OWNER DICHOTOMY

Slavery was an institution that rested on the control of labor. In order to accomplish this goal, planters developed a system that in their view allowed for the optimum use of labor without losing it. In short, it was in the interests of planters to see their slaves survive and reproduce. It was within this margin that slaves were able to negotiate a space for themselves. One part of this negotiable space was the recognition of marriage and some degree of personal freedom outside this owner/slave dichotomy. In effect, slaves in the United States were able to maintain some elements of their cultural heritage, including their beliefs about marriage and the family.

Though you will be studying what slave owners did to your ancestors, this often requires only a literal interpretation of the records that are available. The more creative interpretations arise when you have to infer how your enslaved ancestors maneuvered in this space over time. The following discussion will help you to provide a framework, or "eyes" to see.

SLAVE MARRIAGES AND MATRIFOCALITY

*T*he institution of marriage during slavery was recognized by most slave owners for many reasons. Historians have surmised that planters, because of their own economic interests, encouraged marriage and often found moral justification through their views on religion. This, of course, did not grant slave parents legal rights over their children. Slaves with deep African cultural roots also had their preferences. Thus, slaves recognized extended kinship (both real and adoptive). Planters did not. A case in point is that of Robert Smalls's testimony before the American Freedmen's Inquiry Commission in response to the following question: "When they say parents, what do they mean by the word?" Smalls replied, "They mean relations in general; the same that they mean when they say 'family.' "

Many researchers will come to their task with the view that the family relationships of slaves were structured by the female-headed household, when in fact, such a household was never the norm during slavery. Rather, it is a phenomenon that developed in relatively recent times. What shows up in the records as female-headed households were actually households that had been affected by mortality (which was high), sales, and "broad marriages" where husband and wife were owned by neighboring slave owners. The phenomenon, therefore, may be an artifact of historical record keeping rather than a representation of reality. Records kept by Europeans were based on their notion of family, which was not the same as the notion of family among slaves. In no small measure did the African notion of extended kinship maintain the sense of community among enslaved Africans.

Applying the same arguments as above, nuclear families should also be viewed as the exception rather than the rule. Housing often did not accommodate such an arrangement anyway. Slave families often shared one cabin, common meals, and because of the nature of their enslavement, common supervision of children. Slave life was far more communal than can be imagined today. The context in which Africans found themselves only reinforced their existing values about family rather than radically changing them. It was the slave owner who attempted to impose a different structure, but to no avail because the economic organization of his farm or plantation was frequently based on a communal workforce rather than an individual one. The slave family should, therefore, be viewed as an extended family where children were reared by both parents, grandparents, aunts, and uncles for a good portion of their youth.

THE EXTENT OF FAMILY DISRUPTIONS

*M*arriages and the family were disrupted by frequent death, sales of "recalcitrants," planter migrations to new frontiers, financial instability of the slave owner, and the domestic slave trade. The one prevailing fear within the slave family and community was the fear of being sold and separated from one's family. Slaves could be sold individually or within kin groups of various sizes and compositions (two-parent nuclear family, mother with some or all of her children, especially infants, extended family). The one group that experienced the highest number of individual sales consisted of males between the ages of fifteen and twenty-four. The group least likely to have been affected by sales consisted of older slaves. Of course, during the height of the domestic slave trade, a premium was placed on labor—thus a higher incidence of sales of males and females in their prime. This was eventually offset by sales of whole family units to the Deep South.

TRACING YOUR ANCESTRY THROUGH THE FEMALE LINE

*I*t is often assumed that it will be easier to trace your ancestry through the female line rather than the male line because of the view that slavery created and reinforced matrifocal families. That is not the case. This issue is often confused with the judicial view of slavery, which is based on the belief that because slave men had no legally recognized "rights" to their wives or children, they would, therefore, never appear as parents in records on slavery. Slave owners frequently held men accountable for their families, and their record books as well as estate papers were, more often than not, arranged according to the patriarchal view of the ordered relationships between men and women: men at the head, their wives as helpmates and servants, and their children as servants to both parents. Thus, when you examine slave lists as your primary source

for reconstructing family relationships, you will find such an order "imposed" on slaves whether it reflected reality or not.

The question remains, however, are there more records that tie mothers to children than those that tie fathers to children? The answer depends on the extent to which slave owners kept birth records, and that was probably minimal when compared to the other kinds of events they recorded. Birth lists or, more frequently, notations of births on lists drawn up for other reasons, are to be found, but not necessarily in great quantities. The same applies to deaths, which were kept just as casually. Censuslike lists of all slaves on one plantation, often ordered into family groups, are far more common than birth or death lists.

Another factor to keep in mind is that any record reflects only one point in time over a whole generation. Do not make broad inferences based on one record or one slave list. For full understanding, each and every document has to be placed in perspective. For example, most slave lists were made at critical points in the whole generational cycle of the slave community. A list of slaves before and after a sale or before and after the slave owner's death may show some significant differences. What's more, neither may truly reflect the entire slave population except for that one point in time.

A NOTE ON NAMING PATTERNS

*N*aming patterns are important in reconstructing family ties. You might be surprised to find that surviving records indicate that slaves were able to and did name their children, despite the famous scene from *Roots*. Note that slave owners were more likely to assign names to newly arriving Africans than to those who were born on U.S. soil. The extent to which new slaves, or "saltwater" slaves, had this right is still not known, primarily because it is a complex issue. We do know that African names (original as well as anglicized) formed a significant and recognizable part of the name pool among slaves in nearly every region during the whole of slavery. One scholar estimated that African names constituted at least 25 percent of the name pool in certain areas. A careful reading of the works by Turner, Dillard, Puckett, and Wood (listed in the bibliography) will help you to recognize African-derived names.

When slave parents named their children, they almost always used names of their kin or their own brothers and sisters. A scholar who studied the Ball plantation in South Carolina found that seven out of ten children were named after relatives. In another, a child named "Winter" was actually born in summer—the rationale for his given name being that he was named after a paternal uncle who had recently died. In addition, this researcher found that male children were named after kin more than female children, with sons being named for their fathers more often than daughters being named for their mothers. In fact, all of the naming patterns that she discovered showed a strong attachment to the paternal line. What this means for your research is that you will look for and carefully examine naming patterns for your ancestors from one generation to the next.

The use of surnames by slave families was common, but historians cannot really tell us the extent to which this practice prevailed in different slave communities. Occasionally planters did recognize surnames, and they were duly entered into their record books. These surnames should not be confused with

identification names used by the slave owner to distinguish work assignments or slaves carrying the same first name. What can be said, then, is that records will frequently show surnames, often almost as an afterthought by the person entering the names in the record.

REGIONAL VARIATIONS

*R*esearchers should be aware of the regional variations in slavery. If your ancestors were from the South Carolina low country, think "rice and indigo." If your ancestors were from southern Louisiana, think "sugar cane and a little rice." If your ancestors were from Maryland and Virginia, think "tobacco." If your ancestors were urban slaves, think "domestic servants" or even factory workers. If your ancestors lived near major mining or timber regions, think "mining and timber." All else, think "cotton." Rice and sugar cane are associated with large labor forces. Think large-scale plantation owners. Cotton may vary considerably. Tobacco could be grown with either kind of labor force. These crops were certainly not the only crops to be grown by slave holders, but they were the major crops. Knowing the regional variations in crop production and sizes of slave holdings will help you to define the kind of slave community in which your ancestors lived.

THE QUESTIONS OF COLOR AND MIXING

*E*ntire books have been written about color designations assigned to African American slaves. Terms such as *griffe*, *sambo*, *mustee*, and even *copper* have historical meaning. Mixing frequently occurred between Indians, Blacks, and Whites. Those who claim some Indian ancestry often assume that this ancestry can be proven with documents. But suppose the initial mixing occurred in 1780, or 1680? Is it likely that you can prove your Indian ancestry then? I would say probably not—at least with written records, despite the fact that early records occasionally named enslaved Indians. Or consider the possibility that a slave of African-Cherokee mixture was sold further South to Mississippi and lived near the Chickasaw. You might falsely conclude that your ancestor was part Chickasaw when, in fact, he was part Cherokee. One final caveat: Your ancestors, and their descendants, often claimed Indian ancestry when, in fact, the source of the mixture is European. I have a relative in her nineties who insists that one of our ancestors was "French-Indian." What's more, she won't allow access to any knowledge that she may have about the nature of this question, and I've concluded that she knows less than she pretends about "French-Indians."

However, there are many communities in North Carolina and Virginia and some in New York that consist of descendants of these initial mixtures (Black, White, Indian) and that today represent a wide range of color gradations. If you find that your people lived in or were associated with one of these communities, you may have a stronger case for identifying which Indian ethnic group your ancestors mixed with. Of course, the more recent the mixture (nineteenth century), the more likely that you can identify the specific Indian group.

Also consider the possibility that your ancestors were owned by Indian slave owners. If you identify an ancestor as "Indian" in the 1830s and 1840s living among the five southeastern tribes, often called the Five Civilized Tribes (Creek, Choctaw, Chickasaw,

Cherokee, and Seminole), you may want to assume first that they were owned by the many mixed bloods who lived between the White and Indian communities. When I visited the Alabama archives in Montgomery, the first book I picked from the shelves was a transcription of deeds for Lowndes County. The first entry showed a sale of slaves by an Indian whose name had been phonetically written rather than translated!

Finally, slavery occurred over a very long period of time in very different regions of the country. Think variability in terms of time, regions, slave owners, slave origins, and almost any other variable that comes to mind. No institution is static or simple, though it may rest on the deceptively simple foundation of uncompensated labor. In terms of both slave and free families, learn to think in generational terms.

This overview of some basic definitions and problems should provide a good start. All of the work is worth the effort just to know where your folks came from. In addition, consider yourself a part of a pioneering effort. If African American genealogy remains a viable field, it will depend on researchers like you to make it so. Imagine that within fifty years, beginning African American genealogists will have a lot more assistance because of your efforts. In the subsequent chapters, techniques of researching major record groups created during the period of slavery will be discussed. These techniques will often assume that you have discovered the name of the last owner, the name that you need to get started. However, techniques that do not assume this knowledge will also be pointed out. Again, the research task is an arduous but not unimportant one. Good luck!

Chapter 10

THE LAST SLAVE
AND THE
LAST SLAVE OWNER

To sell cotton in order to buy negroes—to make more cotton to buy more negroes, 'ad infinitum,' is the aim and direct tendency of all the operations of the thorough-going cotton planter: his whole soul is wrapped up in the pursuit.

JOSEPH INGRAHAM, QUOTED IN STEPHEN OAKES, *THE RULING RACE*

Is Slavery Really Dead and Done? Don't Quit Now

Often genealogists and family historians decide, with not much of a valid reason, that there is no point in researching their ancestors beyond the last generation to live in slavery. I suspect that much of this reasoning is based on a fear of dealing with such a touchy subject, particularly if they spent their growing-up years in the South during the pre–Civil Rights era. But slavery is not dead and done. It's true that all of those individuals who were involved as slaves or slave owners or slave merchants are gone. But the impact of what they did survives. Unfortunately, slavery is not dead and done, and it won't be until we find the words to talk about it or until it becomes a part of our cultural memory as well as the nation's.

If you have never sat your children or grandchildren down to tell them the story of their ancestors during slavery, perhaps it is because you don't have the words to do so. Not talking about our ancestors does not make them anonymous—it merely makes our memories filled with anonymous people and blank spaces. Now is your chance to uncover a story that wasn't told to you. Now you can tell it yourself, for you will have the words to do so.

Locating the Last Slave Owner: What to Do When You Haven't a Clue

At one time, I assumed that most African Americans possessed within the family memory some knowledge about their ancestors during slavery. This is an assumption that I had to throw out the window. If you ask any African American this question today, it is very unlikely that a direct answer will be forthcoming. The ties within families and the ties between Blacks and Whites in the South that would have sustained this type of information have long since faded. Nevertheless, some of this knowledge does remain, and this is the knowledge that you will have to tap to make your research a little bit easier at this point.

This chapter outlines some basic techniques in identifying the owner of your ancestor at the time of emancipation. Because the many records that link slaves to their owners have not been indexed or put into a form that is easy to use by genealogists, much of your work during this phase will be done on a "systematic trial and error basis." Under ideal circumstances, finding the name of the last owner should occur during your family interviewing. It often does not, particularly for genealogists whose families migrated from the South between the late 1800s and the early twentieth century. Occasionally, a name given to you as the last owner may turn out to be an owner of land on which your ancestors lived as tenant farmers or sharecroppers. While this person or his parents may also have been slave owners, you can't easily conclude that they owned your ancestors. To add one additional complication, you may have the name of a planter who owned only one of your ancestors and not his or her spouse.

Finally, it is unlikely that you will have the name of every slave owner for those slave ancestors who lived during the last generation of slavery. If you look at my five generation chart in chapter 2, you will see that by the fourth generation, I have to locate the names of at least eight slave owners, and by the fifth, I have to locate the names of sixteen slave owners. It is important for you to begin to imagine two names for every space on your chart past the fourth or fifth generation—your ancestor's and that of his slave owner.

ABOUNDING CLUES

Where you start always depends on how much you know before you start. If you already know the name of at least one slave owner, then this phase of your research will be less difficult when compared to researchers who do not have any. Knowing the last owner or the owner at the time of emancipation takes you directly to probate and other records. Not knowing the name of the last owner will lead you into an intensive search of records and sources with which you are already partially familiar. Clues abound,

but you will need a keen sense of observation to focus and guide your research. The 1870 and 1880 censuses will assume added importance because the families identified therein were probably formed during slavery. These family groups will be the ones that you look for in records left by slave owners.

DEVISING A STRATEGY

Your approach should be based on focusing in on the county where your ancestors lived in 1870 and should include: (1) knowing the history of the county, (2) use of the censuses for 1850, 1860, 1870, and 1880, (3) use of the slave schedules for 1850 and 1860, (4) use of county records like deed books, tract books, and tax lists, (5) use of maps, and (6) creative uses of records from the Civil War period—especially the Freedmen's Bureau records. Much of this effort, of necessity, focuses on information that you already have. The difference is that you will be doing a lot more analytical thinking, whereas before, you had only to locate the records and copy the information into your notebook.

IDENTIFYING THE LAST SLAVE FAMILY

Your ancestors whose lives spanned the period immediately before and after slavery will appear in the 1870 and 1880 censuses. These are the individuals on whom you will focus your efforts, for they were the last slaves. They made that transitional bridge to freedom as an intact family or a reunited family. Follow the example of

THE NOLANS IN THE 1880 CENSUS

Name	Age	Place of Birth*
Nolan, James	50	Georgia, South Carolina, South Carolina
_____, Bettie	44	Virginia, Virginia, Virginia
_____, Susan	20	Georgia, Georgia, Virginia
_____, Hettie	18	Georgia, Georgia, Virginia
_____, Mary	16	Georgia, Georgia, Virginia

*Birthplace for (1) person being enumerated (2) his/her father, and (3) his/her mother

THE NOLANS IN THE 1870 CENSUS

Name	Age	Birthplace
Nolan, James	40	Georgia
_____, Bettie	32	Virginia
_____, Willa	12	Georgia
_____, Susan	10	Georgia
_____, Hettie	8	Georgia
_____, Mary	6	Georgia
Gandy, Annica	60	South Carolina

the Nolan family below to understand how to identify that transitional family.

Assume that your great-great grandmother was Hettie Nolan and you found her in the 1870 and 1880 censuses with her parents, James and Bettie Nolan, a couple whose names you have never heard or seen until this point. You are happy because a line has been extended in a matter of moments, but work through the logic in the following example to see why your happiness will instantly turn into further curiosity.

What assumptions can you make with this information? They are: James and Bettie Nolan had some form of a slave marriage or union which occurred at least by 1858, the year their first child was born. Bettie was about twenty and James was about twenty-eight. This is probably the entire Nolan family unless there were miscarriages, early infant deaths, or a forced separation due to the sale of an older Nolan child prior to emancipation. This can be assumed because spacing between children is relatively even and none would have been of salable age during slavery, particularly since they are all female. (There was a tendency for young black males between the ages of twelve and twenty-five to be sold off more readily than females.)

A PRIVATE BILL OF SALE, 1857

I have this day sold to C T Nelms of Holly Springs Miss for the consideration of Ten thousand five hundred Dollars the Ten following negroes towit

a man Esqine fifteen years old at Twelve hundred Dollars
boy Willis Twelve " " at Eleven hundred Dollars
" Billy Twelve " " at Eleven hundred Dollars
" Solomon Twelve " " at One thousand Dollars
" Pete Eleven " " at Nine hundred & fifty Dollars
Girl Dinah Nineteen " " at Eleven hundred Dollars
" Amanda Thirteen " " at Eleven hundred Dollars
" Cora Thirteen " " at Eleven hundred Dollars
" Ciller Twelve " " at One thousand Dollars
" Anna Twelve " " at Nine hundred & fifty Dollars
which negroes I warrant to be sound healthy and sensible and slaves for life Feb 23. 1857

Chisolm & Adair

Witness

P W Lucas

Bettie's parents may have still been living in 1880, but James's parents probably were not. The way to figure this out is as follows: Assume that the average age at birth of first child for any enslaved female ancestor ranged between eighteen and twenty-two. Then assume that the ancestor you are researching was born the first child. That number will give you an estimated year of birth for the mother. For James Nolan, this rule would indicate that his mother was born between 1808 and 1812. You could also arrive at an estimated date of birth for James Nolan's father by using the same logic. Nolan's father was probably older than his wife by about five to ten years. (Men tended

SALE OF GILES, A SLAVE, FOR $1400 IN 1859

MEMPHIS, TENN.,

[handwritten bill of sale, dated January 6th 1859: "Received of C. C. Nelms Fourteen Hundred Dollars in full, for the Purchase Money of a Negro Man named Giles aged about Twenty one years. Said Negro We warrant sound and healthy in body and mind, and a Slave for life. We warrant also the title to the same good and perfect against all claims whatever. Given under our hand the day and date above written. Test N. B. Forrest — S. W. McCrary & Co"]

to be far older than their wives when compared to contemporary marriages.) If James Nolan's father was five years older than his mother, then his father would have been born between 1803 and 1807. If ten years older, he would have been born between 1798 and 1802. By 1870, he would have been close to seventy years old or more, a somewhat unlikely age when the life expectancy of a slave is considered.

What inferences can be made about Ms. Gandy? Could Ms. Gandy be Nolan's mother? Perhaps—her probable year of birth is 1810, but you will have to explain the difference in surnames. Another inference is that she probably died between 1870 and 1880. A third is that Ms. Gandy was probably related to the Nolans. Ms. Gandy may have been Bettie's mother or aunt, thus a clue to Bettie's maiden name. She may also have been James Nolan's sister or mother since they were both born in South Carolina. There is no absolute way of knowing by using the census alone since the 1870 census does not state relationships, and she was not in the household in 1880 when the census did include that question. Note that Willa was not in the Nolan household for that year either. Suppose Willa got married, and Ms. Gandy is living with her? Hopefully, you have Willa's married name so that you can return to the 1880 census. If not, you'll have to do some more census digging around the area.

The family that you found in the 1870 census will become the family to focus on for further research. For the Nolans, it will be James, Bettie, Willa, Susan, Hettie, and Annica Gandy. This is the family as it would have looked in 1860 if nothing else changed between 1860 and 1870. This is the family that made the transition to freedom, but you must find their slave owner(s) to go back any further in time.

BRIDGING THE GAP BETWEEN 1860 AND 1870

Assume that you discover James Nolan's owner from your great-grandmother. The slave owner's name was Jeremiah Person. Also, assume that you have made great progress because you have also obtained a copy of Jeremiah's will, probated January 5, 1863. Jeremiah's estate papers contained the following names on the inventory filed by the executor for his estate:

Mose, age 80, $100
Annica, age 50, $400
James, age 35, $900
Ned, age 12, $900
Sandy, age 25, $1800

Pompey, age 30, $1200
Sally, age 25, $1000
Lil Sally, age 25, $1200
Big Mary, age 30, $1200
Other names . . .

What inferences can be drawn from this example now that you've at least gotten back to 1863, and now that you have made that significant transition from freedom to slavery? Can you link anyone in the Nolan household of 1870 to the probate record of 1863? If you take the list by itself, it appears to be a random listing of slaves and their market or sale values. The market values reflect how much work can be expected and any special skills that they possessed. Gender is not indicated, but females, the young, and the old were valued less than "prime" male field hands between sixteen and twenty-five. A carpenter, a barrel maker, or a blacksmith was more valued than a field hand. But these values are all relative and reflect the particular market prevailing in a given locality at a given time. Yes, you do have to think like that, so don't be squeamish. You're now looking at things from someone else's perspective. The values assigned to the work that slaves could do were depressed in the slave exporting areas (Kentucky, Tennessee, Virginia, Maryland, North Carolina, coastal Georgia and South Carolina), but they were inflated in the importing areas (Mississippi, Arkansas, Texas, Louisiana, parts of Missouri and other regions).

Although very few inferences can be directly drawn from this inventory, some may be suggested about the linkages between this list and the Nolan family census date of 1870:

- The ages on the inventory are probably estimates.
- James is probably the same person as James reported in the 1870 census despite the slight age difference.
- Bettie, James's wife, and their three daughters (Willa, Susan, and Hettie) were probably not owned by Person. Or, Person may have given Bettie and her three children to one of his children prior to the list being drawn up. Or, Bettie may have been a slave on a neighbor's plantation. That neighbor may or may not have been related to Person!
- The relationship between James and Ms. Gandy is still unclear. Just because they were owned by Person does not mean that they were related. It only increases the possibility. Now you have to add to your list of surnames to look out for the name Gandy.

In this example, several pieces of evidence link these individuals in two records. Six given names, rough estimates of ages, a link to Person according to oral tradition, a location, and the slave marriage between James and Bettie. But further questions arise: How was the name Nolan acquired? Was it a name that had always been used—indeed, was it the surname of James's father, and might there be other Nolans living in the same area where this family was enumerated in the 1870 census?

As you can see, once you find one bit of information, this leads to a whole series of questions that direct you to other records in an attempt to answer them. Of course, not all the questions that you raise can be answered. If you had been told by your great-grandmother how the Nolan name was acquired, then you would be in a far better position to carry on your research. The absence of any "talk" about surnames in the family's oral tradition may mean that the name was always used and that there was no need to ever discuss the question of surnames.

The Nolan case represents a common problem in African American genealogy. At some point, you will encounter the problem of linking families found in the 1870 census to individuals named in records during slavery. What would you do had you not known the name of the slave owner? Note that finding the name expanded your research, but at the same time it compounded your problems. Hopefully, the techniques outlined in this and subsequent chapters will help you to resolve some of these problems as you go along.

THE UTILITY OF SLAVE SCHEDULES

Starting with the slave schedules would seem to be a natural point in identifying the last owner since these schedules enumerated slave owners by name. These schedules should be more appropriately called schedules of slave *owners* and, incidentally, their slaves. They do not name one slave except when, as mentioned previously, the slave had reached the age of one hundred or the census taker made a mistake, as in the case of the 1860 enumeration of slaves in Hampshire County, West Virginia, and enumerated all slaves by name, a bonus for those with slave ancestry in that county. (David Thackery found this case while studying the schedules for another purpose.) The value of slave schedules lies in making available to researchers the names of nearly all slave owners by county and the composition of their slave population. (Each slave was entered by age, sex, and color.) If the number of slave houses on the property is indicated, you can get a good idea of the number of family units. While the 1850 and 1860 schedules ask for number of runaways in the past year, this information was rarely taken by census enumerators.

Because the schedules were compiled county by county, this partly limits the number of potential slave owners that a researcher has to identify in one county, but not entirely so. Shifflett's book on Louisa County, Virginia, *Patronage and Poverty in the Tobacco Belt*, found a total population of 16,701 people in 1860, of which 765 were slave holders, 1,217 were White families, and 10,194 were slaves, plus a few free black families. Such huge numbers of possible slave owners for one county would not give you much to work with unless you wanted to spend the rest of your life trying to find the individual who owned your ancestors. If you want to know the number of slave owners in your county of research, check the statistical report of the Bureau of the Census for the 1860 census. This can be found in those large public libraries designated to receive federal government publications. You can also count them yourself using the slave schedule.

The slave schedules are of utility only if you can narrow down the possible slave owners by using a reasonable method based on elimination. That method requires you to use the 1850, 1860, and 1870 censuses plus the 1850 and 1860 slave schedules. Ask yourself these questions:

1. Who are the Whites who lived in the same enumeration district with my ancestors in 1870?
2. How many are there?
3. Which of them lived closest to my ancestors in 1870, or . . .
4. Which ones have the same surname as that of my ancestors?
5. If a reasonable number (less than fifteen), can I find them in the 1860 census?
6. Can I find them in the 1850 and 1860 slave schedules listed as slave owners?

This process may take some time. You start with a large number and then narrow that number down until you have a manageable project with no more than five to ten names. It is based on the critical assumption that no significant changes occurred in the residence of slaves or slave owners between the onset of the war in 1861 and 1870; your ancestors lived near or on the same place where they were last slaves, and slave owners continued their lives with their former slaves, who had now become employed laborers. This was indeed the case for a great number of people, but there was some local movement between the end of the war and the year of the 1870 census, as your ancestors attempted to negotiate better labor contracts or even to purchase their own land. Furthermore, slave owners may have died, transferred their property to a new owner or a northern lessee, or moved on.

Despite all these possibilities, you may wind up with a list of fifty or even more. If so, you should proceed to identify those living *closest* to your ancestors whose reported personal and real estate values were the highest or those whose surnames your ancestors carried. While a slave owner's wealth in 1870 may not be the same as in 1860 (the difference being the loss of the value of slaves), they still owned sizable amounts of land.

COMPARING DATA FROM THE 1860 SLAVE SCHEDULE WITH 1870 CENSUS DATA

*A*t the outset, it should be stated that this method is only to be used when you have the name of a possible slave owner. Even then, it is filled with pitfalls. I include it here because it is commonly used as evidence that the household in 1870 is the same as a household in the 1860 slave schedule by merely matching age and sex for each individual. It is not really evidence, but a clue, and should be treated as such.

This technique has little utility without names for the same individuals in 1860 or 1850. It is really not recommended except for small-scale slave owners. But even in this case, it proves little. The descriptions in these schedules can, however, allow you to compare changes in ownership between 1850 and 1860 once you have found the name of the owner. This information can then provide an idea of how many slaves to look for in other documents that might name the same slaves.

THE ACCURACY OF SLAVE SCHEDULES

*T*he slave schedules may not be entirely accurate. Compare the information

SLAVE SCHEDULE 1860

Age	Sex	Year of Birth	Age	Sex	Year of Birth*
67	m	1793	11	m	1849
65	f	1795	11	m	1849
40	m	1820	11	m	1849
38	m	1822	9	f	1851
34	m	1826	8	f	1852
30	m	1830	8	f	1852
28	m	1832	7	f	1853
24	m	1836	6	f	1854
22	m	1838	6	f	1854
21	m	1839	5	f	1855
21	m	1839	4	f	1856
19	m	1841	3	f	1857
19	m	1841	2	f	1858
19	m	1841	2	f	1858
16	m	1844	1	f	1860
15	m	1845	1	f	1860
14	m	1846	1	f	1860
14	m	1846	1	f	1860
12	m	1848	1	f	1860
12	m	1848			

*Estimated year of birth calculated using age given in schedule. Color designation of all enumerated was Black.

from the 1860 slave schedule with that from the slave-owning family Bible.

The number of slaves listed in the Bible who were born in 1860 or before is thirty. The number listed in the slave schedule born in or before 1860 is thirty-nine. Only sixteen matches by age and sex were found. This example shows the many foibles of genealogy, but in the context of this chapter, it shows why matching only age/sex descriptions is an unreliable way to verify owner-

DATA FROM BIBLE OF SLAVE OWNER*

Name	Date of Birth	Name	Date of Birth
Pool(21)	12 February 1839	Harriet(6)	12 May 1854
Sukey(20)	2 February 1840	Abram(6)	16 July 1854
Isaac(18)	6 March 1842	Milly(6)	25 December 1854
Burrel(17)	25 January 1843	Loarney(5)	12 February 1855
Amy(16)	11 October 1844	Charles(5)	26 November 1855
Darcas(18)	September 1842	Harbert(4)	25 November 1856
Eliza(15)	1 March 1845	Julius(3)	2 March 1857
Lucinday(15)	7 December 1845	Cornelius(1)	27 March 1859
Joe(14)	1 February 1846	Daniel(1)	17 April 1859
Horace(12)	17 January 1848	Elmyrah	12 August 1860
Martha(12)	2 October 1848	Ann	19 September 1860
Mary Ann(10)	March 1850	E aster	23 January 1861
Solomon(10)	24 July 1850	Kenion	21 May 1861
David(10)	19 November 1850	Rose	5 September 1861
Isaac(9)	7 January 1851	Nancy	17 April 1862
Agnes(8)	24 April 1852	Emeline	21 March 1863
Ross(8)	24 June 1852	Burrell	25 June 1863
Julia(8)	31 October 1852	John	25 August 1863
Henry(6)	25 January 1852	Frank	2 February 1865

*Excludes five born after 1865. The number in parentheses represents the age of each individual in 1860 determined from the Bible entries.

ship or, of more importance, the *identity* of individuals. The obvious—to compare the lists—assumes no changes occurred in the slave population between the time the entries were made and the date the 1860 census was taken.

This example leads to a number of additional questions: Why are no females of child-bearing age reported in the slave schedule when there were twenty-one children twelve and under? Which list would you guess to be more accurate? These anomalies will have to be analyzed by a very astute researcher indeed!

Slave schedules can provide you with a demographic profile of slaves on one farm or plantation. Given certain profiles, as in the example above, it is possible that slaves of marriageable age may have had spouses on neighboring farms or that misinformation was given by the slave owner. Researchers should also examine schedules to see how slaves were grouped. Often, as in the case above, the pattern of enumerating slaves was by sex and then by age. You might also find other patterns such as those listing slaves by obvious family groupings (male, female, children).

One pattern to look for—whether the slaves on one farm or plantation could have formed family groups without selecting mates from neighboring communities—can be accomplished very easily. Simply count the number of slaves for each category: children (under 15); females and males of marriageable age (18+); females in childbearing years (16–40); the elderly (60 and over). This analysis helps you to understand how self-contained each farm or plantation was. As in the list above, you might raise questions about the presence or absence of children or males between the ages of sixteen and thirty. The slave owner above apparently placed great emphasis on males in this age group, and many of them may have been newly purchased *or* he may have sold off or hired out the females. These schedules help you to make some reasonable guesses and judgments beyond the mere name searching to which genealogists can easily become addicted.

Little research has been done on the usefulness of the slave schedules, but their utility will become clearer as more genealogists find creative uses for them. For example, researchers as a matter of course will have to determine whether slave owners are listed in the order that they are listed on the population schedule. If owners do appear in the same order, it can then be assumed that the schedules have additional utility. Slave owners *listed* near each other can be assumed to have also *lived* near each other.

Occasionally, additional owners' names will appear on the schedules, along with the names of legal owners. This occurs when (1) a deceased slave owner's property is being held in trust and is managed by a court-appointed administrator for an orphan, often indicated with the name of the estate;

(2) a planter owns multiple holdings, in which case his name is followed by the name of the overseer with the words "employee" or "overseer"; or (3) a widow is listed as an owner although her husband was the original owner.

Care should be taken to avoid using the name of heirs rather than the owner's name, a name that will appear on official documents.

A RECAP OF METHODS

*H*ere we repeat the methods outlined above so that you can study and apply them to your own situation. If you've done slave research already, probably you've intuitively selected these methods without really thinking about them.

Step 1: Locate your ancestors in family groups or household units in the 1870 census.

Step 2: Examine the 1870 household to determine which of its members were slaves and their probable ages in 1860.

These are the individuals that you will look for *as a group* in any documents that might contain their names as slaves before emancipation or before 1865. Your goal is to match given names, ages, and genders in documents dated prior to this period of time, namely courthouse and plantation records.

Use the profiles below to help you identify which names to look for and to interpret the patterns that you find. The age of each couple at the time of emancipation determines what kind of household you find in the 1870 census.

Profile 1: Young Couples

Suppose you find that the head of household was twenty-three in 1870. This means that he would have been approximately thirteen in 1860 or a child in a household with his parents or other relations. His future spouse may not have been on the same plantation; therefore, you would focus on locating his slave owner. If you do not know anything about this individual, you will have to first determine the names and ages of his siblings and/or the names and ages of his parents. This is the household that you would use to search pre-1860 records.

The emphasis here is on identifying as much descriptive information for your ancestor and others who were associated with him as possible, because you want to look for *groups* of individuals who are associated with each other. This acts as a control in your research. If your ancestor was named John Thomason, it would be difficult to look for one individual named John in documents naming slaves. But, if your ancestor was John, his siblings were Celie, Robert (or Bob), Susan, and Richard, and his parents were Pompey and Marianne, then you could say with some certainty that this is your John because his name appears in a document with the names of his parents or the names of some of his siblings!

Profile 2: Middle-Aged Couples

Here, "middle-aged" indicates couples in their thirties and forties. The same procedure outlined in Profile 1 applies. But here, you are almost certain that the individuals you are looking for were a couple with young children and they were probably on the same farm or plantation. If they were not, then you would look for the wife with small children and possibly some of her relations using the descriptive information from the 1870 census. Use the following couple as an example:

1870 Census

Husband: Jim(51) Wife: Maria(44) Children: Jim(9) Stephen (5)

In this case, Jim and Maria would probably be together on a farm or plantation, and they may have had other children not named in the 1870 census. Suppose that in 1860, their household looked like this:

1860 Household

Jim(41) Maria(34) Sarah(14) Richard(12) Isaac(10)

In this case, you would be looking for either Jim and Maria as a couple (without knowing about Sarah, Richard, and Isaac) or Maria with children whose names you do not know yet. In order to increase your list of names, you would want to know something about their siblings or something about their parents before beginning your search. Note that Richard and Isaac were twenty-two and twenty in 1870. They would probably appear as individual farm laborers living nearby but not necessarily living in their parents' household.

Profile 3: Older Couples

Suppose you find that your ancestor and his or her spouse are relatively old in 1870. Perhaps they have no children in the household. You would still need to go into your pre-1865 search with more names than two.

INCREASING THE NAME POOL WITH OTHER SOURCES

*T*he household found in 1870 existed in a community whose ties were far stronger than we can imagine today. Try to visualize this community as one that contains individuals who, in addition to sharing the same geographical space, are connected by a common past either through sharing the same slave owner, having the same migration patterns, or having a common ancestor. It would not be unreasonable to supplement your name pool with other individuals living in the same household or adjacent to the household listing in the census without knowing their relationship.

Same Surname Searches

You can expand the pool of potential family members by using the 1870 printed census index for your state. You would want to first list all adult individuals carrying the same surname within the same area and perhaps expand to the enumeration district. Consider these possibilities: Those with the same surname are probably related, but they may also be carrying the former owner's name and related only to that extent. This step is optional, but you will find that it is helpful particularly when you are studying a family with a relatively unique surname. Examine again the Longmire lists generated from 1870 and 1880 census indexes in chapter 4. For families with common surnames such as Johnson, Washington, and Smith, you would want to limit your search to the enumeration district at first. This method is called expanding the name pool for research during slavery.

Ancestors Who Carry the Slave Owner's Surname

This is the simplest and most direct technique that all researchers should try, particularly if their ancestors lived in counties characterized by small-scale slave ownership. It is used when one of your ancestors shares the same surname as that of a nearby White head of household in the 1870 census. For those counties characterized by large-scale plantations, this technique is not as relevant. For example, if your ancestors lived on a Mississippi Delta plantation owned by Augustus Pugh with three hundred people, it is very unlikely that you will find many black Pughs in that area. However, if you find this name-sharing pattern, then you could start with the assumption that some of your ancestors took their last slave owner's name, Pugh. (But remember

Caroline Ravenel, who used to be proud of her name.)

This step is equivalent to "going fishing," but almost every genealogist tries it. It is based on "guessing" that the name sharing between your ancestor and a nearby White family in the 1870 census (or the 1880 census for that matter) represents a relationship between them prior to emancipation—namely slave and slave owner. After finding this pattern, consult the 1860 slave schedule and identify all slave owners with that surname. Assume with some *hope* that one of these individuals was your ancestor's last owner. You would then proceed to focus your research on that slave owner. If you do not find this pattern in the 1870 census, also check the 1860 slave schedule to determine whether your ancestors share a surname with any of the slave owners listed. This check is necessary because (1) the slave owner and his family could have left the area before 1870, (2) the slave owner could have died, and (3) the slave owner could have been skipped by the census taker, though this is unlikely.

Another Fishing Technique with Name Matching

Names that "cluster" together in one location often suggest that the people who carry them are indeed related through common ancestry, except in the cases of Johnsons, Smiths, Washingtons, and other common names. Genealogists, because they are addicted to lists of names, will frequently check the printed indexes to the 1870 census to see if the surname they are researching can be found in other states. If, for example, you find that Carrutherses were enumerated only in Louisiana and Virginia, then you

might be tempted to make the assumption that they have to be connected through a common ancestor.

And your argument may be plausible. Part of the Carruthers family, particularly males who would carry the family surname, may have been sold South to Louisiana at some point between 1790 and 1860. Indeed, it is likely that this occurred between 1830 and 1850 at the height of the domestic slave trade. How will you connect these families if you do not know who their previous owners were, if you have no documentation to link them, and there is no surviving oral tradition about Virginia origins? Suppose you find that some of the Carrutherses enumerated in the 1870 Louisiana census were born in Virginia? What then can you make of the connections? The only thing that you can make of these observations is that you have an additional clue and your work is set out for you. You wouldn't assume that the connections between these Carrutherses are through a common ancestor yet.

Therefore, you have to try to find documentation showing that the Louisiana Carrutherses were sold South or migrated South with their owner and that they originated in the same county of Virginia where you found the Virginia Carrutherses enumerated in 1870. You then have to figure out how these Carrutherses were related. That might carry you into the present where, using a copy of the local phone book, you call various Carrutherses in Virginia trying to find out if they know anything about their family history. Sounds implausible? Not at all. I've known genealogists who have tried it with varying degrees of success. Remember, you have no other evidence to go on. Each clue is almost as good as the next one until you eliminate the bad ones and go with the good ones. The following case study shows how using the same surname search might pay off by locating a possible former owner of an ancestor.

CASE STUDY: THE ANCESTRY OF CAL BOGER

*I*n this section, we will revisit Cal Boger, who first appeared in a previous chapter as a post–Civil War migrant to the Chicago area. Boger's case is in many respects a typical one of name sharing with the former owner, but there is a bit of a twist. Examine this case as it unfolds in the rest of this text.

The most critical clues in Boger's story are:

1. Location: His family members were slaves in Hickory Flats, Georgia.
2. Number of siblings: He had twelve.
3. Two surnames are associated with him: McDonough and Boger.
4. He stated that he had adopted the surname Boger.
5. He was a body servant to Dr. Hard of the 8th Illinois Cavalry.

Several strategies come to mind—the most obvious one being research on the 8th Illinois Cavalry to see if any records survive with regard to Boger. The 8th Illinois was a White cavalry unit, and research on that unit should be conducted to determine (1) the nature of the unit's service, (2) whether any private diaries were written by its members, (3) whether a regimental history has been written on the unit, and (4) whether the payrolls for the unit included Boger,

although it appears that he was "adopted" rather than hired. The point of this investigation would be to determine exactly when, where, and how Boger became associated with Dr. Hard and Captain Hattery.

If Boger were your ancestor, you would definitely want to do research on the 8th Illinois, but at the same time, you could take a more direct approach by using some of the strategies outlined in this chapter—namely, searching the 1870 census for Georgia for the names McDonough and Boger. Since there is a printed index for the 1870 census, your research effort is minimal when compared to researching the 8th Illinois Cavalry. This is what I found merely by checking the 1870 census index and the actual census. Note: To make sure that Hickory Flats was not just a local place name rather than an official name, I first checked an atlas to identify its location (Cherokee County).

BOGER SEARCH: 1870 CENSUS INDEX, GEORGIA

Boger, Martha	Cherokee County, page 241
Boger, Charles	Cherokee County, page 241
Boger, Elijah	Cherokee County, page 253
Boger, Martin	Cherokee County, page 254
Boger, Mary	Cherokee County, page 259
Boger, Sarah	Cherokee County, page 259
McDonough, Mary	Cherokee County, page 449
McDonough, M.	Cherokee County, page 229

Most of these individuals were listed in the Hickory Flats District of Cherokee County. While searching for each of these entries in the actual 1870 census, it appeared that the Hickory Flats District had few Blacks. This should automatically suggest to the researcher that this area was not heavily settled by slave owners, *or* the absence of freedmen could also mean that they migrated out. A check of the 1860 slave schedule could answer this question. The following household information was obtained from the 1870 census.

McDonough, McDuffie
22, Male, White, Farm Laborer, Birth Place = Georgia, Personal Property = $100

Boger, Martha Household
65, Female, White, Farmer, Birth Place = Virginia, Personal Property = NA

Boger, Charles Household
Charles: 46, Male, Black, Farm Laborer, Birth Place = North Carolina

Charity: 30, Female, Black, Keeping House, Birth Place = Georgia (Plus 7 children ranging in age between 5 months and 14)

Boger, Elijah Household
Elijah: 22, Male, Black, Farm Laborer, BP = North Carolina

Mary Ann: 20, Female, Black, Keeping House, BP = Georgia

(Plus two children, ages 1 and 3)

Boger, Martin
37, Male, White, Farmer, Value of Real Estate $100, Value of Personal Property $300, BP = Georgia

(Plus his wife and 3 children and a boarder, William Sherman, whose occupation is listed as Physician)

Boger, Mary A.
45, Female, White, Keeping House, Real Estate $1,500, Personal Property $500, BP = Georgia

(Plus two children ages 8, 9)

Boger, Sarah L.
38, Female, White, Keeping House, Real Estate $2,000, Personal Property $400, BP = Georgia

(Plus two children, 14 and 7, and a White resident farm laborer

McDonough, Mary
66, Female, White, Farmer, Real Estate $750, Personal Property $500, BP = Georgia

If you have the necessary genealogical imagination, already you have probably identified some patterns, the most striking one being the absence of heads of household for all of the older white females. Indeed Charles Boger is the only male on this list who is over forty! What this strongly suggests is that these females are widows, and that many of them are possibly recent widows. It is likely that some of their spouses died shortly before or during the war. If this is the case, a check of the various indexes to Georgia wills, and there are many, will easily tell. What you are actually hoping for is that the spouses died before or during the period of the war because their estate papers will contain information on any slaves they owned. The names of slaves generally do not appear in probate records after 1865—unless the slave owner was, indeed, optimistic!

Another obvious pattern is the proximity of Charles Boger's residence to Martha Boger's in the census index, as well as the possibility that he adopted her surname. A third pattern is the place of birth, and it appears that only Charles Boger and Elijah Boger were born in North Carolina while the rest were born in Georgia. This suggests that (1) Elijah may be Charles's son, (2) they were sold together from North Carolina, and (3) Boger possibly took on a new wife since his present wife is too young to have been Charles's mother or Cal's for that matter. We'll assume for now that the ages are correct. You may also assume that one of the absent (and presumed dead) White male Boger spouses, probably one of the older ones, had been born in North Carolina. A final pattern is that some relationship existed between the Bogers and the McDonoughs, though it is not clear what that relationship is yet.

What of Cal Boger's story that he was owned by a McDonough, and the author's story that Boger took that surname to conceal his identity? First, we don't know whether Boger told this story or whether the writer of the article invented his own explanation for how Cal decided to conceal his identity. However, we know that the surname adoption story was probably untrue. To conceal his identity, he would have adopted a name not associated with *any* individual in the area, and though he was young, he certainly wouldn't have adopted McDonough. That would have been a dead giveaway. The most plausible explanation for now is that he was perhaps "hired out" as a slave to one of the McDonoughs. Or, McDonough could have acquired some of the Boger children prior to the war, perhaps to settle a debt owed by Boger.

It appears that the McDonoughs and the Bogers may have been connected through kinship, but that should be determined by locating a genealogy for at least one of the families. It is also possible that Charles Boger is Cal Boger's father, and at the end of the war, he may have chosen to work for his original owner, Martha Boger or her spouse (now presumably deceased). One additional explanation, though farfetched, is just as plausible since we don't know yet. That is, Cal Boger could have claimed that McDonough was his owner when in fact, Martha Boger and her husband were the true owners.

As you can see, the explanations can become as wide-ranging as the information with which you start. The point is to use the information that you have to construct some reasonable assumptions. Working with those assumptions, you would look for additional records, in this case any Cherokee County probate records that may have been filed by the Bogers and the McDonoughs. These records will almost certainly begin to reveal part of the story. *The Handy Book for Genealogists* reveals that Cherokee County deeds are complete except for Book Q, and Will Books A and B are lost. Since you would be concerned with will books first, you should know that Books A and B probably cover the early period of the county's history (1810s). One final tidbit: There is a place called Boger City in Lincoln County, North Carolina, about twenty-five miles northwest of Charlotte and no more than three hundred miles northeast of the Cherokee County seat! With such an unusual name, how could you go wrong?

FINDING THE LAST SLAVE OWNER THROUGH A LAND SEARCH

*T*he land search, using tract books and township plat maps, is one of the best approaches to identifying the names of potential slave owners. As mentioned previously, land descriptions were sometimes used for naming enumeration districts. If you are lucky, you may even find that the enumerator supplied additional information not requested by the Census Bureau, such as the name of the farm or plantation. If you find either of these to be the case, or if you have found that your ancestors owned land, your search is going to be a more direct one. Using tract books along with your map from the state's highway department, you could start your search using a number of approaches. Using the township and range where your ancestors lived in 1870, you could use the names of land owners listed in the tract book as potential slave owners. First, however, you would want to list the names of whites who lived closest to your ancestors in 1870 using the methods above and then follow up by locating their names in the county tract books for 1870 and 1860.

The land search is far more accurate because land records, especially tract books and early plat maps, will show original ownership as well as changes that have occurred over time. This lets you re-create a community by its land ownership, and since slave owners owned land, these records help you to pinpoint where your ancestors were in almost minute detail. Tract books are maintained at the county courthouse. They list ownership of every piece of land in the county by township and range or some other unit if your state of research is one of the original colonies. Note that the land is further divided into sections and then into lots. Plat maps are legal renditions of a tract of land drawn up when the land is officially surveyed.

For every range and township quadrant, the tract book will list approximately 36 sections of 640 acres each, providing the land is not situated near irregularly shaped bodies of water. Because most slave-owner land holdings often exceeded 640 acres, you should find far fewer than 36 slave owners for every quadrant. Two examples are listed below to show how this technique might work. One is for a large plantation region in Mississippi and the other is for Township 7.

Note that the tract book indicates when the land was purchased. That will give you an idea of when the area began to be settled. Note also that for Issaquena County, only five presumed slave owners are listed, and for Township 7, Range 15, only two were listed. You would have to follow the purchase of land in these sections to identify all owners up through 1865. That list will become your list of potential slave owners to research over time.

Historical maps and plat maps for the South that show land ownership are worth locating. Microfilmed tract books can be ordered and used at most LDS stake libraries or state archives and the original can be used in the county courthouse. The Library of Congress houses one of the largest collections of local land-ownership maps in the country. To determine whether a map of your county of research is housed at the Library, check the index to the book *Land Ownership Maps* by Stephenson. A copy of the map can then be ordered from the Library of Congress through its photo duplication department.

OTHER POST-1865 METHODS TO IDENTIFY THE LAST SLAVE OWNER

Most methods to identify the last slave owner are linked to creative uses of census records or the Freedmen's Bureau

ISSAQUENA COUNTY (MISS.) TRACT BOOK: TOWNSHIP 11, RANGE 9, SECTIONS 16–20

Section	Acres	Purchaser	Date of Sale
16, Lot 1	95	McCullough & Duncan	24 June 1831
16, Lots 2, 3	196	Joseph Dunbar	28 Jan 1833
Remaining lots not apportioned—			
17, Fract.	136	William E. Hall	13 Jan 1835
18	306	Duncan & McCullough	13 Jan 1835
18	320	Castleman	28 Dec 1835
19	All	Haynes & Overton	28 Dec 1835
20 (N 1/2)	320	Castleman	13 Oct 1835
	240	Dunbar	28 Jan 1833

records. You will also want to examine courthouse records as a routine matter to determine whether your ancestors owned land or made transactions with local Whites that required recording. These transactions may lead you to adding other possible slave owners to your list to research. Courthouses do not have anything called "Sharecroppers Records"; however, you may find that these transactions were registered in deed books, crop lien records, or mortgage books of all kinds. Do not assume that your ancestors,

BUTLER COUNTY (ALA.) TRACT BOOK, TOWNSHIP 7, RANGE 15, SECTION 14

Section	Acres	Purchaser	Date of Sale
NE 1/4 of NE 1/4	40	Unsold	
NW 1/4 of NE 1/4	40	Unsold	
SE 1/4 of NE 1/4	40	Unsold	
SW 1/4 of NE 1/4	40	Unsold	
NE 1/4 of NW 1/4	40	Unsold	
NW 1/4 of NW 1/4	40	Jas W. Shine	14 Dec 1853
SE 1/4 of NW 1/4	40	Jas W. Shine	18 Dec 1852
SW 1/4 of NW 1/4	40	Jas W. Shine	16 Feb 1849
NE 1/4 of SE 1/4	40	Unsold	
SE 1/4 of SE 1/4	40	Unsold	
W 1/4 of SE 1/4	40	Archibald M. Reid	21 Oct 1839
NE 1/4 of SW 1/4	40	Jas W. Shine	16 Feb 1849
NW 1/4 of SW 1/4	40	Jas W. Shine	5 Jan 1844
South 1/2	40	Jas W. Shine	20 Feb 1844

because they were landless, will not appear in deed books. One of my students showed me a note for a mule that one of her ancestors had mortgaged!

Using the Agricultural Censuses

You may also use the 1870 and 1880 agricultural censuses to reconstruct possible ties between former slave owners and freedmen. By identifying all White farmers enumerated near your ancestors in the 1870 and 1880 agricultural censuses, you may then use the population censuses to identify potential slave owners in a given area. The 1880 agricultural census provides a space for the number of employees in the past year. This will give you an indication of the number of potential freedmen to look for living near that particular farmer. In addition, the agricultural censuses can be used to narrow the number of potential slave owners to look for. Careful! Reconstructing families and relationships over a ten- to twenty-year span is more difficult than it appears. Many changes could have occurred in these households. Therefore, the agricultural censuses represent only an additional tool for you to use—not certain proof that your ancestors worked for a particular individual as tenant farmers or sharecroppers.

Finally, though labor contracts were covered in a previous chapter, it might be important to emphasize their relevance again. While the large body of contracts are not indexed, it might be worth your effort to comb through those for your county of research, particularly after you identify a group of potential slave owners, since a great majority of former slaves did sign contracts with their last owners.

Finding the Name of One Slave Owner Leads to Finding Others

If you identify a couple who married during slavery and you know at least one of the owners but have not found evidence that the spouse was owned by the same slave owner, you will want to make the following assumption: Their slave owners lived near each other. Researching nearby slave owners for the spouse whose owner is unknown will usually turn up a slave owner. (Spouses almost certainly lived within walking distance of each other, generally no more than five miles apart.) Once you have identified one slave owner, you will want to begin to try to reconstruct the relationships that this owner had with neighboring slave owners, some of whom owned your ancestors.

Obstacles to Using These Techniques

These techniques are based on an often tenuous series of clues and many assumptions about the predictability of your ancestors' behavior. They are not guaranteed, partly because so little research has been done on this problem. What you are trying to do is to take one family whose members probably did not exceed seven individuals and match them to one slave owner out of a list of ten to fifteen, with that list being derived through a process of elimination. Imagine that you have a lens focused on a map of the whole county. It is then progressively narrowed until you focus on your ancestors and the individuals who lived around them. You are then making a good guess that these individuals were linked by common ancestry (i.e., they were related to each other) *or* that they were linked as former slave and former owner.

One obstacle that you will encounter is

time. In effect, you may wind up spending a considerable amount of time doing a whole community study because of the limited amount of information that you start with. Another is that conditions found in the 1870 census do not reflect the same conditions that existed prior to the Civil War. In effect, you may wind up falsely assuming that your ancestors and their previous owners did not migrate. You are also partly assuming that the Civil War did not disrupt these relationships. Many things could have occurred between 1861, when the war started, and 1870, when your ancestors were fully enumerated in the 1870 census.

WHEN ALL EFFORTS FAIL

*I*f these techniques do not work for you, then try another line or go directly to the county deed and will books starting with 1865 and work back five years at a time, abstracting transactions involving slaves. Of course, you should check first to see whether someone has abstracted and published these volumes before you begin your own project. While these books do show a lot of activity, it is not likely that the average slave owner had major transactions every six months or every year. It is more likely that his activities

with respect to slaves would have occurred in longer cycles. In this case, published abstracts and indexes of wills and deeds may help you, particularly if the publisher of these volumes included the names of all slaves named in such transactions. However, it is best to use the original records themselves (on site or microfilm). This is recommended for those researchers who are certain that their ancestors were in the county for a long period of time prior to emancipation. Finally, you may wind up with a complete index of slaves and owners before you get to your ancestors, and even then you may not find all of them. You can, however, publish the results from your indexing project, a contribution that equals the research you will have compiled on your own ancestry.

Finally, you aren't finished yet. This chapter was devoted to techniques to use to locate the last slave owner. Now you have to trace the steps of the slave owner and his transactions over his lifetime and that of his ancestors, if they owned slaves. At least you will have supplemented your knowledge about the county and area of research, an aspect of research which is often, though mistakenly, overlooked when the names of slave owners are known. Know the lay of the land!

Chapter 11

THE RECORDS
OF SLAVERY

The records are there;
you just have to make
the connecting links!

FROM AN AFRICAN AMERICAN GENEALOGIST

DEVISING A STRATEGY OF RESEARCH BASED ON THE TYPE OF SLAVE OWNER

*T*he process of identifying a slave owner, discussed in the previous chapter, should help you to understand the type of community in which your ancestors lived prior to emancipation. Those of your ancestors who lived on large plantations led lives that were quite different from those who lived on a small farm with perhaps five to ten slaves or less. Those who lived on large plantations in Virginia or South Carolina also had qualitatively different lives from those who lived on large plantations in the Mississippi Delta or in the sugar-growing regions of Louisiana.

Those who were either sold or migrated with their owners to the Lower South between 1790 and 1860 (Alabama, western Georgia, Louisiana, Mississippi, Arkansas, Missouri, Florida, and Tennessee) lived lives that were also qualitatively different from the lives their parents had led one generation away in the Upper South (Virginia, Maryland, North and South Carolina, Kentucky, parts of Tennessee and coastal Georgia). Those who had experienced northern slavery, most of which had been abolished no later than 1810, lived lives that were con-

siderably different from their fellow slaves in all of the South—from Delaware all the way to New Orleans.

Those owned by the relatively small, educated, planter elite in all states also led lives that may have differed from the rest of their enslaved brethren on small farms and small slave holdings. Finally, those who lived on newly forming plantations and farms had lives that were significantly different from those who had been born into old, stable slave communities. These variations are important to understand because they are connected to nearly every issue that affected the lives of your ancestors as slaves—from the quality of housing in which they lived to their chances for gaining freedom prior to the onset of the Civil War all the way down to the present, and the most essential of your concerns now: the number and quality of records that your ancestors' owners left behind.

Your strategy of research must be based on some idea of the circumstances in which your ancestors lived at each period of their enslavement—principally their locations, their migration experiences, their history of being sold, and most important, the number of slaves owned by the planter or farmer who owned them. Having this information can help you to situate your ancestors in the context of a slave community, a community that may or may not have been stable over time.

There are two types of communities that, though at polar extremes, can give you some idea of how to proceed in reconstructing your ancestors' kinship ties. One type is the slave community on a very large plantation. Such a community may have contained one hundred or more slaves, may have consisted of twenty to thirty families, and may show some generational continuity over time—perhaps not having been affected by the vicissitudes that did beset many planter families. Such communities were rare because the whole logic of slavery fed on what Stephen Oakes called a "continuous cycle of buying more slaves and land to plant more cotton, tobacco, sugar cane or rice to buy more slaves and land . . ." without end. This meant that the children of a large planter frequently set out to establish themselves in new locations, often with the slaves inherited from their father. A slave community that had become stable, perhaps over a one-hundred-year period in Virginia, could have been dispersed over several states in a matter of a few years. Slaves who had grown up in a large community on a Virginia plantation or slaves who had been owned by a small-scale planter in a heavily populated region of Maryland may have found themselves somewhere on the Georgia-Alabama frontier, surrounded by a real frontier with only a few planter families located miles apart.

A second type of community emerged among slaves who lived on several nearby small farms or plantations. This community could also have developed over time, perhaps having been affected by slave sales in only a small way—that is, local sales rather than having their relatives sold far away. In this type of community, kinship, marriage, and other ties existed across plantations and farms rather than being bound on one large plantation. A separate type of analysis is called for in reconstructing the ties between slaves on small-scale farms.

STATISTICS ON SLAVE OWNERSHIP

Once you begin to read widely, you will find one often-cited statistic. In a sense, it is somewhat of an anomaly, but it is used to show how variable the institution of slavery was from the perspective of both the slave and the owner. It is this: the majority of slave owners owned five or fewer slaves, but the majority of slaves lived on holdings where the number of slaves exceeded twenty. What this means for your research is that your ancestors were more likely to have lived on large holdings rather than on small holdings, more likely to have lived in association with other slaves than as isolated slaves on a small farm with a struggling planter. But the regional and historical variations for slave ownership are so great that it would serve you well to know first what type of slave holdings were more likely to exist for the period of time and region on which your research is focused.

By 1860, there were approximately 400,000 slave holders, representing a very small portion of the White adult male population in the South. About 20 percent of this number would have been considered part of the planter class, owning twenty or more slaves each. Ownership of twenty slaves as a cutoff point between being a farmer and a planter seems small, but it was not. Even using $500 as the average value of a slave, a planter with ten slaves was worth $5,000, and a planter with twenty was worth $10,000. That was a lot of money for those times.

Slave ownership during the colonial period was often characteristic of Anglo upper-class settlers, many of whom came to this country with money or endowments already. Because slaves were always expensive relative to individual wealth for all periods of slavery, the tendency to associate slave ownership with that class would not be entirely inappropriate. According to Stephen Oakes, in his study of slave owners, this class had pretty much taken up the most productive land before the close of the eighteenth century. Thus, those entering the slave-owning class after that time were more likely to have inherited their wealth than to have acquired it through some other means. Finally, for those slave owners who inherited slaves, further upward mobility almost always meant migration into new areas beyond the original colonies after 1790.

The Rules

There is one rule that generally applies to the records left by slave owners: The smaller the slave owner, the fewer the surviving records and the greater your reliance on public records. Conversely, the larger the slave owner, the greater the number of records and the greater the reliance on his surviving personal papers (private records). You will spend just as much time in researching the records of small-scale owners as you would with large-scale planters.

For the small-scale owner, you will often have to use wills, deeds, censuses, and other local records, generally housed at the courthouse or the state's archives, to reconstruct the lives of your ancestors in slave communities. For large planters, you will generally rely on surviving personal and business records. These records are often located either at the state's archives or in a major historical collection—generally as part of a university library or historical society. However, researchers should know that small-scale slave owners often had ancestors or relatives who themselves were relatively large-scale owners. Therefore, the number of slaves owned at a particular point in time is only one among many clues that you will have to use.

A second rule about records that you will need to understand is that every step involves two distinct activities: One is the search and the other is the analysis. You will often spend more time searching than analyzing, but even the search involves some analysis, and at the least, a process of eliminating different paths of research. Finding out that the records you need are housed at the University of Texas leads you either to search for a microfilmed version of the records or to plan to look at the records firsthand. Finding out that a planter didn't arrive in Twiggs County, Georgia, until 1845 will prevent you from assuming that records exist on the planter in Twiggs County prior to 1845. (Of course, in this case, slaves who had lived in Twiggs County before he arrived may have been purchased by him after he arrived.)

A third rule is that you will not be analyzing nuclear families (father, mother, children) but lists of slaves in an attempt to reconstruct enough kinship ties to identify with some certainty your own direct line of ancestry.

A fourth rule is that there is no step-by-step process as in the first section of this book. While you will generally follow the rule about working from the present to the past, you may find records dated at widely diverging years, in which case you will have to fill in the gaps. This is in part due to the fact that you are tracing either slave inheritance patterns or slave sales over a long period of time. For example, you might find first a list of slaves dated 1850 and then later search for any bills of sale recorded in the county's deed books. Or, you might find that John Smith inherited one of your ancestors and his sister inherited his spouse.

A fifth rule is that greater reliance will be placed on deed and probate records for the small-scale farmer/planter, the goal being to reconstruct the process of his acquiring slaves and their subsequent establishment of marriage and family ties.

A sixth rule is that the surviving lists of slaves kept by large-scale planters (located in their personal and business papers) should be analyzed first, followed by an analysis of their probate and deed records. The planters' lists should represent the maximum number of slaves owned by the planter, whereas will and deed records, by their nature, may show only partial lists because planters acquired slaves through inheritance or purchase over time. For example, nearly four hundred transactions relating to the affairs of Stephen Duncan were counted in the will and deed books for one county alone. Duncan was one of the largest planters in the history of the United States. This rule assumes that you will be researching both sets of records at the same

time, more or less. The analysis stage is where you will deal with the planters' lists first and then cross-check their contents with what you find in the probate, deed, and other courthouse records using the dates from the planters' lists as markers. This process will ultimately lead you to nearly a complete picture.

A final rule is that the consequences of moving or selling one million slaves South between 1790 and 1860 will be felt in all of your research for the period between 1790 and 1870. The section on the domestic slave trade and the settlement of the Lower South will help you to understand why this is the case.

THE ANONYMOUS SLAVE MYTH

*T*here is no such thing as an anonymous slave or a slave without history. The study of slaves and their descendants is the study of survivors, as your presence attests. There are, however, slaves who cannot be documented. The only way to find out, however, is to do the research and know why the knowledge of some slaves is lost forever. As one genealogist put it, the records are there, but you simply have to make the connecting links through your thorough research. Know that documenting the life of a slave who had a history of being sold is quite different from documenting his root family, which may have remained intact. Blassingame's collection of slave narratives is well worth reading as a source to fertilize your own imagination about the possible experiences that your ancestors may have had, though they remained unwritten and untold to you as a part of your family's collective memory.

The Genealogy of Slaves Is the Genealogy of Slave Owners

*T*he world in which slaves lived started and stopped with the slave owner. That the slave owner was at the center of the slave community's existence was often felt directly and intensely if the slave owner had no more than ten to twenty slaves. On larger farms and plantations, the slave owner's existence could be more remote and mediated through an overseer. On very large plantations, indeed, it was quite possible, though unlikely, never to have seen the individual who owned you. Though large-scale planters may have been remote, every event in their lives affected the slaves they owned, and slaves were often attuned to those events, if not knowing them down to their last detail.

The key events in the life cycle of slave owners also determined in large part the cycle of a particular slave community. As in the example of the Goosby family and their slave Senah, the elder Goosby had, through purchases of slaves from his neighbors or directly from Africa, built up a relatively stable slave community. At the time of his death, this particular community was transformed and fragmented, eventually being dispersed to Georgia and Mississippi where new communities were formed.

Because planters or their children constantly migrated farther West and South, the generational cycle of a slave community could be interrupted by the same migrations, in which case it was often a matter of transplanting the community. In other cases, particularly in the Upper South during the domestic slave trade (1790 to 1860), slave communities often went through a process of whittling away through sales of slaves to traders. The most drastic changes occurred, however, with estate divisions of insolvent or indebted planters, where slave communities were completely broken up. Therefore, slave communities rarely remained intact and in one place over a very long period of time. In sum, the generational depth of a slave community or its age depended in large measure on the stability and endurance of the planter family over time. Those showing the most generational depth would be the communities in the original colonial areas, and even here, slave communities were formed and then dispersed according to the fortunes of slave-owning families.

The Records to Collect

*T*he essential records that should be collected or located for the slave owner under study are his estate records and his surviving personal and financial papers. A summary of the kinds of records and information that you will need on the owner follows:

A basic genealogy of the slave-owning family

Conveyance or deed records over the owner's lifetime

Church affiliation and his practices with regard to the church affiliations of his slaves

Military service including Civil War, Revolutionary War, and War of 1812

A census profile over his lifetime or adulthood

Tax entries for the county of residence

Land ownership (plat map and/or legal description)

Personal papers (account books, day books, diaries, slave lists, etc.)

Estate records (will, inventory and appraisement, annual returns, etc.)

In studying slave-owning families, you want to obtain basic information that will maximize your chances of locating any documentation on your ancestors. Note that the term is *slave-owning family*, and not just one slave owner. Once you locate an owner, you will have to re-create his familial and business ties because these will show the inheritance patterns that you need to focus on. For example, if you find that Wilbert Scott and Tabitha Jones Scott had five sons and three daughters, you will need to know their names, their spouses' names, their children, their places of residence, as well as vital events such as dates and places of birth, marriage, and death. You would also need to know the same information for the parents of both Wilbert and Tabitha. This is the minimum (three generations) that you would need in order to examine the patterns of inheritance in this family. This sounds easy enough; however, it is quite time-consuming, as you will shortly see.

CASE STUDY: THE PARTIALLY RECONSTRUCTED GENEALOGY OF A SMALL-SCALE PLANTER

*I*n the course of doing research on one of my ancestors, Charlotte Nix, I had to use materials collected from various genealogies and local histories to reconstruct a partial genealogy of the slave-owning family. Take note of how complex the study of a family's written genealogy can become, particularly if there is extensive name sharing from one generation to the next. This is what I found by using three sources of information, some of which conflicted and some of which had been recopied (perhaps without verification) from the earliest genealogy of this family.

The Basic Story

One Phillip Perry III of Nancemond County, Virginia, had approximately eleven children. Apparently the family's oral tradition states that in 1746 seven of them, all brothers, arrived in a part of Granville County, North Carolina, which would later become Franklin County, North Carolina. No documentation exists on the three sisters who are occasionally mentioned nor is there any direct proof that all of the seven males were brothers. Proof has often been established using proximity of residence and relationships stated in various land and estate transactions. The seven brothers were Jeremiah, John, Francis, Joshua, Nathaniel, William, and Burwell. Of the seven, lineages had been established for four of them—Jeremiah, John, Nathaniel, and Burwell.

A Rough Chart of Known Lineages

Using the three printed sources, I was able to come up with a rough chart to guide me in my research. The chart follows.

Note that the second generation contains three Johns, three Burwells, and three Jeremiahs, all cousins. This will cause considerable confusion in researching records using names only. However, the Perry family devised a method of distinguishing those with the same given names. In legal records, they used terms such as "redhead" or "red"

Jeremiah (?–1778)	John (?–1796?)	Nathaniel (?–1790)	Burwell (1735?–1803)
Spouse: Unknown	Spouse: ?	Spouse: ?	Spouse: Elizabeth Massey
Willis (1756–?)	Solomon	Drury	Jeremiah (1761–1838)
Jeremiah (1757–?)	Ruth	Ephraim	Joshua
John (1769–1859)	Rebecca	Sarah	Rachel
Burrell (1767–?)	Mary	Miss	Mary
3 sisters, not named	Miss		Burwell
	Burwell		John
	Anna		Edith
	John		
	Abey		
	Jeremiah		
	Abraham		
	Bennett		

to distinguish between them. Care must be taken, because it is easy to place an individual in the wrong lineage or the wrong period of time when you don't have other descriptive information such as dates of birth and death or a spouse's name.

Since I know that John, the son of the elder Jeremiah, owned one of my ancestors, the names of his children and his wife would be of particular interest in my research. John married Ruth Strickland (1779–1843), his second cousin around 1797. Around 1829, he and his family moved to Georgia and eventually settled in Russell County, Alabama. They had ten children, some of whom migrated farther west into Alabama and possibly other states. Those children were Willis, Strickland, John Madison, Jane, Mary, Ruth, Amaryllis, Eliza, Patience, and Frances. Jane, the fifth child, was granted Charlotte and her children in a deed of trust in Russell County, Alabama. Jane and her husband, Edward, eventually settled in Butler County, Alabama.

Some Rules for Locating and Using Published Genealogies of Slave-Owning Families

In general, published genealogies should be evaluated on the consistency of information found therein. Remember the general rule and avoid overreliance on only one source. In addition, if the same information is repeated in all sources, locate the original source and evaluate the evidence used. Identify any inconsistencies in the sources. For example, each source indicated that none of the original brothers fought in the American Revolution since they were Loyalists, but a more recently published source indicated that the first Jeremiah was killed fighting on the American side! No one source can be accepted as an authority until you check the records yourself. Since researchers will often recopy lineages, particularly those not in their direct line, assume that the researcher has done a more thorough job on his own line and has perhaps failed to verify information for other lines.

Locating genealogies on slave-owning families can be difficult, particularly if the family was dispersed throughout the South. So too will be their genealogies, which will appear as branches of a root family from the place of origin. Surname files at state archives, local historical societies, the county's public library, bibliographies of published genealogies, genealogical periodical indexes, various family directories, the Ancestral Data file at your local LDS stake library, and hereditary society files like those maintained by the DAR Library in Washington, D.C., should be checked as a matter of good research. Using the observations about the various Perry genealogies should be a warning to good researchers. At the same time, having access to what the family members have published about themselves is far better than having to start from scratch and reconstruct a genealogy yourself. Your first line of attack, therefore, is to locate as much information as possible about the slave-owning family after you have located the name of the last slave owner.

BUILDING A CENSUS PROFILE OF THE SLAVE OWNER

*T*he genealogy of a slave-owning family will help you to trace inheritance and migration patterns. In effect, the slave owner's genealogy is like a skeletal outline that you will use just as you would use your own family's genealogy during freedom. In addition to the genealogy, there are other things that you will need to do in order to complete the picture. One especially helpful strategy is to build a census profile.

This is perhaps the easiest thing to do,

though it too has its pitfalls. In addition to identifying individuals in the slave owner's household for each census year, you will also want to count the number of slaves owned. Unlike the post-1850 censuses, the 1790 to 1840 censuses enumerate by name only the head of household, thereby making it difficult to identify names of females and children in the household. Other household members and slaves are listed only in age/sex categories. The 1790, 1800, and 1810 censuses list only total number of slaves owned; the 1820, 1830, and 1840 censuses listed slaves by age and sex categories under the name of the slave owner.

You will also want to use the county tax lists for years in between the census to identify number of slaves owned and any changes in that number. This helps you to narrow down to specific years when the slave owner purchased, sold, or lost slaves through other means such as death.

SURVEY TRANSCRIPTIONS OF CHURCH RECORDS

*D*etermining the slave owner's religious affiliation may be difficult unless you have access to a variety of transcribed or indexed church and cemetery records for the county of research. Researchers should be familiar with the presence of major denominations in certain areas and the early role of the Anglican church during the colonial period. This information you will find during the stage when you researched the county history. While Methodists and Baptists were eventually in the majority, places like New Orleans and its surrounding parishes would obviously indicate a strong

EXAMPLE OF A SLAVE INSURANCE POLICY FOUND IN A PLANTER'S PERSONAL RECORDS

LIFE DEPARTMENT. AGENCY AT NEW ORLEANS.

ÆTNA INSURANCE CO., HARTFORD, CONN.

 ANNUITY FUND, $150,000;

Exclusively held, pledged and appropriated, with its reserved accumulations, by the Charter and regulations of the Company, to the payment of annuities and losses connected with Life Assurance only...and in no event to be liable for the other debts, contracts or engagements of the Company.

SLAVE POLICY.

This Policy of Insurance Witnesseth, That THE ÆTNA INSURANCE COMPANY, In consideration of the sum of ...Seventeen and 25/100... Dollars, to them in hand paid by ...Mrs. Mary Raby... DO INSURE THE LIFE OF THE WITHIN-NAMED SLAVE OR SLAVES, for the term of ...One (June) or Twelve... months, in the amount set opposite his or her name. Loss, if any, payable to ...Mrs. Mary Raby... for the benefit of ...herself... amounting to the total sum of ...Six Hundred... Dollars, according to the Application of said ...Mrs. Mary Raby... bearing date the ...Fifteenth... day of ...October... one thousand eight hundred and fifty ...three... and deposited in the Office of this Company.

And the said Company do hereby Covenant and Bind Themselves, well and truly to pay to the said ...Mrs. Mary Raby... of the Parish or County of ...New Orleans... State of ...Louisiana... within ninety days after due proof of the death of the within-named Slave, Slaves, or any of them, the amount insured and set opposite the name or names of the deceased, deducting therefrom all indebtedness on this Policy at that time: PROVIDED, he, she or they die within the period embraced in this Policy, to wit: From twelve o'clock (at noon) on the ...Fifteenth... day of ...October... one thousand eight hundred and fifty ...three... until twelve o'clock (at noon) on the ...Fifteenth... day of ...October... one thousand eight hundred and fifty ...four... for which said payment, the said Annuity Fund, with its reserved accumulations is solely and exclusively pledged and appropriated.

And it is hereby understood and expressly declared to be the true intent and meaning of this Policy, and the same is accepted by the Assured, that if the Application subscribed by the said ...Mrs. Mary Raby... shall be in any respect untrue or incorrectly stated — or if the said Slave or Slaves, or any of them shall die by his, her or their own hands — or by any injury inflicted in an attempt to commit suicide — or by the hands of justice — or in violation of law — or by the hands of a mob — or by a foreign invasion — or by an insurrection — or by the neglect, abuse, or maltreatment of the owner, or any one to whom he, she or they shall be entrusted — or shall be laboring under any chronic disease at the time of issuing this Policy — or shall be forced, permitted or entreated, by his, her or their owner, or by the agent of the owner, to engage in any combat causing his, her or their death — or shall abscond or be kidnapped — or shall, without the consent of this Company previously obtained and endorsed on or attached to this Policy, be taken or permitted to be taken to more Southern localities (if South of the 35th degree North latitude) than that in which insured, between the fifteenth day of July and the fifteenth day of November, or engage the said Slave or Slaves in any more hazardous occupations than those enumerated and set opposite his, her or their name or names — or in the event of any previous Insurance, (or subsequent, without the consent of this Company previously obtained and endorsed on or attached to this Policy,) on the life or lives of the within-named Slave or Slaves — then, and in all such cases, the said Company shall not be liable for the payment of the sum insured and set opposite the name or names of the said Slave or Slaves deceased, or any part thereof; and this Policy, so far as relates to said payment, shall be utterly void.

And it is further Agreed, That in every case where this Policy shall cease, or become, or be, null or void, all previous payments made thereon, shall be forfeited to the said Company. N. B.—*This Policy not assignable without the consent of the Company, previously obtained and endorsed on or attached thereto.*

In Witness Whereof, The said ÆTNA INSURANCE COMPANY have, by their Vice President and

Catholic influence. If you know nothing about the slave owner except that he lived in the New Orleans area, you might want to assume at the outset that he was a member of the Catholic church. If you are researching a slave owner in low-country South Carolina, then the Episcopal church would be the likely affiliation. There are other major denominations that had a clear impact on the status of slaves and slavery. The Moravians and the Quakers are obvious examples. If you know that individual Quakers emancipated many of their slaves and one of your ancestors was owned by a Quaker at some point, then obviously searching Quaker church records would be of extreme importance in your research.

Because slaves were frequently admitted and baptised as members of the slave owner's church, it would be a mistake to assume that no such records exist—even for small rural churches. The records of various Louisiana Catholic parishes have been abstracted, including marriages and baptisms of some slaves. The records of some Episcopal churches, particularly those in low-country South Carolina, contain the names of slave members as well as the dates of their baptisms. Consider the following part of a membership register taken from the microfilm series of early South Carolina churches:

THE SLAVE OWNER'S WILL

*T*here are two approaches to locating a will for the slave owner. One is to rely on a will index that has been compiled for the whole or part of a state, often called a *tes-*

COLOURED BAPTISMS

Names	Masters' Names	Baptised
Wally	Dr. Edward Brailsford	Jan 1, 1837
Sancho	James S. McPherson	Jan 7, 1837
Anthony	James S. McPherson	April, 1838
Renchy	James S. McPherson	April, 1838
Abby	Rev. S. Elliott Se__?	April, 1838
Mary	Rev. S. Elliott Se__?	April, 1838
Hagar	Rev. S. Elliott Se__?	April, 1838
Bella	John Heyward	August, 1838
Sarah	Mrs. Pritchard	August, 1838
Clarissa	James S. McPherson	Jan, 1839
Claudia	James S. McPherson	Jan, 1839
Monday	James S. McPherson	Jan, 1839

Source: Thackery Workshop on African American Genealogy. Original record part of South Carolina Historical Society's microfiche series of low-country (Charleston area) church records.

tators index, and the other is to search through the index of each will book yourself using the slave owner's name (on microfilm or at the courthouse). Note that the statewide indexes do not include all wills for a given state. If you rely on a statewide index, always follow up with an examination of the indexes for individual will books. Once you find the will, your task is not over, as you can see from the following transcription of John Perry's will, which names my great-great-great grandmother Charlotte. (Note that when you transcribe wills, you must copy them just as they appear. Do not correct spellings or grammar.)

When I started researching this line, I knew little about Charlotte Nix except that she was buried in a local United Methodist Cemetery along with some of her children and their spouses. I didn't know that she had been owned by relatives in one family nor that for the last twenty years of slavery, she had been owned by the daughter of her original owner. In fact, Charlotte and her children were being held in trust by John M. Perry (Jane's brother), and in the event of her death, ownership of Charlotte and her children would revert to him rather than to his sister's husband. I didn't know that dower slaves (slaves owned by a wife but not by her husband) are often difficult to trace. What had preoccupied me for most of my early research was that someone in the family had surely heard about her since she had died in 1895. I wasted much time not wanting to believe otherwise. I resigned myself to the possibility that some memories are not for keeps.

I had access to two excellent books, one a Nix genealogy and the other a local history of the area authored by one of the Nix descendants who still lived there). Having

located these materials only underscores the importance of knowing at the outset the local history and having access to genealogies of families who lived in the area. Once I discovered that Charlotte Nix had been owned by John Perry, I then proceeded to locate further documentation on the Perry line.

A search of the records led me to (1) the above mentioned deed of trust held by Perry's son, (2) John Perry's will, (3) an inventory of his estate, (4) a deed of sale to his children in Franklin County, North Carolina, (5) a variety of wills and deeds entered in the Franklin County courthouse books for Perry family members, most of whom had been small-scale slave owners, (6) his father's will, and finally (7) his father-in-law's will. Perry's will is transcribed below in its entirety as an example of what to expect. Names of slaves are in boldface type.

THE WILL OF JOHN PERRY OF RUSSELL COUNTY, ALABAMA

Last Will and Testament of John Perry deceased I John Perry of the county of Russell in the State of Alabama, do make and ordain this to be my last Will and Testament. After the payments of my debts I dispose of my property in the following manner

I give and bequeath to my son Strickland Perry the land I gave him in the State of North Carolina, and also the sum of one dollar.

Item 2nd I give and bequeath to my daughter Jane Nix and the legal heirs of her body, the negro woman **Charlotte and her children** now in her possession.

Item 3rd I give my daughter Mary Brooks the negro woman **Indiana and her children**.

Item 4th I give the heirs of my son Willis

Perry the Five hundred dollars which I advanced to him in Muscogee County Georgia.

Item 5th I give to my son John Perry the five hundred Dollars I advanced to him in Muscogee County Georgia.

Item 6th I give my daughter Ruth Matthews the negro girl **Hannah and her children.**

Item 7th I give and bequeath my daughter Amaryllis Benson the sum of Five Hundred Dollars to be raised and of my estate.

Item 8th I give my daughter Eliza Strand the sum of Five Hundred Dollars

Item 9th I give my daughter Patience Vance the sum of Five Hundred Dollars

Item 10th I give my daughter Frances Lansen the sum of one Thousand Dollars.

It is my will that all my property both real and personal be sold as soon as the law will permit and the above bequests paid and the remainder if any of the proceeds arising from the sale of my Estate be divided equally between the heirs of my son Willis Perry, my son John Perry, and my daughter Amaryllis Benson, Eliza Strand, Patience Vance, Ruth Vance, Ruth Mathews and Frances Lawson (Lansen?)

I hereby constitute and appoint Edgar Garlick and Richard Baker Executors of this my last will and testament.

In testimony whereof I said John Perry, hath hereunto __?__ my hand and affixed my seal on this 5th day of November A.D. 1853.

Signed, sealed and acknowledged
John Perry (His mark)

in presence of the __?__ October

Erased __?__ November interlined before signed

John A. Lims Thomas H. Burch

Frederic C. Slappy

Codicil No. 1   I, John Perry do make the following additions in the foregoing will. Having lost **a negro fellow** by death, I give my daughter

Patience Vance the sum of one Thousand Dollars, instead of Twelve hundred dollars as bequeathed to her. I give and bequeath to my daughter Frances Lansen the sum Eight Hundred Dollars instead of One Thousand Dollars as bequeathed to her. I nominate and appoint Theophilus White and Richard Baker my Executors instead of Edgar Garlick and Richard Baker and give my said Executors full power to sell and dispose of my land(?) at such time and place and on such terms as they may think advantageous to my Estate, without the necessity of allowing an order from the Probate Court to sell.

John (his mark) Perry

Signed, sealed, published and declared this 12th day of December A.D. 1854 in our presence

Thomas H. Burch

R. H. Baker

John A. Lims

The State of Alabama Dismally appeared before me George H. Wardell, Russell County Judge of the Probate Court of Russell County R. H. Baker who after being duly sworn says that is his signature which appears in the Codicil of the will of John Perry dated 12 December 1854. That he has no recollection of the presence of the other two? subscribing witnesses but supposes they must have been present. The codicil was signed in affiants presence by the one John Perry by making his mark according to the best recollection of affiant, at the time the same bears date. In affiants ? belief, the said John Perry was at the time of sound disposing mind and memory.

Sworn transcribed this 9th January 1860 R. H. Baker

George H. Waddell, Judge PC

The State of Alabama, In the Probate Court Russell County, January Term 1860

Personally appeared in open Court Frederic G. Slappy one of the subscribing witnesses to an instrument of writing heretofore filed for Probate in this Court __?__ the last Will and testament of John Perry late of said county now deceased and being sworn saith that said John Perry __?__ and published and declared the __?__ and contain his last Will and testament in the day the same bears date in his presence and in the presence of the other subscribing witness Thomas K. Burch that he signed his name as a witness thereto in the presence of said testator and of such other witness and that such other witness subscribed his name as such in his and the testators presence; and further that in his opinion and belief said testator at the time of executing said will was of sound and disposing mind and memory from last __?__ subscribed this 9th January 1860.

F. C. Slappy

Recorded May 3, 1860 George H. Waddell, Judge of Probate (Russell County, Alabama)

The Inventory

After Perry's death, the will was admitted to probate and entered in the Russell County Will Book by the clerk. Any papers associated with the proceedings were filed as an estate packet with others in the Russell County courthouse. The inventory of his estate should also appear in the packet. It was also recorded in a record book labeled "Inventories, Appraisements and Sales, 1837–1863." Note the dates on each document. On November 5, 1853, Perry wrote and/or signed his will. On December 12, 1854, he wrote a codicil. On December 13, 1859, an inventory of his property was taken. Between the last codicil in 1854 and the date of the inventory in 1859, Perry died. An inventory is taken only after the death of the writer of a will. The will and inventory were then presented at the next term of court which was January 1860. I later found his death recorded in the 1860 Census Mortality Schedule as November 1859 at the age of ninety! The inventory is transcribed below:

INVENTORY AND APPRAISEMENT: ESTATE OF JOHN PERRY DECEASED

Inventory and appraisement of the personal property belonging to the Estate of John Perry, decd late of Russell County, Ala, taken this 13th day of December 1859.

Cash on hand	16.75	1 lot ____? ware & kitchen furniture	2.00
2000? fodder	18.00	1 spinning wheel	1.50
100 Bus. corn	100.00	1 shot gun	1.00
8 pork hogs 1000 lbs.	80.00	1 bed stead & furniture	25.00
1 __ Steer	50.00	1 paid sad. __?	1.00
1 bull	10.00	1 set knives & forks crockery	2.00
1 cow & calf	10.00	1 side board chest tables	2.00
1 do do	10.00	6 cottage chairs	4.50
1 do do	10.00	1 tin safe & tables	2.00
3 heifers	30.00	7 head geese	2.80
1 gray stallion	100.00	**1 negro man Jesse**	100.00
1 Bay Horse	50.00	**1 negro woman Susan**	400.00

1 c__?	10.00	**1 negro man Harry Malone**	1600.00
1 grind stone	50.00	6000 lbs seed cotton	150.00
2 pen stocks plantation tools	3.50		
1 saddle 7 bridle	2.50		
2 Bee Hives	2.00		[total] $2841.30

PROBLEM SOLVING WITH PERRY'S WILL AND INVENTORY

On the face of it, the will is fairly straightforward. The judge of probate, before allowing the will to be probated, had to assure that Perry was of sound mind when the will was signed and amended in the codicil. Thus, the statements from various witnesses to Perry's signature. Perry states that his executors do not have to report to the judge of probate with regard to the disposition of his property! Note also that the inventory does not name the slaves bequeathed to his daughters. Normally, researchers can count on finding subsequent reports by executors in the form of inventories and estate sales. In Perry's case, the will preempts such reports. The judge of probate, however, has the final decision. As in all puzzles, the ability to solve them depends on how much information you have before you start, and that is the case with Perry's will.

Deriving Leads from the Will and Inventory

Listed below are some possible leads to Perry's life and migration path based on the will alone. Assume that you are the researcher, and you know nothing else about Perry except the information contained in the will.

1. Originally from North Carolina. (Search census indexes until his name is located. That will provide county of origin.)
2. Lived in or owned land in Georgia, possibly Muscogee County. (Check Muscogee County deed book indexes—1860 and before.)
3. Had at least ten children. (Try to locate their residence using names of spouses starting with the 1860 Alabama Census Index.)

Identifying Obstacles

A good researcher should make a list of things that the will does not include:

1. No mention of Perry's wife.
2. No indication of place of residence for daughters who inherited slaves nor any dates indicating when they were given.
3. No indication that sons inherited slaves.
4. Children of Hannah, Charlotte, Indiana not named, nor is the relationship between any of the slaves indicated.
5. Very close to the Civil War period—may diminish possibility of any subsequent transactions on slaves inherited by Perry's children.
6. No explanation for the discrepancy in Patience Vance's inheritance.
7. No name for the "negro fellow" who died.

8. He may have owned additional slaves.

9. Most of his personal wealth was in three slaves and not in his household belongings. No mention of the value of his land indicating a further search is needed.

John Perry's 1829 Deed (Franklin County, North Carolina)

Searching the records in Franklin County turned up a deed between Perry and some of his children. Part of the deed appears below:

Property purchased at the sale of John Perry (Sp.) 6th of March 1829 by Eliza Perry, Amaryllis Perry & Willis J. Perry. One Negro woman Holley and her four children Iley, Indiana, Dorcas, & Mason, Susan and her four children Adam, Hartless, Charlotte & Malone, One Negro man Jesse . . .

The first thing that comes to mind is this: If Perry sold his slaves to his children (we assume that the purchasers are his children rather than other adult relatives), how did he reacquire them or, indeed, was this a mere paper transaction to raise money as had been suggested in the Perry genealogies? Some things are resolved while new questions arise. With regard to the ancestry of Charlotte Nix, we now know that her mother was named Susan, and we also know the names of at least three of her siblings, one of whose names Charlotte gave to her oldest son (Adam). We also know that Harry is Harry Malone, but we don't know what happened to Hartless or Adam since they are not named in the will or the inventory.

The two women with children named in this deed are Holley and Susan. Hannah, who is named later in Perry's will, does not appear in this purchase. Perhaps Perry purchased Hannah later. What happened to Indiana's mother, Holley, and her siblings Iley, Dorcas, and Mason? What happened to Adam and Hartless, Charlotte's siblings?

The *1850 Slave Schedule (Russell County)* indicates that Perry owned four slaves: two males, aged sixty and twenty-one, and two females, aged forty-five and eighteen. There is no way of "guessing" at the identity of these slaves until more information is collected. For example, if Charlotte was born in 1805 as her headstone states, she would have been twenty-four in 1829 and forty-five by 1850. However, we know that she was named as a child in the 1829 deed record. Had she been an adult woman of childbearing age, it is very likely that she would have been named separately with at least one child of her own by then given that the average age of slave women at the birth of their first child was generally between nineteen and twenty-one.

Finding these records throws into serious doubt Charlotte's year of birth as listed on her headstone. It is likely that the forty-five-year old female reported in the 1850 slave schedule was Susan, Charlotte's mother. By the year of the inventory nearly ten years later, she would have been very old indeed for a slave woman. Note that she was valued at $400 and Jesse at $100, indicating that he was perhaps older and may very well have been her mate.

Finally, those slaves owned by Perry in 1829 whose names do not appear in his will or inventory may have been sold. A slave named Mason listed as Holley's child on the 1829 document appeared in the will of Phineas Perry of Russell County, Alabama

(1862). No relationship has been established between Phineas and John Perry.

The saga of Perry's estate has included crossing the boundaries of several states and at least four generations. (Perry himself lived from the Revolutionary War to the onset of the Civil War period.) In the process, you have partially documented the separation of slave families and their owning families. Perry's children were spread far and wide by the time the Civil War started. So too were the families of his slaves! There is much more work to be done now, and the 1870 census would be a good starting point before any attempts are made to extend the line back in time—no matter how enticing it seems. Furthermore, your research should focus on Perry's children and the slaves they and their spouses owned both in Alabama and in North Carolina. The idea is to create a maximum list of slaves owned by Perry and his children before focusing on Susan's generation, a generation that would place your research close to finding either an ancestor born in Africa or an ancestor who lived during the Revolutionary War period.

A Note on Searching Deed Books and Inventories and Appraisals

*D*eed books record the transfer of property generally on the basis of sale, gift, or trust. Though there is a preponderance of land transactions in deed books, researchers should know that pre–Civil War deed books included some of the following transactions: slave sales, wills (occasionally), manumissions, apprentice papers, petitions,

depositions, tax lists, slave hires, and miscellaneous documents. The record keeping practices of clerks could often be unique and peculiar to their county. For the southern states, deed books generally recorded the sale or transfer of land and slaves. Like will books, deed books are indexed by grantor (person selling or giving) and grantee (person receiving).

In addition to deed books, counties will have frequently created books that are called "inventories and appraisals" or an equivalent name. Inventories may also be interfiled in deed books depending on the county's record keeping practices. In Perry's case, the executor of his estate reported back to the court that an inventory had been taken and that no irregularities were found. Subsequent entries will indicate when and how the property was disposed of until the file is closed. Researchers should follow transactions until that point.

A Different Kind of Transaction: The $26,900 Sale

*T*he following deed recorded a sale by one Vertrier to the Barclays in Claiborne County, Mississippi. It is included as an example to show how deeds often do name the relationships between slaves as well as other incidental information—in this case, a runaway who was purchased by the buyers despite his absence! It also shows the difference in the scale of operation between a small-scale slave owner in Franklin County and the larger speculative selling of slaves in what was then called the Southwest.

DANIEL VERTRIER TO THOMAS BROCKHURST BARCLAY AND GEORGE P. BARCLAY

Bill of Sale: Claiborne County Clerks Office. This certifies that the written bill of sale was received for record 4th January 1821 and with its acknowledgement duly recorded in Book F, page 291. P.A. __?__, Clerk

  Fee $1.65

  Rec'd for record Jan 4th 1821

  State of Mississippi

  Claiborne County

For and in consideration of the sum of Twenty Six Thousand Nine Hundred Dollars to me in hand paid at and before the sealing and delivery of these presents the receipt whereof is hereby acknowledged, I do grant bargain and sell and by these presents have granted bargained sold and delivered unto Thomas Brockhurst Barclay and George Perares Barclay and to their assigns the Thirty Eight following negroes, mulattos, Slaves to wit—Tom & Nancy (his wife) Isaac & Phoebe (his wife) and Isaac Martha & Solude their children, Buck & Mary, his wife, Antoine & Dinah (his wife) Matilda and Eliza and Jack (her children) Jerry and Puck his wife and Frances their child, Mingo & __?__ Robert and Louisa (his children) Joe & Betsy (his wife) Jess & Hannah, his wife, Harriet Jack Logan and __?__ Nancy—Watson and Till his wife & Ben their child Sam and Milly his wife and Hamilton their child and Fortune and Mary his wife—And I do hereby bond myself my heirs and to warrant and defend the aforesaid Negroes and mulattoes against the law for a claim or claims of all and every person by pardons whatsoever _____? or to claim them or any or either of them and that they are slaves for life. In testimony whereof I have hereunto set my hand and seal the first day of January one thousand and eight hundred and twenty.

  D. Vertrier

Mem. If negro Fortune named on the within bill of sale who is at present run away is not delivered in three months his valuation 1200 dollars is to be deducted from the amount within specified.

Analysis of Vertrier's Sale

That the two Barclay brothers could afford to pay nearly $27,000 cash for slaves suggests not only that they were well off, but that there would be other such transactions to look for, particularly in their surviving personal and business papers. Note, however, that the bill of sale does not actually indicate the form of payment. The receipt would have to be located to determine the form of payment. This deed was registered some forty years before the beginning of the Civil War and some thirteen years after the abolishment of the international slave trade. These slaves probably came from another region of the United States. As with the names of all slaves found in documents, a list should be constructed in the following manner:

FAMILY GROUPINGS: VERTRIER'S SALE OF JANUARY 1, 1820

(Deed Book F, Page 291—Claiborne County, Mississippi)

Family #1	Tom & Nancy (his wife)
Family #2	Isaac & Phoebe (his wife)
	Children
	Isaac
	Martha
	Solude
Family #3	Buck & Mary (his wife)
Family #4	Antoine & Dinah (his wife)
	Children
	Matilda

Eliza

Jack (her children, but not Antoine's?)

Family #5   Jerry & Puck (his wife)
Child: Frances

Family #6   Mingo & __?__ (his wife?)
Children
Robert
Louisa (his children, but not his spouse's?)

Family #7   Joe & Betsy (his wife)

Family #8   Jess & Hannah (his wife)

Singles?   Harriet, Jack, Logan, and __?__, Nancy

Family #9   Watson and Till (his wife)
Child: Ben

Family #10   Sam and Milly his wife
Child: Hamilton

Family #11   Fortune and Mary (his wife)

This list should be supplemented by similar lists found before and after the sale. Vertrier was probably a New Orleans agent who sold slaves upriver after their arrival in New Orleans.

UNDERSTANDING THE MIGRATORY PATHS OF THE SLAVE OWNER

*T*he settlement of the Old Southwest Territory was done with slave labor; when planters and farmers moved out of the original colonial areas of settlement to the Southwest between 1790 and 1860, invariably African American slaves constituted a large contingent. Even the earlier expansions into western Virginia, North Carolina, Kentucky, and Tennessee involved slaves. Travelers' accounts, diaries, and records of frontier settlements and forts attest to the presence of slaves, including records left by American heroes like Daniel Boone.

For researchers with Deep South ancestry, plotting the migratory path of the slave owner is important; clues about his origins should be gathered in the course of reading a local history of the area. Because these early settlers tended to travel in groups, they frequently named their places of settlement after their areas of origin. Once you find that your ancestors were owned or carried away by a migratory farmer-planter, you will have to determine how he arrived and how his slaves arrived (overland, a combination of land and inland water routes using the Ohio and Mississippi rivers, or by the Atlantic coastal water route between Virginia and New Orleans).

PASSPORTS

*I*f your ancestors were brought into areas still unincorporated as part of the state and still occupied by Indians or foreign nations east of the Mississippi River, "passports" were issued to them stating that they were traveling through said territory. Some of the earliest passports were granted to slave owners trying to recover runaway slaves. Generally passports named the slaves who accompanied the migrants, as in the case of Isaac Dubose and his son Peter of Sumpter District, South Carolina, who were issued passports to pass through Georgia in 1804, and his wife who joined them in 1810 along with their fifty-eight slaves. The following passports were abstracted from the Territorial Records (records relating to prestatehood) housed at the Mississippi Department of Archives and History. They were pub-

lished in the *Mississippi Genealogical Exchange*. Additional passport records have been abstracted and published. Note that most documents were issued up to the 1820s.

RECORDS SHOWING MIGRATION OF FREE BLACKS AND SLAVES WITH THEIR OWNERS

Adams County, Mississippi Territory: Personally came Benjamin Orr and being duly sworn deposeth and says that he wishes to take a certain free man of colour through to the state of Ohio, Chillicothe, which said free man of colour is by name Samuel Davis, about five feet nine inches and 3/4 of an inch high, aged twenty-three years

or thereabouts, wooly hair, mulatto complexion, black eyes, a native of Pennsylvania. Sworn to and subscribed this 13th day of May 1813 before me, Robert A. Morrow, J. P.

Adams County, Mississippi Territory: Derrel Martin makes oath before me that Josiah Marting, a citizen of Georgia is at this time detained in the Choctaw Nation with fifteen negroes whom he believes to be exclusively the property of the said Josiah Martin who is desirous and means to bring said slaves to the Mississippi Territory. He states the slaves to be a negro woman Milly with seven children, viz, Ruth, George, Jacob, Nancy, Tempe, Calles, and Patrick; Nelly with these children: Hala, Mary, and Daniel together with Julis, a black fellow, Sarah, a yellow woman and Jurden, a black boy. Witness my hand 13 December 1811. D. Rawlings.

Mississippi Genealogical Exchange, vol. 18 (Summer 1972), vol. 18 (Spring 1972), and vol. 17 (Fall 1971).

Passports exist in various state and territorial archives and they tend to be fairly detailed—identifying slaves by name, age, color, their owners, and the slave owner's origins.

SLAVE IMPORTATION REGISTERS

*T*he State of Georgia passed a law that further prohibited the importation of slaves for sale or resale but not for the migrant's own use. Alabama also passed a similar act in 1832. Most of these laws required registration at the county's courthouse. Part of the Alabama act (3 November 1831—13th Annual Session of the House of Representatives) is reproduced below:

Section 2. And be it further enacted, That all persons emigrating to this State, after the passage of this act, and bringing with them any slaves, shall, within ten days after their arrival in the county in which they intend to reside, and within thirty days after their arrival with said slaves within the limits of this State, make out and file in the office of the clerk of the county court of said county, an account or statement of all slaves so brought with them, designating the name and sex, and as nearly as may be, the age, size, and color of each, and at the same time take and subscribe before the clerk of said court, an oath of the truth of said account or statement. . . ."

The extent to which various counties executed this law is unknown. Records were found in at least one Alabama county. In Perry County, Alabama, the clerk of court seems to have been relatively conscientious about adhering to the law. He maintained a register of slaves and an appearance docket! One Harwood Jones deposed on March 5, 1832, that "Henry, a Negro man about 25 years old, 5´10˝ well proportioned and dark complected without any visible scars or marks and Moses, about 14 years old, 4´7˝, well proportioned and black complected without any visible scars or marks were obtained as a legacy from his father's and mother's estates in Mecklenburg County, Virginia. . . ."

In Georgia, there seems to have been a greater adherence to the spirit of this law. Records survive for several counties. According to the *Slave Importation Register* for Richmond County, Georgia (1820–1821), one James Martin attested in July 1821 that he was bringing the following twenty-five "field hands" into the state: Old Brewster(70), Jack(30), Sau(23), Moses(22),

Sarah(45), Luce(35), Kate(25), Mary(25), Adam(14), Jim(14), Henry(14), Joe(11) with name crossed out, Dicke(10), Tom(10), Jim(11), Jim(14), Mary(30), May(12), Anne(6), Chauncy(7), Lucy(4), Bob(6), Henry(3), Poll(2), Phoebe(1 1/2), Let(4), and March (9 months old). Note that this appears to be an entire plantation moving farther South.

DIARIES: EVEN THEN, THEY TOLD ALL

*Y*ou may often find diaries and letters kept by migrating slave owners. *The Lides Go South and West: The Record of a Planter Migration in 1835* is an example that is often pointed to as a tremendous firsthand account on the history of this migration. There are other diaries and letters to be found in the papers of planters, and they often make references to slaves by name or as a group and to other families who traveled with them. In the case of the Lides, most of their slaves had left ahead to make preparations for their arrival in Alabama. Therefore, not many slaves are named specifically. One Chicago researcher, Belzora Cheatham, obtained a copy of part of a planter's diary, enough to confirm her ancestors' migration path to Texas. Cheatham's findings were reported in an article for the *Journal of the Afro-American Historical and Genealogical Society*. In addition, research on her home community eventually led to state recognition of her ancestors as pioneers, as well as of the community they built. Finally, some diaries can be controversial—even hundreds of years after they were written. Some by their nature are not written to fool but to confess our own inner agonies and ecstasies.

SLAVE "IMPORTATION" RECORD, STATE OF GEORGIA

State of Georgia } Clerk's Office, Superior Court

Richmond County. }

Be it known, That *James Martin*

has this day taken the oath required by the act of the General Assembly of this State, relative to the importation of Slaves therein in regard to *Twenty five* Negro Slaves *who are field hands except the children to wit*

Old Brister 70. Jack 30. Sam 25. Moses 22. Sarah 45. Luce 35. Kate 25. Mary 25. Adam 14. Jim 14. Henry 14. Dick 10. Jonas Jim 11. Jinny 14. Mary 30. Meg 12. Anne 6. Chance 7. Lucy 4. Bob 6. Henry 3. Phebe 1½ Poll 2. Jet 4 years old March 9 morelto old

A diary written between 1848 and 1899 was recently published by a descendant of the diarist. Entitled *The Secret Eye: The Journal of Ella Gertrude Clanton Thomas*, the diary contained extensive references to the slaves owned by Thomas and her husband as well as to their economic demise after the war. Thomas's constant reference to mulatto children on other plantations as well as the dynamics of interpersonal relationships between slave-owning families and their slaves provides an unusual peek into the past. Such diaries are often kept within families, as was the case with Thomas's until recent times.

CARRY ME BACK TO OLD VIRGINNY

In 1860, nearly all adult Mississippi slaves had been either forced migrants to that state or first-generation Mississippi-born slaves. Only 32,814 . . . had lived in that state in 1820.

HERBERT GUTMAN, *THE BLACK FAMILY IN SLAVERY AND FREEDOM, 1750–1925.*

TWO SLAVE SHIP MANIFESTS, DOMESTIC SLAVE TRADE

MANIFEST of Negroes, Mulattoes, and Persons of Color, taken on board the ___ James Monroe of Norfolk, whereof John C Saunders is Master, burthen 111-24 tons, to be transported to the Port of New Orleans — for the purpose of being sold or disposed of as Slaves, or to be held to service or labor.

Number of Entry.	NAMES.	SEX.	AGE.	HEIGHT. feet.	inches.	Whether Negro, Mulatto or Person of Color.	OWNERS or SHIPPERS NAMES AND PLACES of RESIDENCE.
1	Shilly	female	30	5	0	Tawney	
2	Catharine	"	6 mon	1	10		
3	Sarah	"	30	5	1½	black	
4	Rose	"	14	4	9		
5	Merret	male	8	3	10	"	
6	Jack	"	7	3	6		
7	Eliza	female	5	3	0	Yellow	John C Saunders On board
8	Jupiter	male	9 mon			black	
9	Tabby	female	15	4	10	black	
10	Spencer Wilson	male	15	4	9½	Tawney	
11	William Wilson	"	16	4	8½	black to	
12	Warren Wilson		16	5		black	
13	___ Wilson	female	8	3	11		
14	Reuben Ainley	male	13	4	4½		
15	John Grey	s	34	5	9½	Yellow	
16	John C Carter	"	24	5	7½		
17	George Taylor	"	20	5	5	black	
18	Edmond Moore	"	40	5	7	Yellow	

I, John C Saunders do solemnly, sincerely, and truly swear to the best of my knowledge and belief, that the persons above specified, were not imported or brought into the United States, since the first day of January, eighteen hundred and eight, and that under the Laws of the State of Virginia, they are held to service or labor as — Slaves. So help me GOD.

COLLECTOR'S OFFICE, NORFOLK, October 18__
Sworn to before me.
___ Collector.

MANIFEST of Negroes, Mulattoes, and Persons of Color, taken on James Monroe of Norfolk, whereof is Master, burthen 111-24 tons, to Port of New Orleans — for the purpose of being s Slaves, or to be held to service or labor.

Number of Entry.	NAMES.	SEX.	AGE.	HEIGHT. feet.	inches.	Whether Negro, Mulatto or Person of Color.	
1	Shilly	female	30	5	0	Tawney	
2	Catharine	"	6 mon	1	10		
3	Sarah	"	30	5	1½	black	
4	Rose	"	14	4	9		
5	Merret	male	8	3	10	"	
6	Jack	"	7	3	6		
7	Eliza	female	5	3	0	Yellow	
8	Jupiter	male	9 mon			black	
9	Tabby	female	15	4	10	black	
10	Spencer Wilson	male	15	4	9½	Tawney	
11	William Wilson	"	16	4	8½	black to	
12	Warren Wilson		16	5		black	
13	___ Wilson	female	8	3	11		
14	Reuben Ainley	male	13	4	4½		
15	John Grey	s	34	5	9½	Yellow	
16	John C Carter	"	24	5	7½		
17	George Taylor	"	20	5	5	black	
18	Edmond Moore	"	40	5	7	Yellow	

Forced migration to the Deep South, better known as the domestic slave trade, was an abysmal business, and ironically, slave traders as an occupational group were considered less than desirable, if not despicable, by the general population. Though it was a dirty business, it accounted for a large portion of the forced migration of slaves to the Deep South. It is still being debated how much of this movement of nearly one million slaves, primarily the young in their prime, can be attributed to slave traders as opposed to planters migrating with their slaves. But, if you look at the records, it can be easily seen that the majority of the slaves were young men and women who had been sold or carried away from their families, friends, and kin by slave traders, who established an extensive network of local and regional markets and who left behind ledgers, account books, and other such evidence attesting to their activities.

It mattered how you arrived in the Deep South. Being transported by the coastal waterways was significantly different from being transported overland in a slave coffle, for which many vivid accounts remain in the literature on slavery. Alice Walker has recounted the story of how her great-grandmother was taken from Virginia to Georgia. Perhaps you have encountered a similar story; now you will know how to interpret it. Finally, the lyrics to "Carry Me Back to Ol' Virginny" can be read for added meaning. Written by an African American and later appropriated by minstrels, it contains references to slave migration and the Great Dismal Swamp. One scholar has estimated that nearly one half of the one million slaves sold South were sold from Virginia. Note also that the Great Dismal Swamp was home to runaway slave communities, but there seems to be some controversy about how many self-liberated people actually inhabited the place.

There are two large groups of records that link slaves to migrating slave owners and slave traders. They are the coastwise ship manifests for the domestic slave trade and the surviving records of slave trading houses and slave traders. The coastwise ship manifests are housed at the National Archives in Washington, D.C., and slave traders' papers are housed in various repositories throughout the country. Reproduced below is a transcription of a the manifest of a ship that departed Petersburg, Virginia, for New Orleans, a journey that could take one month or less depending on the type of vessel and the number of stops. The coastwise ship manifests are part of National Archives

Record Group 39, Records of the United States Customs Office.

Some researchers will be able to make the connections, particularly those whose ancestors came with an owner to settle in the countless small places that dotted both sides of the Mississippi River, as well as areas in Texas. Records are available for all major southern ports, but remember the story about the beginner who tried to find his one ancestor in these records based on a family story. Though not easy to use because they are not indexed by the names of those involved with the trade (sellers, buyers, brokers, etc.), through careful research they may serve you well.

If you have reached the point in your research where you identify in a planter's records the names of slaves purchased from a trading house in New Orleans as well as the date, you could also consider examining the original manifests housed at the National Archives. Before doing that, however, it might be worth your time to become acquainted with the Notarial Archives of New Orleans, where many such transactions were recorded prior to slaves being "sold up the river."

The manifests are organized by port of arrival or departure and year (early 1800s through 1860). Your research effort should be limited to no more than a two-year period at a time and to a planter's name (either buyer or seller). You should not search for your ancestors' names only. By examining the lists above, you should be able to easily see why this is the case (common given names and the absence of surnames), although many slaves leaving Virginia were listed with their surnames. In addition, it is more difficult to research

TRANSCRIPTION OF A SHIP MANIFEST: DOMESTIC SLAVE TRADE

Ship Name: Planter of Petersburg (A brig)
Date of departure: 13 Feb 1819
Port of Departure: Petersburg, Virginia
Port of Arrival: New Orleans

Slaves owned by Aug Gerard, New Orleans

Name of Slave	Sex	Age	Height	Color	Receiving Party
Ira?	m	21	5-6	All Black	**G. Roche, New Orleans**
Louis	m	14	4-7		
Fanny	f	18	5-5		
Delcey	f	15	4-7		
Patience	f	15	4-11		
Betsey	f	14	4-7		
Fanny	f	10	4-3		
Nelly	f	16	5-2		
Peter	m	22	5-8		

Slaves owned by James Thorborn, Norfolk

Name of Slave	Sex	Age	Height	Color
Reuben	m	18	5-3	mulatto
Nelson	m	18	5-3	black
Sam	f	17	5-7	black
Prosperous	m	42	5-6	black
Anthony	m	5	3-5	black
Clary	f	25	5-0	yellow
Betsey	f	23	5-1	black
Minerva	f	11	5-0	black
Beckey	f	23	5-1	black
Natty	f	19	5-2	black
Judith	f	13	4-8	black
Jenny	f	14	4-10	black
Priscilla	f	15	5-1	black
Nelly	f	15	4-8	black

Slaves owned by Joseph Jerard of New Orleans

Name of Slave	Sex	Age	Height
Eliza	f	11	3-10
Nelly	f	20	5-3
Tom	m	17	5-7
Shadrack	m	2-	5-11
Robert	m	15	4-6

Slaves owned by John Marast of Norfolk

Name of Slave	Sex	Age	Height
Stephen	m	16	5-4
Milly	f	13	4-5
Nancy	f	11	4-4

Slaves owned by John Stiles of Petersburg, Consigned to Daniel C. Forrest of New Orleans

Charles Kenzie	m	27	5-8	
Jane Jones?	f	30	5-7	
Geo Robertson	m	25	5-6	
Poole	m	43	5-9	
David Jones	f	14	4-7	
Scipio	m	14	4-7	
Jack	m	13	4-3	
Syrus	m	10	3-12	
Daniel	m	12	4-5	
Wm Jones	m	9	3-12	
Isham	m	13	4-3	
William	m	11	3-11	
Milton	m	7	3-7	
Lettice	f	12	4-6	
Sampson	m	12	4-2	
Lucy	f	10	4-2	
Polly	f	4	3-2	
Jane	f	10	4-0	
Fanny	f	13	4-2	black
Isabella	f	10	3-12	black
Parmelia	f	15?	3-10	yellow
Rose	f	12	4-3	black
Nancy	f	13	4-10	black
Suey?	f	13	4-7	black
Parmalia	f	13	4-6	black
Oiney	?	10	4-1	black
Polly	f	13	4-7	black
Jane	f	35	5-2	black
Polly	f	24	5-2	black
Minney	f	23	5-6	black
Robert	m	5	3-1	yellow
Paper fold—unable to read next three lines				
Fanny	f	15	4-11	yellow
Patrick	m	22	5-9	black

Slaves owned by Thomas Martin and Jas Reynolds, Consigned to Jackson & Reynolds of New Orleans

Sam'l Brown	m	35	5-3	black
Malache	m	35	5-7	black
Robin	m	21	5-1	black
Paul	m	20	5-11	black
Jos Anderson	m	22	5-2	yellow
Mary Ann	f	22	5-3	mulatto

NOTE: New Orleans custom official notes on arrival that manifest is correct "except that a child has been born."

slaves who were traded as opposed to those who were brought South by a planter transferring his entire operation from Virginia to Mississippi or Louisiana. Most of the surviving manifests start at 1818, when the shipment of slaves South was well under way.

RECORDS OF SLAVE TRADERS AND TRADING HOUSES

Records left by slave traders have not been used by African American genealogists. Surviving records are scattered and many often be buried in the personal papers of a planter or the confiscated Confederate records of a Union soldier, as was the case for two Hector Davis & Co. account books (Richmond, Virginia, 1857 and 1864). These account books are part of a Civil War collection at the Chicago Historical Society. The collection of documents and records related to the trade housed at the Pennsylvania Abolitionist Society should also be noted. The conveyance records (notarial archives) found in New Orleans and other southern courthouses will occasionally show that certain individuals were involved in the trade. To locate these records, genealogists will have to use the subject index to the National Union Catalogue of Manuscript Collections (Slavery and/or Slave Trade as subjects) as well as know something about the trade in the particular state of research. Because slaves were moved overland as well as by the coastwise trade, you will have to design a research strategy based on examining the sources on both of these routes to determine how your ancestors arrived in the Deep South.

Michael Tadman's work *Speculators and*

Slaves documented approximately 157 South Carolina slave-trading firms for the 1850s alone, and this group was believed to underrepresent the total number involved in the trade. Traders may often be identified in local newspapers as speculators, traders, or Negro speculator-traders. The mechanisms of the trade as it operated in South Carolina point out the difficulties that await the unwary researcher. Most slaves were purchased singly in an itinerant fashion for a number of reasons. Traders attempted to avoid family group sales because of the difficulties involved in selling families. They also tended to buy in cash, but many of their local sales involved credit. In some cases, local banks leveraged their funds heavily to provide credit to traders and purchasers of slaves. Tadman found that traders avoided "judicial" (through local probate courts) sales; most slaves sold under this mechanism appear to have remained in the local area.

Your chances of finding a slave sale transaction are relatively high, for despite the preference for cash sales, much of the system operated on credit, thereby making it necessary to create mortgages and other conveyance records. The group at greatest risk of being sold were the young, particularly those in their teens and early twenties. Tadman calculated that had you been born in 1820, there was a 30 percent or more chance that you would have been sold in the domestic trade by 1860, with a slightly greater probability for girls between twelve and fifteen. It was commonly believed that they made better cotton pickers, that they matured faster, and that they could also be used as domestic servants. One final obstacle which may hinder your research: Tadman concluded that most slaves were taken overland rather than by the coastal waterways, thereby decreasing the likelihood of matching sales to the manifests discussed above.

UNUSUAL RECORDS/UNUSUAL FINDS

*I*n the course of your research, if you are thorough and if you read widely, you will encounter many kinds of records that include the names of slaves, particularly in the records of large slave owners. One of the most unusual kinds of records that you might encounter relates to insuring slaves. When I encountered a copy of a slave insurance policy in the Mercer family papers, I decided that it might be worth some investigation. The policy was underwritten by an agent of the Aetna Insurance Company based in New Orleans in 1853. Other companies involved in insuring slaves were the Hartford Life Insurance Company (the practice actually caused their demise), New York Life Insurance and Trust Company, American Life Insurance and Trust Company, and Baltimore Life Insurance and Trust Company.

You wouldn't write to the company's archives to ask whether a slave insurance policy was ever made for one of your ancestors. (The records of defunct companies may be located in various local archives using the usual search procedures.) But you would almost certainly find copies of policies in the personal papers of large slave-owning families. You can also see why insurance companies did not widely issue such policies. Not only was the idea of selling insurance on an individual's life difficult to sell to the general public (probably rank-

ing with slave trading on the scale of public repugnancies of the time), it was contradictory to insure the life of a slave. The idea that slave owners could make money on a slave's life that had been unduly shortened through overuse—even profiting from his death—perhaps proved to be a bit much. Furthermore, most of the insurance companies required a physician's statement of good health as well as information about whether the slave was acclimated to the local area. Whether these policies exist in large quantities is a matter for further research. Note that many of the companies that issued such policies are no longer in business—at least under their original names.

"THEY WERE EXTREMELY LITIGIOUS WHEN IT CAME TO BLACKS"

*T*his statement was made by an attorney who was investigating free ancestry in colonial Virginia. In short, nearly all American court and legislative records at all levels contain plentiful references to and cases regarding slaves or free African Americans during the period of slavery. County courts throughout the history of slavery passed countless laws regulating the activities of slaves as well as activities relating to what their owners could or could not do with them or to them. Many of these laws eventually turned up as cases before various courts, starting with probate courts and culminating in higher-level courts. They all emerged into a body of state laws that came to be known as the Black Codes. And don't forget Agnes Cane Callum's research, which was based on court petitions for freedom spanning one hundred years. To get a good feel for the kinds of court records that are available to researchers, Helen Catterall's documentary collection, *Judicial Cases Concerning American Negro Slavery*, should be consulted.

This chapter has shown how records that name slaves—both common records and uncommon ones—are available and can be used by persistent genealogical researchers. The next chapter will show how to reconstruct family ties from slave lists. Also see Special Topic 1 on locating genealogical and historical sources, without which you will not get very far for this period of research.

AND, WHATEVER HAPPENED TO CAL BOGER?

*T*o convince you that a little bit of knowledge can carry you far if you know the records, we will give you the results of a routine search that all genealogists should do once the name of a potential slave owner is found. Remember that Cal Boger was said to have claimed a McDonough as his last owner, and that we found an African American Boger living near a White Boger in the 1870 census for the Hickory Flats district of Cherokee County. Checking the various indexes to Georgia wills, I did not find a Boger or McDonough. But there is an index called *Georgia Intestate Records*, and I found that one Peter C. Boger's estate was entered in probate in February 1863. Boger died intestate (without a will), but he had substantial property. He was perhaps a casualty of the Civil War. The *Cherokee County Inventories and Appraisements*, which I

ordered through an LDS stake library, contained the following inventory. His wife, Martha H. Boger, was the administrator.

PETER C. BOGER'S SLAVES	
Sam valued at $800	Ruth valued at $500
Charles valued at $1000	Lucinda valued at $750
Willis valued at $900	Gela & Child at $1000
Caleb, a boy, at $700	Emeline at $800
Henrey at $550	Bartenia at $700
Calvin at $550	Lueruth? at $450
Jim at $600	Ladusky at $300
Moses at $500	Lanora at $200
Eliza at $600	Jane at $300
William at $250	Rose at $450

Source: *Book C, Inventory and Appraisements*, Cherokee County, Georgia, 1854–1924, pp. 51–53.

It appears that the Calvin listed in the inventory is probably the same Cal Boger who found his way North after the Civil War. Could it be that Cal was hired out or sold to a McDonough? Indeed, could he have been taken to the war by his owner from whom he ran away to join the Yankees? These questions are all answerable for the diligent researcher.

WHAT IN THE WORLD DO I DO NOW?

*T*his chapter has been dense, but its contents can be reduced to one simple statement: Once you find the last slave owner, you are using his family history and genealogy as a guide to identify his recorded transactions that named slaves he *and* his extended family owned over time using primarily the family's personal records, if you can find them, and any public transactions that they recorded at the courthouse. Later, you will examine some of the other records included in this chapter as examples of the kinds of records that exist.

Once you finish your research, you could very easily publish the information that you found in abstract form, not only your identified ancestors but also the slaves that remain anonymous. Your research may quickly yield the information that you think you want, but there will still be a lot of missing pieces to fill in. What you will generally find is a networked community in a local area, and you will definitely be curious about the other folks that you encounter. Make sure you keep accurate records as you go along, and list your sources so that you won't have trouble finding them again. More often than not, you will have to examine your notes once you find additional links among your slave ancestors.

Chapter 12

RECONSTRUCTING FAMILIES AND KINSHIP IN THE SLAVE COMMUNITY

Some people think that slaves had no feeling—that they bore their children as animals bear their young . . .

JENNIE HALL, FORMER SLAVE, WPA SLAVE NARRATIVES

Searching for and Constructing Lists: A Necessary Step

*Y*ou will be searching for a variety of lists and contextual information that will help you interpret the lives of your ancestors. Since it is likely that nearly all slave owners kept lists of slaves, the question then becomes which lists are best, assuming that they survived at all. There is no standard terminology to describe such lists. A variety of terms have been used, including the simple term "list of slaves." The name of the list does not matter as much as the function of the list as perceived by the individual who compiled it. This chapter discusses lists that you will locate, mainly in the surviving personal papers of planters housed at a number of places dispersed throughout the country—archives, university libraries with manuscript collections, and even in the possession of the descendants of slave owners. This is an analysis chapter, but you will also have to spend some time locating the papers. For that, you should study the Special Topic at the end of the book entitled "Sources for Advanced Research in Slave Genealogy."

The type of list that you are likely to find is based on the scale of the slave owner's operation. Planters and farmers were very much influenced by the plantation management literature of the times, and most read on a regular basis journals and newspaper like *De Bow's Review*, which was filled with suggestions on "slave management." Many suggestions related to record keeping practices of the time. Thus, the use of journals and ledger-type entries filled the same functions that accounting sheets fill today. Large plantations kept lists of slaves out of necessity. Very small planters often had no need for such lists. If it amounted to a question of keeping track of five slaves, the "list" may have been entered in the family Bible.

Two critical types of lists exist for your analysis: lists found in the papers of large-scale planters and lists to be found in estate or conveyance records. For small-scale planters, your list or lists will emerge as you find more information in deeds, inventories, and wills. Consider the case of Perry, where it could have been easily thought that he owned only the slaves named in his will at the time of his death when, in fact, he had already transferred the slaves some years ago. Likewise, had you only counted those listed in the inventory, you perhaps would have never found out that he owned others—especially if he died intestate. Outlined below are the kinds of lists that you may encounter depending on the scale of the planter's operations. Knowing the function of every list that you find helps you to better determine the relationships between the slaves named in it.

- Blanket and/or clothing lists: Such lists may be of more value than others because these items tended to be issued by family groups.
- Cabin Lists: These lists may also indicate family groups. Care is the word here, however, because several families often shared one housing unit. The living arrangements of slaves also varied by region and type of slave owner.
- Task Assignment/Productivity Lists: Some planters maintained records on the amount of work assigned to or performed by each slave. Some simply maintained lists of work crews if the plantation was operated under the system of gang labor. Note also the possibility that plantation operations may have been dispersed (in different areas away from the home plantation), and lists will reflect this with "surnames" sometimes assigned according to the type of labor. Consider the following list taken from the Mercer family records. This list implies that the slaves will be moved around to different plantations.

TRANSCRIPTION OF UNDATED AND UNSIGNED LIST FROM MERCER FAMILY PAPERS

I send a list of the people just as I think will just convenience and the least interfere with cer-

tain operations on G. You of course will need waggoners and one or to (sic) head plowers. I think it would be a good arrangement to moove (sic) Phillis and her family and Ishams wife Lucy to G. and send as many to the new place from G.

1st group: Joe Godwin and Malinda—carpenter and 5 children

2nd group: Friday, Patsey B., Robbin L. (child)—tend the sick and dieing?

3rd group: Dennis, Phebby, Gab? L., Susan (child)—Mind children

4th group: Phibby B. (Cook, one lame hand)—(5 children) Celey, Nathan, Banks, Francis (no account)

5th group: Letty Y, William, Lafayette

6th group: Plesant, Hannah—Waggoners

7th group: Sam Y (good plower), Lucy—

8th group: Amey L, Buckery, Milly L, Martha—2 children

9th group: Elick, Nelson—ox drivers

10th group: George D., Pagey—Stack driver, in place of the new Blacksmith and wife

Note that husband and wife are linked together with their children, and comments are included on each person with regard to the unknown task, probably settlement of a new plantation or a new piece of land in or near Adams County, Mississippi, where the Mercers resided.

- Family Bible Lists: The names of slaves were often listed in the slave-owning family's Bible either by family groups or by dates of birth.
- Birth lists: Some slave owners kept records of births by plantation. Such records will often enable researchers to reconstruct familial ties between mothers and children, but less frequently with fathers.

- Inventories: Estate inventories listing slaves often appear in surviving planters' records. These inventories should also be duplicated in the records of the probate court in the county of death and/or residence. Make sure that they are indeed one and the same document.
- Bills of Sale: Records of the sale or purchase of slaves will also often appear in county courthouse deed books or mortgage books. Such bills of sale will also appear in planters' records on scraps of paper labeled receipts or with no identification at all. Since the purchase of slaves was often done in a piecemeal manner, researchers should not expect to find long lists of purchases or sales of slaves. Again, such transactions were more likely to occur at the time an estate was being divided and sold off or during the expansion of a planter's farming activities. Note, however, that researchers whose ancestors last lived in states like Mississippi, Louisiana, Georgia, and Alabama may often find fairly long lists of purchases for planters who had just begun to establish themselves in the early 1800s. The Vertrier/Barclay list in the previous chapter represented such a list.
- Slave Hiring Lists: Slave hiring was a fairly common practice, particularly for artisans, who eventually formed a large class of skilled slaves about which White workers protested. While it is generally true that slave hiring was most common for the Upper South states, it was also fairly common in other areas, particularly during depressions or during a shift from producing one crop

to another. Slave hiring was done on an annual basis, generally during the first part of any given year, and often recorded in deed books or in account books kept by planters.

Controversial Lists: "Breeding" Records

When the profitability of slaves as capital became that great, as it did very early on, the market economy came to intrude deeply into the most intimate of human relationships.
STEPHEN OAKES, THE RULING RACE

You will not find lists *labeled* breeding lists. However, consider the terminology in the following list from the Mercer papers.

MERCER SLAVE PURCHASES— UNKNOWN YEAR

List of Negroes belonging to W. Moore and raised by him on his own plantations, Albermarle County, Va.

No 1. Phillip—field hand and rough smith, aged 24—	$750
No 2. Thornton—field hand— very likely, 21 years	$725
No 3 Washington—field hand— very likely, 21 years	$725
No 4 Sam—field hand, 17 years	$725
No 5 Tom—field hand, 20 years	$700
No 6 Dec—hunt boy?, 16 years	$575
No 7 Ann—field negress, 17 years	$550
No 8 Charity—field negress, 17 years	$550
No 9 Rosamond—field negress, 16 years	$550
No 10 Lucy, 15 years	$525
No 11 Mary Jane, 13 years	$450
No 12 & 13 Elsy & child, 21 years and 1 year	$600
December 10—purchased for $7000	$7425

The meaning of the term "raised" is not quite clear. It suggests either that the slaves were born and grew up in family units on Moore's plantation (planters often referred to slaves as being part of their families) or literally that he raised them just for sale. If the date of purchase was in the 1840s or after, credibility is lent to the idea that he *raised* them with the *idea* of sale in the Lower South. The handwriting is probably that of a Mercer, part of a class of wheeler-dealers and speculators in the operation of large-scale plantations. This class certainly had come to view the Upper South states like Virginia and Maryland as factories that "raised" slaves just for sale. Indeed, writers of that era, including the abolitionists, also saw it in those terms. Furthermore, planters in the Lower South did have a preoccupation with the types of slaves they purchased and an undying fear that those slaves being bought on the open market were somehow recalcitrants that had been sold away just to get rid of them. Thus the emphasis on "raised by Moore" as a term rather than merely "purchased from" Moore. Moore knew their history, or at least he thought he did. Nevertheless, he was involved in "intruding deeply into the most intimate of relationships."

We include this still controversial issue here for two reasons: It is a painful and controversial part of African American history, and it needs to be treated sensibly so that you can understand where your ancestors really fit into this debate. After all, they are long gone, and what they told us is not often clear about what really happened. The debate on slave breeding is still raging among historians, for it implies that somehow slave women were "forced" or "induced" to bear or "breed" children merely for sale. Obviously no slave woman or man would consent to have children so that the slave owner would sell them, as Jennie Hill asserted in her statement at the beginning of the chapter. Therefore, when the actual records are examined, it is difficult to come to the conclusion that slave owners had the power to breed slaves for resale as you would stock. (Note, however, that forced "marriages" did exist.) The godly terminology claimed in planters' writings certainly indicated that *they* felt they could, for the literature is filled with references to "breeding" and "negro stock."

But slaves lived in two worlds—an outer world in which they were seen as objects and an inner world in which they saw themselves at the center. The differences in frames of reference—the slave owner's and the slave's—should come as no surprise to you. There's another perspective as well, namely what writers of that era said about what they observed, especially the antislavery forces, who had the capacity in their arguments to reduce the most complex of situations into elemental truisms in much the same way as we do today when we talk about the American legacy of racism. You may, however, be led to the wrong conclusions based on whose frame of reference you are using. This is especially the case with the slave owner's necessary, but unhuman, preoccupation with the fertility of slave women or the potency of slave men as partners. Certainly slaves did not see themselves in those terms despite the symbolism and behavior evoked on both sides of the slavery question.

The widespread institution of slave marriage, something rarely mentioned by slave owners themselves, is an example of the differences in frames of reference between owners and slaves. While slave owners did recognize family units—it is apparent in the lists that survive—the profit motive overrode every consideration in this respect. The idea of viewing slave children produced *by* slave marriages as a source of future profit did take hold among many Upper South planters. One final point should be included here. Historians cannot tell us the extent of forced marriages nor the extent of free choice in mate selection. Evidence exists for both. The implication here is that when we use the term *slave family*, we mean just that: a male and a female who produced children and lived together until death or separation due to sale, choice, or other reasons. The point is that they are, centuries later, traceable through your own bloodlines using historical records. Therefore, researchers should not confuse what was said or written or perceived with what was done. In conclusion, the symbolism associated with the language used by slave owners should not lead you to conclude that slaves believed in that symbolism or applied it to themselves.

- Other Lists: Frequently, you will encounter lists for which there is no apparent function, either due to the incompleteness of surviving records or the very real possibility that the lists refer not to slaves but to horses who were given names. A close inspection should suggest that such names are not those that would be found in the slave population. These lists will often appear next to lists of slaves in day books, which recorded transactions on a daily basis, journals kept by the planter or his

overseers, and account books which combined a running account of the planter's purchases with other transactions related to the operation of the farm or plantation.

Contextual Information

Planters' records should be searched for contextual information that will allow you to make some inferences about the slave community in which your ancestors lived. Diaries and journals, medical and doctor's bills, accounts with large trading houses, plat maps showing the plantation in geographical space, correspondence, and anything else found in planters' papers will provide you with key information that may not be found elsewhere.

They Survived All of This: Once You Find the List, What Do You Do?

You might say, "Is this what my effort amounts to?" You are likely to stare at the list and ask yourself this question and more, namely how your ancestors survived all of this. They survived it for many reasons—one of which had to do with the need for their labor, and the other based on their own ability to create a space between their world, about which planters often understood little themselves, and the world in which planters lived, which slaves made a point of understanding for their own survival. But you may ask the question: "How will I find out who was related to whom?" One possible response is clearly that, unfortunately, you may never find the answer.

However, your finding the answer depends on the following factors: (1) the condition of the surviving lists, (2) the number of lists available for different years, (3) the "inferred" function of the lists, (4) the organization of the lists, (5) whether the names on the list(s) can be matched with information that you have found in other types of records, namely the 1870 and 1880 censuses and conveyance records (probate and deed), and (6) whether the named slaves are linked to their owners.

The best list, therefore, is one that is dated, readable, links slaves to their owners, links slaves to each other in kinship groupings, and finally one that had a clear purpose at the time it was created. If these conditions apply to any given list and if the same information appears in other lists at different points in time, your job has already been made easier for you. The Ball family's plantation records contain many of these elements, and historians have frequently used them for that reason. Once you do find a list or lists, routinely submit your analysis to the following questions:

1. Are there regular blank spaces between groups of names, lines or other demarcations such as brackets and wavy lines such that individuals appear to be listed in groups?
2. Are the individuals listed in a sequence: older male, younger female, and children with their ages given in descending order within each group?
3. Is there terminology such as "wife of," "child of," "family," "belonging to the same family"?
4. Do surnames appear on a frequent basis? Do given names appear to be

surnames? Are given names repeated frequently?
5. Are there prefixes or suffixes attached to given names such as "little," "big," "small"? These may also appear as "surnames," though by now, the researcher should know that these are simply identifications attached to names that are shared by several individuals, some of whom may be related.
6. Is there any other consistent pattern that holds for the same list or for several different lists found in the same records?
7. Are there other lists that can be matched—inventories, bills of sale, estate inventories, as well as lists from nearby plantations owned by the same family or the family's relatives?

The following case study offers you an opportunity to analyze lists from a plantation owned by the Duncan family. Using the questions above, try to identify family groups on the following list.

CASE STUDY: THE CARLISLE SLAVE COMMUNITY IN ISSAQUENA COUNTY, MISSISSIPPI

Carlisle Plantation occupied approximately 2,200 acres in Issaquena County in the Mississippi Delta. Stephen Duncan was its owner, and Duncan can lay claim to having been one of the largest slave holders in the history of U.S. slavery. A Northerner from Pennsylvania (born in Carlisle in 1787), Duncan arrived in Natchez in the early 1800s joining other relatives already established in planting.

Though an M.D. by training, he made his money on Mississippi and Louisiana plantations. Unlike many planters of his era, he also invested his earnings in the North, principally in railroad bonds. He was also one of the founders of the Mississippi State Bank, which became defunct before the Civil War, and he was also actively involved in the American Colonization Society, which will be discussed in a subsequent chapter. Perhaps he himself had considered freeing and sending some of his slaves to Liberia.

Duncan or his children had owned at least fifteen plantations at various times in both Mississippi and Louisiana. They were L'Argent, Auburn, Camperdown, Carlisle, Duncan, Duncannon, Duncansby, Ellisle, Homochitto, Middlesex, Oakley, Oxford, Rescue, Reserve, Attakapas, and possibly Chapitoulas. By 1860, he owned 717 slaves and 7,710 acres of land worth over one million dollars in Mississippi alone. Interestingly, Duncan claimed loyalty to the Union during the Civil War in order to protect his investments in the South, as any "Yankee" capitalist would have done. He died in New York (1867) after having moved there in 1863. According to a local informant in Issaquena County, Duncan has no living descendants.

Four lists, some of them incomplete, were copied from one of the Carlisle plantation journals. The two most complete lists were used for this analysis, the first dated 1856 and the second dated 1861. Neither list had marks to show divisions into family groups; however, the internal order of both lists suggested an organization by family groups and/or living units. They followed the order of male/female/children, all in age-descending order. Each individual was numbered, and occasionally birth and death dates were entered. These censuslike lists were generally followed by clothing rations for the year along with a description of the plantation given in township, range, and section format including total number of acres. The 1856 list is reproduced in its entirety on the next page to give you some idea of what you might face. It is then followed by a division into family groups for both 1856 and 1861. Before reading further, get some practice by studying this list to see what kinds of family groups can be identified. Use the suggested criteria above to try to divide this list into family groups.

TRANSCRIPTION OF LIST OF SLAVES OWNED BY STEPHEN DUNCAN DATED DECEMBER 4, 1856

(From *Volume V: Plantation Journal*, 1856–1865)

List of Slaves on Carlisle Plantation

	Name	Age
1.	Isam	45
2.	Winny	37
3.	Mirrida	17
4.	Merriman	5
5.	Vincent	2
6.	Larkin	6 mos Died 1857
7.	Minerva	20
8.	Kiah	1
9.	Catherine	15
10.	Sally Bivans	55
11.	Bill Rankin	60 Died 1858
12.	Sophy	45
13.	Margaret	16
14.	Henry	14
15.	Milton	30

TWO CARLISLE PLANTATION SLAVE LISTS

Carlisle Plantation

		aged				
1	Isam	45	38.	Jacob Biggs - aged -
2	Winny	37	39.	Francis -
3	Merrida	17	40.	Porter - died '5?
4	Merriman	5	41.	Eliza -
5	Vincen	2	42.	Moses -
6	Larkin - Died '57 - 6 mos	43.	Charles G. Jr.
7	Minerva	20	44.	Lorenzo D.
8	Kiah	1	45.	Jim Preston
9	Catherine	15	46.	Maria Preston
10	Sally Bevans	55	47.	Sarah -
11	Bill Rankin Died '58	60	48.	Meck L.

Carlisle Plantation 1st Jan. 1860

		aged				
No. 1.	Isam	58	No. 37.	Spencer aged
" 2.	Winny	50	" 38.	Margaret
" 3.	Merriman	9	" 39.	Dick
" 4.	Vincent	5	" 40.	Jacob B
" 5.	Charles G.	30	" 41.	Henry L.
" 6.	Minerva	23	" 42.	Delphey
" 7.	Kiah	4	" 43.	Sally Bevans
" 8.	Lily Ann	2	" 44.	Lilly
" 9.	King	6 mos	" 45.	Jane Lewis
" 10.	Jackson	20	" 46.	B. Sally
" 11.	Catherine	18	" 47.	Louisa
"	Stephey	58	" 48.	John J.
"	Meck L.	16	" 49.	Fanny Ann
"	Milton	33	" 50.	Rachel
"	Eliza	30	" 51.	William

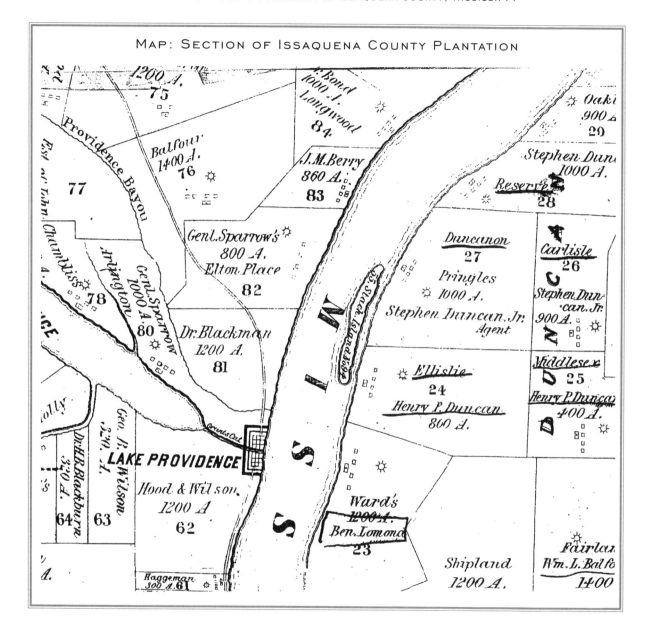

MAP: SECTION OF ISSAQUENA COUNTY PLANTATION

List of Slaves on Carlisle Plantation

Name	Age	Name	Age
16. Eliza	24	57. Harriet	40?
17. Kitty	5	58. Harrison	20
18. Owen	30	59. William	19
19. Sommerville	27	60. Elizabeth	14
20. Henderson	8	61. Taylor	10
21. Warren	5	62. Lloyd	8
22. Julia	4 mos Died 1857	63. Nat L.	5
23. Isaac	40	64. Bob B.	34
24. Mary Anne	30	65. Angelina	16
25. Lavinia	14	66. Maria Bob	25 or 16?
26. George	12	67. Jacob L.	14
27. Isaac	9	68. Andrew Blk.	
28. Jane Lewis	45	69. Malvina	
29. Peter	40	70. Edward	38 (Edmond?)
30. Harriet B.	35	71. Sucky	44
31. Emily Jane	13	72. Phebe	12
32. Dudley	9	73. Thomas	5
33. Mingo	35 Died 1857?	74. Rosana	7 mos
34. Melissa	35	75. Anthony	37
35. Louisa	2	76. Amanda	23
36. Clara	1 mos	77. Betina	3
37. Letty	?	78. Mary Magdalen	1
38. Jacob Biggs	22	79. Wesley	22
39. Francis	14	80. Melinda	20
40. Porter	4 Died 1859	81. Hicks	40
41. Ellen	25	82. Bill Fowler	48
42. Moses	5	83. Sally Fowler	40
43. Charles G. Jr	4	84. Sandy	16 Died 1858
44. Lorenzo	2	85. Ebenezer	15
45. Jim Preston	47	86. Monroe	11
46. Maria ˝	37	87. Abner	7
47. Sarah	19	88. Bass	5
48. Aleck	16	89. Gallatin	4
49. Jim?	5	90. Isaac F	3
50. Randal	Died 1859	91. Amy L.	8
51. Martha A.	5 mos	92. Glora Ann	2
52. Stephen	9 ms	93. Willis	30
53. Amy Granny	70	94. Milly	40
54. Charles G.	27	95. Alexander	20 Sold? 1861
55. Jeferson	20	96. Charles L.	18
56. Nat	45	97. Matilda	11

98.	Susan	4
99.	Stephen	6
100.	Chapman	5
101.	Sabina	2
102.	Jerry	45
103.	Clarissa	40
104.	Isabel	20
105.	Malone	2 (Died 1860)
106.	Archy	21
107.	Bob L.	14
108.	Jonas	11
109.	Davis	45
110.	Rachel	45
111.	Lorenzo	19
112.	Nancy	12
113.	Delphy	40
114.	John T	33
115.	Henry T	37
116.	Harriet	30
117.	Thornton	33
118.	Maria T	40
119.	Patsy	5
120.	Spencer	23
121.	Samuel	25
122.	Emma	33
123.	Henry Blk	30
124.	Maria L	27
125.	Solomon L	7
126.	Barney	11
127.	Violet	4 mos Died 1857
128.	Jack	40
129.	Betsy	35
130.	Jim H	14
131.	Daniel	5
132.	Martin	3 mos
133.	Osborne B	40
134.	Charity	36
135.	Walton	16 Died 1859
136.	John L	13
137.	Osborn L	11
138.	Polly	7

139.	Mary Anne L.	5
140.	Mary	4
141.	Becky	3
142.	Daniel Rollins	60
143.	Amy Brown	55
144.	Simon	12
145.	Solomon	35
146.	Charlotte	60
147.	Sally Blk	35
148.	Louisa	35
149.	Jacobson	14

Carlisle contains according to Kelly's survey, 2208 28/100 acres embracing parts of Section 9: T 12: R: 9 West & Sec 33: T 12: R: 8 W & Secs 15 & 16: T: 11: R: 9 West, All of Sec 19:T:11:R: 9 W, 2/3 of the East half of Sec 18: T: 11: R: 9 W & the W 1/2 of Sec 10: T: 11 R:8 W. And having one hundred and forty nine Negroes as named above. Signed: S. Duncan Jr. Dated 3 December 1856. (Clothing for Plantation follows.)

(Note: A question mark in the age columns indicates that the age was unreadable.)

Identifying the Slave Community's Cycle of Development

Ask yourself this question: What should I do next? Let's assume that you have a set of names and/or households derived from the 1870 census. Suppose Isam is your ancestor, and he entered freedom with the surname Pruitt. Would you ignore the possible kin relationships between him and other individuals on Carlisle? How would you find out who else is related to him on Carlisle? You would try to first place all individuals into family groups by analyzing the patterns found in the list.

Once family groups begin to emerge, your next step would be to locate additional lists with different dates from the planter's papers or from his estate records. Once these lists are collected, you are now ready to compare the lists over time, a procedure that takes some time since changes in the composition of households will have occurred, and that is exactly what you need to know. It is a difficult task and often involves some arbitrary decisions until further information is collected. Always consider your first "divisions" as a working or provisional list until you can compare the families over time. Comparing lists over time shows how the slave community developed in terms of kinship. The original Duncan list, dated December 1856, was compared to a list created in 1861. The 1861 list helped to clarify some of the relationships that were not clear using the 1856 list alone.

Expect your first list to contain some inaccuracies. Some will really be family groups based on kinship, whereas others would be more appropriately called "households," which may or may not have been based on kinship. For example, it is unknown whether the above lists also overlap with cabins or living units, adding to the problem of matching. Notice also that the notations that appear next to some names indicate that Duncan attempted to record vital events (births and deaths) through 1864.

The following list represents how I divided the 1856 list into family groups based on the criteria of rank order (male, female, children). I also used the 1861 list (part of which is reproduced on a previous page). The 1861 list was helpful for those listed near the end. This type of work is not short-term. Plan to do a bit at a time.

Author's Division of the 1856 Carlisle Plantation List into Family Groups

Families in 1856

Family #1

Isam	45
Winny	37 (died 1863)
Mirrida	17
Merriman	5
Vincent	2
Larkin	6 mos Died 1857

Family #2

Minerva	20
Kiah	1

Family #3

Catherine	15
Sally Bivans	55

Family #4

Bill Rankin	60 Died 1858
Sophy	45
Margaret	16
Henry	14

Family #5

Milton	30
Eliza	24
Kitty	5

Family #6

Owen	30
Sommerville	27
Henderson	8
Warren	5
Julia	4 mos Died 1857

Family #7	
Isaac	40
Mary Anne	30
Lavinia	14
George	12
Isaac	9

Family #8	
Jane Lewis	

Family #9	
Peter	40
Harriet B.	35
Emily Jane	13
Dudley	9

Family #10	
Mingo	35 Died 1857?
Melissa	35
Louisa	2
Clara	1 mos
Letty	?

Family #11	
Letty	?
Jacob Biggs	22
Francis	17
Porter	4 Died 1859

Family #12	
Ellen	25
Moses	5
Charles G. Jr	4
Lorenzo	2

Family #13	
Jim Preston	51
Maria	37
Sarah	19
Aleck	16

Jim	5
Randal	Died 1859
Martha A.	5 mos
Stephen	9 ms

Family #14	
Granny Amy	70
Charles G.	27
Jeferson	20

Family #15	
Nat	45
Harriet	40
Harrison	24
William	19
Elizabeth	14
Taylor	10
Lloyd	8
Nat	5

Family #16	
Bob B.	34
Angelina	16

Family #17	
Maria Bob	
Jacob L.	

Family #18	
Andrew Blk.	
Malvina	

Family #19	
Edward	38 (Edmond?)
Sucky	44
Phebe	12
Thomas	5
Rosana	7 mos

Family #20	
Anthony	37
Amanda	23

Betina	3		Archy	21
Mary Magdalen	1		Rob L.	14
			Jonas	11

Family #21

Wesley	22		**Family #27**	
Melinda	20		Davis	45
			Rachel	43

Family #22

Hicks	40		Lorenzo	19
			Nancy	12

Family #23

Bill Fowler	48		**Family #28**	
Sally Fowler	40		Delphy	40
Sandy	16 Died 1858		John T	33
Ebenezer	15			
Monroe	11		**Family #29**	
Abner	7		Henry T	37
Bass	5		Harriet	30
Gallatin	4			
Isaac F	3		**Family #30**	
Amy L.	8		Thornton	33
Glora Ann	2		Maria T	40
			Patsy	5

Family #24

Willis	30		**Family #31**	
			Spencer	23

Family #25

Milly	40		**Family #32**	
Alexander	20 Sold? 1861		Samuel	25
Charles L.	18		Emma	33
Matilda	11			
Susan	4		**Family #33**	
Stephen	6		Henry Blk	30
Cla?	5		Maria L	27
Sabina	2		Solomon L	7
			Barney	11
			Violet	4 mos Died 1857

Family #26

Jerry	45		**Family #34**	
Clarissa	40		Jack	40
Isabel	20		Betsy	35
Malone	2		Jim H	14

| Daniel | 5 |
| Martin | 3 mos |

Family #35	
Osborne B	40
Charit?	36
Walton	16 Died 1859
John L	13
Osborn L	11
Polly	4
Mary Anne L	5
Mary	4
Becky	3

Family #36	
Daniel Rollins	60
Amy Brown	55
Simon	12

Family #37	
Solomon	35
Charlotte	60
Sally Blk	35
Louisa	35
Jacobson	14 (Jackson?)

Once you begin to isolate family groups, certain patterns emerge, and questions arise, such as, Is there a computer program that I can use for several lists? Probably not, but maybe you can get one of your computer wizard friends to develop one. This is your "first cut list." Alone it doesn't tell you much about their social relations, but perhaps it does. One thing that you can do is to create a pool of eligible names for the next generation by simply identifying those who will be of marriageable age in the next five and ten years. You will know that those who have married on subsequent lists are not related.

Then you can return to the first list to examine who was not related to whom as well as speculate about who was related to whom. Sound confusing? It won't be when you find your own ancestors. Another pattern to observe from the above list is those groupings that don't seem to make sense because they are either too large or have no common pattern among them. This is particularly the case near the end of the list. Are they slaves who have just arrived on the plantation and do not share ties with the rest of the group yet? Anything that you surmise will have to be weighed against subsequent lists. If you find only one list, dated in 1856, for example, and no other information up until the 1870 census, you will have to do a huge leap of faith. But this is very unlikely. Remember the labor contracts, the 1866 census (though not very reliable), Freedmen's Bureau records including marriages, and so on.

Duncan's overseers maintained good lists because he ran a huge operation from Adams County, Mississippi, his home. As far as I have been able to discern, he did not live on any of his upriver plantations. That means he had to have periodic reports on his operations. Thus, the lists attain more validity in terms of their accuracy.

Your next step is to look for other lists, and depending on the size of the operation, no doubt you will find them. Listed below are my matches between the 1856 list and the 1861 list (not reproduced in this volume). On the 1856 list, I found thirty-seven units that I defined as families. On the 1861 list, I found forty-two families. Twenty-seven family units remained the same between 1856 and 1861. There were nine new family formations between 1856 and

1861, some due to dissolution by death or perhaps divorce but most due to new family creation, and I was still unable to match four individuals. That is considerable continuity, and the fact that the lists were five years apart helped considerably. There were twenty recorded deaths for the five-year period between the lists.

This represents a 13 percent death rate. We can be more assured that by matching names and relative ages we are talking about the same people. Subsequent information should bear that out. Listed below are examples showing continuity, new family formation, and dissolution. Also note that my method of record keeping was to permanently assign a number to each family for the earliest list dated 1856. If someone moved to a newly created unit between years, I assigned a number to the new unit with a notation indicating the family unit number to which the person originally belonged.

As you examine slave lists, you will notice naming patterns and the use of the terms Big, Little, Yellow, or even letters. Note also that some surnames will appear as in the case of the Fowler name. Did they leave slavery with that surname? is the question to be asked. As I studied the lists collected from the Issaquena plantation, I found that Isam and Winny were always listed at the top of each one, but there was never a surname attached to this couple. Did Isam occupy a special role within the slave community, or was there some valuable role he performed in the context of the plantation's operations? These are the kinds of questions that you will automatically ask yourself as you proceed.

COMPARISON OF FAMILY UNITS BETWEEN 1856 AND 1861 LISTS

Families in 1856

Family #1	
Isam	45
Winny	37
Mirrida	17
Merriman	5
Vincent	2
Larkin	6 mos Died 1857

Family #3	
Catherine	15
Sally Bivans	55

Family #15	
Nat	45
Harriet	40

Families in 1861

Family #1	
Isam	49
Winny	37 (died 1863)
Married Lavinia in HH #7, 1856	
Merriman	10
Vincent	6
—	

New Family #43	
Jackson	21 From HH #37, 1856
Catherine	19 in HH# 3, 1856
Susanna	9 mos died
Sally Devers	Died 1861 (Bivans?)

Family #15	
Nat	49
Harriet L.	44

Harrison	24	Harrison	24
William	19	Married, see HH #16, 1861	
Elizabeth	14	Elizabeth	18
Taylor	10	Taylor	14 (died 1863)
Lloyd	8	Lloyd	12
Nat	5	Nat Little	9
		Polly	Born Jan 8th

Family #7		Family #7	
Isaac	40	Isaac B	44
Mary Anne	30	Mary Anne	32
Lavinia	14	Married Mirrida in HH #1, 1856	
George	12	George	16
Isaac	9	Isaac Little	14

Family #27		Family #27	
Davis	45	Davis	49, see HH #27, 1856
Rachel	43	Unmatched	(Divorced?/Deceased 1864?)
		Isabella	24, see HH #26, 1856
		Lucinda	3
		Matthews	5 mos
Lorenzo	19	Married, see HH #44	
Nancy	12	Nancy	16

		New Family #44	
		Lorenzo	23, see HH #27, 1856
		Frances	21 (died in '63)
		Parmelia	8 mos (dead in '61)

Family #6		Family #6	
Owen	30	Owen	30
Sommerville	27		
Sommerville	31		
Henderson	8	Henderson	12
Warren	5	Warren	9
Julia	4 mos Died 1857	Deceased	
		Sommerville Little	2

		New Family #45	
		Merida	21, in HH #1, 1856
		Lavinia	20, in HH #6, 1856
		Ananias	1

	New Family #46	
	Aleck Little	20, in HH #13, 1856
	Emily Jane	17 in HH #9, 1856
	New Family #47	
	Ebenezer	19, in HH #23, 1856
	Sarah	23, in HH #13, 1856
	Martha	4
	New Family #48	
	Jeff	23, not listed in 1856
	Phoebe	24, in HH #13, 1856
	Rosy Anne	4
Family #11	Dissolved	
Letty	?	See HH #12, 1861
Jacob Biggs	22	See HH #12, 1861
Francis	17	Deceased
Porter	4 Died 1859	Deceased

Transcribed from original record. Note the variation in ages.

Using Marriage Patterns to Determine Kinship

From the above lists, you can also figure out who was not related, an important point to take note of. For example, Isam and Winny's family was not related to Isaac and Mary Anne's family since their children married. Scholars have surmised that as a rule, slaves rarely allowed marriages between relatives—not even distant cousins—a rule of kinship that is partly based on customs brought from selected African groups. There are always exceptions to the rule, however, if you know anything about African ethnic groups.

The next example shows how something as complex as family ties can be resolved, or at least partly resolved, once you expand the number of lists. In this case, I used lists from 1851, 1856, 1860, and 1861. The lists cover a span of ten years and deals with a subgroup related by kinship and marriage. The focus is on a young man named Charles G. and a young woman named Ellen, both of whom start out in the same household in 1851. After 10 years and after analyzing four lists, their relationship begins to emerge, but not with absolute certainty. Here the analysis is focused on one individual at a time to determine which households they were listed in over time.

The Method of Reconstructing Family Ties from Large Lists

As in all genealogical investigations, proximity and position are some of the hidden patterns that underlie kin relations. This too is the case for analyzing lists of slaves, which contain only names, ages, and scanty vital data. Because you have to discover the underlying meaning contained in these lists,

EXAMPLE OF FAMILY RELATIONS RECONSTRUCTED FROM MULTIPLE LISTS

Charles G's Households (1851–1861)

1851		HH #14, 1856		HH #2, 1860		HH #2, 1861	
Charles G.	29	Granny Amy	70	Charles G.	31	Charles G.	31
Letty	50	Charles G.	27	Minerva	24	Minerva	24
Ellen	14	Jeferson	20	Kiah	5	Kiah	5
Jake	18			Cely Anne	2	Cely Anne	2
Moses				Elizabeth	2	Elizabeth	2
Charles Y	born '53						

Ellen's Households (1856–1861)

HH #12 1856				HH #14, 1860		HH #16, 1861	
Ellen	25	William	22	William	23		
Moses	5	Ellen	28	Ellen	29		
Charles G. Jr.	4	Moses	8	Moses	9		
Lorenzo	2	Charles G. Jr.	7	Charles G. Jr.	7		
		L. Lorenzo	6	Lorenzo L.	5		
				Isiah	3		
		Benjamin	8 mos	Deceased?			

Note: Ellen's age was probably recorded incorrectly in 1851.

you must put yourself, comfortably or uncomfortably, in the position of the list maker. For example, would you simply make a list of family groups without regard to where they lived or what role they played in the operation of the plantation? It is unlikely when you have to keep track of well over one hundred individuals whose families may change as a result of marriages, births, and deaths. If you compile a list one year and then check the list a year later, what would you use to remember who was who if you didn't use their surnames?

In the lists above, there was some attempt to distinguish individuals by assigning the terms *big, little, black, yellow, tall, Jr., young,* and *granny.* In a few of the lists, new-borns were assigned the term "baby" without a name. There was also a change in the positioning of the families between 1856 and 1861. The 1856 list gives the order of the slaves on Carlisle as they were entered into the journal, but on the 1861 list, many of the new and younger families were listed at the beginning. In addition, these new families were often listed next to the household of origin, but no clear pattern emerged with regard to whether it was the husband's or wife's household of origin.

The essential method is to start with a workable list, or a list that includes the maximum number of slaves and that clearly has a household or family pattern. Initially, the year of the list does not matter because whatever date you start from, you want to follow the family or household over time. The first thing to do is to transcribe the list as it appeared in the journal assigning a number to each individual, if the list is not numbered. The second thing to do is to break them up into provisional family or household groups, assigning a permanent number to each household.

Note that in 1851, Charles G. and Ellen started out in the household with Letty, but Letty does not appear in any of the subsequent households in which they lived. If the 1851 list had not been discovered, we might not have known that Charles G. and Letty were connected at one point in the past. We will assume that Letty was their mother, but an earlier list will have to confirm this.

In using four lists with separate dates, a reasonable scenario can be constructed. Letty is probably a widow, or perhaps her husband is on another plantation. Duncan's plantations were not far from each other, and based on lists for his nearby plantations, it appears that reassignments did occur. Note that if Letty was the mother to Charles G. and Ellen, without having the list for 1851 you would never have known it. The family as it existed on the first list, presumably drawn up before the others, split and joined or formed three new households over the ten-year period. Note also that the ages for Charles G. and Ellen were inconsistent, but their children's were consistent. You might have first assumed that Ellen and Charles G. were married because Ellen had a child named Charles G., but it is more likely that Ellen followed the practice of naming one of her children after a sibling, a fairly common pattern to watch out for. Finally, a woman named Granny Amy was consistently listed with one or more of these children, presumably siblings, on all lists; it could very well be that she is their grandmother as well as the grandmother of other children on the list. If Letty is the mother, earlier lists would show Letty as a child in Granny Amy's household. Without information from the descendants of these families or lists created prior to 1851, there is little else that can be inferred about their kinship.

Further Inferences

If Duncan acquired this land in the 1830s, as the tract books indicated in a previous chapter, then to extend this group back in time you would focus on locating lists in his personal papers between initial settlement and development of the land by the slaves on this list to 1851. This is roughly a twenty-year period, but a very critical one indeed, because you have to locate the points of purchase for the slaves. That will tell you where they came from. To clear land for a new plantation and settle it was labor intensive. Duncan needed a lot of hands, suggesting the possibility that the number of people on Carlisle was always large.

Many of the slaves on Carlisle will appear in the 1870 and 1880 censuses, and they will report their places of birth. If they consistently report Virginia or South Carolina, then you'll know that Duncan probably purchased them in lots or groups of slaves that had some association prior to being sold South. Duncan was not one of the many planters who moved their entire operations, including slaves, to the South via overland routes or via the coastwise route. He was basically a northern-style businessman, which makes his transactions a little bit more predictable. He may have bought slaves in the Natchez market who had been transported overland from places like Kentucky, Tennessee, or farther-off points like Virginia and Maryland. Or he may have bought slaves from the New Orleans market who were then sent upriver to his plantations. Remember that Duncan lived in Natchez, Adams County, Mississippi, one of the places where a high concentration of absentee planters resided along the Mississippi River. One final possibility is that some of the slaves on Carlisle had been moved from his Adams County plantations, suggesting the possibility that they were not transshipped from anywhere in the United States but were descendants of the first Africans in the New Orleans area, most of whom were shipped straight from Africa.

Extending Households with Other Lists

Because Duncan died in 1867, you wouldn't expect to find slaves named as part of an inheritance for any of his heirs. However, you might find that he deeded his property over to his children. Because Duncan owned plantations in three separate places, you might want to consider hiring a skilled researcher from each of those counties. A hired researcher for Adams County searched the indexes to the deed books and found nearly four hundred transactions associated with the Duncan family between the early 1820s and the post–Civil War period. A similar number of transactions may exist in Issaquena County or in surrounding Louisiana parishes. Of course, Duncan could have transacted all of his

business in Adams County alone. This too is possible.

You would also have to try to identify your ancestors in any surviving labor contracts that Duncan or his managers entered with freedmen. Contracts were not located for Carlisle plantation, but they were located for nearly every other plantation owned by Duncan in Issaquena County. The 1880 census for Issaquena County enumerated individuals by plantation name, suggesting how little things had changed. Under the Holly Ridge plantation, Sharlot Selevin was enumerated at the ripe age of eighty-five; David Chapman, now thirty-two, had married a woman named Rachel; and Merrika and Merriman Pitts were thirty-two and twenty-eight respectively. Merriman and Merrika (possibly Merrida) were children in the household of Isam and Winny in 1856.

CONSTRUCTING LISTS FOR SMALLER PLANTERS

Some of the same methods outlined above apply to lists derived from courthouse records and other sources for small-scale planters. Your goal would be to construct a maximum list of slaves owned by the planter over his lifetime. Since planter families often sold or inherited slaves within the larger family, you will have to view your research as one whose goal is to reconstruct the family ties between the slaves owned by members of a fairly large family over time. Cheryl Ann Cody was able to reconstruct 620 slave families for nine rice plantations owned by the Ball family between 1720 and

1865. The plantations were continuously owned by descendants of the original owner with only two major estate divisions over a period of 160 years.

In the case of John Perry, for example, there were at least six siblings who were slave owners, all of whom lived in Franklin County, North Carolina, between 1746 and 1830. They too had children who eventually became slave owners. Since their land was often adjacent, a reconstruction of the slave community in the area where the Perrys lived will almost certainly answer questions about the ancestry of those slaves who were dispersed as a result of the Perry children migrating to Georgia and Alabama starting, it appears, in the 1790s. The Franklin County deed records and will books are filled with estate and land sales that were attended by the Perrys and their neighbors. This level of activity almost assures the researcher that the task at hand is doable, but complex.

DISMAL LISTS DO TELL DISMAL STORIES

Suppose you find a list that shows seventy-five slaves, of whom forty are males of marriageable age but most do not appear to have mates, ten are children, six are elderly (over fifty), and fourteen are females of marriageable age but few with mates. What would you think? This is what you may face during certain time periods and regions. Slave communities did show these kinds of imbalances, especially during their formative periods. Over time, these communities tended to evolve into "stable" communities or, at the least, communities without gross imbalances in the male/female ratio.

The picture of the Carlisle slave community in 1851 represents a relatively stable slave community with some generational depth (at least twenty years by 1851), but what did the plantation look like in its first five years when it was being developed? Was it nearly all male? It is likely that at some point, you will find a list that shows severe demographic imbalance in the form of a "dismal" list. By now, you should know that the list, like all lists, represents only one point in time—namely the date that it was drawn up. This is why it is important to look at slave communities in terms of cycles, starting with early development all the way through to maturity, where there is generational depth as expressed in family units with grandparents, parents, aunts and uncles and children.

Newly created plantations in the Deep South, unless they were plantations that had been moved in their entirety (planter migrations), will often show these characteristics during the early phases of plantation slavery in the Americas, and such imbalances continued to be a problem in the Caribbean and South American regions of sugar cane production, where mortality was extremely high. Dismal lists tended to shift toward a reflection of how Africans responded to their situation—namely to begin to form families after some time. One scholar found that older men formed unions first—often resulting in large age differences between spouses (ten or more years)—until the pool of females of marriageable age increased.

Finally, whatever list you start with, know that it will take some time to accomplish your goals. While you may have

skimmed through the first phases of your research, you now have to view your task as a more systematic one. You will not have as many instant successes unless a scholar has already done part of the painstaking research for you, something for which you will be grateful. But the work is often far more gratifying if you do it yourself.

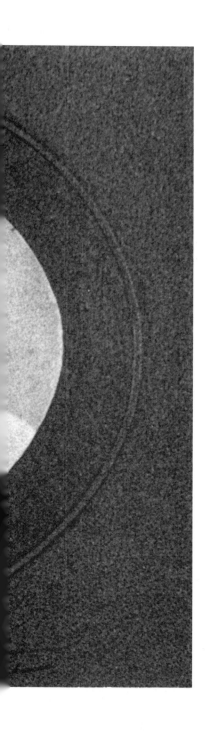

Chapter 13

THE RECORDS
FREEDOM GENERATED

But freedom has frequently had to make its way in the world by serving as a means to an end, and it has often proved a powerful means.

EDMUND S. MORGAN, *AMERICAN SLAVERY, AMERICAN FREEDOM: THE ORDEAL OF COLONIAL VIRGINIA*

*C*onsider the following excerpts that I saved from the Afrigeneas mail list on the World Wide Web. Note that these are postings in the form of e-mail, and they always refer to some source that has to be found in a library. Again, the Web is useful for browsing to see what information is out there and occasionally to connect, but never as a primary source. Though the technology is advanced, human beings are the ones who have to post, and therein lies the problem. Entering data takes a long time!

The world you are about to enter during this phase of research is not cyberspace, however. It is the colonial period, and what a different world it was. If you are a genuine novice, throw off the subconscious belief that there were no Black people in America at that time. I'm not setting up a false argument to knock it down, but the typical American textbook doesn't tell you that in many places in the Americas, Africans outnumbered Whites by a great margin. The colonial world—the New World, the Americas, whatever term you use—was a world filled with slaves in every corner. Seems obvious now that you've read this book, but for the general American public, the colo-

nial world was a world without slavery and Africans.

Excerpts from Original Records Posted on Web Discussion Lists

A Few Postings from Paul Heinegg, Author

From 1677 to 1691, a slave named Mary appears in the Surry County, Virginia Tax Lists of Robert Caulfield. Since slaves were taxable at the age of sixteen, Mary was born before 1662. In the year 1690, a slave named Judith, born before 1674, also appears in Caulfield's tax list. Since Mary was the only female slave in the household, perhaps she was Judith's mother.

John Bass, a white man, married an Indian in Norfolk County, Virginia, in 1638. His grandson, William Bass of Norfolk County, married Sarah Leviner, mulatto daughter of "Negro woman" Jean Lovina in 1729. They lived on a 200 acre farm in Norfolk County next to the free African American Hall and Price families.

John Archer, born about 1645, was a taxable slave in Northampton County, Virginia. "John Archer negro" in Mrs. Grace Robbins' household with her white servants between 1665 and 1675. He was free by 1697 when he appeared in Northampton County Court to bind his eleven year old son Thomas as an apprentice. In 1700 he was sued for failing to deliver a ten-foot mill wheel as promised.

William VENNERS, born about 1701, petitioned the Richmond County, Virginia Court in September 1732 stating that, "he is a Mulatto born of a white woman named Elizabeth Venners who at the time of his birth was a Servt. in Northumberland County, That he is now kept in Servitude by one Arjalon Price." The court ordered him set free [Orders 9:652, 658]. He was probably the ancestor of the following members of the VENA family counted as "other free" in the Richmond County census for 1810 [census p. 413]. . . .

From a Dorothy A. Koenig, Posted to Afrigeneas

RE: Early Black Manhattanites

Those interested in the Black presence in New Amsterdam should consult the article by Dickenson in the *New York Genealogical and Biographical Review* (Volume 116, Numbers 2 and 3) part of which is reproduced below.

"There had been a century-old commerce between Iberia, Africa and Brazil. In reviewing the names of those petitioning for freedom on February 25, 1644, after 18 or 19 years of working for the Company, one can clearly identify the Iberian-Lusitanian-Brazilian-Bantu heritage of the first manumission group. They include:

"Paula Angola, Gratia D'Angola, Little or Cleyn Anthony Van Angola, Jan Fort Orange, Jan Francisco, Big or Groot Manuel, Simon Congo, Willem Anthony Portuguese, Peter Santomee and Manuel de Gerrit de Rues. These earliest freed slaves in New Netherland were collectively known as 'The Eleven.' "

Posting from Lee C.

My name is Lee, I'm brand new to this list. I'm hoping I'll be able to solve some mysteries with the assistance of this forum. I'm specifically researching the ancestors of my maternal grandmother. All my life I'd heard her people were Jews and Cherokees . . . but after a year of intensive searching, I've found nothing to show this to be true. My family is white; entirely of Northern European ancestry. My grandmother, however, looked anything but—curly jet black hair, black eyes, a wide nose, and dark "caramel" colored skin.

She was truly a beautiful lady. I always assumed her complexion and rather non-Anglo features were the result of the Jewish and Indian heritage. Since her death, I've become very interested in genealogy. I've found absolutely no evidence that her ancestors were ever Jews. As a matter of fact, they seem to have been very

Christian! Likewise, I've found a lot of oral history about Indian ancestry, but no documentation. I have found that most of her people had English and Scottish surnames, and a few Germans.

After the 5,000th time someone asked "who's that black lady?" when looking at my family photos, I thought perhaps my family had some African origins. I found that one of my "Jewish" ancestors was listed as "colored" in DAR records, yet white in all other records. I also found some of my family's surnames (and even a few individuals of whom I'm kin) in Paul Heinegg's book "Free African Americans in North Carolina & Virginia." With these clues, I set out looking for any info—grasping at straws.

I was completely unprepared for the hostile replies I received from several individuals. Two persons of distant relation, in particular, sent me the most hateful and vicious e-mails I'd ever read. As a white male, I'd never been attacked in such a manner—racially. Some of these people would rather die than admit they MIGHT POSSIBLY have an African ancestor.

One elderly lady even threatened to "sue for defamation" because I stated I believed a common ancestor might have married a mulatto woman 300 years ago! It was really an eye opening experience.

The Emergence of Free Persons of Color

*T*here are, indeed, some African American families who claim to have never experienced formal slavery. There are some also who prefer to be called "colored" in the historic sense but not the contemporary sense. Though difficult for us to understand today the difference between being Black

and being "colored," at one point in the past, it meant something to a small class of free Blacks, many of whom were once "African" but, we may suppose, became free persons of color through the many admixtures characteristic of the very early colonial period in America. The above excerpts bear witness to this obscured fact of colonial history.

A descendant of one Sarah Madden tells the story of the Madden family of Virginia from the mid-1700s to the present (*We Were Always Free*). According to its author, none of the *traceable* individuals in this lineage was ever formally enslaved, primarily due to a Virginia law which stated that mulatto children of white females were to be bound out as indentured servants for a period of thirty-one years, after which they could be free. The law was later changed to limit the term of years served to eight. That was some kind of freedom!

Based on these and many similar cases to be found in the court records and parish vestry records of Virginia, most scholars have concluded that a sizable portion of the class of free persons of color obtained that status through white female indentured servants who bore children by black male slaves or "servants" during the colonial period. But be careful about claiming totally free ancestry when, in fact, a male slave progenitor cannot be identified. Note that the legal status of the mother determined the status of her children for both slaves and indentured servants.

A well-known genealogist, Elizabeth Mills, has estimated that African American genealogists can expect to find at least one free person for every eight ancestors. With odds as high as this, you cannot afford to ignore the possibility that one of your ancestors may have lived as a "free person of color." Many of those listed in Newman's transcription of free Blacks found in the 1790 census and Carter Woodson's book *Free Negro Heads of Families in the United States in 1830* gained their freedom during the colonial period in both the North and the South. How and where they became free is a question that you will have to answer once you discover your ancestors listed as free persons of color in the pre-1870 censuses.

The first task, therefore, is to be alert enough to consider the possibility of free ancestry in the first place, particularly if you are researching a family line that shares some of the following characteristics, which turn into clues for further research. These clues about free ancestry come in obscure forms for the unwary researcher:

- Family stories about being free or never being enslaved
- Residence in a historically black town or settlement
- Residence in areas known to have a large population of free blacks
- Any Canadian connections, including indication of place of birth as Canada on federal population censuses
- Heavy mulatto ancestry
- Family ownership of mid-nineteenth century (or earlier) memorabilia
- Very early and continuous educational achievement
- Membership in a local social elite
- Pre-1914 migration settlement in major urban centers
- Residence in a particular area outside of the South in 1870

- Residence in southern states or cities known to have had a relatively large class of free blacks

These, however, are only clues, some of which are nevertheless extremely reliable, particularly in the case of mulatto and free ancestry, both of which are closely associated in the Deep South.

In order to determine whether one of your ancestors was freed during or after the colonial period, think about some of the following ways that this may have occurred: (1) They were indentured servants prior to the institutionalization of slavery; (2) they were the children of a free white female indentured servant; (3) they purchased their own freedom; (4) they "stole" their own freedom by running away; (5) they were granted their freedom by a slave owner because they (a) were related by blood, (b) had performed some act deemed "heroic" by their owner or under existing legal statutes such as saving the life of a White, (c) had performed some service deemed faithful enough to warrant freedom either at the time of the owner's death or prior, (d) were granted their freedom based on the owner's moral or religious convictions, or (e) were able to move about freely enough because of some occupational skill or training; (6) they passed or assimilated into the White world because they were light enough to do so; or (7) they served during the Revolutionary War.

PROTECTIVE SLAVERY AND FREE BLACK OWNERSHIP OF SLAVES

*T*his is a complex subject, but it can be dealt with by asking this question: If you were an ex-slave, now freed, and you had the chance to buy one and only one family member's freedom, which one would it be? Obviously, it would be your wife's, especially if she was of childbearing age, because all future children would be free, and she could perhaps earn enough to help purchase the freedom of others. Or, if you were free and wanted to guarantee your mate's absolute freedom, which would be better—to own him or her as a slave or to live with him or her in freedom? In some cases, it was better to own the spouse as a slave, especially if you lived in an area where laws placed pressure on free Blacks. Some states placed head-taxes and occupational taxes on free Blacks. Ironically, it was safer and cheaper to be your spouse's or your parent's slave than to be free. They had enough difficulty surviving as free persons, given the anti-Black proscriptive laws that eventually emerged.

Of course, if you took the risk of keeping your mate in protective slavery, in the event of your demise, he or she could easily have been exposed to being sold to pay your debts, and this did happen. Finally, if you lived during the period when manumissions had to be legislated rather than simply registered (private manumissions), you would have to worry whether your dependents would be reenslaved because it was feared that they would become clients for the county's poor relief fund, a subject which was always a bone of local contention, since the planter elite believed that everyone else's labor should be stolen.

Finally, there were some Blacks who owned slaves as an investment. This seemed to have been particularly the case in Louisiana, Natchez, and South Carolina.

South Carolina produced some of the most interesting examples. One White named Holman, a slave trader, having resided on the West African coast for years, had a mulatto family which carried on his business after his demise, but the children eventually settled in South Carolina to establish a fairly substantial plantation. The Holman family was only one of a surprisingly considerable number documented by Koger in his work on free Blacks in South Carolina.

THE RECORDS

*T*he records generated to document the recognition of freedom are many, but nearly all such instances were documented in courthouse conveyance records (mainly deed books). You may also find the following records helpful in your search:

Censuses: Often those genealogists who research free ancestors will find that racial designations for free persons of color will shift from one census to the next. In one census year, they may have been listed as mulatto, and in the next they may have been entered as White. The tremendous admixture of the three main racial groups (Indian, African, and White) can cause the unwary genealogist to incorrectly assume that a free person of color (as listed in the censuses) was a person of primarily African descent when in fact he or she may have been of Indian and White descent or Indian and African descent or a combination of all three.

Free Papers/Certificates of Freedom: No matter how freedom was obtained, nearly every county judicial body was required to register free persons either in deed books or free registries and to issue certificates of freedom which were then carried by free persons of color. If the individual free man or woman moved out of the state—as many were required to do—they registered their certificates of freedom at the local county courthouse in the state to which they migrated. If they expected to reside in any particular county for a while before settling elsewhere, they still registered themselves as free persons of color at a local courthouse. The original certificates often contained fairly detailed physical descriptions which would have been included if the clerk copied into the local court records the original certificate. Therefore, if you find a certificate of freedom copied into a deed book in Michigan or Indiana or elsewhere, you will often be able to determine the county in which the certificate was originally issued (and the individual's presumed place of origin). Many of these registers and manumission records have been abstracted and published, especially for the states of Ohio, Virginia, and Maryland. Indeed, those researching free ancestry can look forward to a large body of transcribed and abstracted genealogical sources for this group when compared to those who remained enslaved.

Higher Court Petitions: The individual state and local laws on manumission were often complex, changing, and certainly varied form state to state in the South. Early county and state laws contain more than plentiful evidence that European settlers were concerned about the regulation of "unfree" individuals and their labor. Once a codified set of laws emerged on the issue of

slavery for each colony or territory, there was a parallel tendency to limit or remove the power to manumit slaves from individual slave owners. Therefore, manumission of individual slaves often involved petitioning higher-level courts either by the slave owner or by those slaves hwo felt they had a strong enough case to contest the frequent denial of their bequeathed freedom by the heirs of a deceased slave owner. The latter case often occurred when the slave owner willed a sizable portion of his estate to a slave mistress and their children. Such cases appear from the earliest days of legal slavery through its demise.

Runaways, Absentees, and Recalcitrants in Newspaper Advertisements: Running away was so widespread during all periods of slavery that it could be called endemic. So too were plots of slave rebellion—from New York to Louisiana—during the colonial period. Runaways, depending on where they were located, often returned or were recaptured and hardly ever lost their lives as punishment for their acts. Recaptured runaways were often "deported," and those who "imported" them often had fears that they were recalcitrants. Louisiana passed several laws prohibiting the resale of deported slaves in the state.

Runaways were often absorbed into local Indian populations or in the few maroon colonies that developed in Louisiana and Florida prior to their cession to the United States. Researchers will face some problems tracing runaways who were absorbed into local Indian populations. Since their numbers were so great, it would serve your research well to examine surviving colonial newspapers, most of which have been microfilmed. In addition, records of colonial jails, if they survived, would also contain information on "recaptives," including specifics about their owners, rewards given to those who helped to recapture them (including slaves), and physical descriptions.

Church Records: The parish vestry records of the Anglican church, records of Catholic parishes, and records of the Quaker church contain many references to the manumission of slaves or to the legal status of African who may not have been formally enslaved. The further back in time, the more likely that such records will be of importance to you in locating information on the circumstances under which your ancestor became free. Note that Catholic parish records would apply to those areas in which there was a strong Spanish and French presence—namely, Louisiana and the Mobile and Pensacola areas.

Occupational Freedom: Artisan slaves often outnumbered White artisans, and because of their skills they were often hired out for various periods of time. Therefore, they were able to purchase their freedom or sustain their escape by working in a specific trade. Sources that relate to specific occupations, though they are rare, should not be overlooked. One particularly large occupational group consisted of individuals who worked in various capacities aboard whaling vessels and merchant ships, often forming up to 50 percent of the crew, and in some cases working for Black-owned vessels. The book *Black Sailors: Afro-American Merchant Seamen and Whaleman Prior to the Civil War* contains a wealth of sources for those whose

ancestors may have been involved in this trade. Maybe you'll *really* read Melville now. Urban slaves and slave hires had many opportunities to live in a nominally "free" environment.

FREE BLACKS IN THE NORTH AND ON THE FRONTIER

During the recent conflicts between Black and White students at Brown University, Black students often noted that the original bequest for this venerable institution was from dirty money—money earned from the slave trade, no less! Researchers should know that the differences between northern and southern slavery were only a matter of degree. This does much to explain why northern manumission was relatively slow, halting, and gradual. As their southern brothers were to do after the Civil War, the Yankees passed a series of laws after manumission that virtually placed free Blacks in a *prison of laws*. Nevertheless, between 1780 and 1804 all northern states had passed laws leading to abolition, whether through gradual abolition or through rulings of higher courts. In some states like New Jersey, which shared more with Maryland perhaps than with other Mid-Atlantic states, there was considerable resistance to manumission. By 1800, approximately 37,000 northern Blacks were still reported in bondage, and by 1830, some 3,600 remained in bondage, most in the state of New Jersey!

Scattered throughout the North, the Midwest, and the Far West are clusters of African American communities formed during the period which we associate with the post-1790 settlement of the American frontier. Even in places where there may be no surviving physical evidence of these early settler communities, the historical records will often show that free African Americans had, at some point in the past, lived there of their own free will. States like Ohio, Michigan, Pennsylvania, and New York, as well as midwestern states like Illinois, Indiana, and Wisconsin contained such communities. Settlements such as those found in Cass County, Michigan, upstate New York, and Allentown in the San Joaquin Valley of California are examples. Note however that there were many Black towns or settlements formed immediately after the Civil War; these should not be confused with black settlements formed after the early northern emancipation of slaves.

Frontier slavery existed in the territories of Illinois and Indiana as well as Wisconsin. By the early 1820s, free Blacks were able to move through these areas with less fear and trepidation, but they still had to live in fear of collusion between slave-catchers and local law officials, some of whom were easily bribed. Researchers should be aware of the fact that there was always a significant amount of European movement between the New England/Mid-Atlantic states and the southern slave states. (The great divide of the Mason-Dixon line is a relatively recent phenomenon.) Not only were there extensive trade ties between white families fed by the economics of slavery; there were also familial ties. Some researchers may indeed trace their ancestors back to northern slave owners who migrated to the South or who sold their slaves to southern traders prior to the northern abolition of slavery.

In addition to the above sources, you will have to be aware of the fact that free Blacks often had ties to local Whites who acted as patrons in the event that their freedom was contested or in the event of difficulties that may have compromised their freedom. Even when free Blacks settled in the Midwest, it was often necessary to create or maintain such a relationship. Therefore, the names of Whites who appear on certificates of freedom or other documents should not be ignored as leads to locating further documentation. Finally, free persons of color will appear in many of the standard records used by genealogists. Tax records, land records, and surviving military records for all colonial wars are of importance.

WHY CRISPUS ATTUCKS WON'T DIE: THE AMERICAN REVOLUTION

*I*n 1977, a group of Black students was attacked by six White men with bats and clubs during their visit to the Bunker Hill monument in Boston. Four of the students and their teacher required hospital treatment. Whatever the causes of this little war of 1977, it should come as no surprise that slaves and free Blacks fought in the American Revolution and all other colonial and postcolonial wars. If you haven't donated money to help construct the memorial to African Americans who fought in the Revolution, then perhaps it is time. Your donation may help others, like the men at Bunker Hill, to see in true monumental style what happened during this period.

Morgan's quote at the beginning of the chapter with regard to freedom emerging as a means to an end (often someone else's end) has to be considered seriously. In that respect, this war was a rehearsal for the conflagration that the Civil War was. If you've gained experience in using the War Department records for your Civil War research, you will find many similarities between the two—at least from the perspective of the African American experience. Technically, free Blacks and slaves were not allowed to bear arms or serve in the various colonial militias, but as in the Civil War, laws limiting Black enlistment and/or participation often denied the reality of the battlefield. Washington and his council of war, much like Lincoln some years later, issued a policy on slave and free Black recruitment in 1775 preventing the enlistment of "any deserter from the ministerial army, nor any stroller, negro or vagabond, or person suspected of being an enemy to the liberty of America. . . ."

Colonial America had perhaps not fully envisioned the dilemma in which it found itself—wars on two fronts. One was a war for freedom to run its own affairs, including maintaining the institution of slavery. The country was envisioned as one for White men only, and slaves were considered "foreigners" in much the same way as enemies of the country. The other was a full-blown rebellion at home and a war from abroad. Slave rebelliousness was a constant fear among the colonial elite, and it is not surprising that they lumped slaves together with others who were enemies to the country's "liberty."

Imagine, if you will, that your ancestor arrived in the United States during the Revolutionary period—perhaps from a war in his own homeland, where he became a captive, to a war in his new home where, still a captive, he might be used as war

"booty" and tossed from one side to the other. The world surely must have looked like it was falling apart. Although slave imports did fall off during this period, Africans continued to arrive. If newly arriving Africans had trouble figuring out the events taking shape around them, those who had been here for any period of time had no difficulty. The Revolutionary War put a considerable dent in slave ownership, particularly among planters in Virginia and South Carolina.

These were your "choices" if you were a "free agent" slave trying to make your way to freedom during this period:

1. You could have been owned by a Loyalist who had time to "refugee" you and other slaves to Spanish East or West Florida, the Bahamas, Jamaica, Haiti, or Nova Scotia.
2. You could have been "indemnified" or taken from an American and given to a Loyalist as a replacement for slaves lost during the war.
3. You could have gone to battle with your owner who remained loyal to the American side, or you could have fought in one of the contingents of German and French forces that were involved in the war.
4. You could have been in one of the contingents fighting on the American side as part of a state militia unit.
5. You could have served in either the American or British navy.
6. You could have been impressed to work on various fortifications by either side. Impressed slaves were often "public" slaves purchased for wartime use in Virginia.

7. You could have been freed as a result of the confiscation of American property in the North, or when the British waged their southern campaign, you could have been confiscated and then sold.

8. You could have lost your freedom if you were sold by one of the British officers upon evacuating the American mainland.

9. You could have escaped on your own and wound up in East Florida.

10. You could have "found freedom" by making your way to one of the British ships that evacuated from New York, Virginia, or South Carolina, providing you could document your newly acquired freedom.

11. You could have fought in the war but remained enslaved until you petitioned for your freedom, as did James Armistead who became James Lafayette after the Virginia General Assembly granted him his freedom in 1786, five years after having served as a spy.

If these possibilities excite you—as they would any good genealogist—then you have your work cut out for you. The range of possible experiences that your ancestor may have encountered during the course of the war makes all the policy statements from the Continental Army about Black enlistment seem trivial. The barring of Blacks from serving in the military was later lifted to admit free Blacks after the colonial governor of Virginia, Lord Dunmore, offered freedom to Blacks and indentured servants in exchange for their willingness to bear arms against the Americans—again, freedom making its way into the world. It is estimated that 5,000 Blacks served on the American side in all capacities, including leading a few all-Black units, but it is likely that the numbers were much greater since the total number of men who enlisted at one time or another reached 300,000.

Researchers should therefore not ignore the military service of slave owners nor other records associated with raising colonial militia units. For the Revolutionary War, researchers will find many compilations of lists by state as well as for the entire Continental Army. There are several lists of Blacks who served, most notably one compiled by Newman and the other by the Daughters of the American Revolution. There is still no authoritative list of Black Revolutionary War enlistees—primarily because most surviving records do not identify the race of the enlisted men and a name alone, even when it appears to be African as in the case of Cuffee, may indeed turn out to be the surname of a European. Furthermore, because service was often intermittent and an enlisted man could serve in various units raised in the war effort, Revolutionary War research is not always as straightforward as it appears to be. Of course, checking the Revolutionary War service records and pension files housed at the National Archives and also available on microfilm at its federal record centers should be one of your first steps once you locate ancestors who lived during the war and who subsequently show up in postwar records as free persons of color.

One possible clue that researchers may overlook is that many veterans who settled the southern frontier obtained land grants as a result of their service in this and other wars. This also may have been true for some Black veterans except that they would have settled in areas outside the South. A thorough land search for a landowning free ancestor is always in order, although it is not presently known whether many Black veterans of this war applied and obtained land grants. Jeffrey J. Crow identified several for North Carolina. For example, one Valentine Locus received a 228-acre land warrant for his enlistment of thirty months in 1776. Isaac Perkins received 274 acres for thirty-six months of service.

LOYALIST SLAVE OWNERS AND BLACK LOYALISTS

Winning the war was not a foregone conclusion. Because it was a relatively long war (1775 to 1783), the British offer of freedom to slaves caused a great dislocation among the slave population, particularly in Virginia. Again, the same question asked about the Civil War period should be applied once you reach this phase: How did the war affect the area where your ancestors were located? Obviously, your ancestors' experiences could vary widely depending on whether they were owned by a Loyalist or an "American." Years after the war, slave owners tried to retrieve their former slaves, and some, like Pierce Butler, who had sat the war out in Philadelphia, returned to find a loss of two hundred on his South Carolina plantations.

If your ancestor was among the thousands (and perhaps four times more than the number identified as having served on the American side) who were able to board British ships as part of the British evacuation of the American mainland, thereby gaining their freedom, then you will find their names and relatively detailed descriptions, including former owner, entered on inspection rolls which were microfilmed as part of the National Archives series *Miscellaneous Papers of the Continental Congress, 1774–1789*, Roll 7(M332), and *Papers of the Continental Congress, 1774–1779*, Roll 66 (M247). Eventually resettled in Nova Scotia, many of this group migrated to Sierra Leone in 1792, the first large group of African returnees. An estimated 8,000 were brought to what was then East Florida from Savannah and Charleston, including some who were slaves of Loyalists. Note that some, estimated at approximately 2,500, returned along with their owners after Loyalists were permitted to resettle in Georgia and South Carolina. Many also escaped to Seminole country, where they were to fight the Americans in a later war at Fort Mose.

AFRICA ALWAYS ON MY MIND: EMIGRATION MOVEMENTS

It may be a surprise to you to discover that African Americans, though always in a trickle, have returned to Africa over the whole course of American history. Africa has always been in the collective memory of some African Americans. While the image of Africa has changed over time and the reasons for going have changed with them, one constant is that African Americans saw Africa as a land of retreat from American slavery and only secondly as a land of freedom, particularly during slavery. African Americans who returned to Africa during slavery had no choice but to cast their vision of Africa in tragic terms, terms that Africans didn't accept because they were unaware of the global impact of slavery.

1792: BLACK LOYALIST RETURNEES

*T*hose researchers who find that their ancestors wound up in Nova Scotia after the American Revolution will have to continue their search in Sierra Leone. On January 15, 1792, fifteen ships with 1,196 "black loyalists" sailed form Halifax to Sierra Leone. They arrived in March of that year hoping that their denied promises of land in Canada would be met in what was to become Freetown, the present-day capital of Sierra Leone. They joined the survivors of a band of about four hundred Blacks and seventy White women—people the British had essentially deported, some of whom had come from the Americas. Added to this group were Jamaican maroons (many of Asante descent) who, having been defeated in a war with the planters, were deported to Sierra Leone in 1795.

These groups preceded the Liberian returnees by nearly thirty years, and their story, profoundly different from all future returnees, has yet to be told as it deserves to be. Boston King's narrative, *Memoirs of the Life of Boston King, a Black Preacher, Written by Himself, During his Residence at Kingswood School*, is one of the few surviving written records of this experience written from the perspective of a settler. King's story should introduce you to the range of possibilities that await researchers who can document an ancestor during this period.

1820: LIBERIAN RETURNEES

*T*hat the focal point for the largest group of returnees wound up being a settlement off the "Grain Coast" on a little island later called Providence Island, now part of Liberia, has been of no small consequence, particularly as the country of Liberia evolved in the minds of African Americans. Liberia was perhaps one of the most written-about places in Africa through the middle of this century. The trials and tribulations of the African American settlers from both the mainland United States and the Caribbean have captured the imagination, the scorn and the praise of a wide variety of writers. One book written by Charles S. Johnson, former president of Fisk University, was even published posthumously.* Nevertheless, the settlers did survive and thrive, often under nearly impossible circumstances and often with a tenuous partnership with the United States, informally supported by the American Colonization Society.

Despite the controversy, your research wouldn't be complete unless you checked the large body of records left by the American Colonization Society which, founded in 1817, had all but ceased to operate by the turn of the century. The surviving documentation on emigration to Liberia, of which there is much, should always be

---

*Johnson might have been afraid to express his candid views on the state of the country, particularly with respect to the Americo-Liberian ruling elite's political and cultural domination of native Liberians. The book is entitled *Bitter Canaan* (New Haven, Conn.: Yale University Press, 1987).

checked when you encounter the following: (1) a free line of ancestors living in Virginia or Maryland who disappear from the records, (2) any free ancestors during the period when the ACS was most active, or (3) a slave owner who was a member of the ACS. If these conditions sound confusing, perhaps it is because you always thought that the ACS was an independent movement of free Blacks who wanted to return to Africa. That it was not.

RECORDS OF THE AMERICAN COLONIZATION SOCIETY

*H*oused at the Library of Congress, but also available on microfilm, are the voluminous papers left by the American Colonization Society. To give you an idea of their rich potential in your research, consider the following two letters written to the society by free Blacks:

From Reverend Nall of Mobile, Alabama Date: June 24, 1850

The free people of color in our city have, of late, been much excited and alarmed. The grounds of all that you will find in the accompanying notice from our sheriff. Of the state of things, I was not apprised before last week . . . I learned form good authority that about 300 will be affected by the operation of this law. Many have already gone to New Orleans—to the North and wherever else they could. Our churches are seriously affected—especially the Methodist and Baptist. Their best, leading colored members have left—are leaving—and most gone. The question now presently . . . What can be done? What must be done? I have

been asked as to the services of the Colonization Society . . .

From Abraham Camp, Illinois Territory, 1823

I am a free man of colour, have a family and a large conexion of free people of colour residing on the Wabash, who are all willing to leave America whenever the way shall be opened. We love this country and its liberties, if we could share a right to them; but our freedom is partial, and we have no hope that it ever will be otherwise here; therefore we had rather be gone, though we should suffer hunger and nakedness for years. Your ____(?) may be assured that nothing shall be lacking on our part in complying with whatever provision shall be made by the United States, whether it be to go to Africa or some other place; we shall hold ourselves in readiness, praying that God (who made man free in the beginning, and who by his kind providence has broken the yoke from every white American) would inspire the heart of every true son of liberty with zeal and pity, to open the door of freedom for us also.

In order to tackle this voluminous collection, researchers should first review the index to the *African Repository*, the society's monthly publication issued between 1819 and 1892. This was a widely circulated journal, and you may find a complete run in any large urban library. The society's annual reports are often bound with the *Repository*. The annual reports listed subscribers and members of state organizations, and therefore the reports could be used to identify slave owners who were involved in this movement. The *Repository* reprinted many letters from inquiring free Blacks, particularly if they showed a certain type of optimism for colonizing Africa. Ship departures, lists of emigrants, and brief articles on individual emigrants were always featured in the *Repository* on a regular basis. For example, the 1849 volume (#1) reported on a Mr. Cassell who returned to the United States to study; it also lists occasional vital records such as a report issued by the colony's registrar for 1848 which included genealogical information on births, marriages, and deaths and a story about an unnamed man who purchased himself for $2,500 and his wife for $300. The letters from Camp and Nall may not have been reprinted, for they show the fear of indiscriminate laws under which free Blacks often lived as well as their belief that they would never enjoy the nominal freedom they had gained, even on the frontier.

Another relatively easy task would be to examine the *Census of the Colony of Liberia* taken in 1843. This census, oddly enough, appears in the congressional reports called Serial Sets which may also be found at many libraries (Serial Set 458, U.S. Congress, Senate Document 150, 2nd Session, 28th Congress). The 1843 census of the colony was printed as part of a report on Admiral Perry's African expedition to examine conditions on the African coast. Because the census is part of Perry's report, it does not appear in the index to the Serial Sets. It offers quite detailed information on each emigrant, including children, who lived in the five separate Americo-Liberian settlements of the colony. As with all source material, don't assume that this is an exhaustive list. Many of the settlers died and many emigrated to Liberia after the census was taken. A part of the census is reproduced below to show its content.

A third source to check consists of a three-volume series published by the U.S.-based Liberian Studies Association listing emigrants to Liberia for separate periods of time. Schick compiled the list for 1820 to 1843, Brown covered 1843 to 1865, and Murzda 1865 to 1904. When combined, these represent the most exhaustive list compiled to date of settlers from the United States. Those who departed from the Caribbean are not included unless they embarked on ships leaving the United States. Note that some of the families appearing on the lists actually never left the country, and some who did arrive in Liberia returned after a brief stay. There is even the possibility that your ancestor's name may appear on this list but he or she never left the country. Those who were freed as slaves often took the opportunity to use their freedom in the United States, particularly former slaves who were to embark from Virginia, where there was a large enough free Black population in which one could move about freely without being detected and without having free papers, a situation which was always a source of concern with those in the ACS. Nevertheless, the fact that your ancestors may appear on these lists provides information about their experiences that you perhaps did not have before.

The correspondence files of the ACS collection are conveniently separated into letters to the ACS from within the United States and letters from Liberia. The correspondence files were indexed by the ACS, and individuals who were of African descent will often have a note next to their names that reads "col'd." This stands for *colored*, in case you thought it meant "cold." Some of the letters from Liberia have been tran-

CENSUS OF THE COLONY OF LIBERIA—SEPTEMBER, 1843.

Population of the town of Monrovia.

Names.	Age.	No. in family.	Date.	Where born.	Connexions in the colony.	Profession.	Extent of education.	Health.
Samuel Benedict	51	–	August, 1835			Merchant and farmer.	Liberal	Good.
Mary Benedict	44	–	Jan., 1833	–	S. Benedict's wife	–	Reads and writes	Feeble.
James Benedict	13	–	August, 1835	–	S. Benedict's son	–	do	Good.
Jane Drayton	65	–	do	–	None	–	None	Feeble.
Hannah Taylor	14	–	April, 1834	–	–	–	Reads and writes	Good.
M. H. Dones	14	–	July, 1837	–	None	Apprentice	do	do.
Charles Snetter	13	–	June, 1832	–	do	do	do	do.
Nancy Benedict	11	–	–	In the colony	do	do	None	do.
Sadi Benedict	15	–	–	do	do	do	do	do.
John Benedict	15	–	–	do	do	do	do	do.
Peter Benedict	9	–	–	do	do	do	do	do.
William Benedict	14	–	–	–	do	do	do	do.
Benjamin Miller	34	–	Feb., 1838	–	do	Laborer	do	do.
Harry Winkler	22	14	Jan., 1835	–	do	do	do	do.
H. B. Mathews	46	–	Jan., 1833	–		Shoe maker	Reads and writes	do.
Lavinia Mathews	41	–	do	–	H. B. Mathews's wife	–	do	do.
Samuel Mathews	16	–	do	–	H. B. Mathews's son	Shoe maker	do	do.
Martha Mathews	14	–	do	–	H. B. Mathews's daughter	Apprentice	do	do.
J. Johnson	13	–	———, 1833	–	–	do	None	do.
Henry Peal	6	–	———, 1833	–	–	do	do	do.
J. McGill	15	7	Sept., 1839	–	–	do	do	do.
Catharine Jacobs	80	–	Jan., 1833	–	–	Huckster	do	Excellent for her age.
Abraham Jacobs	13	–	do	–	Catharine Jacobs's grandson	–	do	Good.
Emma Mathews	13	–	do	–	Catharine Jacobs's grand-daughter	–	Reads and writes	do.
Catharine Smith	11	4	do	–	C. Smith's daughter	–	do	do.
Francis Payne	30	–	March, 1829	–	–	Merchant	Liberal	do.
David Y. Payne	25	–	do	–	Brother to Francis	do	do	do.
William H. Payne	21	–	do	–	–		do	do.

scribed and published in book form—*Slaves No More, Letters from Liberia, 1833–1869,* and *"Dear Master": Letters of a Slave Family.*

In addition to the ACS papers, you will want to examine the various state colonization society papers and journals, if they are locatable. The largest state societies were those in Maryland and New York. But most southern states also had societies, including Mississippi. Of all the state groups, the records left by the Maryland society are the most prolific and worthy of examining, particularly if your ancestors are from that state or nearby states. Both the ACS and the Maryland society's records have finding aids, and you will be surprised to find the extent to which free Blacks are documented in these collections, both of which often include slave owners' wills, their correspondence, and of particular interest, comments on the conditions under which free Blacks lived in communities throughout the country written and submitted by the field agents of the society. Agents, in their correspondence to the ACS, unwittingly revealed the true purpose of the society. They frequently reported on their meetings with local freedmen, often wondering how they could remain in their more or less miserable conditions rather than taking a chance to repatriate to their ACS-designated homeland, Liberia.

Finally, a search would not be complete without checking the standard indexes to articles appearing in historical journals. There are many such articles which report on specific emigrant families and slave owners who were involved in the society. There are also articles that report on unsuccessful tries at emigration, as in the case of the rejection of Marcus Garvey's plan of emigration in 1924. Because Americo-Liberians always maintained cultural ties with the United States, many emigrant families maintained contact with their families in the United States. You may, indeed, find letters written by emigrants to their families here in the United States.

There have been other emigration movements, but the American Colonization Society's efforts to remove the free Black presence in the United States stands out as the most successful one and the one that generated the most records during the nineteenth century. Note that this movement gained its momentum through free Blacks in the North—Cuffee and Russwurm—but they later severed their ties with the ACS and joined forces with the abolitionists. One, Edward Wilmot Bylden, remained in Liberia and made a significant contribution to the emergence of African and African American written history.

ABOLITIONISTS AND THE UNDERGROUND RAILROAD

*T*racing individual ancestors who stole their freedom can be one of the most problematic aspects of your research, particularly if they were slaves in some of the Deep South states. Free Blacks often lived without the benefit of community if they escaped individually and without much help until arriving in the North. Those who managed to escape and arrive in communi-

ties where there was an established community of free Blacks—especially places like Richmond, Baltimore, Boston, New York, and Philadelphia—were able to reestablish themselves, though always living in fear of being ensnared by slave-catchers and sold South or redeemed for an award. The accounts of Harriet Jacobs and Frederick Douglass indicate that living under the fear of recapture often necessitated not being documented or changing one's identity, and particularly one's name.

However, as in all things, the acorn doesn't fall far from the tree. Escaped slaves did not completely sever their ties to the past, and these ties, no matter how tenuous, are the ones that you will have to use as clues. In addition, escaped slaves often had to solicit the help and protection of Whites and/or established Blacks in a particular area. Note that Cal Boger, though he appeared to have severed his ties with the past, really didn't change his name or his identity very much. But in Boger's case, we started out with specific information on former owner and place of residence. For escaped slaves, that will often not be the case.

While running away was endemic, recall that it was often followed by recapture. Those who succeeded often had the support and connections of the Underground Railroad. And, for those sources, researchers should review the possibilities that exist in the voluminous documents and papers left by the abolitionist movement, particularly those of the Pennsylvania Abolition Society and the Black abolitionists. The latter have been collected and microfilmed, but researchers should first carefully read the guide to the microfilm edition. Note that the five-volume set entitled *The Black Abolitionist Papers* reproduced only about 10 percent of the documents contained in the microfilm series. The role played by Black abolitionists has been underestimated. To give you an example of what you might find in this collection, a Baltimore painter named Jacob R. Gibbs maintained a file of free papers from Blacks who had died. These he gave to some of the approximately two thousand runaways that he helped to escape. This perhaps explains why such documents do not survive within your family—they may have been recycled. A well-reasoned search strategy should be used before you take the plunge.

Also, consider the stories recorded by William Still in his important work, *The Underground Railroad*, which should be consulted if your free ancestors lived anywhere on the Eastern Seaboard near Philadelphia. Most of the slaves documented in Still's work escaped after 1852, and most had escaped from Delaware, Maryland, Washington, D.C., and Virginia. Few had come from Deep South states, primarily because the routes on the Underground Railroad varied from region to region.

INDIAN VERSUS EUROPEAN ANCESTRY: WHAT'S A TRI-RACIAL ISOLATE ANYWAY?

Americans are fascinated with their Indian ancestry, but less so with their African, particularly when they don't know they have any. But all things must and do change, and things are indeed changing with regard to the old American notions of ancestry. This, of course, is all for the good. Keeping pedigrees honest applies to both sides of the fence. This statement applies to African Americans, who often attribute Indian ancestry as the source of their mixed blood when in fact it is European, or who mistakenly claim European ancestry when in fact it may have been Indian depending on when it occurred, the latter point often not being known. This argument is equally applicable to Whites who fear having some African ancestry or who don't know they have some African ancestry. A well-informed archivist once told me that no White family whose ancestors lived in southern Louisiana during the French and Spanish period can be absolutely certain that they do not have at least some African and Indian ancestry. Additionally, White genealogists, like Black genealogists, often have the Pocahontas syndrome—claiming Indian ancestry when there is none. According to the records, Pocahontas was childless!

Recently, an article entitled " 'Verry Slitly Mixt': Tri-Racial Isolate Families of the Upper South—A Genealogical Study" was published in the journal of the National Genealogical Society. This article, written by Virginia Easley De Marce, states in its first paragraph:

Since the eighteenth century, communities with a mixed ancestry and an uncertain ethnic identity have been scattered throughout the Upper South. Originating in Virginia and North Carolina, they spread significantly into South Carolina, Kentucky, and Tennessee, then developed offshoots into the Deep South and states North of the Ohio River. Journalists in the nineteenth and twentieth centuries have called them "mystery people" and advanced incredible legendary stories to account for their origins. Anthropologists usually refer to them as tri-racial isolates.

De Marce's research lays the basis for a clear understanding of the possibilities and impossibilities of tracing Indian, African, and European ancestry, particularly as those families emerged from the colonial period, when a great portion of the initial mixtures occurred. It also clarifies what is knowable and what is not. De Marce's article, as well as her sources, stand as must reading on a subject that is often complicated and, in many cases, ultimately unknowable.

African American genealogists who claim Indian ancestry should be prepared to at least speculate about when the initial mixture occurred and how it changed over time. Many African Americans have pictures of or can describe ancestors who "looked" Indian and were said to be Indian. Intermixing, alliances, and all other arrangements between free and enslaved Indians and African Americans existed over the entire period of American history—even down to the present day. Know what the possibilities are before making assumptions; my first look at records housed at the Alabama Department of Archives was an abstract of probate records for Lowndes County in which an Indian slave owner was selling a slave.

Many mixed-bloods, products of the so-called Five Civilized Tribes of the Southeast and Europeans, were slave owners. Many free Blacks joined Indian nations in the North, as Bernice Guillaume documented for her ancestors who became affiliated with the Indians on Long Island, New York. Many migrated with the Cherokee, one of the most extensively documented of the group of the five. Indeed, the complex relationship between Africans and Indians in any genealogical reconstruction is a project unto itself. Before you begin your search for Indian ancestry, unless of course your ancestors were resident among one of the isolated communities in the East, complete the African American line and then return to sources that prove or disprove one of your ancestors was Indian. If you follow this approach, your research skills will be well honed enough to make your search a successful one.

Freedom came in many forms and in many different ways for African Americans. Some cases are easily documented, particularly if your ancestor was formally manumitted by a slave owner. But freedom was not always a matter of manumission; some slaves "stole" their freedom while others seized an opportunity in those almost insane moments of chance that present themselves in life, generally as a means to another end.

WHAT DO I DO NOW?

*T*his chapter covered a phase of research that is often overlooked by genealogists because we assume that we have no free ancestry. We may also assume erroneously that once our research takes us back to this period, the records will be too difficult to research. Just the few examples cited in this chapter should lead you to conclude otherwise. The records for this period of time are essentially no different from those to be found during the postcolonial period in both the original colonies and in other parts of the South where settlers began to expand.

Once you reach this period, your skills should be at a level where you can easily navigate the territory. What you must do now is to put on your agenda the task of understanding how your own ancestors' experiences fit into the colonial period. The next chapter will help you to continue to clarify this question.

Chapter 14

THE LAST AFRICAN
AND THE FIRST
AMERICAN

I am not a ward of America; I am one of the first Americans to arrive on these shores.

JAMES BALDWIN, *THE FIRE NEXT TIME*

Until the 1820s, more than twice as many people of African descent crossed the Atlantic Ocean as Europeans.

The first object which saluted my eyes when I arrived on the coast was the sea, and a slave ship which was then riding at anchor and waiting for its cargo. These filled me with astonishment . . . I was now persuaded that I had gotten into a world of bad spirits and that they were going to kill me . . . At last we came in sight of the island of Barbados . . . and we soon anchored off Bridgetown . . . We thought we should be eaten by these ugly men, as they appeared to us . . . at last the white people got some old slaves from the land to pacify us. They told us we were not to be eaten but to work, and were soon to go on land where we should see many of our country people . . . and sure enough . . . there came to us Africans of all languages.

FROM *THE INTERESTING NARRATIVE OF THE LIFE OF OLAUDAH EQUIANO OR GUSTAVUS VASSA, THE AFRICAN* (1789; BORN AN IBO CIRCA 1745)

THE LAST AFRICAN

*B*y the time Olaudah Equiano set sight on the American shore at Bridgetown sometime in 1755, the island of Barbados had been settled for nearly 128 years. Equiano, in some respects, was a late arrival. Indeed, he had known nothing of American slavery prior to being kidnapped from his village, though based on his account, his village must have known of *its effects*, for they lived in a fortified settlement, a certain indication that his village had experienced kidnappings. The world Equiano left, though dear to his heart, had finally been drawn into the orbit of Europe and slavery, perhaps without really knowing it, some three hundred years after the first Europeans reached the shores of West Africa. But, from a child's viewpoint, this world was filled with innocence, unlike the world of the Traore family dynasty, which lived and suffered from the dual encroachments of Islam and Christianity in Segu (Mali), the story Maryse Conde recounted in her two epic historical novels, *Segu* and *Children of Segu.*

Once your research reaches the colonial period, you will encounter many Equianos and many "children of Segu." They were the first Africans to arrive on the shores of the Americas, the first Africans that you may encounter in your own lineage, and the last African to live in Africa. While one of these forced migrants, unknown to you now, initiated your lineage on this side of the Atlantic, you might also want to think of him or her as representative of a lost lineage in Africa.

You will be dealing with an experience that was very different from the world in which your ancestors lived between the years 1790 and 1860. Your research will cover the seventeenth and eighteenth centuries, the formative period of American history. You should be prepared to view the world in a more international context, where planters in the original thirteen colonies had extensive trade and family ties with Caribbean planters and their European counterparts. It was a world where sugar, tobacco, and indigo were of far more importance than cotton. It was a world in which native-born Africans lived side-by-side with Africans born in America. It was a world in which a sizable population of free Blacks had begun to emerge, partly as a consequence of private manumissions and later as a result of the post-Revolutionary surge of formal abolition in the North. It was also a world of war, either with native-born Americans or between European powers in their scramble for territorial domination. It was a world that had begun to be characterized by constant migrations farther inland and away from the original colonial seaboard settlements. Finally, it was a world where African slaves lived alongside free Africans who could have been listed in one of America's first blue books, *A List of Persons of Quality.*

This chapter should be viewed as a thinking chapter—designed for you to understand the kinds of processes that you will need to go through in order to understand the pre-1790 period when the total number of Africans in America barely exceeded one-half million. In many ways, your research will simply be an extension of the research you have conducted in tracing slave owners. Essentially, the same methods apply, and the same kinds of public and private records are available. Your research will continue to focus on records left by slave owners—their transactions at local courthouses, their religious practices with regard to their slaves and church membership, the land and slaves they bought and sold, the places to which they migrated, and their surviving personal and business papers. What differs is the historical context in which slaves and slave owners lived, and this chapter should help you to (1) plan a strategy for this period and (2) anticipate possible sources that you may not have thought about. Many guidebooks and genealogical sources exist for this period, and they will help you as you encounter the standard stumbling blocks of colonial handwriting, archaic English, the conversion from the Julian to the Gregorian calendar, and strange names such as Etheldred.

REMEMBER 1790

*T*he year 1790 should be treated as an important transition point in your research. Once you reach this point, and that can happen quite easily when you find an ancestor whose estimated year of birth is placed in this decade, it is likely that the geographical focus of your research will be found in one of the original thirteen colonies or foreign-held territories that would eventually become part of the United States. This was the year of the first United States census. By 1790, nearly all Africans to be imported into this country had already arrived. (Indeed, the Virginia legislature had passed an act closing the slave trade in 1778!) In addition, by 1790 the number of American-born slaves *exceeded* the number of slaves who had been born in Africa. This also marked the year when population began to spill over into the frontier farther west and farther south. It is also the point at which a sizable number of slave owners had begun to move from being small-scale farmers to being large-scale planters. With the invention of the cotton gin in 1793, the further spread of large-scale slavery from the original colonies of the South to this new frontier was made certain. It was also the end of an era in which the majority of slaves had lived on small farms in relatively densely populated areas not too far from the Atlantic coast. Finally, it was the end of the Revolutionary era, whose result was the failure to resolve the status of African Americans beyond that of slavery. The following table provides a brief look at the slave and free Black population in 1790 by area of residence.

THE FORMATIVE PERIOD OF SLAVERY: ON THE GENDER OF VIRGINIA

*T*he early colonial period was one in which the legal status of Africans

UNITED STATES AFRICAN POPULATION, 1790

State	Slave	Free
Upper South	521,169	30,158
Delaware	8,887	3,899
Kentucky	11,830	114
Maryland	103,036	8,043
North Carolina	100,572	4,975
Tennessee	3,417	361
Virginia	293,427	12,766
Lower South	152,902	3,502
Georgia	29,264	398
Louisiana	16,544	1,303
South Carolina	107,094	1,801
North	40,370	27,109
Total	1,388,512	94,429

Source: Berlin, *Slaves Without Masters*, Table 2, p. 46, and Appendix 1, Table A. Excludes population figures for Spanish and French territories that eventually became a part of the United States.

evolved to one of perpetual slavery over time. Virginia, followed by Maryland, set the pace. In the historical literature, Virginia is always referred to as female, but beware. The experiences of Africans in Virginia determined to a great extent what would happen to Africans in the rest of the colonies yet to be settled on the North American mainland. If "Carry Me Back to Ol' Virginny," written by African American James Bland, has any meaning, it certainly must rest on the perception that perhaps the character of Virginia was a type of female not understood by the men who created her.

Despite the unclear status of the first Africans to arrive at Jamestown in 1619, the very existence of the international slave trade made the introduction of formal slavery in Virginia and other North American colonies merely a question of time. Scholars like to quibble about whether the early settlers intended to "import" slaves. According to one scholar, by 1675, more Africans had arrived in Brazil than would ever arrive in North America throughout the course of the slave trade. Though trade ties between Britain and the other European slave-trading nations were hidden behind great political struggles between their nations, the realities of labor scarcity in their American colonies eventually led them all to behave in the same way—that is, to enter the business of "importing" Africans. If the first Africans to arrive in Virginia were "curious," the Virginia merchants certainly knew what they were there for. They were well aware of the uses of slavery in Portuguese and Spanish America.

The Virginians used the device of extending the terms of indentured servitude for Africans, particularly as White indentured servants gained either their freedom and upward mobility or succumbed to the elements, as many of them did. By 1690, Virginia formally institutionalized slavery. As grants, trusteeships, lord proprietorships, and every manner of device used to own and settle land was thought of by the English, other colonies followed suit. Therefore, good researchers should be aware of how slavery and settlement evolved in a particular colony, when slaves were formally introduced, where they came form, and the types of relationships that evolved between Africans and Indians. *Not knowing the history of a colonial settlement will seriously hamper your research.*

This information, all part of the necessity of placing your ancestors' experiences in historical context, should guide your research endeavors. For example, researchers whose ancestors lived in those mainland colonies owned and settled by the Spanish and French along the Gulf will sometimes encounter added difficulties—namely, records written in Spanish or French and records located in countries of the Caribbean and Europe.

THE FIRST AFRICAN AMERICANS: LOST MEMORIES OF AFRICA

*I*t is often stated that one William Tucker, who was born and baptized at Jamestown, Virginia, in 1624, was the first African American to be born on American soil. Because you know a lot about records now, you would want to modify that assertion by stating that Tucker's may have been the first

recorded African American birth in what was to become the United States. But whether this was indeed the case cannot be proven or disproven. Africans had arrived on the mainland of what was to become the United States way before 1619. One of the earliest permanent settlements was at St. Augustine, where the Spanish had disembarked Africans in the sixteenth century. One scholar found that part of Francis Drake's famous Roanoke arrival in June 1586 included a group of "Cimarrons" (escaped slaves) from a maroon colony in Panama.

The process of arrival or importation, adaptation, and the formation of an Afro-European culture among slaves in the United States (often called creolization) effectively occurred over a relatively short and intense period of time, mainly during the eighteenth century. You may wonder why your ancestors failed to pass down more knowledge than you now have about your African ancestors—at least the last African or the first African to arrive or the first African American in your line, depending on how you view it. The simplest answer is that the last Africans had arrived before 1790, and even by then, there were more native-born people of African descent in the United States than African born.

But this is only part of the answer. Other reasons are:

1. There was an extremely high rate of mortality among the first Africans brought to the Americas.
2. Most who came were from an age group least likely to maintain traditions—the young.
3. Creolization started during the first decade of their arrival.

4. Early settlement patterns (small farms and relatively small plantations with dispersed quarters for slaves) generated isolation and division rather than the communalism needed to maintain the continuities with Africa so evident (even to the naked eye) in the Caribbean and South America.

5. North American planters used specific methods to sever any ties that would encourage revolt—often prohibiting singing, drumming, and the use of African names.

6. The North American slave population began to reproduce itself early on.

7. Unlike in the South American and Caribbean slave populations, there was not a continuous infusion of new slaves from Africa. Note that formal slavery ended in Brazil in 1888, and that between 1800 and abolition nearly three million Africans were brought to Brazil!

The reasons could continue, but the slave brought to North America found himself or herself far more isolated from other Africans and far more "supervised" than the slave taken to Jamaica or Brazil. Indeed, supervision and interaction were constant—whether from an overseer or the planter himself or through interaction with indentured servants and hired White workers. In the Caribbean, the world continued to be essentially an African one, but in the British colonies on the mainland, the world was red, white, and black. However, memories of Africa passed down through the oral tradition may have continued to exist under certain conditions. Those are: (1) late arrival after or near the year when importation of

slaves had been abolished (1808) and through the illegal trade that continued; (2) older slaves who occupied important positions in their group of origin (religious figures, herbalists, ancestry in a ruling lineage); and (3) residence in the few maroon colonies or in places characterized by large-scale plantations as in the case of low-country South Carolina.

For those researchers who are interested in exploring memories of Africa or Africans in the African American oral tradition, the narratives contained in volumes of *The American Slave* compiled by Rawick would be a good place to start. Indeed, when you interviewed your relatives, you may have found a few surviving stories as did Robert L. Hall, a scholar who reported a conversation with Richard McKinney at Live Oak's African Baptist Church. McKinney related that his farthest back African ancestor was an African born around 1820 who, illegally imported into the United States, passed down knowledge of his ethnic identify as Ashanti (Asante).

Even if you have no idea who the first African was, you may have an idea of who the first African American was. He was born of African or African-Indian or African-European parents sometime between the 1620s and 1790. He became a slave relatively late in the history of slavery in the Americas. His parents were relatively young and may indeed have died prior to his reaching maturity, all circumstances that kill family and collective memory. He lived in only a few places in the United States—in any of the original colonies both North and South. He was a slave in areas that produced tobacco, rice, indigo, sugar cane, and cotton along with other crops. Though his life expectancy may have been relatively short, he did live long enough to produce your lineage. African American genealogy tells the story of survivors.

SEARCHING FOR AFRICA'S IMPRINT

As you begin to explore documents that place you close to the time of arrival of large numbers of Africans, you should be alert to the often hidden clues that suggest the continuance of African practices. This would especially apply to the use of names, one of the most persistent and obvious links with Africa found among African Americans in the United States. Other practices are often referred to in the journals and day books left by planters, particularly those who had leisure time to write. Rather than assume the perspective of the writer/planter and pass these practices and behavior off as strange, be prepared instead to consider the possibility that they were practices found in Africa during that period of time and that have continued through today. Examples are the use of glass and shell decorations on graves, the practice of divination with roots and other devices, speech patterns, and of course, the more obvious ones in dance and music.

WHAT REALLY IS IN A NAME?

Often given names assume more importance during this phase of your research. In some cases, you will find that African names persisted, while in others, your ancestors may carry names assigned by their owners—names that were derived from their own worldview. Names from the classical period of Greek and Roman history, place names such as London and Bristol, and shortened names of English given names were all assigned to Africans. Indeed, some of these names were eventually used as surnames by Africans, as in the case of Pompey. What these names reflected other than their imposition by a slave owner was often the worldview of the planters themselves, for it has been noted that the early elite and literate Virginians tended to be preoccupied with studying the classics, reading and studying in Greek, Hebrew, and Latin.

The Persistence of Day Names

My grandfather's given name is Quessie, which in present-day Twi means "born on a Sunday." We'll have to assume here that the name preceded the adaptation of the European seven-day week among the Akan of Ghana, in which case, the name will have yet another meaning. I have often been enticed to think that the place of origin for one or more of his ancestors may have been Ghana because Twi is the language spoken by the Fante and Asante, both ethnic groups of the Akan cultural group in present-day Ghana. (Note that the Akan extend into the Ivory Coast.) When I saw all of his relatives, the Crittendens, sitting on his first cousin's porch, I had the overwhelming feeling that, indeed, they had to be from somewhere in Ghana. Whether I'll be able to identify his ancestors' region of origin depends on a series of contingencies, the first one being that I have to document the line as far back as I can. His ancestors were owned by a slave owner with Virginia roots, but perhaps he bought slaves in Georgia or elsewhere as he migrated to Alabama. Furthermore, the custom of using Akan day names was probably adopted by other Africans or applied to Africans by Europeans, often in a derogatory sense, as in the use of "Quash" in the islands to refer to a lazy person. The point is that a name is not sufficient evidence, at least for me, to state that my ancestors came from Ghana.

You May Carry an African Name Already

A variety of African names have survived and are still being used, perhaps without the name-bearer's knowledge. The current trend of naming children with African or "African-sounding" names has been bashed by a variety of comics and serious writers as well. One writer in a well-known women's magazine lambasted African American mothers for giving their children names which she argued can neither be pronounced nor phonetically spelled and for which there are no "meanings." She concluded by saying that she gave her son a name whose meaning she located in a dictionary of names so that he could be proud to say what his name means. She even believed the story that circulated about children being named after certain diseases. This lack of historical perspective is unfortunate, to say the least. This pseudo-scientific approach to names should be avoided, as should the standard name dictionaries when you encounter "African sounding" names.

But those African Americans who give their children these "unusual" names are simply carrying on the silent tradition of assigning more importance to the given name than to the surname. The given name speaks to a specific meaning and identity, whereas the surname is always somebody else's name. It seems fairly obvious, doesn't

it? But there are as many explanations for assigning a given name as there are people. I once met a woman named Valencia who firmly but politely told me, after I suggested that she was named after a city in Spain, "No, that's the name my mother gave me."

One does not have to invent an African name or even borrow one. All it takes is knowing a little history and accepting the fact that given names carry considerable importance among African Americans. Many African American given names are actually anglicized African names. Consider the name Annica, which is still being used. Sounds very contemporary, but it was one of the most common African names to be used from the very beginning of slavery in the United States. Names like Mahalia, Phoebe, Zack or Jack, Abba, Ola, Pecola, Teneh, and even names that White Southerners may carry often have African origins. The reason they survived? They could be easily spelled and pronounced in English. That is, the sounds were familiar enough to be intelligible to those writing. But the version of an African name that you may encounter is only part of a series of names given to a child. Careful here: An African name only indicates the ethnic group in which it was most commonly used. The name itself, particularly for Africans in North America, may not indicate ethnic origins but the adaptation of the naming practices of another African ethnic group, as in the widespread use of Akan (Asante and Fante) day names. To find lists of African names that survived, see the bibliography for this chapter, but here are a few more: Mingo, Cuffee, Sambo, China (N'China), Cato, Jacco, Hagar, Job, Rinah, Neicee, Genie, Jemima, Juba, Cuba, and Arminta.

Finally, the importance of given names

is often not in their meaning but rather in their use from one generation to the next. Valencia's name was given to her by her mother. While name usage among enslaved Africans has not been studied enough to know what patterns existed for most regions, it is known that there was a tendency to assign male names from one generation to the next more frequently than female names. You should therefore study the patterns of given name assignment in your lineage. From observing how the names reappear over several generations, there is a possibility that you can figure out the rules for name assignment in your lineages.

UNDERSTANDING COLOR DESIGNATIONS AND OTHER TITLES

Grif, sambo, mustee, mulatto, woolly, quadroon, negro, negre, negress, copper, brown, black, light complexion, dark, octaroon, yellow, white, free person of color, new negro, outlandish, saltwater negro, Coramantee, creole, country marks, ship mates, country man or *woman, the mark of Ham,* and *Sabian* are all terms that were used to describe persons of some African ancestry that originated during the colonial period. Failure to know what they meant—often they had different meanings from region to region and from one period of time to the next, or meanings known only to the person writing the description—may cause you some difficulties, particularly if you rely on dictionary definitions to describe color designations when you examine a line known to have been tri-racial (Indian, African, and European). The following brief dictionary should help you. The more common appellations such as *maroon, quadroon, octaroon, creole,* and *mulatto* can be found in a standard dictionary. Those with an asterisk are based on definitions suggested by Jack Forbes.

New negro—An African-born slave, generally just arrived.

Outlandish—A slave from another region or country or recently from Africa.

Saltwater—An African-born slave or an African born in passage.

Country marks—Scarification patterns on face, stomach, or back; also an indication of being African born.

Ship mates—Term commonly used in Jamaica and perhaps rest of Caribbean to indicate that individuals made the passage on the same ship. May or may not indicate same ethnicity.

Free person of color*—An ambiguous designation that may have included individuals of undetermined quantities of African, Indian, and European ancestry. Often refers to non-White without indicating racial identity. May have also included non-European "whites" such as individuals from the Middle East and North Africa or dark individuals of Spanish origin. Most important, included Indians in many public records including censuses.

Mustee*—White and Indian mixture, but in some areas such as South Carolina, it meant Indian/African ancestry. A person of combined yellow, brown, and copper complexion.

Sambo/Zambo*—African and Indian mixture with some amount of undetermined European ancestry and marked Indian features.

Grif/Griffe*—Most common in French-speaking (New Orleans and elsewhere) areas and used to refer to three-quarters Indian and one-quarter African. Equivalent to sambo. More or less equivalent to mustee.

"People of That Nation": Understanding Descriptions of African Nations

*D*escriptions of African ethnic groups are bound to be confusing for the unwary. They have even been confusing to many present-day American scholars who are writing about the survival of African culture in the Americas. They were also confusing to the first Europeans who wrote these descriptions into the records. Let's just take a little example of a group commonly known throughout West Africa, the Fulani. In English-speaking countries, they are referred to as Fulani. In French-speaking countries, they are referred to in a variety of ways. The various names that have been assigned to this one ethnic group include Toucouleur, Fula, Tukulor, Peul, Fulfulde, Fulbe, and even Mandingo. You should know that what you call yourself and what others assign to you represent two separate realities. According to one scholar, Toucouleur is used in Senegal, Fula in Gambia, and Fulani in Nigeria (the name assigned to them by the Hausa, a people whom they conquered and with whom they intermarried). Tukulor means "the sedentary ones," Peul or Fula "the nomadic cattle keepers," Fulfulde refers to their language in Nigeria. And what do they call themselves? Hal Pularen, or speakers of the Pular language.

This exercise could be extended, and there is one additional precaution. There seems to be some confusion between the terms *Mande* and *Mende*. Because this will be important to you if you explore this part of your research, the term *Mende* refers to an ethnic group located in Sierra Leone, while *Mande*, depending on how it is used, refers to a language classification of the Mande-speaking people who belong to many different ethnic groups in West Africa, the Mende of Sierra Leone being one of them. In addition, the term *Mande* is applied to an ethnic group that is also called Mandinka or Maninka, who originated in the heartland of the Mande-speaking peoples' homeland in present-day Mali. Mande speakers later dispersed throughout West Africa.

The point is that the names used for African ethnic groups, particularly during the period of the slave trade, have varied over time and have sometimes been confused with the name of the language they spoke. Finally, these names may not be the name they called themselves. Consider excerpts from various documents that describe the origins of Africans, noting how their ethnic identity is treated:

Philadelphia (September 1799)

This indenture witnesseth, that Fidel a Negro boy of the nation of Mozambique aged 15 years and a slave to John Rene Granville in consideration of his having this day granted letters of emancipation to him . . .

SOURCE: PENNSYLVANIA ABOLITION SOCIETY PAPERS, *INDENTURES AND MANUMISSIONS OF AFRICANS*, THE HISTORICAL SOCIETY OF PENNSYLVANIA

Baltimore (June 1, 1784)

To all those to whom it may belong: I Augustus Montoroy, inhabitant of the Parish of Port au Prince: certify having freed the Negress Genie of the Nation Congo aged about 28 years . . .

SOURCE: PENNSYLVANIA ABOLITION SOCIETY PAPERS, *INDENTURES AND MANUMISSIONS OF AFRICANS*, THE HISTORICAL SOCIETY OF PENNSYLVANIA

Quamine (or Quamino) was brought to Rhode Island from Anomabu on the Gold Coast in 1754 or 1755 at about ten years of age. . . . Quamine retained his Fanti tongue and the English-educated Fanti missionary Philip Quaque confirmed Quamine's family connections were still strong on the Gold Coast. . . .

WILLIAM D. PIERSEN, *BLACK YANKEES*, P. 76

Fidel was described as being from Mozambique, Genie from the nation of Congo, and Quamine from Anomabu, Gold Coast (Ghana). Your optimism may rise when you discover that, indeed, there are documents that attribute a particular nation of origin or ethnic group to an African. At least you know that you've found the first African because most documents do not refer to American-born Africans as being of a particular nation. However, how sure can you be that the information is correct? You can be sure only to the extent that satisfactory documentation exists on the individual so named in the document. In the case of Fidel and Genie, you only have some idea of the region of origin. For Quamine, you have not only a name, but also a place of origin and language spoken. If you had just the name and Gold Coast as an origin, you could have incorrectly guessed that he was Asante, when in fact he was Fanti, since both groups use the name Quamine. Forget about the spelling—Europeans wrote what they heard; the phonetic spelling of names is a recent development.

In short, the more your ancestor's case was a unique one, the more likely that you will find some reference to nation of origin and, as in the case of Quamine, specific village or area. Finding specific information on place of origin for Africans in North America is fairly rare, but for the Caribbean region and places influenced by the Caribbean (New Orleans), there is a greater likelihood that ethnic identity can be found in the records. The naming of "New Africans" or "New Negroes" or "Saltwater" Africans as they were called was often done by their owners. Thus, even in cases where ethnic and or regional identity can be reasonably established, the essential clue of having a name is often missing. There are many pitfalls awaiting the unwary when it comes to the names of African ethnic groups, particularly since even today, there are thousands of them to know about.

REGION OF ORIGIN VERSUS ETHNIC IDENTITY

*I*n the records that do survive, nation of origin can refer to a unit as broad as Guinea or as narrow as Quamine's village of "Anomabu." Furthermore, a specific ethnic group can be named in a record when, in fact, the person so named as belonging to that group may have come from an ethnic group farther inland. Therefore, it is impor-

MANUMISSION OF GENIE OF THE CONGO NATION, 1784

In the Name of the King

To all those to whom it may belong: I — Auguste Montoroy
Inhabitant of the Parish of Port au Prince: Certify having freed the Negress
Genie: of the Nation Congo: aged about ÷ 28 Years ÷ ≈ after behaving
well — as a Subject ought to behave towards a Master. and in parting.
I give — to the said — Negress — named Genie. of the Congo Nation:
Liberty. & an Assurance — in a writing of Power: in case of Need
to serve her: in case of Difficulty; & trouble that she ÷ may — have
with time: I pray — the Council — ≈ superior — to pay attention
to the said — writing — done & performed — with my own hand ÷
for the said Negress. Behaving. as she to behave herself toward me
I give her a double Assurance — in parting — for Port of France): —
to rejoin my Relations: whom I desire to see ÷ A sight which
the intervening Distance prevents: And certify with Truth — and
swear with all Assurance. that — the above named Genie — merits
every possible Attention: from all Persons — of Character ÷ ÷ she
may enjoy every right — when she. may deem it necessary ÷
in case of Difficulty: to the Truth whereof I swear: ÷ Baltimore
this 1st June 1784 the said writing signed & sealed on the Date
ensuing — . Signed — and — Date — — placed — below

At Baltimore   this 1st June 1784.

Auguste Montoroy
3d ÷

Seals — 4th
Known Truth:
proved sincere:
just — Necessary: —
&c &c &c

Indorsed

Copy of an Object of Merit. Freedom given to
the within named Genie of the Congo Nation — for her
Assurance   Baltimore this 1st June 1784

Auguste Montoroy
3rd

Auguste Montoroy
3rd

tant for researchers to know that nation of origin, region of origin, and ethnic group origin are three different perceived realities that Europeans attempted to describe. Listed in descending order of inclusiveness, your ancestors may have been described in the records as follows:

- Cultural region of origin (Guinea versus Congo, for example)
- Slave trade region (Bight of Benin versus Windward Coast)
- Port of origin (Whydah versus Mesurado)
- Nation of origin (Senegal Nation versus Congo Nation)
- Ethnic group (Mandingo versus Nago)
- Village/town of origin (rare unless from area surrounding port)

The records will interchange these six concepts without ever giving you a clue, unless you know what they refer to for that particular period of the slave trade. Usages tended to change over time, and it is clear that the Europeans themselves did not understand African customs. For example, the records frequently refer to Guinea as a place of origin, but by now you will know that this does not refer to the present-day country of Guinea but rather to the northern coastal area of the slave trade, or for that matter any person who is of African origin. As for those thousands of ship manifests that simply indicate the places slave ships stopped before eventually landing in South Carolina or Virginia, I would say that this evidence is less than sufficient to identify region of origin. Slave ships often stopped at several places before setting sail across the Atlantic. It wasn't easy to buy slaves, after all. That's why one slave owner named Littlejohn equipped a ship that set sail from Boston just to acquire slaves from the Gold Coast. As reported in Dorothy Spruill Redford's *Somerset Homecoming*, the ship master's diary has yet to be located to verify that the ship did not stop anywhere else. However, many diaries and logs do survive, and some will indicate that they stopped at El Mina one day, remained for one week and then set sail for Calabar, and waited at Bonny for a month before setting sail—without having acquired any slaves at the last port.

Based on statistics recently published by scholars, each American colony "imported" different proportions at different times, depending on: (1) the country that monopolized the trade to that particular colony at any given time, (2) the occasional preferences of planters if and when they had a choice, and (3) the extent of internal strife within certain African regions. For the South Carolina port of Charleston, the majority of slaves who arrived were mainly from Angola/Congo (40 percent), Senegambia (19 percent), the Windward Coast (16 percent), and the Gold Coast (13 percent), with most arriving at differing times (that is, decades). At Virginia ports, the Bight of Biafra was the region of origin of the greatest number of Africans who arrived there (38 percent), followed by the Gold Coast and Angola/Congo at 16 percent each, and then Senegambia at 15 percent. In colonial New Orleans, a trade almost totally monopolized by the French and later by the Spanish, there was a decided preference for inland slaves from the Senegambia region, many of whom were Bambara captives from the incessant warfare in the interior.

Most statistical figures represent, at most, the region from which Africans were shipped and not necessarily their true ethnic identity. Note that none of the figures are firm and the numbers debate continues among scholars. However, region of origin can suggest a broader cultural identity. Slaves from Angola/Congo, though sharing in an underlying African cultural identity with other Africans that would, ironically, be discovered on the shores of the Americas, were culturally distinct from slaves arriving from the Senegambia region. While knowing the region of origin of slaves for a particular colony will help you in your research, it will not tell you what your ancestor's ethnic identity was. Equiano probably departed from the Bight of Biafra at either Bonny or Calabar. Had we not known the ethnic identity he claimed, we could have guessed that it perhaps was Ibo, or any one of the many other ethnic groups to the north and east of the Niger Delta.

Therefore, when you encounter references to region of origin, you should assume one or a combination of the following:

1. Place of embarkation, but not necessarily place of origin
2. Region of origin somewhere from the coast up to no more than two hundred miles inland, and occasionally farther
3. A region of origin sharing a common culture, but containing many different ethnic groups and languages, some of which were mutually intelligible

One final example will help you to understand why European descriptions of political, geographical, and ethnic groups are generally not sufficient to pinpoint an area of origin. Some of the best descriptions of specific place of origin may be found in the records associated with the Amistad mutiny. Barber's book, *A History of the Amistad Captives*, contains results of interviews with the thirty-six captives who recounted their stories through a translator named James Covey. Covey was able to comprehend most of the languages that the captives spoke because, like them, he came from the same Mendi country, an area that occupies parts of present-day Liberia and Sierra Leone. Note that Covey did not speak all of the languages, but he was able to understand most of them. Covey's story itself is instructive of how conditions among the small coastal kingdoms led to his capture. More dominant groups acted as predators on smaller groups, often starting wars, and ultimately fighting for control of trade between the coast and the interior, which also included control of the roads between settlements. Most of the captives had been kidnapped and taken through Vai country, one of the groups that struggled for control of the trade with Europeans. Below are several examples of what the captives said their origins to be, along with their stated names:

Fawni (Foni): He was born at Bum-be, a large town in the Mendi country: the name of his king was Kabandu . . . He was seized by two men as he was going to plant rice . . . carried to Bem-be-law, in the Vai country, and sold to Luiz, who kept him there two months, before he took him to Lomboko. From Bem-be-law to Lomboko is one day's walk.

Burna . . . was taken when going to the next town by three men. In his country are high mountains, but no rivers; has seen elephants and leopards. He was six weeks in traveling to Lomboko, where he was kept three and a half moons.

Sing-gbe (Cinque) The Leader: Was born in Mani, in Dzhopoa, i.e. in the open land, in the Mendi country. The distance from Mani to Lomboko, he says, is ten suns or days . . . His king, Kalumbo, lived at Kawmendi, a large town in the Mendi country.

Gilabaru (Grabeau): (Second in command to Cinque) Was born at Fulu, in the Mendi country, two moons (months) journey into the interior. In his country has seen people write—they write from right to left. Besides Mendi, he speaks Vai, Konno and Gissi.

Here, when the interviewer refers to king, it is most likely a chief. The so-called Mendi country really refers to the interior of the coastal area known as the Mendi country. Those who came from further inland referred to their places of origin that, at best, represented small clusters of ethnic groups, loosely affiliated with each other in political units. Some of these places no longer exist in modern times, yet people who belong to those ethnic groups are still in existence, for the most part, and they still live in the area, but perhaps not in those specific villages.

The following geographical regions were standard ones as used by Europeans and as described in Curtin's *The Atlantic Slave Trade*. (Use a modern map of Africa with this exercise.) In the European worldview, these terms applied only to the coast and the forts they had built, for it wasn't until the nineteenth century (the age of formal imperialism) that Europeans developed sustained contact with inland groups.

Senegambia—The coast between present-day Senegal and Gambia. Often called the Upper Guinea Coast.

Sierra Leone—The coast from the Casamance River to Cape Mount, or roughly including Guinea, Guinea-Bissau, and Sierra Leone.

Windward Coast—The coast from Cape Mount to Assini, or present-day Liberia and Ivory Coast—some parts also called the Grain Coast (rice) or the Malaguetta Coast (pepper).

Gold Coast—The coast from Assini to the Volta River, or most of present-day Ghana.

Bight of Benin—The coast from the Volta River to the Benin River, or most of present-day Togo and Benin (formerly Dahomey). Also called the Slave Coast.

Bight of Biafra—The coast from the Benin River to Cape Lopez or most of present-day Nigeria, Cameroon, Equatorial Guinea, and Gabon. Also includes Bight of Biafra.

Angola/Central Africa—The coast from Cape Lopez to the Orange River, or most of present-day Gabon, Congo, Zaire, Angola, Namibia (formerly South West Africa), and South Africa up to the Orange River.

Mozambique—The southeastern African coast from the Cape of Good Hope to Cape Delgado, or present-day Mozambique and Madagascar.

From Philip D. Curtin, *The African Slave Trade* (1969), p. 130.

PORTS OF DEPARTURE, REGIONS OF ORIGIN, AND PORTS OF ARRIVAL

*A*fricans who arrived as slaves in what was to become the United States departed from what Equiano called "that part of Africa known by the name of Guinea . . . which extends along the coast above 3,400 miles from Senegal to Angola, and includes a variety of kingdoms." The port of departure can tell you something about the region of origin if it can be verified that the slave ship stopped at only a few ports.

Port of arrival, unlike the port of departure, is far more specific because most Africans arrived in only a few areas on mainland United States: Sullivan's Island off the coast of Charleston, South Carolina (often called the Ellis Island of Africans because at least 40 percent of all Africans arrived through here), the various ports in Virginia, a few at Savannah, Georgia, and some finally at New Orleans. Early in the trade, some, but not all, slaves were "seasoned" in the Indies—an obvious step to decrease the high mortality experienced during the first year—but by the time the trade was well under way to the American colonies, they were arriving directly from Africa. Scholars now estimate that well over 80 percent of all slaves arriving in North America came directly from Africa, and for some regions it was more. Note that few arrived at North Carolina ports because there were no natural harbors.

By the formal abolition of the international slave trade, which went into effect in 1808, the African stock that had become African American was formed for the most part by slaves shipped from the following regions: Senegambia (13 percent), Gold Coast (16 percent), Bight of Biafra (23 percent), the Windward Coast (11 percent), and finally from the region between Angola and Congo (25 percent). Again, these are estimates which have been slightly modified by historians since they were first published by Curtin.

THE RECORDS OF THE SLAVE TRADE

I am looking for any information on a slave ship that was shipwrecked off the coast of Cape Hatteras North Carolina in 1767. The ship was said to have been carrying about 300 Africans. The name of the ship was Good Intent, and the name of the captain of the ship was Copland. This was an English slave ship en route from Africa. My ancestor, Elizabeth Jennett, was said to have been on this ship.

SUBMITTED BY "BILL" TO
AFRIGENEAS WEB SITE

If you have been able to trace your ancestry back to the 1700s, the period in which most slaves arrived in the United States, you may want to "thrash around" in the records and documentation that have survived. A reasonable strategy would depend on the area where your ancestors lived during that period. If your ancestors were in Tidewater Virginia, for example, a number of records exist for you to possibly pinpoint the ship of arrival. There are, however, a series of contingencies or "ifs" that would apply to your efforts. They are:

1. If you have the name of a specific slave owner and you have traced your ancestors back to his ownership

2. If the slave owner kept a diary that listed or made mention of his purchases (giving specifics like month, date, and year as well as vessel or merchant from whom he purchased slaves)

3. If the merchant's account books survived

4. If the slave owner also assigned names shortly thereafter

5. If the naval shipping lists have survived, and many have

6. If the ship master or a member of his crew left a diary or ship log detailing the voyage

If these conditions are met, in varying degrees, then perhaps you can state that your ancestors arrived at a specific time and from a specific area—including from the Caribbean. It is interesting to note that Jamaican slaves commonly referred to other slaves who made the slave voyage with them from Africa as "shipmates." No such affinities have been reported among Africans in North America.

The first line of attack on locating a slave ship is the archives from the state in which the ship was assumed to have landed. Records that document the trade to Virginia have been transcribed and written about by several scholars. One volume, entitled *Virginia Slave-Trade Statistics 1698–1775*, lists all key information found on surviving naval shipping lists, including the earliest slave traders. Part of this transcription was also based on Donnan's *Documents Illustrative of the History of the Slave Trade to America*. Before going to London, however, you might find that the records have been microfilmed. In addition, researchers should closely examine the South Carolina records.

Remember the previous discussion of Sullivans Island, South Carolina, as well as the discussion on New Orleans as a major destination port for French slavery.

Because the purchase of a slave, even during colonial times, was an expensive venture, members of the early planter elite of Virginia were the most extensive slave holders and traders. They also belonged to that class which was able to own its own leisure time—time enough to write diaries and keep records which, hopefully, have survived for you to use wisely in your own research. Note that planters who occupied land near the major ports often served as factors or traders for planters and farmers living upriver. Their activities are frequently reported in the literature, and this should alert you to the possibility that you may find your ancestor was purchased by a "gentleman" planter with cash reserves to engage in trading activities who later sold your ancestor to a plantation upriver. Some of America's most illustrious names—Landon Carter and Richard Byrd of Virginia, Henry Laurens, Thomas Middleton, and the Butlers of South Carolina—all combined land speculation and slave trading, or the "Guinea business," as Laurens called it.

THE TRANSATLANTIC SLAVE TRADE, 1527–1867: A DATABASE

This database is in CD-ROM format, and it contains information on 27,233 transatlantic slave voyages for the period 1527–1867. There are twenty-two maps that will assist you in visualizing the trade. Because the CD-ROM had not been released when this book went to press, there is no way to evaluate the content of the database except to say that it is the only publication of its type with such massive amounts of information, and it will serve genealogists well. It is important to note that the database is organized around each voyage. In general, ships took more than one voyage. Information for each voyage could yield up to 226 discrete kinds of information (variables or fields of information) such as dates, names of captains and crews, number of slaves, ports of arrival and departure, and ship owners. The directors of this project emphasize, however, that most of the voyages do not have this amount of information.

For researchers who have gotten to the point of looking for a slave ship this database will serve as an excellent source. The database was developed at Harvard, and its primary intended use is of course for academic research. But you know by now that as many genealogists as scholars will eventually use it, a point the project developers may not have thought about very much. The genealogical use will be based on whether you've found information in records indicating that the person is "saltwater" or a new slave arriving from Africa, or, as in the case of the individual who posted the listing to Afrigeneas, if you already have the name of the ship, the year, and some evidence that your ancestor was on a certain ship.

According to Professor Eltis, one of the project developers, "The database contains no names except for owners and captains, among whom there were certainly a few Blacks. There are, however, 65,000 to 70,000 names of Africans who entered the slave trade, but were diverted to Sierra Leone and Havana between 1819 and 1845 on account of their ships being captured (as a result of the abolition of the international slave trade). These names are not part of the set, but will be put into a separate database. We have nothing at all on African translators. There are separate records on who bought the slaves, but these are from the Caribbean, not the mainland (U.S.)."

Note that the database is a compilation or consolidation of other databases that historians have developed, plus information that the project itself collected. For researchers, this is an added bonus, because you can go to the original database (in most cases, if it's in English and published) to explore for yourself. The editors of the CD-ROM publication indicate that the voyages contained in the set represent the majority of voyages for the British for the period 1650 to 1807, the French for the period from 1700 to the 1830s, the Dutch for the period 1680 to 1802. The gaps are: the Portuguese trade, largely for Brazil, the French trade for the United States during the late 1700s, and the Spanish trade for the nineteenth century, largely for the Caribbean. There are also gaps for the first century-and-a-half of the trade (1520s to 1670s). Finally, the editors caution that the African locations indicate only point of departure and not region of origin, a distinction that is pointed out above.

BRINGING CLOSURE TO YOUR RESEARCH: YOUR MULTICULTURAL AFRICAN HERITAGE

*E*ven if you find a region of origin and a specific "nation" or ethnic group for your first African or American ancestors, you should know by now that you carry more than their blood in your veins. Most African Americans are an amalgamation of different African ethnic groups—the first people of African descent among all previous African diasporas to create a pan-African cultural identity outside Africa, something that hasn't happened in Africa yet. Understanding how this process occurred is enough to keep you busy for a long time, for it involves understanding the cultures your ancestors probably came from and how they blended with other cultures, changed, and survived to reinvent themselves and tell the story here in the Americas.

Chapter 15

CONCLUSION

Family Reunions and Regaining
a Collective Memory

A ship
A chain
A distant land
A whip
A pain
A white man's hand
A sack
A field
of cotton balls—
The only things
Grandpa recalls.

JIMMIE SHERMAN, *FROM THE ASHES: VOICES OF WATTS*

The African American Family Reunion

African American cultural traditions are really quite resilient, and this is no more evident than in the countless reunions that are held each year throughout the country, particularly in the South, where family reunions tend to merge into community-wide homecomings. This celebratory aspect of African American culture occurs when hundreds of relatives gather in one location each year or every two years to meet and greet, to honor and respect their elders, and to re-create a past with a new—indeed a northern—vision. The recent rituals that have been introduced into these gatherings guarantee that this growing movement of "returning home" will indeed survive. The older rituals which can only be seen by a keen observer are age-old ones, not just invented for reunions.

When the descendants of Steven Miller and his siblings held their reunion in Leflore County, Mississippi, during the summer of 1990, nearly 300 people dutifully attended. They had good reasons not to miss it. While many came individually, 125 came on a chartered bus from Chicago. The Miller reunion had grown so large that relatives were unable to house all who attended. At

their nineteenth reunion, they paid homage to the Miller family, which came up with the tax money to prevent foreclosure on the property years ago. The year 1990 was a special one because the family, as a corporation, was officially opening its newly constructed private park with a swimming pool, tennis court, basketball court, and other facilities. Named the Miller Park, it is located just a few paces away from the remains of the Stenson Plantation and its old slave cabins, where no less than five generations ago, the Millers were slaves. It is also in sight of the Shiloh Baptist Church. Though its membership now consists of a mere fraction of the original membership, it once served as the family church. Still standing next to the church is the old schoolhouse where one of the Miller ancestors once taught.

Reunions and homecomings are really an old southern tradition. What is new about Black family reunions is their level of organization, including the emergence of family corporations whose vision reaches beyond the annual reunion itself. The Bustill family (descendants of William Still) of Philadelphia has been holding reunions since the Civil War. In 1989, the Payne family reunion held in Richmond, Virginia, reunited for the first time one line of the

349

family which had migrated to Liberia in 1829! The Hairston family has its origins on the Cooleemee Plantation near High Point, North Carolina. This remarkable family of 1,400 calls itself "The Hairston Clan." The stories literally go on and on.

Remembering when times were simpler, when even brutality was simpler but nonetheless painful, reunion celebrants care little about the rage that brews over their very existence. This is all forgotten when cars drive up and down old dirt roads, when guests rotate from house to house to eat heavy southern meals and imbibe cold water or iced tea, when children play freely in yards and on porches, and yes, when women can complain about how many guests they had to serve, whose children had lost their manners up North, and how lonesome it would be when everyone left. This after all is the late twentieth century, and the collective memory has forced a distance between the dreadful past and the present—so great a distance that the idea of ancestry can be contemplated without trepidation.

These reunions are intimate affairs where the world often turns Black—if only for a weekend. For many celebrants in the past, that reunion week was needed to renew an inner strength and to affirm one's existence and ties to a concrete place in an otherwise unfriendly and frequently threatening world. One wonders why such fond memories have remained when, in fact, the reality was always quite different. It is because families impressed upon the young at a very early age a sense of the bountifulness of existence.

Reunions are occasions for reaffirming generational continuity between the family and its ancestors. Many African Americans still have a strong sense of place even though, ironically, many never owned one parcel of land in the South. It is as if the annual return is haunted with questions that are linked to the places where our ancestors once lived and died. We mark that place by being there every year in the same place, at the same time, on the same grounds where our ancestors once stood and worshiped.

As the concrete ties to our ancestors recede with time, we ask more questions than can ever be answered. We begin to supplement ritual with the written word to make sure that the important things are preserved. That is why you probably started your genealogical project in the first place. Seeing so many people in one room or in one church, all of whom share common ancestry but perhaps without knowing exactly how or when, made you want to fit the pieces together.

THE PURPOSES OF REUNIONS

Reunions essentially speak to three aspects of the family as a collective group: celebration, heritage, and continuity. Celebration is the reunion itself. Banquets, barbecues, dances, and fish fries are the order of the day, followed by a concluding church service. Throughout this celebration, reunion participants often hold ceremonies that emphasize heritage and continuity. Generally a family historian reports the latest information on family research, a ceremony is held to honor ancestors, and various committees meet to guarantee a smooth transition to the next reunion. The historical consciousness of ancestry depends to a great extent on how much of the family story is emphasized at each reunion.

ENSURING A CONSCIOUSNESS OF HERITAGE

*T*he family historian plays a key role in helping reunion members to understand their heritage. If that task falls to you or your committee, every member of the family should know, at least, the following: (1) a story about the founding couple or the earliest documented ancestors, (2) their accomplishments as well as those of other ancestors, (3) special family traits and names that repeat themselves from one generation to the next, (4) family folklore or wisdom passed down, (5) some knowledge of the ancestral home, and finally, (6) every family should have a genealogical chart or table that is accurate and complete.

Most large reunions have a historical committee rather than one family historian, primarily because the task of reconstructing the family's genealogy and history cannot really be handled by one person alone. The larger the size of the reunion, the more important it is to document the family's distant past as well as to begin to document current generations. The Harrisons of South Carolina, presumably not related to the Hairstons, held their most recent reunion in Philadelphia, where at least one thousand descendants of Peter and Harriet Edmunds Harrison assembled for this weekend event. This number is enough to start a whole town, and it certainly would qualify the family as a clan. The Harrison family directory lists nearly five hundred families spread over the United States, but mainly clustered in South Carolina, Philadelphia, New York, and New Jersey. That such a large family, consisting of descendants of Peter and Harriet Harrison, has kept an identity for so many years shouldn't be a surprise. The family's history has been fairly well researched and written by a member who is an archivist and historian. Part of that history is reproduced below as an example of what might appear in your own reunion program book to ensure a consciousness of heritage.

Excerpt from Harrison Family Reunion Souvenir Book

Prior to 1865, Peter and Harriet Harrison were both slaves of John Harrison, Sr. He was one of the largest slave owners in Fairfield County. In 1843 he was taxed on 223 slaves. His father, Reuben Harrison, had moved down from Virginia before the Revolution and acquired thousands of acres stretching from Ridgeway to Longtown. John Sr. was one of several large planters in the area who raced horses for sport. Harriet Edmunds Harrison and her two oldest children had been purchased by John Harrison, Sr. for $1240.

Harriet first shows up in 1835 as a small child valued at $75 in a slave inventory of the property of the Estate of Robert Edmunds of Richland District. Her mother appears to have been a slave named Mary. They were listed together on the slave inventory, and they were both among the eleven slaves of Robert Edmunds transferred by his Estate to his daughter, Mary Edmunds, the wife of Richard B. Harrison. Mary died in 1847 and Richard shortly thereafter. Harriet and Mary were next transferred to their minor children, Mary Harrison and John Harrison, Sr. of Fairfield, was appointed by the Richland District, Court of Equity as their legal guardian and he took control of their slaves by 1851. He brought all eleven slaves to his plantation where they lived together with his slaves. Harriet and Peter probably met at this time at the Harrison plantation and may have married shortly thereafter.

In April of 1865, Peter and Harriet Harrison, like hundreds of other slaves in Fairfield County were free to begin new lives. Already the parents of five children, Reuben, Mary Ann, Richard, Robert and Letta, they decided to remain in Fairfield County. Much of the property in the county, both buildings and crops, had been destroyed earlier in the year as the Union troops moved north from Columbia to Charlotte. Little food remained in the county; times were exceedingly difficult for all.... January 1, 1874 was a red letter day for the Harrison family. Peter purchased for $1000 a farm consisting of "200 acres more or less" in Township 5 from Edward P. Mobley.

THE REUNION PROGRAM BOOK: CREATING A PROGRAM BOOK FOR KEEPS

*R*eunion program books vary from the simple to the elaborate. Whatever your reunion can afford, be mindful that a keepsake book that is artfully and accurately presented should be your goal. After looking through many such books, I've listed a few tips to help you create something worth keeping.

Clear Ancestral Charts

A good chart should include some genealogical data on all family members. To avoid confusion in relationships, the chart should be a good piece of graphic work that includes complete names and dates as well as places of birth, marriage, and death. The standard generations chart exhibited in chapter 2 should be used. If you do not have enough information yet, you should at least have some estimated dates to show the sequence of generations. Don't assume that everyone will know which line of the family they belong to. Some of this information can be requested when you send out the reservation packets. Design a simple form and ask each family to complete and return it.

Photographs and Memorabilia

Include photographs and documents that reproduce well. Avoid using color photographs unless they can be converted to black-and-white prints. At some point, a formal group photograph or a series of photographs of all reunion attendants should be taken and included in the program book for the following year.

Other Items to Include

Some families include a directory organized by city. Others include newsworthy items of family accomplishments from the previous year. Birthdays, obituaries, scholarships and prizes, vacations taken, and church activities are things that can easily be placed in a program book.

Finally, you might want to consider using a printer for a special program book. If it is your tenth annual reunion, you could celebrate it by having the program book professionally printed as opposed to using a quick printer. To economize on printing costs, include the cost of each book in the annual reunion fee.

CONTINUITY

*T*he continuity of the reunion process will often be tested when generational transitions are made. To guarantee continuity, think of it as a process which connects the past to the present and the present to the future. Guaranteeing continuity with the past may involve researching the family's genealogy, purchasing land as a corporate body where your ancestors lived in the South, or simply keeping the memories of your ancestors alive by holding a ceremony to honor them. As your family reunion becomes more organized and larger, you will want to think about ensuring that communication is maintained between the branches of the family in each city during the rest of the year. One family may hold

monthly family meetings while another may issue a quarterly newsletter. Make sure that your communication is deeper than seeing each other for Christmas and Thanksgiving celebrations.

Do not underestimate the resources that can be tapped when you pool your finances and skills to meet the current and future needs of family members. Savings and investment programs, small loan programs and other help for families in crisis, informal counseling for younger family members by matching the old with the young, scholarship funds or a college book fund, renovation of the old home church, land purchases, and the construction of a retreat center or recreational center are probably all within your family's reach once you pool your financial resources. If you add up all the money that is spent by each family to attend the reunion (travel, hotel, food, etc.), you may be surprised to find out how much of an investment has already been made.

CREATING AND MAINTAINING A FAMILY ASSOCIATION

*F*amily associations are organized just as you would organize any other not-for-profit organization. Officers are elected, a constitution and by-laws are written, and a bank account is established which requires the signature of at least two individuals. The officers or the board should communicate frequently enough to monitor the affairs of the family, and they should always issue a written financial report, preferably in your program book.

EMPHASIZING THE GENERATION OF COUSINS

*I*t is the generation of cousins to which the reunion organization should look to maintain the tradition. If cousins grow up together in the same town or the same neighborhood and if they share many experiences together, the family organization has a better chance of maintaining the tradition. Unfortunately, many cousins don't have a chance to really experience this stage in the life cycle with kin, particularly since families continue to be dispersed throughout the country. Therefore, the reunion organization should seriously consider institutionalizing programs that emphasize the young

members of the family. Mentoring the young, offering rewards or prizes for accomplishments, visiting throughout the year, and even closely monitoring this generation's progress are all called for.

A FAMILY OF INCLUSION

*T*he bigger the better. If your reunion has under one hundred people each year, it's time to find those lost family members and bring them back into the circle. The more members you have, the more resources you will have to share. Of course, you may wind up attending more than one reunion each year since families do branch off. Have fun!

TWO CONCLUSIONS

Conclusion 1

Jimmie Sherman's poem represents a certain alienation from the past which many African American families are now trying to change. Indeed, Jimmie's perspective might be based on how he viewed his grandfather's experiences, rather than on how his grandfather viewed them himself. On the other hand, his poem speaks to how he, as a young person, viewed the African American past—the collective experience of a people to which he is attached by kinship. If for no other reason, think about the Jimmies of this world when you tell the collective story of your family at the next family reunion or when you tell your part of the story of the African American family.

Doing family history research and having family reunions is all about reviving a

lost collective memory. It is true that the American family is under tremendous stress, and the African American family seems to be getting a double dose of it. These are perilous times for families, and for the children produced by families. Your research will not do anyone any good if, taking it as a hobby, you fail to pass to the current generation a sense of how their ancestors overcame the obstacles and struggles that are a part of the human condition.

Unless you can share in a meaningful way how your ancestors "fought the good fight," the results of your research will remain on the shelf. Hopefully, this book has helped you not just to connect with the past but, of more importance, I hope that it has helped you to reconnect with your own ancestors, to connect with your family, with future generations, and, perhaps of most importance now, with the young Jimmies of this world.

Conclusion 2

Loss of personal historical memory is not just an African American problem, particularly with regard to the most painful parts of the past. With regard to slavery, you will begin to wonder how dead and done it really is. The role of slavery in American history has yet to be appreciated—nor have its consequences in contemporary America. Slavery has not been written into the historical consciousness of most Americans. It needs to be. Steps made by major Protestant denominations to publicly acknowledge the sins of slavery are positive ones. Without continued forward movement, Americans will continue to wonder what it was all about. After all, the scramble for tobacco, sugar, and rum, and slaves to produce them, in retrospect turned out to be bad for everybody.

Special Topic 1

SOURCES FOR
ADVANCED RESEARCH IN
SLAVE GENEALOGY

Be prepared.
No one knows
you're coming.

AFRICAN AMERICAN GENEALOGIST

HISTORICAL AND GENEALOGICAL GUIDEBOOKS

*T*here exists a large body of guidebooks that will direct you to important sources in your state of research. The two principal types are general historical and/or genealogical guidebooks, and guides to specific collections. General guidebooks may be guides to research at a state's archives or guidebooks for the whole state or specifically for one ethnic group. *Black Genesis*, the *Ohio Black History Guide*, and *Afro-American Sources in Virginia* are just a few titles that specifically cover African Americans. Examples of genealogical and historical guidebooks are *Research in Georgia*, an example that deals with a specific state, and the DAR's *Lest We Forget: A Guide to Genealogical Research in the Nation's Capital*, a book that deals with libraries and archives in the capital. Titles such as *The Southern Historical Collection*, *A Guide to Manuscripts*, *Guide to the Heartman Manuscripts on Slavery* (actually a published inventory of holdings at Xavier University), and the *Guide to Private Manuscript Collections in the North Carolina State Archives* are examples of guidebooks to specific manuscript collections that contain the surviving family and business papers of individuals. Guidebooks to research in a specific county are occasionally published, and the WPA (Works Projects Administration) series, part of the Depression-era Historical Works Commission, often contains specific information on county records. If you are using a large genealogy library, or if you are using a database search at a local library, you would want to use the following search format in order to identify additional guidebooks for your state of research:

Name of State—History—Sources
Name of State—Genealogy—Sources

GENEALOGIES OF SLAVE-OWNING FAMILIES (PUBLISHED AND UNPUBLISHED)

*F*inding genealogical and biographical information on a slave owner can take some time, particularly if you are not using a library with a large genealogical collection. The following kinds of sources can help you either to locate a published genealogy or to construct a partial genealogy sufficient for you to carry out your research:

1. Bibliographies of genealogies
2. Biographies
3. Biographical compendia

4. Clippings files and genealogical folders located at public libraries, state archives, and other libraries
5. Local newspapers and county histories
6. Scholarly studies or popular books on individual planters and slave holders as a class
7. Genealogical publications like the *Genealogical Helper* or the *Directory of Family Associations*

You will frequently come across genealogical titles that are too obscure for you to make a judgment about whether the family you are researching appears in the publication. This situation arises especially with titles such as "The Genealogy and Complete History of the Ansons and Allied Families from Colonial Times to the Present." This title merely gives you the surname Anson, but it doesn't tell you where the Ansons originally lived, nor who the allied families are—critical information that most genealogists would need in order to determine whether an extended search for a copy is necessary. If any uncertainty arises about the identity of families, try to determine whether the information you need is contained therein by requesting that the library make a photocopy from the pages that contain the families you are researching.

Once you find a genealogical study or a biography, be careful in evaluating how the kin ties were documented. If sources for these ties are not listed, then you will have to worry about the accuracy of the study. A common term in genealogy is "false pedigrees," or lines that have not been sufficiently documented to verify a kin connection. This can arise when individuals are anxious to join a hereditary society or when some other pressure is brought to bear on the individual's search.

USING LOCAL SOURCES TO LOCATE INFORMATION ON PLANTERS

One of the first things that you might want to do is to simply write a letter of inquiry to the following institutions: local public libraries and small college libraries located in the county where the slave owner and his family lived, the largest state university library, the state's archives, and state and local historical societies. This letter should be brief and to the point, as in the following sample letter of inquiry:

TO: Manuscript or Reference Librarian

I am conducting genealogical research on the following family:

Benjamin Lasswell and allied families (Albemarle County, Virginia, 1790–1830)

Does your library have a file or papers for any members of the Lasswell family? If so, I would like to know the cost of having the index or inventory copied.

Thanks for your assistance.

Sincerely,

This sample letter allows librarians or archivists to quickly determine what is on file and then respond to your letter. If, however, you go into great detail, you will receive a standard form letter indicating that the library does not conduct research for individuals. Therefore, the information that you are soliciting should be considered preliminary information to be used in preparation for a visit or for a more detailed inquiry once you receive the initial information. Small genealogical files can be copied for a nominal fee, however.

USING THE NATIONAL UNION CATALOGUE OF MANUSCRIPT COLLECTIONS

*T*his catalogue attempts to provide basic, but brief, descriptions of manuscript collections housed in the United States. This is the catalogue that you would use to identify the surviving personal papers of large-scale planters or planters who were literate and had the leisure time to keep a written record of their activities. It cannot claim to be comprehensive because institutions have to report their holdings voluntarily, yet it is the one most convenient sources for finding basic information on the personal papers of planters and slave owners, including their location. Researchers should know that the catalogue is actually a multiple-volume series, and many larger public libraries will have them in the reference section. To save yourself time in checking every volume, ask first for the *Index to Personal Names*, a surname index to all entries for the years between 1959 when the first volume was published and 1984. Examine the following entry (78-2151) found for the surname Massenburg. Note that the entry number, 78–2151, tells me to look for entry number 2151 in the 1978 volume.

NUCMC ENTRY FOR NICHOLAS MASSENBURG

Massenburg, Nicholas Bryar, d. 1867.
Papers, 1823–95. 41 items and 3 v.
In U of NC at Chapel Hill, Library,
Southern Historical Collection (908).
Daily records of agricultural activities on a Franklin Co.. N.C., plantation, including slave lists, accounts, and family records; and family correspondence (chiefly 1866–84) of Massenburg's wife and daughters.

This entry, translated, indicates that Nicholas Bryar Massenburg, deceased in 1867, left papers dated between 1823 and 1895 of which the University of North Carolina at Chapel Hill has forty-one items, including three volumes, and that the number assigned to his papers by the university library is Record Group 908. The fact that slave lists and account books are in this collection should indicate its value, but now some contact with the library is necessary. A basic letter requesting a further description or a copy of the inventory would be appropriate. The address for the library can be obtained from the *American Library Directory*, found in the reference section of your library. The University of North Carolina library sent a short series description, part of which is reproduced below. Compare this entry, which is more detailed, to the entry from the NUCMC.

MASSENBURG DESCRIPTION— UNIVERSITY OF NORTH CAROLINA

Series 1. Correspondence
1823–1895. 76 items.

Arrangement: chronological
(4 paragraphs describing letters.)
Series 2. Other Material
1852, 1866–1867. 3 items.
(1 short paragraph including mention of a diary.)
Series 3. Volumes
1834–1851. 2 manuscript volumes and 1 reel of microfilm. The volumes include detailed daily records of family and agricultural activities, slave lists, plantation accounts, and miscellaneous notes. Typed copies of the first two volumes are available. Vol 1, 1834–1839; Vol 2, 1840–1846; Vol 3, 1847–1851 (microfilm copy).

Biographical Note: Nicholas Bryar Massenburg married Lucy Henry Davis in December 1831. They owned "Woodleaf," a plantation located on Halifax Road, two miles northeast of Louisburg on Fox Swamp in Franklin County, North Carolina. They also owned another home on Sandy Creek, also in Franklin County, referred to as "Egypt" in the journals. The Massenburgs had nine children who lived to maturity, among them, Lucy Cargill Massenburg.

Subsequent correspondence indicated that I could obtain microfilm copies of the plantation journals through the library's reproduction services. This did not include reproductions of the typed copies, because they were transcriptions done later and technically not part of the papers. At this point, researchers would have to make a decision whether it is worth it to pay the cost, hire a local researcher, or make a visit. Hiring a local researcher would probably be your best bet at the beginning. Remember, the university library may have a list of researchers, *or* through the state's archives, you might be able to obtain a list of qualified researchers who live in or near Chapel Hill.

SOURCES AT THE STATE ARCHIVES

State archives house a variety of information on individuals. An initial letter is appropriate so that you can obtain needed information for a successful first visit. If the individual was an important figure in the state, you will often find a significant amount of information. If the individual was known only locally in his county of residence, you may not immediately find what you need. Resources at most state archives are:

- Surname files or indexes
- Biographical compendia including the Goodspeed series
- Original or microfilmed copies of county courthouse records
- Abstracts of county records
- Higher court records (district and supreme court)
- Territorial papers (papers relating to the prestatehood period)
- Genealogy books and genealogies
- Land records (original patents)
- Personal papers of state residents
- Military records (pension applications for Civil War and other wars)
- Maps, plats, gazetteers, atlases
- Censuses for the state and the region

Many archives have made some attempt to index certain records by surname and type of record (surname files). The names along with some brief information about the records in which the names appear may be filed in a card catalogue, master reference books, or in some cases, they may have been computerized. These are the most helpful finding aids for an initial visit to your archives. Know, however, that this information can also be requested by mail, by making a simple request: Does the archives have material on John Doe who lived between 1808 and 1896 in Smith County? If so, can you provide a short description of this material?

The following summary is from a brochure on records and sources at the South Carolina Department of Archives and History which was obtained by writing a general letter of inquiry with regard to their holdings for genealogical research.

MATERIAL LISTED IN BROCHURE OBTAINED FROM S.C. DEPARTMENT OF ARCHIVES

Indexes to: Wills to 1853, Land Grants and Plats, Memorials of Land Titles (1732–1775), Audited Accounts for Revolutionary Services, Records of Confederate Service

Combined Alphabetical Index (1680–1865), a Department of Archives finding aid covering the following records:

> Plats, Grants, Memorials, Conveyances
> Court Records including Petitions to Practice Law and Renunciations of Dower
> Summary and Process Rolls for South Carolina Court of Common Pleas
> Tax Returns (1824)
> Property Sales—Bills of Sales for 1773–1840 and 1843–1872
> Accounts Audited Growing Out of the Revolution (1778–1804)

South Carolina's surname index, called the *Combined Alphabetical Index (1680–*

1865), was compiled from records housed at the archives, thereby making your task much easier in locating information on slave-owning families. Based on this description, however, a beginning researcher would not know that these records contain records of genealogical importance because terms such as wills, deeds, and so forth do not appear. This example shows how important it is to know about local records and records specific to the state. Original county records or transcriptions and abstracts of such records are often housed at state archives under headings that do not necessarily correspond to those used at the county level. Thus, reading a research guidebook or articles on various records housed at the archives is a preliminary necessity. These articles will always appear in the state's historical journal. Consider the explanation of these records taken from the same packet of information:

County and city records make up a major part of the Department's holdings. To find the records of a particular county or town, consult *A Guide to Local Government Records in the South Carolina Archives* (1988). The following post-emancipation local records are most useful in African American genealogical research:

Courts of Equity and Common Pleas: South Carolina abolished the court of equity in 1868 and transferred its functions to the court of common pleas. Records from both these courts are good sources for the names of litigants in cases involving sharecropping contracts and in suits involving debt. Of particular value in cases involving agricultural contracts and debts is the record series, Transcripts of Judgments, which begins in 1870. Records from the Court of Equity also hold information on cases concerning the legal determination of color involving persons of mixed race.*

*FROM PAUL R. BEGLEY AND STEVEN D. TUTTLE, *AFRICAN AMERICAN GENEALOGICAL RESEARCH* (AT THE SOUTH CAROLINA DEPARTMENT OF ARCHIVES AND HISTORY), PAGES 7–8. THIS PAMPHLET MAY BE OBTAINED BY WRITING THE ARCHIVES DIRECTLY.

USING SCHOLARLY SOURCES

Suppose a scholar has studied the plantation (both slaves and owners) on which most of your ancestors lived for a very long time, and you discover the publication at the *end* of your research. This has happened, and as a good researcher, you are urged to try to answer this question: *Have any books, dissertations, or journal articles ever been published on the slave-owning family that I am researching?* Many major studies on plantations have been published in the last twenty years. Consider some of the following titles:

Myers, Robert M. *The Children of Pride: A True Story of Georgia and the Civil War.* New Haven: Yale University Press, 1972.

Cody, Cheryl Ann. "Slave Demography and Family Formation: A Community Study of the Ball Family Plantations, 1720–1896." Ph.D. dissertation, University of Minnesota, 1982.

Riley, Franklin L. "Diary of a Mississippi Planter, January 1, 1840 to April, 1863." *Publications of the Mississippi Historical Society* vol. 10 (1909), 305–481.

Hamilton, William B., and William D. McCain. "Wealth in the Natchez Region: Inventories of the Estate of Charles Percy, 1794 and 1804." *Journal of Mississippi History*, vol. 10, no. 4 (October 1948).

Phillips, Ulrich B., and James D. Glunt, eds. *Florida Plantation Records from the Papers of George Noble Jones.* St. Louis: Missouri Historical Society, 1927.

House, Albert Virgil, ed. *Planter Management and Capitalism in Ante-Bellum Georgia: The Journal of Hugh Fraser Grant, Rice Grower.* New York: Columbia University, 1954.

The importance of locating scholarly studies can only be understood when you examine the papers of planters, some of which are voluminous. *The Children of Pride,* all 1,845 pages of it (an unusual publication in and of itself), reproduces *part* of the vast amount of correspondence between a few families in Georgia—namely the families of the principal subject, Dr. Charles Colcock Jones (Liberty County), and his heirs, the Kings, the Wests, and the Robarts. Note in this case that the author removed names from some of the letter writers in a few cases. An index to the slaves mentioned in the correspondence as well as biographical profiles of members of the slave-owning family are included, some with multiple entries.

The only way to be comprehensive in your search of scholarly publications is to:

- Always check local libraries and historical societies where the slave-owning family was established. These may be in more than one state.

- Next check the standard indexes and bibliographies on American historical publications.
- Check the indexes to the state's journal of history.
- Next check bibliographies on slavery, plantation life, and local history.
- Next consider running a computer search through a local university or college. This generally involves a fee, and there is no guarantee that the data bank being used contains all references. You will often need help with defining your keywords for this kind of search.
- Keep abreast of more recent publications by reading book reviews in the state's journal of history or in the established historical journals.
- Do a year-by-year search of *Dissertation Abstracts International* to locate possible dissertations, starting with the present and working back, or use *A Bibliography of Doctoral Research on the Negro, 1933–1966*. Look for subjects relating to slavery, planters, and plantations.

To conduct your search, either in a library or on-line, use the following search terms for beginners:

Specific Search Terms
The name of the slave owner or slave-owning family
The name of the geographical place (city, county, state, region)
The name of the plantation

Broader Search Terms (Keywords)
Plantation Life/Plantations/Slavery/Diaries/Journals/Plantation Records/Estate Records

A Note on Using Indexes, Transcriptions, and Abstracts of Courthouse Records

*R*esearchers will find a profuse amount of this material in good genealogical libraries, state archives and historical societies, and local (county) historical societies. Generally, abstracts and indexes should be your first line of attack for transactions in which the slave owner was involved. If you start out with microfilmed copies of county records, you will have to rely on the indexes to each record book, which will also have been filmed as part of filming the book. Caution: This approach can be taxing if you are not systematic in keeping track of the order in which the records were filmed.

Therefore, it is recommended that you first try to locate printed (in book form) indexes, transcriptions, and abstracts to courthouse records. Caution again—these books do contain many errors, if for no other reason than it is a massive undertaking to abstract records from the time of a county's settlement through 1860. For example, many North Carolina county records have been abstracted or indexed. In some ways, the North Carolina researcher is in "research heaven." On the other hand, two of the standard sources are said to contain many errors, including differing information for the same wills. One important fact that researchers of African American genealogy should keep in mind when using abstracts and indexes is that only recently have the names of slaves been included. Examine the following excerpt from a work that does include the names of slaves. Then read it without the names, considering the problems that arise if you do not have information on which slaves were given to which parties.

EXAMPLE OF AN ABSTRACTED WILL NAMING SLAVES

(21) Will of Richard Richards. To brother (no first name given) Richards three negroes Frank, Kame, Gilbert; a saddle and bridle. To brother Jesse Richards 2 negroes Broom, Fanny; a bed and furniture left at Martha Harlow's. To Martha Harlow during her life a bed and furniture, a pot and other household possessions she already has in hand. To Thomas Harlow a set of farmer's tools. To Williamson Richards a bed and furniture. To Willis Richards "my gun and shot moulds." Remainder of tools and other property and debts owed to estate and the hire of a negro to Josiah Smith to be used to pay debts of estate. To John Richards a note on Peter Callum for 20 pounds. To John and Jesse Richards "all that can be attained by a lawsuit between myself, Jones & Capt. Perry." To John Richards another note on Peter Callum for 33 dollars. Executors: Joseph Dickins, William Dickins. July 7, 1795. His mark. Witnessed: John Strother, Elizabeth Dukes. Proved in September Court, 1795, by oaths of John Strother and Elizabeth Dukes.

Having an abstract or index to records saves you, the researcher, the time that it would take to examine the indexes to each will or deed book. Since the compiler of this information has done a lot of the preliminary work, you simply have to follow through by writing directly to the courthouse or the state archives for a copy of the original. You will need the specific book number or title and the page number of the document. Because of the differences in record keeping practices between clerks over time in one county as well as the differences in practices from county to county, you will have to check to see what other record books exist.

MAJOR MICROFILMED COLLECTIONS OF FAMILY AND BUSINESS PAPERS OF SLAVE-OWNING FAMILIES

Records of Antebellum Southern Plantations from the Revolution Through the Civil War, *Microfilm Edition*

This microfilmed series is an ongoing microfilming project which, when completed, will constitute a major source for research on southern slave-owning families. Researchers will be able to have access to these records without having to visit the archives and libraries where the original records are housed. However, because of its cost, you may find that only a few major public and academic libraries will have the complete series. Therefore, your best bet is to obtain a copy of the descriptive guide, which many libraries will purchase without purchasing the microfilmed copies of the records.

If you are researching Deep South ancestors, the first thing you should realize about this series is that it covers the period 1783 to 1865, approximately eighty-two years. In terms of historical time, eighty-two years is not a lot, but you should also realize that this is the period when there was a major shift of the slave and free population from the oldest settled regions of the South to the states we now call the Deep South.

The second point to understand is that the families included in this series were generally large plantation holders whose impact and family ties reached from Virginia to Texas.

Thorough familiarity with the guide is important. The series is not organized by place of residence of planters. Rather, it is organized by libraries or archives where the records are presently housed. The residence of the planter and the location of his surviving papers are not the same. The papers of a Virginia planter might be in the same series with the papers of a Louisiana planter, both of which are housed at Louisiana State University. You would, therefore, want to obtain a complete listing of the planter's records for each series. Finally, you would want to determine how to obtain the reels that you need through interlibrary loan or a visit to the library. Even if the records of the slave owner that you are researching were not included in this series, you would want to closely examine the guide to determine whether any planters for your area or county of research were included as associates of the individual planter under question. This is recommended because planters rarely lived in isolation, particularly if they were wealthy. This point, though it has been emphasized previously, cannot be ignored by researchers. The following case study of Alexander K. Farrar's papers, which form a part of this project, should be examined from the perspective of your having an ancestor who was owned by Farrar.

Case Study: Alexander K. Farrar's Papers

The guide provides a brief biographical and genealogical statement on the family. From that, we learn that Alexander Farrar was a descendant of the founders of Kingston in Adams County, Mississippi, that he had two wives, and that he was a lawyer having clients in Natchez, Kingston, and other parts of Louisiana. He was also a member of the state legislature, and he served as chairman of the Vigilance Committee of Adams County, a committee that concerned itself with the possibility of slave revolts. The following excerpt was taken directly from the guide. It is reprinted here to show the format for describing the personal papers of an individual.

Contents of Papers

Papers of Alexander K. Farrar (1814–1878) contain rich documentation of plantations, law, finance, education, travel, family, society, and politics in the Natchez area from the 1840s through 1860s. Slave records from plantations in Adams County, Mississippi, and Catahoula Parish, Louisiana, are augmented by correspondence and business and professional records relating to overseers and the regulation of slaves in these localities. The five series in the collection include Daniel Farrar's business records, correspondence and papers, professional and business records, plantation records, and miscellaneous papers. Records in these series often overlap, as the personal, legal, plantation, and miscellaneous affairs of Farrar and his father are inseparable.

Information Pertaining to Slaves and/or Slavery

Daniel Farrar business records, 1834–1850, include bills, receipts, invoices, and deeds of Alexander K. Farrar and his father Daniel Farrar (d. 1845) in Adams County. Accounts pertain to the sale of cotton and purchase of supplies including accounts with William

Harper, of Avalanche Plantation, and with William Ferriday & Co. Incidental records document the purchase and sale of slaves and the jailing of runaway slaves. Accounts also reflect the hiring of slaves by Avalanche Plantation, which was run in partnership by Harper and Farrar.

Major themes among the letters include plantation management, miscellaneous neighborhood events, the activities of slaves, slave hire arrangements, and potential investments in slaves and plantations. One letter dated July 22, 1856, is from John E. Beck, a slave in Pike County, Mississippi, to Farrar and the slaves on his plantation, including a note to the slave's ex-wife with comments on a later marriage of Beck in Pike County. A letter from Ann (Dougharty) Farrar to Alexander while he was attending the legislature in 1857 recounts the attempted murder of a planter by a slave in Adams County following the planter's punishment of the slave's wife. Letters of 1858 discuss the apprehension of runaway slaves . . . . A letter from a woman in 1854 urges Farrar's support for the emancipation of her son so he can take possession of his property. . . . Other undated personal correspondence includes correspondence and an unidentified estate inventory including extensive slave lists.

Legal practice records include correspondence, slave lists, bills of slave and hire agreements for slaves, and jail receipts for runaway slaves. Also included are overseers' receipts, prices current, . . . deeds, plats, and indentures . . . . A subseries also relates to the murder of Duncan Skinner, an overseer at Bon Ridge Plantation, and the murder of McBryde, an overseer at a nearby plantation. Both murders occurred in 1857. Lengthy memorandums recount the discovery of the murders and the questioning of the slaves on the plantations . . . .

Miscellaneous documents include undated land surveys and maps. A resolution outlining a census of Natchez shows the aggregate number and sex of whites, slaves, and free blacks in the city in 1856. Additional information on the Farrar family can be found in: *Biographical and Historical Memoirs of Mississippi*, vol. 1 (Chicago, Illinois: Goodspeed, 1891); Henry Blackburn Eaton, *Descendants of the Jersey Settlers of Adams County, Mississippi*, 2 vols. (Jackson, Mississippi: Society of the Descendants of the Jersey Settlers, 1981); and *Virginia Magazine of History and Biography*, vols. 7–10.

The above excerpts offer only a small peek at the wealth of information to be found on the Farrar family, their slaves, and even the slaves of neighbors. Therefore, even though your ancestors may not have been slaves on the Farrar plantations, they may have been slaves on one of the plantations owned by one of his clients, neighbors, or relatives (Stephen Duncan, Absalom Sharp, Lewis H. Swayze, William Holliday, and John Ford). Alexander Farrar's legal papers contain important probate and business documents left by these and other slave-owning families in the region. This you would not have known unless you had read the guide.

Problems with Using the Guide and the Microfilmed Records

For every set of papers, the guide provides a rather extensive general introductory description as indicated above. However, the *contents* of each reel are not described in any great detail. Enough information is provided to give the researcher an idea of which reel to examine for slave lists or probate records or personal correspondence, or for plantation records and account books.

INDEX: FARRAR'S PAPERS

Reel 6:	Introduction*, Business Records	233 frames
Reel 7:	Personal Correspondence	963 frames
Reel 8:	Professional & Business Records	948 frames
Reel 9:	Plantation Records	965 frames
Reel 10:	Plantation/Miscellaneous Records	227 frames
Total Frames	(Pages for Farrar Papers)	3336 frames/pages

*Note that the introduction contains a description of the papers as compiled by the staff of the library where it is housed.

Farrar's papers occupy approximately five reels of film. Each reel is numbered by frames. (The number is imprinted at the bottom of the film frame and not on the document.) Therefore, each frame number is equivalent to a page number. To give you an idea of how many frames you will have to go through, the following list of the Farrar papers is provided:

Going through 3,336 pages of handwritten manuscript material is time consuming. Researchers should plan first to locate those reels that contain slave lists, maps, and any estate papers. This should then be followed by a closer examination of the family's correspondence and business transactions that do not appear to deal with slaves. The quality of the filming is fairly high; however, researchers should note that old historical documents can often be difficult to read on microfilm because most documents are handwritten and most are in various stages of decay. Occasionally, you will find a few preprinted documents (legal forms, for example), but these will not be as important as the handwritten ones. Finally, papers for several individuals may run together on one reel of film. Farrar's papers begin with frame 233 of Reel 6 for this series and end with frame 227 of Reel 10, followed by the Ellis-Farrar family papers (starting with frame 228 of the same reel), also of Adams County. Despite these minor drawbacks, which can be solved by thoroughly reading the guides to each series, researchers should know that these microfilmed records can provide a major breakthrough for those with ancestors who lived on large plantations throughout the South.

The Louisiana State University–Greenwood Press Project

This series was published in microfiche format before *Records of Antebellum Southern Plantations*. It is a *sampling* of the LSU collection, and does not represent its entire collection of plantation and family papers housed at the university's Department of Archives. Its formal title is *Plantation Records from the Louisiana State University Department of Archives*, and it is likely that it can be found only at larger university libraries in the country. Although it is not widely available, it would be important to those researchers who had ancestors on plantations in Mississippi and Louisiana. Because the average researcher is unlikely to find a comprehensive list of the content for this series, descriptions are included below:

Family Papers of Norbert Badin (1829–1900)—Free Black planter of Melrose, Mississippi.

Diary of Mary Bateman, 1856 (Argyle Plantation near Greenville, Mississippi).

Priscilla Munnikuysen Bond Diary (1857–1869)—Diary and other items on a Louisiana sugar plantation.

Louis Amedee Bringier Papers (1876–1901)—Personal and business papers of a French Louisiana planter.

John C. Burruss Family Papers (1825–1882)—Mississippi family covering three generations.

Eli J. Capell Family Papers (1817–1900)—Pleasant Hill Plantation of Amite County, Mississippi.

Samuel A. Cartwright Family Papers (1826–1864)—Cartwright was known as a "Doctor" of Negro Medicine.

Atala Chelette Family Papers (1819–1900)—A Free Black family of Natchitoches Parish, Louisiana.

Stephen Duncan Family Papers (1846–1899)—Papers of Duncan family of Adams and Issaquena counties, Mississippi.

Mrs. Isaac H. Hilliard Diary (1849–1859, 1866)—Wife of an Arkansas planter with descriptions of her travels in Louisiana, Mississippi, and Kentucky.

John C. Jenkins Family Papers (1840–1900)—No location given for this planter.

Moses Liddell (St. John R.) Family Papers (1813–1900)—Extensive collection (6,261 items plus 49 bound volumes) of a Mississippi and Louisiana family.

Louisiana State University Slavery Collection (1804–1860)—38 items of miscellaneous materials.

Eliza A. Magruder Diary (1846–1857)—Young girl's diary of a plantation near Natchez.

William J. Minor Family Papers (1748–1898)—Mississippi banking and planter family covering three generations.

James Monette Diary (1848–1863)—Diary of activities on Bellview and later named Pleasant Hill Plantation, Louisiana.

Leonidas P. Spyker Family Papers (1856–1900)—1 volume of records, Northwestern Louisiana.

Clarissa E. Leavitt Town Diary (1853)—Life near Baton Rouge.

In addition to the above series, researchers should be aware of the possibility that other planters' records may be available in microfilm or microfiche format. As mentioned previously, the Library of Congress and state archives routinely microfilm the papers of individuals who have been important in the history of the country or their state of residence. This would include planters' papers, particularly if they achieved some national or statewide prominence. If you are certain that you need to study a planter's papers in great detail, the institution can microfilm them for you, generally at a cost that is prohibitive for the average researcher's pocketbook. Inquire anyway!

Various archives and libraries will also film manuscript collections for individual researchers, but this can be a costly venture if you are unsure of what you are looking for.

Libraries with major collections of planters papers are: Louisiana State University, South Carolina Department of Archives, University of North Carolina at Chapel Hill, North Carolina Department of Archives and History, University of Virginia Library system, the Virginia State Library and Archives, and the Perkins Library at Duke University. But there are others, as you will see once you examine the *National Union Catalogue of Manuscript Collections*.

Once you locate the records of a planter family, your best bet is to research these records yourself rather than hiring a researcher. While it is okay to hire a local researcher for courthouse records, plantation records—as in the case of Farrar above—require too much time to examine. However, in the case of Massenburg's records, where slave lists are clearly identified, it would not be too difficult for a researcher, with very specific instructions, to find slave lists for you to evaluate on a preliminary basis only. You will still have to examine the records yourself.

It would be good to close this chapter with the statement made by the genealogist at the beginning: *Be prepared.* No one knows you're coming. What that means is you should have some familiarity with what you are searching for prior to visiting any institution, particularly since African American genealogy is still a new field. Your correspondence and reading should have prepared you to ask the kinds of questions you need to have answered prior to visiting any facility that houses manuscript collections or genealogical materials.

Special Topic 2

AFRICAN
AMERICAN
INSTITUTIONAL
RECORDS

Our educational institutions were collecting and preserving the records of our history long before there was a National Archives. . . . An archives is like the mind—a repository. The records therein like the memory. Surely it is a terrible thing to neglect and waste our cultural legacy as it is to waste the potential of the mind. Preserving archives is an act of wisdom.

THOMAS C. BATTLE, HISTORIAN AND CURATOR,
MOORLAND-SPINGARN COLLECTION, HOWARD UNIVERSITY

Overview

*T*he untapped resources found in the holdings of the major repositories of African American colleges, libraries, and archives throughout the country have not been discussed fully. People like Dorothy Porter, Arthur Schomburg, Monroe Work, Vivian Harsch, and Carter G. Woodson have actively built collections of material in Black institutional settings. Many of these resources will remain unexplored until genealogists begin to actively compile needed indexes and abstracts of material that pertain to individual African Americans. As you explore these sources, be mindful that the policy for all archives and repositories in the country is that only you, the researcher, can do your own research. The value placed on preservation of historical records in this country does not allow for high-paid staff nor for adequate staff to effectively deal with the public.

In addition to learning how to identify African American sources for this period, you will also become aware of the need to locate and preserve the many records on African American life that still lie waiting for a good researcher like you to unearth. Church records probably constitute the single most important body of records in this category.

While they are extremely important, many historical researchers and archivists are aware that personal papers now in the possession of African American families are just as important. Historians and the staff of libraries with manuscript collections are constantly looking for the surviving papers of local and national public figures. Even items such as letters written by migrants back home constitute a critical source in documenting the African American experience.

In the course of your research, you will inevitably find cases of gross negligence in the preservation of family papers, church records, and even public records. In other cases, you will find that unavoidable fires and other catastrophes have wiped away forever written documents that could have helped you in your research. You might even be tempted to attribute these losses to the undeveloped awareness of the importance of records within the African American community. Before you do that, you should know that the disregard for "old" records is an All-American disease, exhibiting itself at the highest levels. Indeed, failure to recognize their value and to preserve such records was characteristic of American record keeping practices until early in the twentieth century, when historians and other scholars began to encourage the development of an archival system at the national and state levels. Nevertheless, records continue to be destroyed due to negligence or even administrative policy. Archivists and historical preservation agencies have to decide what is important to preserve as well as what needs to be discarded. These are difficult decisions to make; records not considered valuable now may at some point in the future become important for reasons that cannot be presently identified.

You will also become thankful for those African Americans, especially librarians and collectors, who silently collected items for years, items that now constitute the basis of acclaimed collections on African American life. Nevertheless, the effort to preserve African American history is still often an uphill struggle. In the late nineteenth and early twentieth centuries, the creation and preservation of records depended heavily on the existence of a literate and educated African American community free to consider matters other than its day-to-day survival. Such communities did exist, though they were small. Philadelphia's black community played such a role, and its viability is evidenced by the work of individuals like William Still and William Adger.

The reasons that you will find it difficult to conduct genealogical research using African American sources (that is, sources generated by African Americans) are summarized below:

- Dispersal of records and sources
- Inadequate indexing of large record groups
- Lack of detailed catalogues and guidebooks describing major collections
- Inadequate staffing at major libraries

Despite these obstacles, existing sources are plentiful enough to keep good researchers busy for a long time.

Major Sources

The following section provides a review of possible sources that African American genealogists might find helpful in building a genealogical and biographical profile for individuals. The focus here is on those major sources created by African Americans or records kept on African Americans between 1865 and 1910, a period in which public records (vital records and census records) are often uneven or nonexistent with regard to African Americans. You should remember that this period was one in which African Americans began to migrate out of the South or to new locations in the South. Therefore, you will want to consider the possibility that an ancestor moved from a local area before concluding that census takers missed him or her due to negligence. This makes African American sources even more important in your research for this period. If you encounter difficulties for this period of time, the following types of records should be located. These records are, however, not just for locating information not found in other sources. They should also be used when you want to expand your research by building biographical profiles of some of your ancestors.

Surviving Black Newspapers, particularly those with longer runs, have been microfilmed. Early African American newspapers contain extensive information on individuals, particularly those who had occupations that allowed for upward mobil-

ity—teachers, ministers, and even Pullman porters. Researchers should attempt to locate microfilm editions of any local Black newspapers that were published in the areas where their ancestors lived. The local area should be defined rather broadly, particularly if your ancestors lived in a rural area. Early Black newspapers covered a wide range of issues, but their significance for genealogists lies in their fairly extensive coverage of individuals, including obituaries or death notices.

Researchers should not only look for information on individuals; they should also take note of articles that cover other issues, particularly those that relate to employment, migration, and politics. One researcher, Lori Husband, found that the *Chicago Defender* regularly printed names of World War I draftees from predominantly Black wards. She also found query letters (sometimes written by former slaves still looking for their separated relatives). These columns appeared in almost every major Black newspaper. Because early papers are relatively easy to skim, your research will not be as difficult as you might anticipate. Few of these papers have been indexed for genealogical data, and James Abajian's work (see Bibliography) is still the most comprehensive source. Other smaller newspaper indexing projects have been undertaken by genealogists, and there is a dire need for more such efforts.

African American Insurance Company records should represent a tremendous resource to genealogists because many were founded after the turn of the century. At present, little is known about their availability, but a standard letter of inquiry should be directed to the individual in charge of the company's records stating your purpose and requesting information on the company's policy with regard to releasing information on deceased individuals.

Early Published Biographical Sources are extremely helpful if your ancestor was active in local and national African American institutional life. African Americans were particularly anxious to show their progress by the turn of the century, and the products of the early Black press attest to this effort. Titles such as *Men of Mark: Eminent, Progressive and Rising* are typical of such publications. Do not overlook "strange-sounding" titles. This publication contained 1,138 pages profiling African Americans throughout the country, including photographs! A number of these *Who's Who*-type directories—or "mugbooks," in genealogical parlance—were published by the early Black press, and some are more difficult than others to locate. However, a recent publication, *Black Biographical Dictionaries, 1790–1950*, claims to have located all surviving biographical dictionaries. Researchers should know, however, that despite all good efforts, the vast number of papers still in private hands in the African American community may indeed unearth new additions to this work. One major source that was never published is Daniel A. P. Murray's compilation of biographies under the tentative title, "Murray's Historical and Biographical Encyclopedia of the Colored Race." Murray was the first African American bibliographer at the Library of Congress.

One major source of biographical information that every genealogical researcher should use is the forty-two-volume series *The American Slave: A Composite Autobiogra-*

phy, compiled by George P. Rawick. This series of oral interviews conducted by WPA workers in the late 1930s is probably the most exhaustive effort ever to compile life histories of former slaves. The quality of the genealogical data recorded by interviewers, however, varied considerably, since there was no emphasis placed on family relations and ancestry during the defining stages of this project. Despite this drawback, locating such recent memories of events that occurred during slavery will help those who do find ancestors in this compilation.

Researchers should also look for additional oral history compilations of former slaves. Though the Rawick compilation is the most exhaustive, there is always the possibility that additional interviews exist in such local facilities as state archives and libraries with manuscript collections. A number of publications have extracted interviews from the original WPA typewritten manuscripts. Though the same interviews appear in the Rawick series, these publications should not be ignored because they often extract the best interviews centered around one particular state or subject. A fairly extensive evaluation of the WPA project was written by Tony Burroughs (see chapter 2 bibliography). Burroughs underscores the possibility that each interview may exist in several forms and in separate locations, a point researchers need to know once an ancestor's interview has been located.

Local oral history projects have been conducted for a number of years. An inquiry through the major public library or the state's archives in your area of research may yield additional biographical information in the form of oral interviews. Oral history projects are also routinely reported in the journal *Oral History*.

College and Training School Records are often untapped by genealogists partly because some of the early training schools established after emancipation are now defunct. A prodigious effort at locating any surviving records will benefit individual researchers; furthermore, once these records are found, some effort should be made to find an archive that will accept them as part of their collection. Locating the records of the early training schools is best done in the local area unless you know that all surviving records exist in a particular collection. Because these schools were often supported by one of the religious denominations, you might also find that the school's papers were transferred to that denomination's archive.

Black colleges should be contacted through the registrar's office and the library. The registrar's office may copy your ancestor's application and correspondence with the institution depending on the school's policy. The library may have yearbooks and other information about students who attended the school. In writing to the registrar and the library, you should explain the purpose of your research and its use. You should also indicate that you are willing to submit a fee for their efforts including copying. A recent historical exhibit at Atlanta University's library revealed that files on students at Black colleges may contain quite a bit of correspondence. The exhibit reproduced a number of letters from applicants or their parents covering details such as the family's economic condition and the student's academic performance.

Associational and Club Records (Unions, Social Clubs, etc.): These records are often hard to find, if they are extant. Social, civic, community improvement, and mutual benefit societies were widespread in urban Black communities at the turn of the century and later. If your ancestor belonged to one of the nationally based organizations such as the Masons, you are more likely to find information on his activities. For example, Masonic lodges offered burial policies to their members. These policies may contain genealogical information not to be found elsewhere. The Eastern Star societies would have similar data. In order to determine whether a search for these records would be beneficial, you should start with some evidence that your ancestor was a member. This evidence should have been collected in the course of conducting your interviews. You may also write to the organization's headquarters or to the local lodge to which your ancestor belonged.

Political Records: Included in this category are records of various political and social movements that either involved Blacks or had a direct impact on Blacks. Most of these records are now housed in manuscript collections, and many have been microfilmed. If you had an ancestor who was politically active and you are seeking a wide range of information on his or her life, it would definitely pay to check these sources.

The back-to-Africa movements, from the American Colonization Society to the Garvey movement, contain a wealth of data on individuals. The activities of the American Colonization Society (ACS), though they were aimed at removing the perceived threat of Free blacks to the slave population, did generate a lot of interest within the African American community. As mentioned in a previous chapter, the papers of the ACS and its state organizations, particularly the Maryland State Colonization Society contain a large body of correspondence from free Blacks interested in migrating and slave owners desiring to manumit their slaves for emigration to Liberia.

Membership rosters of national organizations such as the early NAACP might provide information on place of residence for some of your ancestors, particularly when that information is needed to trace a migrating ancestor at the turn of the century. The same applies for obscure records maintained by various branches of the federal government. For example, one scholar cited a circulation list for the *Chicago Defender* that was collected by the FBI in the 1920s! The *Defender* was more nearly a national African

American newspaper than any other at the time. Therefore, researchers should not discount the possibility that an ancestor's address could be located on this roster collected by the FBI.

Because genealogical information can often become difficult to locate for certain areas and periods of African American history, researchers should leave no stone unturned, particularly when large sets of records are available. That is the case with records associated with lynching. One compilation that may prove to be helpful in this area, particularly if you have a family story that suggests one of your ancestors was lynched, is the Tuskegee Institute Lynching records.

AFRICAN AMERICAN CHURCH RECORDS

Church records are voluminous, and they often contain the most important kind of information that genealogists are looking for—evidence of births, marriages, and deaths. African Americans have belonged to every existing religious denomination in this country; furthermore, they have created their own independent religions and religious movements. African American churches are no different from many small Euro-American churches in the United States; they have not been careful about preserving historical records. Only the better-organized churches and those in large cities are likely to have a continuous set of records that could be properly termed "historical." Exemplary record preservation exists at Mother Bethel A.M.E. Church (Philadelphia) and Bethel A.M.E. Church in

Baltimore, where archives have been established. Unfortunately, the records of Quinn Chapel, founded in Chicago in the 1840s, have not been located. My own personal experience with trying to locate records on my family's church, discussed in a previous chapter, should serve as a guiding lesson.

Characteristics of African American Church Records

- *Dispersed*—Church records are housed in a variety of places—from the church secretary who has all the old records to major repositories.
- *Plentiful*—As the major institution in African American life, such records are plentiful, believe it or not. The earliest publishing efforts among African Americans were those of the various church bodies known as the Sunday School Publishing Board or by other names.
- *Severely underutilized*—Church records are not a prominent part of African American genealogy as in Euro-American genealogy. This is partly a function of the above two factors plus the lack of indexing activity among African American genealogists.
- *Difficult to access*—Many records are still uncatalogued and housed in archives, manuscript collections without adequate resources and staff. Funds are often not available for even the simplest preservation efforts, such as microfilming.
- *Undervalued*—Such records are often taken for granted, particularly at the church level. Some denominations have only begun to recognize the importance of preservation. The Black Methodists

have been more careful about this than have the Baptists.
- *Sometimes unlocatable*—Consider the following statement made by Professor Albert J. Raboteau in a bibliographic essay on Black church sources:

Consulting all the pertinent denominational archives cited below would not locate more than a fraction of the relevant materials. Some valuable items seem to have been lost. Some pamphlets, church minutes, and private diaries that were available to nineteenth-century black denominational historians have subsequently disappeared. The personal journal of Joseph Cox . . . (AME) was for example a century ago in the possession of AME historiographer Daniel A. Payne. Today it can no longer be located.

A Strategy of Research for Using Church Records

1. Decide what is the focus of your research. That will determine what kinds of records to look for and where to find them. If the focus of your research is an individual who was not a church leader, then you will be looking for the types of records generated by the church itself. These records are primarily genealogical in nature (birth, marriage, death). If, however, you are searching for information on a lay leader, the church itself, or an organization of the church such as the missionary society, then your search will lead you to organizational records that have been generated by both the local church and the national organization.

2. Be aware of the historical context of your research. African American church records were generated as people

became literate and more organized. By the 1880s, such records achieved phenomenal growth. It was during this period that the church publishing industry really took off.

3. Be aware of the function of church records in your research. Do you need records of marriage, birth, and death for the period before statewide registration? Church records, if they were preserved, may fill the gap left by uneven registrations of African American vital events between 1866 and the turn of the century. If you need information about an ancestor's role in the local church and its organizations at the regional and national levels, then records preserved in various archives will be of help.

4. Know the likelihood of finding records for your particular area of the country or the region, particularly the farther back in time you go.

5. Know the history of the denomination that you are researching.

6. Know the types of records available. Use the chart below to do some problem solving.

Records to Expect

1. Expect to find few transcriptions and indexes of records. When you find them, they are likely to be adjuncts to indexes of White church records, as in the case of the Parish Registers of Christ Church.

2. Church journals, papers, and magazines have been published since the 1890s.

3. Registers of birth, baptism, marriage, and death tend to be rare for certain periods and certain kinds of churches.

The Catholic church has a long tradition of maintaining an institutional system for vital records of parish members. On the other hand, small rural church records, though these are the ones you will most likely be looking for, are far less available. Researchers should not ignore the records relating to the period when freedmen, formerly members of the slave owner's church, left to establish their own churches, sometimes with the assistance of the former church. Or consider the example found in Pauli Murray's book *Proud Shoes*, where a baptismal record crucial to reconstructing her family line was housed at the Chapel of the Cross Episcopal Church in Chapel Hill, North Carolina, where she delivered the Holy Eucharist after becoming a deacon and priest of the church!

Therefore, for the period near the end of slavery, it would be extremely necessary for researchers to know either the church to which the last slave owner belonged or the name of the church of which the present Black church is an offshoot. Slave attendance in White churches was fairly widespread and has been documented in the historical record. Therefore, check for any surviving records at the local historical society or the church itself.

4. Early registers of birth, marriage, and death for Black churches established immediately after the Civil War are probably difficult to find. This, however, should really be the focus of your genealogical research. The simple reason: collecting and preserving. Nearly every denomination is now

YOUR CHURCH HISTORY RESEARCH

WHO/WHAT	Information	Records	Location
Individuals/ Members	Genealogical Data	Baptism Marriage Death Membership	Local Church Record System (Secretary)
Active Lay	Genealogical	See above	Church/Archives & Mss. Collections
Members & Leaders	Biographical Activities	Obituaries	Bio. Publications
Religious Leaders	Correspondence Biographical & Genealogical Career & Service Sermons & Speeches	Same Personal Papers	Same as above
Church	General History Organizations Membership & Growth Pastors, Priests Org. Leadership Buildings & Locations Cemeteries	Probate-Deeds Tax Rolls WPA File Pastor's Records Registers/Rolls Correspondence	Same as above + Church Members Former Pastors
Church Conferences	Organizational Records Meetings Conferences	Minutes Programs Journals	Same as above
Central Body	Publications Financial Records Member Churches National Meetings Religious Leaders Schools & Colleges Political Activities	Magazines Correspondence Minutes Library/Archives	Same as above

trying to collect such records. State and local historical societies may also be interested in them, particularly if they can be shown to be of some historical value. Your collecting should, of course, include cemetery records, often the only surviving records for your home area church. Individual church records may also be tucked away in a manuscript collection. Consider entry #6725 from Howard University's *Bibliography of African and Afro-Religious Study*. The entry notes that *The Baptist Meeting House Church Book*, May 3, 1818, to August 3, 1856, for Casey's Fork, Kentucky, contains a list of its members.

5. Encyclopedias or cyclopedias are important for those researching ancestors who were lay or religious church leaders. Titles like *The Encyclopedia of African Methodism*, published in 1916, are quite common.

6. Conference minutes are also of genealogical importance. They contain lists of delegates to meetings, ministers, licentiates, and officers. In addition, most association minutes will contain obituaries for its members.

7. Written church histories may appear as formal published histories, short histories in religious and historical journals, or as part of the church's annual celebration souvenir book, or even in dissertations, particularly for historically important churches. A history of Chicago's Olivet Baptist Church exists in the form of a master's thesis that was done in 1922 at the University of Chicago!

Other kinds of records appear to exist in abundance, particularly for lay and religious leaders of churches, but the problem is one of access. How does one access church records, particularly when they are so scattered? If you have exhausted possibilities of locating surviving records for your ancestor's particular church, then your next best bet is to try to locate records on that church in various manuscript and archival collections.

Archival and Manuscript Holdings at Black Institutions for Church Research

Following is a brief review of several major collections housed at black institutions. Researchers should be mindful of the fact that librarians and archivists cannot do research for you, but they can answer standard questions with regard to their collections.

Schomburg: The Schomburg Center's Preservation of the Black Religious Heritage Project was designed to collect and preserve (microfilming and conservation) the records of major churches in ten metropolitan areas in the country. Of more importance, however, is the center's willingness to collect local Black church records. Examine the following statement:

The types of materials needed include: the minutes of church governing bodies, committees, societies and clubs; pre-twentieth-century birth, marriage and death records; materials from outreach and community service ministries; printed and recorded music; audio and video recordings of sermons, programs and special events. . . . The Project is prepared to make, preserve and provide access to microfiche reproductions of these materials in cases when it is not possible to secure original records. The center has published two pamphlets that are available upon request: *Preservation of the Black Religious Heritage* and *Preserving African-American Religious Documents: A Guideline for Churches and Other Religious Institutions.*

Amistad Research Center: This center has also been collecting church records. In addition to the American Missionary Association collection, their largest collection relating to African American religious history, Amistad also has sizable holdings for the Central Congregational Church, the AME, and the UCC. Two select bibliographies on religion have been compiled, and can be obtained by request. Note that the AMA collection would be helpful if you had ancestors who attended one of the many schools the organization established after the Civil War or if you had an ancestor active in the abolitionist movement. A very detailed index to the correspondence in the AMA collection exists.

Wilberforce University: The official repository for AME records; however, there is no active collection policy at present. The collection primarily contains General Conference minutes, State Conference reports and minutes, and other such publications for the AME Church. A few records also exist for the AME Zion and CME churches. A finding aid to the collection may be obtained by writing directly to Wilberforce's Carnegie Library. Because the AME Church has a strong tradition of record keeping and publishing, researchers should expect to find nearly all conference reports and minutes. In addition, those interested in initiating projects to preserve church records should obtain a copy of the brochure published by the official historiographer for the church (Dennis C. Dicker-

son's *The Past Is in Your Hands: Writing Local A.M.E. Church History*). This brochure could also be used by other denominations for it offers a comprehensive approach to reconstructing the history of local churches.

Livingston College: Hood Theological Seminary is the official repository for the AMEZ Church. An index of rare materials and records is currently being prepared. Most of the material in this collection consists of membership rolls, conference reports and minutes, personal letters, historical books, and biographical records. Finally, some of the more important materials in the collection will be available on microfilm.

American Baptist Historical Society: Before using this collection, researchers should check the guide *Afro-American Baptists: A Guide to Materials in the American Baptist Historical Society*. The society does have a sizable collection of church annuals and Black Baptist periodicals, some of which are on microfilm. None of the Baptist denominations has a major archival center; however, the National Baptist Convention, USA, Inc., recently opened the Baptist World Center. According to Professor Raboteau, this collection is of major importance, but it is presently uncatalogued. As a substitute, records of the Historical Commission of the Southern Baptist Convention should be checked.

The Howard University Research Center on Black Religious Bodies recently published *The Directory of African American Religious Bodies: A Compendium* by the Howard University School of Divinity. This directory is indispensable to researchers, and it should be consulted prior to starting your research on church records. The Moorland-Spingarn Research Center recently acquired the papers of Joseph H. Jackson, longtime president of the National Baptist Convention and minister of Olivet Baptist Church in Chicago. These papers will supplement the growing collection efforts in African American Baptist records. As with all new acquisitions, researchers should not expect to have access to them until they have been processed.

WPA: The WPA's published and unpublished materials include quite a bit of material on Black churches. In order to access this material, researchers should first read "A Guide to the Unpublished Inventories, Indexes, and Transcripts" of the WPA. This guide will indicate where the material is housed. For example, the WPA created inventories of Alabama church records for both Black Methodist and Baptist churches for all counties. This material will indicate what records did exist at the time the inventory was taken, and it is housed at the Alabama Department of Archives and History. This information forms a baseline of what to look for once you do start searching for records. Note that some of this information may also be published. The WPA also transcribed cemeteries, and the guide identifies them. Similar publications for your state of research are likely to be available.

As with all research that involves extensive use of manuscript collections, researchers should follow some simple rules of courtesy:

1. Identify any finding aids on a particular collection.

2. Write the archivist for the collection before visiting, stating as specifically as possible what you are looking for.
3. Become familiar with the collection before visiting so that you won't waste time looking.

Researchers should also identify and write to the individual in charge of the denomination's historical records or any libraries affiliated with the denomination's theological schools.

A Note on Slaves and Islam

*T*here are documented cases of slaves who maintained their Islamic faith. If your family's oral tradition includes stories that relate to Muslim religious practices such as praying to the East, praying on a mat, refusal of Christianity as a doctrine, or the use of names derived from Arabic, then you might want to consider the possibility that one or some of your ancestors maintained their faith. This is a fascinating and little understood aspect of the African American religious tradition, but one major documentary publication essential to exploring this question has been recently published (Allan D. Austin, *African Muslims in Antebellum America*). Researchers should review this work to understand how Islam manifested itself in the slave community.

Conclusion

*I*n this chapter, an attempt has been made to acquaint researchers with the importance of records generated primarily by

African American institutions after emancipation. In addition, some attempt has been made to point to family patterns and clues from oral traditions that might point to records to consult in the course of your research. Many of these records are housed in library manuscript collections and therefore require added effort to locate. Indexing and abstracting of school and church records are in their infancy among African American genealogists. Therefore, researchers will have to be fairly diligent in locating and using such records until they become more accessible.

Special Topic 3

CARIBBEAN
ANCESTRY

Mus tek cyear a de root fal heal de tree.

(You must nurture the root to heal the tree.)

FROM *THE LEGACY OF IBO LANDING: GULLAH ROOTS OF AFRICAN AMERICAN CULTURE,* MARQUETTA L. GOODWINE

OVERVIEW

*R*ecords of Caribbean countries are just as plentiful as those of the United States, particularly records left by planters. Because African Americans of the Caribbean have migrated to the United States at different times and under differing circumstances, it is important to focus on when the migration occurred. For example, if you are researching ancestry during the seventeenth century in Virginia, Maryland, South Carolina, or Georgia, it would be important to know that a sizable portion of the United States slave population arrived in the Caribbean prior to being "transshipped" to the United States during that period of time. Later, the majority would come from Africa. In addition, many planters (British, French, and Spanish) migrated to the United States with their slaves from the Caribbean at different periods of time. As early as the 1730s through the American Revolution, planter families like the Winthrops, one of whom became the governor of Massachusetts, migrated from the Caribbean islands. Another slave-owning family, the Vassalls, arriving from Jamaica, settled in the Boston area.

Barbados planters were among the first to settle in South Carolina. One particu-larly large migration occurred after the Haitian Revolution, when French planters and a large contingent of free Haitian Blacks and slaves who had settled in Cuba eventually migrated to southern Louisiana in 1809 and 1810. There was considerable controversy surrounding this event because by then, United States law prohibited the importation of slaves, and furthermore, there was considerable fear among planters who believed that importing slaves from Haiti was an invitation to rebellion. Never-theless, about nine thousand Haitian refugees arrived from that country via Cuba, among whom about three thousand were free Blacks and three thousand were slaves. Many of the free Blacks did settle in the New Orleans area despite the prohibi-tion on their remaining. Others settled in the Charleston, South Carolina area. Planters, with their slaves, settled in both places.

By 1834, slaves in the British Caribbean had been formally emancipated but contin-ued to live under British colonial rule and labor indentures similar to Reconstruction-era sharecropping arrangements in the American South. While U.S. laws discour-aged the immigration of freed slaves from other parts of the world, freedmen from the Caribbean area probably began to migrate to the United States in small trickles, later followed by extensive migration to the northeastern states and Florida during the 1920s.

PLENTIFUL CARIBBEAN RECORDS

Whenever and however your British, Spanish, or French Caribbean ancestry was formed, you should become familiar with the tremendous number of resources available to researchers. British Caribbean records, especially for the nineteenth century, include plantation records, slave registrations, church records generated by missionaries, and abolitionists' records. If your ancestors are recent immigrants to the United States, make sure you read the chapters on slavery in this book. Don't assume that they won't apply to you. At the least, they will provide you with a frame of reference with which to attack your own research problems.

One good place to start, of course, would be the archives of the particular country in which your research will take place, followed by obtaining material on the holdings for the Caribbean at the Archives of the West Indies. In addition, since some of the genealogical material has been microfilmed by the Genealogical Society of Utah, you will be able to order what is available through a local LDS stake library. Indeed, some of the material that you may need is housed at the British Public Records Office, but before hopping a plane to London, try to communicate by mail and by all means make sure that you have exhausted all local materials including, of course, your family's oral tradition. Given the heavy influence of African cultural traditions in the Caribbean, an oral interview should definitely include questions relating to African ancestry, traditional religious and healing practices, and ethnic identities.

CENSUSES OR SLAVE REGISTRATIONS, 1812–1834

Between 1812 and 1816, the local colonial legislatures of the British Caribbean, under pressure from the British Parliament, passed laws that required the triennial registration of slaves in all localities or parishes. For Jamaica, these censuses, called Returns of Registrations of Slaves, were taken in 1817, 1820, 1823, 1826, 1829, and finally, in 1832 when slave owners were compensated for their losses in view of the proposed emancipation of slaves. Other colonies registered slaves at different dates. The returns contain the names of slave owners and for slaves, the following information: name, sex, color, country of birth (often identified as Africa with no further distinctions), and mother's name if the mother was alive and lived on the same holding. A remarks column contains notations on any changes that occurred between registrations such as sale, desertion, shipment or sale out of the colony, death, birth, and the like. Because these records were generated locally, there will be some differences in how inclusive the registrations were from one colony to the next. For example, in Jamaica, those living in the maroon colonies were not registered.

In order to use these records, you would have to know the place and plantation where your ancestors last served as slaves. Because the actual information entered into the registrations varied so much from one colony to the next, it is difficult to make generalizations about their overall content, particularly the inclusion of surnames, the methods of entering slaves in family groups or individually, the assigning of surnames that may differ from post-emancipation names, and the identification of kin relations. Researchers might find, despite the lack of uniformity in registrations, that ethnic identification will frequently appear, particularly if the person being registered was of African birth. One historian counted at least five hundred different "ethnic" labels applied to Trinidadian registrants.

Researchers should therefore use these registrations along with all subsequent censuses since 1834 to trace their ancestry in much the same way that was described in the chapter on censuses. Once the period of slavery is reached, the records left by planters and the parish registers of the Church of England should be consulted. Though many planters were absentee, they nevertheless did the same things that all other planters during the era of slavery did—they bought, sold, and conveyed slaves in perpetuity. Some of these records have been abstracted. For example, the eight-volume series called *Barbados Records* con-

tains probate documents covering the period 1639 to 1725. Another volume, *Genealogies of Barbados Families*, would also serve researchers well—especially those whose ancestors were brought to the United States by various planters migrating to the mainland.

For those with ancestry in the French Caribbean, similar records exist. A check of materials filmed by the Genealogical Society of Utah (LDS) indicated that the Haitian Notarial Archives (most dating from the mid-1700s through the early 1800s), parish registers of individual churches, a few emancipation records, and censuses of planters are available. Indexes exist for the notarial records and court records. Winston De Ville has transcribed some census records in a volume entitled *St. Domingue Census Records and Military Lists, 1688–1720*. In addition, a genealogical magazine published in Paris, *Généalogie et histoire de la Caraïbe*, covers genealogical and historical topics pertaining to Haitian planters and, no doubt, their slaves.

This necessarily brief review of Caribbean sources excludes the Spanish Caribbean, but researchers should know that similar sources exist for Cuba and Puerto Rico, particularly in the parish records of the Catholic church.

Special Topic 4

AMERICAN INDIAN
ANCESTRY

Racism keeps people who are being managed from finding out the truth through contact with others.

SHIRLEY CHISHOLM

INTRODUCTION

No person shall be eligible to a seat in the General Council but a free Cherokee male citizen, who shall have attained to the age of twenty-five years. The descendants of Cherokee men by all free women, except the African race, whose parents may have been living together as man and wife, according to the customs and laws of this Nation, shall be entitled to all the rights and privileges of the Nation as well as the posterity of Cherokee women by free men. No person who is of Negro or Mulatto parentage, either by the father or mother's side, shall be eligible to hold any office or profit, honor or trust under this Government.

ARTICLE III, SECTION 4, CHEROKEE
CONSTITUTION OF 1827
QUOTED IN *BLACK INDIAN
GENEALOGY RESEARCH* BY ANGELA Y.
WALTON-RAJI

You have probably heard that Indian-Black relations were far better than Black and European relations. In general, most scholars agree that they were, particularly for groups like the Seminole Indians. On the other hand, the politics of racial identity and assimilation have definitely come into play between these three groups, and as you explore the meaning of Indian ancestry, you will come to a deeper understanding of the complexity of ethnic group relations in the United States as well as elsewhere. Some African Americans strongly identify with their Indian ancestry even though they don't know the specifics, while others are rather more suspicious of people who claim such ancestry, wondering why African American group identity isn't enough to get along with. As you explore possible Black-Indian relations, whether by blood or association, you will hopefully come up with your own answers.

On balance, Indian tribes throughout American history have been in a besieged state—from the early Indian wars during the Colonial period down through the massive removal of members of the so-called Five Civilized Tribes to Oklahoma Territory during the 1830s. Even partial assimilation and adoption of European culture (inter-marriage, customs, names, attire, religion, etc.), did not eliminate the one issue that caused conflict between these two groups. That issue was land. Put simply, the policy from earliest colonial times through the nineteenth century was one based on the idea of "Indian removal." Indeed some states declared Indians into nonexistence by legislative fiat despite the presence of remnant groups. Such was the case in Virginia, for example, where those Indians who wanted to have their tribal identities recorded on official birth records would have to do it in a neighboring state pursuant to a 1924 state law.

In addition to the policy of removal, there was a policy of nonrecognition of unaffiliated Indians or those individuals not living with their tribal groups. For example, the Choctaws, the first tribe to remove to the Oklahoma Territory, left behind 7,000 in Mississippi who refused to migrate. The remaining Mississippi Choctaws lost their tribal status as well as the benefits paid to those who agreed to migrate. The point here is that the policy only recognized as Indians those who lived within their groups or those who remained affiliated with the tribe. The rest, those who had assimilated, or those who became citizens of the United States, were often not recognized as "Indian" in the record. These are individuals who, in effect, lost their identities, perhaps not by choice, but through policy. This policy will have some impact on your research. It will become difficult to find an Indian ancestor named as a member of a tribal group or simply called "Indian," a designation that won't help you very much anyway—especially in those regions that had many smaller Indian groups.

THE SHIFTING SANDS OF RACIAL IDENTITY: IDENTIFYING AN INDIAN ANCESTOR

Many researchers (both European and African American) prematurely look for Indian ancestry, often without much evidence at hand and with the expectation that the records will be readily available. Proving Indian ancestry is easy for those who have continuously maintained a tribal identity. For all others, proving Indian ancestry will be difficult. Note as mentioned earlier that it would be inappropriate to simply say you have an "Indian" ancestor. The term "Indian" was a creation of European contact that was forced on Indians as a collective group, much in the same manner that the term "African" was used as a global term to apply to groups on that continent that had never heard the term before. That is, the first time they knew they were "African" was when they met a European.

African American researchers might encounter at least three circumstances that would warrant a closer look at the voluminous records that document contact between Africans and Indians. The stage of slave research is the point at which you are most likely to encounter this contact, and it is a stage at which you should be alert to the possibility of an Indian slaveowner and/or free Indian ancestor. Slavery was not the only kind of relationship that existed between Africans and Indians, but it is the one that is the most documentable. In sorting out a relationship between an African ancestor and an Indian ancestor, ask yourself these questions:

1: Do I know when the contact occurred?
2: Do I know where the contact occurred?
3: Do I know whether contact was between an affiliated Indian (living with his or her tribe) or nonaffiliated living among Europeans?
4: Do I know the relationship (slaveowner/ slave; husband/wife, etc.)
5: Do I know the name of the tribe and band that my ancestor belonged to?

If you can't answer these questions with any accuracy, then you have a lot of research to do. Not being able to answer, however, should not prevent you from exploring the possibilities that exist, particularly during the phases of slave research where (1) escaping slaves often sought protection (successfully and unsuccessfully) from Indian groups for all periods prior to emancipation, (2) assimilated Indians or mixed-bloods often owned slaves, and Europeans, as they pressed into Indian occupied land, brought their slaves with them. For the period of early contact when a great deal of mixing occurred between Indians and Africans, the Colonial period, additional possibilities exist because (1) some Indians were actually enslaved and lived alongside African slaves, (2) Indians, like early Africans, were often indentured for a certain term of service, (3) Europeans and their slaves, by implication, fought Indian groups during the period of the Indian Wars, and (4) Indians fought Indians yielding slave captives.

The Blood and the Name: Tribal Rolls & Tribal Identity

One of the easiest ways to determine Indian ancestry is to write to the tribe, assuming that it is a tribe that still exists and is recognized by the Bureau of Indian Affairs. For this of course, you must know the name of the tribe as well as the name of the Indian ancestor. The Bureau of Indian Affairs maintains a list of recognized tribes as well as tribes that are applying for federal recognition.

Each tribe maintains an original roll of its members and each has established clear criteria for membership. If you are able to complete the required form, then it is likely that you have recognized Indian ancestry. That is, the tribe has on file evidence that a CDIB (a certificate of degree of Indian blood) was issued. This certificate is used by all Indian groups to determine tribal membership, official enrollment, and eligibility for federal allotments and other services. For an ancestor who lived at the turn of the century, the tribal office would examine its rolls to determine whether the ancestor was ever enrolled or recognized as a member of that group. Note that official enrollment could have occurred by being married to an Indian or by being an Indian freedman (former slave) of a particular tribe.

Note, however, that you can have Indian ancestry and not be recognized on any tribal rolls. Such are the anomalies of official determination of who is and who is not a member of an ethnic group. Therefore, going the route of official tribal rolls maintained by the various groups is not a good approach for those who have no documentation with respect to Indian ancestry. Tribal councils are often deluged with requests for enrollment by Americans who may or may not have Indian ancestry and who may also have intentions of cashing in on the real and perceived benefits that accrue to Indians who remain in their groups.

Thus, you really are not likely to receive an answer for a query based on having an Indian ancestor if that is all the evidence you have. Further, each tribe's constitution determined who was to be recognized as a member and who was to be officially enrolled. Criteria for membership were not uniform across all groups. The essential requirements are that an ancestor appear on the tribe's rolls and that the individual have a recognizable blood quantum or degree of Indian blood. The degree of blood would exclude many Indians who have lived away from their own tribal communities though their ancestors might appear on the roll. Additional criteria include residency in the tribal home and continued social contact with the tribe. This would appear to be a question of both blood and cultural identity.

African Americans are even less likely to get information through this route, nor are they likely to gain tribal enrollment even if they could prove direct descent from a full-blooded Indian, especially for the Five Civilized Tribes that were removed to Oklahoma. Walton-Raji has stated this problem in a rather succinct way for African American researchers: "For many blacks with Indian ancestry, there is sometimes a misconception that the first ancestor to be found will be one who is a full blood Indian. It is important to note that race was a significant factor with the Indians of the Five Civilized Tribes, and if there was any association with blacks the blood line was frequently discounted by the time of official enrollment (1890s to 1907). Despite possible mixed heritage, the Black citizen and his family were more likely to have been listed among the Freedmen."

The bottom line is that following this route is not advised. Put succinctly, if you or current family members are not presently on the tribal rolls, you should probably not begin searching Indian sources until you have first researched the family in the same fashion you would any other American family from the present back to the late nineteenth century. This advice is the standard advice given to researchers at most genealogical libraries and it is paraphrased from research sheets used by the Newberry Library of Chicago.

EVALUATING THE EVIDENCE

The first circumstance that should lead you to consider Indian ancestry is having a strong oral tradition that an ancestor was indeed Indian. Oral traditions tend to be about three to five generations deep, so having such a tradition would place your ancestor during the period of slavery. This oral tradition might not be specific as to name of Indian nation or what the term "Indian" meant to those sharing the tradition, but it nevertheless should not be ignored. The oral tradition is often accompanied by photographs of an ancestor who "looked Indian." Researchers should know by now that "looking Indian" could actually mean a number of interracial combinations. It could first mean that actually the mixture occurred between a European and an African and just so happened to produce features that look "Indian." It could refer to a combination of all three racial groups, each of which may have uncertain lineages with respect to previous mixing. So, "looking Indian" should be thrown out the window just like "having the mark of Ham," a term that whites often used to refer to indeterminate mixtures of Black and white.

The second circumstance would be having direct knowledge that your ancestors were associated with Indians who were removed to the Oklahoma Territory in the 1830s and thereafter. This would come about as you research your Oklahoma heritage. How would you know that? Well, if you remember that one of the cardinal rules is to start from the present and work back, the first stages of your research would most likely include knowledge of ancestry in those places that once formed a part of the Oklahoma Territory, now more or less the state of Oklahoma. Of course you must also remember that many African Americans from nearby states settled in independent communities and towns in Oklahoma during the Oklahoma land rush of the 1890s.

The third circumstance is as difficult as the first. This circumstance would involve doing research in a local area unaware that your ancestor had any type of relationship with a member of one of the Indian nations. In effect, evidence would be ignored. In the course of your research, you will need to know the local history of the area where your ancestors served as slaves or lived as free persons prior to the abolition of slavery. Knowing the state and local history of your research area has been underscored throughout this work, but it becomes even more important now. For example, the Southern states formed part of a frontier in which the relationships between Indian and European were constantly being tested despite the presence of a large number of mixed-blood Indians who were traders and intermediaries between the two groups and who had also taken on European names. When the various nations were moved, they took with them their slaves who had connections with slaves owned by European settlers. While slave research is already difficult enough, imagine facing a dead end because you didn't know that the slaveowner and the slaves were part of the Indian removal to the Oklahoma Territory in 1838–40. Knowing the names of slaveowners who were Indian or mixed-blood in that area would help.

The bottom line is that if you know the local history, then you might automatically understand that finding a slaveowner named MacIntosh in Alabama rings a bell. MacIntoshes were a large class of mixed and assimilated Indian-Europeans who owned slaves, lived in those areas Americans once called the Old Southwest (Alabama, Georgia, Mississippi, etc.), and served as middle men in trading and other affairs between settler Europeans and the various Indian nations that lay claim to the land. Some even supported the Confederate side in the Civil War. As an aside, some of the leaders who encouraged their nations to move to the Oklahoma Territory were executed once they arrived. This was essentially a genocidal trek and forced removal of five major Indian groups from North Carolina, Georgia, Alabama, Tennessee, Arkansas, Mississippi, and Florida. The groups were and still are, ironically, called the Five Civilized Tribes and the trek became known as the Trail of Tears.

Examples of the third case might also occur when you are researching free African Americans in Virginia, North Carolina, and the New England states, all of which had significant populations of Indians who did not participate in the removals. This also relates to the emergence of mixed groups of indeterminate African, Indian, and European ancestry who tended to migrate as groups to remote areas of the country and intermarry among members of similar communities. The so-called Redbones, Melungeons, Portuguese, etc. have been written about in popular literature as if they came from space. Often white in appearance, they carry indeterminate amounts of Indian, African, and European blood lines. These groups are often called tri-racial isolates. The term literally means what it says—groups of individuals whose lineages include African, Indian, and European ancestry and who migrated together throughout the South but maintained a kind of group identity. Some, however, did remain in the East, primarily in North Carolina.

Adding to this already shifting sand of complexity and changing racial identities is the possibility that you may trace your ancestry back to some of the groups in North Carolina, Virginia, and New York who essentially no longer carry an Indian cultural identity (language, customs, oral history), but who claim Indian ancestry and have applied for recognition to the Bureau of Indian Affairs. Often these groups can be identified as African American, using the famous eyeball method of determining ethnicity. The Lumbees of North Carolina are a notable example. Still there are others who are applying for state and federal recognition as an Indian nation or tribe.

Yet another factor that adds to research difficulties is that Indians living outside their tribal communities were enumerated as mulatto or as free persons of color in many public records, including the censuses. Indians were not part of the American census taking effort until the year 1900. However, separate tribal rolls were taken at fairly consistent intervals by the Bureau of Indian Affairs and their agents starting with enumerations before their removal to Oklahoma.

UNDERSTANDING THE RECORDS THROUGH GUIDEBOOKS

*A*t this stage of research, it is essential that you use reliable guidebooks for research. At a minimum, you will need the chapter entitled "Native American Family History" in *The Source* and Angela Y. Walton-Raji's *Black Indian Genealogy Research*. Additional sources, including historical works, are included in the bibliography.

There are three major repositories of records relating to Indians in this country. They are located at the National Archives in Washington, D.C., the Oklahoma Historical Society, and the Federal Record Center in Fort Worth, Texas. These sources should be supplemented by sources at the state level for those tribes that have state recognition rather than federal recognition. In addition to these records, the usual records that most researchers use may or may not apply depending on the period of time and location. Censuses and census studies near Indian reservations are especially appropriate, as are local courthouse records (including probate and deed records).

FREEDMEN'S RECORDS OF THE FIVE CIVILIZED TRIBES

*R*esearchers who should search these records would be (1) those with known ancestry in Oklahoma for any period of time and (2) those who are looking for slaves or freedmen who might have migrated to the Oklahoma Territory for the period of removal (1830–1836). Note that if your ancestors migrated to Oklahoma as part of the land rush of the 1890s, which included many Blacks migrating from Mississippi and Louisiana, then you are not likely to find your ancestors on these rolls unless one of them married one of the freedmen of the Five Civilized Tribes.

In order to understand how to use the records, researchers should understand how they were created. In this case, there was an enrollment process which took place between 1898 and 1914 to determine tribal citizenship. Enrollment was under the supervision of the Dawes Commission which was originally charged with negotiating several major changes to the constitutions of these groups, namely abolition of tribal government and changing land ownership from a tribal basis to individual allotments. The negotiations included apportioning individual land allotments to both tribal members and the former slaves of tribal members.

In order to allot lands individually, an official roll of members or citizens for each tribe had to be prepared. Approximately 250,000 enrollment applications were received nationwide, but the final rolls contain only 101,000 actual enrollments. Individuals were enrolled under several categories—citizens by blood, citizens by marriage, newborn citizens by blood, minor citizens by blood, freedmen (freed slaves), newborn freedmen, and minor freedmen. To determine whether a person was legally entitled to a land allotment, individual hearings were held which required presenting proof of relationship within the nation. In addition, each of the five nations had separate processes and separate land allotments. Note that only an estimated 25 percent of the final enrollees were recognized as full-bloods. Note also

that the officials of the Dawes Commission used previous rolls that had been compiled to determine a person's status.

The goal of your research is to locate the following records: (1) enrollment cards and (2) applications for enrollment. A word of caution here. Enrollment cards, dated 1899–1907, are often called census cards because they provide a wealth of information on family groups, even more detailed than census entries. For freedmen, the last slaveowner is identified. Note that the enrollment cards were of three types—straight cards for those who were admitted to tribal citizenship, "D" cards for those whose applications were considered doubtful, and "R" cards for rejected applications. The enrollment cards contain the following information for each individual listed in the family group: name, official enrollment number (roll number), age, sex, degree of Indian blood, relationship to the head of the family, parents' names, and any references to enrollment on earlier rolls. Note that Walton-Raji's examination of enrollment cards indicates that the degree of Indian blood is generally not indicated on the cards. Additional notations of genealogical value may also appear. Enrollment cards are numbered and arranged in numerical order under each category. To obtain the enrollment or census card number, you will first need the final rolls for each tribe.

The applications for enrollment often contain detailed narratives or testimony given to the Dawes Commission in person with regard to the applicant's life as well as that of family members. These two sources, when combined, can be a genealogical gold mine. In order to access these records, however, one needs to examine (1) the index to the enrollment cards, (2) the index to the final rolls, and (3) the final rolls (1914) themselves for the appropriate index numbers.

Note that the enrollment cards and applications are on National Archives microfilm. Researchers should check all categories and not just those labeled "Freedmen." Records relating to rejected applicants should also be examined, particularly for their genealogical value.

Final rolls and the index can be found in printed format under the following title in those larger public libraries that serve as federal repository libraries. The title follows:

The final rolls of citizens and freedmen of the five civilized tribes in Indian territory / prepared by the Commission and Commissioner to the Five Civilized Tribes, and approved by the Secretary of the Interior on or prior to March 4, 1907 . . .

INDIANS AND FREE BLACKS

*I*n researching possible Indian ancestry, location and time are obviously key to understanding the nature of any assumed relationship between an African and an Indian ancestor. For those groups in places like Virginia, North Carolina, and New York, mixtures occurred early on and continued, often forming groups that were no longer identifiable as Indian. In some cases, these groups lost or almost lost their Indian status by legislative fiat because of a significant and obvious infusion of African American blood. Virginia E. DeMarce cited at least three such cases—the Ginagaskin of

Virginia's Eastern Shore, the Nottoway of Southampton County, Virginia, and the Pamunkey of Virginia. DeMarce's article appears in the bibliography, and is essential for understanding the shifting racial identities that emerged as African, Indian, and European mixed from the earliest points of contact up through the present.

Given the early policies toward Indians, researchers will find that for the Colonial period, nontribal Indians were often entered into the public records as mulattos, including all federal censuses. Thus when you are researching early free Black ancestry, you may indeed have no way of identifying an Indian ancestor unless court and other civil records, such as tax lists, identified them as such. Note that one significant source on early free Blacks, Paul Heinegg's series of abstracts of colonial records, indicates a fairly frequent reference to free and enslaved Africans as well as Indians in the original records. Anyone researching free Black ancestry must consider the possibility that those ancestors listed as mulatto may very well have been Indian.

Adding to the difficulty of identifying Indian ancestry for this period is the phenomenon of tri-racial isolates or groups of families with indeterminate mixtures of Indian, African, and European blood who tended to migrate together westward and southward, marry similar groups that emerged from the Colonial period and ultimately wound up sharing a recognizable pool of surnames that have continued to the present. Groups like the Melungeons and Redbones actually do have identifiable origins and are believed to have emerged from just a few Indian groups in the Chesapeake (Chickahominy, Gingaskin, Mattapony, Nansemond, Pamunkey, Rapa-hanocks, etc.). For a detailed exploration of this issue as well as a list of names, re-searchers should study closely Virginia E. DeMarce's article, listed in the bibliography.

This all too brief review is only sugges-tive of what lies ahead for the researcher who sets out to discover an Indian ancestor, especially those who gave up their tribal affiliation at some point, if not their tribal identities. Those who will be most success-ful are those who know the local history of the research area, know how to use guide-books, and have the mobility to pursue the quest wherever the records might lead them. Good luck!

Special Topic 5

WORLD WARS I & II

We negroes love our country. We fought for it. We ask only that we be treated as well as those who fought against it.

PAUL LAURENCE DUNBAR

INTRODUCTION

*R*esearchers may think that records on an ancestor who served in one of these wars will yield plentiful information. For example, a military service record from World War I may provide vital information not to be found elsewhere since the generation of men who served would have been born during the 1890s, a time when registration of vital records was uneven and often lacking. Before making this assumption, read the following official policy statement with regard to obtaining individual military personnel records for these and other twentieth century wars.

On July 12, 1973, a disastrous fire at National Personnel Record Center (Military Personnel Records) destroyed approximately 16–18 million Official Military Personnel Files. The affected record collections are described below.

Branch	Personnel and Period Affected	Estimated Loss
Army	Personnel discharged November 1, 1912, to January 1, 1960	80%
Air Force	Personnel discharged September 25, 1947, to January 1, 1964	75%

No duplicate copies of the records that were destroyed in the fire were maintained, nor was a microfilm copy ever produced. There were no indexes created prior to the fire. In addition, millions of documents had been lent to the Department of Veterans Affairs before the fire occurred. Therefore, a complete listing of the records that were lost is not available. Nevertheless, NPRC (MPR) uses many alternate sources in its efforts to reconstruct basic service information to respond to requests.

You will read this short statement many times just to make sure that it really did happen as well as to speculate on the possibility that the records you want survived the fire. Note that most men who served in the military during both wars were in the Army, but if your ancestor was in another branch of the military that was not affected by the fire, then you should be able to locate a military service record.

It is estimated that about 25 million records were "affected by the fire" and about 5 million were recovered. It may take the personnel at the Military Personnel Records Center some time to reconstruct these records—another reason why there is no clear official policy statement about whether plans exist to try to reconstruct all records. Assume that the records you need were destroyed along with your chances of tapping into a record group that was especially important, not just for genealogists but for general historical research. Indeed, the burden of proof of service for some unlucky veteran may often rest on his having documents in his personal possession. This is why you won't find much mention of these records in the standard guidebooks except to indicate that they were destroyed in a fire. But all is never lost in genealogy, and what you are able to uncover often depends on how skillful and persistent a researcher you are.

ALL NOT LOST

*E*ven though the above statement is discouraging, note that you can still request whatever information is available on an individual veteran. At the least, completing standard form 180 will yield verification that the individual did serve—if you can meet the standards for privacy required by the federal government. Genealogists can request an alternate form from the Personnel Records Center (Form R6-7231) if they cannot meet the requirements for release of information on standard form 180. Alternatively, submission of a death certificate with form 180 should be sufficient to overcome the hurdles that require proof that you are next of kin or have legal authority to obtain information.

Actually, the form itself asks for as much information as you are seeking (veteran's complete name used while in service, service number or Social Security number, branch of service, and dates of service, date and place of birth, place of discharge, last unit of assignment, and place of entry into the service, if known). You can still try without hav-

ing all of the requested information, especially if the veteran's name was unique, you have a Social Security number, branch of service and date and place of birth and death. But if you did not have your ancestor's division and company or his serial number, obtaining that information will form the basis of your subsequent research. On the other hand, if your ancestor's county of residence did indeed register returning veterans (see page 115 for an example), you will perhaps get more information from this source than you would from the Military Personnel Record Center.

If you started your genealogy project without interviewing veterans about their military experiences, now is the time to do it. The surviving records will not allow you to gain the same perspective that you would gain from interviewing your own relatives. Of course, many veterans of both wars are now deceased, and to reconstruct their experiences during the course of the war would be a formidable but doable task for experienced researchers. Now that you are familiar with some of the standard genealogical guidebooks, you will note that very little is said about how to reconstruct this experience. This special topic will give you a starting point.

African American researchers are especially encouraged to explore the possibility of reconstructing an ancestor's military experience because the military was a point of departure for migration to Northern and other cities. In addition, men often left the military with skills as well as a new view of the world. It is important to understand how the military widened the horizons of those millions of veterans who left both wars with a new optimism. Incidentally you might want to read a recent novel by Guy Johnson, *Standing at the Scratch Line*, which is remarkable in depicting the experiences of men who served in the 369th Infantry Division during World War I.

A CHECKLIST OF SUPPLEMENTARY AND ALTERNATIVE RECORD SOURCES

Discharge Records

Discharged servicemen were directed to register at the local courthouse in their counties of residence. These records are quite detailed, and should form the first line of attack in the absence of any other sources of information on the veteran.

World War I Draft Registration Cards

These records were discussed earlier under censuses. Located at the Atlanta branch (Federal Record Center) of the National Archives, the World War I draft registration cards of approximately 24 million males between the ages of eighteen and forty-five can reveal the following information: name, address at time of registration, date of birth, age, race, citizenship, birthplace, occupation and employer, dependent relatives, marital status, father's birthplace, and name and address of nearest relative. Note however that there were three rounds and information asked varied from one round to the next. This information does not include actual service information, however, it helps to pinpoint an ancestor between 1914 and 1918. In addition, the card for an ancestor can provide vital data that may appear in no

other place for that period. Recall the discussion on availability of vital records for the early twentieth century. Most states had just begun to keep these records during the same period as the draft registration process occurred.

World War I: Local Newspapers

Newspapers often published the names of men who had been drafted. Lori Husband's transcription of draft data from the *Chicago Defender* for draftees who lived in the principal African American sections of Chicago is an unusual source, but insightful with regard to what local papers might yield. Since papers during this period were rarely lengthy, a check of a four- to five-year run should not be difficult.

World War II Draft Registration Cards and Selective Service Registration

Draft registration cards also exist for men born between 28 April 1877 and 16 February 1897. Note that these men would have been quite old to actively serve; however, as part of war preparedness, this final round of registrations took place in 1942. These records have been microfilmed and may be on file at the various federal record centers. You may also write to the Atlanta federal record center to obtain a copy. (Request the form and try to provide as much information on the individual as possible since your ancestor's name may not have been unique.) A similar process was used between 1940 and 1975 to call up and identify draft-eligible men. Each individual who was called up was eventually given an eligibility number. These records (1940 to 1970) are available through the National Archives in Washington, D.C.

Unit Histories and Other Information on Unit of Service

By writing to the Military Reference Branch of the National Archives in Washington, D.C., you can request information on your ancestor's unit of service. Occasionally, unit photographs may exist. Rosters may be found in these records as well as returns and morning reports (essentially rosters created over the course of service of a particular unit to chart the presence/absence of a soldier).

Headstone Applications

If your ancestor is buried in a private cemetery, there is a chance that his headstone was provided by the Monument Service of the Veterans Administration. Applications for headstones include basic data about the deceased (name, place and date of burial, military organization, rank and years in service) plus the name and address of the individual or organization who applied for the headstone. These records are located at the National Archives in Washington, D.C.

Final Pay Vouchers

While perhaps not normally requested by genealogists, the Military Personnel Record Center has used 19 million final pay vouchers as a baseline from which to begin to reconstruct a soldier's service history. The vouchers provide basic data which can be found in other records. The vouchers are used with other surviving records to issue individual veterans a Certification of Military Service which stands in the place of the original discharge record. Individual veterans who need such a record can order it from the Military Personnel Record Center in St. Louis.

Office of the State Adjutant General

Information on your ancestor's military service can often be obtained through the adjutant general's office for his state of residence. Frequently, rosters and service information are published by these offices for men who were recruited while residents of the state.

Locator Services and Veterans Organizations

If you wish to find a veteran, the military branch under which he served (Army, Navy, Air Force, etc.) offers a locator service. A letter will be forwarded to the veteran at his last known address. Similar services may be offered by active veterans organizations through their publications.

Veterans organizations are also a great source for informal histories of the unit of service. For example, I located the National Headquarters of the 92nd Infantry Buffalo Division Association, World War I and II through a listing of such organizations at a web site. The historian of the organization has been compiling information and records for a number of years—to the extent that a nationally recognized African American institution offered to house them. At the time of writing, I'm waiting for his reply with regard to one of my relatives who is now deceased. The key is to contact the national headquarters of the unit and then locate the historical material. For World Wars I and II units, most of the individuals that you will contact are African American since military units were segregated.

Classes

Classes offered by the regional branch of the National Archives are often taught by experienced archivists who have worked with the records in one way or another. These classes provide many inside tips that you won't find in any publications. Classes are especially recommended for military research for all wars because the sources are varied, located in many libraries and archives, and are difficult to access without expert help.

Libraries

Obviously a source of general histories on specific wars, famous units and individuals, the specialized military libraries offer a wealth of additional information in print or manuscript form.

The Army Military Research Institute, located in Carlisle, Pennsylvania, for example, has an online catalog that allows the researcher to determine what exists on a particular unit. In addition, an onsite visit for the more avid researcher may yield memoirs of commanding officers, personal papers of officers, and more technical literature on specific battles throughout history. The library at Carlisle does not participate in interlibrary loan, but your library will be able to assist you in locating copies of works that appear in lending libraries. Note that the keywords for a library search are based on the standard terms or subject headings used by the Library of Congress. To identify books relating to African Americans during both world wars, use the following search terminology. World War I should be: *World War, 1914–1918 Afro-Americans*. World War II should be: *World War, 1939–45 Afro-Americans*.

Conclusion

*I*f you are able to collect just the basic information on a veteran (unit of service, branch of the military, and name of war), you can easily reconstruct your ancestor's story without having to regret the loss of records at the Military Personnel Record Center in St. Louis. Beyond the minimal data that can be found in the above sources, it will be up to you to provide the context of your ancestor's service. For that, many sources exist.

Special Topic 6

WHAT TO DO
WITH YOUR RESEARCH

Writing Family Memoirs or the Family Story, and 101 Genealogy Research Projects Waiting to Be Done

African American genealogy tells the story of survivors.

INTRODUCTION

*C*ollective memory tells a people's story in epic form—a story which everyone can repeat and which offers an explanation of major historical experiences. The epic of Sundiata is one example of collective memory in oral form, for it tells the story of the Mande people of Mali. Every Mande person knows the epic and the genealogy of the founding family of Old Mali. Similarly, every African ethnic group has stories of origin that tell the story of their clan, village, or group over long periods of time. These stories generally include an explanation about the founding family and its genealogy with which every member of the clan or village can identify through his or her own kinship.

African Americans do not have one epic story to explain their capture from Africa, their enslavement and subsequent freedom in the Americas. Nor do many of us have family stories that tell the story of our ancestors in epic form. What we have are bits and pieces of stories, or many individual stories based on individual achievements. *Roots* came closest to telling a collective story in epic form, for it was the story of nearly every African American family. Kunta Kinte was a symbol of the first African to arrive in America, and for many of us, it was the first time

that public legitimacy was given to the historical experience of the African American family in America. In a major way, *Roots* is our epic story. Yet, your family has an epic story waiting to be told. It just takes a storyteller, a story writer, and some means to disseminate it to your family.

At some point, you will have to decide how your results will be presented or shared with an audience (family, friends, the genealogical community, or the general reading public). Whether your goal is to write a family memoir or to do a genealogical study only, you will need to have some idea of what has been published and what works. As your research results unfold, you will discover what is unique about your family's experiences as well as what is typical. Perhaps a story will emerge that is dramatic enough to be told to a wider audience. Your ability to present your results in written form will, therefore, depend on identifying the type of presentation you want.

This chapter will provide you with some guidelines to follow, although it is likely that you already have a good sense of your family's traditions and what kind of presentation you want to follow. Knowing when to begin to write is a big part of your research. For example, should you begin to write as soon as you complete research for one generation, or should you begin to write immediately? Should you include information on the research process or should you exclude it? Should you use any of the many computer programs now available to structure your writing or should you attempt to design your own? How important is it to present a formal genealogical table, for example, or will you really care? Some of these questions can be answered by examining family histories and genealogies that have already been published.

In chapter 1, it was suggested that any documentation that shows continuity between generations in African American families, particularly over a long period of time, is a welcome addition to the existing body of publications on the African American family. What has been missing from many of the now-classic studies of African American families can begin to be corrected because many genealogists and family historians are researching and publishing their results, most of which contradict the stereotypical notions about the history of the black family. As this book goes to print, some attempts have been made to debunk *Roots* as the classic or representative African-American family story.* Because of these problems, I would urge all genealogists and family historians to begin writing family histories and memoirs based on their genealog-

---

*One *Village Voice* writer, calling *Roots* a hoax, apparently confused the representativeness of the story with questions about Haley's character, which, in the end, are two entirely separate matters. The story and the storyteller(s) should never be confused—we would never have any great literature if the writer's personal life and habits mattered.

ical studies. In the world of family history, generational continuity counts!

SOME MODELS TO THINK ABOUT

*T*he following outline shows what can be done with genealogical studies and source materials used by genealogists. Once you become an advanced researcher, you will already have some idea of the direction your publication will take. The examples below show how genealogy inspires a wide range of publications.

Genealogical Studies

A genealogical study includes all the basic data on each family in your pedigree or generations chart. It follows a standard notational system that has been adapted by the genealogical community. Other notational systems are offered in computer programs, and many writers follow the standard notational system used in the *National Genealogical Society Quarterly*. Because African American genealogists will often have missing data, the standard genealogical charting systems may need to be modified. However, most standard notational systems do account for missing data, multiple marriages, and adopted children.

Family and Personal Memoirs

This is a type of family story that is written from a personal perspective, generally by a family member or descendant, which interweaves the personal, the anecdotal, as well as genealogical and historical information. Family memoirs, because they are personal, do not have to follow a chronological order; nor do they have to follow a standard genealogical format. Additionally, the term covers a wide range of publications—from family oral history to full-fledged academic-style studies.

Clifton Taulbert's *Once Upon a Time When We Were Colored* is a marvelous example of a personal memoir whose story revolves around the relationship between the author and the adults in his childhood. Kathryn Morgan's *Children of Strangers*, a family memoir based on sayings or family folklore from a great-grandmother whose stories survived, reflects the way in which humor was used in African American families to deflect the essentially negative experience of slavery. The Delany sisters' *Having Our Say: The Delany Sisters' First 100 Years* is written in a similar style where their strong personalities are presented against a background of a supportive family. Unlike genealogical studies, family memoirs allow writers to focus on familial lines and ties that are most important in their own personal development. One of the best examples is that of Carole Ione's *Pride of Family*, in which Ione isolated a line of female ancestors whose lives and actions allowed her to gain a deeper understanding of what shaped her own identity. Leslie Alexander Lacy's *The Rise and Fall of a Proper Negro* is another example, filled with wry humor and insightful observations about his life growing up in an unusual middle class family.

Failure to take advantage of family history or to understand its importance is a fault of the storyteller and not the family's history. Gayle Pemberton, in her book *The Hottest Water in Chicago*, underrated the impact that generational ties may have. Most writers of memoirs generally come to a resolution about the importance of their ancestors' struggles in history. Pemberton's great-great-grandmother lived between 1787 and 1895. Of Agnes Bledsoe, who was born free, it was said that when she was a child of five, she was taken to see George Washington, who not only shook her hand but picked her up and kissed her! Pemberton discounts this as a bit of "Americana fame," but for the genealogist such evidence represents many years of toiling research just to know who their ancestors were. Pemberton's failure to reconstruct family lines as a rudimentary exercise no doubt led her to undervalue her ancestors' experiences in historical time. Of more importance than the George Washington story is the fact that the account of Agnes Bledsoe's life was taken from an obituary that was in the possession of Pemberton's father, a Chicago "race man," or political activist.

Historical Novels and "Faction"

These terms refer to essentially fictionalized accounts of one's family history, using details and facts from historical sources. *Roots* and *Jubilee* fall into this category, although when *Jubilee* was published there was no ambivalence about the correct category in which it should be placed (a historical novel). Alex Haley's work, on the other hand, was surrounded with so much ambivalence due to its marketing and subsequent TV serialization as a "true" story. However, it should be noted that Haley consistently described the work as "faction," a fictionalized account of his family's history using free interpretations of the family's partial genealogy and oral history. A less well known, but equally interesting work is Madrue Chavers-Wright's book *The Guarantee*, in which her ancestors are given narrative lines. This also makes Chavers-Wright's book "faction," although the genealogical and historical data is essentially factual. Lessons for the unwary family historian: Know whether you're writing a novel based on your family's genealogical data, and tell your readers up front which parts are factual and which are not. Of course, if you become as lucky as Haley, you will likely abandon your genealogical research in favor of a megabucks contract. Since *Roots* was marketed so well, and since it told the story of the African American family in such broad epic proportions to the extent that we can say it is a representative story, it is very unlikely that anyone else will get such a great book contract.

Jubilee is highly recommended for those who want to understand how adherence to the facts of one's family history can be used as the overall plot for a historical novel. When reading Margaret Walker's work, genealogists can immediately recognize the records she used to reconstruct her family history as well as how she wove the bare facts into a historical novel.

Biographies

Biographies come in many forms, but those that tell the story of an individual's life work set in the context of family dynamics and the generational impact of family founders or ancestors are those that concern the genealogist-turned-historian. Donald Stone's *Fallen Prince: William James Edwards, Black Education and the Quest for Afro-American Nationality* is such a work. It is the kind of story that is told when a genealogist discovers an ancestor whose life's work is worthy of full historical treatment. Biographies, of necessity, must include genealogical data, but it is often left up to the writer to determine which generations are important. Michael P. Johnson's *Black Masters* tells a tragic story of generational discontinuity in the life of William Ellison and his family, a free Black slave-owning family in South Carolina. Biographies, because they can be told from different perspectives, should always be evaluated based on the perspective the writer uses. Tragedy in African American biographical and autobiographical writing is often seen as a school for learning.

Autobiographies

Autobiographies tell the life story of the writer. Those that draw on family history to show how ancestry had some impact on their own lives can be highly readable. The first chapters of the *Autobiography of Malcolm X* are indeed profound, for they show how generational influences often ultimately win out. Though Malcolm never directly attributes his father's early political activism as an influence, he was in so many ways the reincarnation of his own father, an active Garveyite. Autobiographical writings are, therefore, some of the best genealogically based approaches.

General and Academic Family Histories

African American scholars and professionals have begun to mine their own family histories as subjects worthy of study. Two examples stand out. One is *Free Frank* and the other is *Ambiguous Lives: Free Women of Color in Rural Georgia, 1789–1879*. Both authors, Juliette Walker and Adele Logan Alexander, are historians who with the assistance of surviving family memorabilia and personal papers were able to tell some very unusual stories with regard to the origins of free Blacks. In the former case, Free Frank purchased not only his freedom but that of fourteen additional family members over a ten-year period. Alexander's work documents the status of women of African and European descent, some of whom were never manumitted but who lived as the unofficial spouses of planters in Middle Georgia. Pauli Murray's *Proud Shoes: The Story of an American Family* is another good example.

Genealogies and Family Histories Combined

Many genealogists, not satisfied with the cut-and-dry formula of genealogical charts, tables, and other formats, choose instead to combine genealogy and family history with an emphasis on the search for one's ancestors. Examples of this genre are *Somerset Homecoming, In Search of Kith and Kin*, and *The Seed of Sally Good'n: A Black Family of Arkansas, 1833–1953*. Dorothy Spruill Redford's *Somerset Homecoming* still stands out as one of the best publications in African American genealogy because it artfully combines the excitement of the search with revealing and surprising stories.

Community Histories

Most often the result of collaborative projects or scholarly studies, community histories tell the story of a neighborhood, small town, or rural area within one county or region. Most community histories written about African Americans have been done by scholars. Elizabeth Bethel's *Promiseland: A Century of Life in a Negro Community* combined oral history with an intimate knowledge of the area. Two fine examples of

community history that weave personal family history into the history of a larger community are Joyner's study of his family in South Carolina and Philadelphia, Charles W. Joyner's *Down by the Riverside*, and Allen Ballard's *One More Day's Journey: The Making of Black Philadelphia*. *We the People Tell Our Story* by Mildred Pratt is a good example of a collaborative effort in telling the history of African Americans in a small town in Illinois.

Church and Institutional Histories

These are some of the most important kinds of histories that need to be written in the African American community, particularly for the period between emancipation and the 1930s. As you do your genealogical research, this type of history should most immediately come to you as an opportunity to write and publish. If you are shy of writing, be assured that the church and institutional history need not be book length, but rather as accurate and inclusive as possible.

Oral Histories

A compilation of oral histories of older Black residents in a community along with photographs is a doable project for many genealogists. Again, this type of project is the kind that you can easily design as you interview individuals, first in your family, then later members of other families. A scholarly study based on oral history is Theodore Rosengarten's *All God's Dangers, the Life of Nate Shaw*. Unfortunately, all of the names in this book were changed because the approach was done from the perspective of a sociologist. The story has rarely been told from the perspective of sharecroppers themselves! My genealogy students had wonderful stories about how their ancestors left Louisiana and Mississippi. One student shared with me a story about an ancestor and his wife who owned property inherited from a former slave owner. Because they were involved in a losing struggle to hold on to their land, they decided simply to leave rather than face life-threatening circumstances. They bought their train tickets to Chicago, put on their best clothes, and over them they wore coveralls and work clothes. Once on the train, they took them off!

This review of the possibilities that exist for you when you start genealogical research is not all-inclusive. Nevertheless, it should give you an idea of what can happen once you start your research. Genealogical research can form the basis of all these approaches because the research methods and the source material that you use should prepare you well to expand and apply your skills to these broader areas of history.

PRESENTING YOUR RESEARCH

*I*t is assumed that what you write will be nonfiction rather than fiction. Nonfiction writing is just as difficult—perhaps more so than fiction—because you have to keep the reader's attention through description rather than plots, action, and dialogue. The following discussion should help you to sort out some of the basics in presenting your research in a written form.

Every Story Is Worth Telling—Maybe
Every family is unique, but families share many common historical experiences, a fact which places most of our families in the cat-

egory of the not-so-unusual. Dudley Randall's poem "Ancestors" asks the question, If your ancestors were not princes, kings, and queens, is the story worth telling? The answer is yes, but it depends on how good a story you can tell without relying on those very props that make other stories so well liked. In effect, the story is only as good as the storyteller—in this case you.

Starting out with a trunk full of old documents, letters, photos, and other memorabilia definitely helps. But, if you haven't a clue on how your family's experiences fit into the broader patterns of history or what message can be conveyed using your family as an example, you won't be able to tell a good story. The worth of the story starts with your own deep sense of appreciation for how your slave and free ancestors "got over."

Conceptualization and Outlining
This stage will form the basis of your writing. In many ways, the decisions made now will affect every step in the writing process. Once you've decided what kind of presentation you will do, make sure that you create an outline. For each topic in your outline, write a brief paragraph stating what you plan to include as well as the estimated number of pages you plan to write.

Understanding Major Themes in the African American Experience
Because you've done extensive genealogical research by the time you reach this point, you will already be familiar with some major themes in the history of African American families. In writing your presentation, you should avoid stereotypes and loaded terms, particularly those associated with slavery

and the contemporary Black family. Your use of major themes should be guided by telling the story in a direct and clear manner.

Know the Difference Between Facts and Speculation

As you write, make sure you alert the reader that a particular passage is your own interpretation by using qualifying terms and phrases such as *probably, perhaps, in my opinion, this cannot be verified in the records, but it seems...*

Because your family is counting on you to tell the story correctly and accurately, you should let them know when you are stating a fact (an event that occurred and was documented) and when you are speculating by using the suggested qualifying terms. Some speculations are reasonable and some are not. In genealogical terms, surmise is used often to refer to a conclusion that is drawn from examining several documents which alone do not contain the facts that we want to establish. We can conclude by surmise that James and Ethel were married even though the documents used to establish this conclusion did not include a specific date of marriage. They had children, lived in the same house over a period of years, and each of their death certificates indicates that they had been married to each other for forty years.

Give Credit Where It's Due

Always, always let your readers know the sources that you used. If you are quoting directly from a book or a document, indicate complete information on the source. For a book, include the author's name, the book's title, the year of publication, and the publisher. For a document, you must identify the document, name the record group,

name the place where the original may be found, and indicate whether you used a microfilm copy of the original record. References to documents should always include a date or an estimated date. If the document is in your personal collection, as in the case of oral interviews, indicate the year the interview was taken, who did the interview, the name of the person interviewed, and that it is in your personal collection. A manual on citing your sources is worth having in your library.

Finding Your Style

The style of writing that you select is directly related to the type of publication you plan. The best way to find your own voice and style is to study some of the models outlined above. The style with which you feel most comfortable is the one you should rely on. No need to struggle with a biography when your own style says it's best to write a memoir. If you are writing a biography or a person's life story, you wouldn't use the same style as that used in an autobiography. Your own style is the one with which you feel most comfortable. Know that straight nonfiction writing is the most difficult, but it can become less difficult if you rely on the device of *telling* people's stories rather than *describing* people's stories. Though it is easy to rely on the device of writing in chronological order, know that this can be boring unless you use other devices to draw out the story.

Finding Your Audience

Your audience will, in large part, determine the style of writing and the overall presentation of your work. You probably decided early on who your audience would be.

Often, genealogists write a brief family history with charts for the family reunion program. This is good practice if you plan to write a more detailed publication. But writing for the family and writing for publication in a genealogical journal represent very different styles. Ask yourself this set of questions: Who do I want to read this? Will I need some help? Is it good enough to share with the audience that I want to reach? Knowing your audience will help you on questions such as the length and style of your work.

Publishing Your Work

Here's another set of questions to think about: Do I want to publish? Do I want to publish the work myself? Do I want to have a genealogical publishing company publish my work? Do I want to have it published in a genealogical journal? Do I want a major commercial publisher to publish my work? These questions are intimately tied up with your decisions about the audience to whom you are writing, the style and voice of your writing, and ultimately, who will publish your work.

Before you answer these questions, it is important to know that there are only a few genealogical publishers. A simple query letter to the publisher is a must: Are you interested in publishing a genealogical study of XYZ? You should also examine the publisher's catalogue to know what kinds of works are being accepted. If you are doing a formal genealogical study, you should automatically know that the audience and the publication will be limited to those who read genealogical journals and other publications. This is a very limited audience, mainly libraries and family members. If you write a memoir or family history, your audience is broadened but the subject matter has to be sufficiently interesting and well written so that the publisher can justify investing money in your work.

If you self-publish, you lose the benefit of good editorial advice. However, many genealogical publications are self-published. This is a high risk to take, particularly when you find that self-publishing is more costly than you think. If, however, you still decide to self-publish, always have at least three people read the manuscript and make comments. At least one person should have good grammar skills, and another should have good comprehension skills. If you can afford to pay a professional who has good editing skills, do so. It is almost impossible to detect all of your own errors. Also avoid hastily putting together your results. In the end, you will not be the judge of your work, but your audience will. One final reminder if you want a major genealogical publishing company to publish your work—know which ones carefully edit their manuscripts and which do not.

Presenting Characters Versus Inventing Characters

At some point you will have the urge to "lend" one of your ancestors words which you cannot verify that he or she ever spoke. One way to avoid this is to avoid using dialogue and avoid the format of fictionalizing your family's history. Your ancestors' lives were dramatic enough, and a story told with your opinions and your own perspective is better than a story told with invented lines and dialogues, unless, of course, you are writing historical fiction based on your family's story.

Avoiding Confusing Presentations

A well-structured approach to your publication is important. If you write for one audience only, then you will avoid a confusing presentation. Your family members may not be interested in a formal genealogical presentation, but they can easily see its importance when you use graphics such as a descendant's chart and photographs. If you use the format of a formal genealogical study and your audience consists of family members only, provide some explanation of how to read the charts in your publication. By all means, avoid a hodgepodge of genealogical bits and pieces that force your audience—your readers—to wonder what your work is for. The best approach, in the end, is to write a straight and direct narrative first and later embellish it.

Fictive and Real Alliances with Old European Families of the South

Sometimes, the proof is in the pudding and there is no need to go any further. One pitfall that should be avoided, if for no other reason than it is in bad taste these days, is to overstate the frequently obvious—blood ties to famous Whites of the Old South—and to include in your publication European genealogical lines back to one of the kings of England, for example. A reading of Birmingham's *Certain People* should give you a good dose of this perspective. Failure to adequately evaluate the family's oral tradition is evident in many family publications, particularly with respect to European ancestry. Equally passé, of course, is inventing African kings and queens as ancestors. Hopefully, by the time you bring closure to your research, you will understand that the history of African American families is pri-marily a history of slave and nominally free families who survived and made their "marks" despite the odds. That is a heroic enough story to tell.

OTHER APPLICATIONS: 101 GENEALOGICAL PROJECTS WAITING FOR YOU

Once you finish your research and write your results, you will still want to do genealogy. Your research skills can easily transfer to many other projects that African American researchers and genealogists ought to be doing right now. Remember when you had so much trouble using works that had not been adequately indexed? Well, your work is cut out for you. Since you know the pitfalls to avoid in compiling indexes, abstracts, and other genealogical source material, you can now apply your knowledge to a number of projects yourself, being careful to let your readers know the sources you used, where they are located, possible errors, the method used to transcribe or abstract the information, and whether the sources or documents cover the entire set of records or only a part.

If, for example, you decide to abstract records pertaining to slaves in collections housed at your state's archives, you should list the collections so that researchers will know which collections were not included and where to look for other records. If you compile lists of slaves without including the marks on slave lists, what good will your research be to others who come along? Finally, avoid misleading titles that suggest your publication contains information that, in fact, it does not. And remember, you are doing this to help other researchers and to further the state of African American genealogy. Following is a list of projects that individuals and genealogical societies can and should do to advance the state of the field.

Indexing Projects

- *Early African American newspapers*—an everyname index
- *Post-1890 African American newspapers*—obituaries, marriages, missing relatives advertisements
- *Freedmen's Bureau Records*—Careful here. Start with microfilmed editions and index one set of records on one reel at a time, if they contain significant genealogical information such as marriages, lists of pupils, and labor contracts. Check to see whether the records you want to index are being done now or have already been published.
- *Black College Yearbooks*—index photos, if names are given, as well as class members, particularly for the earliest years found through 1930.

Abstracting Records

- Slaves and their owners named in any set of probate records for one county or in microfilmed planters' records.
- Your local funeral home records, particularly those for the turn of the century.
- Your local church records, particularly obituaries, anniversary programs, baptismal lists, membership lists, and marriages for older rural churches in the South and North.
- Family Bibles in the possession of fellow church members.

- Membership lists and other data from fraternal organizations such as the Masonic orders, social clubs, sororities, and fraternities from their origins through the 1920s.

Transcriptions

- A Black cemetery in a large city, starting with records kept by the sexton's office.
- Headstones found in Black cemeteries in your county, if you live in the South.

As you can see, most of these projects guide you to records in the Black community. Start there and advance to larger record groups, preferably with a partner or as a group project.

PRESERVATION

*I*f you are more interested in preservation, there are many buildings, places, and individuals worthy of your research and documentation. Collecting life stories that focus on migration experiences, work experiences, family memories, and the like can form the basis of an oral history of your neighborhood or town. Identifying significant historical sites in your local area, particularly in the South, is also important. A survey of the oldest Black churches in your county, old plantations, a compilation of names used for places that do not appear on a map are all doable projects. When you drive through your county of residence or your neighborhood, don't think of it as a level, nonhistorical field. If people lived there before, there is some history to be discovered. Work with various local and state historical preservation agencies and landmark commissions if you plan to become involved in a major project.

A NOTE TO PROFESSIONAL HISTORIANS

While historical research on African Americans is "wonderfully plentiful," historians sometimes do make mistakes. One of the biggest occurs when the records used to research and write a publication are not discussed clearly and in detail, including what information is found in the group of records and what is not. Often, historians assume that the reader is already familiar with the records. When genealogists read historical material, they do it for two reasons—to know more about the records and to know the story.

Recent scholarly publications have begun to index the names of slaves, a welcome addition to say the least, particularly if the named slave is discussed extensively in the original records. Finally, databases that include slaves, but not their names or their owners, are disheartening to say the least, and if those databases that do include names are not made known to the African American genealogical community or noted in the journal of the National Afro-American Historical and Genealogical Society, they can't be of much use until the next graduate student comes along and starts to do something with them. Other than that, we owe historians a huge debt for all of their painstaking work, something you will come to understand and appreciate once you are able to reconstruct the family ties among your ancestors who lived in slavery.

A FURTHER NOTE ON COUNTY COURTHOUSE RECORDS

INTRODUCTION

While it is relatively easy to locate wills and deeds, courthouses contain more than these records. For example, Anne Malone, who studied slave families in Louisiana, suggests that in addition to the slave owner's will, inventories, appraisements, estate divisions, bills of sale, mortgages of land and slaves, conveyances of land and slaves, and inventories from divorces and separations were equally important. Therefore, a courthouse search has to be planned, and it has to cover more than the routine will and deed book searches.

The most essential step, the step to take before expanding your research at the courthouse, is first to read about the records. Much of the genealogical literature assumes that you, the researcher, already know about these records. This discussion assumes that you know little about them, primarily because your ancestors did not record many transactions at local courthouses until they were free, and even then, if they did not own property, their importance in the family's surviving personal records would be diminished. You will not find in your family's personal papers an abundance of old wills, deeds, and other kinds of legal transactions that date back to the nineteenth century, unless of course your ancestors were members of that almost minuscule part of the Black population that was both free and propertied. While you may not need a grasp of the American legal system to do courthouse research, you will need to have some basic knowledge of what was and was not recorded at the courthouse in your local area of research.

For the beginning steps, researchers should answer the following questions:

1. Is there a publication on how the local court system is/was organized for my state of research?
2. Is there a publication that describes the contents of local records as well as the dates they cover?
3. Have there been any county boundary changes? Do I have the correct county for the period of my research?
4. Are there any maps of the local area that would help me?
5. Have the records I need been indexed or abstracted? If so, where can I find the indexes or abstracts? Can I count on them to be fairly accurate and inclusive?
6. What terms do I need to know about to do a successful search?

Your first line of attack is to obtain from the state's archives a description of local or county courthouse records. Names for the same records may vary from state to state depending on the period of time that the records were created, as indicated in the example on South Carolina discussed in Special Topic 1. Your state archives will be able to describe the records, their function, whether they have been abstracted or indexed, whether the original volumes have been microfilmed, if the records have been lost or destroyed due to fires (of which there were many), and finally, whether they have been called in by the state's archives for historic preservation reasons.

A second step would be to read a general description of these and other records in an all-purpose guidebook such as Greenwood's *Researcher's Guide to American Genealogy, The Handybook for Genealogists,* or *The Source. The Handybook* provides useful information in a capsule form, and it is recommended as a basic source. It contains a brief summary of each state's history, a list of counties with any county boundary changes indicated along with dates, maps showing county boundaries by state, and a suggested reading list for further research. Next to each county entry, a star or an asterisk will tell you if a local history of the county has been published and whether the county records were part of the WPA Project. For a more lengthy discussion of county courthouse records and legal records in general, the guidebook entitled *The Source* contains two chapters, one entitled "American Court Records," and the other entitled "Land and Tax Records." The discussion of probate records in the chapter on American court records contains essential information, perhaps not readily available elsewhere. Greenwood's work goes into greater detail, devoting at least three chapters to probate records including providing basic legal definitions of terminology that every genealogist needs to know, and for that reason it is recommended as a basic tool on probate records.

THE RECORDS

*T*he farther back in time, the more likely that you will find records that cover a broad scope of local activities—everything from maintaining roads to collecting taxes on anything that moved (from ships landing at a harbor to head taxes on slaves to taxes for maintaining the county poor house). The only kind of tax you are not likely to find is the income tax, but note that some early taxes, in one form or another, could be considered a disguised form of the income tax. What you find ultimately depends on your state of research. States comprising the original thirteen colonies will have very old records showing more diversity than states settled and incorporated after the 1810s (Deep South states). With regard to slavery, you have to be aware of just how many types of transactions could occur with regard to ownership of a slave and whether those transactions were recorded. As mentioned previously, a slave could be sold outright, held in trust, hired out to another planter or even to timber companies and industrial works for a period of time (generally on a year-to-year basis), mortgaged for a set period of time, assigned to work on local road maintenance and construction, taxed, owned jointly by more than one individual, owned by a company, church, or other institution rather than a planter/farmer, jailed and tried for an offense (running away, murder, and other violence) and finally, manumitted by the owner; a slave or group of slaves could also be the subject of long legal battles between members of the same family, confiscated as part of a bankrupt planter's property and sold at a sheriff's sale, transferred without record to another individual, or brought into a marriage by a wife and never recorded until years later when one of the partners died. The point to understand about the records is that slaves as property could appear in a variety of records, all located in the countless courthouses where slavery existed. Knowing how individual counties named record books where these transactions were recorded is the researcher's task, a task that can be accomplished once you locate the will, which will contain good evidence about the slave owner's possible transactions. Of course, at the same time that you search for the will, you will also learn more about the slave owner's standing in the local community and the type of wealth that he may have accumulated over his lifetime. That alone will be a good indicator of the types of records that might be located.

BURNED COUNTIES

Sometimes, you will find that records have been destroyed due to fires (natural and arson) or due to "deaccession," where archivists or institutions decide to discard records based on a variety of reasons, most of which relate to a formal evaluation of their historical usefulness. Rarely are records destroyed because they relate to slavery. In one instance, however, William G. LeFurgy noted in his book *The Records of a City: A Guide to the Baltimore City Archives*, that very detailed records relating to slaves and free Blacks in Baltimore were discarded as late as the 1950s. Whatever the reason, burned counties or those counties where courthouses have been destroyed by fire or other causes will present stumbling blocks in your research, perhaps early on. For example, if you find the name of a slave owner, and the courthouse was burned in 1868 or during the Civil War as were some counties in Virginia, Georgia, and elsewhere, your search for estate records will be terminated very quickly. It would seem then that the only possibility would be to locate the descendants of the slave owner to determine whether they have copies of the original records (wills, bills of slave sales, inventories, etc.). While this approach might work and has often worked for African American genealogists, another approach would be to search for some of the records in adjacent counties. Examine the map of Alabama that the Department of Archives and History issues to researchers. It appears that south-central Alabama had a rash of fires, and surely most people in these counties developed their own protective measures to guarantee that land titles were publicly registered. In a case like this, researchers should be aware that multiple registrations of certain transactions, especially land transactions between individuals, were often made across both counties and states as a measure of insurance against willful and natural destruction of courthouses. I have a copy of a land deed for one of my ancestors that reads:

Sloss and DuBarry Trustees Deed to Cary Nix
State of Alabama, Jefferson County

Know all men by these presents: That for and in consideration of the sum of ($200.00) Two hundred Dollars in hand paid by Cary Nix to J. W. Sloss and J. N. DuBarry both Trustees, under and by virtue of a declaration of Trust, duly recorded in the offices of the Judges of Probate of Montgomery County in Book Seven (7) of Deeds page Three Hundred and Seventy-Two (372), Crenshaw County in Book Ten (10) of Deeds page One Hundred and Forty-One (141), Conecuh County in Book "G" of Wills and Deeds pages One Hundred and Three (103), Escambia County in Book B of Wills and Deeds page One Hundred and Seventeen (117), Covington County in Book (5) five of Wills and Deeds on pages Four Hundred and Twenty Three (423) to Four Hundred and Twenty-Seven (427) inclusive, Monroe County in Book Eleven (11) of Wills and Deeds on pages Five Hundred and Fourteen (514) to Five Hundred and Sixteen (516) inclusive, and of Butler County in Book marked "FF" of Mortgages and Deeds on pages Two Hundred and Two (202) to Two Hundred and Five (205) inclusive, the counties aforesaid lying and being in the State of Alabama . . .

This deed was registered in seven counties in 1880, for good reason too. Only one of the counties, Montgomery, was not a burned county, and furthermore three of them burned after this deed was registered, one for the fourth time!

Facing a burned county does not mean all is lost, however. It does diminish your chances of locating bills of sale for slaves, but for other kinds of transactions, a burned courthouse does not always spell the end of your research. If transactions in neighboring counties are not located for the slave owner, the next step would be to focus on the slave owner*s place of origin as a possible source of information. The place of origin should have been found during the course of your research about the individual slave owner and the history of migration to the local area. For research in Deep South states, this kind of backward search would generally mean a search in one of the original thirteen colonies. Since most Deep South states obtained statehood in the 1810s and thereafter, the gap between 1865 and 1810 is fifty-five years, a long time, but certainly not like one hundred and fifty years. Additionally, some slave owners often practiced stepwise migration where residence was taken up in various counties for short periods of time before eventually settling in one specific location. They often left their mark along the way, and a prodigious search of the available records along the migration path might help to locate additional records.

Note on the map that sometimes the parent county of a burned county might have records that predate the fire, assuming that it was not burned also. Parts of Crenshaw County, for example, belonged to Butler County before it was created in 1866. Presumably, records for those parts of Crenshaw County that belonged to Butler County before 1866 would be filed in Butler County Records. In effect, the researcher who is looking for a slave owner in that part of Crenshaw County that once belonged to Butler County will possibly find records dated between 1853, the year of the Butler County fire, and 1866, the year Crenshaw County was created. Finally, burned counties are not always entirely burned. Tax and land records may have been salvaged or kept in another location. Always check with the local courthouse to verify what "burned" really means. It is clear that it does mean that some records will not be available for your research, and that you will have to devise alternative strategies to locate the information you need, perhaps in substitute records.

ORIGINAL VERSUS MICROFILMED VERSIONS

Microfilmed versions of courthouse records, particularly estate records (wills, inventories), can be extremely useful, and if they are available to you, by all means use them. However, it is always recommended that you use records on site when possible because of the nature of historical records. Kinship is a web; therefore, so are the records. Finding one individual's estate records will lead to questions about the same records for other individuals named in the record under question. Furthermore, microfilmed courthouse records do not always tell you what was not filmed. Loose estate papers contain more than just inventories, for example. Furthermore, since you will have to use the index for each book, and since each index is filmed with the book, you can easily lose track of your search. If, for example, the record book that you are looking for was filmed as part of a whole series of records books, zooming back to the index for Book C and then back to the index for Book W can take a lot of your time. If you are on site, it is a lot easier to simply pull the volume from the shelf and run through the index for the years that your search covers. In addition, the descriptive information used to categorize the microfilm edition of

wills or deeds often does not correspond to the way they are arranged at the courthouse. The best measure is to know what was filmed and what was not filmed.

THE WILL IS ONLY A FIRST STEP

Though the will is only the first step, it is one of the most critical documents on the slave owner that you can locate. The will can serve as a map to lead you to further searches in local records. Before you locate the will, you will have to determine whether the slave owner died testate or intestate. If you do not locate the name of the slave owner in a will index or in various books at the courthouse between approximately 1840 and 1865, then it is possible that the slave owner died intestate, as in the case of Calvin Borger's owner. That is, the slave owner did not write a will before his death, and for many small-scale planters, that is a good possibility. Historians who have studied these records have noted that for various regions of the country, up to 50 percent or more of propertied males in certain regions died without leaving written wills. However, for slave owners, this figure is certainly lower because ownership of slaves automatically put them in a class of individuals who had wealth. Though a propertied person may have died intestate, this does not mean that you will not find a probate record in local courthouse records. Depending on the local customs for keeping records, there might exist separate volumes for intestate records. Certainly, you would want to check to see whether an intestate index exists for the county or for the state, as in the case of Calvin Boger.

"BURNED COURTHOUSES," STATE OF ALABAMA

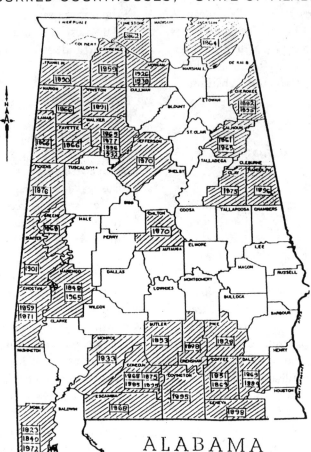

ALABAMA

If an individual slave owner died intestate, you will find that the court appointed an administrator (administratix). Note that the will writer appoints his own executors, mainly male relatives or in-laws or a local person who is financially solvent and respected in the community. The executor and the administrator serve the same function; they oversee directions issued by the will writer or the judge of probate respec-

tively. The standard procedure was to conduct an inventory and appraisement of the person's property and report back to the judge of probate at the next term of court. (Courts in local rural areas did not meet continuously.) Once the judge of probate was satisfied that requirements for this process satisfied the law, the records from the inventory and appraisement were generally entered into separate volumes under that name, but you should also know that these records are also referred to as "conveyance records." Subsequent transactions on the individual's estate will appear in either the will book or the inventory and appraisement book until all property is sold or received by the heirs. As these transactions occurred, the clerk of court entered names in the index to each book in which a transaction was entered. Again, depending on local custom, names of all heirs were entered as well as the deceased's name. The deceased, the writer of the will, is termed the *devisor*, and the index is often simply called a *devisor's index*. Likewise, names of devisees or heirs were entered into a *devisee's index*, often following the devisor's index, and this is where things could have gotten sloppy. Nevertheless, because errors could occur, you might find a devisee listed and not the devisor. Therefore, knowing the names of possible heirs would also help. (This is one of the reasons that you need to locate a genealogy and conduct a census search of the slave owner for 1850 and 1860 before or during your search for the will.) Searching devisee indexes is often as important as searching devisor indexes! Finally, because wills can become more complicated than this description, it is important to read the above sources before you start your search.

ANALYZING THE WILL

Once you locate the will, your troubles may really begin. Wills often hide as much as they reveal. The process of identifying slaves in probate records is often a messy one, because individual circumstances are always unique. You may, for example, find slaves named in a will during the period 1840 to 1865 and never find them again unless you know how to really "work" the records. Listed below are just a few problem-solving questions that you need to use to analyze the will:

1. Does the will reveal how the deceased acquired your ancestors?
2. Who was designated to acquire or inherit your ancestors?
3. Can you verify that they actually "took possession" of your ancestors?
4. If the wife retained ownership, how long did she live?
5. If a child was named as an heir, who was the child's guardian?
6. Are there any leads to slaves who were inherited prior to the will and referred to only as gifts that were given prior to the will?
7. For the named heirs, do the records indicate current residence?

These questions are necessary because even if an individual inherited a slave, that does not mean that he or she "took possession" of that slave and went home. Slaves could have been sold to pay off remaining debts, sold to raise cash to be divided among children, divided by the administrator at his own discretion, or divided equally among all dependent children, in which case the widow "took possession." Though the will is a fair predictor of what will happen, at least in the view of the deceased, anything may have happened after the individual's death. Thus a will is only a statement of intent by an individual who will not have control after his or her death but who attempts to control certain events nevertheless.

PERSONAL
RECORDKEEPING WITH
EXERCISES FOR
BEGINNERS

INTRODUCTION

*E*very family historian needs a chart system and a set of basic forms to record information and data collected on family members. Charts should be used as your worksheets. They can tell you what information you need to obtain to complete documenting each person's life cycle from birth to death.

As you progress in your research, you will eventually want to purchase a software program that keeps track of all of your data. Indeed, a software program can guide you in your research. Before purchasing, seek advice from other genealogists. Note that the programs can't do your research for you, but they can definitely guide you and help you to organize and present your family data in the correct manner. Even if you use a software program, you still need to keep charts as a back-up system. Your compiled charts will eventually fill a large three-ring binder.

There are two basic charts that you will need to keep on hand all the time. They are the descendants' chart or pedigree chart and the family group sheet. As you collect information, be sure to enter it on these charts. That makes it easy to glance back and see what missing information needs to be found.

Once you complete one lineage, your software program can be used to present your research in a formal genealogical chart called an *ahnentafel* (ancestor table). The ahnentafel will start with the last ancestor that you traced and it will give the lineage in the following manner—The Descendants of John and Amanda Smith. The ahnentafel is a special numbering system that is universally used for presenting formal genealogies.

Charts also help you to think about your family as a group larger than your immediate family. You will begin to see the whole web of family relationships that existed in the past and that continue to exist through your generation. Some families are the size of clans while others are smaller, but note that very few extended family groups die out. In order to discover this web of family relationships, don't forget that you need the two basics.

Charts and forms included in this section are:

1. Five Generations Chart
2. Family Group Sheet or Record
3. Descendants' Chart Starting with Your Grandparents
4. Individual Data Card
5. Research Record

You may also devise your own forms for recordkeeping as you progress.

BEGINNING WITH YOURSELF:
ARE YOU THE REPOSITORY OF FAMILY MEMORY?

Part 1: Answer Yes or No to the following questions.

1. _____ I am the oldest child of my parents.

2. _____ I am female.

3. _____ I am male.

4. _____ I grew up in a single-parent household.

5. _____ I grew up in a two-parent household.

6. _____ I grew up with one of my grandparents.

7. _____ I know where my folks come from.

8. _____ I have all of our reunion programs and address books.

9. _____ I am on good terms with most people in my family.

10. _____ I grew up listening to family stories about people long since gone.

If you wrote yes for 8 of these, then you are off to a good start.

If you wrote yes 5–7 times, then you too are off to a good start, but you will have to put a little more effort into your project.

If you answered yes to less than 5, you have challenges ahead, but they are not insurmountable. This is why you are doing this project.

INDIVIDUAL DATA CARD

*T*he data card is envisioned not so much as a card but as a sheet with two of them so that the person economizes on paper use. So there will be two per sheet of paper or two on a page.

Use these data cards to record research notes and other information, including phone numbers and follow-up. This helps you keep track of each person that you are researching. Once home, enter the information in your family history software program or your genealogical recordkeeping system. Then file the cards in a three-ring binder that can be easily carried to a library or research facility.

INDIVIDUAL DATA CARD

Surname _____
Given Name _____
Birth Record _____
Location or Source _____
Content:
_____
_____
_____

Marriage Record
Location or Source _____
Content:
_____
_____
_____

Death Record
Location or Source _____
Content:
_____
_____
_____

Burial Information
Cemetery _____
_____
Funeral Home _____
Address: _____

Census Information
1920: County _____ State ____
ED _____ Page _____ Line _____
1910: County _____ State ____
ED _____ Page _____ Line _____
1900: County _____ State ____
ED _____ Page _____ Line _____
1880: County _____ State ____
ED _____ Page _____ Line _____
1870: County _____ State ____
ED _____ Page _____ Line _____

Use back for schools attended, city directory information and other notes.

Surname _____
Given Name _____
Birth Record _____
Location or Source _____
Content:
_____
_____
_____

Marriage Record
Location or Source _____
Content:
_____
_____
_____

Death Record
Location or Source _____
Content:
_____
_____
_____

Burial Information
Cemetery _____
_____
Funeral Home _____
Address: _____

Census Information
1920: County _____ State ____
ED _____ Page _____ Line _____
1910: County _____ State ____
ED _____ Page _____ Line _____
1900: County _____ State ____
ED _____ Page _____ Line _____
1880: County _____ State ____
ED _____ Page _____ Line _____
1870: County _____ State ____
ED _____ Page _____ Line _____

Use back for schools attended, city directory information and other notes.

FIVE GENERATIONS CHART

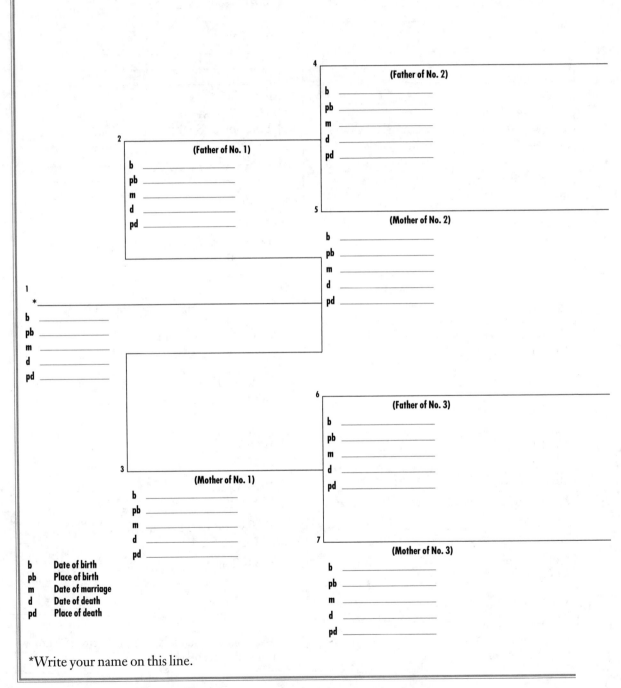

4 (Father of No. 2)
b _____
pb _____
m _____
d _____
pd _____

2 (Father of No. 1)
b _____
pb _____
m _____
d _____
pd _____

5 (Mother of No. 2)
b _____
pb _____
m _____
d _____
pd _____

1
*
b _____
pb _____
m _____
d _____
pd _____

6 (Father of No. 3)
b _____
pb _____
m _____
d _____
pd _____

3 (Mother of No. 1)
b _____
pb _____
m _____
d _____
pd _____

7 (Mother of No. 3)
b _____
pb _____
m _____
d _____
pd _____

b	Date of birth
pb	Place of birth
m	Date of marriage
d	Date of death
pd	Place of death

*Write your name on this line.

(See page 26 for instructions on filling out this chart.)

FIVE GENERATIONS CHART

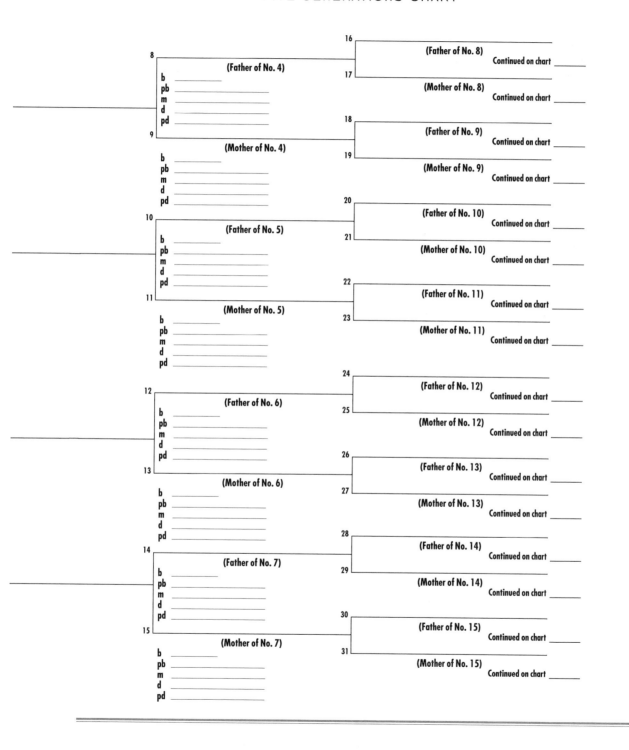

16	(Father of No. 8)	Continued on chart _____

8

(Father of No. 4)

b _____
pb _____
m _____
d _____
pd _____

17	(Mother of No. 8)	Continued on chart _____

18	(Father of No. 9)	Continued on chart _____

9

(Mother of No. 4)

b _____
pb _____
m _____
d _____
pd _____

19	(Mother of No. 9)	Continued on chart _____

20	(Father of No. 10)	Continued on chart _____

10

(Father of No. 5)

b _____
pb _____
m _____
d _____
pd _____

21	(Mother of No. 10)	Continued on chart _____

22	(Father of No. 11)	Continued on chart _____

11

(Mother of No. 5)

b _____
pb _____
m _____
d _____
pd _____

23	(Mother of No. 11)	Continued on chart _____

24	(Father of No. 12)	Continued on chart _____

12

(Father of No. 6)

b _____
pb _____
m _____
d _____
pd _____

25	(Mother of No. 12)	Continued on chart _____

26	(Father of No. 13)	Continued on chart _____

13

(Mother of No. 6)

b _____
pb _____
m _____
d _____
pd _____

27	(Mother of No. 13)	Continued on chart _____

28	(Father of No. 14)	Continued on chart _____

14

(Father of No. 7)

b _____
pb _____
m _____
d _____
pd _____

29	(Mother of No. 14)	Continued on chart _____

30	(Father of No. 15)	Continued on chart _____

15

(Mother of No. 7)

b _____
pb _____
m _____
d _____
pd _____

31	(Mother of No. 15)	Continued on chart _____

FAMILY GROUP SHEET

HUSBAND _____

Town   State

    Birth date _____   Place _____

    Marriage date _____   Place _____

    Death date _____   Place _____

    Burial date _____   Place _____

    Father _____   **Full Maiden Name of Mother** _____

    Other Wives of the Husband _____

  WIFE _____

    Birth date _____   Place _____

    Marriage date _____   Place _____

    Death date _____   Place _____

    Burial date _____   Place _____

    Father _____   **Full Maiden Name of Mother** _____

    Other Husbands of the Wife _____

#	Sex	Children in order of birth	Born Day/Month/Year	Where born	Died Day/Month/Year	Where died
Date Married & Spouse						

Chart compiled by _____

(See page 29 for instructions on filling out this chart.)

GRANDPARENTS: THE TEN ESSENTIAL QUESTIONS

1. Where were you born?

2. When were you born? (Month, day and year.)

3. Who were the most important relatives to you when you were growing up? Where are they now? (List them as the person names them.)

4. Did you know your grandparents? What were their names, where did they live, and when and where did they die?

5. What church did your family go to when you were growing up?

6. When relatives started moving to the North and elsewhere, what cities did they go to? (Include Southern cities also.)

7. Did anyone keep family Bibles? If so, who did and do you know where the Bible is now?

8. When did you get married to ___ and where did his or her family live when you got married? Also ask for the names of all children.

9. Did anyone in the family ever talk about slavery and sharecropping? If so, what did they talk about and who were the people they talked about most?

10. Can you tell me about your own life, starting from when you were in your youth through today? (Cover birth through childhood, young adult years, adult years including marriage, aging.)

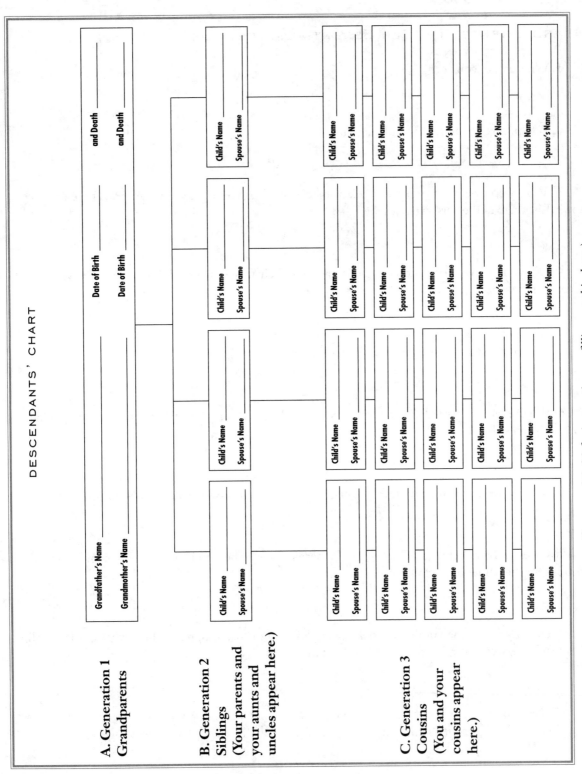

DESCENDANTS' CHART

A. Generation 1 Grandparents

Grandfather's Name ——— Date of Birth ——— and Death ———

Grandmother's Name ——— Date of Birth ——— and Death ———

B. Generation 2 Siblings
(Your parents and your aunts and uncles appear here.)

Child's Name ———
Spouse's Name ———

C. Generation 3 Cousins
(You and your cousins appear here.)

Child's Name ———
Spouse's Name ———

(See pages 26–29 for instructions on filling out this chart.)

WHERE DO YOU FIT IN THE BIG PICTURE? AN EXERCISE USING A DESCENDANTS' CHART

    This exercise may require additional boxes. In that case, add them or create your own chart adding as many boxes as needed. Use either your mother's or father's side of the family (whichever you feel you know most about) for this exercise. Because this is an exploratory exercise, use approximate dates if you don't have precise ones.

    1. Write the names of either your paternal or maternal grandparents below and in the box on the chart labeled "A."

        Grandfather _____ Date of Birth _____ and Death _____
        Grandmother _____ Date of Birth _____ and Death _____

    2. Next list the names of your grandparents' children and their spouses. Make sure you list them in the order of oldest to youngest. Enter their names in the boxes labeled "B." This is actually your parent's generation, and he or she would appear here along with siblings (brothers and sisters) and a spouse. Your parent's siblings and their spouses are the people you call aunts and uncles. Make sure you list them from the oldest to the youngest.

    3. For each couple that appeared in #2 above, list their children from the oldest to the youngest. Enter their names in the boxes labeled "C." Your name will appear here, and these are your first cousins or your generation of cousins.

Couple #1	Couple #2	Couple #3 etc.
_____	_____	_____
_____	_____	_____
_____	_____	_____
_____	_____	_____
_____	_____	_____
_____	_____	_____

    4. How many people did you enter? _____Even if you are missing information, how many people total should appear on this chart? _____

    5. Examining the generation of cousins, answer these questions:
        1: Who is the oldest cousin?_____ Estimated Age _____
        2: Who is the youngest cousin? _____ Estimated Age _____
        3: Where do you fit in?

    6. For each generation, list all of the oldest adults who are still living and their ages.

    These are the people who probably have the big picture of your family, just like the picture that emerged in your mind as you did this exercise. These are the people that you interview first!

    Note: This exercise may be extended to get a picture of more than three generations, but before you do that, know that genealogy software programs can do it for you even more easily. Try extending the exercise by starting with your great-grandparents listed in the boxes for generation one and work down. Here you will get an even larger picture of your family as well as a picture of how your own parent might have seen his family.

Research Calendar

SURNAME _____

Month & Year _____

	A Date	B Time	C Phone Number	D Work	E Follow-up?
1	/				
2	/				
3	/				
4	/				
5	/				
6	/				
7	/				
8	/				
9	/				
10	/				
11	/				
12	/				
13	/				
14	/				
15	/				
16	/				
17	/				
18	/				
19	/				
20	/				
21	/				
22	/				

This is an absolutely essential form. Use the model to devise your own as you progress.

COMPILING YOUR PERSONAL RESOURCE GUIDEBOOK USING THE WEB

*B*ecause many researchers are already on the Net, this exercise has been included to help you explore in a time-efficient manner. This exercise is a variation on an interactive beginner's exercise that I did for www.Afrigeneas.com. Visit the site and explore further.

Each of these steps has a link for further assistance. Follow the links, download key information, print it out and file in a three-ring binder with subject dividers. This notebook will be your own personal resource guidebook, something that every genealogist needs throughout the duration of a research project.

Finding Guidebooks
www.amazon.com
www.cushcity.com
www.barnesandnoble.com

To explore further, use the following keywords for your Web search. Caution: don't forget that the point of this exercise is to compile your own personal resource guidebook. It's easy to get sidetracked on the Web.

Web search key words:

Genealogy   Genealogy Guidebooks
African American Genealogy   American Genealogy   Caribbean Genealogy
Canadian Genealogy   Roots   Family Tree   Family History

Finding Beginners' Exercises on the Web
You will find beginners' exercises on many sites. Some are fee-based while others are free. Explore as many as you can for preliminary information. The following sites contain some basic information to get you jump-started:

www.Afrigeneas.com
www.ngsgenealogy.org
www.nara.gov/genealogy
www.cooklib.org/genmain.html

Join a Local Genealogy Society
It's time to get hooked up. As your research begins, join one of the many African American genealogy societies that exist, including the national AAHGS. Examine both listings.

http://soc.genealogy.africanFAQ1.3.5#societies
www.rootsweb.com/~mdaahgs

Find Your County of Research
County locator website: http://mapping.usgs.gov/www/gnis/gnisform.html

Visit Popular Genealogy Websites
www.afrigeneas.com www.familysearch.com
www.ancestry.com www.rootsweb.com/
    caribgw/ (For Caribbean Genealogy)
www.Cyndi'sList.com/hispanic.htm
    (For Caribbean Genealogy)

Visit Sites for Your State of Research
You will need to know what genealogical sources exist in your state of research. Names, addresses, and hours for libraries and the state's archives will appear at this site as well as lists of materials and guidebooks on doing research in the state:

www.usgenweb.com

Click on your state and download information about how to do research in that state, including the address of the state's archives, genealogical societies in that state, and other useful information.

Visit Sites for Your County of Research
www.usgenweb.com (click on county)

Note that African American genealogy groups may also appear on usgenweb. Feel free to follow the links for African American special interest groups. Then go to the message boards and post your first query (see next step). Bookmark the county site and plan to visit it frequently because new information is being posted every day.

Join and Post Your First Query to an E-Mail Discussion Group
Go to: www.afrigeneas.com or usgenweb.com (your county site) and post a query. Use the following model:

RE: JAMES, THORNTON, RILEY in GEORGIA Seeking living descendants and information on Andrew James (born 1901) and his wife, Elizabeth Thornton, who left Greene County, Georgia, around 1930 and moved to Detroit. They lived near a place called Shady Grove in Greene County. Elizabeth's maiden name was possibly Riley. Would also appreciate any contact with Rileys or Thorntons from that area.

Start Ordering Vital Records
How to obtain vital records:
www.vitalrec.com
SSDI—Social Security Death Index: www.ancestry.com. This is an important tool when you don't know the date of death for one of your ancestors. The SSDI is online at Ancestry.com. You can also write a letter to the Social Security Administration requesting a copy of the original application. The response time for receiving copies varies, but plan to wait at least one month.
IGI—International Genealogical Index: www.familysearch.org First read about the IGI. Then try to locate some of your ancestors by entering their names.

Find a Good Genealogy Library
www.mcpl.lib.mo.us/
www.newberry.org/geneal/isc346.htm
http://lcweb2.loc.gov/resdev/ess

AFRICAN AMERICAN AND GENEALOGY
WEB SITES

These sites are examples of the many that you will find. My selection of them carries no endorsement except that they are representative and sometimes essential.

Free Sites
www.usgenweb.com/ (Links to all states and counties that have web sites.)
www.rootsweb.com

African American Genealogy
www.Afrigeneas.com (Here you will find the largest African American genealogy website with an active e-mail list.)
Christine Charity's Web site: ccharity.com
Cyndi's List of Web sites: www.cyndislist.com/african.htm

American Indian Research
Bureau of Indian Affairs: www.doi.gov/bureau-indian-affairs.html
www.nara.gov/nara/nail.html

Archives and Historical Societies
Addresses for All States: ils.unc.edu/archives/archive7.html

American Association for State and Local history: www.aaslh.org
Georgia: www.sos.state.ga.us/Archives/
Louisiana: www.dhh.state.la.us/
Louisiana: dhh.state.la.us/OPH/vrinfo.htm
Mississippi: www.mdah.state.ms.us/
National Archives Home Page: www.nara.gov/nara/nail.html
National Archives (Genealogy Homepage): www.nara.gov/genealogy/

Canadian Research
www.islandnet.com/~jveinot/cghl/cghl.html
www.niagara.com/~acavasin/nj/njhl.htm#001

Caribbean Research
www.nypl.org/research/sc/sources/caribsubjects.html
www.ourworld.compuserve.com/homepages/vroyal
www.rootsweb.com/~caribgw/ourworld. compuserve.com/homepages/vroyal/ (Caribbean Discussion List)

Census Research
www.mindspring.com/~smothers/dallas.htm (1866 Census Dallas County)

www.mindspring.com/~smothers/wilcox.htm
(1866 Census Wilcox County)

www.genealogy.org/~bcg

www.censuslinks.com

www.census-online.com

www.censusmicrofilm.com (Microfilm rental/purchase cheaply)

Free Blacks

www.freeafricanamericans.com (Virginia, North Carolina)

www.TDN-NET.com/rossville (Ohio)

Freedmen's Bureau

www.nara.gov/guide/rg105.html

Genealogy Databases

www.Afrigeneas.com

www.ancestry.com

www.familysearch.org

Genealogical Societies

www.genhomepage.com/societies.html

National Genealogical Society: www.ngs.genealogy.org

Federation of Genealogical Societies: www.fgs.org/~fgs/

Genealogical Certification

www.genealogy.org/~bcg/

Historical Societies

www2.cybernex.net/~`manty/new.html

Land Descriptions, Geographic Locations, Maps

Bureau of Land Management: www.glorecords.blm.gov

Geographic Place Name Search: www.mit.edu:8001/geo

Township/Range System Described: www.outfitters.com/genealogy/land/twprange.html

Libraries and Private Manuscript Collections

Locating Libraries: www.libraryspot.com/librariesonline.htm

American Library Association: www.ala.org

Cook Memorial Library Online Genealogy Resources: www.cooklib.org/genmain.html

Family History Center Stake Library Addresses: www.lds.org

Catalogue—African American Sources: www.upress.virginia.edu/plunkett/mfp.html

Library of Congress: http://lcweb2.loc.gov

National Union Catalogue of Manuscript Collections: lcweb.loc.gov/coll/nucmc/nucmc.html

Newberry-Library (Chicago): www.newberry.org/geneal/isc346.htm

New Orleans Public Library www.gnofn.org/~nopl/nutrias.htm

OCLC (Online Computer Library Center): www.oclc.org

Local History

Gullah-Geechee Sea Island's Coalition: http://users.aol.com/queenmut/GullGeeCo.html

Military

CIVIL WAR, UNITED STATES COLORED TROOPS

www.itd.nps.gov/cwss/usct.html (Index to USCT)

www.itd.nps.gov/cwss/ (Explanation of Index)

www.genealogy.org/census/1890.html

www.rootsweb.com/~ncusct/usct.htm (N.C. Regiments)

DEPARTMENT OF VETERANS AFFAIRS:

www.va.gov

FEDERAL PERSONNEL RECORDS CENTER
(WORLD WAR I TO VIETNAM)
www.nara.gov/regional/stlouis.html
Military-Library:
    carlisle-www.army.mi/usamhi/
     (Army Military History Institute)
Military Personnel Records Center:
    www.nara.gov/regional/mpr.html

NATF80 AND NATF180 FORMS
www.nara.gov/regional/mprsf180.html (World
    War I and After)
Order Veterans Records:
    www.nara.gov/research/ordering/milodr.html

SAILORS
www.hup.harvard.edu/Featured/BlackJacks/

Slave Narratives
xroads.virginia.edu/~hyper/wpa/index.html

Slave Trade
Atlantic Data Base:
    www.cup.org/electron.html
Domestic Slave Trade:
    www.Afrigeneas.com/slavedata/

Slaveowners' Papers
National Union Catalogue of Manuscript Collec-
    tions (NUCMC):
    lcweb.loc.gov/coll/nucmc/nucmc.html
Louisiana State University Library-Special Col-
    lections:
    www.lib.lsu.edu/special/plantations.html

Underground Railroad
www.ugrr.org/research.htm

AFRICAN AMERICAN GENEALOGY
SOCIETIES IN THE UNITED STATES
AND CANADA

Canada

Africville Genealogical Society
2349 Maynard St
Halifax, Nova Scotia
Canada B3K 3T8

Black Cultural Centre of Nova Scotia
POB 2128
East Dartmouth, Nova Scotia
3Y2 Canada B2W

Buxton Historic Site & Museum
North Buxton, Ontario
Canada N0P 1Y0
(519) 352-4799

Historical Society of St. Catherines
Box 1101
St. Catherines, Ontario
Canada L2R 7A3

Niagra Historical Society
Box 208
Niagara on the Lake, Ontario
Canada L0S 1J0
(416) 468-3912

North American Black Historical Museum
277 King St
Amherstburg, Ontario

Canada N9V 2C7
(519) 736-5433

Ontario Black History Society
Ontario Heritage Center
10 Adelaide St East, Suite 202
Toronto, Ontario
Canada M5C 1J3

Uncle Tom's Cabin Historical Site
RR#5 Highway 21
Dresden, Ontario
Canada N0P 1M0

Alabama

AAHGS* Freedom Trail
220 Oak Dr
Lowndesboro, AL 36752
Bob Mants, President

African Ancestored Family Studies
PO Box 4250
Anniston, AL 36204

Black Heritage Council of the Alabama Historical
    Commission
468 South Perry St
Montgomery, AL 36130-0900
(334) 242-3184

Arizona

AAHGS Tucson
PO Box 58272
Tucson, AZ 87554
Emily Ricketts, President

Arkansas

AAHGS* Little Rock
PO Box 4294
Little Rock, AR 72214

California

African American Genealogical Society of North-
  ern California
PO Box 27485
Oakland, CA 94602-0985
Ranie George Smith, President

AAHGS* Bay Area
Electra Kimble Price
KimbleP@aol.com

California African American Genealogical Society
PO Box 8442
Los Angeles, CA 90008-0442
Ronald Higgins, President

San Diego African American Genealogy Research
  Group
PO Box 740240
San Diego, CA 92174-0240
Milton Hines, President

Colorado

Black American West Museum
7474 East Arkansas
Denver, CO 80231

Black Genealogical Research Group
4605 E. Kentucky Ave #5F
Denver, CO 80222

The Black Genealogy Search Group of Denver,
  CO
PO Box 40674
Denver, CO 80204-0674
Iris Agard Hawkins, President

Connecticut

Connecticut Afro-American Historical Society
444 Orchard St
New Haven, CT 06511

Delaware

African American Genealogy Association of
  Delaware
c/o Ezion Mt Carmel United Methodist Church
800 N. French St
Wilmington, DE 19801-3590

Harriet Tubman Historical Society
PO Box 146
Wilmington, DE 19899

District of Columbia

AAHGS* James Dent Walker Chapter
PO Box 34683
Washington, DC 20043
Cornelius L. Cooper, President

National AAHGS*
PO Box 73086
Washington, DC 20056-3086
Barbara D. Walker, President

Florida

AAHGS* Central Florida
2586 South Conway Rd
Orlando, FL 32812
Stuart W. Doyle, President

Ft. Mose Historical Society
PO Box 4230
St. Augustine, FL 32085

Illinois

African American Genealogical Research Institute
PO Box 637
Matteson, IL 60443-6370
Lori Husband, Director

Afro-American Genealogical & Historical Society
of Chicago, Inc.
PO Box 37-7651
Chicago, IL 60637
Saundra Brown, President

AAHGS* Little Egypt IL
207 Lendview Dr
Carbondale, IL 62901
Mary Farris, President

AAHGS* Chicago, Patricia Liddell Researchers
PO Box 438652
Chicago, IL 60643
Thelma Strong Eldridge, President

Indiana

AAHGS* Gary
567 South Vermillion Pl #303
Gary, IN 46403
Leslie Green, President

Kentucky

Kentucky African American Heritage Commission
3014 Petty Jay Rd
Louisville, KY 40220

Louisiana

African American History Alliance of Louisiana
PO Box 51715
New Orleans, LA 70151-1715

Louisiana African-Americans
University Station
PO Box 16726
Baton Rouge, LA 70893

Maryland

AAHGS* Baltimore
PO Box 9366
Baltimore, MD 21229-3125
Roland N. Mills
Louis S. Diggs

AAHGS* Central Maryland
PO Box 2774
Columbia, MD 21045
Sylvia C. Martin, President

AAHGS* Prince George's County
PO Box 44722
Ft. Washington, MD 20744-9998
Carolyn C. Rowe, President

AAHS Maryland
Afro-American Heritage Society of Charles
County
Highway 925 N Box 316
Waldorf, MD 20601

Eastern Shore Historical Association
5731 Mt Holly Rd
East New Market, MD 21631
Arvel Johnson, President

Harriet Tubman Afro-American Genealogical
Society
508 Woodbride Cir
Cantonsville, MD 21228-1126
Angela Walton-Raji, President

Massachusetts

AAHGS* New England
PO Box 3266

Saxonville, MA 01705-3266
Joseph Smith, President

Michigan
The Fred Hart Williams Genealogical Society
Burton Historical Collection
Detroit Public Library
5201 Woodward Ave
Detroit, MI 48202

Mississippi
Vicksburg African American Historical Preservation Foundation
PO Box 821956
Vicksburg, MS 39182

Missouri
AAHGS* Landon Cheek
PO Box 23804
St. Louis, MO 63121-0804
Margaret Durham
Ivory Spiller, President

AAHGS* MAGIC
PO Box 300972
Kansas City, MO 64139-0972
Joan B. Fletcher, President

The Black Archives of Mid-America, Inc.
2033 Vine
Kansas City, MO 64108

Nebraska
Great Plains Black Museum Library
2213 Lake St
Omaha, NE 68110

Nevada
The Walker African-American Museum
705 West Van Buren Ave
Las Vegas, NV 89106
Gwen Walker, Founder & President

New Hampshire
African American Resource Group
PO Box 5094
Portsmouth, NH 03801

New Jersey
AAHGS* New Jersey
758 Stirling Dr East
South Orange, NJ 07079-2425
Lucius A. Bowser, President

Afro-American Historical and Genealogical Society
1841 Kennedy Blvd
Jersey City, NJ 07305

New York
The African-American Genealogy Society of Rochester (TAAGS-R-US)
123 Wisconsin St
Rochester, NY 14609

Afro-American Historical Association of the Niagara Frontier, Inc.
PO Box 63
Buffalo, NY 14207

AAHGS* Jean Sampson Scott Greater New York
PO Box 022340
Brooklyn, NY 11202
Elvin Montgomery, Jr., President

Buffalo Genealogical Society of the African Diaspora
c/o Sonia Walker
PO Box 2534
Buffalo, NY 14240-2534

North Carolina
AAHGS* Charlotte
PO Box 32664

Charlotte, NC 28232
Alvin A. Ricks, President

AAHGS* Piedmont Triad
PO Box 32664
Greensboro, NC 27416
Mary Lane, President

The Heritage of Blacks in North Carolina
c/o Linda Simmons-Henry
PO Box 26334
Raleigh, NC 27611

North Carolina Afro-American Historical
   Genealogical Society
PO Box 26785
Raleigh, NC 27611-6785

Ohio

African American Genealogical Society of Cleve-
   land
PO Box 200382
Cleveland, OH 44120-9998
Dr. Deborah A. Abbott, President

Pennsylvania

African American Genealogy Group
PO Box 1798
Philadelphia, PA 19105-1798
Charles Dorsey, President
John Logan

AAHGS* Western Pennsylvania
PO Box 5707
Pittsburgh, PA 15208
Gladys L. Nesbit, President

Rhode Island

Rhode Island Black Heritage Society
46 Aborn St
Providence, RI 02903

South Carolina

AAHGS* Columbia
PO Box 8836
Columbia, SC 29202

The Black Family Reunion Institute
PO Box 280515
Columbia, SC 29228
E. Gail Anderson Holness, President

Tennessee

African American Heritage Society Museum
PO Box 222
Franklin, TN 37064

African Genealogical & Historical Society of Ten-
   nessee
PO Box 171124
Nashville, TN 37217
Tommie Morton-Young, Ph.D., President

Texas

African American Genealogical and Historical
   Society of San Antonio, Inc.
PO Box 200784
San Antonio, TX 78220
Johnnie Davis, President

African American Genealogy Network of DGS
   (Dallas Genealogical Society)
PO Box 12648
Dallas, TX 75225-0648
Emille Betterson, President

AAHGS* Houston
PO Box 750877
Houston, TX 77275-0877
Eleanor F. Caldwell, President

Tarrant County Black History & Genealogical
   Society
1020 East Humboldt
Fort Worth, TX 76104

Virginia

AAHGS* Hampton Roads
PO Box 2448
Newport News, VA 23609-2448
Selma Stewart, President

AAHGS* Richmond
7723 Granite Hall Ave
Richmond, VA 23225
Timothy Wilson, President

AAHGS* Tidewater
PO Box 10522
Virginia Beach, VA 23450
Essie Dozier, President

Alexandria Black History Resource Center
638 North Alfred St
Alexandria, VA 22314

Fauquier County Afro-American Historical Asso-
   ciation
PO Box 268
Midlands, VA 22728
Karen White, President

Washington

Black Heritage Society of Washington State, Inc.
PO Box 22565
Seattle, WA 98122

Wisconsin

African American Genealogical Society of Mil-
   waukee
PO Box 24094
Brown Deer, WI 53224-0094
Julia Saunders, President

Wisconsin African American Preservation Committee
6302 Mineral Point Rd #311
Madison, WI 53705

Wisconsin Black Historical Society
2620 West Center St
Milwaukee, WI 53206
Clayton Benson, President

BIBLIOGRAPHY

Chapter 1: Regaining Our Collective Memory, Reclaiming a Lost Family Tradition

The sources cited below are representative of the types of works that have been written about African American families and communities. Most have been written by African Americans, and are therefore told from the perspective of the African American experience. They are included as examples of how African American families and communities have dealt with personal and family memory from a historical perspective.

Alexander, Adele Logan. *Ambiguous Lives: Free Women of Color in Rural Georgia, 1789–1879.* Fayetteville: University of Arkansas Press, 1991.

Ballard, Allen. *One More Day's Journey: The Making of Black Philadelphia.* Philadelphia: Institute for the Study of Human Issues, 1984, 1987.

Bennett, Katie Brown. *Soaking the Yule Log.* Decorah, Iowa: privately printed, 1995.

Berry, Leonidas H. *I Wouldn't Take Nothing for My Journey: Two Centuries of an Afro-American Minister's Family.* Chicago: Johnson Publishing, 1981.

Bethel, Elizabeth R. *Promiseland: A Century of Life in a Negro Community.* Philadelphia: Temple University Press, 1981.

Birmingham, Stephen. *Certain People: America's Black Elite.* Boston: Little, Brown, 1977.

Brady, Paul L. *A Certain Blindness: A Black Family's Quest for the Promise of America.* Atlanta: ALP Publishing, 1990.

Chavers-Wright, Madrue. *The Guarantee: P. W. Chavers, Banker, Entrepreneur, Philanthropist in Chicago's Black Belt of the Twenties.* New York: Wright-Armistead, 1985.

Clifton, Lucille. *Generations.* New York: Random House, 1976.

Cornish, Sam. *1935: A Memoir.* Boston: Ploughshares Books, 1990.

Delany, Sarah, and A. Elizabeth Delany, with Amy H. Hearth. *Having Our Say.* New York: Kodansha, 1993.

Engs, Robert F. *Freedom's First Generation: Black Hampton, Virginia, 1861–1890.* Philadelphia: University of Pennsylvania Press, 1979.

Fields, Mamie G., with Karen Fields. *Lemon Swamp and Other Places: A Carolina Memoir.* New York: The Free Press, 1983.

Frost, Olivia Pleasants. "The Journey of Five Generations of a Freedman's Family in Their Quest for Higher Education." *Journal of the Afro-American Genealogical and Historical Society,* vol. 3 (Summer 1982), 54–64.

Gatewood, Willard B. *Aristocrats of Color: The Black Elite, 1880–1920.* Bloomington: Indiana University Press, 1990.

Greenberg, Jonathan. *Staking a Claim: Jake Simmons Jr. and the Making of an Afro-American Oil Dynasty*. New York: Atheneum, 1990.

Gwaltney, John Langston, ed. *Drylongso: A Self-Portrait of Black America*. New York: Random House, 1980.

Haizlip, Shirlee Taylor. *The Sweeter the Juice: A Family Memoir in Black and White*. New York: Simon and Schuster, 1994.

Haley, Alex. *Roots*. New York: Doubleday, 1976.

Ione, Carole. *Pride of Family: Four Generations of American Women of Color*. New York: Summit Books, 1991.

Jacobs, Harriet. *Incidents in the Life of a Slave Girl, Written by Herself*. Cambridge, Mass.: Harvard University Press, 1987. Reprint.

Joyner, Charles W. *Down by the Riverside: A South Carolina Slave Community*. Urbana: University of Illinois Press, 1984.

Jupiter, Del. *Augustina of Spanish West Florida and Her Descendants with Related Families of Egan, Kelker, Palmer and Taylor*. Franklin, N.C.: GPS, 1994.

Lacy, Leslie Alexander. *The Rise and Fall of a Proper Negro: An Autobiography*. New York: Macmillan, 1970.

Lewis, Elizabeth Clark. *Living In, Living Out: African American Domestics in Washington, D.C. 1910–1940*. Washington, D.C.: Smithsonian Institution Press, 1994.

Lightfoot, Sara Lawrence. *Balm in Gilead: Journey of a Healer*. New York: Addison-Wesley, 1988.

Madden, T. O. *We Were Always Free: The Maddens of Culpeper County, Virginia: A Two-Hundred-Year History*. New York: Norton, 1992.

Marcere, Norma. *The Fences Between*. Canton, Ohio: Daring Publishing, 1993.

Merritt, Carole. *Homecoming*. Atlanta: Afro-American Family History Association, 1982.

Morgan, Kathryn. *Children of Strangers: Philadelphia*. Philadelphia: Temple University Press, 1980.

Murray, Pauli. *Proud Shoes: The Story of an American Family*. New York: Harper & Row, 1956.

Patterson, Ruth Polk. *The Seed of Sally Good'n: A Black Family of Arkansas 1833–1953*. Lexington: University Press of Kentucky, 1985.

Pemberton, Gayle. *The Hottest Water in Chicago*. Boston: Faber & Faber, 1992.

Pinkard, Olivia T., and Barbara C. Clark. *The Descendants of Shandy Wesley Jones and Evalina Love Jones: The Story of an African-American Family of Tuscaloosa, Alabama*. Baltimore: Gateway Press, 1993.

Pratt, Mildred, comp. *We the People Tell Our Story: Bloomington-Normal Black History Project*. Normal, Ill.: McLean County Historical Society, 1987.

Quander, Rohulamin. "The Quander Family 1684–1910." *Journal of the Afro-American Historical and Genealogical Society*, vol. 3, no. 2 (Summer 1982).

Redford, Dorothy Spruill, with Michael D'Orso. *Somerset Homecoming: Recovering a Lost Heritage*. New York: Doubleday, 1988.

Still, William. *The Underground Railroad*. Chicago: Johnson Publishing Company, 1970. Reprint.

Stone, Donald P. *Fallen Prince: William James Edwards, Black Education, and the Quest for Afro-American Nationality*. Snow Hill, Ala.: The Snow Hill Press, 1990.

Taulbert, Clifton. *Once Upon a Time When We Were Colored*. Tulsa: Council Oaks Books, 1989.

Walker, Juliette. *Free Frank: A Black Pioneer on the Antebellum Frontier*. Lexington: University Press of Kentucky, 1983.

Walker, Margaret. *Jubilee*. New York: Bantam Books, 1966.

Chapter 2: Beginning Your Genealogical Pursuit

Blassingame, John W. *Slave Testimony: Two Centuries of Letters, Speeches, Interviews and Autobi-*

ographies. Baton Rouge: Louisiana State University Press, 1977.

Brecher, Jeremy. *History from Below: How to Uncover and Tell the Story of Your Community, Association or Union.* New Haven, Conn.: Advocate Press, 1986.

Burroughs, Tony. "Slave Oral History." In Paula K. Byers, ed., *African American Genealogical Sourcebook.* Detroit: Gale Research, 1995.

Clark-Lewis, Elizabeth. "Oral History as a Research Tool." Speech, Afro-American Historical and Genealogical Society, 1991 Annual Conference, Washington, D.C. (cassette tape).

Gwaltney, John Langston, ed. *Drylongso: A Self-Portrait of Black America.* New York: Random House, 1980.

Havlice, Patricia P. *Oral History: A Reference Guide and Annotated Bibliography.* Jefferson, N.C.: McFarland & Company, Inc., 1985.

Morgan, Kathryn. *Children of Strangers: Philadelphia.* Philadelphia: Temple University Press, 1980.

Rawick, George P., ed. *The American Slave: A Composite Autobiography.* Westport, Conn.: Greenwood Press, 1979. (42 volumes including name and subject index)

Smith, Allen. *Directory of Oral History Collections.* Phoenix: Oryx Press, 1988.

Tucker, Veronica. *An Annotated Bibliography of the Fisk University Library's Black Oral History Collection.* Nashville: Fisk University, 1974.

Wilson, Emily. *Hope and Dignity: Older Black Women of the South.* Philadelphia: Temple University Press, 1983.

PRESERVATION OF RECORDS AND PHOTOGRAPHS

Eastman Kodak Company. *Care and Identification of 19th-Century Photographic Prints.* Rochester, N.Y.: Eastman Kodak Company, 1984.

Elkin, Lisa. "Unearthing of Freed-Slave Cemetery May Put Dallas Road Project on Hold." *New York Times* (National), Aug. 13, 1990.

Merritt, Carole. *Historical Black Resources: A Handbook.* Atlanta: Georgia Department of Natural Resources, 1994.

Chapter 3: Techniques and Tools

DIRECTORIES

The following directories will provide accurate addresses for libraries and other institutions. The reference section of your local public library should have the general directories while a genealogy library would have those relating to that subject.

American Library Association. *American Library Directory,* 1992–93 edition. Chicago: American Library Association, 1990.

Bentley, Elizabeth P. *County Courthouse Book.* Baltimore: Genealogical Publishing Company, 1990.

Filby, William, comp. *Directory of American Libraries with Genealogical or Local History Collections.* Wilmington, Del.: Scholarly Resources, 1988.

Makower, Joel, ed. *The American History Sourcebook.* New York: Prentice Hall, 1988.

Meyer, Mary K., ed. *Meyer's Directory of Genealogical Societies in the U.S.A. and Canada.* Mt. Airy, Md.: The Author, 1990.

Wheeler, Mary B., ed. *Directory of Historical Organizations in the United States,* 14th ed. Nashville: American Association for the Study of State and Local History, 1993.

GUIDE BOOKS AND RELEVANT ARTICLES: SPECIFIC STATES

Alabama

Barefield, Marylin D. *Researching in Alabama: A Genealogical Guide.* Chattanooga: Southern Historical Press, 1988.

Arkansas

Wagoner, Claudia. *Arkansas Researcher's Handbook.* Fayetteville, Ark.: Research Plus, 1986.

District of Columbia

Washington Chapter, Daughters of the American Revolution. *Lest We Forget: A Guide to Genealogical Research in the Nation's Capital.* Washington, D.C.: DAR, 1989.

Florida

Robie, Diane C. *Searching in Florida: A Reference Guide to Public and Private Records.* Costa Mesa, Calif.: Independent Research Consultants, 1982.

Georgia

Davis, Robert S. *A Researcher's Library of Georgia History, Genealogy, and Record Sources.* Easley, S.C.: Southern Historical Press, 1987.

Louisiana

Boling, Yvette G. *A Guide to Printed Sources for Genealogical and Historical Research in the Louisiana Parishes.* Jefferson, La.: The Author, 1985.

Hebert, Donald J. *Resources in Louisiana Libraries.* Baton Rouge: Louisiana State Library, 1971.

MacDonald, Robert R., John R. Kemp, and Edward F. Haas, eds. *Louisiana's Black Heritage.* New Orleans: Louisiana State Museum, 1979.

Ricard, Ulysses S., comp. *African Americans in Louisiana: Selected Works Along with Some Genealogical References.* New Orleans: The Chicory Society of Afro-Louisiana History and Culture, 1989. (Available from Amistad Research Center, New Orleans.)

Maryland

Heisey, John W. *Maryland Research Guide.* Indianapolis: Heritage House, 1986.

Jacobsen, Phebe R. *Researching Black Families in the Maryland Hall of Records.* Annapolis, Md.: Maryland Hall of Records, 1984.

Meyer, Mary K. *Genealogical Research in Maryland: A Guide.* Baltimore: Maryland Historical Society, 1983.

North Carolina

Leary, Helen F., and Maurice R. Stirewalt. *North Carolina Research: Genealogy and Local History.* Raleigh: North Carolina Genealogical Society, 1980.

McBride, Ransom. "Searching for the Past of the North Carolina Black Family." *North Carolina Genealogical Society Journal*, vol. 32 (May 1983).

South Carolina

Begley, Paul R., and Steven D. Tuttle. "African American Genealogical Research." Columbia: South Carolina Department of Archives and History, 1991.

Cote, Richard. *Local and Family History in South Carolina: A Bibliography.* Easley, S.C.: Southern Historical Press, 1981.

Easterby, J. H. *Guide to the Study of South Carolina History.* Spartanburg, S.C.: Reprint Company.

Moore, John H. *Research in South Carolina.* Columbia: University of South Carolina Press, 1967.

Tennessee

Fulcher, Richard Carlton. *Guide to County Records and Genealogical Resources in Tennessee.* Baltimore: Genealogical Publishing Company, 1987.

Johnson, Clifton H. "Some Archival Sources on Negro History in Tennessee." *Tennessee Historical Quarterly*, vol. 28, no. 4, 1969.

Schweitzer, George K. *Tennessee Genealogical Research.* Knoxville, Tenn.: George K. Schweitzer, 1986.

Texas

Kennedy, Imogene K., and J. Leon Kennedy. *Genealogical Records in Texas.* Baltimore: Genealogical Publishing Company, 1987.

Woolfolk, George R. "Sources for the History of

the Negro in Texas with Special Reference to Their Implications for Research in Slavery." *Journal of Negro History*, vol. 42, no. 1 (January 1957).

Virginia

Plunkett, Michael. *A Guide to the Collections Relating to Afro-American History, Literature and Culture in the Manuscripts Department of the University of Virginia Library*. Charlottesville: University of Virginia, 1990.

Chapter 4: Your Ancestors on Record

This section suggests some basic sources for beginning your research. Both the sources specific to African American research and to American genealogy in general should be used. Titles with an * may be ordered for a nominal fee from the institution.

BASIC SOURCES FOR BEGINNING AFRICAN AMERICAN GENEALOGY

Journals and Magazines

Journal of Negro History and *The Negro History Bulletin*

Journal of the Afro-American Historical and Genealogical Society

American Visions Magazine

Quarterly Journal of the National Genealogical Society

Books and Articles

Begley, Paul R., and Steven D. Tuttle. "African American Genealogical Research." (South Carolina) Columbia: South Carolina Department of Archives and History, 1991.*

Blockson, Charles. "Black American Research and Records." In Jessie Carni Smith, ed., *Ethnic Genealogy: A Researcher's Guide*. Westport, Conn.: Greenwood Press, 1983.

Blockson, Charles, with Ron Fry. *Black Genealogy*. Englewood Cliffs, N.J.: Prentice-Hall, 1977.

Gutman, Herbert. *The Black Family in Slavery and Freedom, 1750–1925*. New York: Pantheon, 1976.

Jacobsen, Phebe R. *Researching Black Families in the Maryland Hall of Records*. Annapolis, Md.: Maryland Hall of Records, 1984.*

Lawson, Sandra. *Generations Past: A Select List of Sources for Afro-American Genealogical Research*. Washington, D.C.: Library of Congress, 1988.

McBride, Ransom. "Searching for the Past of the North Carolina Black Family." *North Carolina Genealogical Society Journal*, vol. 32 (May 1983).

Nordman, Chris. "Basic Genealogical Research Methods and Their Application to African Americans." In Paula K. Byers, ed., *African American Genealogical Sourcebook*. Detroit: Gale Research, 1995.

Redford, Dorothy Spruill. *Somerset Homecoming: Recovering a Lost Heritage*. New York: Doubleday, 1988.

Rose, James, and Alice Eichholz. *Black Genesis*. Detroit: Gale Research, 1978.

Szucs, Loretto D., and Sandra H. Lubking, eds. *The Source: A Guidebook of American Genealogy*, rev. ed. Salt Lake City: Ancestry Publishing, 1996.

Thackery, David. *A Bibliography of African American Family History at the Newberry Library*. Chicago: The Newberry Library, 1988 + updates. (This is an essential bibliography. To order, write to: The Newberry Library, 60 W. Walton, Chicago, IL 60610.)

Thackery, David. "Tracking African American Family History." In *The Source: A Guidebook of American Genealogy*, rev. ed. Salt Lake City: Ancestry Publishing, 1996.

Thackery, David, and Dee Woodtor. *Case Studies in Afro-American Genealogy*. Chicago: The Newberry Library, 1988.

Walker, James D. *Black Genealogy: How to Begin*.

Athens: University of Georgia Center for Continuing Education, 1977.

Witcher, Curt Bryan. *A Bibliography of Sources for Black Family History in the Allen County Public Library Genealogy Department.* Fort Wayne, Ind.: Allen County Public Library, 1989.*

Woodtor, Dee Parmer. "African American Genealogy: A Personal Search for the Past." *American Visions*, vol. 8, no. 6 (Dec./Jan. 1994), 20–25.

Young, Tommie M. *Afro-American Genealogy Sourcebook.* New York: Garland, 1987.

BASIC SOURCES IN AMERICAN GENEALOGY

Eichholz, Alice. *Ancestry's Red Book: American State, County and Town Sources*, rev. ed. Salt Lake City: Ancestry, Inc., 1992.

Everton, George. *The Handy Book for Genealogists*, rev. ed. Logan, Utah: The Everton Publishers, 1991.

Greenwood, Val D. *The Researcher's Guide to American Genealogy*, 2d ed. Baltimore: Genealogical Publishing Company, 1990.

Mills, Elizabeth S. "Ethnicity and the Southern Genealogist: Myths and Misconceptions, Resources and Opportunities." In Ralph J. Crandall and Robert M. Taylor, eds., *Generations and Change: Genealogical Perspectives in Social History*. Macon, Ga.: Mercer, 1986.

U.S. Department of Health and Human Services. *Where to Write for Vital Records*. Washington, D.C.: U.S. Government Printing Office, 1990.

Chapter 5: A Place Called Down Home

SOURCES TO HELP YOU UNDERSTAND MIGRATION AND IMMIGRATION FROM THE SOUTH

Ballard, Allen B. *One More Day's Journey: The Story of a Family and a People*. New York: McGraw-Hill, 1984.

Bigglestone, William E. *They Stopped in Ohio: Black Residents and Visitors of the Nineteenth Century*. Oberlin, Ohio: The Author, 1981.

Bryce-Lamport, Ray Simon. "Black Immigrants: The Experience of Invisibility and Inequality." *Journal of Black Studies*, vol. 3, no. 1 (1972), 29–56.

Crew, Spencer R. *Field to Factory: Afro-American Migration 1915–1919*. Washington, D.C.: Smithsonian, 1987.

Crockett, Norman L. *The Black Towns*. Lawrence: Regents Press of Kansas, 1979.

Gottlieb, Peter. *Making Their Own Way: Southern Blacks' Migration to Pittsburgh, 1916–1930*. Urbana: University of Illinois Press, 1987.

Holmes, William F. "Labor Agents and the Georgia Exodus, 1899–1900." *South Atlantic Quarterly*, vol. 79 (Autumn 1980).

Larrie, Reginald R. *Makin' Free: African-Americans in the Northwest Territory*. Detroit: Blaine Ethridge Books, 1981.

Marks, Carole. *Farewell—We're Good and Gone: The Great Black Migration*. Bloomington: Indiana University Press, 1989.

Newby, I. A. *Black Carolinians: A History of Blacks in South Carolina from 1895 to 1968*. Columbia: University of South Carolina Press, 1973.

Painter, Nell I. *Exodusters: Black Migration to Kansas After Reconstruction*. New York: Norton, 1976.

Redkey, Edwin S. *Black Exodus: Black Nationalists and Back to Africa Movements, 1890–1910*. New Haven: Yale University Press, 1969.

Stewart, Roma Jones. "The Migration of a Free People: Cass County's Black Settlers from North Carolina." *Michigan History*, vol. 71, no. 1 (Jan.-Feb. 1987).

Woodson, Carter G. *A Century of Negro Migration*. New York: Russell and Russell, 1969. Reprint.

Chapter 6: Unraveling the Ties That Bound

Bureau of the Census. *Twenty Censuses: Population and Housing Questions, 1790–1980.* Washington, D.C.: U.S. Government Printing Office, 1979.

Cummings, John. *Negro Population in the United States, 1790–1915.* Washington, D.C.: U.S. Bureau of the Census, reprinted 1969 by Kraus Reprint, New York.

Dubester, Henry J. *State Censuses: An Annotated Bibliography of Censuses of Population Taken After the Year 1790 by States and Territories of the United States.* New York: Burt Franklin, 1969. Reprint.

Greene, Evarts B., and Virginia B. Harrington. *American Population Before the Federal Census of 1790.* New York: Columbia University Press, 1932.

National Archives and Records Service. *Guide to Genealogical Research in the National Archives,* 1985.

Chapters 7–8: Finding Freedom's Generation and Close to Kin, but Still Waiting for Forty Acres and a Mule

Note: Articles and books on Reconstruction and the Civil War in specific states are plentiful. As a general rule, those published after 1960 attempt to accurately reflect the African American experience.

Berlin, Ira, et al., eds. *Freedom: A Documentary History of Emancipation, 1861–1867.* 4 vols. New York: Cambridge University Press, 1985. (This series should appear in many local libraries. Its accessibility is a benefit to you because each volume contains examples of documents that can be located on your African American ancestors in various National Archives records: Series I, Volume I: The Destruction of Slavery; Series I, Vol. II: The Wartime Genesis of Free Labor: The Lower South; Series I, Vol. III: The Wartime Genesis of Free Labor: The Upper South; Series II: The Black Military Experience.)

Brewer, James H. *The Confederate Negro: Virginia's Craftsmen and Military Laborers, 1861–1865.* Durham, N.C.: Duke University Press, 1969.

Cornish, Dudley. *The Sable Arm: Negro Troops in the Union Army.* New York: Longmans Green & Co., 1956.

Davis, Ronald L. F. *Good and Faithful Labor: From Slavery to Sharecropping in the Natchez District, 1860–1890.* Westport, Conn.: Greenwood Press, 1982.

Dyer, Frederick H. *A Compendium of the War of the Rebellion.* Dayton, Ohio: Morningside Press, 1978.

Everly, Elaine C. "Marriage Records of Freedmen." *Prologue,* vol. 5 (1973).

Litwack, Leon F. *Been in the Storm So Long: The Aftermath of Slavery.* New York: Knopf, 1979.

McPherson, James M. *The Negro's Civil War.* New York: Ballantine Books, 1991.

Mobley, Joe A. *James City: A Black Community in North Carolina, 1863–1900.* Raleigh: North Carolina Department of Cultural Resources, 1981.

Newman, Debra. "Depositors in the Freedman's Savings and Trust Company, 1865–1874." *Journal of the Afro-American Historical and Genealogical Society,* vol. 3, no. 3 (Fall 1982).

Osthaus, Carl R. *Freedmen, Philanthropy, and Fraud: A History of the Freedman's Savings Bank.* Urbana: University of Illinois Press, 1976.

Oubre, C. F. *Forty Acres and a Mule: The Freedmen's Bureau and Black Land Ownership, 1865–1868.* Baton Rouge: Louisiana State University Press, 1978.

Quarles, Benjamin. *The Negro in the Civil War.* Boston: Little, Brown, 1953.

Richardson, Joe. *Christian Reconstruction: The American Missionary Association and Southern Blacks, 1861–1890.* Athens: University of Georgia Press, 1986.

Roark, James L. *Masters Without Slaves: Southern Planters in the Civil War and Reconstruction.* New York: Norton, 1977.

Rose, Willie Lee. *Rehearsal for Reconstruction: The Port Royal Experiment.* New York: Oxford University Press, 1976. Reprint.

Rothrock, Carol K. *The Promised Land: The History of the South Carolina Land Commission, 1869–1890.* Columbia: University of South Carolina Press, 1969.

Sterling, Dorothy, ed. *The Trouble They Seen: Black People Tell the Story of Reconstruction.* New York: Doubleday, 1976.

Wiley, Bell I. *Southern Negroes, 1861–1865.* Baton Rouge: Louisiana State University Press, 1965. Reprint.

GUIDES TO RECORDS, NATIONAL ARCHIVES PUBLICATIONS, AND OTHER FINDING AIDS.

A Guide to Civil War Maps in the National Archives, rev. ed. Washington, D.C.: National Archives and Records Service, 1991.

Beers, Henry Putney. *The Confederacy: A Guide to the Archives of the Confederate States of America.* Washington, D.C.: National Archives and Records Service, 1991.

Black Studies: A Select Catalog of National Archives Microfilm Publications. National Archives and Records Service, 1984.

Boatner, Mark. *The Civil War Dictionary.* New York: D. McKay Co., 1959.

Burroughs, Tony. "Records Specific to African Americans." In Paula K. Byers, ed., *African American Genealogical Sourcebook.* Detroit: Gale Research, 1995. (A good discussion of Freedmen's Bank and Freedmen's Bureau records.)

Davis, George, et al. *Atlas to Accompany the Official Records of the Union and Confederate Armies.*

National Archives and Records Service. (See O'Reilly citation below for the index.)

Everly, Elaine. *Preliminary Inventory of the Records of the Field Offices of the Bureau of Refugees, Freedmen and Abandoned Lands.* Washington, D.C.: NARS, 1973.

Guide to Genealogical Research in the National Archives. National Archives and Records Service, 1985.

Munten, K. W., and Henry P. Beers. *The Union: A Guide to Federal Archives Relating to the Civil War.* Washington, D.C.: National Archives and Records Service, 1986.

National Archives Microfilm Resources for Research: A Comprehensive Catalog. Washington, D.C.: National Archives and Records Service, 1991.

Newman, Debra Ham. *Black History: A Guide to Civilian Records in the National Archives.* Washington, D.C.: National Archives Trust Fund Board, 1984.

O'Reilly, Noel S., et al. *A Graphic Index to the Atlas to Accompany the Official Records of the Union and Confederate Armies.* "Prologue: The Journal of the National Archives (1969 +)."

Walker, Jimmie. "The National Archives and Records Service." In Jessie Carney Smith, ed., *Ethnic Genealogy.* Westport, Conn.: Greenwood Press, 1983.

POST–CIVIL WAR LABOR RECRUITMENT

Burton, Vernon. "Race and Reconstruction: Edgefield County, South Carolina." *Journal of Social History,* vol. 12 (Fall 1978).

Holmes, William F. "Labor Agents and the Georgia Exodus, 1899–1900." *South Atlantic Quarterly,* vol. 79 (Autumn 1980).

Chapters 9–12: Slavery

Note: Because they are widely available, the standard histories of slavery for various states and other geographical areas which you should use are not included in this bibliography.

AFRICAN AMERICAN FAMILY DURING SLAVERY

Gutman, Herbert G. *The Black Family in Slavery and Freedom, 1750–1925*. New York: Pantheon, 1976. (An academic study that you will need as your research progresses.)

Mintz, Steven, and Susan Mintz. "The Shaping of the Afro-American Family." In *Domestic Revolutions: A Social History of American Family Life*. New York: Free Press, 1988.

Schweninger, Loren. "A Slave Family in the Antebellum South." *Journal of Negro History*, vol. 60, no. 1 (1975).

BASIC REFERENCE SOURCES AND BACKGROUND READING

Berlin, Ira, and Ronald Hoffman, eds. *Slavery and Freedom in the Age of the American Revolution*. Charlottesville: University Press of Virginia, 1983.

Hefner, Loretta L. *The WPA Historical Records Survey: A Guide to the Unpublished Inventories, Indexes, and Transcripts*. Chicago: Society of American Archivists, 1980.

Hoffer, Peter C. *Africans Become Afro-Americans: Selected Articles on Slavery in the American Colonies*. New York: Garland, 1988.

Howell, J. B., ed. *Special Collections in Libraries of the Southeast*. Jackson, Miss.: Howick House, 1978.

Index to Personal Names in the National Union Catalog of Manuscript Collections (1959–1984). Alexandria, Va.: Chadwyck, Healey.

Library of Congress. *National Union Catalog of Manuscript Collections*. Washington, D.C. (1959–).

Merritt, Carole. "Slave Family History Records: An Abundance of Materials." *Georgia Archives*, vol. 6 (Spring 1978), 16–21.

Miller, Joseph C. *Slavery: A Worldwide Bibliography, 1900–1982*. White Plains, N.Y.: Kraus International, 1985.

Miller, Randall M., and John D. Smith. *Dictionary of Afro-American Slavery*. New York: Greenwood Publishing Group, 1988.

Oakes, James. *The Ruling Race: A History of American Slaveholders*. New York: Knopf, 1982.

Olson, James Stuart. *Slave Life in America: A Historiography and Selected Bibliography*. Lanham, Md.: University Press of America, 1983.

Rattray, R. S. Ashanti. *Law and Constitution*. London: Oxford University Press, 1929.

Smith, John D. *Black Slavery in the Americas: An Interdisciplinary Bibliography, 1865–1985*. Westport, Conn.: Greenwood Press, 1983.

Thompson, Edgar T. *The Plantation: An International Bibliography*. Boston: G. K. Hall, 1983.

Vlach, John M. *Back of the Big House: The Architecture of Plantation Slavery*. Chapel Hill: University of North Carolina Press, 1993.

LOCATING GENEALOGIES AND STUDIES OF SLAVE OWNERS

Bentley, Elizabeth. *Directory of Family Associations*. Baltimore: Genealogical Publishing Company, 1991.

Kaminkow, Marion J. *Genealogies in the Library of Congress*. Baltimore: Magna Charta Book Co., 1972.

Kaminkow, Marion J., ed. *U.S. Local Histories in the Library of Congress*. Washington, D.C.: Library of Congress, 1988.

Library of Congress. *Genealogies Catalogued by the Library of Congress Since 1986*. Washington, D.C.: Library of Congress, 1991.

Menn, J. K. *The Large Slaveholders of Louisiana, 1860*. New Orleans: Pelican Publishing Company, 1964.

New York Public Library. *Dictionary Catalog of the Local History and Genealogy Division*. Boston: G. K. Hall, 1974.

Swem, Earl G. *Virginia Historical Index*. 2 vols. Gloucester, Mass.: P. Smith, 1965.

Towle, Laird C., ed. *Genealogical Periodical Annual*

Index, Key to the Genealogical Literature (Volume 26). Bowie, Md.: Heritage Books, 1981.

MIGRATION AND MOVEMENTS OF SLAVES AND PLANTERS

Daniels, Jonathan. *The Devil's Backbone: The Story of the Natchez Trace.* New York: McGraw Hill, 1962.

Rohrbough, Malcolm J. *The Trans-Appalachian Frontier: People, Societies, and Institutions, 1775–1850.* New York: Oxford University Press, 1978.

Southerland, H. *The Federal Road Through Georgia and the Creek Nation.* Chattanooga: Historic Chattanooga Press, 1989.

Wells, Tom H. "Moving a Plantation to Louisiana." *Louisiana Studies,* vol. 6 (1967).

SLAVE SALES AND SLAVE TRADERS (DOMESTIC)

African-American Family History Association. *Slave Bills of Sale Project.* Atlanta: African-American Family History Association, 1986.

Bancroft, Frederick. *Slave Trading in the Old South.* Baltimore: J. H. Furst Co., 1931.

Clark, Thomas D. "The Slave Trade Between Kentucky and the Cotton Kingdom." *Mississippi Valley Historical Review,* vol. 21, no. 3 (Dec. 1943).

Stephenson, Wendell H. *Isaac Franklin: Slave Trader and Planter of the Old South.* Baton Rouge: Louisiana State University Press, 1938.

Tadman, Michael. *Speculators and Slaves: Masters, Traders, and Slaves in the Old South.* Madison: University of Wisconsin Press, 1989.

RUNAWAYS AND THE UNDERGROUND RAILROAD

Carter, George E. *The Black Abolitionist Papers, 1830–1865: A Guide to the Microfilm Edition.* (Index included.) Sanford, N.C.: Microfilming Corporation of America, 1981.

Headley, Robert K. *Genealogical Abstracts from 18th Century Virginia Newspapers.* Baltimore: Genealogical Publishing Company, 1987.

Mullin, Gerald W. *Flight and Rebellion: Slave Resistance in Eighteenth-Century Virginia.* New York: Oxford University Press, 1972.

Smith, Billy G., and Richard Wojtowicz. *Blacks Who Stole Themselves: Advertisements for Runaways in the* Pennsylvania Gazette *1728–1790.* Philadelphia: University of Pennsylvania, 1989.

Still, William. *The Underground Railroad.* Chicago: Johnson Publishing Company, 1970. Reprint.

Tregillis, Helen Cox, comp. *River Roads to Freedom: Fugitive Slave Notices and Sheriff Notices Found in Illinois Sources.* Bowie, Md.: Heritage Books, 1988.

Windley, Lathan A. *Runaway Slave Advertisements: A Documentary History from the 1730s to 1790.* 4 vols. Westport, Conn.: Greenwood Press, 1983.

NON-PLANTATION SLAVERY

Dew, Charles B. "David Ross and the Oxford Iron Works: A Study of Industrial Slavery in the Early 19th Century." *William and Mary Quarterly,* vol. 31, no. 2 (1974).

Eaton, Clement. "Slave-Hiring in the Upper South: A Step Toward Freedom." *Mississippi Valley Historical Review,* vol. 46 (1960).

Hodge, Jo Dent. "The Lumber Industry in Laurel, Mississippi at the Turn of the Nineteenth Century." *Journal of Mississippi History,* vol. 35 (1973).

Hughes, Sarah S. "Slaves for Hire: The Allocation of Black Labor in Elizabeth City County, Virginia: 1782–1820." *William and Mary Quarterly,* vol. 35 (1978).

Starobin, Robert S. "Privileged Bondsmen and the Process of Accommodation: The Role of the House-servants and Drivers as Seen in Their

Own Letters." *Journal of Social History*, vol. 4 (Fall 1971).

Starobin, Robert S. *Industrial Slavery in the Old South*. New York: Oxford University Press, 1970.

TECHNIQUES IN SLAVE GENEALOGY

Cody, Cheryll Ann. "Naming, Kinship and Estate Dispersal: Notes on Slave Family Life on a South Carolina Plantation, 1786–1833." *William and Mary Quarterly*, vol. 39 (1982).

Cody, Cheryl Ann. "Kin and Community Among the Good Hope People After Emancipation." *Ethnohistory*, vol. 41, no. 1 (1994).

Hall, Gwendolyn Midlo. *Africans in Colonial Louisiana: The Development of Afro-Creole Culture in the Eighteenth Century*. Baton Rouge: Louisiana State University Press, 1982.

Harris, J. William. "Plantations and Power: Emancipation on the David Barrow Plantations." In Orville Vernon Burton and Robert C. McMath, Jr., eds. *Toward a New South: Studies in Post–Civil War Southern Communities*. Westport, Conn.: Greenwood Press, 1982.

Malone, Ann Patton. "Searching for the Family and Household Structure of Rural Louisiana Slaves, 1810–1864." *Louisiana History*, vol. 28, no. 4 (1987).

Malone, Ann Patton. *Sweet Chariot: Slave Family and Household Structure in Nineteenth-Century Louisiana*. Chapel Hill: University of North Carolina Press, 1992.

Streets, David H. *Slave Genealogy: A Research Guide with Case Studies*. Bowie, Md.: Heritage Books, Inc. 1986.

GUIDEBOOKS: MANUSCRIPT COLLECTIONS

Neagles, James C. *The Library of Congress: A Guide to Genealogical and Historical Research*. Salt Lake City: Ancestry Pub., 1990.

Beers, Henry P. *French and Spanish Records of Louisiana: A Bibliographical Guide to Archive and Manuscript Sources*. Baton Rouge: Louisiana State University Press, 1989.

Sullivan, Larry E., et al. *Guide to the Research Collections of the Maryland Historical Society*. Baltimore: Maryland Historical Society, 1981.

Davis, Richard C., and Linda Angle Miller. *Guide to the Catalogued Collections in the Manuscript Department of the William R. Perkins Library, Duke University*. Santa Barbara, Calif.: Clio Books, 1980.

Tilley, Nannie. *Guide to the Manuscript Collections in the Duke University Library*. Santa Barbara, Calif.: ABC-CLIO, 1980.

Guide to Research Material in the North Carolina State Archives. North Carolina Department of Cultural Resources, 1988.

Society of North Carolina Archivists. *Archival and Manuscript Repositories in North Carolina: A Directory*. Raleigh, N.C.: The Society, 1987.

Cain, Barbara T. *Guide to Private Manuscript Collections in the North Carolina State Archives*. Raleigh: North Carolina Division of Archives and History, 1981.

Stokes, Allen H. *A Guide to the Manuscript Collection of the South Caroliniana Library*. Columbia: South Carolina Library, 1982.

Guide to the Microfilmed Manuscript Holdings of the Tennessee State Library and Archives. Nashville: Tennessee State Library and Archives, 1983.

Guide to the Manuscript Collections of the Virginia Historical Society. Richmond: Virginia Historical Society, 1985.

Duncan, Richard R. *Theses and Dissertations on Virginia History: A Bibliography*. Richmond: Virginia State Library, 1986.

Mansfield, Stephen. *Collections in the Manuscript Division, Alderman Library, Containing References to Slavery for the Period from 1820 to 1865*. Univ. of Virginia, Charlottesville.

Xavier University. *Guide to the Heartman Manuscripts on Slavery*. Boston: G. K. Hall, 1982.

LAWS AND LEGAL RECORDS

Catterall, Helen H., ed. *Judicial Cases Concerning American Slavery and the Negro*. 5 vols. Washington, D.C.: Carnegie Publications, 1926–1937.

McPherson, Robert G. "Georgia Slave Trials, 1837–1849." *American Journal of Legal History*, vol. 4 (1960).

Miller, T. Michael. *Murder and Mayhem: Criminal Conduct in Old Alexandria, Virginia* 1749–1900. Bowie, Md.: Heritage Books, 1988.

NAMES, NAMING PRACTICES, AND NAME ORIGINS

Cody, Cheryl Ann. "There Was No 'Absalom' on the Ball Plantations: Slave-Naming Practices in the South Carolina Low Country, 1720–1865." *American Historical Review*, vol. 92, no. 3 (June 1987).

Dillard, J. L. "West African Day Names in Nova Scotia." *Names*, vol. 19, no. 4 (1971).

Dillard, J. L. *Black Names*. The Hague: Mouton, 1976.

Inscoe, John C. "Carolina Slave Names: An Index to Acculturation." *Journal of Southern History*, vol. 49 (1983).

Puckett, Newbill N. (comp.), and Heller, Murray (ed.). *Black Names in America: Origins and Usage, Collected by Newbill Niles Puckett*. Boston: G. K. Hall, 1975.

Thomas, Kenneth. "A Note on the Pitfalls of Black Genealogy: The Origins of Black Surnames." *Georgia Archives*, vol. 6 (Spring 1978).

Turner, Lorenzo. *Africanisms in the Gullah Dialect*. Ann Arbor: University of Michigan Press, 1974. Reprint.

Chapter 13: The Records Freedom Generated

COLOR DESIGNATIONS/MISCEGENATION

De Marce, Virginia E. " 'Verry Slitly Mixt': Tri-Racial Isolate Families of the Upper South—A Genealogical Study." *National Genealogical Society Quarterly*, vol. 80 (1992).

Forbes, Jack D. "The Evolution of the Term 'Mulatto': A Chapter in Black–Native American Relations." *Journal of Ethnic Studies*, vol. 10, no. 2 (1982).

Forbes, Jack D. *Black Africans and Native Americans: Color, Race and Case in the Evolution of Red-Black Peoples*. New York: Blackwell, 1988.

Gordon-Reed, Annette. *Thomas Jefferson and Sally Hemings: An American Controversy*. Charlottesville: University Press of Virginia, 1997.

Johnston, James H. *Race Relations in Virginia and Miscegenation in the South, 1776–1860*. Amherst: University of Massachusetts Press, 1970.

Jordan, Winthrop. "American Chiaroscuro: The Status and Definition of Mulattoes in the British Colonies." *William and Mary Quarterly*, vol. 19 (1962).

Mills, Gary. "Miscegenation and the Free Negro in Antebellum 'Anglo' Alabama: A Reexamination of Southern Race Relations." *Journal of American History*, vol. 68 (June 1981).

Williamson, Joel. *New People: Miscegenation and Mulattoes in the United States*. New York: Free Press, 1980.

FREE BLACKS AND MANUMISSION

Berlin, Ira. *Slaves Without Masters: The Free Negro in the Antebellum South*. New York: The New Press, 1974.

Brown, Barbara W., and James Rose. *Black Roots in Southeastern Connecticut, 1650–1900*. Detroit: Gale Research, 1980.

Bumbrey, Jeffrey Nordlinger. *A Guide to the Microfilm Publication of the Papers of the Pennsylvania Abolition Society at the Historical Society of Pennsylvania*. Philadelphia: Pennsylvania Abolition Society, 1976.

Carvalho, Joseph. *Black Families in Hampden County, Massachusetts: 1650–1855*. Boston: New England Historical and Genealogical Society, 1984.

Dickenson, Richard B. *Entitled! Free Papers in Appalachia Concerning Antebellum Freeborn Negroes and Emancipated Blacks in Montgomery County, Virginia*. Washington, D.C.: National Genealogical Society, 1981.

Franklin, John Hope. *The Free Negro in North Carolina, 1790–1860*. New York: Russell and Russell, 1943.

Greene, Lorenzo J. *The Negro in Colonial New England, 1620–1776*. New York: Atheneum, 1974. Reprint.

Jacobs, Donald M. *Antebellum Black Newspapers*. Westport, Conn.: Greenwood Press, 1976.

Koger, Larry. *Black Slaveowners: Free Black Slave Masters in South Carolina, 1790–1860*. Jefferson, N.C.: McFarland & Company, 1985.

Mills, Elizabeth Shown, and Gary B. Mills. *The Forgotten People: Cane River's Creoles of Color*. Baton Rouge: Louisiana State University Press, 1977.

Mills, Elizabeth Shown, and Gary B. Mills. "Slaves and Masters: The Louisiana Metoyers." *National Genealogical Society Quarterly*, vol. 70 (Sept. 1982).

Mills, Elizabeth Shown, and Gary B. Mills. "Tracing Free People of Color in the Antebellum South: Methods, Sources, and Perspectives." *National Genealogical Society Quarterly*, vol. 78 (Dec. 1990).

Morgan, Lynda J. *Emancipation in Virginia's Tobacco Belt, 1850–1870*. Athens: University of Georgia Press, 1992.

Piersen, William D. *Black Yankees: The Development of an African-American Subculture in Eighteenth-Century New England*. Amherst: University of Massachusetts, 1988.

Russell, John H. *The Free Negro in Virginia: 1619–1865*. New York: Dover Press, 1969.

Schafer, Judith K. " 'Open and Notorious Concubinage': The Emancipation of Slave Mistresses by Will and the Supreme Court in Antebellum Louisiana." *Louisiana History*, Spring 1987, vol. 28, no. 2.

Senese, Donald J. "The Free Negro and the South Carolina Courts, 1790–1860." *South Carolina Historical Magazine*, vol. 68 (1967).

Winks, Robin. *The Blacks in Canada: A History*. Montreal: McGill-Queens University Press, 1971.

Woodson, Carter G. *Free Negro Owners of Slaves in the United States in 1830: Together with Absentee Ownership of Slaves in the United States in 1830*. New York: Negro Universities Press, 1968. Reprint.

Woodson, Carter G. *Free Negro Heads of Families in the United States in 1830*. Washington, D.C. Association for the Study of Negro Life and History, 1925.

REVOLUTIONARY AND PRE-REVOLUTIONARY WARS

Bowman, Larry G. "Virginia's Use of Blacks in the French and Indian War." *Western Pennsylvania History Magazine*, vol. 53 (1970).

Crow, Jeffrey J. *The Black Experience in Revolutionary North Carolina*. Raleigh, N.C.: N.C. Dept. of Archives and History. 1996.

Farley, M. Foster. "The South Carolina Negro in the American Revolution, 1775–1783." *South Carolina Historical Magazine*, vol. 79 (1978).

Greene, Robert E. *Black Courage, 1775–1783: Documentation of Black Participation in the American Revolution*. Washington, D.C.: National

Society of the Daughters of the American Revolution, 1984.

Heinegg, Paul. *Free African Americans of North Carolina: Including the Family Histories of More Than 80% of Those Counted as "All Other Free Persons" in the 1790 and 1800 Census.* Abqaiq, Saudi Arabia: Paul Heinegg, 1992, 3rd ed.

Jones, George F. "The Black Hessians: Negroes Recruited by the Hessians in South Carolina and Other Colonies." *South Carolina Historical Magazine*, vol. 83 (1982).

Newman, Debra L. *List of Black Servicemen Compiled from the War Department Collection of Revolutionary War Records.* Washington, D.C.: National Archives and Records Service, 1974.

Newman, Debra L., and Marcia Eisenberg. "An Inspection Roll of Negroes Taken on Board Sundry Vessels at Staten Island Bound for Nova Scotia, 1783." *Journal of the Afro-American Historical and Genealogical Society*, vol. 1, no. 2 (1980).

Quarles, Benjamin. "The Colonial Militia and Negro Manpower." *Mississippi Valley Historical Review*, vol. 45 (1959), 643–652.

Quarles, Benjamin. *The Negro in the American Revolution.* Chapel Hill: University of North Carolina Press, 1961.

Saunders, Gail. *Bahamian Loyalists and Their Slaves.* London: Macmillan, 1983.

Walker, James Dent. *Afro-Americans in the American Revolution.* Salt Lake City: National Genealogical Conference, 1985. (Cassette tape.)

Walker, James W. St. G. *The Black Loyalists: The Search for a Promised Land in Nova Scotia and Sierra Leone, 1783–1870.* New York: Africana Publishing, 1976.

Wright, Esmond. "Red, White and Black Loyalists." In Kenneth Pearson, *1776: The British Story of the American Revolution.* London: Times Books, 1976.

AFRICAN ORIGINS AND EMIGRATION/COLONIZATION AND EMIGRATION

The African Repository. Washington, D.C.: American Colonization Society. (1825–1892)

Campbell, Penelope. *Maryland in Africa: The Maryland State Colonization Society, 1831–1857.* Urbana: University of Illinois Press, 1971.

Grant, John N. "Black Immigrants into Nova Scotia, 1776–1815." *Journal of Negro History*, vol. 58 (1973).

Hoyt, William D. "The Papers of the Maryland State Colonization Society." *Maryland Historical Magazine*, vol. 22 (1937).

Jenkins, David. *Black Zion: The Return of Afro-American and West Indians to Africa.* London: Wildwood House, 1975.

"Letters of Negroes Addressed to the American Colonization Society, 1818–1856." *Journal of Negro History*, vol. 10, no. 2 (April 1925).

Library of Congress—Manuscript Division. *The American Colonization Society: A Register of Its Records in the Library of Congress.* Washington, D.C.: The Library, 1979.

McDaniel, Antonio. *Swing Low, Sweet Chariot: The Mortality Cost of Colonizing Liberia in the Nineteenth Century.* Chicago: University of Chicago, 1995.

Miller, Floyd J. *The Search for a Black Nationality: Black Emigration and Colonization, 1787–1863.* Urbana: University of Illinois Press, 1975.

Schick, Tom W. "A Catalog of the National Archives of the Liberian Government." *History in Africa*, vol. 3 (1976), 193–202.

Staudenraus, P. J. *The American Colonization Movement: 1816–1865.* New York: Columbia University Press, 1975.

Wiley, Bell I. *Slaves No More: Letters from Liberia 1833–1869.* Lexington: University Press of Kentucky, 1980.

Chapter 14: The Last African and the First American

Austin, Allan D. *African Muslims in Antebellum America: A Sourcebook.* New York: Garland Publishing, 1984.

Curtin, Phillip. *The Atlantic Slave Trade: A Census.* Madison: University of Wisconsin Press, 1969.

Dalgish, Gerald M. *A Dictionary of Africanisms: Contributions of Sub-Saharan Africa to the English Language.* Westport, Conn.: Greenwood Press, 1982.

Donnan, Elizabeth, comp. *Documents Illustrative of the History of the Slave Trade to America.* 4 vols. New York: Octagon Books, 1965. Reprint.

Higgins, W. Robert. "Factors Dealing in the External Negro Trade." *South Carolina Historical Magazine,* vol. 65 (1964).

Higgins, W. Robert. "The Geographical Origins of Negro Slaves in Colonial South Carolina." *South Atlantic Quarterly,* vol. LXX (1971).

Holloway, Joseph E. *Africanisms in American Culture.* Bloomington: Indiana University Press, 1991.

Howard, Thomas. *Black Voyage: Eyewitness Accounts of the Atlantic Slave Trade.* Boston: Little, Brown, 1971.

Klein, Herbert S. "Slaves and Shipping in Eighteenth-Century Virginia." *Journal of Interdisciplinary History,* vol. 3 (Winter 1975).

Mannix, Daniel P., and Malcolm Cowley. *Black Cargoes: A History of the Atlantic Slave Trade, 1518–1865.* New York: Viking Press, 1962.

Minchinton, Walter E., ed. *Virginia Slave Trade Statistics, 1698–1775.* Richmond: Virginia State Library, 1984.

Olsberg, Nicholas R. "Ship Registers in the South Carolina Archives." *South Carolina Historical Magazine,* vol. 74 (1973).

Rawley, James A. *The Transatlantic Slave Trade.* New York: Norton, 1981.

Wood, Peter. *Black Majority: Negroes in Colonial South Carolina from 1670 Through the Stono Rebellion.* New York: Knopf, 1974.

Wood, Peter. " 'More Like a Negro Country': Demographic Patterns in Colonial South Carolina, 1700–1740." In Stanley L. Engerman and Eugene D. Genovese, *Race and Slavery in the Western Hemisphere.* Princeton, N.J.: Princeton University Press, 1975.

Special Topic 1: Sources for Advanced Research in Slave Genealogy

PLANTATION RECORDS: COMPILATIONS ON MICROFILM/MICROFICHE

Genovese, Eugene, and John Milton Price, comps. *Original Plantation Records in the Collection of Louisiana State University, Department of Archives* (Microfiche). Manuscripts Selected by E. Genovese and John Milton Price. (Baton Rouge). Westport, Conn.: Greenwood Press, 1973.

Stampp, Kenneth M., ed. *Records of Ante-Bellum Southern Plantations from the Revolution Through the Civil War.* Frederick, Md.: University Publications of America, 1985.

DETAILED STUDIES: PLANTATIONS, PLANTER FAMILIES, AND SLAVERY IN LOCAL AREAS

Bell, Malcolm Jr. *Major Butler's Legacy: Five Generations of a Slaveholding Family.* Athens: The University of Georgia Press, 1987.

Burton, Orville. *In My Father's House Are Many Mansions: Family and Community in Edgefield, South Carolina.* Chapel Hill: University of North Carolina Press, 1985.

Clifton, James M., ed. *Life and Labor on Argyle Island: Letters and Documents of a Savannah River Rice Plantation 1833–1867.* Savannah, Ga.: Beehive, 1978.

Davis, Edwin Adams. *Plantation Life in the Florida Parishes of Louisiana 1836–1846 as Reflected in the Diary of Bennet H. Barrow.* New York: Columbia University Press, 1943.

Easterby, J. H. *The South Carolina Rice Plantation as Revealed in the Papers of Robert F. W. Allston.* Chicago: University of Chicago Press, 1945.

Hairston, Peter W. *The Cooleemee Plantation and Its People.* Lexington, N.C.: Davidson County Community College, 1986.

House, Albert Virgil, ed. *Planter Management and Capitalism in Ante-Bellum Georgia: The Journal of Hugh Fraser Grant, Rice Grower.* New York: Columbia University Press, 1954.

Klein, Rachel N. *Unification of a Slave State: The Rise of the Planter Class in the South Carolina Backcountry, 1760–1808.* Chapel Hill: University of North Carolina Press, 1990.

Miller, Elinor, and Eugene D. Genovese. *Plantation, Town and County: Essays on the Local History of American Slave Society.* Urbana: University of Illinois Press, 1974.

Morton, Louis. *Robert Carter of Nomini Hall: A Virginia Tobacco Planter of the Eighteenth Century.* Charlottesville, Va.: University Press of Virginia (reprint), 1964.

Myers, Robert M. *Children of Pride: A True Story of Georgia and the Civil War.* New Haven, Conn.: Yale University Press, 1972.

Otto, John Solomon. *Cannon's Point Plantation, 1794–1860: Living Conditions and Status Patterns in the Old South.* Orlando: Academic Press, 1984.

Rosengarten, Theodore. *Tombee: Portrait of a Cotton Planter.* New York: Morrow, 1987.

Smith, Julia Floyd. *Slavery and Plantation Growth in Antebellum Florida, 1821–1860.* Gainesville: University of Florida Press, 1973.

Special Topic 2: African American Institutional Records

AFRICAN AMERICAN SOURCES

Note: The sources listed herein are only suggestive of genealogical information that might be found in publications by and about African Americans.

Abajian, James de T. *Blacks in Selected Newspapers, Censuses, and Other Sources: An Index to Names and Subjects.* Detroit: Gale Research, 1977. (3 volumes and 2 supplements)

Bigglestone, William E. *They Stopped in Ohio: Black Residents and Visitors of the Nineteenth Century.* Oberlin, Ohio: The Author, 1981.

Brignano, Russell C. *Black Americans in Autobiography: An Annotated Bibliography of Autobiographies and Autobiographical Books Written Since the Civil War.* Durham, N.C.: Duke University Press, 1974.

Bryl, Susan, and Erwin K. Welsch (compilers). *Black Periodicals and Newspapers: A Union List of Holdings in Libraries of the University of Wisconsin and the Library of the State Historical Society of Wisconsin.* Madison: University of Wisconsin Memorial Library, 1975.

Burkett, Randall, et al., comps. *Black Biographical Dictionaries, 1790–1950.* Alexandria, Va.: Chadwyck-Healey, Inc., 1990.

Burkett, Randall, et al., comps. *Black Biography, 1790–1950, Cumulative Index.* Alexandria, Va.: Chadwyck-Healey Inc., 1990.

Clayton, Ralph, comp. *Black Baltimore: 1820–1870.* Bowie, Md.: Heritage Books, 1988.

Crockett, Norman L. *The Black Towns.* Lawrence: Regents Press of Kansas, 1979.

Dunnigan, Alice Allison. *The Fascinating Story of Black Kentuckians: Their Heritage and Traditions.* Washington, D.C.: Associated Publishers, 1982.

Goode, Kenneth G. *California's Black Pioneers: A*

Brief Historical Survey. Santa Barbara, Calif.:
McNally and Lofton, 1974.

La Brice, Henry G. *The Black Newspapers in America: A Guide.* Cambridge, Mass.: Harvard
University Press, 1973.

Larrie, Reginald R. *Makin' Free: African-Americans in the Northwest Territory.* Detroit:
Blaine Ethridge Books, 1981.

Merritt, Carole. *Historical Black Resources: A Handbook.* Atlanta: Georgia Department of Natural Resources, 1994.

Newby, I. A. *Black Carolinians: A History of Blacks in South Carolina from 1895 to 1968.* Columbia:
University of South Carolina Press, 1973.

Pennsylvania Historical Museum Commission.
Blacks in Pennsylvania History: Research and Educational Perspectives. Harrisburg: Pennsylvania Historical and Museum Commission,
1983.

Rice, Lawrence D. *The Negro in Texas, 1874–1900.*
Baton Rouge: Louisiana State University
Press, 1971.

Schatz, Walter, ed. *Directory of Afro-American Resources.* New York: Bowker, 1970.

Sinnette, W. Paul Coates, et al. *Black Bibliophiles and Collectors: Preservers of Black History.*
Washington, D.C.: Howard University Press,
1990.

Stewart, Roma Jones. "The Migration of a Free People: Cass County's Black Settlers from
North Carolina." *Michigan History,* vol. 71,
no. 1 (Jan.-Feb. 1987).

Thornbrough, Emma Lou. *The Negro in Indiana Before 1900: A Study of a Minority.* Indianapolis: Indiana Historical Bureau, 1957.

Thurmond, Michael L. *A Story Untold: Black Men and Women in Athens History.* Athens, Ga.:
Clarke County School District, 1978.

Tindall, George B. *South Carolina Negroes,
1877–1900.* Chapel Hill: University of North
Carolina Press, 1952.

Tolson, Arthur L. *The Black Oklahomans: A History,
1541–1972.* New Orleans: Edwards Printing
Company, 1972.

Williams, Ethel L., and Clifton F. Brown (compilers). *The Howard University Bibliography of African and Afro-American Studies.* Wilmington: Delaware Scholarly Resources, 1977.

Work, Monroe N. *The Negro Year Book.* 10 vols.
1912–1947. Washington, D. C.: Associated
Publishers.

CHURCH SOURCES: BACKGROUND
INFORMATION

Clarke, Nina H. *History of the 19th Century Black Churches in Maryland and Washington, D.C.*
New York: Vantage Press, 1983.

Frazier, E. Franklin. *The Negro Church in America.*
New York, 1964.

George, Carol V. R. *Segregated Sabbaths: Richard Allen and the Rise of the Independent Black Churches.* New York, 1973.

Gravely, William B. "The Social, Political, and Religious Significance of the Foundation of the Colored Methodist Episcopal Church
(1870)." *Methodist History,* vol. 18 (Oct. 1979),
3–25.

Gravely, William B. "The Rise of African Churches in America (1786–1822): Re-Examining the Contexts." *Journal of Religious Thought,* vol. 41 (Spring/Summer 1984).

Irvin, Dona L. *The Unsung Heart of Black America:
A Middle Class Church at Midcentury.* Columbia: University of Missouri Press, 1992.

Leffall, Dolores, comp. *The Black Church: An Annotated Bibliography.* Washington, D.C.:
Minority Research Center, 1973.

Payne, Wardell, ed. *Directory of African American Religious Bodies: A Compendium by the Howard University School of Divinity.* Washington,
D.C.: Howard University Press, 1991.

Payne, Wardell, ed. *Howard University Dictionary*

of Afro-American Religious Studies. Washington, D.C.: Howard University Press, 1991.

Raboteau, Albert J. *Slave Religion: The "Invisible Institution" in the Antebellum South*. New York: Oxford University Press, 1978.

Raboteau, Albert J. "The Black Church: Continuity Within Change." In David W. Lotz (ed) *Altered Landscapes: Christianity in America, 1935–1985*. Grand Rapids, Mich.: Eerdmans, 1989.

Raboteau, Albert J., et al. "Retelling Carter Woodson's Story: Archival Sources for Afro-American Church History." *Journal of American History*, vol. 77, no. 1 (June 1990).

Sernett, Milton C. *Black Religion and American Evangelicalism: White Protestants, Plantation Missions, and the Flowering of Negro Christianity 1785–1865*. Metuchen, N.J.: Scarecrow Press, 1975.

Sobel, Mechal. *Trabelin' On: The Slave Journey to an Afro-Baptist Faith*. Westport, Conn.: Greenwood Press, 1979.

U.S. Catholic Historian. "The Black Catholic Community, 1880–1987." *U.S. Catholic Historian* (Special Issue), vol. 7 (Spring/Summer 1986).

Walker, Clarence E. *A Rock in a Weary Land: The African Methodist Episcopal Church During the Civil War and Reconstruction*. Baton Rouge: Louisiana State University Press, 1982.

Washington, James M. *Frustrated Fellowship: The Black Baptist Quest for Social Power*. Macon, 1986.

Williams, Ethel L. *Biographical Directory of Negro Ministers*. Metuchen, N.J.: Scarecrow Press, 1965.

Wills, David D., and Richard Newman. *Black Apostles at Home and Abroad: Afro-Americans and the Christian Mission from the Revolution to Reconstruction*. Boston: G. K. Hall 1982.

Woodson, Carter G. *The History of the Negro Church*. Washington, D.C.: Associated Publishers, 1921. Reprint.

CHURCH INSTITUTIONAL HISTORIES WRITTEN BY AFRICAN AMERICANS

Note: The following titles represent examples of sources that African American researchers might use to reconstruct the history of a church, church leaders, and active lay leaders.

AME Church

Bradley, David H. *History of the AME Zion Church*. 2 vols. Nashville, AMEC (African American Episcopal Church) 1956–1970.

Cannon, N. C. W. *History of the AME Church*. Rochester, N.Y.: 1842.

Gregg, Howard D. *History of the AME Church: The Black Church in Action*. Nashville: 1980.

Payne, Daniel A. *The Semi-Centenary and the Retrospection of the African Methodist Episcopal Church in the United States of America*. 1866, reprinted Freeport, N.Y.: Books for Libraries Press, 1972.

Payne, Daniel A. *History of the African American Episcopal Church*. 1891, reprinted Nashville: A.M.E. Sunday School Union-Johnson Reprint Corp., 1968.

AME Zion Church

Moore, John J. *History of the African Methodist Episcopal Zion Church*. New York: 1884.

Rush, Christopher. *Short Account of the Rise and Progress of the AME (Zion) Church*. New York: 1843.

Walls, William J. *AME Zion Church: Reality of the Black Church*. Charlotte, N.C.: A.M.E. Zion Pub. House, 1974.

Wood, James W. *One Hundred Years of the AME Zion Church*. New York, 1895.

CME Church

Hamilton, Fayette. *Conversation on the Colored Methodist Episcopal Church*. Nashville: 1884.

Hamilton, Fayette. *Plain Account of the CME Church*. Nashville: 1887.

Lakey, Othal H. *History of the C.M.E. Church*. Memphis: 1985.

Phillips, Charles H. *The History of the CME Church*. 1898, reprinted 1972. Expanded version, 1925.

Other Methodists

Baldwin, Lewis V. *Invisible Strands in African Methodism: A History of the African Union Methodist Protestant and Union American Methodist Episcopal Churches, 1805–1980*. Metuchen, N.J.: Scarecrow Press, 1983.

Bragg, George F. Jr. *History of the Afro-American Groups of the Episcopal Church*. New York: Johnson Reprint Corp. 1922; reprinted 1968.

Gravely, Will B. "African Methodisms and the Rise of Black Denominationalism." In *Rethinking Methodist History: A Bicentennial Historical Consultation*, ed. Russell E. Richey and Kenneth E. Rowe. Nashville: Kingswood Books, United Methodist Pub. House. 1985.

Baptists

Fitts, Leroy. *A History of Black Baptists*. Nashville: Broadman Press, 1985.

Jordan, Lewis G. *Negro Baptist History, U.S.A., 1750–1930*. Nashville: 1931.

Special Topic 3: Caribbean Ancestry

Brandow, James C., comp. *Genealogies of Barbados Families*. Baltimore: Genealogical Publishing Company, 1983.

Bryce-Lamport, Ray S. "Black Immigrants: The Experience of Invisibility and Inequality." *Journal of Black Studies*, vol. 3, no. 1 (1972).

Caribbean Historical and Genealogical Journal. San Luis Obispo, Calif.: TCI Genealogical Resources.

Covington, Paula H., et al. *Latin America and the Caribbean: A Critical Guide to Research Sources*. New York: Greenwood Press, 1992.

Craton, Michael. "Changing Patterns of Slave Families in the British West Indies." *Journal of Interdisciplinary History*, vol. 10, no. 2 (Summer 1979).

Craton, Michael, with Garry Greenland. *Searching for the Invisible Man: Slaves and Plantation Life in Jamaica*. Cambridge, Mass.: Harvard University Press, 1978.

Craton, Michael, and James Walvin. *A Jamaican Plantation: The History of Worthy Park, 1670–1970*. Toronto: University of Toronto Press, 1970.

De Verteuil, Anthony. *Seven Slaves and Slavery: Trinidad, 1777–1838*. Port of Spain, Trinidad: Republic of Trinidad and Tobago, 1992.

Gaspar, David B. *Bondmen and Rebels: A Study of Master-Slave Relations in Antigua*. Baltimore: Johns Hopkins Press, 1985.

Higman, B. W. *Slave Populations of the British Caribbean, 1807–1834*. Baltimore: John Hopkins University Press, 1984.

Higman, B. W. *Slave Society in the Danish West Indies: St. Thomas, St. John and St. Croix*. Baltimore: John Hopkins University Press, 1992.

Kiple, Kenneth F. *The Caribbean Slave: A Biological History*. New York: Cambridge University Press, 1984.

Lamur, H. E. "The Production of Sugar and the Reproduction of Slaves at Vossenburg, 1705–1863." *Caribbean Studies*, vol. 3 (1987).

McDonald, Roderick. *The Economy and Material Culture of Slaves: Goods and Chattels on the Sugar Plantations of Jamaica and Louisiana*. Baton Rouge: Louisiana State University Press, 1993.

Meredith, John. *The Plantation Slaves of Trinidad, 1783–1816*. New York: Cambridge University Press, 1988.

Munford, Clarence J. *The Black Ordeal of Slavery and Slave Trading in the French West Indies, 1625–1715*. Lewiston, N.Y.: E. Mellen Press, 1991.

Patterson, Orlando. *The Sociology of Slavery*. London: MacGibbon and Kee, 1967.

Peters, Thelma. "The Loyalist Migration from

East Florida to the Bahama Islands." *Florida Historical Quarterly*, vol. 40, no. 2 (Oct. 1961).

Ragatz, Lowell J. *A Guide for the Study of British Caribbean History, 1763–1834*. Washington, D.C.: U.S. Government Printing Office, 1932.

Sanders, Joanne M. *Barbados Records*. Baltimore: Genealogical Publishing Company, 1984.

Special Topic 4: American Indian Ancestry

Blumer, Thomas J. "Practical Pointers in Tracing Your Indian Ancestry in the Southeast." *Journal of the Afro-American Historical and Genealogical Society* (Spring/Fall, 1994).

Byers, Paul K. *Native American Genealogical Sourcebook*. Detroit: Gale Research, 1995.

DeMarce, Virginia E. " 'Very Slitly Mixt': Tri-Racial Isolate Families of the Upper South— A Genealogical Study." *National Genealogical Society Quarterly* (March 1992).

Dewitt, Donald L. *American Indian Resource Materials in the Western History Collections, University of Oklahoma*. Norman: University of Oklahoma Press, 1990

Forbes, Jack D. *Africans and Native Americans: The Language of Race and the Evolution of Red-Black Peoples*. Chicago: University of Illinois Press, 1993.

Haliburton, R. Jr. *Red over Black: Black Slavery Among the Cherokee Indians*. Westport, Conn.: Greenwood Press, 1977.

Heinegg, Paul. *Free African Americans of North Carolina and Virginia*. Baltimore: Clearfield Co., 1994.

Hill, Edward E. *Guide to Records in the National Archives of the United States Relating to American Indians*. Washington, D.C.: National Archives and Records Services Administration, 1981.

Kirkham, E. Kay. *Our Native Americans and Their Records of Genealogical Value*. Logan, Utah: Everton, 1980–1984.

Littlefield, Daniel F. Jr. *Africans and Creeks: From the Colonial Period to the Civil War*. Westport, Conn.: Greenwood Press, 1979.

Littlefield, Daniel F. Jr. *Africans and Seminoles: From Removal to Emancipation*. Westport, Conn.: Greenwood Press, 1977.

Littlefield, Daniel F. Jr. *The Chikasaw Freedmen: A People Without a Country*. Westport, Conn.: Greenwood Press, 1980.

Newman, Debra L. *List of Free Black Heads of Families in the First Census of the United States, 1790*. Washington, D.C.: National Archives and Records Administration, 1973.

Olexer, Barbara. *The Enslavement of the American Indian*. Monroe, N.Y.: Library Research Associates, 1982.

Perdue, Theda. *Slavery and the Evolution of Cherokee Society 1540–1866*. Knoxville: University of Tennessee Press, 1979.

Porter, Kenneth W. *Relations Between Negroes and Indians Within the Present United States*. Washington, D.C.: Association for Negro Life and History.

Spindel, Donna. *Introductory Guide to Indian-Related Records (to 1876) in the North Carolina State Archives*. Raleigh: North Carolina Division of Archives and History, 1977.

Walton-Raji, Angela Y. *Black Indian Genealogy Research: African American Ancestors Among the Five Civilized Tribes*. Bowie, Md.: Heritage Books, 1993.

Wissler, Clark. *Indians of the United States*. New York: Anchor Books, 1966.

Witcher, Carl B., and George J. Nixon. "Tracking Native American Family History." In Szuchs, Loretto Dennis and Sandra Hargreaves Luebking, *The Source: A Guidebook for American*

Genealogy. Salt Lake City: Ancestry, Inc., 1997.

Woodson, Carter G. *Free Negro Heads of Families in the United States in 1830, Together with a Brief Treatment of the Free Negro.* Washington, D.C.: Association for the Study of Afro-American Life and History, 1925.

Special Topic 5: World Wars I & II

Barbeau, Arthur E., and Florette Henri. *Unknown Soldiers: Black American Troops in World War I.* Philadelphia: Temple University Press, 1974.

Dryden, Charles W. (Charles Walter). *A-Train : Memoirs of a Tuskegee Airman.* Tuscaloosa: University of Alabama Press, 1997.

Francis, Charles E. *The Tuskegee Airmen: The Men Who Changed a Nation.* Boston: Branden Pub. Co., 1993.

Hall, Gwendolyn Midlo (ed.). *Love, War, and the 96th Engineers (Colored): The World War II New Guinea Diaries of Captain Hyman Samuelson.* Urbana: University of Illinois Press, 1995.

Heaps, Jennifer Davis. "World War II Prisoner of War Records." *Prologue: Journal of the National Archives* (Fall 1991).

Heywood, Chester D. *Negro Combat Troops in the World War: The Story of the 371st Infantry.* Pen and ink drawings by D. Lester Dickson. New York: Negro Universities Press, 1969.

Holway, John. *Red Tails, Black Wings: The Men of America's Black Air Force.* Las Cruces, N.M.: Yucca Tree Press, 1997.

Humphries, Bruce. *The Tuskegee Airmen: The Story of the Negro in the U.S. Air Force.*

Hunton, Addie W., and Kathryn M. Johnson. *Two Colored Women with the American.* New York: AMS Press, 1971.

Husband, Lori. *Chicago World War I Draftees: Districts 3, 4, 5 and 70.* Oak Forest, Ill.: Husband, 1990.

Johnson, Gay. *Standing at the Scratch Line: A Novel.* Random House, 1998.

Johnson, Richard S. *How to Locate Anyone Who Is or Has Been in the Military.* Fort Sam Houston, Tex.: Military Information Enterprises, 1991.

Knapp, Michael. "World War I Service Records." *Prologue: Journal of the National Archives* (Fall 1990).

Lee, Ulysses. *The Employment of Negro Troops.* Washington, D.C.: Center of Military History, U.S. Army, 1994.

Little, Arthur W. *From Harlem to the Rhine: The Story of New York's Colored Volunteers.* New York: Covici, Friede, 1936.

McGuire, Phillip. *Taps for a Jim Crow Army: Letters from Black Soldiers in World War II.* Santa Barbara, Calif.: ABC-Clio, 1983.

Nalty, Bernard C. *The Right to Fight: African-American Marines in World War II.* Washington, D.C.: History and Museums Division, Headquarters, U.S. Marine Corps (USGPO) 1995.

Potter, Lou. *Liberators: Fighting on Two Fronts in World War II.* New York: Harcourt Brace Jovanovich, 1992.

Putney, Martha S. *When the Nation Was in Need: Blacks in the Women's Army Corps During World War II.* Metuchen, N.J.: Scarecrow Press, 1992.

Reddick, Lawrence Dunbar. "The Negro in the United States Navy During World War II." *Journal of Negro History* (April, 1947).

Sandler, Stanley. *Segregated Skies: All-Black Combat Squadrons of WW II.* Washington, D.C.: Smithsonian Institution Press, 1992.

Scott, Emmett Jay. *Official History of the American Negro in the World War.* New York: Arno Press, 1969.

Sims-Wood, Janet. "We Served America Too! Black Women in the Women's Army Corps During World War II." *Journal of the Afro-*

American Historical and Genealogical Society 3–4 (1994).

Smith, Graham. *When Jim Crow Met John Bull: Black American Soldiers in World War II Britain.* New York: St. Martin's Press, 1988.

This Is Our War; Selected Stories of Six War Correspondents Who Were Sent Overseas by the Afro-American Newspapers: Baltimore, Washington, Philadelphia, Richmond and Newark. Original drawings by Francis Yancey. Baltimore: The Afro-American Company, 1945.

U.S. Army Military History Institute. "Proceedings of the First Conference on Black Americans in World War II. Conference on Black Americans in World War II (1st, 1992, Carlisle Barracks, Pa.)." U.S. Army Military History Institute, 1992.

Examples of a Search Using the Military History Research Institute: Using the search term "92nd Infantry Division," commonly called the Buffalo Soldier Division, I was able to identify many sources. The site has working bibliographies for each division or unit. Following are examples of what I found:

WORLD WAR I

U.S. Army War College. Hist. Sect. *Order of Battle of the United States Land Forces in the World War: American Expeditionary Forces, Divisions.* Wash, DC: CMH, 1988, pp. 428–35.

U.S. Army War College. "The Ninety Second Division, 1917-1918." Study, 1923.

WORLD WAR II

Arnold, Thomas St. John. *Buffalo Soldiers: The 92nd Infantry Division and Reinforcements in World War II, 1942–1945.* Manhattan, Kan.: Sunflower, 1990. 245 pp.

Goodman, Paul. *A Fragment of Victory in Italy During World War II, 1942–45: The 92nd Infantry Division in World War II: A Special Study Concerned with the 92nd Infantry Division and Its Principal Attachments, Including the 473rd and 442nd (Japanese American) Infantry Regiments.* Nashville: Battery Press, 1993.

Hargrove, Hondon B. *Buffalo Soldiers in Italy: Black Americans in World War II.* Jefferson, N.C.: McFarland, 1985.

Hunter, Jehu C., and Major Clark. *The Buffalo Division in World War II.* n.p., 1985.

Martin, Ralph. "Negroes in Combat." *Yank* 3 (23 Feb 1945): pp. 6–7.

Raymond, E. A. "Black Buffalo." *FA Jrnl* 36 (Jan 1946): pp. 14–16. Per. 598th FA Bn in Italy, Dec 1944.

Stanton, Shelby L. *Order of Battle, U.S. Army, World War II.* Novato, Calif.: Presidio, 1984.

U.S. Dept of Army. "History, 92nd Infantry Division." 5 vols. Photostat, 1945. #05-92.1945/2.

v.1–February 1945, Part 1, ca 200 p.

v.2–February 1945, Part 2, ca 400 p.

v.3–April 1945, Part 1, ca 200 p.

v.4–April 1945, Part 2, ca 150 p.

v.5–May 1945, ca 200 p.

U.S. Dept of Army. Hist Div. *Combat Chronicle: An Outline History of U.S. Army Divisions.* Wash, DC: 1948.

U.S. War Dept. AGO. "Historical Documents, World War II."

Wilson, Dale E. "Recipe for Failure: Major General Edward M. Almond and Preparation for the U.S. 92nd Infantry Division for Combat in World War II." *Journal of Military History* (July 1992).

Special Topic 6: What to Do with Your Research

(See also Chapter 1 Bibliography.)

Barnes, Donald, and Richard S. Barnes. *Write It Right: A Manual for Writing Family Histories and Genealogies.* Ocala, Fla.: Lyons Press, 1983.

Dickerson, Dennis C. *The Past Is in Your Hands: Writing Local AME Church History.* 1990.

Draznin, Yaffa. *The Family Historian's Handbook.* New York: Jane Publishing, 1978.

Note: Consult chapter 1 sources for a list of family memoirs that have been written by African Americans. In addition, the following books provide information on what is preservable in the African American past.

Calder, Loth, ed. *Virginia Landmarks of Black History.* Charlottesville: University Press of Virginia. (Covers sites on the Virginia Landmarks Register and the National Register of Historic Places.)

Merritt, Carole. *Historical Black Resources: A Handbook.* Atlanta: Georgia Department of Natural Resources, 1994.

Wright, Roberta Hughes. *Lay Down Body: Living History in African American Cemeteries.* Detroit: Visible Ink Press, 1996.

Special Topic 7: A Further Note on County Courthouse Records

(Also see guidebooks listed in Chapter 5.)

Civil Works Administration. *South Carolina Will Transcripts, 1782–1868.* Columbia: S.C. Department of Archives and History.

Guide to Local Government Records in the South Carolina Archives. Columbia: University of South Carolina Press, 1988.

Guide to Research Material in the North Carolina State Archives, Section B: County Records. North Carolina Department of Cultural Resources, 1988.

Historical Records Survey, Works Projects Administration (WPA). *Guides to County and Local Records Series.* (May be found at the National Archives, Library of Congress, state archives, and large public libraries.)

Lucas, Silas E. Jr. *An Index to Deeds of the Province and State of South Carolina 1719–1785 and Charleston District 1785–1800.* Easley, S.C.: Southern Historical Press, 1977.

Merritt, Carole. *Homecoming.* Atlanta: Afro-American Family History Association, 1982.

Moore, Caroline T. (compiler) *Abstracts of Wills of the State of South Carolina, 1783–1850.* Columbia, S.C.: 1974.

Stephenson, Richard W., comp. *Land Ownership Maps: A Checklist of Nineteenth Century U.S. County Maps in the Library of Congress.* Washington, D.C.: Library of Congress, 1967.

Taylor Foundation. *Index to Probate Records of Colonial Georgia, 1733–1778.* Atlanta: Taylor Foundation, 1991.

INDEX